THE JEW
IN THE
AMERICAN
WORLD

THE JEW
IN THE
AMERICAN
WORLD

A Source Book

Edited by
JACOB RADER MARCUS

WAYNE STATE UNIVERSITY PRESS   DETROIT

ISBN-13: 978-0-8143-2548-3   ISBN-10: 0-8143-2548-3

See pages 618–621 for complete
copyright and acknowledgments.

Library of Congress Cataloging-in-Publication Data
The Jew in the American world : a source book / edited by
Jacob Rader Marcus.
p.   cm.
Includes bibliographical references and index.
ISBN 0-8143-2547-5 (alk. paper).—ISBN 0-8143-2548-3
(pbk. : alk. paper)
1. Jews—United States—History—Sources. 2. Jews—Canada—
History—Sources. 3. United States—Ethnic relations—Sources.
4. Canada—Ethnic relations—Sources.
I. Marcus, Jacob Rader, 1896–
E184.J5J465   1996
973′.04924—dc20   95–22271

Book design by Joanne Elkin Kinney

Grateful acknowledgment is made to
The Leonard and Harriette Simons Endowed Family Fund
for financial assistance in the publication of this volume.

To
My beloved dear ones

Contents

❧

PART V
Emerging American Period, 1925–1960

Preface

❧

In 1938 I published a documentary history entitled *The Jew in the Medieval World, A Source Book: 315–1791;* it is still in print, still employed as a textbook in many colleges and universities. Now I have written a new work patterned on my medieval documentary. This work, too, is a documentary accompanied by detailed introductions; it has been written for use in lecture courses or seminars. It is my hope, on the basis of my experience with *The Jew in the Medieval World*, that this new book will be welcomed in the some 300 colleges that teach Judaic subjects and in the thousands of synagogs and Jewish cultural institutions that devote themselves to the furtherance of Jewish life.

It is now my privilege to thank those who have helped me prepare this work. The librarian and staff at the Hebrew Union College–Jewish Institute of Religion in Cincinnati have always been most helpful; Abraham J. Peck, the administrative director of the American Jewish Archives and his associates have all rallied to assist me; this is true too of the Public Library of Cincinnati and Hamilton County; whenever I turned to the Cincinnati Historical Society the personnel were most gracious. The librarians at the American Jewish Historical Society in Waltham, Massachusetts, never failed to respond when I directed my inquiries to them. Let me hasten to thank those who have worked closely with me. Mrs. Etheljane Callner, my secretary for more than forty years, has been—as she always was—a tower of strength. Judith M. Daniels of the University of Cincinnati has labored with me to make *The Jew in the American World* a sound and accurate textbook. Rabbinical student Raymond Schklar has spent long hours bringing his technical computer skills to my aid. My beloved friend and disciple, Stanley F. Chyet, professor of American Jewish History on the Los Angeles campus of the Hebrew Union College–Jewish Institute of Religion, has vetted this work as he has all my writings for more than thirty years. I am grateful to Etheljane Callner, Judith M. Daniels, Raymond Schklar, and Stanley F. Chyet for their constant helpfulness. I do not delude myself; any work of substance owes much to a few who are distinguished by their courtesy, their learning, their high academic standards. All this I appreciate most keenly in these my years as a nonagenarian.

And, finally, there are the many who at some time or another have aided me in the preparation of this documentary but whom, for a variety of reasons, I am regretfully obliged to leave unnamed. My most heartfelt thanks to them all.

Jacob R. Marcus

American Jewish Archives
On the Campus of the Hebrew Union College–
Jewish Institute of Religion
Cincinnati, Ohio

Jacob Rader Marcus saw the manuscript of this book into production but did not live to see the final proofs or the index. I have performed those last services for him. He died on November 14, 1995, in his hundredth year. In his lifetime and largely because of his efforts American Jewish history was transformed from amateur apologetics into a professional discipline. Born in Pennsylvania and raised in West Virginia, he traveled to Germany for his professional historical training (Ph.D., University of Berlin, 1925). He not only wrote many volumes of American Jewish history, but also rescued many of the records of American Judaism and founded a place where they could be preserved and studied—the American Jewish Archives of Hebrew Union College. Appropriately this, his last work, gives to other scholars and the public many of the documents from which he worked.

His death leaves a very large empty space in the minds and hearts of his students and his friends. It was a privilege to assist him with his work during the last decade.

Judith M. Daniels
December 1995

PART I

The North American
Colonial Jew
1585–1775

Though individual Jews had been coming to North America since 1585 the first Jewish community was not established until 1654 when twenty-three refugees hailing from Brazil landed in Dutch New Amsterdam. By the time the Americans broke with the British in 1775 the Jews here had founded six communities of their own: Montreal, Newport, New York, Philadelphia, Charles Town (South Carolina), and Savannah. The synagog was the community; it held services, conducted a Hebrew school—with or without secular studies—made provision for the impoverished, and aided other Jewish communities both here and abroad. It even maintained strong ties with pious Jews in Palestine.

The handful of Spanish-Portuguese Jews here imposed their ritual on American Jewry, though by the 1720s the Ashkenazim—Central and East Europeans—were in the majority. Under the English the Jews acquired civil rights and were even granted a limited form of naturalization. The privileges they acquired only whetted their appetite for more; they wanted complete equality. Though most Gentiles here never fully foreswore their invisible baggage—their anti-Jewish prejudices—Jews got along well with their Christian neighbors.

In economic matters they were given free rein. Most of them were shopkeepers, even the artisans. Successful businessmen in the larger towns were merchant-shippers, protoindustrialists. They exported raw materials and imported consumer wares. The richer merchants engaged in the buying and selling of huge land tracts; some others manufactured candles, imported an occasional cargo of slaves, and served as army purveyors; one even participated in a large-scale whaling expedition. On the whole, American Jews were part of an extended middle class.

The Jews on this continent succeeded in transporting many of the values of the European Jewish community to America. Acculturation took place at a rapid rate. Despite their European origins they speedily became "Americans," developing also a Jewish culture that was distinctively their own. Social controls were weak; Judaism as a religion and as a way of life prospered through a policy of salutary neglect, yet these Jews were loyal to their people and their faith.

1

THE COMING OF THE JEWS TO
BRITISH AND DUTCH NORTH AMERICA
1585–1655

I n 1585, thirty-five years before the Pilgrims landed at Plymouth, Joachim Gaunse, a Bohemian Jew and mining expert, made his way down the gangplank at Roanoke Island; he was a member of Sir Walter Raleigh's first colonizing expedition. In 1581, Gaunse (Ganz) had been invited to Elizabethan England despite the fact that Jews had been expelled from the country at the close of the thirteenth century. He remained in North America, in "Virginia," until June 1586 when he returned to London with the other Roanoke settlers. Three years later he was arrested in Bristol for blasphemy, charged with denying that Jesus was the Son of God. The Bristol authorities dispatched the prisoner to the Privy Council in London. This is the last we hear of him; his fate is unknown.

Sixty years after Gaunse was arrested, Solomon Franco, a supercargo, walked the streets of Boston in a day when John Alden and Miles Standish were still alive; but one man, one Jew, cannot establish a community. In late August or early September 1654, twenty-three Jewish refugees landed in the town of Dutch New Amsterdam (a decade later English New York). If they had ten males over thirteen they may have constituted North America's first Jewish community. In all probability they had come from Dutch Brazil, which had just been reconquered by the Portuguese. They were not welcomed. On September 22, Peter Stuyvesant, the governor, dispatched a letter to the West India Company expressing the desire of the Dutch colonists to expel the newcomers. Fearing they might be driven out, the refugees asked their compatriots in Old Amsterdam (Holland) to intervene. The Amsterdam Jews turned to the board of the company requesting that its North American colony be opened to Jewish trade and settlement; the company acquiesced. Before the favorable decision of the company was reported in New Amsterdam, the Reverend Johannes Megapolensis, a local clergyman, wrote the governing board of the Dutch Reformed Church in Amsterdam, Holland, requesting that it use its influence to secure the expulsion of these "godless rascals." On April 26, 1655, the West India Company, answering Stuyvesant's letter of September 22, 1654, ordered him to let these Jews stay in Manhattan. This reluctant decision of the company members—bigots also—was influenced by their mercantilism. They needed settlers to manufacture raw materials and to buy consumer goods; profits were all important. The company was a commercial enterprise and not primarily a colonizer. Stuyvesant was unhappy with the members' decision. On October 30 of that year he wrote them somewhat curtly, saying that if they admitted Jews it would be difficult to exclude Lutherans and Catholics!

Selection I, parts A and B, are the affidavits testifying to Gaunse's "blasphemy"; selection II is Stuyvesant's letter urging his board to expel the Jews from New Amsterdam; and selection III is the "charter" of New Amsterdam Jewry. The Jewish community of Amsterdam, Holland, requested that the New Amsterdam Jews be accepted as permanent settlers; the West India board endorsed its petition (selection III). Selection IV is Dominie Megapolensis's appeal to his clerical colleagues in Amsterdam urging them to work for the expulsion of the refugees in New Amsterdam. Selection V is a letter of the board to Governor Stuyvesant instructing him to permit the Jews to remain, and the sixth and final selection is a brief comment of Stuyvesant expressing his misgivings if the Jewish newcomers are permitted to stay on.

I. Joachim Gaunse Denies
the Divinity of Jesus, September 12–16, 1589

A

On Fridaie, beinge the twelfthe daye of September 1589 I, Richard Curteys, mynister, came into the howse of Mr. Richard Mayes, inholder [innkeeper] in the cytie of Bristoll, where one Joachim Gaunze of Prage [Prague] vsed conference [talked] with me in the Hebrue tonge, at which tyme one of his companye, whose name I knowe not, enformed me that the said Joachim Gaunze was an infidell, for he holdeth that Christe Jesus is not the sonne of God. At which tyme of our secret speeche the said Joachim came into our companye unto whome I, the said Richard Curteys, spake in the Hebrue tounge to this effect: that Jesus of Nazareth, the kinge of the Jewes, whome the Jewes crucyfied was and is the sonne of God. At which tyme he answered me in the Hebrue tounge; he is not the sonne of God, whose replie beinge so odious I spake in the Englishe tonge to the ende that others, beinge there present, might heare it and witnes his speeche: What, do you denie Jesus Christ to be the sonne of God? At whiche tyme he awnswered: What needeth the almightie God to have a sonne, is he not almyghtie?

By me

Richard Curteys

Mynister

Enformed [reported] before the worshipfull Mr. maior & the justices of the citie of Bristoll, the xvth daie of September, 1589, vppon myne othe [oath], taken vppon the Holye Evangelye

B

Civistas [sic] Bristoll, Coram maiore et Ald'ri's xvi die Septembris Anno Rne Elizabethe xxxi 1589 [City of Bristol, before the mayor and aldermen, on the 16th day of September, in the 31st year of the reign of Queen Elizabeth, 1589]

Jeremye Pierce of the cytie of London, Joyner [carpenter], inhabitinge neere the Lorde Riches house in greate St. Barthomewes, informeth the saide mayor and aldermen, upon his othe [oath] taken upon the Holye Evangilistes of God, that he being in companye w'th Jeachim Gaunz, at the cytie of Bristoll, on Fryday last, being the xiith of this instante monethe, fallinge into communicac'on [discussion] of the Oulde Testam't and the Newe, this exam't [examinant] demaunded of the said Jeochim whether he did not beleeve in Jesus Christe, the Sonne of God? Whereunto the saide Jeochim aunswered that there was noe suche name, and that there was but one God, whoe had noe wife nor chielde.

Robert Kitchen, Mayor, et al. . . .

(Endorsed) The informac'ons [facts] againste the Jewe.

II. Peter Stuyvesant, Manhattan,
to the Amsterdam Chamber of Directors,
September 22, 1654

The Jews who have arrived would nearly all like to remain here, but learning that they (with their customary usury and deceitful trading with the Christians) were very repugnant to the inferior magistrates, as also to the people having the most affection for you; the Deaconry [which takes care of the poor] also fearing that owing to their present indigence [due to the fact that they had been captured and robbed by privateers or pirates] they might become a charge in the coming winter, we have, for the benefit of this weak and newly developing place and the land in general, deemed it useful to require them in a friendly way to depart; praying also most seriously in this connection, for ourselves as also for the general community of your worships, that the deceitful race—such hateful enemies and blasphemers of the name of Christ—be not allowed further to infect and trouble this new colony, to the detraction of your worships and the dissatisfaction of your worships' most affectionate subjects.

III. Amsterdam Jewry's Successful Intercession for the Manhattan Immigrants, January 1655

To the Honorable Lords,
Directors of the Chartered West India Company,
Chamber of the City of Amsterdam
     The merchants of the Portuguese nation [the Sephardic Jewish community] residing in this City [of Amsterdam] respectfully remonstrate to your

Granted [February 15, 1655] that they may reside and traffic, provided they shall not become a charge upon the Deaconry or the Company.

Honors that it has come to their knowledge that your Honors raise obstacles to the giving of permits or passports to the Portuguese [Sephardic] Jews to travel and to go to reside in New Netherland, which if persisted in will result to the great disadvantage of the Jewish nation. It can also be of no advantage to the general Company but rather damaging.

     There are many of the nation who have lost their possessions at Pernambuco and have arrived from there in great poverty, and part of them have been dispersed here and there. [Pernambuco, or Recife, the stronghold of Dutch Brazil, was captured by the Portuguese, January 1654.] So that your petitioners had to expend large sums of money for their necessaries of life, and through lack of opportunity all cannot remain here [in Holland] to live. And as they cannot go to Spain or Portugal because of the Inquisition, a great part of the aforesaid people must in time be obliged to depart for other territories of their High Mightinesses the States-General [the Dutch government] and their Companies, in order there, through their labor and efforts, to be able to exist under the protection of the administrators of your Honorable Directors, observing and obeying your Honors' orders and commands. [The West India Company owned the young Dutch colony of New Netherland.] It is well known to your Honors that the Jewish nation in Brazil have at all times been faithful and have striven to guard and maintain that place, risking for that purpose their possessions and their blood. [The Jews distinguished themselves in the defense of Pernambuco, remaining there until its fall in 1654.]

Yonder land [New Netherland] is extensive and spacious. The more loyal people that go to live there, the better it is in regard to the population of the country as in regard to the payment of various excises and taxes which may be imposed there, and in regard to the increase of trade, and also to the importation of all the necessaries that may be sent there.

Your Honors should also consider that the Honorable Lords, the Burgomasters of the City and the Honorable High Illustrious Mighty Lords, the States-General, have in political matters always protected and considered the Jewish nation as upon the same footing as all the inhabitants and burghers. Also it is conditioned in the treaty of perpetual peace with the King of Spain [the treaty of Muenster, 1648] that the Jewish nation shall also enjoy the same liberty as all other inhabitants of these lands.

Your Honors should also please consider that many of the Jewish nation are principal shareholders in the [West India] Company. They having always striven their best for the Company, and many of their nation have lost immense and great capital in its shares and obligations. [The Company lost heavily through the capture of Brazil by the Portuguese.]

The Company has by a general resolution consented that those who wish to populate the Colony shall enjoy certain districts of land gratis. Why should now certain subjects of this State not be allowed to travel thither and live there? The French consent that the Portuguese Jews may traffic and live in Martinique, [Saint] Christopher, and others of their territories, whither also some have gone from here, as your Honors know. The English also consent at the present time that the Portuguese and Jewish nation may go from London and settle at Barbados, whither also some have gone. [Martinique, Saint Christopher, and Barbados are in the West Indies.]

As foreign nations consent that the Jewish nation may go to live and trade in their territories, how can your Honors forbid the same and refuse transportation to this Portuguese nation who reside here and have been settled here well on to about sixty years, many also being born here and confirmed burghers, and this to a land that needs people for its increase? [Jewish "New Christians" from Portugal had settled in Holland as early as 1593.]

Therefore the petitioners request, for the reasons given above (as also others which they omit to avoid prolixity), that your Honors be pleased not to exclude but to grant the Jewish nation passage to and residence in that country; otherwise this would result in a great prejudice to their reputation. Also that by an Apostille [marginal notation] and Act the Jewish nation be permitted, together with other inhabitants, to travel, live, and traffic there, and with them enjoy liberty on condition of contributing like others. . . .

IV.   Rev. Johannes Megapolensis, New Amsterdam, to the Classis, the Governing Board of the Dutch Reformed Church, Amsterdam, Holland, March 18, 1655

... Last summer some Jews came here from Holland, in order to trade. Afterwards some Jews, poor and healthy, also came here on the same ship with D[omine Theodorus] Polheijmis. It would have been proper that these had been supported by their own nation, but they have been at our charge, so that we have had to spend several hundred guilders for their support. They came several times to my house, weeping and bewailing their misery, and when I directed them to the Jewish merchant [Jacob Barsimson?] they said that he would not lend them a single stiver. Now again in the spring some have come from Holland, and report that a great many of that lot would yet follow and then build here their synagogue. This causes among the congregation here a great deal of complaint and murmuring. These people have no other God than the unrighteous Mammon, and no other aim than to get possession of Christian property, and to win all other merchants by drawing all trade towards themselves. Therefore, we request your Reverences to obtain from the Lords Directors that these godless rascals, who are of no benefit to the country, but look at everything for their own profit, may be sent away from here. For, as we have here Papists, Mennonites and Lutherans among the Dutch; also many Puritans or Independents, and many Atheists and various other servants of Baal among the English under this Government, who conceal themselves under the name of Christians; it would create a still greater confusion, if the obstinate and immovable Jews came to settle here.

V.   The West India Company to Peter Stuyvesant, April 26, 1655

Honorable, Prudent, Pious, Dear, Faithful [Stuyvesant] ...

We would have liked to effectuate and fulfill your wishes and request that the new territories should no more be allowed to be infected by people of the Jewish nation, for we foresee therefrom the same difficulties which you fear. But after having further weighed and considered the matter, we observe that this would be somewhat unreasonable and unfair, especially because of the considerable loss sustained by this nation [the Jewish community], with others, in the [Portuguese re-]taking of Brazil, as also because of the large amount of capital which they still have invested in the shares of this company. Therefore after many deliberations we have finally decided and resolved to apostille [to note in the margin] upon a certain petition presented by said Portuguese Jews [January 1655] that these people may travel and trade to and in New Netherland and live and re-

main there, provided the poor among them shall not become a burden to the company or to the community [in the future poor Jews would not be supported by the Manhattan churches], but be supported by their own nation. You will now govern yourself accordingly.
[The Directors of the W[est]. I[ndia]. Co. Department of Amsterdam.]

VI.   Peter Stuyvesant, New Amsterdam, to the Board of the West India Company, Amsterdam [October 30, 1655]

To give liberty to the Jews will be very detrimental there, because the Christians there will not be able at the same time to do business. Giving them liberty, we cannot refuse the Lutherans and Papists.

2

POLITICAL RIGHTS AND
DISABILITIES UNDER THE ENGLISH
1669–1762

When the English conquered New Amsterdam in 1664 and re-named it New York they did not immediately abolish the disabilities that had been imposed on the Jews by the Dutch. Originally all thirteen English colonies denied Jews many rights. Still, in the course of time—by the turn of the century, 1700—Jews were allowed to hold religious services publicly, to sell at retail, and to practice crafts.

Many towns and provinces in British North America soon made Jews freemen or allowed them to vote. In a limited sense they were citizens. But no Jew in any of the fourteen colonies—which, after 1763, included Canada—could legally hold any honorific office. If a Jew chanced to hold office, it was probably because he had become a formal convert to Christianity or had not hesitated to take a Christian oath. Often Jews were chosen as constables but that was an onerous job, an unwelcome burden as a rule. In one respect Jews were better off than some Quakers and Baptists; they were not beaten and jailed.

In 1740, desirous of furthering trade and settlement in the colonies, Parliament enacted a law in mercantilist England making "naturalization" possible for foreign-born Protestants and for Jews residing in the overseas dependencies. No concessions were made to Catholics by the terms of this act. (A later attempt to extend the benefits of this law to Jews living in England itself failed.) The civic position of foreign-born Jews in the colonies was improved by this law, for they could now become citizens of a sort after seven years' residence in the colonies. (Native-born Jews were deemed Englishmen though of limited political rights.) This new citizenship meant that they had the right to trade anywhere in the British empire under the terms of the Navigation and Trade Acts. The enactment of 1740 constituted an improvement over the past, for colonial Jews, hitherto naturalized or denizened by colonial governors or colonial provincial legislatures, had not been automatically and as of right permitted to trade in the English possessions. As Article VI of the 1740 act makes clear, however, even under the terms of this new law, no Jew could hold office, serve in Parliament, or accept grants of land from the Crown.

Not many Jews sought naturalization in the American colonies. They were not impressed by the privileges granted, for they had managed to carry on trade successfully and own land without benefit of any formal recognition of their civic and political status. British America needed settlers too desperately to ignore them or to concern herself with legal proscriptions. Nonetheless, despite the obvious intent of Parliament's 1740 Plantation Act, Roger William's Rhode Island set out deliberately to deny Jews naturalization. A victim of this prejudice was Aaron Lopez (ca. 1731–1782), one of America's most notable merchant-shippers.

Jews were not to receive full political rights in America's thirteen colonies until the era of the Revolution. New York gave its Jews equality in 1777; the remaining twelve states emancipated their Jewish subjects slowly, even grudgingly.

Selection I was framed in large part by John Locke, the seventeenth-century English philosopher. It was never fully put into operation and was abrogated in 1693. Article XCVI was inserted over his protest and without his knowledge. Selection II is the Frame of Government granted by William Penn to Pennsylvania in 1682; selection III, the Charter of Massachusetts Bay, was authorized by William and Mary in 1691; selection IV, the act passed in 1740 by George II of England and Parliament, provided for the naturalization of settlers in the American colonies. The final selection, V, is a reprint of the 1762 decision of the Superior Court of Rhode Island denying naturalization to Aaron Lopez and Isaac Elizer, Jews, despite the explicit affirmative provisions of the 1740 parliamentary statute.

I.   The Fundamental Constitution of Carolina, 1669

Ninety-five. No man shall be permitted to be a freeman of Carolina, or to have any estate or habitation within it, that doth not acknowledge a God, and that God is publicly and solemnly to be worshipped.

Ninety-six. As the country comes to be sufficiently planted and distributed into fit divisions, it shall belong to the parliament to take care for the building of churches, and the public maintenance of divines, to be employed in the exercise of religion, according to the Church of England; which being the only true and orthodox, and the national religion of all the King's dominions, is so also of Carolina; and, therefore, it alone shall be allowed to receive public maintenance, by grant of parliament.

Ninety-seven. But since the natives of that place, who will be concerned in our plantation, are utterly strangers to Christianity, whose idolatry, ignorance, or mistake gives us no right to expel or use them ill; and those who remove from other parts to plant there will unavoidably be of different opinions concerning matters of religion, the liberty whereof they will expect to have allowed them, and it will not be reasonable for us, on this account, to keep them out, that civil peace may be maintained amidst diversity of opinions, and our agreement and compact with all men may be duly and faithfully observed; the violation whereof, upon what pretence soever, cannot be without great offence to Almighty God, and great scandal to the true religion which we profess; and also that Jews, heathens, and other dissenters from the purity of Christian religion may not be scared and kept at a distance from it, but, by having an opportunity of acquainting themselves with the truth and reasonableness of its doctrines, and the peaceableness and inoffensiveness of its professors, may, by good usage and persuasion, and all those convincing methods of gentleness and meekness, suitable to the rules and design of the gospel, be won ever to embrace and unfeignedly receive the truth; therefore, any seven or more persons agreeing in any religion, shall constitute a church or profession, to which they shall give some name, to distinguish it from others. . . .

One hundred. In the terms of communion of every church or profession, these following shall be three, without which no agreement or assembly of men, upon pretence of religion, shall be accounted a church or profession within these rules:

1st. That there is a God.

II. That God is publicly to be worshipped.

III. That it is lawful and the duty of every man, being thereunto called by those that govern, to bear witness to truth; and that every church or profession shall, in their terms of communion, set down the external way whereby they witness a truth as in the presence of God, whether it be by laying hands on or kissing the Bible, as in the Church of England, or by holding up the hand, or any other sensible way.

One hundred and one. No person above seventeen years of age shall have any benefit or protection of the law, or be capable of any place of profit or honor, who is not a member of some church or profession, having his name recorded in some one, and but one religious record at once.

One hundred and two. No person of any other church or profession shall disturb or molest any religious assembly. . . .

One hundred and six. No man shall use any reproachful, reviling, or abusive language against any religion of any church or profession, that being the certain way of disturbing the peace, and of hindering the conversion of any to the truth, by engaging them in quarrels and animosities, to the hatred of the professors and that profession which otherwise they might be brought to assent to. . . .

One hundred and nine. No person whatsoever shall disturb, molest, or persecute another for his speculative opinions in religion, or his way of worship.

II.   Frame of Government of Pennsylvania, 1682

XXXIV. That all treasurers, judges, masters of the rolls, sheriffs, justices of the peace, and other officers and persons whatsoever, relating to courts, or trials of causes, or any other service in the government, and all members elected to serve in provincial Council and General Assembly, and all that have right to elect such members, shall be such as possess faith in Jesus Christ, and that are not convicted of ill fame, or unsober and dishonest conversation, and that are of one and twenty years of age, at least, and that all such so qualified, shall be capable of the said several employments and privileges, as aforesaid.

XXXV. That all persons living in this province, who confess and acknowledge the one Almighty and eternal God, to be the creator, upholder and ruler of the world, and that hold themselves obliged in conscience to live peaceably and justly in civil society, shall, in no ways, be molested or prejudiced for their religious persuasion, or practice, in matters of faith and worship, nor shall they be compelled, at any time, to frequent or maintain any religious worship, place or ministry whatever.

III.   The Charter of Massachusetts Bay, 1691

Wee doe by these presents for us, our heires and successors, grant, establish, and ordaine that for ever hereafter there shall be a liberty of conscience allowed in the worshipp of God to all Christians (except Papists [Roman Catholics]) inhabiting or which shall inhabit or be resident within our said province or territory. . . .

IV.   The British Naturalization Act, 1740

An act for naturalizing such foreign Protestants, and others therein mentioned, as are settled or shall settle, in any of His Majesty's colonies in America (Anno 13 Geo. II, Cap. VII).

Whereas the increase of people is a means of advancing the wealth and strength of any nation or country;

And whereas many foreigners and strangers, from the lenity of our government, the purity of our religion, the benefit of our laws, the advantages of our trade, and the security of our property, might be induced to come and settle in some of His Majesty's colonies in America, if they were made partakers of the advantages and privileges which the natural born subjects of this realm do enjoy;

Be it therefore enacted by the King's Most Excellent Majesty, by and with the advice and consent of the Lords Spiritual and Temporal, and Commons, in this present Parliament assembled, and by the authority of the same, that from and after the first day of June, in the year of our Lord one thousand seven hundred and forty, all persons born out of the legiance of His Majesty, his heirs or successors, who have inhabited and resided, or shall inhabit or reside for the space of seven years or more, in any of His Majesty's colonies in America, and shall not have been absent out of some of the said colonies for a longer space than two months at any one time during the said seven years, and shall take and subscribe the oaths . . . shall be deemed, adjudged, and taken to be His Majesty's natural born subjects of this kingdom, to all intents, constructions, and purposes, as if they and every of them had been or were born within this kingdom. . . .

III. And whereas the following words are contained in the latter part of the oath of abjuration, *videlicet*, "upon the true faith of a Christian";

And whereas the people professing the Jewish religion may thereby be prevented from receiving the benefit of this act;

Be it further enacted by the authority aforesaid, that whenever any person professing the Jewish religion shall present himself to take the said oath of abjuration in pursuance of this act, the said words—"upon the true faith of a Christian"—shall be omitted out of the said oath in administering the same to such person, and the taking and subscribing the said oath by such person, professing the Jewish religion, without the words aforesaid . . . shall be deemed a sufficient taking of the said oaths, in order to intitle such person to the benefit of being naturalized by virtue of this act. . . .

VI. Provided always, and it is hereby further enacted, that no person who shall become a natural born subject of this kingdom by virtue of this act, shall be of the Privy Council, or a member of either house of Parliament, or capable of taking, having, or enjoying any office or place of trust within the kingdoms of Great Britain or Ireland, either civil or military, or of having, accepting, or taking any grant from the Crown to himself, or to any other in trust for him, of any lands, tenements or hereditaments within the kingdoms of Great Britain or Ireland, any thing hereinbefore contained to the contrary thereof in any wise notwithstanding.

V.   Why the Court Refused to Naturalize Aaron Lopez, Superior Court Rhode Island, Newport, SS. March Term, 1762

The petition of Messrs. Aaron Lopez and Isaac Elizer, persons professing the Jewish religion, praying that they may be naturalized on an act of Parliament made in the 13th year of His Majesty's reign George the Second, having been duly considered, and also the act of Parliament therein referred to, this court are unanimously of opinion that the said act of Parliament was wisely designed for increasing the number of inhabitants in the plantations, but this colony being already so full of people that many of his Majesty's good subjects born within the same have removed and settled in Nova Scotia and other places, [the petition] cannot come within the intention of the said act. [This act of 1740 permitted Jews in the colonies to be naturalized.]

Further, by the charter granted to this colony, it appears that the full and quiet enjoyment of the Christian religion and a desire of propagating the same were the principal views with which the colony was settled; and by a law made and passed in the year 1663, no person who does not profess the Christian religion can be admitted free of this colony. [This proviso is not found in the original charter of 1663, but was added about 1699.] This court therefore unanimously dismiss the said petition as absolutely inconsistent with the first principle upon which the colony was founded and [inconsistent with] a law now of the same in full force.

3

LIVING AS A JEW IN A CHRISTIAN COMMUNITY
1658–1760

On the whole, though Jews living in the British North American colonies were tolerated, Judaism certainly was not respected; the masses—with exceptions—tended to look askance at Jews because of their religion and its practices. In 1658 Jacob Lumbrozo (d. 1666), a Maryland Jew, was accused of having denied the divinity of Jesus—a capital crime under the terms of the 1649 Act Concerning Religion, the so-called Toleration Act. Lumbrozo, a native of Lisbon, was obviously a Marrano or New Christian; he very probably came from Holland where he left a sister. In Maryland, living as a Jew, he was a merchant, landowner, physician, and surgeon. On February 23, 1658, Lumbrozo was charged with "uttering words of blesphemy against our Blessed Saviour Jesus Christ." He was freed, though it is not known why he was not punished or executed. He may have enjoyed the benefits of a general amnesty issued in London. It is also possible that as a physician and surgeon his skills were valued in a frontier community. It is not improbable also that he may have secured his freedom by conversion, for later he was known only as John Lumbrozo. One thing is sure: Jews were not welcomed in Maryland; the very existence of the Act Concerning Religion was a threat even if its punitive terms were rarely enforced. An antiblasphemy law remained on Maryland's law books as late as the 1920s.

The good doctor was anything but a solid citizen. He was charged with attempting a rape, performing an abortion, and receiving stolen goods, but somehow survived these accusations. It must be born in mind constantly: seventeenth-century frontiersmen were not always of heroic stature.

The persecutions that Jews always experienced in Christian states in the past had convinced them that Christianity was an inferior religion. Marriage to a Gentile was dreaded, for the children were rarely reared as Jews. This was deemed a calamity; unity in the Jewish family was severely impaired. On the other hand, despite the fact that in colonial days Jews and Christians moved in different social circles, there were numerous exceptions; individuals, Jews and Christians, developed intimate friendships.

Selection I describes the arrest of Jacob Lumbrozo for blasphemy (1658); selection II, a letter, records the traumatic impact of an intermarriage on a New York Jewish mother (1743). The writer, Abigail Franks, was the wife of a prominent merchant and army purveyor. Abigail—a woman of culture—writing to her son Naphtali (Heartsey), then in London, told him that Phila, his sister, had eloped with Oliver DeLancey, a New York aristocrat. Selection III documents the friendship between a Jew and a non-Jew. Friendships frequently surmounted religious restraints. Manuel Josephson (d. 1796) was one of colonial America's few learned Jews; he was an excellent Hebraist and, apparently, interested in contemporary European literature to judge from the fact that he also owned a general library. An observant religionist, he served as president of Shearith Israel in New York and Mikveh Israel in Philadelphia. During the French and Indian War while working as a sutler at Fort Edward, he made the acquaintance of a young soldier, a Boston Gentile, John Maylem. They became fast friends. A biographer has referred to Maylem as "a poet of small talent and a warrior of little distinction." In this letter Maylem, still only twenty-one years of age, bared his soul to his friend and confidant.

I. Jacob Lumbrozo Denies the Divinity of Jesus, February 23, 1658

Att a Provinciall Court held att St. Marie's on Wednesday, this 23th Ffebruary, 1658 . . .

Was called afore the board Jacob Lumbrozo, and charged by his L[ordship]s attorney for uttering words of blesphemy ag[ain]st our Blessed Saviour Jesus Christ.

The depos[itio]n of John Ffossett, aged 44 yeares or thereabouts, sayth this 19th day of Ffebruary 1658:

Th[a]t about halfe a yeare since, this depon[en]t being att the howse of Mr. Richard Prestons, and there meeting w[i]th Jacob Lumbrozo, hee, this depon[en]t and the s[ai]d Lumbrozo falling into discourse concerning our B[lesse]d Saviour Christ, his resurrection, telling the s[ai]d Lumbrozo th[a]t hee was more then man, as did appeare by his resurrection; to w[hi]ch the s[ai]d Lumbrozo answered that his disciples stole him away.

Then this depon[en]t replyed th[a]t noe man ever did such miracles as hee; to w[hi]ch the s[ai]d Lumbrozo answered that such works might be done by negromancy, or sorcery, or words to th[a]t purpose. And this depon[en]t replyed to the s[ai]d Lumbrozo th[a]t hee supposed that the s[ai]d Lumbrozo tooke Christ to be a negromancer; to w[hi]ch the s[ai]d Lumbrozo answered nothing but laughed, and further this depon[en]t sayth not. . . .

I, Richard Preston, Jun[io]r, doe testify th[a]t about June or July last past, comming from Thomas Thomas, in company w[i]th Josias Cole and the Jew doctor, knowne by the name of Jacob Lumbrozo, the s[ai]d Josias Cole asked the s[ai]d Lumbrozo whether the Jewes did looke for a Messias? And the s[ai]d Lumbrozo answered yes. Then the s[ai]d Cole asked him what hee was that was crucifyed att Jerusalem? And the s[ai]d Lumbrozo answered, hee was a man. Then the s[ai]d Cole asked him how hee did doe all his miracles? And the s[ai]d Lumbrozo answered, hee did them by the art magick. Then the s[ai]d Cole asked him how his disciples did doe the same miracles after hee was crucifyed? And the s[ai]d Lumbrozo answered, hee taught them his art, and further sayth not. . . . [Deposition taken 21 February 1658 by Henry Coursey.]

The s[ai]d Lumbrozo sayth th[a]t hee had some talk w[i]th those persons and, willed by them to declare his opinion, and being by profession a Jew, he answered to some perticular demands then urged. And as to that of miracles done by art magick, he declared what remaines written concerning Moses and the magicians of Egipt, but saed not any thing scoffingly or in deroga[ti]on of him [whom] Christians acknowledge for their Messias.

It is ordered that the s[ai]d Lumbrozo remaine in the sheriff's custody untill hee putt in security body for body to make answere to what shall be layd to his charge, concerning those blasphemous words and speeches, att the next Provinciall Court, and th[a]t the persons be there present to testify viva voce in Court. . . .

II. The Dread of Intermarriage, June 7, 1743

Flatt bush, June 7th, 1743

Dear Heartsey:

My wishes for your felicity are as great as the joy I have to hear you are happily married. May the smiles of Providence waite allways on y'r inclinations and your dear [wife] Phila's whome I salute with tender affections, pray'g kind Heaven to be propitious to your wishes in makeing her a happy mother. I shall think the time teadious untill I shall have that happy information, for I don't expect to hear it by the return of these ships, and therefore must injoyn your care in writting by the first oppertunity (after the birth or wathever it shall please God to bless you with) either by via Carrolina, Barbadoz, or any other.

I am now retired from town and would from my self (if it where pos-siable to have some peace of mind) from the severe affliction I am under on the conduct of that unhappy girle [your sister Phila]. Good God, wath a shock it was when they acquainted me she had left the house and had bin married six months. I can hardly hold my pen whilst I am a writting it. Itt's wath I never could have imagined, especialy affter wath I heard her soe often say, that noe consideration in life should ever induce her to diso-blige such good parents.

I had heard the report of her goeing to be married to Oliver Delancey, but as such reports had offten bin off either of your sisters [Phila and Richa], I gave noe heed to it further than a generall caution of her conduct wich has allways bin unblemish'd, and is soe still in the eye of the Chris-tians whoe allow she had disobliged us but has in noe way bin dishonora-ble, being married to a man of worth and charector.

My spirits was for some time soe depresst that it was a pain to me to speak or see any one. I have over come it soe far as not to make my concern soe conspicuous but I shall never have that serenity nor peace within I have soe happyly had hittherto. My house has bin my prisson ever since. I had not heart enough to goe near the street door. It's a pain to me to think off goeing again to town [lower Manhattan] and if your father's buissness would premit him to live out of it I never would goe near it again. I wish it was in my power to leave this part of the world; I would come away in the first man of war that went to London.

Oliver has sent many times to beg leave to see me, but I never would tho' now he sent word that he will come here [to Flatbush]. I dread seeing him and how to avoid I know noe way, neither if he comes can I use him rudly. I may make him some reproaches but I know my self soe well that I shall at last be civill, tho' I never will give him leave to come to my house in town, and as for his wife, I am determined I never will see nor lett none of the family goe near her.

He intends to write to you and my brother Isaac [Levy] to endeavour a reconcilation. I would have you answer his letter, if you don't hers, for I must be soe ingenious to conffess nature is very strong and it would give me a great concern if she should live un happy, tho' it's a concern she does not meritt. . . .

Your affectionate mother,

Abigaill Franks. . . .

III.   Manuel Josephson Befriends
a New England Poet, October 15, 1760

My very good friend Mr. J-s-phs-n,

I take this opportunity to avow my gratitude to you and your wife, in a most sincere manner for the many favours receiv'd when reduc'd to the most contemptible state of indigence, and should tax myself with the highest injustice, was I deficient in making my acknowledgements.

That unlucky afternoon when I came home to your house with my senses totally absorb'd in liquor, prov'd one of the luckiest in my life. I awoke next morning in such a shocking condition, that to have any idea of my situation you must form a picturesque of the horrors of the damn'd. I got up, and without seeing any one, ran directly to Whitehall, embark'd in the ferry boat and in 2 days (solely on foot) arriv'd at Philadelphia, with all the horrors of indigence and poverty having but 2 coppers in my pocket, and ate nothing for 36 hours, and laying in the woods one night, I determin'd to put an end to my being, and striking farther into the woods, took out the shirt out of my pocket and fixing a noose in each sleeve, make [sic] a slip, hung one of the nooses on the remainder of a broken bough and stretching open the slip thrust my neck in and swung off, when, the cloth giving way, I came with a full sweep upon the ground, the shirt being rent fairly in two. I began then to reflect with all the horror of suicide and could scarcely help thinking it otherwise than an interposition of divine Providence. However, I made good use of it, refrain'd from all intemperance, alter'd my conduct and have since enjoy'd a tranquillity to which I have been a stranger this many years. My principles of religion, however, is not alter'd in regard to what they were, but yet allowing there was no such thing as futurity yet the pleasures of a temporal life by the 3 weeks experience I have had can make of earth a heav'n.

I went into the city, found several of my friends, embark'd for R.I. where I am now arriv'd, and shall settle immediately into some steady business.

Beg Mr. J-s-phs-n you will be kind enough to deliver Mr. Hawxhurst that favour of the bag wig which you was kind enough to present me—he will see it safely convey'd me—mine is all off my head—and I am (you know) little able to buy—the favour will be gratefully acknowledged among the already innumerable receiv'd by
Y'r very much oblig'd
John Maylem.

Hope your books prove right. Pray mention nothing to no one concerning that same hanging affair, you are (except myself) the only person in the world that knows it. Pray Mr. J-s-n send the wig.

Due respects to y'r spouse, Mr. J-d-h and his spouse. Mr. Hawxh— will send the wig by Cap'n Gibbs with my lac'd hat, which is a Taylors, an odd place to leave a hat, as bad as to leave a watch at a shoemakers.
Newport 15 Oct'r, 1760
vessel just going off

4

Culture and Acculturation
1722–1770

The typical Jewish artisan or shopkeeper in a North American town or village was not well educated. This was particularly true if he had been born abroad in Germany, Poland, or Russia. Settlers of Iberian birth or descent were more at home in matters literary. Children born in the British colonies were, as a rule, given a good grounding in the three R's, either in a Jewish all-day school or through tutors employed by their parents. Since many Jews were in business, some education was imperative. In every town of size there was always an individual or two who had a good library, and, even from our modern vantage point, may be deemed a person of considerable culture. Most male Jews, though they read Hebrew with a mechanical fluency, as a rule did not know the meaning of the words. They were in no sense academicians; they learned to read the Hebrew alphabet because the entire religious service was in Hebrew (and some Aramaic). Those who were adept in the classical tongue were, occasionally, employed as teachers by Christians. The American Jew did not go to college; an academic degree buttered no parsnips. A diploma would not help Jews make a living, admit them to the civil service, or permit them to practice law; officers of the king had to take a Christian oath. Medicine in colonial days was not a lucrative field; therefore very few Jews became practitioners.

New England pietists loved Hebrew but not Hebrews. That may explain why no synagog was established in Boston until almost 200 years after the first Jew walked the streets of the city. Hebrew, however, was God's tongue, the language of what Christians called the Old Testament, especially of the Psalms. A century after Harvard was founded Hebrew was still a required subject. Hebraists were respected and sought after even

45

if they were Jews. Thus in 1720, when Judah Monis, an Italian Jew, appeared with the manuscript of a Hebrew grammar, Harvard gave him an honorary Master of Arts degree. Two years later, after his conversion to Christianity, he was appointed to the faculty as instructor of the Hebrew tongue. Monis remained an observant Christian but did insist on celebrating the seventh day of the week as the Sabbath—not Sunday the first day —for God himself had rested on that day from the labors of creation. In the following letter—selection I—Monis accepts the appointment to teach but asks for a living salary. He certainly recalled that his ancestor, the Patriarch Jacob, had stipulated with God that he receive bread to eat and a garment to wear.

How long does it take to acculturate a European immigrant who lands on American soil? As we know, the process was often a very speedy one. The following account—selection II—by Peter Kalm, a Swedish subject who visited the colonies in the mid-eighteenth century, proves that the newcomers and their children were often quick to adapt themselves to the Gentile way of life (1748). Kalm was somewhat surprised; back in Sweden Jews were few and barely tolerated. They were not given equal political rights until 1951.

In 1769, Moses Lindo of Charles Town, South Carolina, an indigo exporter, met the Reverend Hezekiah Smith who was raising money for Rhode Island College—later to be called Brown University. Lindo contributed liberally to the new school because the institution welcomed Jewish students; they would be subject to no disabilities because of their Jewish religion (selection III). In 1771 the trustees and fellows of the college informed Lindo that they would provide a Jewish tutor if the number of students justified it, and, if the Jews so desired, they could establish their own chair of Hebrew. Nothing came of this proposal. In 1928, 157 years later, the president of Brown University refused to allow Jewish fraternities on campus although the existing fraternities would admit no Jews. American Jewry protested and the university trustees backed down. Poor Roger Williams!

I. Harvard Honors and Appoints
Its First Jewish Member of the Faculty, May 22, 1722

Cambridge, May 22th, A.D., 1722

To the Rev[eren]'d President and the Other Rev'ds,
Members of the Corporation of Harvard College.
Rever'nd Gentlemen:
    I have been inform'd of the honour you have put upon me in chusing me to be a teacher of the Hebrew language in your College. The respect

you have shown to me in this choice I heartily and thankfully acknowledge, and I hope you will interpret these lines as testimonies of my gratitude. Tho' I believe I could betake myselfe to such secular business as by
ordinary blessing of Providence would promote my worldly interest and
estate more than w[ha]'t I can expect by instructing youth in the Hebrew,
yet I finde my selfe steadily inclined and willing to spend my time (if Providence favour the design) in giving the best instruction I can in the aforesaid language to all such members of the College as shall be desirous to
learn of me.

I think the more acquainted the ministers of the gospel are w'th the
Hebrew tongue, and so w'th the Old Testament, the better able they will
be to understand the New Testament and so preach our glorious *Lord Jesus
Christ* who was ever spoken of by all the Old Testament prophets.

But however necessary I may apprehend the knowledge of the Hebrew language to be, and however willing and disposed I may be to teach
it, yet rev'd gentlemen, I hope you will give me leave to say that the salary
you have voted as an incouragement or reward for my labour is not sufficient to support me. It is not sufficient to support me in my single state,
much less if I should enter into a married state (w'ch I have some hope of
doing). If I should speedily enter on the service you have chosen me to,
[the] necessary furniture for a chamber in College can't cost me much less
than thirty-five pounds. But if I had such furniture by me already (w'ch
certainly I have not), yet the salary you have voted would not suffice to
support me thro' the year.

I hope, gentlemen, you will candidly interpret this representation of
my case, and if you continue to desire my being an instructor in the Hebrew in the College, I hope you will please to think of some methods
wherby a proper support and maintainance may be afforded to me, and I
shall count my selfe greatly oblig'd if you will let me know your minds in
this matter as soon as you conveniently can.

I am, rev'nd gentlemen, w'th great gratitude and respect,
One of your humble servants,
Judah Monis.

II.   The Jews of New York City, November 2, 1748

November the 2d. Besides the different sects of Christians, there are
many Jews settled in New York, who possess great privileges. They have a
synagogue and houses, and great country-seats of their own property, and
are allowed to keep shops in town. They have likewise several ships,
which they freight and send out with their own goods. In fine, they
enjoy all the privileges common to the other inhabitants of this town and
province.

During my residence at New York, this time, and in the next two years, I was frequently in company with Jews. I was informed, among other things, that these people never boiled any meat for themselves on Saturday, but that they always did it the day before; and that in winter they kept a fire [going continuously] during the whole Saturday [for kindling fire anew on the Sabbath is prohibited by Jewish law]. They commonly eat no pork; yet I have been told by several men of credit, that many of them (especially among the young Jews), when traveling, did not make the least difficulty about eating this, or any other meat that was put before them; even though they were in company with Christians.

I was in their synagogue last evening for the first time, and this day at noon I visited it again, and each time I was put into a particular seat, which was set apart for strangers or Christians. [This synagogue, Shearith Israel, was then on Mill (South William) Street.] A young rabbi [Benjamin Pereira] read the divine service, which was partly in Hebrew, and partly in the rabbinical dialect [Aramaic]. Both men and women were dressed entirely in the English fashion; the former had all of them their hats on, and did not once take them off during service. The galleries, I observed, were appropriated to the ladies, while the men sat below. During prayers, the men spread a white cloth [the praying shawl, the talit] over their heads, which perhaps is to represent sackcloth. But I observed that the wealthier sort of people had a much richer sort of cloth than the poorer ones. Many of the men had Hebrew books, in which they sang and read alternately. The rabbi stood in the middle of the synagogue, and read with his face turned towards the east; he spoke, however, so fast, as to make it almost impossible for any one to understand what he said.

III.   Rhode Island College Welcomes Jewish Students,
April 17, 1770

Charlestown, 17 April, 1770

Mess'rs Sampson & Solomon Simson,
Gentlemen:
       You will be so kind as to order your correspondent in Rhode Island to pay unto the trustees of the new college the sum of five pounds York currency on my account, and to transmit me th'ir receipt in my name.
       As the Rev'd Mr. Smith will inform th'm, the reason th't induces me to be a benefactor to this college is th'ir having no objection of admitting the youth of our nation without interfereing in principals of religion. If so, my donation shall exceed beyond the bounds of th'ir imagination.
       I presume the college is like Merchant Taylor's School in London where I went every day for three years, as well as two of my brothers, from

9:00 to 1:00 o'clock. There was at th't time about 800 boys, sons of the principal merchants and trading people in the city. I have lived to see two Lord Mayors and seven aldermen, and many toping [excellent] merchants my school-fellows, which, I assure you, was no small service to me when I was a broker on the Royal Exchange.

I have sent yo' by the bearer two of our gazettes wherein I believe there is more news from London than at y'r place.

I sincerely wish you well, and remain, with regard, gentlemen,
Your obliged humble serv't,
Moses Lindo.

5

How They Made a Living
1754–1763

With very few exceptions the colonial Jews under the British were engaged in commerce. Even the artisans were businessmen; they made something to sell. They were a nation of shopkeepers. A few may have farmed or owned cattle that grazed in the fields and woods, but that was always a sideline. A handful peddled . . . till they opened a tiny shop. Some were privateers; that was a speculation; others bought and sold land; some were merchants or merchant-shippers. In the 1760s, some Jews of means joined a cartel and manufactured candles made of whale oil; the Rhode Islander Aaron Lopez, the most enterprising of the lot, helped organize a huge whaling expedition to South American waters and the Falkland Islands in search of raw material for his candle factory (1775).

Six selections are printed here; they reflect the diverse interests typical of the North American Jewish businessman during this period. The first selection is a reprint of advertisements of two Boston tobacconists, a Jew and a non-Jew. They were business rivals and, apparently, enjoyed vilifying each other. Selection II is an indenture whereby a metal refiner, Isaac Moses, became a covenant servant. It was his good fortune to be redeemed from what was actually a form of "slavery" by a Jew, Mordecai Sheftall of Savannah. Isaac Moses signed his indenture in May 1758. That very year Barnard (Issachar Ber) Gratz wrote a Yiddish letter (selection III) to his teenage brother Michael (Yehiel), who was preparing to come to Pennsylvania after a brief excursion that took him to India. The Gratz brothers, as B. and M. Gratz, would one day become a respected Philadelphia mercantile firm. In 1760 the Savannah shopkeeper, Isaac Delyon (De Leon) sent an order for goods (selection IV) to his wholesaler Barnard Gratz. Delyon was trading rice and hides for groceries. The English of this Savannah merchant left something to be desired although he was probably a native American. In 1762 Isaac Elizer and Samuel Moses of Newport sent a ship to pick up a cargo of slaves in Africa (selection V). Not many Jews were in this business; the capital required was huge. They had no scruples in buying and selling slaves; blacks were a commodity. There were to be no Jewish abolitionists till the second quarter of the nineteenth century. Not many Jews went West to trade with the Indians and buy furs. Mr. Abram (Abraham, Abrahams, Abrams) Chapman (Chapman Abraham) was an exception. He was a Canadian Jew who was working out of Detroit in 1763 when he was captured during Pontiac's Rebellion. According to the following account he barely escaped being burnt at the stake. Another version informs us that he was exchanged for a Pottawatomi chieftain (selection VI).

I. Rival Boston Tobacconists, a Jew and a Gentile, Trade Verbal Blows, October 21, 29; November 5, 1754

Whereas Emanuel Abrams, a Jew, has of late had the notorious impudence to go thro' the town imposing on the inhabitants, to the disadvantage of all honest traders and sellers of snuff, a certain kind of trash of his own making; which in order to make it sell quick, he is pleased to give in the name of Kippen's. And as he has had the front to say he bought it of me, the subscriber, I would therefore inform the publick that I never sold that person snuff of any kind to my knowledge, nor so much as know such a fellow existing.
Allan Melville.

N.B. This may also serve to inform the above-named snuff merchant, that if he does not leave off his villainous practice of fathering of his musty trash upon me, I will certainly make it turn out the dearest snuff that ever he bought.
Boston, October 21, 1754.

Whereas Mr. Allan Melville, merchant, has made free with my character in last Tuesday's paper; and I value my credit and reputation, equal as he himself, or any other gentleman; therefore notify the publick that said advertisement is without foundation, and as I always treated my customers with the utmost civility and the best of goods, hope they'll continue their favours, and shall always be as ready to receive their command.
Ema. Abrahams.

N.B. As Mr. Melville is pleased to give my goods the character of trash and musty trash, with an intent to hurt the sale of my goods, this may serve to acquaint him, as also the publick, I have as good snuff as he, or any imported, and customers may have samples on trial.

E. A.

II.   Isaac Moses Becomes
an Indentured Servant, May 19, 1758

This indenture, made the nineteenth day of May, in the thirty-first year of the reign of our Sovereign Lord, George the Second, King of Great-Britain, etc., and in the year of our Lord, one thousand seven hundred and fifty eight, between Isaac Moses of Hanover, gold and silver refiner of the one part, and Edward Somerville of London, merchant of the other part, witnesseth:

That the said Isaac Moses, for the consideration herein after-mentioned, hath, and by these presents doth covenant, grant, and agree with [the said] Edward Somerville, [his executors or] assigns, that he, the said Isaac Moses, shall and will, as a faithful covenant servant, well and truly serve the said Edward Somerville, his executors or assigns, in the plantation of Georgia beyond the seas, for the space of three years next ensuing his arrival in the said plantation, in the employment of a gold and silver refiner.

And the said Isaac Moses doth hereby covenant and declare himself now to be the age of thirty years, a single person, and no covenant or contracted servant to any other person or persons.

And the said Edward Somerville, for himself, his executors or assigns, in consideration thereof, doth hereby covenant, promise, and agree to and with the said Isaac Moses, his executors and assigns, that he, the said Edward Somerville, his executors or assigns, shall and will, at his or their own proper costs and charges, with what convenient speed they may, carry and convey, or cause to be carried and conveyed, over unto the said plantation, the said Isaac Moses, and from henceforth, and during the said voyage, and also during the said term, shall and will, at the like costs and charges, provide for and allow the said Isaac Moses [all?] necessary cloaths, meat, drink, washing, lodging [meet?] and convenient for him as covenant servants in such cases are [provided?] for and allowed.

And [for himself?] the said Edward Somerville [doth promise?] and agree that, provided the said Isaac Moses pays him [or his assigns?] for his voyage within one month after his arrival in Georgia aforesaid, then this indenture to be void, or else to remain in full force.

And for the true performance of the premises, the said parties to these presents bind themselves, their executors and administrators, the either to the other, in the penal sum of twenty pounds sterling, firmly by the[se] presents.

In witness whereof, they have hereunto interchangeably set their hands and seals, the day and year above-written.

Isaac Moses.

Sealed and delivered in the presence of Thos. Hayes. . . . [The following receipt appears on the back of the document.]

Received of Mr. Mordecay Sheftall the sum of eight pound eight s[h]ill[ings] in full for the within mentioned Isack Moses' servitude. Savannah, December 11, 1758.

Edward Somerville.

III. Barnard Gratz Writes to Brother Michael Who Was about to Come to America, November 20, 1758

[Philadelphia, November 20, 1758].

Greetings to my dearly beloved brother who is as dear to me as my own life, the young man, Yehiel—long may he live—that princely, scholarly, and incomparable person:

I report that I am in good health, and I hope you are too.

I learn, dear brother, from the letter of our relative Solomon [Henry] to our relative Koppel [Jacob Henry] that you have returned from India. I am very much surprised, but I cannot say much because I do not know the reason [for your return].

Only if you are satisfied to live in the country and keep a shop—if you are at all able to do that—or to live with my employer, Mr. David Franks, would I advise you to come here in the spring by the first boat. But you must agree to follow our advice while you are here. In that case I hope everything will turn out satisfactorily to you. My plan would be that you come here and stay with my employer two or three years until you learn the business. Meanwhile you will get the same wages that I got.

[In that case] You might turn your money over to Mr. Moses Franks and take an order on Mr. David Franks [his brother], to be paid here when you arrive. I think this would be better than keeping a shop in the country. Mr. David Franks is a very good man, and you will be able to make some money with your capital here. Otherwise, "do as is good in thine own eyes," do what you want, but do let me know through someone what you have in mind. And don't be too proud. From me,

Your brother,

Issachar Ber[Barnard].

Remember me to everybody in our family.

P.S. Dear brother, if you intend to come here and live with Mr. Franks, you should not bring with you any merchandise whatsoever. You will be able to earn more with your money here. Will you please, therefore, do me the favor of paying our relative Solomon [Henry] nineteen pounds, i.e. £ 19 ster. on my account. When you arrive, I shall return the sum at once. The rest you ought to give to Moses Franks, and have him issue an order on Mr. David Franks here. Come over by the first boat, as I have already spoken to my employer about you, and he will wait for you until the month of Nisan or Iyyar [April/May]. However, you may do as you please.

I have just reconsidered the matter with our relative Jacob. If you have some money, you might bring with you about eighteen or twenty silver watches, worth from forty-five to fifty-five dinars [shillings?] a piece, some new-fashioned watchchains, about twenty dozen of women's shoes made of calamanco and worsted damask of all colors, a few dozen of women's mittens of black worsted, and a few other articles. In this case you can invest your money [in these articles] and not turn it over to Moses Franks. You might ask him what he thinks you ought to bring here, if you have more money than you need for the articles mentioned above. Let them be insured.

IV.   Isaac Delyon of Savannah
Ships Barnard Gratz of Philadelphia
Rice and Hides in Exchange for Groceries,
September 24, 1760

Savannah, 24 Sept., 1760.

To Mr. Barned Gratz,
Marchant in Philadelphia.
Mr. Gratz,
Sir:

By Capt. Joseph Howard I have inclosed you an invoiice of sundry [goods] shiped you on my one [own] account; four barrels rice; four bundles of drear [deer] skins, one hundread dressed ones, fifteen onery [ordinary], six in the heir [undressed], which [you] will be good enuph to seal [sell] them to the best advantage. Please to seal them so that I may git the remittence by this schooner, because I don't know when the[re] will be a nother opertunity. Even if you should be oblige to seal them something cheepor than the common rate, I should be glad if you would send me an account of the seals [sales] of which I have shiped you in all.

I should be glad if you have received the money of what you sould for me. If you have, you will be good enuph to remit it by this.

You rote me by Capt. Nezbet to let you know if starch seals heir [here]. It is now from 30s. to 40s [shillings].

Pleas to send me the following artcles. You will mutch oblige me if you do send theme this time, becaus it will be mutch to my advantage. Pleas to inshure what you send. From
Your most humble servant,
Isaac Delyon

> 25 lb. chokolet
> 1 barrel linced [linseed] oil
> 1 doz best black grane [grain] calf skins
> 9 barrels makarels
> 1 ditto herrings
> 150 lb. gingerbread
> 2 barrels cranberys
> 10 barrels of apples

If there is any thing remaing, pleasd to send it in milk and butter bread if the wether is not low. Could send me 15 barrels ables [apples], but do let them be the last you put on board, for fear of the frost.

V.   Isaac Elizer and Samuel Moses of Newport Dispatch a Ship to Africa for a Cargo of Slaves, October 29, 1762

Newport, Octo'r 29, 1762.

Captain John Peck:

As you are at present master of the sloop "Prince George" with her cargo on board and ready to sale, you are to observe the following orders:

That you imbrace the first fair wind and proceed to sea and make the best of your way to the windward part of the coast of Africa, and at your arrival there dispose of your cargo for the most possible can be gotten, and invest the neat proceeds into as many good merchantable young slaves as you can, and make all the dispatch you possibly can.

As soon as your business there is compleated, make the best of your way from thence to the island of New Providence [Bahamas] and there dispose of your slaves for cash, if the markets are not too dull. But if they should [be], make the best of your way home to this port, takes pilates and make proper protest [before the authorities as to the state of your cargo of vessel] where ever you find it necessary. You are further to observe that all the rum on board your sloop shall come upon an average in case of any misfortune, and also all the slaves in general shall come upon an average in case any casualty or misfortune happens, and that no slaves shall be brought upon freight for any person, neither direct nor indirect.

And also we allow you for your commission, four slaves upon the purchase of one hundred and four, and the privilege of bringing home three slaves, and your mate, one.

Observe not neglect writing us by all opportunitys of every transaction of your voyage. Lastly be particular carefull of your vessell and slaves, and be as frugal as possible in every expense relating to the voyage. So wish you a good voyage, and are your owners and humble servants.

But further observe, if you dispose of your slaves in Providence [Bahamas], lay out as much of your neat proceeds as will load your vessel in any commodity of that island, that will be best for our advantage, and the remainder of your effects bring home in money.
Isaac Elizer,
Samuel Moses.

VI. Abraham Chapman [Chapman Abraham] Escapes Being Burnt at the Stake in Pontiac's Rebellion, 1763

About the commencement of the Indian war in 1763, a trading Jew, named Chapman, who was going up the Detroit river with a batteau-load of goods which he had brought from Albany, was taken by some Indians of the Chippeway nation, and destined to be put to death. A Frenchman impelled by motives of friendship and humanity, found means to steal the prisoner, and kept him so concealed for some time, that although the most diligent search was made, the place of his confinement could not be discovered. At last, however, the unfortunate man was betrayed by some false friend, and again fell into the power of the Indians who took him across the river to be burned and tortured. Tied to the stake and the fire burning by his side, his thirst from the great heat, became intolerable, and he begged that some drink might be given to him. It is a custom with the Indians, previous to a prisoner being put to death, to give him what they call his last meal; a bowl of pottage or broth was therefore brought to him for that purpose. Eager to quench his thirst, he put the bowl immediately to his lips, and the liquor being very hot, he was dreadfully scalded. Being a man of very quick temper, the moment he felt his mouth burned, he threw the bowl with its contents full in the face of the man who handed it to him. "He is mad! He is mad!" resounded from all quarters. The bystanders considered his conduct as an act of insanity, and immediately untied the cords with which he was bound, and let him go where he pleased.

This fact was well known to all the inhabitants of Detroit from whom I first heard it, and it was afterwards confirmed to me by Mr. Chapman himself, who was established as a merchant at that place.

6

THE COLONIAL JEWISH COMMUNITY
1728 TO CA. 1770

During the colonial Jewish period, 1654–1775, the synagog was the community. It was simple and uncomplicated. There was but one organization in town, the synagog; its officiants were the community officers. (New York's Shearith Israel may have appointed a committee—a hevrah—to care for the sick and bury the dead.) Up to 1775 there were but six congregations in all of British North America: Montreal, Newport, New York, Philadelphia, Charleston, and Savannah. They were all small and weak, struggling to survive; there were periods—sometimes decades—when there were no services, no requisite quorum of ten males. On the frontier, communities rose, died, and rose again.

New York City's Shearith Israel, the Remnant of Israel, is the oldest congregation on the North American mainland. Religious services were held in New Amsterdam in the 1650s, although by the time the English conquered New Netherland there was no religious quorum in the newly named town of New York. We do not know exactly when Shearith Israel —the Spanish-Portuguese synagog—was established. It is not improbable that the religious community had one or more constitutions—or congregations—before 1706, but they have not survived. Selection I is an amended form of the rules adopted in 1706. In 1728, when Shearith Israel began to expand, its leaders wrote a new set of rules and raised money to build a sanctuary on Mill Street. The synagogal officers, a self-perpetuating board of three, supervised all phases of the religious, charitable, and Jewish educational life of local Jewry. Ultimately the first-class members, the *yehidim*, controlled the administration; after a fashion, therefore, there was democracy. Shearith Israel had three salaried functionaries: a hazzan or minister, a ritual slaughterer, called a shohet or *bodeck*, and the shammash, or beadle (selections IIIA–C). The *hatanim*—the *hatan torah* and the *hatan bereshit*—the "bridegroom of the Law" and the "bridegroom of Genesis"—were officers who were given the honor of closing and beginning the annual cycle of Pentateuchal readings. Inasmuch as voluntary offerings were not sufficient to support the community, additional funds were raised by pew rentals. As early as the 1720s the majority of the Jews who attended services were Central and East Europeans, Ashkenazim; the community, however, was dominated by Jews of Spanish-Portuguese—that is Sephardic—origin; the differences between these two elements may explain the dissension that seems to have been present and is alluded to in the third article of selection I.

There were few if any Jewish social controls in the hinterland in colonial days. Frequently there was never more than a family or two in a town or a village. Assimilation, de-Judaization, was rapid. Shearith Israel, the mother congregation for the New England and the mid-Atlantic provinces, was disturbed by the report that Jews were ignoring basic religious customs and laws. Thus it was that on the eve of the Day of Atonement, 1757, when the villagers flocked to town for the High Holy Days, the leaders of the New York congregation publicly admonished those Jews who were flouting Jewish practices (selection II).

Philadelphia Jews first met for religious services no later than the 1740s. They had a cemetery as early as 1738, but it was probably around the year 1770 that the attempt was made to organize formally. Selection IV may have been a draft constitution. At that time the prime concern of the founders was the resolution of personal hostilities; enemies did not want to be seated near one another. Since most of the members were born in Central and Eastern Europe this draft was written in a German Yiddish; the ritual adopted was very probably Sephardic, the standard then in all American synagogs. By 1776 the congregation had hired a religious factotum; by 1782, a reconstituted society made its appearance; it called itself Mikveh Israel, the Hope of Israel.

I. The Oldest Extant Constitution of a North American Jewish Community, September 15, 1728

In the Name of the Blessed God, Amen [In Hebrew]

Whereas, on or about the year 5466 [1706], certain wholesome rules and restrictions have been made by the then elders of our holy congregation, to preserve peace, tranquility, and good government amongst th'm, and those after them; and as they have been neglected to be put in due force for some time past, wee now meet with common consent and resolve to revive the same with some amendments and additions, which are as follows:

F[irs]tly There shall be elected a parnaz [president] and two *hatanim* [officers], w'ch shall like wise serve as assistants [board members] for the good government of our holy congregation, and in order to w'ch we have now, this year of 5489 [1728–29] elected Mr. Mosses Gomez for parnaz, to whom we gave power that he might elect two *hatanims* and as assistants for this present year. And accordingly, he did elect Mr. Daniel Gomez for *hatan torah* and first assistant, and Mr. Binj[ami]n Mendez Pacheco as *hatan bereshit* and second assistant, and for the future, the parnaz and his assistants, then in being, has power to chuse another parnaz and assistants in their roome yearly.

2ndly We give authority to the gent'[le]m[en] that shall be elected yearly, as is customary in the Jewish congregations, that with the fear of God they may act as their conscience shall dictate [to] them for the well governing of our said congregation.

3dly If any person or persons whatsoever shall offer to give any affront or abuse, either by words or action to any person or persons within the said sinagog, he or they so offending shall be obliged to pay to the parnaz, then in being, the sum of twenty shillings, if it be adjudged by the said parnaz and assistants that he or they have offended, which money shall be applyd for the use of the sinagog. And if refus'd to pay the said fine, the whole congregation shall assist the said parnaz and assistants to recover the same.

4thly Whoever shall be elected parnaz and refuse to serve shall pay the sum of three pounds. Alsoe those *hatanims* that shall be elected and refuse to act in the s'd post shall pay a fine of foarty shillings, each one [of] which sums shall be apply'd as in the 3d article is specified.

5thly In case any disputes may arise so that the parnaz and his assistants cannot agree, an indifferent [impartial] person whom they shall chuse shall decide the difference between them.

6thly No unmarried man shall be elected parnaz, nor a married man before he has served eitheir for *hatan torah* or *hatan bereshith*.

7thly If any poor person should happen to come to this place and should want the assistance of the sinagog, the parnaz is hereby impowerd to allow every poor person for his maintainance the sum of eight shillings p'r week, and no more, not exceeding the term of twelve weeks. And the parnaz is also to use his utmost endeavours to despatch them to sum othere place as soon as possible, assisting them with necessarys for their voyage, that is, for a single person fourty shillings. But if it be a family, then the parnaz shall call his assistance [assistants] and consult with them, both for their maintainance whilst ashore and also for their necessarys when they depart. Those poor of this congregation that shall apply for *sedaca* [charity] shall be assisted with as much as the parnaz and his assistants shall think fitt.

8thly The offerings [donations] shall be gather'd every three months by the parnaz. As likewise, it not being convenient the selling of misvots [religious honors], it's resolved for the future that in lieu thereof the parnaz w'th his assistants shall tax the men's seats in the sinagog, as they are now seated, but not exceeding fifteen shillings each seat p'r annum, nor less than five shillings. And the misvots shall be given out by the parnaz as the whole year.

9thly We, now prezent, and those that shall hereafter be admitted as yechidims [first-class members] into this congregation, do and shall submit to the foregoing articles.

10thly The parnaz shall be obligded twice a year to cause these articles to be read in the sinagog both in Portugues and English. Sign'd. In New Yorck in the *Kl Ks* [*Kahal Kodesh* or Holy Congregation] of Sheerit Israell, the 12 of Tisry a. [in the year] 5489 [September 15, 1728].

Here fallows the articles for the officers, vizt.:

And that the officers of this holly congregation may not at any time pretend ygnorance of what is at their charge to observe, we have with concorde [resolved] *that*

1stly The hazan [minister], Mosses Lopez de Fonseca, shall be obligded to atend at the sinagog at the custumary hours twice every week day, and three times on the Sabath and feasts, to preform prayers, and what more belongs to his function, as is custumary in othere congregation[s] and that he also, in case the *bodeck* [slaughter inspector] be indispos'd, shall assist in his room, for the which he shall have his selary of fifety pounds and six cords of wallnut wood [for fuel] per annum, also Passover cakes [matzos] for his family, all which shall be payd him out of the *tsedaca* [treasury].

2ndly That Benjamin Elias shall have twinty pounds salary per annum, in concideration of his haven [having] served as *bodeck*, and his age and circumstance requiring assistance. And we give authority unto the parnaz that he may receive such sums w'ch divers persons perticulerly have subscrive for that perpose. He shall also have two cords of wood and passover cakes.

3dly That Semuel Bar Meyr [H]aCohen, *bodeck* of this *kahall* [congregation], shall be obligded to kill at severall places [for different butchers], and sufficiently for the whole congregation, and that every six months he shall submit to be exameend in the dinimz [ritual laws] by the hazen and any other *bodeck* said hazan shall choose, for which he shall have twenty pounds salary per annum.

4thly That Valentin Campanall *shamaz* [beadle], shall be obligded to atend at the sinagog and shall call the yechidimz that they may assemble togeathere at the usuall hours; and he likewise be obligded to call to *selichot* [penitential prayers] such persons as shall be given him by the parnaz in [a] list. That he shall keep the synagog candlesticks and lamp clean, and make the candles; also shall keep the sestern [cistern, for washing hands] supplyed with watter, for which he shall have sixteen pound[s], two cords of wood, and masot [matzos] p'r annum.

5thly If any whatsoever of the officers, above said, shall neglect in not doeing what he ought, and what is aforesaid, the parnaz and his assistants have power to fine him or them in the sum they shall judge fitt, not exceeding three pounds, and in case the offence shall be great, the parnaz and assistants shall not discharge any of said officers out of their place without first call'g all the yechidimz for to give their vote, and the major part shall carry it, the parnaz haveing two votes.

6thly That the afores'd salarys are to be understood for this present year of 5489 [1728–29], and that on the begining of the year 5490 [1729–30] the parnaz and assistants that shall then be named they are to declare if they confirm or anull these articules, so farr as concerns the officers and their salarys or any part of them. And if confirmed they shall subscribe their names on foot of this, and the same shall be done by those that then shall follow,
Moseh Gomez, parnas, et al.

II. Religious Laxity in the Backcountry, September 14, 1757
In the Name of the God of Israel [In Hebrew]

The parnasim [presidents. There were two presidents; each served for several months.] and elders having received undouted testimony that severall of our bretheren that reside in the country have and do dayly violate the principles [of] our holy religion, such as trading on the sabath, eating of forbidden meats, and other henious crimes, and as our Holy Law injoins us to reprove one another agreeable to the commandments in Liviticus . . . thou shalt surely reprove thy neighbour and not suffer sin upon him, the consideration of this divine precept has induced the parnasim and elders to come to the following resolution in order to check the above mentioned growing evil, and as our *hachamim* [sages] observe . . . that is no one is to be punished unless first admonished:

Therefore whosoever for the future continues to act contrary to our Holy Law by breacking any of the principles command will not be deem'd a member of our congregation, have none of the mitzote [honors] of the sinagoge confered on him, and when dead will not be buried according to the manner of our brethren. But like Nehemiah [chapter 13], who treated those of old that transgressed, in the same manner he ordered the gates to be shut against them, so will the Gates of our Community be shut intirely against such offenders, but those that repent and obey the precepts of the

Almighty, we beseech the divine goodness to open to them the gates of mercy, and all their enterprizes be attended with the blessing of haven . . . *All who obey will be blessed* [Hebrew].

At the meeting of the parnasim and elders of the congration it was unanimously agreed that the foregoing should be read on the holly day of Kipoor [Yom Kippur] 5518 [1757] which was accordingly don in the Sinagog. . . .

III.   Hired Officiants in New York City, Slaughterer, Beadle, Minister, 1765–1768

A

JONAS PHILLIPS APPOINTED SHOHET (SLAUGHTERER) FOR CONGREGATION SHEARITH ISRAEL, NEW YORK CITY APRIL 22, 1765 TO MARCH 23, 1767

1st Yair [Iyyar], 5525 [April 22, 1765] The former sochet [slaughterer] having resign'd the place and due notice having been given, after proper examination, Jonas Philips was unanimously elected sochet for this kaal [congregation] under the following regulations: The said elected sochet is to use his best endeavors to keep the markets sufficiently furnish'd with meats for supplying of this congregation, and conform to all the rules and restrictions of former sochets. He is not to make any quantity of beef without first obtaining the consent of the parnassim and adjuntos [board members], and is to be allow'd thirty-five pounds salary p'r annum. . . .

On the 22d Veadar, 5527 [March 23, 1767] By particular desier of the parnas residente, Mr. Isaac Adolphus, there was called a meeting of the parnasim and ajuntos, to complain of the bodecks [slaughterer] leaving the pinchers at the buchers, and it was resolved that it should be looked into, and the bodeck suspended till farther orders, and adjourn the ajunta [board] till 12 o'clock the next day, which was accordingly done. And then it was resolved by the s'd parnasim and ajuntos, that the bodeck, Mr. Phillips, shall continue to kill, and no other person. If ever he does leave the pinches with any buchers, then, to be suspended, and the K.K. [*Kehillah Kedoshah*, the Holy Congregation] summonsed immediately. [Irresponsible butchers, using the pincers, could make false seals, certifying ritually unfit meat as kosher and thus make a big profit. Phillips served as slaughterer till 1769. Later as a merchant in Philadelphia he became one of the leaders of the Jewish community. He was the grandfather of Mordecai M. Noah, the dramatist, and "Commodore" Uriah P. Levy.]

B
CONGREGATION SHEARITH ISRAEL, NEW YORK CITY, PRESCRIBES THE DUTIES OF THE SHAMMASH, THE BEADLE MARCH 6, 1768

The 17th day of the month Adar, year 5528 [in Hebrew, March 6, 1768]. At a meeting of the parnasim and Mr. Daniel Gomez, Joseph Simon, Hayman Levy, assistants: Resolved that Judah Israel, who, at the last meeting of the parnasim and assistants was suspended for his unbecoming behavior, now appeared and making proper concessions for his past misconduct, entreated to be reinstated in his office, and it was accordingly agreed by the gentlemen present that the said *samas* [beadle] should have the keys of the synegouge and execute his office. And to prevent any of the like complaints hereafter, it was agreed that it should be here inserted, in the presence of the said *samas*, what matters particularly relates to his office and what he is faithfully to perform, vizt:

First	That he shall give constant attendance in synegouge at prayer times,
Second	Make the candles,
Third	Keep the *tamid* [eternal light] continually light,
Fourth	Clean the lamps and the silver and all the brasses twice in every year,
Fifth	Keep the synegouge clean allways, and be carefull of every thing that belongs to the synegouge,
Sixth	That he shall attend at marriages, circumcissions and funeralls, and shall conform to every thing, that the parnasim and assistants shall think the duty of the *samas*, and shall at all times stricktly obey the orders of the parnas for the time being,
Seventh	That he shall not at any time lay out, use, or expend any moneys for the use of the synegouge to amount of more than eight shillings without the leave and approbation of the parnas for the time being,
Eighth	And for all which services he is to receive his sallary and perquisites, as agreed, formerly, to which the said *samas* chearfully agreed, and returned thanks. [Israel was to serve Shearith Israel as shammash, beadle, for decades.]

C

GERSHAM SEIXAS HIRED AS HAZZAN (MINISTER) OF
SHEARITH ISRAEL, NEW YORK CITY
JULY 3–25, 1768

Tamuz the 18th, 5528 [July 3, 1768].

At a meeting of the parnasim and Mr. Joseph Simson, Daniel Gomez, Hayman Levy, assistants, the parnasim [presidents] informed the gentlemen present that Mr. Gershom Seixas had made application for the office of hazan [cantor and minister] to this kaal. Mr. Seixas then attending made a personall application for said office, when it was resolved that publick notice should be given in the synegouge on Sabath next, that the yaheedim [full members] would attend the parnasim and assistants [board] on Sunday next at the hebra [vestry room] at 3 o'-clock in the afternoon, to choose and nominate a hazan in room and place of Mr. Silva, discharged, and at same time all persons who would choose to offer them selves candidates for the office of hazan, to give their attendance.

Tamuz the 25th, 5528 [July 10, 1768].

At a meeting of the parnasim, assistants, and yaheedim agreable to the resolution of the 18th instant
    The parnasim acquainted the gentlemen present that Mr. Gershom Seixas, and no other person, appeared as a candidate for the office of hazan, when he was unanimously, and without one negative, voted by the parnasim, assistants, and all the present yaheedim to the said office of hazan, under the proper regulations and restrictions to be fixed by the parnasim and assistants. [Gershom Seixas, later the patriot "rabbi" of the Revolution, was a cultured gentleman.]

Menahem [Ab], the 11th, 5528 [July 25, 1768].

At a meeting of the parnasim and Mr. Joseph Simson, Daniel Gomez, assistants.
(Mr. Jacob Franks, one of the assistants, not being able to attend, signified his sentiments in writing that the hazan, Mr. Gershom Seixas, should have his full salary and all perquisites, as his predecessors heretofore had.)
    Resolved that the hazan, Mr. Gershom Seixas, should have the sallary of eighty pounds, per annum, with firewood, and other perquisites as the late hazan had, and that he may, if he pleases, have the use of the house belonging to the synegouge where Mr. Cohen now

lives. But that he shall have no allowance for house rent this year, that the said hazan is elected and fixed during his decent and good behavior, and under all restrictions as hazans heretofore have been.

IV. Philadelphia Sets Out to Establish a Synagog, ca. 1770

Since we are concerned about the matter of creating an organized community, it is important that we exercise prudence in selecting communal leaders.

The members who select the Board of Five are hereby warned to be careful to choose people who will dispense justice. And when the Board of Five choose a president, the ruling is that he must first have served as *hatan torah* and *hatan bereshit*. In addition, the Board of Five shall be careful, when they select a president, to see that he is neither quarrelsome nor tyrannical, but that he is a God-fearing man who is desirous of according justice to everyone.

If it should happen that a person has been a *hatan torah* and a *hatan bereshit*, and his turn arrives to become president, and it is known that he is quarrelsome and tyrannical, then that man is not to be made president. The Board of Five shall then elect another person, one who is respected here, to serve as president, even though he has not been either *hatan torah* or *hatan bereshit*.

Every householder is obliged to pay heed to what the president orders in the synagogue and, God forbid, not offer him any affront.

If there is a quarrel among the members, then the one in whom the quarrel centers must go to the president and to the Board of Five, and they must settle the matter. If, however, the litigant will not present himself, then the president has no right to give him a seat nor show him any religious courtesy in the synagogue, not to him, nor even to his children (as long as the children are subject to the litigant), until he submits to the president's decision. For the president is required to rent out the seats in order to support the synagogue. If, however, a person does not want to pay for his seat, then he has no right to a seat, nor to any congregational religious courtesy, not even to make a single donation in public.

If a person has insulted the synagogue and does not wish to submit, and the president decides that man has done wrong, and that the affronter is to have no religious courtesy as long as he, the president, is in office, when, later on, another president comes to power, the new president is not to accord that man any religious courtesy until that offender has been examined by the new president and the Board of Five, to determine whether he was guilty or not.

Every householder is obligated to do that which is right, to submit to any orders of the president in the synagogue.

The president has the right to summon the Board of Five together whenever the need arises.

If a householder is of the opinion that the president has done him an injustice, then that man has the right to go to the Board of Five and to lay his case before them, and the Board of Five shall listen to both disputants to determine who is right. If, however, the Board of Five cannot settle the matter, then they are to summon a number of householders in order to settle the dispute between the parties.

If it is known that a person has desecrated the Sabbath, that person has no right to receive a religious courtesy in the synagogue until he hears what his sentence is to be.

If the president accords a religious courtesy to anybody in the synagogue, that person is obligated to accept [and make an appropriate donation]; if not, he has to pay a fine.

If a person has a religious obligation to fulfill at a morning service, he is obligated likewise to come to the afternoon service. If not, he has to pay a fine. [If the community has arranged a special weekday service in the morning for a man, others may want his presence for a religious quorum in the afternoon. Let him appear!]

If a stranger comes to town, he is not immediately to be accorded a religious courtesy in the synagogue. He has to be here in town for at least several weeks, unless it happens that there are people here in town who know him. Then he is entitled to religious courtesies at once.

If there are people in the community who do not want to make any contribution, and separate themselves from the group, and do not want to help to support the community, when they die they [their heirs] have to pay for the cemetery lot, as much as the president and the Board of Five think that the lot is worth. They can demand much or little.

If a stranger [dies in town] and has means, he [his heirs], too, must pay for his burial lot. [Strangers who were impoverished itinerants were not expected to pay for their burial lots.]

7

Jewish Education
1755–1762

There can hardly be any question that children—boys only—were taught Hebrew by tutors no later than the third quarter of the seventeenth century. The teachers, "ribbis," were often recruited from the ranks of the financially incompetent. In 1731 a wealthy London army contractor, Jacob Mendes da Costa, memorialized his family by endowing a Hebrew school and building in New York City. It was called the Evening Meal Offering (*Minhat Areb*, a Gift to the West). The British colonies were clients of the empire. Indeed U.S. Jewry was receiving financial help from Europe as late as the 1890s. By 1755 Shearith Israel set out seriously to establish an all-day school conducted by the minister, the hazzan. Children of the indigent paid no tuition; the hazzan collected fees from all others; it was one of his important perquisites (selection I). In 1760 there was talk of bypassing the minister and hiring a schoolmaster (selection II); in 1762 the congregation employed Abraham Isaac Abrahams for the job. He was also a constable, shopkeeper, distiller, tobacconist, and the community's mohel, circumciser (selection III). All things considered the school did surprisingly well. Nothing was attempted, so it would seem, to further the Jewish education of adults before the second quarter of the nineteenth century.

The following are the records documenting this educational progression.

I.   The First All-Day School [December 7, 1755]

K.[ehillah] K.[edoshat] Sheerith Israel the 3 Tebet 5516 [December 7, 1755].

At a meeting of the parnasim [presidents] and elders of the congregation it was resolv'd, that twenty pounds p'r annum be added to the salary of the hazan on condition that he open a school at his own house every day in the week (Fryday afternoon, holy days, and fast days excepted) and teaches such poor children gratis that shall have an order from the parnas presidente, the Hebrew, Spanish, English, writting and arithnetick.

In the summer from 9 to 12 in the forenoon and from 5 in the afternoon, and in the winter from 10 to 12 in the forenoon and from 2 to 4 in the afternoon and that the children may be strictly kept to their learning, the parnasim and the elders, according to their seniority, engage to visit s'd school monthly to examine the children and judge if the scholars, under the hazan's care, advance in their learning. The above additional salary to commence from last Rosh a Shanah [Jewish New Year] and to continue whilst the hazan discharges the duty above expressed.

II.   The Search for a School Teacher, December 16, 1760

New York, Dec'r 16, 1760

Mr. Benj. Pereira,
Sir:
    After our compliments to you and your family wee take this opper'y to acquaint you that at a meeting of the elders of this K.K. it was agreed that wee should apply to you and that you will be good enough to engage a suitable master capable to teach our children the Hebrew language. English and Spanish he ought to know, but he will not suit unless he understands Hebrew and English at least. This must require your particular care. A single, modest, sober person will be most agreeable. However, on your good judgment wee shall depend as you very well know our minds and tempers and can make choice of such as will be suitable and capable of the undertaken.
    He must oblige himself to keep a publick school at the usual hours of the forenoons on every customary day at our *jesiba* [yeshiva, school]. Children whos parents are in needy circumstances he must teach gratis. His salary shall be first at forty pounds, New York money, p[e]r year, and shall commence from the day of his arrival here, and all other children he teaches must and will pay him as has been done heretofore. Wee flatter

ourselfs you will excuse the trouble wee give you as it will very much
oblige our whole congregation and in a more particular manner the *parna-
sim* who are, s'r,
Your most ob't humble [serv'ts,
Daniel Gomez,
Samuel Hart.]

III.   Mr. Abrahams Must Teach
the Three R's [April 25, 1762]

Iyar 2nd 5522 [April 25, 1762] The Parnassim, and Assistants [board
members] agreed with Mr. Abraham Is. Abrahams to keep a publick school
in the Hebra [vestry room], to teach the Hebrew language and translate
the same into English, also to teach English reading, writing, and cypher-
ing.

The congregation to allow him twenty pounds per annum with liberty of having offerings made him in synagogue. He is to teach all such
children gratis that can not afford to pay; all others are to be paid for quarterly, as he may agree with those who send them to school.

In case the hazan should be absent or indisposed, said Abrahams is to
perform in that function, and if the fore-mentioned allowance should happen to fall short of expectation or his deserts, upon application to the parnassim and assistants they are to take it into consideration.

Sivan 3 5522 [May 25, 1762] At a meeting of the parnassim and assistants Mr. Abram. Is: Abrahams declared he could not undertake keeping
school for the sum above mention'd. The majority therefore resolved to
allow said Abrahams forty pounds per annum out of the sedaka.

8

Jewish Culture in British North America
1766

There was very little Hebrew or Jewish literary culture in the British North American colonies in pre-Revolutionary days. Even as late as 1775 there were at the most 500 Jewish householders in the fourteen colonies, many of whom had no families. American Jewry was small and obscure; there was to be no ordained rabbi officiating on the continent until 1840. Judah Monis, an instructor at Harvard, published his *Grammar of the Hebrew Tongue* in 1735; in the 1750s and 1760s enterprising Gentile American publishers printed English and German editions of a sermon preached in Berlin by a rabbi after a victory of Frederick the Great. For reasons now unknown it seems to have become a best-seller. Haim Isaac Carigal, a Palestinian rabbi who was visiting Newport in 1773, preached in the local synagog. His sermon was speedily translated into English by a member of the Lopez clan. After the conquest of Canada in 1760, New York's hazzan delivered an original Hebrew prayer of thanksgiving for the victory of the British over the French. It was translated into English by a Friend to Truth.

The translator was, very probably, Isaac Pinto (1720–1791), undoubtedly one of the most learned Jews on the continent. This immigrant—a West Indian?—spent most of his time in New York making a living as a shopkeeper and language teacher. He was a linguist of capability and in the 1780s was employed by various departments of the new United States government as a translator. In 1766 Pinto had published an English translation of many of the Hebrew Sephardic prayers read on the Sabbath, various holidays, and the Days of Awe, Rosh Hashanah and Yom Kippur. For some of his translations Pinto leaned on the 1740 Spanish work of Isaac Nieto, *hakham* (rabbi), of the Sephardic congregation in London. Pinto's was the first English rendition of these prayers by a confessing Jew. His book was not part of the service, which was all in Hebrew or Aramaic; it was used by the men and the women in the pews the better to understand the prayers rattled off by the officiants.

In the following selection Pinto explains his reasons for publishing his 194-page liturgical work in English.

I. Isaac Pinto's Translations of Various Sephardic Hebrew Prayers, 1766

PREFACE

A veneration for the language *sacred* by being that in which it pleased Almighty God to reveal himself to our ancestors, and a desire to preserve it, in firm persuasion that it will again be re-established in Israel, are probably leading reasons for our performing divine service in Hebrew. But that [language], being imperfectly understood by many, by some, not at all, it has been necessary to translate our prayers in the language of the country wherein it hath pleased the Divine Providence to appoint our lot. In Europe, the Spanish and Portuguese Jews have a translation in Spanish, which, as they generally understand, may be sufficient, but that not being the case in the British Dominions in America has induced me to attempt a translation in English, not without hope that it will tend to the improvement of many of my brethren in their devotion, and if it answer that good intention, it will afford me the satisfaction of having contributed towards it. In justice to the learned and Reverend . . . Ishac Nieto, I must acknowledge the very great advantage I have received from his elegant Spanish translation of the prayers of Rosh-Hashanah [New Year] and Kippur [Atonement], from which, by particular desire, I have taken the liberty of translating his Exhortation, and prefixing it to these sheets. Notwithstanding my utmost care, I make no doubt this translation has its errors, and the stile, I am sensible, has its defects, which I hope will meet with indulgence from the candid reader.

EXHORTATION

Mortal man! Consider that thou art going to present thyself before the Eternal, Omnipotent, and Omniscient Being who hath created and formed thee, that supports and governs thee, on whose providence all this grand system of the universe depends. Consider that he is infinite, and is every where present, and that he beholds and observes thee. Consider that if thou adorest him as thou oughtest, and as is thy duty, thou obtainest salvation; if not, thou bringest condemnation on thyself. If thou behavest devoutly, thou pleasest him; if not, thou offendest him. Consider that adoration is a most essential part of religion and of the divine service. That, and no other is the exercise of this sacred house, which if thou performest according to thy duty, thou sanctifiest his Holy Name; if not thou profanest it. Observe that thou effectest thy ruin, with that by which thou oughtest to make thy gain, and destroyest thyself with the same act whereby thou oughtest to obtain salvation. Offer him then thine heart; clothe thyself with a true devotion; dedicate thyself entirely to his service; divest thyself of every wor[l]dly consideration; and intreat him to grant thee that which is convenient for thee, and confide in his divine providence; for if thou art not wanting thereto, that will never fail thee.

9

CHARITY, SOCIAL WELFARE, COMPASSION
1755–1773

The colonial congregation was concerned with worship, education, charity. Shearith Israel of New York City took care of the sick and buried the dead; it pensioned its poor, made provision for visiting mendicants, and contributed to Jewish causes and institutions in North America, the Caribbean, and abroad. Philanthropy to Palestine Jewry was a religious obligation, almost a privilege. The Hebrew word for charity is zedakah, righteousness. Because the colonials gave liberally, this word became a synonym for the synagogal treasury. Though individuals like Aaron Lopez and his father-in-law, Jacob R. Rivera, were good givers, providing for the needy was primarily the job of the organized kehillah, the community. The synagog, on the whole, was generous despite the fact that no colonial congregation could boast of even 100 members; many worshipers were poor. When the presidents and board members ran out of money and patience they dispatched their importunate clients—claimants! —to the nearest town or put them on the next ship leaving for the West Indies or South America.

The following selections from 1755–1773 tell their story with an eloquence all their own.

I.   Obras Pias: Pious Works

A

K.[ehillah] K.[edoshah. Holy Congregation] Sheerith Israel, the 3 Tebet, 5516 [December 7, 1755]. . . .

73

At the same time it was also resolvd that forty shill[ing]s shall be given in small sums to the poor shoe-maker and the forty shill's in the like manner be given to Isaac Navarro.

K. K. Sheerith Israel 18 Nissan, 5516 [April 18, 1756]

At a meeting of the parnasim [presidents] and elders of this congregation, Mr Joseph Simson, in behalf of the Wid[o]w Mrs. Hays that she declined taking her allowance from the tsedakah [treasury] for the future, with thanks for what already received.

B

K. K. Sheerith Isr'l, 8th Sivan, 5516 [June 6, 1756]

At a meeting of parnasim and elders of this congregation.
Apply'd, the Wid[o]w Mrs Hanah Louzada, for a maintainance for her and one son. Resolved. She be allowed support for four weeks only. . . .

C

New Brunswik [New Jersey] 9 November, 1761.

Sir:
I take the liberty to wright to yow now. I think the at [that] is time for yow to get my wenters [winter's] . . . provisions, likewise a little money to bay some wood for the wenter. I woud a come down my self to feetchet [fetch it], but ben desebled, my legs heving swelds [swellings]. But y[d] hope, sir, that at ensent [that ancient proverb] not aut a sigt aut of mind [will apply to me]. Sir, hier y [I] lay sufering for the vant of wood and provisions. Y [I] remende, sir,
Your most humble servent
Hanne Lezade [Lous(z)ada]
Remember my love to your espowse . . . and the reste of your familly. . . .

D

Shebat 30th, 5523 [February 13, 1763]

At a meeting of the parnasim and assistants [board], agreed to allow the Widdow Solomons five pounds towards house rent, to commence the first day of May ensuing.

E

5524, the 1st day of *Tammuz* [July 1, 1764]

At a meeting of the parnasim and assistants it was agreed that the sedaka should allow a sufficiency for lodging and boarding the sick man now at the widow Solomons, and twenty shillings to be given to Mrs. Andrews.

F

5526 Hesvan, the first [October 16, 1765]

At a meeting of the assistance [assistants] with the parnassim the following articles were agreed and resolved. . . .
2nd That Aaron Pinto shall be dispacht as soon as possible [sent out of town].
3d That the foll'g persons shall be allowed for wood: the hazan, ten pounds, the samas [beadle], seven pounds, ten shillings, the rabbi [teacher], seven pounds, ten shillings, Rachel Campanel, three pounds, Hannah Louzada, three pounds, Rebeca Navaro, three pounds, Mr. Sexias famley, six pounds, together forty pounds. [Perquisites and charity are mixed.]
4th That Mrs. Navaro be allowed a doctor.
Benja Gomez
Samuel Judah

G

4th Kisleu, 5526 [November 17, 1764]

At a meeting of the parnassim and assistance [assistants] the following was agreed to and resolved:
That three corse shirts be made and sent to Aaron Pinto as he is almost naked and that after Rabby Joseph Israel [a respectable mendicant] has preached his sermon, he is to be dispacht by first opp'ty to Newport in order to take passage for Surinam, and if he will not go is to remain at his own expence.

H

[1765?]

To the president and elders of the synagoga in the City of Newyork:
The petition of Levy Micheals of the city of Mountreal in the province of Cannada most humbly sheweth:

That the petitioner, being alarmed with the unexpected and disagree-
able situation of his daughter in this city, induced him to leave home and
come to Newyork in the month of November last, and being unhappyly
detained here beyound the time he had fixed, has caused his money to become nearly exhausted.

Labouring under the most pressing diffeculties and a heavy expence
for his support, and the great distance he has to travel home, lays him under the necessity of takeing this method to lay his diffeculty before you,
and humbly prays you to take his case into consideration and grant him
such a sum of money, upon loan, as you in your wisdom shall see meet,
and, as in duty bound, etc., which sum shall be returned as soon as possible
after his ariveal home.

Levy Michaels

[Michaels was a merchant and fur trader.]

I

The fourth day of the month of Adar, year 5528 [Hebrew. February 22, 1768].

At a meeting of the parnasim, and Mr. Daniel Gomez, Joseph Simson,
Hayman Levy, assistants, it was resolved and agreed:

First That Rachell Campanall, making application for an addition to
her yearly allowance, complaining that from her infirmities and advanced
age she is not capable of doing any kind of work and cannot subsist from
her allowance of twenty pounds p'r annum,

Wherefore the parnassim and assistants having considered her condition do agree that the allowance for said Rachell Campanall shall be augmented to the sum of twenty five pounds p'r annum to be paid to her quarterly, and commence from the approaching *Pesach* [Passover], and that the
three pounds allowed her for firewood shall still be continued. [Some New
England Campanals, later Christians, may have changed their name to
Campbells.]

J

Newport, May 21st, 1770.

Messrs. Nicholas Brown & Co.
[Providence, R.I.]
Gentlemen:

There is one of our [religious] society who arrived here yesterday from
St. Eustatious, in order to git a passage for Surinam [South America] where
he has very able relations that have sent for him. His family I knew well in
the West Indias, and [they were] some of the principal [members] of our

society, but by the frowns of fortune are reduced [in circumstances]. I am informed you have a vessel bound to Surinam. I shall be glad [if] you'll let me know by first boat if he can have a passage in her, when she will sail, and whither she is to stop here before she sails, or if he must goe to Providence.

If you can oblige me in this, I shall thankfully acknowledge the favour, and am very respectfully, gentlemen,
Your humble servant,
Jacob Rodrigues Rivera

K

Newport, May 25th, 1770.

Messrs. Nicholas Brown & Co.
Gentlemen:
Mr. Lindsey sent me word that you had desired him to inform me that your vessel would sail for Surinam next Sunday, and that you was so obliging as to allow the bearer a passage in her, but must be there by Sunday. He therefore goes up with this boat and will wait on you. He carries his [kosher] provissions with him, and [you] will add greatley to the favour if you recommend him to your captain. I cannot but return you my thanks for this favour, and would return the same whenever you put it in my power.

I am with great respect and regard, gentlemen,
Your most obliged servant,
Jacob Rodrigues Rivera

L

May 29th, 1770.

Mr. Rivera.
Sir:
Yours of the 25 instant is before us. Captain Sheldon in our brigg sailed last Sunday for Suranam, by whome your friend went passenger.
We are your humble servants,
[Nicholas Brown & Co.]

M

Newyork, July 26, 1770.

[Aaron Lopez, Newport, R.I.]
Dear Sir:

I take the liberty once moor of troubling you in the letter way, which I hope you'l pardon. Necesseaity drives me to it. I am now in years and unable to do anny thing for my self. It's comeing to quarter [rent] day, and I am affraid I shall be troubled. I am helpt by my friends, but it is not sufficent to keep me from disstress. So, dear sir, I hope your heart, which is naturly tender, will be moved with kind compassion for a poor fellow creature who is labouring under greater distress then it's possible to express. What ever you do for me, I hope God will doubly return.

So, remain with great respect,
Your obedient servant,
Hannah Paysaddon.

N

5531, Tisrey 4th [September 23, 1770]. . . .

On the same it was agreed by the parnassim and assistance [assistants] to allow Saml Israel for the use of Rachael Campanal 20 shillings p'r week and have two p'r of sheets made and sent her.

Also to pay Levy Marks 40 shillings and discharge him from the *sedaka* [treasury. No more grants.]

O

City of New York,
New Goal [jail], 9th September, 1773.

To Mr. Solomon Simson of the City of New York, merchant. The petition of Michael Jacobs, of the said city, shopkeeper, most humbly sheweth:

That your poor distressed petitioner has been confined in this goal [probably for debt] for upwards of twenty-six weeks, which has so reduced him that he is no longer able to support under it, and connot afford himself the common nessary's of life.

Your petitioner, therefore, most humbly prays that you and the congregation will be favorably pleased to take it into your generous consideration and grant him such relief in the premises as to you shall seem meet.

And your petitioner, as in duty bound, shall ever pray, etc.
his Michael *Meir* [Hebrew] Jacobs
mark
[Jacobs signed in Hebrew and in English. He was not illiterate. The congregation gave him back the money he had once contributed.]

10

Jewish Social Life in the North American English Colonies 1761–1773

No cinema, no radio, no television existed in early America, but there were weddings, circumcisions, social visits, and religious services where Jews could gossip . . . and quarrel. Dining was important in those days; the Spanish-Portuguese as well as the Central and East European Jews had their own "Jewish soul foods." To top everything off, there were the pleasures of ale, porter, wines, spirits, brandy, gin, rum. The New World was often a rough world; people "took the spirits down to keep the spirits up."

Colonial America held its own in sociability, if not culture, with the Old World. The larger towns abounded in social organizations for the joiners who could afford them. There were all kinds of associations: Irish, French, and Hungarian clubs; Masonic fraternities; dancing assemblies; even musical, philosophical, and literary societies. Philadelphia had its Schuylkill Fishing Club; New York, its Friendly Club; Boston, its Merchant's Club; Newport, its Fellowship Club and its Redwood Library.

There was also at least one Jewish social organization—Newport's Jewish club of 1761. Although the Newport association was the only colonial Jewish club of which record or mention survives, it may have had counterparts in other towns. Aaron Lopez was not listed among the charter members of the Newport society. While later to become one of America's most prominent merchant-shippers, Aaron was in 1761 still a relative newcomer to Newport's tiny Jewish community of some ten families. His brother, Moses (ca. 1706–1767), belonged, but Aaron, apparently, was not yet able to afford the cost of eating and gambling—prime features of almost all the clubs of the time.

Three selections follow: the first is the constitution of Newport's Jewish club; the second is a friendly note from Miriam Gratz to her brother-in-law, Barnard Gratz, then on a visit to London; the third is a letter of Esther Hart, a Charles Town, South Carolina, teenager to Aaron Lopez, the Newport merchant-shipper.

I.   Newport's Jewish Club,
November 25 to December 16, 1761

RULES NECESSARY TO BE OBSERVED AT THE CLUB VIZ:

Newport, R.I., November 25th, 1761.

First. The club is to be held every Wednesday evening during the winter season. The members to be nine in number; and by the majority of votes a chairman to be elected to serve one month only.

Second. After one month, or four club nights, a new chairman to be elected in the manner aforesaid.

Third. No person to be admitted as a member of said club without approbation of the members.

Fourth. Each of the members shall have liberty to invite his friends to the club, and well understood, one at a time only.

Fifth. The hours of club to be from 5 to 10, in the manner following: From 5 to 8 each member is at liberty to divert at cards, and in order to avoid the name of a gaming club, the following restrictions shall be strictly observed, viz.: That no member shall presume or offer to play for more than twenty shillings at whist, picquet or any other game besides his club [his share for the evening supper]; on proof of gaming for any more, the member or members so offending shall pay the value of four bottles good wines for the use and benefit of the ensuing club night.

Sixth. At eight of the clock the supper (if ready) to be brought in. At ten the club [each one's share] to be adjusted and paid, and no cards or any other game shall be allowed after supper.

Seventh. After supper if any of the members have any motion to make relating to the club he must wait till the chairman has just drank some loyal toast.

Eighth. That none of the members shall [say anything?] during [their?] conversation relating to synagogue affairs, on the forfeit of the value of four bottles good wine for the use as aforesaid. [Religion and politics were taboo in clubs.]

Ninth. If any of the members should behave unruly, curse, swear or offer to fight, the chairman shall lay such fine as he sees fit, not exceeding, for each offence, four bottles good wine for the use of aforesaid.

Tenth. If any of the members happen to be sick or absent [from town], by acquainting Mr. Myer [the steward] with the same, shall be exempt from paying anything towards the club, but if no notice given as aforesaid, shall pay his quota of the supper only.

Eleventh. If any of the members does not meet at club nights, and can't offer sufficient reason for so doing, the chairmain with the members shall determine if he or they are to pay the proportion of the whole club, or the quota of supper only.

Twelfth. If any of the members neglect coming to club three nights successively without being sick or absent [from town] shall be deemed unwilling, consequently his name shall be erased from the list, not to be admitted during the season without the consent of the chairman and all the members.

Thirteenth. Every member, after signing the articles, and not willing afterwards to conform to the same, his or their names shall be erased out of the list, and no more to be admitted during the season.

In witness whereof the members of said club have signed their respective names the day and year above written. Moses Lopez, Isaac Polock, Jacob Isaacs, Abr'm Sarzedas, Nap't. Hart, Moses Levy, Issachar Polock, Naph't. Hart Jr., Jacob Rods. Rivera.

Fourteenth. At a club held the 16th day of December, 1761, it is resolved and agreed by the chairman and the majority of all the members that these articles be inserted amongst the rules of said club, viz:

That in case the chairman is not at the club, the secretary, for the time being, shall take his place, and the same obedience shall be paid him as if the chairman was present, and to be invested with equal authority. As also the said secretary is hereby empowered to nominate with the concurrence of the members then present, a secretary to supply his place for the time being; and that every month a secretary shall be elected in the same manner and form as the chairman is elected.

II. Miriam Gratz, Philadelphia, to Barnard Gratz, London, Her Brother-in-Law, August 26, 1769

Philadelphia, August 26, 1769

My dear Brother:

As I have just now heard of this opportunity [to forward this letter], I do myself the pleasure of dedicating a few lines to you, and I hope to be excused for not doing my duty before, but I can assure you that it was not neglected for want of regard for my dear brother. Therefore, as I know your goodness, I need not make any further apologies.

I have the happiness of acquainting you that our family enjoys perfect health. Dear little Rachel [your five-year-old daughter] has escaped the small pox and is hearty. She often talks of her "dear little Daddy" and wishes to see him, as, indeed, we all do. But how could it be otherwise when a person whom we all love and esteem, is at so great a distance from us.

Would it was spring. Then should we be in expectation of a new happiness [Miriam gave birth to a son in April, 1770]. But, alas, a long winter is before us, though I can assure you there is nothing wanting but your presence to make us completely happy. I have a dear, good, and kind husband and a dear little prattling niece, which is a great comfort. I pray that the Almighty may prosper you in all your undertakings and conduct you safe over the wide ocean to your dear friends here.

I hope you'll make yourself entirely easy about Rachel and be assured she'll be as well taken care of by us as she possibly can be. Becky [the nurse?] is the same kind body she always was. She desired me to remember her kindly to you and to let you know that she is much pleased in living as she does. I can assure you that I do everything in my power to render everything agreeable to her.

Rachel gives her love to you and hopes that you won't forget her London doll. I hope after the receipt of this, I shall be favored with a few lines from you. I could not expect it before, as it was my place to write first. My dear Michael [my husband, your brother] joins me in love to you. I must conclude, wishing you every felicity this world can afford. From
Your ever loving and affectionate sister,
Miriam Gratz

P.S. I should be much obliged to you if you would make my kind love acceptable to my Aunt [my father's relative] and to my new cousin, Mr. Solomon Henry.

"You must make haste home," Rachel Gratz. (This is Rachel writing. As she begged me to let her write, I was obliged to guide her hand to please her.)
For Mr. Barnard Gratz, London.

III.   Teenager Esther Hart of Charles Town, South Carolina, Writes to Aaron Lopez, the Newport Merchant, September 3, 1773

Charles Town, 3d Sept., 1773.

Mr. Aaron Lopez
Sir:

Your much esteem'd favour came safe to hand with the assurances of your kind wishes towards my papa and mama and family, which you have our greatfull acknowledgements in return for them. If my papa was presant he would with a great deal of pleasur answare his worthy friend's esteem'd favour, but as he [is] not, is deprived of that satisfaction, as [he] is gone to Philadelphia for the benefit of his helth, for he has been very much indisposed this summer. [Philadelphia was the country's metropolis. It had a hospital and a medical school.]

My papa had thoughts of paying your place [Newport] also a visit if he found himself better, which I hope kind providence will grant him. I hope my friend will excuse the liberty I have taken in addressing him with this scrall, but as papa being absent was the reason of my being so bold.

My mama joines with me in congratulating you and my dear Mrs. Lopez on her safe delivery. It also renders us happy to think she is so brave with all your dear branches [children]. A continuance of that blessing we sincerely wish you all.

Good sir, you will pleas to make mama and selfs respects acceptab[l]e to Mrs. Lopez and Mrs. Mendez [your daughter], and Miss Ester [Lopez], and the rest of the family. You will pleas to accept the same from one that subscribes herself.
Your obliged humble serv't,
Esther Hart.

11

The Concept of *Kelal Yisrael* in Colonial America
1759–1774

Christians are bound together by the mystical concept of the body of Christ. Christ is within them, and they are within him. He is their Savior; they and their God are one indivisible whole. The Jewish concept, *kelal yisrael*, betokens the Community of Israel; every Jew is responsible for every other Jew. Unlike Christians, Jews are not united in the hopes for salvation in a world to come. Jews share common hope, common ideals; more important, common fears. They have a categorical imperative: aid one another. Jews actually respond when fellow Jews cry out; this may be less true of Christians.

The several selections that follow reflect the various aspects of *kelal yisrael*. In 1759 a handful of Newport Jews set out to build a beautiful and expensive sanctuary. These Jews turned to Shearith Israel in New York City. Help us! This, too, is *kelal yisrael*. We are Jews; you are Jews. Implicit here is the conviction that Jews are not petitioners but claimants. Don't let us down. What New York sent was equal to a minister's salary for about two years; this was no trifle. In addition it sent religious ornaments and a reading desk (selection I). In 1770 Henry Isreall of Jamaica turned to Aaron Lopez in Rhode Island. What he is really saying is: We are both Jews; I know you will respond to my needs (selection II). When in the years 1728–1730 New York Jewry was building its first synagog, it had appealed to fellow Jews in three continents and received gifts from Jamaica, Curaçao, Barbados, London, and even from two or three isolated Jews who had managed to survive in Puritan Boston. When in 1772 a devastating hurricane destroyed the congregation on the Dutch island of St. Eustatius, the congregation turned to New York's Jews and not in vain. The appeal of these stricken Caribbean Jews is reprinted in selection III.

As early as 1759 a Palestinian Jew had turned up in North America with outstretched palms. He was from Safed, one of the holy cities. In the 1760s Hebron, almost crushed by the extortion of Turkish pashas, appealed to North American Jews for monetary aid; in 1770, it received sizeable sums from New York, Philadelphia, and Newport, amounting in total to over £100. In June of 1775 Rabbi Samuel Cohen of Hebron landed in Newport; he was an authentic "messenger," authorized to collect funds for suffering Hebron. He preached in the beautiful new synagog and probably prayed for peace. A war was going on. The continentals were about to issue their Declaration of Independence. Rhode Island and New York Jews got together, raised a large sum of money, and sent Cohen back to Europe, out of the war zone. As a Palestinian evangel he was cherished and protected. Two letters follow: one is from London's Sephardic leaders; the other is from a Barbados merchant. Both assure American Jews that Cohen's cause is a worthy one (selections IV and V). All this is *kelal yisrael*.

I. Newport Jews Ask New York's Jews to Help Them Build a Synagog, March 21, 1759

Newport, R.I., Adar 22d, 5519 [March 21, 1759].

Gent.:

The pious intentions of a congregation yet in its infancy, we desire, may plead a sufficient excuse for this address. Sincerely desirous to establish a regular congregation in this town, we therefore have lately purchased a suitable lot of land whereon we design to build a sinaguogue. And for furthering our said intentions we have likewise by subscription raised a small fund wherewith to begin and carry on the work and which in due time we hope to see fully compleated. At present, finding our abilities not equal to our wishes for finishing the work in so short a time as we desire, we have resolved to crave the assistance of the several congregations in America, and as the Feast of the Passover is near at hand, a time when there will be the greatest appearance of our brethen at New York, we embrace this opportunity to acquaint you with our proceedings and intentions relative thereto, intreating you to commuinicate the same to the congregation at New York and to supplicate for us their charitable assistance towards carrying on this work, either by a freewill offering in the sinagogue, or subscription, or in any way which may be agreable to you.

When we reflect on how much it is our duty to instruct children in the path of vertuous religion, and how unhappy the portions must be of those children and their parents, who are thro' necessity educated in a place where they must remain almost totally uninstructed in our most holy and divine law, our rites and ceremonies, and from which place they may perhaps never have it in their power to depart; when we farther reflect on how much it is our duty to assist the distressed, and when we consider the extensive usefullness of a charity, like this for which we now supplicate assistance; we can entertain no doubt of your zeal to promote this good work.

That God Almighty will be pleased to direct your councils, prospect your vertuous actions and intentions, give us peace, and very soon send the Redeemer to Zion, is and shall be the devout prayer of, gent.,
Your obedient and very hum[bl]' serv'ts,
Jacob Rod's Rivera, Jacob Isaacs, I. Hart, Aaron Lopez. etc., etc.

To the gent., the parnassim of the K.[ehillah] K.[edoshah] Holy Congregation] Seherit Israel, in New York.

II.   Henry Isreall of Jamaica Wants Aaron Lopez of Newport to Send Him Kosher Meat, July 8, 1770

Jamaica. St. Anns, July 8th, 1770

Sir,

Meeting with this favourable opportunity have embraced it. I am hopefull you'll excuse my taking the liberty in troubling of you in this let-ter. I live in the country and we are obliged to live very hard as we cant gitt such sort of provisions as is suitable to our religion without sending to the towns in Jamaica. It is then a great length and chargeable and what we gett is very poor stuff and dear. I would therefore be kindly oblige to you if you would be so kind as to take the trouble found in sending by the return of Captain Potter for Saint Anns, two good large barrell of good *kashar* beeff (fatt and prime pieces) and will send you the payment by the return of the same vessell. I must also beg you'll send me it as reasonable as possible, as I have a large family, and I have enough to do to support 'em genteelly. If you'll please enquire of Capt. James Potter of me, or of Captain Hefferon, they will tell you, or of any other of the captains that trades here. I have been in this parish going on forty-two years. Captain John Freebody, Jun'r, who was here in the year fifty-three at a circumcission of one of my sons, can tell you. I am onacquainted with your person or family but I hope they enjoy their health. I am with esteem, Sir, your most obedient servant
Henry Isreall.

N.B. If you can, or if it would be agreeable, I would be much [obliged] to you to have packed up in one of the barrells a few tongues.

III.   After a Devastating Hurricane in the West Indies, the Congregation in St. Eustatius Turns to New York Jewry for Help, September 7, 1772

To the most dignified gentlemen, Parnasim Gabay [presidents, treasurer] and Trustees of the Congregation Shearith Israel.

Our Most Dignified Gentlemen:

With aching hearts with the greatest agony of our incomparable feeling, we address to you these lines hoping you will accept them and be aware of the great destruction from which the Almighty miraculously saved some of the inhabitants and dwellings when in the morning of August 31st, the sky being covered with dark clouds and raining, little by little a great hurricane appeared doing great disaster to all of those who were out and in doors and it looked as not only the Island, but the whole world would come to an end of that day. The roofs of the houses were flying all over, the families were found under the ruins having no one to help them, and all were in a very dangerous condition, with thunder, lightning, and stones flying everywhere.

With great sorrow we relate to you the great misfortune with which the Lord punished us, causing us to witness the synagogue destroyed by the storm and trying to take the sefarim [Scrolls of the Law] out of the ruins, which, thank God, we succeeded in doing, and now we are in the greatest misery known. Still we are holding services in the home of the Lady Hannah, widow of Leon Benjamin and we resolved to observe this day of Monday, September 7th [1772] as a solemn day of fasting for the preservation of our lives and those of our dear families, praying to the Almighty that we should never again experience such a misfortune, our sins having caused us to see our holy synagogue destroyed. And now we ask of you with humble supplication to assist us and that without your aid it will be impossible to rebuild our holy synagogue.

We hope you will grant our petition, and pray to the Almighty for the existence of his holy synagogue, and may the Lord reward you and your families with happiness and prosperity.

Respectfully yours,

Parnasim, Gabay and Trustees of the Congregation Honen Dalim [Generous to the poor]. . . . St. Eustatius, 1st October, 1772

IV.   Congregation Gate of Heaven, London, Asks American Jews to Aid the Oppressed Jews of Hebron in Palestine, May 5, 1773

Most worthy gentlemen, parnessim [presidents], gabaim [treasurers] of the holy kehilot [congregations] of America:

Having seen the contents of the letter which was signed by the gentlemen, hahamim [rabbis] of the city of Hebron in the Holy Land and addressed to us, and since it is clear to us that the wretchedness and misery
are true which are happening to our brothers in Palestine, caused by the
civil wars, which, also for those regions, as also for their safety.

Now you will please take note that we have granted the request which
the same gentlemen made of us in the above-mentioned letter, and we recommend to all our brothers, the gentlemen parnassim deputes [officers]
and *yehidim* [members] of the various kehilot of America, that the Great
God have mercy on the misfortunes and miseries of our brothers of Hebron, and that they respond to this call for aid with their generous assistance to their messenger, the gentleman R.[abbi] Samuel Cohen, bearer of
this letter, for the relief and refuge of the said people of Hebron. And may
He [God] reward this pious work with an increase in His good gifts as the
culmination of His goodness bestowed upon this *K. K.* of Saar Asamaim
[Holy Congregation, Gate of Heaven] in London, the 5 of May, of Sivan
5533 [1773].

Signed by the following gentlemen:
Abraham Aboab Osorio, President,
Isaac Israel Nunes
David Abarbanel
Charles Serra
Isaac Serra, Gabay [treasurer]

V.   An Apostle from the Holy Land, April 17, 1774

Barbados, April 17th, 1774.

Mr. Aaron Lopez.
Dear Sir:

Your kind and polite letter I had the pleasure to unfold the lst [last] instant per Capt. [John Peters]. The contents [I] have duely noticed, and for
the many very kind expressions I stand greatly indebted. Should any thing
offer this side the water that I can render you or my good friend Mr. Ri-
berro [Jacob Rodriguez Rivera] any services, shall be glad to be commanded.

Dear sir, pardon the liberty I've taken in recommending the bearror,
Mr. Samuel a[Ha] Cohen who is on an embasy from Hebron. His deportment with us has been praysworthy, and make not the least doubt but his
person will be sufficient to recommend. Could you render him any service
for and towards that kaal [community of Hebron], as it now labours under
many difficulties, such favours bestowed shall ever be acknowledged by
him who subscribes himself to be, dear sir,
Your honoured and very humble servant.

N.B. My compliments are respectfully offered Mrs. Lopez and family.

July 1st, 1775.

Since the above, have taken my passage for England per Capt. Blackburne. Shall be glad on my arrival to execute any your commands [to serve as your business agent], and are very respectfully, dear sir,
Yours very affectionately,
Isaac Lindo.

PART II

The Early National Period, 1776–1840

In the year 1775 there were no more than 2500 Jews in the North American British colonies; by 1840 there may have been 15,000 souls, living for the most part in sixteen towns, all, except one, east of the Mississippi. In 1777 Jews, for the first time, were to receive equal rights in one state; by 1840 only four states still denied them high office; the federal government, however, had always accorded them all privileges and immunities. On the whole, most Americans accepted Jews; few Gentiles were openly hostile. Not many of the Children of Israel were well educated in the secular disciplines, yet every town had its individual intellectuals; only a handful among the Jews had received a good Hebrew education; on the other hand, illiteracy was rare. As in colonial days, the Jew was still primarily a shopkeeper, a petty businessman. By the end of this period the privileges accorded Jews made it possible for the enterprising among them—few in number to be sure—to turn to transportation, insurance, banking, the stock exchange, and the professions. There were one or two outstanding lawyers, doctors, journalists, and engineers.

The monolithic community of colonial days began to dissolve. Though Jews were clannish, yet fissiparousness was the order of the day; there were multiple congregations, each of them autonomous; nonsynagogal independent charities emerged; some of them were mutual-aid societies; the women, too, went out on their own establishing societies that responded to the needs of the indigent. By the 1840s we have the first intimations of secularism in the field of philanthropy; synagogs were no longer the chief source of good works. Orthodoxy was threatened in 1824 when dissidents in Charleston, South Carolina established the first liberal religious society. Jewish education in Philadelphia broke with tradition when it opened Sunday schools based on Christian models; the paltry few day schools limped along until the public schools—free, lay, and more or less compulsory—displaced them in the next few decades. Despite the constant secessions in the congregations and the rise of rival and competing welfare societies, the pull of kinship, the concept of *kelal yisrael*, was very strong; Jews helped one another locally, responded on a nationwide basis when asked for aid, and rarely closed their ears to the appeals of oppressed foreign Jewish communities.

America's was the first completely free Jewish community in all Diaspora history, yet living in an open society Jews managed to survive as Jews.

12

POLITICAL RIGHTS OF AMERICAN JEWS
1776–1809

U nder the English, Jews in the American colonies had not been permitted to hold any honorific office; they were second-class citizens. Great changes came when the Americans rebelled. The Declaration of Independence said "that all men are created equal." This was the Great Promise of better things to come (selection I), but no state constitution or retained colonial charter gave Jews political equality in 1776. Although a Whig, a patriot, Moses M. Hays of Rhode Island refused to sign a loyalty oath; he was convinced that the new regime was discriminating against Jews (selection II). The 1776 Maryland constitution was in a way typical of the new organic statutes; by virtue of their religion Jews in this state were disqualified from holding office (selection III). The first state to emancipate its Israelites was New York in 1777; though the emancipatory paragraphs were implicit, they were never questioned (selection IV). Rabbi Seixas of New York City, however, was disabled politically; no clergyman, Jew or Christian, could hold office; this was Deism with a vengeance. Catholics, it would seem, were denied office in New York until the next century.

In 1783 Philadelphia's Jews wrote the Pennsylvania authorities that they resented the passage in the 1776 state constitution which disqualified them from holding office; their protest contained an implied threat that in the future Jews might not settle in that commonwealth and prefer the rival to the north, New York (selection V).

In twenty-eight words Congress's Northwest Ordinance made it clear that religious beliefs and differences would bar no one politically in any new territory that was established (1787). This law thus guaranteed Jews rights in all future states (selection VI). That same year, Jonas Phillips, a leader in the Philadelphia synagog, wrote the delegates to the Constitutional Convention asking them to put Pennsylvania's Jews on a plane of equality with others (selection VII). Phillips imagined that the delegates had the authority to modify Pennsylvania's organic statute; he was in error; the thirteen states were almost autonomous in that period. When the Constitutional Convention finished its work on September 17, 1787, in effect it granted Jews all rights on a federal level. This was no great help, since a Jew might not be able to become a lawyer in a county court—Maryland, for instance—even though there was no law to stop him from becoming president of the United States (selection VIII). Sunday laws, too, disabled Jews politically and economically; they had to close their shops on that day. The first Sunday closing statute had been enacted in Virginia in 1610; such laws have persisted down to the present moment. Typical of the restrictions imposed on Jews is a New York state law passed in 1788 (selection IX).

In 1809 it was disclosed that the Jew Jacob Henry, a member of the North Carolina House of Commons, had not taken the oath of office as a Protestant Christian. This was a constitutional requirement. There was a motion to disqualify him. Henry made a spirited defense, either in the form of a letter or an address (selection X). His colleagues permitted him to retain his seat. They rationalized that he was constitutionally allowed to fill a legislative office but not an executive one! This was casuistry; they liked the man and they kept him. His letter or address was either written or polished by two Catholic friends. Catholics, too, were legally disqualified in that state. Henry's appeal was republished in the *American Orator* as an exemplary piece of literature. There is more than one version of the Henry appeal; the differences are not significant.

As late as 1840, four—possibly five—states still refused to grant political rights to Jews: New Hampshire, Rhode Island, New Jersey, North Carolina, and, probably, Connecticut.

I.   The Unanimous Declaration of the Thirteen United States of America, In Congress, July 4, 1776

When in the course of human events, it becomes necessary for one people to dissolve the political bands which have connected them with another, and to assume, among the powers of the earth, the separate and equal station to which the laws of nature and of nature's God entitle them, a decent respect to the opinions of mankind requires that they should declare the causes which impel them to the separation.

We hold these truths to be self-evident, that all men are created equal, that they are endowed by their Creator with certain unalienable rights,

that among these are life, liberty, and the pursuit of happiness. That to secure these rights, governments are instituted among men, deriving their
just powers from the consent of the governed. That whenever any form of
government becomes destructive of these ends, it is the right of the people
to alter or to abolish it, and to institute new government, laying its foundation on such principles and organizing its powers in such form, as to
them shall seem most likely to effect their safety and happiness.

II.   Moses M. Hays Refuses to Sign a Discriminatory Test Oath, July 11, 1776

He refused to sign the test and called for his accusers. He was then told
there was a number present whom he there saw. He likewise called for his
accusation which was read. I have and ever shall hold the strongest principles and attachments to the just rights and privileges of this my native
land, and ever have and shall conform to the rules and acts of this government, and pay as I always have my proportion of its exigencies. I always
have asserted my sentiments in favor of America and confess the
[Revolutionary] war on its part just. I decline subscribing the test at present
from these principles: First, that I deny ever being inimical to my country
and call for my accusers and proof of conviction. Second, that I am an Israelite and am not allowed the liberty of a vote or voice in common with the
rest of the [Rhode Island] voters, though consistent with the constitution
[Rhode Island's colonial charter] and the other colonies. Thirdly, because
the test is not general and consequently subject to many glaring inconveni-
ences. Fourthly, Continental Congress nor the General Assembly of this
nor the legislatures of the other colonies have never in this contest taken
any notice or countenance respecting the society of Israelites to which I
belong. When any rule, order or directions is made by the Congress or
General Assembly, I shall to the utmost of my power adhere to the same.

III.   The Maryland Constitution Permits Christians Only to Hold Office, November 11, 1776

XXXIII. That, as it is the duty of every man to worship God in such manner as he thinks most acceptable to him; all persons, professing the Christian religion, are equally entitled to protection in their religious liberty;
wherefore no person ought by any law to be molested in his person or estate on account of his religious persuasion or profession, or for his religious
practice; unless, under colour of religion, any man shall disturb the good
order, peace or safety of the State, or shall infringe the laws of morality, or
injure others, in their natural, civil, or religious rights; nor ought any person to be compelled to frequent or maintain, or contribute, unless on con-

tract, to maintain any particular place of worship, or any particular ministry; yet the legislature may, in their discretion, lay a general and equal tax, for the support of the Christian religion; leaving to each individual the power of appointing the payment over of the money, collected from him, to the support of any particular place of worship or minister, or for the benefit of the poor of his own denomination, or the poor in general of any particular county. . . .

XXXV. That no other test or qualification ought to be required, on admission to any office of trust or profit, than such oath of support and fidelity to this State, and such oath of office, as shall be directed by this convention, or the legislature of this State, and a declaration of a belief in the Christian religion. . . .

LV. That every person, appointed to any office of profit or trust, shall, before he enters on the execution thereof, take the following oath, to wit: "I.A.B., do swear, that I do not hold myself bound in allegiance to the King of Great Britain, and that I will be faithful and bear true allegiance to the State of Maryland"; and shall also subscribe a declaration of his belief in the Christian religion.

IV.   New York State Is the First State to Emancipate Jews, April 20, 1777

XXXV . . . That all such parts of the said common law, and all such of the said statutes and acts aforesaid, or parts thereof, as may be construed to establish or maintain any particular denomination of Christians or their ministers, or concern the allegiance heretofore yielded to, and the supremacy, sovereignty, government, or prerogatives claimed or exercised by the King of Great Britain and his predecessors, over the colony of New York and its inhabitants, or are repugnant to this constitution, be, and they hereby are, abrogated and rejected. . . .

XXXVIII. And whereas we are required, by the benevolent principles of rational liberty, not only to expel civil tyranny, but also to guard against that spiritual oppression and intolerance wherewith the bigotry and ambition of weak and wicked priests and princes have scourged mankind, this convention doth further, in the name and by the authority of the good people of this State, ordain, determine, and declare, that the free exercise and enjoyment of religious profession and worship, without discrimination or preference, shall forever hereafter be allowed, within this State, to all mankind: *Provided*, that the liberty of conscience, hereby granted, shall not be so construed as to excuse acts of licentiousness, or justify practices inconsistent with the peace or safety of this State.

XXXIX. And whereas the ministers of the gospel are, by their profession, dedicated to the service of God and the care of souls, and ought not to be diverted from the great duties of their function; therefore, no minister of the gospel, or priest of any denomination whatsoever, shall, at any time hereafter, under any pretence or description whatever, be eligible to, or capable of holding, any civil or military office or place within this State.

V. Philadelphia Jewry Asks for Political Equality, December 23, 1783

[December 23, 1783]

To the honourable, the Council of Censors, assembled agreeable to the constitution of the State of Pennsylvania.

The memorial of Rabbi Ger. Seixas of the synagogue of the Jews at Philadelphia, Simon Nathan, their *parnass* or president, Asher Myers, Bernard Gratz, and Haym Salomon, the *mahamad*, or associates of their council, in behalf of themselves and their bretheren Jews, residing in Pennsylvania, most respectfully sheweth:

That by the tenth section of the Frame of Government of this commonwealth [adopted in 1776], it is ordered that each member of the general assembly of representatives of the freemen of Pennsylvania, before he takes his seat, shall make and subscribe a declaration which ends in these words, "I do acknowledge the Scriptures of the Old and New Testament to be given by divine inspiration," to which is added an assurance that "no further or other religious test shall ever hereafter be required of any civil officer or magistrate in this state."

Your memorialists beg leave to observe that this clause seems to limit the civil rights of your citizens to one very special article of the creed, whereas, by the second paragraph of the declaration of the rights of the inhabitants, it is asserted without any other limitation than the professing the existence of God, in plain words, "that no man who acknowledges the being of a God can be justly deprived or abridged of any civil rights as a citizen on account of his religious sentiments." But certainly this religious test deprives the Jews of the most eminent rights of freemen, solemnly ascertained to all men who are not professed atheists.

May it please your Honors: Although the Jews in Pennsylvania are but few in number, yet liberty of the people in one country, and the declaration of the government thereof, that these liberties are the rights of the people, may prove a powerful attractive to men who live under restraints in another country. Holland and England have made valuable acquisitions of men, who, for their religious sentiments, were distressed in their own countries.

And if Jews in Europe or elsewhere should incline to transport themselves to America, and would, for reason of some certain advantage of the soil, climate, or the trade of Pennsylvania, rather become inhabitants thereof, than of any other state, yet the disability of Jews to take seat among the representatives of the people, as worded by the said religious test, might determine their free choice to go to New-York, or to any other of the United States of America, where there is no such like restraint laid upon the nation and religion of the Jews, as in Pennsylvania.

Your memorialists cannot say that the Jews are particularly fond of being representatives of the people in assembly or civil officers and magistrates in the state, but with great submission they apprehend that a clause in the constitution, which disables them to be elected by their fellow citizens to represent them in assembly, as [is] a stigma upon their nation and their religion, and it is inconsonant with the second paragraph of the said bill of rights. Otherwise, Jews are as fond of liberty as other religious societies can be, and it must create in them a displeasure when they perceive that for their professed dissent to a doctrine, which is inconsistent with their religious sentiments, they should be excluded from the most important and honourable part of the rights of a free citizen.

Your memorialists beg farther leave to represent that in the religious books of the Jews, which are or may be in every man's hands, there are no such doctrines or principles established as are inconsistent with the safety and happiness of the people of Pennsylvania, and that the conduct and behaviour of the Jews in this and the neighbouring states, has always tallied with the great design of the Revolution; [they beg farther leave to represent] that the Jews of Charlestown, New-York, New-Port, and other posts occupied by the British troops, have distinguishedly suffered for their attachment to the Revolution principles; and their brethren at St. Eustatius, for the same cause, experienced the most severe resentments of the British commanders.

The Jews of Pennsylvania, in proportion to the number of their members, can count with any religious society whatsoever the Whigs [the patriots] among either of them. They have served some of them in the Continental army; some went out in the militia to fight the common enemy; all of them have chearfully contributed to the support of the militia and of the government of this state.

They have no inconsiderable property in lands and tenements, but particularly in the way of trade, some more, some less, for which they pay taxes. They have, upon every plan formed for public utility, been forward to contribute as much as their circumstances would admit of, and as a nation or a religious society, they stand unimpeached of any matter whatsoever against the safety and happiness of the people.

And your memorialists humbly pray that if your honours, from any other consideration than the subject of this address, should think proper to call a convention for revising the constitution, you would be pleased to recommend this to the notice of that convention.

VI.   The Northwest Ordinance Implicitly Emancipates Jews in All New States, July 13, 1787

ART. 1. No person, demeaning himself in a peaceable and orderly manner, shall ever be molested on account of his mode of worship or religious sentiments, in the said territory.

VII.   Jonas Phillips Asks the Constitutional Convention to Emancipate Pennsylvania's Jews, September 7, 1787

Sires:

With leave and submission I address myself to those in whom there is wisdom, understanding, and knowledge; they are the honourable personages appointed and made overseers of a part of the terrestrial globe of the earth, namely the 13 United States of America in convention assembled, the Lord preserve them, amen.

I, the subscriber, being one of the people called Jews, of the city of Philadelphia, a people scattered and dispersed among all nations do behold with concern that among the laws in the constitution of Pennsylvania, there is a clause, sect. 10 to viz., "I do believe in one God the creatur and governor of the universe and rewarder of the good and the punisher of the wicked and I do acknowledge the Scriptures of the Old and New Testiment to be given by divine inspiration." To swear and believe that the New Testment was given by divine inspiration is absolutely against the religious principle of a Jew, and is against his conscience to take any such oath. By the above law a Jew is deprived of holding any publick office or place of government which is a contridictory to the [Pennsylvania] Bill of Right, sect. 2 viz.:

That all men have a natural and unalienable right to worship Almighty God according to the dictates of their own conscience and understanding, and that no man ought or of right can be compelled to attend any religious worship or [accept a] creed, or [erect or] support any place of worship, or maintain any minister, contrary to, or against his own free will and consent. Nor can any man who acknowledges the being of a God be justly deprived or abridged of any civil right as a citizen on account of his religious sentiments or peculiar mode of religious worship. And that no authority can or ought to be vested in or assumed by any power whatever that shall in any case interfere, or in any manner controul the right of conscience in the free exercise of religious worship.

It is well known among all the citizens of the 13 United States that the Jews have been true and faithful Whigs, and during the late contest with England they have been foremost in aiding and assisting the states with their lifes and fortunes. They have supported the cause, have bravely fought and bled for liberty which they can not enjoy.

Therefore if the honourable convention shall in their wisdom think fit and alter the said oath and leave out the words to viz.: "and I do acknowledge the Scripture of the New Testiment to be given by divine inspiration," then the Israelites will think themself happy to live under a government where all religious societys are on an equal footing. I solicit this favour for myself, my children, and posterity, and for the benefit of all the Israelites through the 13 United States of America.

My prayers is unto the Lord. May the people of this states rise up as a great and young lion; may they prevail against their enemies; may the degrees of honour of his Excellency, the president of the convention, George Washington, be exhalted and raise up. May everyone speak of his glorious exploits.

May God prolong his days among us in this land of liberty. May he lead the armies against his enemys as he has done hereuntofore. May God extend peace unto the United States. May they get up to the highest prosperitys. May God extend peace to them and their seed after them so long as the sun and moon endureth; and may the almighty God of our father Abraham, Isaac and Jacob indue this noble assembly with wisdom, judgment and unanimity in their counsells; and may they have the satisfaction to see that their present toil and labour for the wellfair of the United States may be approved of through all the world and particular by the United States of America, is the ardent prayer of sires.

Your most devoted obed. servant,

Jonas Phillips

Philadelphia, 24th Ellul, 5547, or Sep'r 7th 1787.

VIII.   Constitution of the United States, 1788–1791

PREAMBLE

We the people of the United States, in order to form a more perfect union, establish justice, insure domestic tranquility, provide for the common defence, promote the general welfare, and secure the blessings of liberty to ourselves and our posterity, do ordain and establish this constitution for the United States of America. . . .

Article VI

. . . The senators and representatives before mentioned, and the members of the several state legislatures, and all executive and judicial officers, both of the United States and of the several states, shall be bound by oath or affirmation, to support this constitution; but no religious test shall ever be required as a qualification to any office or public trust under the United States.

Amendments to the Constitution
November 3, 1791
Article I

Congress shall make no law respecting an establishment of religion, or prohibiting the free exercise thereof; or abridging the freedom of speech, or of the press; or the right of the people peaceably to assemble, and to petition the government for a redress of grievances.

IX. Sunday Legislation in New York State, February 12, 1788

Be it enacted by the people of the State of New York, represented in Senate and Assembly, and it is hereby enacted by the authority of the same, that there shall be no travelling, servile labour, or working (works of necessity and charity excepted), shooting, fishing, sporting, playing, horse-racing, hunting, or frequenting of tipling-houses, or any unlawful exercises or pastimes, by any person or persons within this state, on the first day of the week, commonly called *Sunday;*

And that every person being of the age of fourteen years or upwards, offending in the premises, shall, for every such offence, forfeit and pay to the use of the poor of the city or town where such offence shall be committed, the sum of six shillings;

And that no person shall cry, show forth, or expose to sale, any wares, merchandise, fruit, herbs, goods, or chattels, upon the first day of the week, commonly called *Sunday*, except small meat, and milk and fish, before nine of the clock in the morning, upon pain that every person so offending shall forfeit the same goods so cried, showed forth, or exposed to sale, to the use of the poor of the city or town where such offence shall be committed;

And if any person offending in any of the premises shall be thereof convicted before any justice of the peace for the county, or any mayor, recorder, or alderman of the city where the offence shall be committed, upon the view of the said justice, mayor, or recorder, or alderman, or confession of the party offending, or proof of any witness or witnesses upon oath, then the said justice, mayor, recorder, or alderman, before whom such conviction shall be had, shall direct and send his warrant, under his hand and seal, to some constable of the city or county where the offence shall have been committed, commanding him to seize and take the goods so cried, showed forth, or exposed to sale, as aforesaid, and to sell the same, and to levy the said other forfeitures or penalties, by distress and sale of the goods and chattels of such offenders, and to pay the money arising by the sale of such goods so seized, and the said other forfeitures or penalties, to the overseers of the poor of the city or town where the said offence or offences shall have been committed, for the use of the poor thereof;

And in case no such distress can be had, then every such offender shall by a warrant, under the hand and seal of the said justice, mayor, recorder, or alderman, be set publicly in the stocks for the space of two hours.

X.   Jacob Henry Pleads for Political Equality, December 6, 1809

I certainly, Mr. Speaker, know not the design of the Declaration of Rights made by the people of this state [of North Carolina] in the year 1776, if it was not to consecrate certain great and fundamental rights and principles, which even the [state's] constitution cannot impair; for the 44th section of the latter instrument declares that the Declaration of Rights ought never to be violated, on any pretense whatever.

If there is any apparent difference between the two instruments, they ought, if possible, to be reconciled; but if there is a final repugnance between them, the Declaration of Rights must be considered paramount; for I believe it is to the constitution, as the constitution is to law; it controls and directs it absolutely and conclusively. If, then, a belief in the Protestant religion is required by the constitution to qualify a man for a seat in this house, and such qualification is dispensed with by the Declaration of Rights, the provision of the constitution must be altogether inoperative; as the language of the Bill of Rights is, "that all men have a natural and inalienable right to worship Almighty God according to the dictates of their own consciences." It is undoubtedly a natural right, and when it is declared to be an inalienable one by the people in their sovereign and original capacity, any attempt to alienate either by the constitution or by law, must be vain and fruitless. . . .

If a man should hold religious principles incompatible with the freedom and safety of the state, I do not hesitate to pronounce that he should be excluded from the public councils of the same; and I trust if I know myself, no one would be more ready to aid and assist than myself. But I should really be at a loss to specify any known religious principles which are thus dangerous. It is surely a question between a man and his maker,

and requires more than human attributes to pronounce which of the numerous sects prevailing in the world is most acceptible to the Deity. If a
man fulfils the duties of that religion, which his education or his conscience has pointed to him as the true one, no person, I hold, in this our
land of liberty, has a right to arraign him at the bar of any inquisition; and
the day, I trust, has long passed, when principles merely speculative were
propagated by force, when the sincere and pious were made victims, and
the light-minded bribed into hypocrites.

The purest homage man could render to the Almighty was in the sacrifice of his passions and the performance of his duties, that the ruler of the
universe would receive with equal benignity the various offerings of man's
adoration, if they proceeded from the heart. Governments only concern
the actions and conduct of man, and not his speculative notions. Who
among us feels himself so exalted above his fellows as to have a right to
dictate to them any mode of belief? Shall this free country set an example
of persecution, which even the returning reason of enslaved Europe would
not submit to? Will you bind the conscience in chains and fasten convictions upon the mind in spite of the conclusions of reason and of those ties
and habitudes which are blended with every pulsation of the heart? Are
you prepared to plunge at once from the sublime heights of moral legislation into the dark and gloomy caverns of superstitious ignorance? Will
you drive from your shores and from the shelter of your constitution, all
who do not lay their oblations on the same altar, observe the same ritual,
and subscribe to the same dogmas? If so, which, among the various sects
into which we are divided, shall be the favored one?

I should insult the understanding of this House, to suppose it possible
that they could ever assent to such absurdities; for all know that persecution in all its shapes and modifications is contrary to the genius of our government and the spirit of our laws, and that it can never produce any other
effect than to render men hypocrites or martyrs. . . .

Nothing is more easily demonstrated than that the conduct alone is
the subject of human laws, and that man ought to suffer civil disqualifica-
tion for what he does, and not for what he thinks.

The mind can conceive laws only from Him of whose Divine essence
it is a portion; He alone can punish disobedience; for who else can know its
movements, or estimate their merits? The religion I profess inculcates
every duty which man owes to his fellow men; it enjoins upon its votaries
the practice of every virtue, and the detestation of every vice; it teaches
them to hope for the favor of heaven exactly in proportion as their lives
have been directed by just, honorable, and beneficent maxims. This, then,
gentlemen, is my creed; it was impressed upon my infant mind, it has been
the director of my youth, the monitor of my manhood, and will, I trust, be
the consolation of my old age. At any rate, Mr. Speaker, I am sure that you

cannot see anything in this religion, to deprive me of my seat in this house. So far as relates to my life and conduct, the examination of these I submit with cheerfulness to your candid and liberal construction.

What may be the religion of him who made this objection against me, or whether he has any religion or not I am unable to say. I have never considered it my duty to pry into the belief of other members of this house. If their actions are upright and conduct just, the rest is for their own consideration, not for mine. I do not seek to make converts to my faith, whatever it may be esteemed in the eyes of my officious friend, nor do I exclude anyone from my esteem or friendship because he and I differ in that respect. The same charity, therefore, it is not unreasonable to expect, will be extended to myself, because in all things that relate to the state and to the duties of civil life, I am bound by the same obligations with my fellow-citizens, nor does any man subscribe more sincerely than myself to the maxim, "Whatever ye would that men should do unto you, do ye so even unto them, for such is the law and the prophets." [Matthew 7:12].

13

Jews in the General Community
1780–1816

J ews as businessmen had high visibility on Main Street in some of America's large east coast cities. Culturally they were a minuscule group. In 1790 in a country of about four million souls they numbered, at the most, about 2500, less than one in a thousand. On the whole they were regarded benignly; there was no anti-Jewish violence; they were certainly better off than their relatives in Europe.

The first selection is a letter which Frances (Fanny) Sheftall, a Southerner, wrote to her husband, Mordecai, who was about to be paroled (1780). He and his son had been prisoners of the British for well over a year. During the Revolution this merchant and his teenage boy served as quartermasters for the Continental Georgia forces. The second selection is an appeal to the "Enlightened Citizens" of Philadelphia for gifts to help pay the mortgage on Mikveh Israel, the local synagog (1788). Benjamin Franklin responded generously. The third selection is an exchange between George Washington and the "Hebrews" of Newport; Washington's letter was in answer to a congratulatory note which they had sent or handed to the president (1790). Washington was traveling in New England mending fences; the Yankees resented the dominance of the Virginians in the new administration. The final selection is the bitter answer of Mordecai Manuel Noah who had been summarily dismissed from his post as consul at Tunis, primarily because he was a Jew. Noah was very angry (1816).

I. Frances Sheftall Writes to Her Husband, July 20, 1780

Charls Town [South Carolina], July 20th, 1780

My dear Sheftall:

I have now the pleasure to inform you that I received your letter on the 19 instn., dated May the 5, and sincerly congratulate you and my dear childe on your enlargement [impending release], hoping that we may once more meet again in a great deal of pleasure, for I can assure you that we have been strangers to that for some time past. But I still hope that our troubles will now be soon at an end.

I make not the least doubt, but ere thise comes to hand that you have herd that thise place [Charleston] was given over to the British troops on May 12th by a caputalation after three longe months sige. During that time I retier'd into the country with my family, and a great many of our people [Jews] ware at the same place. During the sige thare was scarce a woman to be see[n] in the streets. The balls flew like haile during the cannonading.

After the town was given over, I returned to town and have hierd a house in St. Michael's Alley belonging to Mrs. Stephens at the rate of fifty pounds sterlinge a year. And whear the money is to come from God only knows, for their is nothing but hard money goes here, and that, I can assure you, is hard enough to be got.

I am obliged to take in needle worke to make a living for my family, so I leave you to judge what a livinge that must be.

Our Negroes [slaves] have every one been at the point of death, so that they have been of no use to me for thise six weeks past. But, thankes be to God, they are all getting the better of it except poor little Billey; he died with the yellow fever on the 3 of July.

The children have all got safe over the small pox. They had it so favourable that Perla had the most and had but thirty [pockmarks]. How I shall be able to pay the doctor's bill and house rent, God only knowes. But I still trust to Providence knowing that the Almighty never sends trouble but he sends some relife.

As to our Adam [a free servant?], he is so great a gentleman that was it to please God to put it in your power to send for us, I do thinke that he would come with us.

I wrote to you about three weeks agoe by way of St. Austatia [Eustatia] to Antigua [where you were held by the British] whare I mention every particular to you, but must now refer it untill it shall pleas God that we see you again. You[r] brother Levy went out of town during the sige toward the northward and has not returned as yet. Thise day his youngest baby, Isaac, was buried. The poor baby was sicke for about three weeks and then died.

We have had no less than six Jew children buried since the sige, and poor Mrs. Cardosar [Cardozo], Miss Leah Toras that was, died last week with the small pox. Mr. DeLyon has lost his two grand children. Mrs.

Mordecai has lost her child. Mrs. Myers Moses had the misfortune to have her youngest daughter, Miss Rachel, killed with the nurse by a cannon ball during the sige.

Perla begs that you will excuse her not whriting by thise oppertunity as she has been with her Aunt Sally for several nights and is very much fatigued, and the flag [of truce ship] goes immediately [with my letter], but hopes that she will be the bearrer of the next [letter] herselfe. But havinge so favourable an oppertunity as the flag [I] was willing to let you no [know] some little of our family affairs.

I have nothing more at present but wish to hear from you by the first oppertunity.

The children joine me in love to you and their brother, and I remain
Your loving wife,
Frances Sheftall.

II. The Gentiles of Philadelphia Help the Synagog, April 30, 1788

To the humane, charitable, and well disposed people, the representation and solicitation of the good people of the Hebrew society [community] in the City of Philadelphia, commonly called Israelites.

Whereas, the religious order of men in this city denominated Israelites were without any synagogue or house of worship untill the year 1780 [1782], when, desirous of accommodating themselves and encouraged thereto by a number of respectable and worthy bretheren of the Hebrew society then in this place [who generously contributed to the design], they purchased a lot of ground and erected thereon the buildings necessary and proper for their religious worship.

And whereas many of their number at the close of the late war returned to New York, Charleston, and elsewhere their homes (which they had been exiled from and obliged to leave on account of their attachment to American measures), leaving the remaining few of their religion here burthened with a considerable charge consequent from so great an undertaking;

And whereas the present congregation, after expending all the subscriptions, loans, gifts, etc., made the society by themselves and the generous patrons of their religious intentions, to the amount of at least £2200, were obliged to borrow money to finish the building, and contract other debts that is now not only pressingly claimed, but a judgment will actually be obtained against their house of worship, which must be sold unless they are speedily enabled to pay the sum of about £800; and which, from a variety of delicate and distressing causes they are wholly unable to raise among themselves;

They are therefore under the necessity of earnestly soliciting from their worthy fellow-citizens of every religious denomination their benevolent aid and help, flattering themselves that their worshipping Almighty God in a way and manner different from other religious societies will never deter the enlightened citizens of Philadelphia from generously subscribing towards the preservation of a religious house of worship. The subscription paper will be enrolled in the archives of their congregation, that their posterity may know and gratefully remember the liberal supporters of their religious society. Philadelphia, April 30th, 1788.

III. Newport Jews Exchange Letters with President George Washington, 1790

A

ADDRESS OF THE NEWPORT CONGREGATION TO THE
PRESIDENT OF THE UNITED STATES OF AMERICA
AUGUST 17, 1790

Sir, Permit the Children of the Stock of Abraham to approach you with the most cordial affection and esteem for your person and merits—and to join with our fellow-citizens in welcoming you to New Port.

With pleasure we reflect on those days—those days of difficulty and danger, when the God of Israel, who delivered David from the peril of the sword—shielded your head in the day of battle:—and we rejoice to think that the same Spirit, who rested in the bosom of the greatly beloved Daniel, enabling him to preside over the Provinces of the Babylonish Empire, rests, and ever will rest upon you, enabling you to discharge the arduous duties of Chief Magistrate in these States.

Deprived as we have hitherto been of the invaluable rights of free citizens, we now, (with a deep sense of gratitude to the Almighty Disposer of all events) behold a Government (erected by the Majesty of the People) a Government which to bigotry gives no sanction, to persecution no assistance—but generously affording to All liberty of conscience, and immunities of citizenship—deeming every one, of whatever nation, tongue, or language equal parts of the great governmental machine. This so ample and extensive federal union whose basis is Philanthropy, mutual confidence, and public virtue, we cannot but acknowledge to be the work of the Great God, who ruleth in the armies of Heaven, and among the inhabitants of the Earth, doing whatsoever seemeth him good.

For all the blessings of civil and religious liberty which we enjoy under an equal and benign administration we desire to send up our thanks to the Antient of days, the great Preserver of Men—beseeching him that the Angel who conducted our forefathers through the wilderness into the promised land, may graciously conduct you through all the dangers and difficulties of this mortal life—and when like Joshua full of days, and full of honor, you are gathered to your Fathers, may you be admitted into the heavenly Paradise to partake of the water of life and the tree of immortality.

Done and signed by order of the Hebrew Congregation in New Port, Rhode Island, August 17th, 1790.

Moses Sexias [sic] Warden

B

George Washington Writes the Hebrew Congregation in New Port, Rhode Island
1790

Gentlemen:

While I receive with much satisfaction your address replete with expressions of affection and esteem, I rejoice in the opportunity of assuring you that I shall always retain a grateful remembrance of the cordial welcome I experienced in my visit to New Port from all classes of Citizens.

The reflection on the days of difficulty and danger which are past is rendered the more sweet from a consciousness that they are succeeded by days of uncommon prosperity and security.

If we have wisdom to make the best use of the advantages with which we are now favored, we cannot fail, under the just administration of a good government to become a great and happy people.

The Citizens of the United States of America have a right to applaud themselves for having given to mankind examples of an enlarged and liberal policy, a policy worthy of imitation. All possess alike liberty of conscience and immunities of citizenship.

It is now no more that toleration is spoken of, as if it was by the indulgence of one class of people, that another enjoyed the exercise of their inherent natural rights. For happily the government of the United States, which gives to bigotry no sanction, to persecution no assistance, requires only that they who live under its protection should demean themselves as good citizens, in giving it on all occasions their effectual support.

It would be inconsistent with the frankness of my character not to avow that I am pleased with your favorable opinion of my administration, and fervent wishes for my felicity.

May the children of the Stock of Abraham, who dwell in this land, continue to merit and enjoy the good will of the other inhabitants, while every one shall sit in safety under his own vine and fig-tree and there shall be none to make him afraid.

May the Father of all mercies scatter light and not darkness in our paths, and make us all in our several vocations useful here, and in his own due time and way everlastingly happy.

G. Washington.

IV. Mordecai M. Noah's Dismissal from Office because of His Jewish Religion, April 25, 1816

The squadron lay off Cape Carthage [near Tunis], arranged in handsome order; the "Guerriere," bearing the broad penant of the commodore [Stephen Decatur], was in the centre, and the whole exhibiting a very agreeable and commanding sight. In less than an hour, I [Noah] was alongside of the flagship and ascended on the quarter-deck. The marines were under arms and received the consul of the United States with the usual honours. Commodore Decatur and Capt. Downs [Master Commandant John Downes], both in uniform, were at the gangway, and most of the officers and crew pressed forward to view their fellow-citizen. After the customary salutations and a few inquiries, Commodore Decatur invited me into the cabin, where, after being seated, he went to his *escrutoire* [escritoire], and from among a package of letters he handed me one, saying that it was a despatch from the Secretary of State, and requested me to use no ceremony, but to read it. It had the seal of the United States, which I broke, and, to my great surprise, read as follows:

Department of State, April 25, 1815. Sir:

At the time of your appointment as consul at Tunis, it was not known that the religion which you profess would form any obstacle to the exercise of your consular functions. Recent information, however, on which entire reliance may be placed, proves that it would produce a very unfavourable effect. In consequence of which, the President has deemed it expedient to revoke your commission. On the receipt of this letter, therefore, you will consider yourself no longer in the public service. There are some circumstances, too, connected with your accounts, which require a more particular explanation, which, with that already given, are not approved by the President.

I am, very respectfully, sir,

Your obedient servant.

(Signed) James Monroe.

Mordecai M. Noah, Esquire, etc., etc. . . .

I paused to reflect on its contents. I was at a loss to account for its strange and unprecedented tenor: my religion an object of hostility? I thought I was a citizen of the United States, protected by the constitution in my religious, as well as in my civil, rights. My religion was known to the government at the time of my appointment, and it constituted one of the prominent causes why I was sent to Barbary. If, then, any "unfavourable" events had been created by my religion, they should have been first ascertained, and not acting upon a supposition, upon imaginary consequences, have thus violated one of the most sacred and delicate rights of a citizen. Admitting, then, that my religion had produced an unfavourable effect, no *official* notice should have been taken of it. I could have been recalled without placing on file a letter thus hostile to the spirit and character of our institutions. But my religion was not known in Barbary; from the moment of my landing, I had been in the full possession of my consular functions, respected and feared by the government, and enjoying the esteem and good will of every resident.

What injury could my religion create? I lived like other consuls; the flag of the United States was displayed on Sundays and Christian holidays. The Catholic priest, who came into my house to sprinkle holy water and pray, was received with deference and freely allowed to perform his pious purpose. The barefooted Franciscan, who came to beg, received alms in the name of Jesus Christ. The Greek bishop, who sent to me a decorated branch of palm on Palm Sunday, received, in return, a customary donation. The poor Christian slaves, when they wanted a favour, came to me. The Jews alone asked nothing from me. Why then am I to be persecuted for my religion? Although no religious principles are known to the constitution, no peculiar worship connected with the government, yet I did not forget that I was representing a Christian nation. What was the opinion of Joel Barlow [U.S. consul to Algiers, 1795], when writing a treaty for [Tripoli, 1797] one of the Barbary States? Let the following article, *confirmed by the Senate of the United States*, answer:

Article 11th—As the government of the United States of America is not, in any sense, founded on the Christian religion—as it has, in itself, no character of enmity against the laws, religion, or tranquillity of Mussulmen [Moslems]; and as the said States never have entered into any war, or act of hostility against any Mahometan nation, it is declared by the parties, that no pretext *arising from religious opinions*, shall *ever* produce an interruption of the harmony existing between the two countries. [Actually, the Arabic of Article 11 says nothing about Christianity. It does, however, ask for reciprocally good treatment for Americans and Tripolitans in the respective two lands.]

If President Madison was unacquainted with this article in the treaty, which in effect is equally binding in all the States of Barbary, he should have remembered that the religion of a citizen is not a legitimate object of official notice from the government. And even admitting that my religion was an obstacle, and there is no doubt that it was not, are we prepared to yield up the admirable and just institutions of our country at the shrine of foreign bigotry and superstition? Are we prepared to disfranchise one of our own citizens to gratify the intolerant views of the Bey of Tunis? Has it come to this, that the noble character of the most illustrious republic on earth, celebrated for its justice and the sacred character of its institutions, is to be sacrificed at the shrine of a Barbary pirate? Have we then fallen so low? What would have been the consequence, had the Bey known and objected to my religion? He would have learnt from me, in language too plain to be misunderstood, that whoever the United States commissions as their representative, he must receive and respect, if his conduct be proper. On that subject I could not have permitted a word to be said.

If such a principle is attempted to be established, it will lay the foundation for the most unhappy and most dangerous disputes. Foreign nations will dictate to us the religion which our officers at their courts should profess. With all the reflection, and the most painful anxiety, I could not account for this most extraordinary and novel procedure. Some base intrigue, probably one who was ambitious of holding this wretched office, had been at some pains to represent to the government that my religion would produce injurious effects, and the President, instead of closing the door on such interdicted subjects, had listened and concurred. And after having braved the perils of the ocean, residing in a barbarous country, without family or relatives, supporting the rights of the nation, and hazarding my life from poison or the stiletto, I find my own government, the only protector I can have, sacrificing my credit, violating my rights, and insulting my feelings, and the religious feelings of a whole nation [the Jews]. O! shame, shame! . . .

It was not necessary for a citizen of the United States to have his faith stamped on his forehead. The name of freeman is a sufficient passport, and my government should have supported me, had it been necessary to have defended my rights, and not to have themselves assailed them. There was also something insufferably little, in adding the weight of the American government, in violation of the wishes and institutions of the people, to crush a nation [the Jews], many of which had fought and bled for American Independence, and many had assisted to elevate those very men who had thus treated their rights with indelicate oppression. Unfortunate people, whose faith and constancy alone have been the cause of so much tyranny and oppression, who have given moral laws to the world, and who receive for reward opprobrium and insult! After this, what nation may not oppress them?

That the subject of religion should ever have commanded the *official* notice of the government of the United States cannot fail to create the greatest surprise when a reference is had to the Constitution of the United

States, and equally so to the enlightened state of the times. In the War for Independence the Jews were unanimous in their zealous co-operation, and we find them holding a high rank in the army and fighting for liberty with a gallantry worthy of the descendants of Joshua, David, and the Maccabees. After the adoption of the constitution, we see them on the bench as judges, in the legislatures as members, and assisting the government, in gloomy periods, to regulate and strengthen the financial system. In all the relations of life as fathers, husbands, and citizens, I persuade myself that they yield to no sect, and they have ever been distinguished for their liberal sentiments towards every denomination of Christians. . . .

Surely it is not too much to expect that under all these circumstances, the officers of government will conform to the wishes of the people and treat them with a delicacy becoming freemen. It is not, however, to satisfy the Israelites in this country that I notice this subject. They are capable of defending their own rights, but it is done to prove to the Jews in Europe, who have great commercial connexions with the United States and are capable of serving or injuring us, that this act of intolerance, of which I have had so much reason to complain, is not the act of the people, is not warranted or approved by them, but it is the simple mandate of the Executive Officer [the President] or the Secretary of State, acting either under an imaginary right, or gratifying a prejudice which I reluctantly believe has had some small influence in dictating the measure. . . .

I will defend my rights and measures at every hazard, and will not permit the government to treat them lightly without a full and clear explanation. I have no reason to believe, neither would I wish to insinuate, that either the President or Secretary of State are desirous, by any official act, to disqualify a citizen, [and, to paraphrase George Washington in a letter to the Jews, to] "give a sanction to bigotry," or awaken the most unhappy and unfortunate prejudices that can possibly exist, those of religion. It would be very inconsistent with their character, but the experiment is too dangerous to countenance. . . .

If we once establish distinctions of religion in the appointment of our officers abroad, we shall not dare to send a Catholic to England, a Protestant to France, or a Jew to Spain. Instead of shaming, by our liberality, and by the force of our noble institutions, these unworthy and destructive prejudices, we shall nourish them by the example unworthy [of] freemen and shall, in time, forget that distinction in religion, rank, rights, opinions, and privileges, are all absorbed in the honorable name of American. That should be the only passport which he should bear about him, who serves his country on a foreign mission. His conscience should be shielded from the dark scrutiny of bigoted power, and considered as a private affair, between God and himself.

The institutions of the United States are the property of the nation. The faith of the people is pledged for their existence. The most distinguished feature in our compact, the brightest link in our chain of union, is religious liberty, is the emancipation of the soul from temporal authority. We cease to be free when we cease to be liberal. From the height of fame and honor we shall fall like "a bright constellation in the evening, and be seen no more!"

14

THE CULTURAL LEVEL OF AMERICAN JEWRY
1810–1839

T he cultural level of American Jews in the early national period was not high. A very large number were immigrants; some came from Eastern Europe where they had received very little secular training. Practically all, however, had somehow acquired sufficient learning to conduct a business; many were shopkeepers. Cohen & Isaacs of Richmond wrote English, but employed the Hebrew, not the Roman alphabet. There was no Jewish community, where there was not an individual—often an autodidact—who was not well educated. Some had fine libraries. Native-born Americans—men and women—had gone to Jewish all-day schools and were versed in the three R's, reading, writing, and 'rithmetic. Others attended private schools and were encouraged to read the English classics. Mordecai Manuel Noah—a student at New York's Jewish all-day school —became a distinguished editor and dramatist. Several men and women wrote poetry; others enjoyed writing doggerel. Women intellectuals were not uncommon. By 1800 Charleston, South Carolina, was a center of secular culture; it sheltered the country's largest Jewish community in those years.

The first selection contains a few verses of Grace Seixas Nathan (1752–1831), the ancestor of the Nathan clan, men and women distinguished for eminence in the fields of law, literature, and education. The second selection includes some poems written by Penina Moïse (1797–1880). This Charlestonian published a volume of verse in 1833, *Fancy's Sketchbook*. She was also a prolific hymn writer. The following sentence is her graphic definition of neuralgia from which she suffered: "Neuralgia, a fugitive from purgatory, who having served as an apprentice in Lucifer's penal laboratory, acquired such proficiency in the art of torturing that, having excited the jealousy of her master, quitted the Satanic institute, and established a patent rack and screw factory, distancing all nerve-racking competitors—not excepting the familiars of the Inquisition." Rachel Mordecai Lazarus (1789–1838) of Warrenton, North Carolina, and Wilmington, Delaware, carried on a correspondence for years with Maria Edgeworth (1767–1849), the Anglo-Irish educator and novelist. Rachel expounds her views on slavery in the third selection.

Isaac Gomez, Jr. (1768–1831), a fourth generation scion of a New York Spanish-Portuguese family, was at home in the Old and New Testaments. A decade or two before his death he wrote a polemical work—unpublished—attacking trinitarianism and defending the Jewish concept of monotheism. Gomez was also the author of a published anthology of literature that brought him high praise from former president John Adams. Gomez called his book *Selections of a Father for the Use of His Children, in Prose and Verse* (1820). In 1829 he wrote a love letter of sorts to his cherished wife Abigail Lopez. He was now sixty-one; they had been married for almost forty years. He was eager, after all the happy years with his wife, to give her an unusual gift which would be truly his own. What would be more fitting than a manuscript prayer book. He sat himself down and spent long weary hours copying the first volume of David Levi's English translation of the daily Hebrew liturgy according to the Sephardic rite. When he was done with his labor of love he bound it in leather, marbled its edges, and handed it to her with the letter which is the fourth selection.

The fifth selection is a poem written by Joseph Lyons (1813–1837), born in South Carolina, probably in Columbia. He received an excellent education in Charleston, and at the age of twenty-two passed the bar examination at Savannah. Lyons was a very unhappy young man. He died of consumption in Paris, France. Octavia Harby Moses (1823–1904), daughter of the Charleston religious reformer Isaac Harby, spent most of her life in Sumter, South Carolina. She began writing poetry at the age of thirteen. The sixth selection is a sample of her art; it was written the year she was married; she was all of sixteen (1839).

I.   Grace Seixas Nathan, Poet, 1810 and on

A

**Written on a geranium plant
which a severe frost blasted.
Jan'y 1810.**

Oh how keenly the sharp air has blown;
It has stript my fair plant of its bloom,
And its life with its beauty has flown,
Ere yet it had reached to its noon.

I had raised it from infancy's bud;
I had made it a daily delight,
Yet a breath that was piercing rude
Destroyed my fair plant in a night.
Now withered and blasted to view,
I behold it with anguish severe.
I recall both its fragrance and hue,
And I pensively shed the sad tear.
I received the fair plant from a friend,
And I would not have lost it so soon,
For I said when my being should end,
I would have it placed nigh to my tomb.
Like the cypress it there might have grown
And marked out the [sod?] for my head,
For sweet friendship was ever my own.
And I would still embrace it when dead.

B

I had a bud so very sweet—its fragrance reached the skies.
The angels joined in holy league—and seized it as their prize.
They bore it to their realms of bliss—where it will ever bloom,
For in the bosom of their God they placed my rich perfume.

Written on the death of my grandchild, Jan'y 19th, 1819.

II.   Penina Moïse, Poet, 1820 and on

To Persecuted Foreigners

1820
If thou art one of that oppressed race,
Whose name's a proverb, and whose lot's disgrace,
Brave the Atlantic—Hope's broad anchor weigh,
A Western sun will gild your future day.

Stanzas.
Oh! hide those eyes of violet hue,
Wild passion they inspire;
They beam too fiercely to be blue,
Their dew is lost in fire.

Yet in thine heart eternal snow
The torch of love destroys;
Long have I felt affection's woe,
But never felt its joys.

I saw thee cull a lovely rose
And place it near thy heart;
I knew its languid leaves would close,
Its fragrance would depart.

In sorrow I beheld the flower
On thy cold bosom lie;
I knew t'would languish there an hour,
I knew it then would die!

I traced my doom reflected here,
My bloom is fading fast;
I live but in thy beauty's glare,
I'll die in it at last!

III. Rachel Mordecai Lazarus, an Intellectual, 1827–1838

A

Wilmington, January 6th, 1827.

My dear Madam [Rachel to Maria Edgeworth]:
    The more I learn of the actual state of Ireland, the more am I inclined to wonder at the mistaken policy of a wise and enlightened government [Great Britain] in pursuing a system so glaringly oppressive, and, I should say, injurious to their own interests. Much has been humanely urged in the British Parliament on the subject of Negro slavery; yet is the condition of the Irish poor incomparably worse than that of the slave, either here, or as far as I am informed, in the [West India] Islands. I do not mean to defend the Slave System, of which I feel and acknowledge all the evils; but where is the consistency of practising, without even a similar shadow of apology, a system which wants but the name to render it more than equally odious?

B

Wilmington, October 6th, 1831.

[Rachel Mordecai to her brother George W. Mordecai, Raleigh]
    I can readily conceive the alarm and anxiety which must have been excited in your mind by the shocking reports of us which were so groundlessly circulated far and wide [after the Nat Turner Negro insurrection]. During the period of the first and greatest commotion among our townsfolk, I thought the accounts (as they eventually proved) so vague that I felt merely a state of discomfort from the scene of indefinable terror and con-

fusion around me without realizing sufficiently to partake of them, and as [our brother] Washington no doubt informed you, we remained quietly at home during the day and night (a very inclement one), when many were exposing themselves in the streets or crowding into the bank and other houses on the front street. The horrible disclosures which have subsequently been made have made a total change in my feelings, and I view the condition of the Southern states as one of the most unenviable that can be conceived. To be necessarily surrounded by those [slaves] in whom we cannot permit ourselves to feel confidence, to know that unremitted vigilance is our only safeguard, and that soon or late we or our descendants will become the certain victims of a band of lawless wretches who will deem murder and outrage just retribution is deplorable in the extreme. The United States government might possibly find a remedy by rendering some equivalent to slave owners and exporting the slaves in as large numbers as practicable to Africa. But I do not know whether if such a plan were proposed it would be acceded to by any considerable majority; people are too short sighted, too unwilling to relinquish present convenience from the fear of future ill or for the prospect of future good. Mr. L[azarus] regrets holding so much property here, and if not actually tied down to the place, would gladly remove to the north, and I cannot help hoping that we may at some period be enabled to do so.

C

Wilmington, January 10th, 1836.

[Rachel to Maria]

If you see our papers you must have remarked the efforts that are making for the abolition of slavery, an end to be desired by all, tho' the means too inconsiderately adopted are in every point of view unjustifiable. The excellent, the philanthropick [William] Wilberforce [the English abolitionist] who spent his best years in the advancement of this labour of love viewed the subject with wisdom and humanity. But what can be said of men who blindly, madly urge the slave to seek his freedom through a sea of blood, who promise to aid him in the commission of crime, without even glancing at the too-certain consequences, and who, while pledging themselves in the cause of suffering humanity, would spread horror and devastation among their brethren and over one half of their mother land? Their mischievous purposes will I trust in Heaven be averted, and the removal of this mighty evil, of which we of the South are not insensible, be left to our own legislators whose wisdom will find means gradually but surely to effect the end. . . .

D

Wilmington, March 18th, 1838.

[Rachel to Maria]

Now to turn to the slave question. I and very many others agree with you and Miss [Harriet] Martineau [the anti-slavery English writer], on the inconsistency of slavery with American liberty, but before we condemn in toto we must attend to the arrangement of historical facts. Was it the American states proud of their freedom and boasting of their rights who employed slave ships to go to Africa and bring to them hewers of wood and drawers of water? No it was English colonies planted in America under grants from the king of Great Britain who entailed this curse upon our land. In process of time these colonies, being denied what they deemed their rights by the mother country, laboured successfully, to throw off her government, and declared themselves an independent people. They were free from the rule of any other nation and they set about forming a government of their own. Could they at that time have loved liberty for itself alone and looked with an equally humane and philosophic eye on the miseries of the slave and the slave holder, all had now been well, but such ideas had not then entered into the mind even of a Wilberforce, and it would have been expecting too much from poor human nature that a people, an infant people, impoverished by war, uncertain of the issue of a newly formed constitution and employing all their faculties to maintain the advantages so hardly gained, should say, the South to the North, we would be wholly free, give us half the worth of our slaves and we will relinquish the other half and labour and till the ground with our own hands (a Utopian supposition), but the North must have replied, we are ourselves bankrupt, our continental money is worse than blank paper and our common country has no treasury and is involved in debt; we cannot assist you nor can you relinquish the only medium by which your shattered fortunes can hope to be repaired.

Will you not allow that this true statement does in part excuse the inconsistency? That the system is an evil, that by it are produced a host of minor evils, is a point readily conceded; whether it is criminal in us to retain our slaves is yet to be considered, and to proceed reasonably and deliberately I would ask what would be their condition were they to be freed tomorrow? Ignorant and inconsiderate as they are, they would for the most part be unable to support or take care of themselves; they would be most uncomfortable as well as a burden to the community. Miss Martineau presents a true picture in the note which she extracts from a Southern publication in which the lady is described as giving medicines to her servants and dressing their wounds with her own hands. There are few of them who will perform these offices of kindness for each other, tho' without compulsion they will, I scarce know why, shew an inclination to attend on the whites under similar circumstances.

But to return, those who are most earnest on the subject of abolition cannot point out the necessary means for its accomplishment; it would not surely be by rendering slaves discontented and instigating them to rise up in arms against their masters. They must then be exterminated in self defence. Yet this has been the means, Miss Martineau's assertion notwithstanding, by which many of those mistaken enthusiasts at the North sought to irritate the minds of our slaves. Eastern pedlars were commissioned to carry pamphlets to distribute among them filled with prints of slaves suffering under the lash and degraded in various ways with which they themselves were unacquainted. These tracts were of a most mischievous nature and calculated only to do harm....

I do hope that means will be adopted for the gradual and judicious emancipation of slaves. The legislature of Kentucky, a wealthy slave holding state west of and adjoining Virginia, have a bill for considering means for this purpose now under consideration; the result will be important to all its sister states. I have long averred that I would willingly undergo the hardship and inconvenience of waiting on myself were that the only alternative, to be freed from the charge and responsibility of living in a slave state....

IV.   Isaac Gomez, Jr., Anthologist, 1829

Mrs. Abby Gomez,
My angelic wife:
Permit me to request your kind acceptance of this book. Having written it for your use, I flatter myself you will use it with pleasure, it being the work of him who has the honour of having been your loving husband for upwards of nine and thirty years, during which time it's a pleasant thing to know that domestic happiness has been our lot, and I make no doubt but it will continue during our journey through life, and I feel the happiness so great that I may say with truth "That I thank my God for having created thee for me and me for thee." And may we be permitted by "The Great Monarch of the Universe" to be together for many years yet to come of uninterrupted felicity is my sincear wish, and I trust you are well convinced that did I possess the riches of Peru, my greatest happiness would be to lay them at your feet. With those sentiments sincearly expressed I take lieve to say that I am truly
Your devoted and loving husband
Isaac Gomez Jun'r

V.   A Poem by Joseph Lyons, May 23, 1834

May 23, Friday. A fool told me today she was sorry for me, and I thought what I here write:

You are sorry for me!!!
Eternal God am I then that *thing*
As to excite pity!
Give me deep scorn, without disguise,
Most rancorous hate, abhorrence,
Anything but pity!
By heaven, 'tis what you feel
For the unresisting worm you've carelessly crushed,
And you pity it for its impotence
To escape or to retaliate.
Am I so gifted—Am I a poor,
Crawling, weak, despicable reptile?
If I am, *then* be *sorry* for me.
But whilst I feel in my capacious soul
A comprehensive power to enfold
Passions that in their expansion
Would shatter your pigmy soul
Into indiscernible atoms,
Dare not to reduce me
To your petty pitiful size,
And be sorry for me, as
You would for your fellows.

VI.   Octavia Harby Moses, Poet, 1839

Impromptu.
On receiving a parting kiss from my husband.

Thou hast left me, beloved, but the touch of thy lip
    Still lingers in fragrance on mine,
More sweet than the nectar which honey-bees sip
    From roses, or wild eglantine!
How slight was the pressure, how brief the caress,
    How fleeting that moment of bliss,
Yet the treasures of monarchs with me did they rest
    Would be worthless, compared with that kiss.

15

MAKING A LIVING IN THE UNITED STATES
1782–1840

It was during the early national period that Jews slowly inched their way into the new economy. A few individual entrepreneurs were involved in banking, stock exchanges, toll roads, canals, railroads, industry, large-scale land speculation, and town building. In the Kentucky of the 1780s Daniel Boone was kept busy surveying thousands of acres of land for Cohen & Isaacs of Richmond, Virginia. Kentucky was still part of Virginia. With the growth of industry and the cities, Jews in small numbers began to turn to the professions: law, medicine, and even engineering. There were a few plantation owners in the South. Still adhering to the colonial patterns, most Jews were shopkeepers, artisans, brokers, auctioneers (jobbers), blockade runners, privateers—in time of war—and aspiring merchants. At the ends of the spectrum there were merchant-shippers and peddlers. By 1840 there were only twenty-some Jewish "communities" in fifteen or sixteen towns. There may have been 15,000 Jews in all the states and territories of the Union.

The first selection is a 1782 advertisement of Haym Salomon (1740–1785). It reflects the business activities of this brilliant Polish immigrant who served as a broker for the Continental Office of Finance and as an agent for the French and Dutch, who were advancing funds to help crush the British. If the English enemy was to be bottled up at Yorktown in 1781, it was imperative to find the funds to equip the Continental forces. Salomon, the alchemist, turned "paper"—bills of exchange—into gold, thus providing the necessary sinews of war. In turn the defeat at Yorktown moved the English to recognize the independence of the rebel colonies. Salomon was not an unimportant cog in the final push for victory.

The second selection is also an advertisement—in doggerel—of a Charleston broker who lent money, sold lands and securities, and emphasized the skills of the slaves he had in stock. Slaves were a commodity. This merchant was Abraham Seixas (1750/51–1799), a Revolutionary War veteran, a brother of the New York clergyman. The third selection recounts one of the business promotions of Aaron Levy (1771–1852), a New York merchant, art dealer, auctioneer, and real estate speculator. Levy staged a Fourth of July celebration near Caldwell, now Lake George, New York, in 1821; he combined patriotism and business. His new promotion was Mount Levy. The Lieutenant Colonel, an officer in the militia, also served in the War of 1812. (Thirty-five years earlier another Aaron Levy—no relative—had founded the town of Aaronsburg in Pennsylvania; it is still in existence.) The fourth selection is a letter of Sally Etting (1776–1863) to her nephew Benjamin Etting (1798–1875). "Poor old Aunt Sal"—all of forty-nine—combined business and family gossip. She was interested in lozenges, china, tea, crepe cloth. Obviously she was a petty shopkeeper operating out of her home.

Lewis H. Polock (1819–1851) is the picaresque hero in the fifth selection. As a teenager he joined a whaling expedition to the Pacific in the 1830s, probably jumped ship, and settled in Yerba Buena in Upper California where he opened a clothing and dry goods store. Polock was involved in an aborted coup d'état in 1840, and was imprisoned by the Mexican authorities. The story of his incarceration and claim for damages is the burden of this selection. During the Mexican War he served as a top sergeant in the infantry. Later he made a living as a professional gambler. Just about a year after his claim was approved, he was assassinated in a bordello. The man who killed him got off with a fine and a three-week jail sentence; he had a Jewish lawyer, the later California Supreme Court judge, Solomon Heydenfeldt. Please note that Polock listed 200 pairs of pantaloons in his inventory, a very substantial stock for a tiny village which, years later, was to become the town of San Francisco. He was a protoargonaut.

I.   Haym Salomon, Broker to the Office of Finance, November 16, 1782

Haym Salomon, Broker to the Office of Finance, to the Consul General of France, and to the Treasurer of the French Army, at his office in Front Street, between Market and Arch streets. *Buys* and sells on commission *bank stock, bills of exchange* on France, Spain, Holland, and other parts of Europe, the West-Indies, and inland bills, at the usual commissions.

He buys and sells *loan office certificates, continental and state money,* of this or any other state, paymaster and quarter-master generals notes; these, and every other kind of paper transactions (bills of exchange excepted) he will charge his employers no more than *one half per cent,* for his commission.

He procures *money on loan* for a short time and gets notes and bills discounted.

Gentlemen and others, residing in this state, or any of the United States, by sending their orders to the office, may depend on having their business transacted with as much fidelity and expedition as if they were themselves present.

He receives tobacco, sugars, tea, and every other sort of goods, to sell on commission, for which purpose he has provided proper stores.

He flatters himself his assiduity, punctuality, and extensive connection in his business, as a broker, is well established in various parts of Europe, and in the United States in particular.

All persons who shall please to favour him with their business may depend upon his utmost exertion for their interest, and part of the *money advanced*, if desired.

II. Abraham Seixas Advertises His Wares, 1794

Abraham Seixas,
All so gracious,
Once again does offer
His service pure
For to secure
Money in the coffer.

He has for sale
Some negroes, male,
Will suit full well grooms.
He has likewise
Some of their wives
Can make clean, dirty rooms.

For planting, too,
He has a few
To sell, all for cash.
Of various price,
To work the rice
Or bring them to the lash.

The young ones true,
If that will do,
May some be had of him,
To learn your trade
They may be made
Or bring them to your trim.

The boatman great,
Will you elate
They are so brisk and free;
What e're you say,
They will obey,
If you buy them of me.

He also can
Suit any man
With land all o'er the State
A bargain, sure,
They may procure
If they don't stay too late.

For papers he
Will sure agree,
Bond, note or publick debt;
To sell the same
If with good name
And buyer can be met.

To such of those
As will dispose
He begs of them to tell;
By note or phiz,
What e'er it is
That they have got to sell.

He surely will
Try all his skill
To sell, for more or less,
The articles
Of beaux and belles,
That they to him address.

III.   Lt. Col. Aaron Levy, Land Promoter, July 4, 1821

The following communication is taken from the paper called *The Guardian*, printed at Caldwell [New York], giving an accurate account of the manner the 4th of July, 1821, was celebrated there. The expenses of the dinner I provided and much was I pleased at the same.

4th of July, 1821 was celebrated at Caldwell by the inhabitants of the patent [real estate plot] formerly known as Smith & Mitchell's patent in a style never before witnessed in this northern clime and for simplicity of manners, correct deportment, and true patriotism we can venture to say it was not surpassed in any part of the Union. At 10 o'clock the inhabitants of the patent with a few visitors from the adjacent country began to collect and to the heart of philanthropy a more interesting sight could not be exhibited. Among the number were to be seen a few of our revolutionary patriots whose toil and ardor in defense of our independence were recounted by them with many original anecdotes relative to our struggle both interesting and amusing; also the old and the young of both sexes amounting to nearly three hundred free souls. The exercises of the day commenced with a prayer from Rev. Abm. J. Switz of Schenectady, a hymn suited to the occasion sung by a choir of the inhabitants, the declaration of American Independence together with an address delivered by Lieutt. Colonel Aaron Levy, an oration by Mr. Switz, a moral and patriotic hymn by the choir. The service concluded with an impressive prayer by the Rev. Mr. Eastwood, resident preacher of the patent, after which at the request of the inhabitants Mr. Eastwood in a complimentary manner named the patent *Mount Levy* with appropriate benedictions to the same. The company then sat down to a dinner prepared under a bower decorated with laurel and evergreen, where the produce of the country was displayed in the greatest profusion. The scene was animated with a number of very handsome young ladies. Several songs were sung, and many patriotic toasts drank. After fully enjoying the refreshments the party formed a procession, of both sexes, and marched around the adjacent hills to music when the company dispersed in the most perfect order and harmony each satisfied with both the service and the repast of the day. The day was uncommonly fine and a stage covered with greens was previously prepared for the orators and deacons of the Mount and it may be with truth asserted, it was the feast of reason and the flow of soul.

Mem'd: I notice here the preceding publication in consequence of my being the principal projector and one of the actors in its scene, and as it is a new settlement under my direction and the day or anything like it never before celebrated, I leave this as a future memorandum for another generation to look at, when I am, as I hope to be, enjoying in another and better world more solid and everlasting blessings. Amen.

IV.   Aunt Sally, Businesswoman, May 19, 1825

Balt., May the 19, 1825.

My dear Ben:

With pleasure I heard from the girls you are about to make us a visit, my dear son, and we shall expect you every day untill we see you. I wrote a few lines Monday by Miss Alexander to your dear parents. I hope they rec'd it. Mr. Cohen was *kind* enough when he was on his way to the boat to call and say he was just going; too late for any one to write a line by him. Have you sold all your goods and have you done well by them. I want to know all your concerns, for I believe no one takes a more sincere interest for your than your poor old Aunt Sal. Have you many chests of tea such as my brother got from you and what is the price? He tells me he dont know as the chest was a present from you to Rachel. If they are not too high I think it likely I could dispose of them. You have not yet let us know what we owe you on the china. Tis very beautifull and every time I look at it, I see something new to admire. My dear Ben, bring down a little black tea for we cannot get such as you have been drinking, and I wish you to be fed as well here as at home. Tis a high joke to invite company and request them to find their own provisions. Do you think it possible to find out the person that makes mint lozenges? I should be very glad if you can get me two pound. Please pay for them and forward them by first opportunity. The crape and them I will settle with you for.

Our little garden looks beautifull. Tell your dear father it is worth while to come down and see it. I am writing at a window surronded by roses. How often do we wish to have him and your dear mother with us. Your uncle talks of moving next week. I have no news to tell you for in the literal translation of the word I am a very homely girl. To all friends, give my love; the girls all send theirs to our dear brother, sister, and the children. God bless and protect you all, prays your affectionate friend
Sally Etting

Mrs. Caton requested me to ask you the price of the first quality silk damask in Canton.

V.   Lewis Polock, Pantaloon Prince of the Peninsula, 1840

To the Commissioners appointed under the Act of March 3, 1849, entitled "An Act to carry into effect certain stipulations of the treaty between the United States and the Republic of Mexico of the 2d of February, 1848."

The memorial of Lewis Polock respectfully represents that your memorialist is now a citizen of the United States, that he is a native of the same having been born in the State of Pennsylvania, that his present domicil is in the Territory of Upper California, that when his claim, hereinafter to be stated, had its origin, he was a citizen of the United States and his domicil was in the State of Pennsylvania where he was born. Tho' he was for the purposes of trade and business residing in and near San Francisco in Upper California, yet he was no subject of the Mexican Republic, its then owner, and took no oath of allegiance to said Republic. . . .

Previous to and on the 9th day of April, 1840, your memorialist was residing at said San Francisco in Upper California with a stock of manufactured clothing and also of goods not made up such as cloths, calicoes, cottons, silks, etc., and he also owned a stock of horses and cows and household furniture and utensils. That on the evening of said 9th of April, 1840, while he was at supper, one Francisco Guerrero "Juez de Paz" [justice of the peace] at that place called out your memorialist and told him he was a prisoner in the name of the Mexican Nation. Your memorialist asked the cause of his arrest and was answered by said Guerrero that he did not know, but he had orders from [Governor] Jose Castro to take up all the foreigners. Your memorialist was then marched off to the mission about 4 miles off and there kept and detained untill ten o'clock of the following day when he was called to the house of said Guerrero and was asked by said Guerrero how long he had been in the country, whether he had a passport in his possession, what was his religion, and other questions of like import.

Your memorialist was then marched to the Mission of Santa Clara where he was searched and with four other persons thrown in a dungeon, about six feet square, having scarcely room to lie down, and with nothing to eat untill ten o'clock of the next day, thus remaining thirty-eight hours without any sustenance. From this place he was removed to San Juan about eighteen leagues distant, and from thence to the town of Monterey where he arrived in one day. As soon as he arrived there he was taken in front of the prison and again searched and then committed to said prison along with forty or fifty other prisoners, and there kept for three days; that during the nights he had to take turns with his fellow prisoners for the purpose of getting a little rest, the prison being so small that they could scarcely move in it. After remaining for three days in this horrible situation he was removed with twenty-two of the other prisoners into another apartment and there kept untill the 22d day of the month when they were all taken out in front of the Governor's door and were called in one by one into the presence of the Governor and not allowed to speak to each other. On your memorialist being called in in his turn he was asked the same questions as had before been put to him by the "Juez de Paz" at the Mission of San Francisco. They were then all taken back to prison and on the following day were put on board the barque Roger Williams (Joseph Snook, Master), put in irons and thrown into her hold and forbidden to speak to each other on pain of death. The vessel put to sea on the same evening by order of Jose Castro and the prisoner's irons were examined every two hours during the nights.

She arrived at the Port of Santa Barbara on the 26th or 27th of said month of April. Your memorialist and the other prisoners were landed and marched up to the Mission, a mile and a half distant or thereabouts. While there they were kept in such close confinement as not even to be allowed to go out to attend to the calls of nature, but were compelled for that purpose to dig a hole in one corner of the room and cover it up with dirt.

They were kept in this situation until May 9th when they were all re-embarked and taken to San Diego where they remained part of a day and then sailed for San Blas and they were again put in irons, not allowed to go on deck even to attend to the calls of nature. About two days before arriving at San Blas your memorialist was taken out of irons and set to work at tailoring. On May 19th they arrived at San Blas, were landed and marched up to the fort on the hill. Here they were kept two nights and one day in close confinement and then marched off to Tepic where they arrived on the 23d day of May. During their journey from San Blas to Tepic each one was only allowed four small biscuits, that he was there detained as a prisoner untill the latter end of October in that year, and then discharged, his bodily health greatly impaired from his protracted sufferings and his property in San Francisco thoroughly despoiled by the Mexican authorities.

And your memorialist proceeds to state in detail the nature, character, and extent of his losses, viz.:

35 cows worth 7 dollars each	$245.00
7 horses worth 20 dollars each	140.00
Outstanding debts due him by different persons and the evidences of his debts and other vouchers scattered, but good if he had been permitted to remain, estimated at	450.00
Saddle, bridle spurs, etc. worth	40.00
200 pair pantaloons at 6 dollars per pair	200.00
15 yards blue cloth at 10 d's [dollars] per yard	150.00
22 d'o [ditto] green cloth at 8 d's per yard	176.00
2 pieces calico at 16 d's per piece	32.00
2 pieces cotton at 18 d's per piece	36.00
2-1/2 lbs sewing silk at 16 d's per lb.	40.00
2 lbs white thread at 4 d's per lb.	8.00
2 lbs black thread at 4 d's per lb.	8.00
Needles, shears, etc.	14.00
Stock of ready made clothing	350.00
Memorialist's wearing apparel	100.00
Bed and bedding	30.00
	$3,019.00

16

AMERICAN JEWISH COMMUNITIES
1810–1812

In 1776 there were five Jewish communities—all of them on the coast and all Sephardic, Spanish-Portuguese in ritual: Newport, New York, Philadelphia, Charleston, and Savannah. In 1840 there were about twenty synagogs in some sixteen towns; the westernmost in St. Louis, Missouri. Many of these conventicles were Ashkenazic, "German" in ritual. The first American Ashkenazic synagog was organized in Philadelphia in 1802 as the Hebrew German Society, Rodeph Shalom (Seeker of Peace). Its cemetery was purchased in 1801; the constitution (selection I) was adopted in 1810; the charter was granted in 1812. There were twenty-five founding fathers. It is not improbable that the prime motive impelling the Ashkenazim to establish their own synagogs was ethnic-cultural, not simply an insistence on their own worship ritual. Immigrant newcomers nearly always looked askance at the older settlers. The numerous Ashkenazic congregations were all different despite their common prayer book. Every congregation delighted in fashioning its own bylaws. Two congregations even welcomed donations from Gentiles! Some tolerated bond servants as members; a few specifically excluded Jews who had married out. New York's Shearith Israel, always conservative, frowned on those who violated the Sabbath and the dietary laws. No child under three was permitted in its synagog during services; decorum was essential. This New York Jewry, Sephardic in style, was to have no dissident Ashkenazic congregation till 1825. The Sephardim in this town—who looked upon themselves as an elite—had no regrets when the German and English immigrants, Ashkenazim, established a congregation of their own, Bnai Jeshurun (Children of Israel); the older pioneer group did not want to be swamped by newcomers; the "patrician" members felt threatened by the

Ashkenazic influx. After 1802 the autocratic one synagog-community was on its way out; from now on there would be multiple synagogs, each an autonomous community, in all the larger towns. This was inevitable in free America where the Protestants were constantly proliferating.

In 1812, the Christian Hannah Adams (1755–1831)—seeking to make a living through her writings—published a two-volume history of the Jews in which she summed up her knowledge of American Jewry. (Americans apparently never tired of reading about God's Chosen People.) She had garnered data on American Jews from Gershom Seixas of New York and Philip Cohen of Charleston. The latter was a prominent citizen of the city, a merchant, militia officer, and a member of the Nullification Convention of 1832. In 1811, Charleston's Jewish community was the largest in the country. Hannah Adams's survey of American Jewry is reprinted as selection II.

I.   Constitution and Charter of Rodeph Shalom, Philadelphia, 1810–1812

THE COMMONWEALTH OF PENNSYLVANIA

To all to whom these presents shall come, greeting. Know ye that the persons whose names are hereunto subscribed, citizens of the Commonwealth of Pennsylvania, having associated themselves together as a religious society and being desirous of acquiring and enjoying the powers and immunities of a corporation and body politic in law, it is hereby declared that they the said subscribers and their successors being citizens as foresaid be, and they are hereby created and declared to be, one body politic and corporate in law and by the name style and title of the Hebrew German Society (Rodeph Shalom). . . .

PREAMBLE

Whereas, on the tenth day of October, in the year one thousand eight hundred and two, the German Hebrews formed themselves into a society in the city and county of Philadelphia which was denominated the Hebrew German Society, Rodeph Shalom, and whereas this society having met, as usual, in the middle days of their Passover Feast in the year one thousand eight hundred and ten, which was at the time of their yearly meeting, it was moved and seconded that the old articles of association should be abolished and to frame a new constitution or articles of association, and after due consideration on the same it was found that the former constitution or articles of association had been violated in the most part so much that it was not possible to keep any regulation and nearly past maintaining, therefore, the society have agreed after due deliberation to the following:

ARTICLES OF ASSOCIATION

Article 1. This society shall be denominated the Hebrew German Society, Rodeph Shalom. Prayers shall be performed according to the [Ashkenazic] German and Dutch Rules and shall not be altered.

Article 2. The officers shall consist of a president, a cashier and a junto [board] of two members. The president shall have the ruling over the congregation in the synagogue; he shall keep strict order during the time of public worship. He shall appoint the time for prayers in the synagogue; and he shall likewise have the power *to let act as forereader* [cantor] whom he pleases during the year; and to appoint the time and place where our Passover bread shall be baked.

Article 3. The cashier shall preside in case of the absence, death, or resignation of the president; and in case of such vacancy it shall be filled by ballot at the succeeding meeting.

Article 4. The election for officers shall be annually in the middle days of our Easter [Passover] by ballot and no vote shall be taken by proxy; the president and cashier to serve one year; one of the junto at the first election to serve one year and the other to serve two years; and all succeeding juntos to be elected for two years so that the junto will always be composed of a new and an old member.

Article 5. No member shall be qualified to be president unless he shall have belonged three years to this society, and be a resident of the city and county of Philadelphia at the same time, nor under the age of thirty years and a married man of unimpeachable character.

Article 6. The cashier to be qualified must be a married man of reputed good character, who has never failed in making payments, by bankruptcy or has taken the benefit of the Insolvent Act. He shall give to the president and junto his judgment bond with approved security for the monies he shall receive, and pay lawful interest for the same, but for any surplus money not amounting to one hundred dollars, he shall pay no interest, reserving the same to defray the expenses of the current year, and as soon as there shall be one thousand dollars in the cashier's hands, then shall the money be laid out in bank stock.

Article 7. The president shall not retain more than ten dollars of the money of the congregation in his possession, but deliver it to the cashier, taking a receipt for the same, which shall be subject only to the drafts of the president and junto, or a majority of them, and the president shall in all expenditures consult the junto.

Article 8. It shall be the duty of the junto annually to settle and adjust the accounts of the president and cashier in the presence of the new officers and exhibit in writing a statement of the receipts and expenditures of the preceding year, as well as of the stock in the hands or possession of the president and cashier.

Article 9. The members of this society shall be entitled to all privileges and honours customary in any of our synagogues.

Article 10. Each member shall subscribe annually a specific sum, not less than four dollars, one-half to be paid at the end of every six months to the president who shall give a receipt for same. All offerings or donations made by a member or a subscriber during the year shall be deducted from the amount of his subscription, but no allowance shall be made to any person whose offerings or donations do not amount to the sum subscribed by him, but he shall pay fully the sum indebted. [Offerings made while the Scroll of the Law is read are free if they do not exceed the annual dues. Any offering more than the amount over the dues must be paid.]

Article 11. Any member refusing to pay his proper dues to the society at the end of the year (the middle of our Passover) shall not have the right to vote in the same and any member who shall not pay his dues in two years, shall be expelled, unless such members shall be too poor, and in such case shall give information thereof to the president, stating his inability, of which the president shall make a memorandum on the subscription paper with the words "poor" opposite to the member's name, which shall be kept private by the officers, and such poor members shall, notwithstanding, be entitled to and enjoy all the immunities of other members.

Article 12. Each member shall attend meeting [services] every Friday evening and Saturday morning, and at different Holydays at our synagogue in due time, which will be appointed by the presiding office. Any member absenting himself shall pay a fine of twenty-five cents for every time he shall not attend, for which fine or fines there shall be no allowance made in settling the yearly subscription, but such money shall be paid separately, and an account of all the fines shall be kept by one of the officers in a book appropriated for that purpose. No fines shall be taken of members who are absent from the city or county of Philadelphia, likewise sickness always to be an exception.

Article 13. The members and subscribers [second-class members] shall at our respective meetings behave in a decent orderly manner, keeping their several seats or places in the synagogue, hold no discourse foreign to the duties before them during the time of public worship or service. Any member or subscriber transgressing shall for the first offense pay a fine, and shall be expelled for the second like offense. Any member suffering himself to be sued for a fine or fines shall, when sued, be expelled from the society for three months.

Article 14. Any member or subscriber, absenting himself from our meeting, at our Sabbath or Holydays, and shall attend any other society or congregation, or keep a meeting at his house, if proved, shall be expelled from our society and nevermore become a member, likewise shall no member or subscriber leave the synagogue until the prayers are over or he or they shall

pay a fine of twenty-five cents. But in case a person has to go out, and requests the president for leave and it is granted such person shall not pay a
fine. [If a member leaves during the service, there might not be a quorum!]
Article 15. It shall be the duty of the president or presiding officer, on report of any sick member, to make the same known with the least possible
delay to the congregation, and where the necessity of the case shall require
it, the presiding officers or junto shall draft two of the members, whose
duty it shall be to sit up and attend such sick member all night, and the
drafts shall continue every night until each member in the society shall
have served a tour, and to commence again with the first members if necessary. Every member refusing to sit up and attend shall for every such neglect pay a fine of two dollars. But members may appoint substitutes in
such cases out of the society. It shall not be obligatory on a member to attend where the disease is contagious.
Article 16. If a member or subscriber should die out of the city of Philadelphia and not exceeding eighty miles therefrom, the president on receiving
information thereof, shall convene the congregation on the same day, to
consult whether or not the deceased member or subscriber can be brought
to the city for interment in our burial ground, and if decided in the affirmative, the president shall appoint two members to bring the body of the
deceased to be interred, and the said two members shall receive for their
services two dollars per day, independent of their expenses, which expense
shall be paid out of the estate of the deceased, but if the deceased was poor
the expense shall be paid out of the funds.
Article 17. The society shall receive no more than one dollar for the
ground of a deceased member or subscriber, or for any one of the family of
a member who is entitled to our ground, but no stranger shall be buried in
our ground without authority of the president and junto.
Article 18. The officers of this society shall receive no compensation for
their services. No money shall be paid at any of the extra meetings, but any
expenses occurring not exceeding five dollars at each time at our half
yearly meetings (namely in the month of April and September) to be paid
out of the funds. [The expense went for food; burial societies held dinners.]
Article 19. Any person wishing to become a member of this society shall
make application to the president and junto in writing which shall be read
at the first meeting after the receipt of such petition, which shall not be
acted on until the end of six months, when if he should receive by ballot a
majority in his favour, and pays his entrance money, the amount of which
to be determined by the president and junto, he shall then be considered as
a member of this society.
Article 20. The president shall preside at all meetings, and a secretary shall
be chosen to keep a correct copy of all the transactions; any member hav-

ing business to offer to the society shall address and lay before the chairman such business. One member only to speak at a time, who shall not be interrupted while adhering to the subject before the society and shall be permitted to speak twice only on the same subject. Any business, by consent of a majority, shall be determined by a committee, and no subscriber shall have a right to speak or vote at any of our meetings, and all business of the congregation shall be recorded in a book for that purpose, dated, signed by the chairman and attested by the secretary.

Article 21. Any member being called to order by the president or presiding officer, and shall not accordingly come to order, shall pay a fine of one dollar, and be deprived of a vote on the business then depending. [signed] Isaac Marks, et al., et al., et al.

II.   Hannah Adams Surveys American Jewry, 1812

A respectable rabbi of New York [Gershom Seixas] has given the following account of his brethren in the United States:

> There are about fifty families of Jews in New York, which, with a number of unmarried men, make from seventy to eighty subscribing members to the congregation *Sherith Israel*, which is incorporated by an act of the legislature of the state, empowering all religious societies to hold their property by charter, under the direction of trustees chosen annually by the communicants of the society, according to certain rules prescribed in the act. The trustees have the management of all the temporalities, as is customary in other societies. They have one synagogue established conformably to the customs and forms of prayer used among the Portuguese Jews in Europe. Their publick service is altogether in the Hebrew language, excepting in particular cases provided for in the constitution of the society. There were some Jewish families in the city when it was owned by the Dutch, but the documents which are among the archives of the congregation do not extend farther back than about one hundred and fifty years. Some of the Jews who settled in New York were of Portuguese, others of German extraction, besides Hollanders. There are also the descendants of those who arrived after New York became an English colony. The Jews had the right of soil under the Dutch government, and the English never attempted to deprive them of it; on the contrary, they granted letters patent to several Jewish families in the time of Queen Anne, who had arrived in London from France among the Huguenots, to settle in North America. In Philadelphia there may be about thirty families of Jews. They have two synagogues, one for those who observe the Portuguese customs and forms of prayer, and the other for those who adhere to the German rules, customs, etc.; neither of them are incorporated. There may be about from eighty to one hundred men, in the whole state of Pennsylvania, who all occasionally attend the synagogues in Philadelphia.

There is in Charleston (South Carolina) a large society incorporated, (with their laws). They have an elegant synagogue established on the Portuguese customs, etc. They also have different institutions with appropriate funds for benevolent and charitable purposes likewise incorporated.

A more particular account of the Jews in South Carolina has been given by [Philip Cohen] one of the principal members of their congregation in the capital of the state, the substance of which is as follows:

The first emigration of the Jews to Charleston took place long before the revolution. The spirit of commerce can never be extinct in them; and their wealth increased with their numbers, which were augmented from time to time, both by marriages, and acquisitions from Europe. The present number of Jews may be estimated at about a thousand. Charleston alone contains about six or seven hundred individuals. The present number of Hebrews in the city are chiefly Carolinians, the descendants of German, English, and Portuguese emigrants, who, from the civil and religious tyranny of Europe, sought an asylum in the western world. While the contest for freedom and independence was carried on, the majority distinguished themselves as brave soldiers and gallant defenders of the cause of a country which protected them. This spirit still actuates them; and as it is but natural that a people, who for ages have groaned under the impolitic barbarity and blind fanaticism of Europe, should inhale the breath of freedom with delight, the Hebrews in this city pay their hearty homage to the laws, which guarantee their rights and consolidate them into the mass of a free people. The religious rites, customs, and festivals of the Jews are all strictly observed by those of this nation in Charleston, but ameliorated with that social liberality, which pervades the minds and manners of the inhabitants of civilized countries. Indeed the seats in a Jewish synagogue are often crowded with visitors of every denomination. The episcopal [clerical] functions are now discharged by the Rev. [Emanuel N.] Ca[r]valho, late professor of the Hebrew language in the college of New York. The Jews in Charleston enjoy equal literary advantages with the other members of the community. Most of the parents being rich, the prejudice is here despised which confines the important object of education to the tenets of religion; and the Hebrews can boast of several men of talents and learning among them. Those Jewish children who are intended for professions receive a handsome classical education. There is now in the city an academy where the French, Italian, Latin, and Greek languages are taught together with other branches of learning. The Rev. Ca[r]valho, mentioned above, also teaches the Hebrew and Spanish languages. The dress and habits of the Jews in Charleston do not distinguish them from the other citizens. Open and hospitable, as Carolinians generally are, they unite, with considerable industry and knowledge of commercial affairs, rather too much of that love of ease and pleasure which climate, as well as national character, tends to nourish. Individuals, however, among those in this country, for their enterprize and judgment, have been entrusted with municipal offices; and one has held a seat with honour to himself and his constituents among the representatives of the state. The institutions which the Jews have established in Charleston are chiefly religious and charitable. They have built an elegant synagogue; and what strongly exhibits the liberality of the city is that the Roman Catholic church is directly opposite to it. They have also societies for the relief of strangers, for attending the sick, and for administering the rites of humanity and burial to the dying and the dead. The most modern institution is a society for the relief of orphans. The capital is already considerable, and it is yearly increasing. The children receive every advantage which is necessary to enable them to be well informed and honourable citizens of their country.

In Richmond, Virginia, there are about thirty Jewish families, who are now building a synagogue; but they are not as yet incorporated. The number of unmarried men is unknown, though there may be about an hundred scattered throughout the state who are and will become members of the congregation. At Savannah in Georgia there are but few Jewish families who assemble at times and commune with each other in publick prayers. The United States is, perhaps, the only place where the Jews have not suffered persecution but have, on the contrary, been encouraged and indulged in every right of citizens.

The Jews in all the United States, except Massachusetts, are eligible to offices of trust and honour; and some of them in the southern states are in office. They are generally commercial men, and a number of them considerable merchants. [Miss Adams did not know that New Hampshire, Rhode Island, New Jersey, Maryland, and North Carolina had not yet completely emancipated their Jews.]

17

RELIGIOUS LIFE IN THE UNITED STATES
1787–1826

The first selection is a description of a traditional Jewish wedding. This account has been preserved for us in a letter which Dr. Benjamin Rush (d. 1813) sent his wife Julia in 1787. Rush, a Revolutionary War notable, was one of America's most famous physicians. The bride was the daughter of Jonas Phillips, a Philadelphia militiaman, blockade-runner, and congregational leader; the groom was to become the father of the later "Commodore" Uriah P. Levy.

The overwhelming majority of America's Jews were tradition-true, in sympathy at least. In almost every town there were always a few liberals and radicals, but they maintained a low profile; they did not want to stir up the Protestant evangelicals or the conforming Orthodox. In the second selection Rebecca Samuels of Petersburg, Virginia, wrote—in Yiddish— to her parents in Hamburg, Germany, describing Jewish life in her remote community (ca. 1792). She was eager to move to a larger town where Jews were more observant. Rebecca was shocked by the disregard for Jewish practices. Apathy in maintaining the age-old customs and rituals was common in early America. The Sabbath, the dietary laws, synagog attendance, the prohibition against intermarriage—all these were frequently neglected and flouted. Social controls were weak; America was Jewishly very much a "frontier."

Jacob Mordecai (1762–1838) was a cultured autodidact who was firmly entrenched in Orthodoxy. In 1822 he was invited by Richmond's Sephardic congregation, Beth Shalome (House of Peace), to dedicate its new sanctuary. Excerpts of his long address constitute the third selection. These Virginia Jews were apologetic; there were Gentiles in the audience; Jefferson and Madison were still alive.

It was in this same decade that Jacob Mordecai—and the cultured Rebecca Gratz, too—took time out to attack Charleston's Reformed Society of Israelites. That Carolina city then sheltered the country's most cultured Jewry. The new society broke with the Charleston Orthodox, Beth Elohim (God's House), in 1824 and established a radical religious fellowship which in essence rejected tradition that reached back for well over 2000 years. This was indeed a revolutionary act. Why radical action now? By the 1820s Reform Judaism had begun to organize itself in Germany; Charleston Jewish intellectuals were embarrassed when Gentiles visited the synagog with its "exotic" service in a foreign tongue. Because they wanted to save the younger generation moving toward assimilation, they set out deliberately to integrate the Jew into the fabric of American life. They were determined to break with the past, with "bigotry and priest craft"! The goals of the new group are described in the fourth selection, an appeal for funds to build a "temple." Deistic influence is obvious. The Reformed Society, never really successful, managed to stay alive until it emerged victorious in 1841 in the somewhat liberalized Beth Elohim congregation, the first permanent Reform synagog in the United States.

I. Dr. Benjamin Rush Describes a Jewish Wedding,
June 27, 1787

Philadelphia, June 27, 1787.

My dear Julia,

Being called a few days ago to attend in the family of Jonas Phillips, I was honored this morning with an invitation to attend the marriage of his daughter to a young man of the name of LEVY from Virginia. I accepted the invitation with great pleasure, for you know I love to be in the way of adding to my stock of ideas upon all subjects.

At 1 o'clock the company, consisting of 30 or 40 men, assembled in Mr. Phillips' common parlor which was accommodated with benches for the purpose. The ceremony began with prayers in the Hebrew language, which were chaunted by an old rabbi [Jacob R. Cohen] and in which he was followed by the whole company. As I did not understand a word except now and then an Amen or Hallelujah, my attention was directed to the haste with which they covered their heads with their hats as soon as the prayers began, and to the freedom with which some of them conversed with each other during the whole time of this part of their worship. As soon as these prayers were ended, which took up about 20 minutes, a small piece of parchment was produced, written in Hebrew, which contained a deed of settlement [the ketubah] and which the groom subscribed in the presence of four witnesses. In this deed he conveyed a part of his fortune to his bride, by which she was provided for after his death in case she survived him.

This ceremony was followed by the erection of a beautiful canopy [the huppah] composed of white and red silk in the middle of the floor. It was supported by four young men (by means of four poles), who put on white gloves for the purpose. As soon as this canopy was fixed, the bride, accompanied with her mother, sister, and a long train of female relations, came downstairs. Her face was covered with a veil which reached halfways down her body. She was handsome at all times, but the occasion and her dress rendered her in a peculiar manner a most lovely and affecting object. I gazed with delight upon her. Innocence, modesty, fear, respect, and devotion appeared all at once in her countenance. She was led by her two bridesmaids under the canopy. Two young men led the bridegroom after her and placed him, not by her side, but directly opposite to her. The priest now began again to chaunt an Hebrew prayer, in which he was followed by part of the company. After this he gave to the groom and bride a glass full of wine, from which they each sipped about a teaspoonful. Another prayer followed this act, after which he took a ring and directed the groom to place it upon the finger of his bride in the same manner as is practised in the marriage service of the Church of England.

This ceremony was followed by handing the wine to the father of the bride and then a second time to the bride and groom. The groom after sipping the wine took the glass in his hand and threw it upon a large pewter dish which was suddenly placed at his feet. Upon its breaking into a number of small pieces, there was a general shout of joy and a declaration that the ceremony was over. The groom now saluted his bride, and kisses and congratulations became general through the room. I asked the meaning, after the ceremony was over, of the canopy and of the drinking of the wine and breaking of the glass. I was told by one of the company that in Europe they generally marry in the open air, and that the canopy was introduced to defend the bride and groom from the action of the sun and from rain. Their mutually partaking of the same glass of wine was intended to denote the mutuality of their goods, and the breaking of the glass at the conclusion of the business was designed to teach them the brittleness and uncertainty of human life and the certainty of death, and thereby to temper and moderate their present joys.

Mr. Phillips pressed me to stay and dine with the company, but business . . . forbade it. I stayed, however, to eat some wedding cake and to drink a glass of wine with the guests. Upon going into one of the rooms upstairs to ask how Mrs. Phillips did, who had fainted downstairs under the pressure of the heat (for she was weak from a previous indisposition), I discovered the bride and groom supping a bowl of broth together. Mrs. Phillips apologized for them by telling me they had eaten nothing (agreeably to the custom prescribed by their religion) since the night before.

Upon my taking leave of the company, Mrs. Phillips put a large piece of cake into my pocket for you, which she begged I would present to you with her best compliments. She says you are an old New York acquaintance of hers. [Her father was Hazzan David M. Machado of Shearith Israel of New York City].

During the whole of this new and curious scene my mind was not idle. I was carried back to the ancient world and was led to contemplate the passovers, the sacrifices, the jubilees, and other ceremonies of the Jewish Church. After this, I was led forward into futurity and anticipated the time foretold by the prophets when this once-beloved race of men shall again be restored to the divine favor and when they shall unite with Christians with one heart and one voice in celebrating the praises of a common and universal Saviour. . . .

Adieu. With love to your Mama, sisters, and brothers, and to our dear children, I am your affectionate husband.
B: Rush. . . .

II. Orthodox Rachel Lazarus Seeks a More Jewish Community, 1792(?)

Petersburg, 1792(?)

Dear Parents:

I hope my letter will ease your mind. You can now be reassured and send me one of the family to Charleston, South Carolina. This is the place to which, with God's help, we will go after Passover. The whole reason why we are leaving this place is because of [its lack of] *Yehudishkeit* [Jewishness].

Dear Parents, I know quite well you will not want me to bring up my children like Gentiles. Here they cannot become anything else. Jewishness is pushed aside here. There are here [in Petersburg] ten or twelve Jews, and they are not worthy of being called Jews. We have a shohet [slaughterer of animals and poultry] here who goes to market and buys terefah [nonkosher] meat and then brings it home. On Rosh Ha-Shanah [New Year] and on Yom Kippur [the Day of Atonement] the people worshipped here without one sefer torah [pentateuchal scroll] and not one of them wore the tallit [a large prayer shawl worn in the synagogue] or the *arba kanfot* [the small set of fringe worn on the body], except Hyman and my Sammy's godfather. The latter is an old man of sixty, a man from Holland. He has been in America for thirty years already; for twenty years he was in Charleston, and he has been living here for four years. He does not want to remain here any longer and will go with us to Charleston. In that place there is a blessed community of three hundred Jews.

You can believe me that I crave to see a synagogue to which I can go. The way we live now is no life at all. We do not know what the Sabbath and the holidays are. On the Sabbath all the Jewish shops are open; and they do business on that day as they do throughout the whole week. But ours we do not allow to open. With us there is still some Sabbath. You must believe me that in our house we all live as Jews as much as we can.

As for the Gentiles [?], we have nothing to complain about. For the sake of a livelihood we do not have to leave here. Nor do we have to leave because of debts. I believe ever since Hyman has grown up that he has not had it so good. You cannot know what a wonderful country this is for the common man. One can live here peacefully. Hyman made a clock that goes very accurately, just like the one in the Buchenstrasse in Hamburg. Now you can imagine what honors Hyman has been getting here. In all Virginia there is no clock [like this one], and Virginia is the greatest province in the whole of America, and America is the largest section of the world. Now you know what sort of a country this is. It is not too long since Virginia was discovered. It is a young country. And it is amazing to see the business they do in this little Petersburg. At times as many as a thousand hogsheads of tobacco arrive at one time, and each hogshead contains 1,000 and sometimes 1,200 pounds of tobacco. The tobacco is shipped from here to the whole world.

When Judah [my brother?] comes here, he can become a watchmaker and a goldsmith, if he so desires. Here it is not like Germany where a watchmaker is not permitted to sell silverware. [The contrary is true in this country.] They do not know otherwise here. They expect a watchmaker to be a silversmith here. Hyman has more to do in making silverware than with watchmaking. He has a journeyman, a silversmith, a very good artisan, and he, Hyman, takes care of the watches. This work is well paid here, but in Charleston, it pays even better.

All the people who hear that we are leaving give us their blessings. They say that it is sinful that such blessed children should be brought up here in Petersburg. My children cannot learn anything here, nothing Jewish, nothing of general culture. My Schoene [my daughter], God bless her, is already three years old; I think it is time that she should learn something, and she has a good head to learn. I have taught her the bedtime prayers and grace after meals in just two lessons. I believe that no one among the Jews here can do as well as she. And my Sammy [born in 1790], God bless him, is already beginning to talk.

I could write more. However, I do not have any more paper.

I remain, your devoted daughter and servant, Rebecca, the wife of Hayyim, the son of Samuel the Levite. I send my family, my . . . [mother-in-law?] and all my friends and good friends, my regards.

III.   Jacob Mordecai Dedicates Beth Shalome, Richmond's Synagog, September 15, 1822

. . . Act righteously, act justly, towards all men, whether he be thy brother, or whether he be a stranger unto thee. Restrain every propensity to acts vicious and abandoned. Our happiness depends on our virtue; our virtue depends on the conformity of our hearts and conduct to the rules of right prescribed to us by our beneficent creator whose attributes are perfect holiness, inflexible justice. The virtuous man stands in a relation to God which is peculiarly delightful—his divine perfections are all engaged in his defence; he feels powerful in God's power—wise in his wisdom; good in his goodness. Worship him in holiness of spirit. Approach this house of prayer erected to his service in lowliness of mind. Observe a serious, devout, and respectful demeanor whilst performing your solemn duties; bear in your minds that all your present and future happiness depends on his merciful, kindness. Let your external behaviour evince your inward reverence. Leave for the short period devoted to the praise of your God, all worldly thoughts at the threshhold of his house. Bear in remembrance that a repetition of words, unless accompanied by the heart and mind, cannot be acceptable to your Father who is in heaven. Be assur'd that that devotion which is mechanical availeth nought. An irreverent behaviour in this house, dedicated to his holy name, is an offence to the great author of our being. Watch over your hearts, and guard against even an appearance of levity and disrespect. Be assured that none can feel the power of Godliness without having the external form of it too. A negligent performance of prayer, a loose observance of ceremonies, are but indignities, offered to the father of mercies. Promote a spirit of kindness, forbearance and brotherly love. Guard against an intolerant, persecuting spirit. Who hath made you judges between man and his maker! Who among you is so perfect as not to have trespassed against the laws of God. Hath he not borne with your iniquities and winked at your backslidings, and shall ye be severe with your brother, to mark his errours and to punish his perverseness! The Lord thy God is a jealous God and judgment belongeth only unto him; vain is your oblation of thanksgiving without a lowly heart; as a bulrush may ye bow down the head; and lift up your voice like a trumpet, but ye obey not the ordinance of your God if your worship be for strife and debate [Isaiah 58:4–5]. As members of a nation distinguished for its religious customs and ceremonies, it is incumbent on us, so to conduct ourselves, as to manifest obedience to the laws of the country which God has been pleased to allot to us, under the shadow of whose government we enjoy comfort and security.

Ye are commanded to "seek the peace of the city whither ye have been caused to be carried away captive" [Jeremiah 29:7]. To consider the whole human family, however diversified by religious faith, all our fellow beings who believe in God and observe the commandments delivered to the sons of Noah: "Everyone who walketh uprightly and worketh righteousness, and speaketh not with his tongue nor doeth evil to his neighbour" [Psalm 15:2–3] equally entitled to salvation with ourselves. For these are called by our wise men "the pious among the nations," and they have a share in the world to come [Tosefta, Sanhedrin, 13]. The Creator of the Universe is not the god of a sect. This charitable doctrine is in strict unison with your religious creed. So long as you hold charity and justice to be essential, integrant parts of your faith, mankind has nothing to censure in your attachment to its tenets. Adhere to that faith as the anchor of your hope in futurity. Avoid all interference with the religious opinion of others. Proselytism is *not* congenial to our maxims. Application for admittance within our pales have long ceased to be a novelty. They are uniformly discouraged from motives pure and benevolent. Those born under a different dispensation are not required to observe our laws. On us alone devolves the punishment for disobeying them. . . . "This law was given by Moses to the children of Israel; it is an inheritance of the congregation of Jacob" [Deuteronomy 33:4].

Now may the God of our fathers, in his infinite goodness, incline our hearts to keep this law "and fear this glorious and awful name, the Lord our God who has brought us out of Egypt to be unto him a people of inheritance" [Deuteronomy 4:20].

IV. Goals of America's First Reform Synagog, 1826

Nearly two years have now elapsed since a large and respectable meeting of Israelites was held in this city, for the purpose of endeavoring to effect some changes, and eradicating many acknowledged errors in the mode of worship at present observed in the synagogue. For the attainment of these objects a society was soon after organized called *The Reformed Society of Israelites*, which has since been incorporated by the legislature. The ends proposed to be attained were chiefly these:

First. To introduce such a change in the mode of worship, that a considerable portion of the prayers be said in the English language, so that by being *understood*, they would be attended with that religious instruction in our particular faith, essential to the rising generation, and so generally neglected; and which, by promoting pious and elevated feelings, would also render the service solemn, impressive and dignified—such as should belong to all our addresses to the Divine power.

Secondly. To discontinue the observance of such ceremonies as partake strongly of bigotry, as owe their origin only to *rabbinical* [i.e. postbiblical] institutions, as are not embraced in the *moral* laws of Moses, and in many instances are contrary to their spirit, to their beauty and sublimity, and to that elevated piety and virtue which so highly distinguish them.

Thirdly. To abolish the use of such portions of the Hebrew prayers as are superfluous and consist of mere *repetitions*, and to select such of them as are sufficient and appropriate to the occasion.

Fourthly. To follow the portions of the *Pentateuch* which are to be said in the original Hebrew, with an English discourse, in which the principles of the Jewish faith, and the force and beauty of the moral law, may be expounded to the rising generation, so that they, *and all others* may know how to cherish and venerate those sublime truths which are emanated from the Almighty Father, and which acknowledged as the first and most hallowed principles of all religion.

Such were, with a few other minor alterations, the principal objects that led to the institution of "The Reformed Society of Israelites" in the city of Charleston. This explanation we deem due to those whose assistance may be extended towards erecting this new temple to the service of the Almighty. It is an appeal to all who are influenced by tolerant and unprejudiced feelings, and who can properly appreciate the conduct of those who are actuated in their wish for the above changes, by a desire to disencumber their religion of what disfigures instead of ornamenting it, and by the religious instruction which distinguishes the present age. It appeals to no sectarian spirit, as it directs itself solely to the bosoms of those that respond to the pure and uncontaminated feelings of an enlightened piety. Exclusive principles belong, more or less, to all sects, but the virtue of benevolence may belong to *all* of every sect. Impressed with these sentiments, we therefore make our application general, and to such as are influenced by the spirit of true religion, and by a manly and discriminating feeling of what is really good and ennobling in human charity.

Donations will be thankfully received, and all communications noticed by either of the subscribers.

Aaron Phillips, President; Michael Lazarus, Vice-President; Isaac

18

EDUCATING YOUNG JEWS
1821–1850s

With one exception—to be discussed—the education provided Jewish children in the early national period differed little from that available in colonial days. For a brief time in the 1790s Shearith Israel of New York maintained an afternoon Hebrew school where the children of members were taught to read and translate the sacred tongue. The same synagog also sponsored an all-day school, the Polonies Talmud Torah, which limped along for many years. It was not very successful in its effort to teach Hebrew and secular subjects.

This congregation did assume responsibility for teaching Hebrew to the children of the poor. There was much talk in those days of the importance of Jewish education; indeed New York had a male and a female association to provide education for the children of the indigent. Little is known of the accomplishments of these two societies. We do know that the synagogal leaders gave Shearith Israel's "ladies" very little encouragement as they strove to aid the children of the poor.

It is not difficult to summarize the educational efforts of Jewry in the years 1776–1840. Many children—boys and girls—were taught Hebrew by a private teacher, the "rebbe," or by the minister himself. Children of the poor received their secular training in the non-Jewish charity schools; middle-class Jews sent their youngsters to private academies most of which were conducted by Gentiles; there were, however, a few schools which were established by Jews. Very few Jews were illiterate. Most Jews read Hebrew script, though it is difficult to determine how many knew the meaning of the words they read. Congregational minutes reveal that New York's Sephardic Jews made few if any sacrifices to further Jewish educational programs. It was the firm conviction of that generation that all forms of education were the responsibility of the family, not the religious community.

In the 1820s individuals like Jacob S. Solis (1780–1829) of Mt. Pleasant, Westchester County, New York, and Moses Elias Levy (b. 1781) of Florida attempted to establish academies for the training of Jewish boys and girls. Solis wanted to open a school to train adolescents in the mechanical arts, trades, sciences, and agriculture. Orphans and European refugees were welcome (1826). Five years earlier Moses E. Levy had set out to found a colony in the West, in Illinois, where young men and women would be taught the arts and encouraged to return to the soil; they were to be given an intense Jewish training and "instructed in the universal of love for mankind, in principles of patriotism, and the defense of their country." Religion in its "purity" was to be promoted. Levy wanted a spiritual and cultural revolution; he was strongly influenced by the teachings of Johann Heinrich Pestalozzi (d. 1827) and Philipp Emanuel von Fellenberg (d. 1844), the Swiss educational reformers. M. E. Levy and Jacob S. Solis accomplished nothing; there were then fewer than 5000 Jews in all of the United States! The prospectus for Levy's new school is reprinted here as selection I. In 1835, Isaac Leeser, American Jewry's most distinguished religious and educational leader, entreated Philadelphia Jewry to create a modern all-day Jewish school. His appeal is selection II. The Sunday school of Rebecca Gratz (b. 1781) and her associates was an immediate success. It had enthusiastic teachers; the hours of instruction were few; its classes were held on the Christian Sunday. We Jews are just like everyone else; the Sunday school is an American institution! Yet it was very Jewish; Rebecca was a pious Jewess.

> Let me like Israel, hope in God;
>   This name alone implore.
> Both now and ever trust in Him
>   Who lives for evermore.

Rosa Mordecai (b. 1839) a grandniece of Rebecca, was a student in the early Sunday school. Rosa's reminiscences of Miss Gratz and the classes are selection III. It is an informative account.

I. Moses Elias Levy's New Style Community, May 9, 1821

Whereas, Mr. M. E. Levy has submitted to us a plan for the education of Jewish youth, and ameliorating the condition of the Jews generally, which, among many advantages, promises to promote the perpetuity of our religion, and prove in a high degree beneficial to our brethren, we have, in the furtherance of such an object, associated ourselves with Mr. Levy, and have adopted the following resolutions:

1. *Resolved*, That to carry into effect the important objects of this institution, the education of Hebrew youth of both sexes, should be the care and concern of the Hebrew community at large.

2. *Resolved*, As a cardinal object of this institution, that Hebrew youth are to be instructed in the Hebrew language and laws, so as to comprehend both letter and spirit, and duly to estimate their character and principles.

3. *Resolved*, That in addition to a course of religious instruction, the scholars and students of this institution shall be taught the elementary branches of education, and such branches of the useful arts and of science, as their capacities may warrant.

4. *Resolved*, That a portion of time of such students shall be devoted to practical lessons in agriculture and horticulture, with a view of promoting health and industry, and in order to qualify them for such pursuits.

5. *Resolved*, That suitable persons shall be selected to preside over the various interests and duties of this institution, who are distinguished for their intelligence, integrity, and moral and religious virtues.

6. *Resolved*, That the observance of simple and economical habits, the love of truth, and all virtues, religious and moral, which tend to ennoble the Israelite and the man, shall be inculcated in the minds of the students of this institution. That they be instructed in the universal love of mankind, in principles of patriotism, and the defense of their country.

7. *Resolved*, That a tract of land of suitable magnitude shall be purchased in a healthy and central part of the Union, for the accommodation of a certain number of families, and the establishment of this institution; and that each scholar, after having completed his studies, shall be entitled to a piece of land, if he think proper to settle thereon.

8. *Resolved*, That three distinguished persons of religion and morality shall be appointed inspectors of this institution, whose duty it shall be to see that the laws for its government are faithfully executed, that religion in its purity is promoted, and to do all which to them may seem proper for its interest, safety, and permanency, and, in their character of censors, to see that no measure is adopted, which may even remotely have a tendency to injure the character and spirit of the institution.

9. *Resolved*, That the name of this institution shall be *Chenuch* [Training] or Probationary; and efforts shall be made to establish societies in different parts of the Union with a view of carrying it into successful operation.

10. *Resolved*, That the members of this institution must be Israelites, men who have confidence in the covenant, and are zealous in support of their religion and its perpetuity, as a sacred duty; who will take an interest in forwarding the institution, and promoting harmony and good will among its members.

11. *Resolved*, That the societies in the different cities in the Union, shall consist of only four members each, and who shall at an appointed time meet (by delegates) in order to devise suitable plans for carrying the institution into operation, and each society shall appoint a corresponding secretary from its members.

12. *Resolved*, That Judah Zuntz be corresponding secretary.

M. L. M. Peixotto
M. E. Levy
M. M. Noah
Judah Zuntz

New York, 7 Eaar, 5581—May 9, 1821

II.   Isaac Leeser's Proposed School, March 8, 1835

To the Jewish Inhabitants of Philadelphia

March 8, 1835

Having been frequently urged by various respectable residents of this city to establish a school, where the children might acquire a correct knowledge of Hebrew, together with a thorough English education; and being at the same time fully impressed with the conviction that our children would be greatly benefitted if they were early instructed in a public school in the precepts of the holy religion which was handed down to the children of Israel, as the best gift God could bestow on His people: I have come to the resolution to offer my services to both congregations of Israelites (and also to such Christians as might be willing to send their children to such an institution) to open a school—as soon as sufficient encouragement is held out—wherein are to be taught Hebrew reading (both Portuguese [Sephardic] and German [Ashkenazic]) *Minhag* [pronunciation], translating from Hebrew into English, the Principles of the Jewish Religion (on the basis of [Joseph] Johlson's Instruction, translated by me about five years ago), English Grammar, Geography, History, Arithmetic, and Writing. For the present these are the only branches which I intend teaching; but at a future time, instruction in Latin, Greek, German, French, Spanish, Italian, Natural History, Natural Philosophy, Drawing, Singing, &c. may be added, if the capacity of the scholars will admit of it, for which extra compensation will of course be expected.

A school like the one herewith proposed, is very much needed in this country, since there is not one, in any city of this extensive land, where a Jewish child can obtain a knowledge of its religious duties. If therefore our people are really alive to the importance of a religious education, which I am afraid many are not, they will eagerly seize the present opportunity to establish a school upon a permanent foundation, which is not to depend upon my continuing to reside in Philadelphia; for it is my candid opinion, that if a teacher should hereafter be wanted, it will be no difficult thing to find one. The first beginning alone is difficult; and as my object is not one of gain, I think it undeniable, that, all things considered, this is the favourable moment when the experiment should be tried, whether Israelites in this country are not able, not willing, to establish for themselves, like their brethren have done in many towns in Europe, a seminary, whence the seeds of righteousness are to be scattered far and near. I do not appeal to sectarian feelings. I possess none myself, for the truth, which our religion upholds, is no sectarian thing; but as Jews we are to observe many little ceremonies, are to acquire many details of religious duties, which none other but a Jew can impart. But, my friends, let it not be said, that Jews in oppressed Europe, where the name of an Israelite exposes the possessor to many vexatious restrictions, should accomplish whenever attempted, what the inhabitants of free and enlightened America failed even to attempt. To the work then! with a confident reliance upon the Giver of all good, and you must succeed! and in place of a decrease of pious and strict Jews, in place of empty benches in the house of worship, in place of public profanation of all our religion holds sacred: there will be an increase of righteousness and religious knowledge; the synagogues will be crowded with worshippers who delight to call on God in their own—dear—national tongue, to them not a dead language; and the reproach of lukewarmness will not be any more uttered against us. I am not unconscious of my being but an individual, one whose life is not to be supposed irreproachable, still it is not to be said, that even by one so weak as I am much may not be done.

It is to be hoped, that persons having the means, will show their approbation of the undertaking, by bestowing as much as they can afford for the purpose of endowing the school, so that even poor children may enjoy the same advantages of education with the rich ones. All moneys given shall be faithfully applied towards obtaining school furniture, books, maps, &c., and the remainder be handed over to trustees, to be laid out in stock bearing interest, which is to be expended solely for the purpose of educating poor children. The furniture obtained with the proceeds of donations is to be likewise the property of the school, and also be vested in trustees. All this, however, can be best settled when the school has once gone into operation.

The terms for tuition in the branches first named, will be ten dollars per quarter, payable quarterly, with the exception of children under five years, who will be charged at the rate of twenty-five dollars per annum. Persons unable to pay these amounts will please notify me of their inability, and every consideration shall be given to their case, and their children shall receive the same advantages as those paying full prices. The government of the school shall be paternal, but I beg that parents will not think of interfering with me, as no unnecessary punishment will be resorted to, yet, on the other hand, firmness is absolutely necessary to insure regularity of behaviour and industry in studying.

Persons receiving this prospectus will please notify their willingness or unwillingness to forward what I have proposed as soon as convenient, by personal application or by a few lines addressed to me, at 86 Walnut Street. At all events I trust that the matter will receive from all Israelites due consideration. Persons having children to send will please to state their names and ages, and for how long a time they intend keeping them at school. Those willing to contribute money, books, &c., having or not having children, will be kind enough to state specifically in writing what they intend contributing.

The plan of teaching I shall adopt may be somewhat different from the one usually pursued, but I hope that parents will permit me to make a fair trial of its utility before they find fault. Persons residing at a distance may rest assured that children entrusted to my care shall be carefully watched over, and their advancement in morals as well as information, strictly attended to.

In conclusion I have to state that for the present I intend to begin with boys only; but if the number of girls offered should be sufficient to pay an assistant teacher, a school for females will also be commenced. Girls are also to be instructed in needle-work, &c.

Invoking the blessing of God upon the undertaking, I subscribe myself

Your obedient servant,

Isaac Leeser,

86 Walnut St. Philadelphia.

March 8th,

Adar 7th 5595.

N.B. Persons sending children or giving donations will please sign this circular and return it to me.

Subscribers names.	Children's names.	Ages.	Donations.
	Boys. Girls.		

III.   Rosa Mordecai's Recollection of the First Hebrew Sunday School, 1850s

My first distinct impression of going to the Hebrew Sunday School was some years after it was organized by my great aunt, Miss Rebecca Gratz, and while she was still its moving spirit (sometime I think in the early fifties). The room which the school then occupied was on Zane Street (now Filbert Street) above Seventh Street, over the Phoenix Hose Company. This was prior to the days of the Paid Fire Department. Before mounting the stairs, I would linger, as many of the girls and all the boys did, to admire the beautifully-kept machines, with the gentlemanly loungers, who never wearied of answering our questions. The sons of our most "worthy and respected" citizens ran after the Phoenix in those days. But I catch a glimpse of Miss Gratz approaching, and we all scatter as she says "Time for school, children!"

The room in which we assembled was a large one with four long windows at the end. Between the centre windows was a raised platform with a smaller one upon which stood a table and a chair. On the table was a much worn Bible containing both the Old and the New Testaments (Rev. Isaac Leeser's valuable edition of the Hebrew Bible had not then been published), a hand-bell, Watts' Hymns, and a penny contribution box "for the poor of Jerusalem."

Here Miss Gratz presided. A stately commanding figure, always neatly dressed in plain black, with thin white collar and cuffs, close-fitting bonnet over her curled front, which time never touched with grey, giving her, even in her most advanced years, a youthful appearance. Her eyes would pierce every part of the hall and often detect mischief which escaped the notice of the teachers.

The only punishment, I can recall, was for the delinquent to be marched through the school and seated upon the little platform, before mentioned, under the table. Sometimes this stand would be quite full, and I was rather disposed to envy those children who had no lessons to say. But, her duties over, Miss Gratz would call them by name to stand before her for reproof, which, apparently mild, was so soul-stirring that even the most hardened sinner would quail before it. She was extremely particular to instill neatness and cleanliness. A soiled dress, crooked collar, or sticky hands never escaped her penetrating glance and the reproof or remedy was instantaneous.

The benches held about ten children each; they were painted bright yellow, with an arm at each end; on the board across the back were beautiful medallions of mills, streams, farm-houses, etc., etc.

The instruction must have been principally orall in those primitive days. Miss Gratz always began school with the prayer, opening with "Come ye children, hearken unto me, and I will teach you the fear of The Lord." This was followed by a prayer of her own composition, which she read verse by verse, and the whole school repeated after her. Then she read a chapter of the Bible, in a clear and distinct voice, without any elocution, and this could be heard and understood all over the room. The closing exercises were equally simple; a Hebrew hymn sung by the children, then one of Watts' simple verses, whose rhythm the smallest child could easily catch as all repeated "Send me the voice that Samuel heard," etc., etc.

Many old scholars can still recall the question: "Who formed you child and made you live?" and the answer: "God did my life and spirit give"—the first lines of that admirable "Pyke's Catechism," which long held its place in the Sunday School, and was, I believe, the first book printed for it. The "Scripture Lessons" were taught from a little illustrated work published by the Christian Sunday School Union. Many a long summer's day have I spent, pasting pieces of paper over answers unsuitable for Jewish children, and many were the fruitless efforts of those children to read through, over, or under the hidden lines.

I could recall the names of many who sat on the long benches as scholars, or in the chairs as teachers, but they have all scattered—some to far distant homes, others to the eternal home. And those who are left are now all men and women, advanced in age—some of them grandfathers, some grandmothers of the present generation. Yet all still bear a grateful recollection of the Zane Street Sunday School, over the Phoenix Hose Company.

The Sunday School was removed in 1854 from Zane Street to the lower floor of the building of the Hebrew Education Society, then situated on Seventh Street, below Callowhill. This kindness has never been withdrawn and the Sunday School has ever since enjoyed the free use of the rooms of the Society, wherever located.

Miss Gratz was still superintendent, president, treasurer and secretary —the powerful and most capable factotum. I, with many others, was soon promoted from the ranks of the scholars to the dignity of teacher, owing to the great increase of very young children. The room was by no means as suitable as the old one, having a very low ceiling and small windows, affording insufficient light and air in summer, while two large stoves at the entrance heated only a small area on a cold winter's day. But economy was most strictly observed by Miss Gratz in all her dealings, and it was very necessary in the management of such a limited revenue as the school has always possessed. The saving of rent however enabled her to spend more liberally for the growing wants of the school.

The benches were low and semi-circular; the teacher sitting in much closer contact with the pupils was thus supposed to be able to maintain better order, and little restless feet were not so often seen dangling under the Superintendent's table. The platform was much larger and had a kind of alcove behind, in which were seated the pupils of the graduating class, taught by Miss Sim'ha C. Peixotto, who struggled with the difficulties of [Joseph] "Johlson's Catechism" until Mr. Leeser wrote his valuable "Catechism" for the school, and dedicated it to Miss Gratz. The articles on the table were also slightly changed; a handsome copy of Rev. Isaac Leeser's large edition of the Holy Scriptures replaced the old [Protestant] "King James's Version."

A roll book was added, and a fine gong bell rang for order, instead of the little tinkling one of the old school room. Maps of Palestine, the Ten Commandments, and other more appropriate emblems adorned the walls, and resolutions of the members of the Phoenix Hose Company.

A few changes had also crept into the weekly routine. The psalm, read one Sunday, was repeated the next week, by the older classes, a certain number of verses being assigned to each scholar. It sometimes happened that the succession would be broken by the absence of one or two pupils, but good marks, pretty cards, and a general desire to improve or get a prize made attendance very regular.

There were various devices used to amuse the very young children, before Miss Rebecca Moss started her infants' class, attended with such marked success. Both Hebrew and English primers were resorted to, in the vain attempt to teach reading, but if the least progress was made one Sunday, it would be entirely forgotten before the next lesson; particularly as the books were not allowed to be taken home. I can still recall my despair when a bright little boy spelt with triumph *N-a-g—Horse*, and *S-l-a-t-e— Looking Glass*, out of a thin, red covered, much illustrated book, which I think has evolved into "reading without tears" that many of you may remember to have wept over.

About this time Miss Sim'ha C. Peixotto, of grateful memory, saved us the trouble of pasting over objectionable passages, by undertaking to write the Scriptural questions, and published the first volume of her excellent Catechism, which held its well-deserved place in the school for many years.

"Pyke's Catechism" was freely distributed, and instead of being taught, parrot-fashion, by the teacher, the tiny green books went home to many Jewish households, with a penalty of five cents attached if injured or lost; and this fee was strictly exacted by the young librarian, who was a great disciplinarian. Books were not very often allowed by him, to be taken home, but were read, after the lessons were recited by the scholars, or aloud by the teacher, if it so happened that all her class studied in the same book, or the same lesson. Generally, however, owing to private reasons, kinship or popularity, a class would be composed of eight or ten boys and girls of different ages and ability, and consequently these were taught out of several books, or even different parts of the same book.

Both Rev. Isaac Leeser [1806–1868] and the Rev. Dr. (then Mr.) [Sabato] Morais [1832-1897] were constant visitors. The former with his strongly marked face, gold spectacles and inexhaustible fund of ever-ready information was a most welcome sight to the young teachers, puzzled by the questions of their big, clever scholars. He knew every child and teacher, called each by name, and nothing was too trivial or too intricate to claim his clear explanation.

Mr. Morais was then young, active, and full of enthusiasm, always ready to lead the Hebrew hymns or take the class of an absent teacher. Tradition says it was in Sunday School that he was first attracted to his beautiful young wife, who was one of the most beloved teachers. Be that as it may, most certainly, "courting" was openly encouraged both by Miss Gratz and Miss Hart, who having never "tasted the delights of matrimony," naturally wished all their young charges to enjoy "connubial bliss." My own teacher has often told me since, how her husband was first drawn towards her, by her gentle manners to her young pupils. Other successful and unsuccessful lovers will always retain pleasant memories of the old Sunday School, and of their walks to and from it.

The annual examination was held about Purim time. Why, at that time, I could never find out—as the work of the class had to be immediately recommenced—unless it was a sort of anniversary, as the school was first opened March 4th, which, by a curious coincidence, was Miss Gratz's birthday.

Can any of you recall the dear old Cherry Street Synagogue, on those March Sundays? I can see it so distinctly with its circular benches and deep gallery facing the large open space between the *tebah* and the *hechal* [the reading desk and the ark], with its broad steps and light doors that raised like a window. It was with something like awe that on these anniversaries we women took possession of the ground floor. [Women were not allowed on the ground floor with males.] A small table was placed in front of the reading-desk for Miss Gratz. The classes were all arranged in the men's seats and were called up to "stand and recite," by Mr. Abraham Hart [the publisher], who presided at the desk; his own clever children invariably making the best recitations and carrying off the prizes. The classes were arranged in a semi-circle, according to the part of the book they studied, the pupils returning to their seats when the limit of their lessons had been reached. One teacher stood in the centre, giving the questions, or, if the classes were numerous, walked gradually around the circle. Thus every child was really examined, and each book recited in whole or in part. The monotony was varied by monologues and dialogues; then came the distribution of prizes, which were called out by Mr. Hart, giving the name of the teacher with the three best scholars. The first prize was always a Bible; or, rather, a Bible and two books were given to each class. These books were most carefully selected by Miss Gratz herself, and handed by her to each child with a kind, encouraging word, often with a written line on the fly-leaf. As the happy children went out orderly by class, through the back door, each was given an orange and a pretzel.

Simple days of our youth, where are you now?

19

Jewish Culture
1820–1840

Of the 15,000 Jews, men, women, and children, in this country in 1840, a few were at home in the Hebrew Bible, the Talmud, the codes, Jewish history. A handful had even gone to European universities and were conversant with the new scientific methodology taking shape in the early nineteenth century. Isaac Nordheimer, for instance, had received his doctorate at the University of Munich and here in the United States issued three volumes on Hebrew grammar (1838). His critical approach left little to be desired.

In 1820 "An Israelite" published *Israel Vindicated*, primarily an attack on missionizing Christians who were importuning Jews to leave their faith. One of the targets of the author was the American Society for Meliorating [Evangelizing] the Condition of the Jews, a national association of Christians utterly devoted to the challenge of converting American Jews. This "Israelite" was probably Abraham Collins, the publisher, a militant Deist and Jew who had little use for Christianity. Some scholars believe that the prime author of the anonymous Jewish work may have been George Houston, a Gentile, a radical anti-Christian polemicist. The work itself, *Israel Vindicated*, followed the format adopted by Montesquieu in his *Lettres Persanes*. Two make-believe people correspond and analyze current events and conditions. In *Israel Vindicated*, the fictitious Nathan Joseph of New York writes to his friend Jacob Isaacs in Philadelphia. In general the author or authors of this book lash out at intolerance and orthodox Christianity. Deriding Christian orthodoxy was a flank attack on the missionaries who were harassing Jews. In selection I the "Israelite" questioned the existence of a historical Jesus.

157

Selections II and III were written by the Reverend Isaac Leeser (1806–1868), the minister of Congregation Mikveh Israel in Philadelphia. He was America's most illustrious Jewish clergyman in antebellum days. The accomplishments of this Modern Orthodox leader were important: he wrote catechisms, a Hebrew primer, works on Judaism; he published a Hebrew Bible, translated it into English, issued Sephardic and Ashkenazic prayer books, organized a Jewish publication society, edited the first permanent Jewish periodical, established the first American Jewish theological seminary, and pioneered as a preacher; his sermons fill ten volumes. In the second selection Leeser instructed his congregants how to educate their daughters (1835). Obviously he believed in the cult of true Jewish womanhood. In his *Claims of the Jews to an Equality of Rights*—selection III —Leeser attacked writings denigrating Jews and Judaism. Most churchgoing people in those early days were encouraged to have nothing but contempt for Jews and their religious practices. In general Jews were deemed social and cultural inferiors. Leeser defended his people and their beliefs.

I. *Israel Vindicated*: The Historicity of Jesus, 1820

Dear Isaacs,

Before entering upon an investigation of the particular dogmas of the Nazarene [Christian] religion, there are two points of considerable importance which require consideration; first, is it clear that the person called Jesus of Nazareth, really existed? Secondly, are the books, which the Nazarenes say contain the true particulars of the life and maxims of the founder of their sect, genuine, as well authenticated writings?

You will, perhaps, think with me, dear Isaacs, that if these questions are not answered in the affirmative, the whole Nazarene system must fall to the ground. If, indeed, there is reason to believe that the person, whom they call the Messiah, never appeared on the earth, and that the books containing his history are fabrications, it is impossible that any one, persuaded of these facts, can be "desirous to receive Christian instruction" at the hands of men, however respectable their rank in life, who attempt to rear a fabric upon so weak a foundation.

How could the learned of our nation defend themselves against the attacks of infidels, who might deny that our legislator Moses ever existed, if the fact was not established by other evidence than what is contained in our sacred books?. . . . How very different, dear Isaacs, is the evidence brought forward by the Nazarenes to establish the existence of the founder of their religion. Four unlettered and interested men of our nation, "pass for the faithful authors of memoirs containing the life of Jesus Christ; and it is on their testimony that Christians believe themselves bound to receive the religion they profess and adopt, without examination, the most contradictory facts, the most incredible actions, the most amazing prodigies, the most unconnected system, the most unintelligible doctrine, and the most revolting mysteries." [*Ecce Homo*, introduction, p. 9]. Surely, if as the Nazarene "Ameliorating Society" assert three kings came from the East, guided by a star, and worshipped Jesus; if at his birth, Herod and all Jerusalem was so "troubled" as to order the massacre of all the infant children in Bethlehem; if Jesus so openly restored the blind to sight, and raised people from the dead; if he was crucified, and, at the time of his death, the sun was totally eclipsed, the earth quaked, and the dead, who were in their graves, came forth and walked publicly through the streets of Jerusalem; surely, I say, if all these most extraordinary and wonderful events, together with the resurrection of Jesus himself from the dead, took place, as is said, in open day and in sight of thousands of the Roman people, besides many of our nation, it would have been impossible to have prevented the former, at least, from placing on record events of so notorious and unheard a nature. Were it even acceded to the Nazarenes, that our forefathers had reasons for overlooking altogether the person of Jesus, it cannot be imagined that a Roman historian, like Tacitus, who has, in so convincing a manner, demonstrated the antiquity of our nation, and who could have no possible interest in concealing the truth, would have entirely overlooked these astonishing occurrences, if they had really taken place. Yet Tacitus has not only taken no notice of them, but even, as to the *person* called Jesus, whom the Nazarenes worship, his history is wholly silent.

With regard to [the first-century Jewish historian] Josephus, I can see no reason to suppose, that he, any more than Tacitus, would have wilfully neglected to notice Jesus in his writings. Our historian faithfully records a thousand events which occurred among our nation, of much less importance than the most trifling miracle said to have been performed by Jesus. He even details, with no sparing hand, the numerous crimes of which Herod was accused. But, from beginning to end of the "History of the Jews," there is not one word to be found respecting the Messiah of the Christians, of the massacre of the innocents, of the three kings, or of the other wonderful events said to have occurred during his life time. Aware of the formidable and unanswerable objection arising from this silence, the Nazarenes endeavoured to get over it by inserting a passage, which they forged, into the text of Josephus, by which they wished to make it appear, not only that he actually recognised the person of Jesus, but that he entertained a high opinion of his character. The forgery, however, was detected, and has been ably exposed by [David] Blondel [d. 1665], L'Abbe de Longuerus, and other good critics.

Besides the histories of Tacitus and Josephus, we have the numerous works of [the Egyptian Jewish writer] Philo, who wrote in the apostolic age in which there is not the slightest allusion to Jesus of Nazareth, nor to any of the opinions said to have been then maintained by his followers.

Can it be expected, dear Isaacs, that a system offered to the consideration of our nation, so defective in its most essential features, should engage
the attention of a single individual among us? Had only one contemporary
and disinterested writer been named, who merely spoke of Jesus as a person of whose existence there was no doubt, I should, for one, have been
"desirous to receive Christian instruction"; but when there is a total absence of all rational proof, as to a point of such vast importance, I feel myself bound to reject the whole as a fable.

Nor can it be said, that the existence of Jesus is as well attested as any
fact in profane history, because we believe in the existence of Scipio, of
Caesar, and of Alexander, on the testimony of innumerable disinterested
historians, who have asserted the fact; but when Titus Livius, and other
writers speak of miracles having been performed, we reject these as improbable events. The case is very different with the Messiah of the Nazarenes. No writers but those who were interested, have recorded any thing
respecting him, and the books which it is pretended they have written are
filled with accounts of wonders and of marvellous events which it is impossible for any man in his senses to believe.

Adieu, dear Isaacs; live comfortably and happy.

Nathan Joseph

II.   Isaac Leeser's Views on the Education of Jewish Girls, 1835

How then is the child to become religious? How is he to read the Bible understandingly if instruction upon the most essential subject of life is
to be withheld from him? Some however may say: "That they will admit
that male children should be carefully instructed, that it is perfectly
reasonable that those who are to become, as it is called, 'the lords of creation' should be qualified for their stations by practical training, that their
morals should be carefully attended to and their mental culture strictly
watched over. But females, they aver, need not that knowledge; theirs
being a more dependent lot it is immaterial whether they are high-learned
in sacred literature or versed in the holy tongue. In short for them superficial reading is enough, for them it will be sufficient if the lighter branches
of elegant learning are cultivated by them." As usual, this reasoning contains with some sprinkling of soundness a great share of fallacy which will
be apparent upon a slight review of the question. It is not to be denied that
it is almost entirely useless for the female to become learned in the strictest
sense of the word; it would indeed unsex her, if she were to study the legal
profession; if she were to step abroad as a physician; if she, forgetful of
feminine decorum, would lay on the harness of war and wage a mortal
combat with the enemy. Well has it been commanded: "There shall not be

man's apparel upon a woman" [Deuteronomy 22:5]; for the female's sphere is not the highway, not the public streets, not the embattled field, not the public halls. . . .

Our daughters then should learn early, even whilst yet infants, that they as well as the other sex are creatures and dependents of God; they too should be early told of the greatness, the mercy and the unending goodness of the Almighty; they should be taught to direct their hopes in affliction and their confidence in prosperity to the Giver of all good. They should be informed that beauty is perishable, wealth is fleeting, joy evanescent, and wisdom fallacious; they should be impressed with the conviction that flattery is a pernicious gift dangerous to the receiver; that the world will crouch and cringe to the prosperous and turn away with disgust and loathing the confiding one whom they themselves have corrupted. Above all the father should betimes commence to teach his daughter the way she should go; he should, so to say, be her guide on the road to eternal life; he should bid her look into the sacred page to gather wisdom and hope from the undying words of Holy Writ; and he should admonish her to cull the antidote to affliction from those records where it is taught to us that the virtuous are never forsaken. Especially however he should inform her how becoming is meekness and how lovely is modesty in the beautiful woman, how much more commanding her loveliness must be if she bears it as a gift of Heaven, not as some gaudy jewel of which the wearer may be proud.

Think you that an education based upon such principles can be otherwise then beneficial? Even if the time consumed in this training should preclude the acquisition of accomplishment; still far better will it be that our daughters grow up religious women and excellent housewives than that they be elegant musicians, skilful painters, graceful dancers or pretenders to sciences which to the great majority of females must be quite useless. If time is left, if the parent's means will permit it, then some of the more showy branches might with advantage be added; but care should always be taken that they be viewed as secondary and that religious instruction and useful solid information should be the first, the most important pursuit.

Whilst on the subject I cannot dismiss it without adding a few words as to the books which are generally considered fit for female reading. I allude to the whole class of fictitious writings, by which I mean romances, novels, and dramas. That some are good, others harmless, is not to be denied; but the majority of them contain false views of morality; a perverted philosophy, and a mawkish sensibility are generally their chief pervading characteristics; and, when, as it is often the case, the young mind has not been stored with sound religious knowledge, this kind of literature destroys almost entirely all sound principles, and it may well-nigh reduce one to the awful state on which the prophet pronounced the curse: "Wo to those who say to the good evil, and to the evil good" [Isaiah 5:20].

It were therefore far better, if the whole of such works were banished or set out of the reach of the young; but if this cannot be done, at least do teach the females, at least prepare them with that kind of information which may act as the antidote to the poison they so plentifully imbibe. In this manner then let us proceed in the education of our children: let religion form the basis both for males and females on which the superstructure of useful and ornamental knowledge can afterwards be profitably built; for without the former, as has been shown, the latter can never produce good and wholesome fruits.

III.   Isaac Leeser Pleads for Equality of Rights for Jews, December 8, 1840

. . . we may freely leave it to others to answer, whether we have not effectually fulfilled the object of our mission. The Omniscient wanted to plant his law in the hearts of men by imperceptible steps towards a gradual fulfilment; He therefore chose a nation of priests to be always ready and perpetual witnesses of his power, whom no force, no bribery, no persuasion should ever wholly cause to swerve from the line of duty He had pointed out to them. The world has beheld this constant, silent exhibition of a pure, unadulterated faith; and though mankind drew the sword, like the valiant warrior on the day of strife, to extirpate these heroic witnesses: it availed not any farther than for a time diminishing the number of the defenders; but the law itself, the noble testimony of God's power, remains untouched. . . .

We now maintain that evil enough has been entailed on us from a long course of malevolence exhibited in many varying shapes for many centuries; we maintain, that in the constitutional and enlightened countries of Europe and America human rights are now better understood than formerly; we maintain, that every man has, or ought to have, the right to worship his Maker in a manner consonant with the dictates of his conscience, saving only that such manner cannot become injurious to society at large, such as atheism and anti-social institutions (although these too should be combatted by reason more than by the force of civil power). We maintain that whilst a man does nothing to injure his neighbour in the enjoyment of liberty, the pursuit of happiness, and his lawfully acquired possessions, he ought not to be restrained from worshipping in the manner just specified, or have his rights abridged for so doing, or to be enticed by any means whatever to yield his opinions, or to be exposed to public scorn for maintaining such views and following a course of conduct based upon them which cannot injure those differing from him in their worldly and spiritual possessions. In short, we claim, as children of one Father, as followers of his law, as supporters of a highly social system, to remain Jews, without the interference of our Christian neighbours and fellow-citizens; just as we act towards them. You may say that we preach toleration because we are in the minority; but that we would speak differently if we were to obtain dominion. But we deny this supposition. You cannot point out a single period in our history where the Jews acted unfriendly to the strangers that dwelt among them. . . .

At the present time we are at all events powerless as a people; we live amongst you, and under your control; you have tried our extermination long enough; you have caused bitterness on your side and heartburning on ours; in some parts of the world you tolerate us, in others you oppress us, and in others again you declare that we are your equals in political rights. Now we appeal to you, to extend your liberality to our opinions also; and to tolerate these as you tolerate our bodies; let them live or die as they can of their own intrinsic value, and leave us their silent enjoyment till we get tired of them, which time will never arrive, as we are promised in the prophecies contained in Scripture. And you, as Christians, must acquiesce in the justice of these remarks, for the founder of your faith himself declared: "Think not that I am come to destroy the law or the prophets: I am not come to destroy but to fulfil. For verily I say unto you: till heaven and earth pass, one jot or one tittle shall in no wise pass from the law, till all be fulfilled. Whosoever, therefore, shall break one of these least commandments and shall teach men so, he shall be called the least in the kingdom of heaven: but whosoever shall do and teach them, the same shall be called great in the kingdom of heaven" (Matthew 5:17–19). . . .

20

Social Welfare Activity
1819–1837

There were always generous individuals in every Jewish community. Aaron Lopez was distinguished in colonial Newport for his generosity; in the early nineteenth century Harmon Hendricks of New York City was known for his gifts to good causes. The basic Jewish welfare institution in the colonial period was the synagog, the congregation, but when Jews began to come to the new United States in goodly numbers special societies arose to meet their needs. From the 1780s on there were immigrant societies, relief, sick-care, and burial organizations; there were other associations eager to provide for orphans and the children of indigents. Actually the first Ashkenazic congregation in America, Rodeph Shalom of Philadelphia, offered sick-care and burials to its constituents before it offered regular religious services. One of the very early New York Jewish charities even talked of a hospice and hospital almost fifty years before Jews' Hospital (Mount Sinai) opened its doors. In the 1830s no Jewish community of size was without one or more social welfare organizations. They were fellowships, *hevrot*. During the sad depression days of the post-Jackson period, 1837 and on, Jewish charity and mutual aid societies multiplied.

The federation concept in philanthropy was foreshadowed vaguely as early as 1822 when the *United* Hebrew Beneficent Society was founded in Philadelphia. A federation of sorts existed in embryo in New York City in 1837 when several local Jewish charities pooled their resources to aid arriving impoverished German Jewish immigrants.

Jewish women—Mikveh Israel members—established the first Jewish female charity; this was the Female Hebrew Benevolent Society of Philadelphia (1819). It was called into being by Rebecca Gratz and a number of her friends. Jewish women—Rebecca, too—had been active in Gentile women's social-welfare societies for just about two decades. They may have been prompted to start a Jewish women's charity because of the long-continuing depression that began in 1815. Families were in dire need. The new organization set out to help women of good family "in reduced circumstances." Relatively very few were helped; the poverty-stricken proletariat was ignored. If the improvident were impoverished it was their own fault! This society also provided access to general dispensaries; Jewish doctors offered their services, and an employment bureau of sorts was envisioned. The largest gift to the society came from the estate of a Gentile. Was the individual member impelled by her gender consciousness to be somebody, to do something? We do not know. Excerpts from the constitution and reports of this early women's society appear in selection I.

Another of Philadelphia's early philanthropies was the Hebrew Society for the Visitation of the Sick and Mutual Assistance (1813). This was a mutual aid organization. Newcomers, usually with no financial reserve, were desperate for "insurance" to provide for their families in the event of sickness or, God forbid, death. The United Hebrew Beneficent Society of Philadelphia was a general relief congeries that included members from both the Sephardic and the Ashkenazic congregations; in a way it was a communal organization, not closely tied to Mikveh Israel as was the 1813 group. Excerpts from the 1822–1837 constitution appear in the second selection.

I.   The Female Hebrew Benevolent Society of Philadelphia, 1819–1837

Preamble, etc.

In all communities, the means of alleviating the sufferings of the poor are considered of high importance by the benevolent and humane. The ladies of the Hebrew Congregation of Philadelphia, sensible to the calls which have occasionally been made in their small society, and desirous of rendering themselves useful to their indigent sisters of the house of Israel, agree to establish a charitable society; and in order to make the benefit permanent, adopt the following:

Constitution

ARTICLE I

The society shall be established and known by the title of the Female Hebrew Benevolent Society of Philadelphia. . . .

RULES AND REGULATIONS

For the government of the Female Hebrew Benevolent Society of Philadelphia. . . .

VISITING COMMITTEE

A committee of managers shall be appointed monthly to investigate the situation of applicants and administer to their relief. They shall visit the pensioners, make inquiries respecting their characters and conditions, and in all cases provide them with necessaries, rather than with money.

PENSIONERS

The pensioners of the society shall be Israelites, residents of the city or county of Philadelphia, of good moral character. Assistance may also be given to sojourning Israelites in clothing or small sums of money.

To educate the children of indigent families, will be a desirable object of the society, when their funds will permit. . . .

REPORT . . .

From the organization of the society in November until the present meeting, the board have met once a fortnight, and every application for assistance has been attended to by the visiting committee. One or two cases may have been attended with disappointment to the applicants, as upon investigation it was thought necessary to reject one altogether, and to give but little to another. The board would not trouble the society with these particulars, but they are desirous to explain the principles on which they act. The funds elicited by charity they consider a sacred trust, to be distributed only where the purposes of charity can be effected. They could not consistently with this, bestow upon the idle and improvident, although their poverty may excite to pity. An indigent family, who are frugal, industrious and grateful, have been assisted during the winter. They bless the society for many comforts, which had else been strangers to their dreary habitation.

It is to modest worth, pining in obscurity, to the indigent who are "ashamed to beg," to the sick, and to the infirm, that the assistance of this society will be most freely given. And that every delicacy may be secured to those who have "seen better days," a select committee will be formed at the next session, through whose hands relief may be secretly bestowed on reduced families, should such unhappily be found in our congregation.

The board, likewise, desirous of establishing a reciprocal service to the industrious and the infirm, propose that persons willing to attend on the sick or to assist in performing the last charitable offices for the deceased, should leave their names with the president of the society; that when occasions among our poor occur, they may be called on and remunerated by the society. Females who wish employment as seamstresses, and those who want them, may also make application to the president, who will keep a register for their accommodation. The board have the pleasure to state, they have received and accepted the offer of professional services from Drs. [Manuel] Phillips and [Isaac] Hays, for the sick among the pensioners, and also the use of the Hebra's [the 1813 men's sick-care society] contributions to the city and Northern Liberties dispensaries. They have expended by the visiting committee forty-one dollars and thirty cents, and deposited in the savings bank three hundred dollars until a purchase of United States six per cent stock can be made on favourable terms, reserving at the disposal of the board, fifty-four dollars and seventy cents for present purposes.

In making this first communication to their patrons [1820?] the board are duly impressed with the importance of the trust reposed in them; and feeling the deepest interest in the success of the institution, they pray that the God of Israel may give them understanding equal to their zeal, so to conduct its concerns as to benefit the distressed and do credit to those who have "stretched forth their hands to the poor and needy" [Proverbs 31:20].

REPORT

November 1, 1837

Ladies:

Since the last anniversary meeting, the Female Hebrew Benevolent Society has become incorporated, and now, under the sanction of the laws, takes its place among those associations with which our city abounds, whose object is the relief of the poor, and to improve the condition of those whom God, for his own wise purpose, has left to the care of their fellow men. "The rich and the poor meet together, and God is the maker of them all" [Proverbs 22:2]; he has endowed them each with the qualities their conditions require, and placed them in stations where they may be mutually serviceable to each other. The hardy labourer brings out the riches of the field, and while he fills the granaries of his employer, earns the portion that supplies the wants of his own family, and furnishes abundance that others may partake, or convert into fabrics of usefulness and beauty. Thus is the goodness of Providence manifested in enabling man to find in the products of nature the means of satisfying all his wants, of acquiring happiness by his own labour; by his intelligence subdoing the earth, traversing the ocean, and making the winds his messengers. And yet, with all his power, during a large portion of his life, man is a feeble being, dependent on the care and aid of his fellow creatures, in the years of childhood and decrepid age; in periods of sickness and adversity, and when the stranger's widow is left destitute in a foreign land, without energy or means to rear her young progeny. To the Jews, who have no country, and whose brethren come from every clime, it is incumbent wherever a few are collected together in a community, to form societies for the relief of the wayfarer, the poor, and the stranger; for in all their borders God has blessed them; the exhortation that encouraged Joshua [1:9], "Be strong and of good courage; be not terrified or dismayed, for the Lord thy God is with thee, whithersoever thou goeth," is daily on our lips and in our hearts; and in all the trials of life, a pious Israelite draws consolation from the same fountain of mercy for his individual sorrow.

The treasurer's account will inform you of the receipts and expenditures of the past year.

During the summer and autumn several poor Jew families arrived in this city from Europe, who required aid, and will be still more destitute in the severity of winter, if your charity is not extended to them. Let them not plead in vain. At your comfortable firesides think of the habitations of the poor; for them no glowing anthracite or blazing wood sends out a genial heat; their hearths are mocked by smoking shavings, and even these but scantily supplied; nor is the winter storm excluded from their dwellings.

By procuring a charter, the Female Hebrew Benevolent Society have made themselves responsible for the permanence of the charity and the faithful discharge of their duties; they are capable of inheriting estates or legacies, and invite those who would make their good deeds live after them attend to the form of bequest; and those who would witness the effects of their compassion, come and give in that spirit of mercy which twice blesseth—blessing those that give and those that receive [*Merchant of Venice*, Act 4].
November 1st, 1837.

II. United Hebrew Beneficent Society of Philadelphia, 1822–1837

CONSTITUTION

PREAMBLE

To provide in the best manner possible for the relief of our unfortunate and indigent brethren, and to ameliorate their sufferings to the utmost of our abilities, is the performance of an obligation which strengthens the bonds of society, by the endearing ties of benevolence and gratitude.

Impressed with these truths, we whose names are hereto subscribed, citizens of the State of Pennsylvania, hereby united in a benevolent association, and for our government, as members thereof, adopt the following rules and regulations; each of us pledging himself to the others to observe them with honour and good faith.

ARTICLE I

The name of the society shall be ... "The United Hebrew Beneficent Society of Philadelphia."

ARTICLE II

The funds of the society shall be appropriated to the following purposes:

1. Relief to the poor and sick of the Jewish persuasion.

2. To procure attendance, medicine, &c., for such sick as are unable to provide for themselves; and in case of death to bury them with decency.

3. To bind poor children apprentices to mechanical trades, with the concurrence of their parents or guardians.

4. Whenever the funds will admit—to encourage the acquirement of the Holy Tongue among the children of the members of our persuasion. . . .

ARTICLE VIII

Section 1. Any Jew residing in the state of Pennsylvania, desirous of becoming a member of this society may apply in writing at any meeting, which application shall lie over until the next stated board meeting, at which time, or at a subsequent stated board meeting, the applicant shall be balloted for; and if he shall receive the voices of two-thirds of the members present, shall be admitted to membership, provided he signs this constitution and pays one dollar on entrance to the treasurer within three months after his election.

Sect. 2. No person who shall be married otherwise than according to the Jewish rites can apply for or be admitted to membership in this society; and if any member shall marry otherwise than according to the Jewish laws, he shall, by the vote of a majority at any board meeting, forfeit his membership—from which vote an appeal may lie to the next general yearly meeting of the society, whose decision thereon shall be final. . . .

ARTICLE IX

Every member shall contribute four dollars annually to the society in quarterly payments; and every member who shall on entrance pay forty dollars shall be exempted from all contributions during his continuance in the society.

ARTICLE X

Sect. 1. The president shall, at his discretion, on application by any person professing Judaism, whom he may deem an object worthy of charity, have the power to relieve such applicant with a sum not exceeding five dollars; if, however, he thinks any applicant entitled to more, he shall in that case consult the board, and whatever sum may be voted to such applicant shall be drawn from the funds by an order signed by the president and attested by the secretary. Weekly allowances may be given to poor resident families applying in writing to the president, who shall lay the same before the board to decide thereon, and order such amount as the applicants are to receive, these orders being also signed by the president and attested by the secretary; *provided always*, that the aforesaid weekly allowances and all other expenditures, shall never exceed three-fourths of the yearly income of this society.

Sect. 2. It shall be the duty of the board of managers to visit the sick, order medical assistances, nurses, and other necessaries required. They shall call on poor applicants, inquire into their distresses, and see that the society is not imposed on by false representations. They shall employ proper persons to sit up with the dying and the dead, who are unable to procure such attendants at their own expense, and to watch their remains at the *beth hayyim* [cemetery].

In every instance where a child of a poor person may be bound an apprentice by this society, it shall be the duty of the board to see that he is bound out in such a manner as to keep his Sabbaths and Holy-days, and in all other respects to adhere as nearly as possible to his religion, agreeably to the Jewish laws. They shall also inquire, previously to such binding, as to the moral character of the intended master, as well as to his capacity to teach the child his trade in a workmanlike manner; and they shall exercise a kindly guardianship over such child, so far as they may with propriety, and see justice done him in every respect. And no person shall have any claim to the charity of this society, unless when applied to by the board, he will agree to their binding his child or children apprentices to learn mechanical trades, unless he shall give a satisfactory reason why he will not comply with their wishes.

Sect. 3. The board may, if they think proper, form themselves into committees on charity, on the sick and dead, on education and apprentices, and such other committees as may facilitate and more fully carry into effect the objects of this institution.

Sect. 4. The board shall elect a messenger and fix his salary; his duties shall be to collect moneys due, attend the society and board at all meetings, keep the place of meeting in order, visit the sick, and make report to the board, attend all funerals and deliver all notices of meetings, of attending *kevurah* [burial], *taharah* [cleansing], and *minyan* [services], and such others as may be delivered to him by the proper officers of the society; give the female relatives of the members notice to attend sewing [of the shrouds] and report to the secretary every member who has subjected himself to a fine.

21

A Jewish Family in the Old South
1812–1837

Raphael Jacob Moses (1812–1893)—a native of Charleston, South Carolina—was a lawyer, orator, and politician. A contemporary historian of the Jews wrote that Moses was "the foremost Hebrew at the bar and in the politics of the Southern States." His home was in Columbus, Georgia. During the Civil War he served the South as a quartermaster officer with the title of major. Though not an ardent religionist he was a proud Jew and never hesitated to defend his "race." Moses was a fifth generation American; his great-great-grandfather—a refugee from the Inquisition—came to Georgia just a few months after Col. James Edward Oglethorpe had landed with the first English settlers (1733). Deborah Cohen Moses (1776–1848), his mother, was the daughter of Jacob R. Cohen, a North African who had served Montreal, New York, and Philadelphia as "rabbi," as an omnibus religious factotum. In the first selection Major Moses described his youth in Charleston; he was as American as "mom and apple pie"; America worked wonders for this descendant of a Portuguese notable and a North African clergyman. In the second selection the major's mother made provision for her burial in an ethical will; her simple piety is startling in its freshness, in its appeal.

I. Childhood in South Carolina,
By Raphael Jacob Moses, 1812–1825

What you want, I suppose, is an anti[e]-mortem diary, a sort of retrospective glance at my life from the cradle to the grave, or sufficiently near the latter to leave it an easy matter for you or anyone else to fill out the few blank pages that may remain.

Well, then, to begin, I was born on the night of January 29th, 1812, in Beaufain St., Charleston, South Carolina. Like most babies, I suppose I entered upon life with a cry. I was born an ugly baby, remained an ugly boy, and lived an ugly man. My mother had two other children, both handsome, but they died in infancy. Death loves a shining mark; they shone, I didn't, and so I was left to become the pet of my mother and the pest of everybody else, "a spoled child," and I went through an extraordinary share of spoiling, and nothing saved me from utter ruin except good luck or some undeveloped innate virtue.

At two years old, I have heard, I knew my letters, and my dear mother thought she saw the germs of a concealed genius which has remained invisible ever since. She kept a school, and I was one of her scholars, cutting a figure in her classes when I should have been cutting my teeth!

My boyhood may be condensed into one word: I was the impersonation of mischief; my pranks were without limit and much to the annoyance of a maiden cousin, Bell Cohen, who had charge of me in the occasional visits paid by my parents to Philadelphia and New York. At school I never took a very high stand as I was much more given to play than to study. I had the reputation at school of having excellent capacity, but lacking industry in my classes. I was seldom "head," and if I got there by accident, I seldom remained there more than a day or two at a time. When the examinations came on annually, I crammed for them, and as I could acquire very rapidly, I generally took a stand with the boys that were up with their lessons all the year round.

The first school that I have any recollection of after leaving my mother's school was kept by a Mr. Southworth. He was an excellent teacher and a severe disciplinarian. I improved very much under him, but one day one of the boys who shall be nameless, but who belonged to the South Carolina aristocracy and was the bully of the school, undertook to whip a little boy, and I interfered. And though I have never been much of a fighter, being neither active or particularly strong, I found my adversary like many other bullies, not much of a hero when put to the test; and it was my good fortune to come off victor in the fight. But alas! as we fought in the schoolyard, which was against the rules, Mr. Southworth was even more victorious than I was, for he whipped us both. I, of course, complained to father, and he went with me to the teacher, justified my course, denounced his inflexible rules, and withdrew me from school. I was then between ten and eleven.

From there I went to Bishop England, a celebrated Catholic divine! He had a very large school. All the teachers were priests; the bishop did not teach, but visited the school about once a week. There was no discipline at all; the boys "ruled the roost" and ruled it with a high hand. I remember on one occasion I loitered by the way, having become much more interested in a game of marbles than in heathen mythology, which was the lesson for the afternoon. Arriving late, Mr. Monk, the priest and teacher, gave my companions and myself a sharp lecture on our being tardy!

At that time, the fashion prevailing were Wellington boots and Wellington coats; in fact, everything was Wellington, and when the priest asked me how some heathen god's feet were covered, for want of a more historical answer I replied: "In Wellington boots!" Monk, already outraged at our late arrival, lifted his rattan, a kind of cane, and was about to come down on me, when I presented a pistol minus a cock, which deficiency being unknown to the priest, his rattan remained suspended in midair. And instead of the whipping, I was ordered to leave the class and informed that I would be reported to the bishop, which being done, on the bishop's next visit, I was summoned to his room for a confessional, not to be absolved by payment of Peter's pence.

I trembled in my shoes for the consequences and wilted before the bishop's steel-grey eyes; they were the greyest eyes I ever saw in any human head, I was, of course, very penitent, and I think the cockless pistol which I exhibited to show how utterly harmless it was and that there was therefore no malice prepense, that the action was the result of a sudden impulse and as the darkies say, done "unthoughtedly," for all of which I was very sorry. The bishop let me off with a well-deserved lecture on the impropriety of my conduct and require that I should express my regrets to Mr. Monk before the class, which I did, resolved in my own mind henceforth and forever, or as long as boyhood lasted, to be a model boy.

I don't think, however, it was many moons before some of the boys, one of which was your little reformer, ripped up the flooring of the schoolrooms. Why or how we did it, I do not remember. The big boys were the masterminds in this escapade, and the perpetrators of the diabolical act were never discovered.

The next thing on the tapis was the examination. I remember it well; it was in the cathedral. At one end of it there was extemporized a platform about five feet high, all around which there were benches, and the priests seated thereon, their legs encased in knee breeches and black silk stockings. The bishop occupied a seat in the center of the platform. The cathedral was crowded. The recitations were made on the platform. I recited with eclat "Aurora Fair Daughter of the Dawn," [from Pope's *Odyssey*] but in the intervals we boys, who were not "tickling" the public for the time being, stationed ourselves around the platform and tickled with pins the underpinning, not of the platform, but the priests, and when the signal was given, "stick a pin there," priests' legs were rubbed and lifted as if mosquitoes were gathering a harvest, and none of us boys ever knew whether a Catholic priest knew the difference between the point of a pin lightly inserted or the bill of a mosquito perseveringly presented.

I remained at the bishop's school about a year, and not being entirely without conscience, nor unlike [Cowper's] *John Gilpin*, who although on pleasure bent yet had a frugal mind, I actually acknowledged to my parents that I was not learning anything but mischief at the bishop's, in which, by the way, you will see I was pretty well graduated, and requested them to send me to another school! Alas, for the change!

They sent me to Isaac Harby [the founder of the Reformed Society of Israelites], father of Octavia Moses, a splendid teacher who believed as "the twig is bent the tree's inclined" and "spare the rod and spoil the child." He bent the twig but never spared the rod. I remember a mulberry tree that grew in the yard. I remember it denuded of many limbs. I remember further the use they were put to, and the further fact that the boys, with whose backs they were to be made familiar, were, with a quizzical look (I think I can see it now), ordered to go and cut a bunch and be sure to get good ones, too. . . .

I continued with Mr. Harby untill I was twelve and a half years of age. I was studying Latin and just about to commence Greek when it suddenly occurred to me that I had absorbed through the skin as much knowledge as I cared to acquire in that way, and I proposed to my overindulgent parents to consider my education finished, and they so considered it. I then left school and entered on the business of life, of which more anon.

I ought not to omit from my boyhood memories as illustrative of my father's character the mortal dread I always had of a butcher boy named Coagley. He was a sort of John L. Sullivan among the boys. He looked to me as tough as a lightwood knot and was certainly as pugnacious as a bull-dog. I have, many a time, gone a square out of my way to avoid meeting Coagley; I had a mortal dread of him, and my father, one day seeing me trying to shirk him, came out with a coachwhip, which in his hands was as formidable a weapon to me (he weighing over 300 pounds) as was Sampson's [Samson's] historical jawbone to the Philistines.

He said: "I see you are afraid of that boy. Now you have either got to whip him or I will whip you." The choice of two evils in this instance was full of difficulties, but when I looked at little Coagley and my big father with his threatening whip and flashing eye, supplemented by an oath or two indicating his determined purpose, I think if Goliath had stood before me, I would have sailed in, by no means regardless of consequences, but wisely considering the blows of the butcher boy the lesser evil of the two. And with the consequences of the defeat present to my mind, I came out victorious, but so battered and bruised that it would have taken a very short argument to satisfy me that "ten such victories would be equal to a defeat." The boy never troubled me again, but I always thought his peaceful bearing was attributable more to his vision of the father of the boy who conquered him than to any apprehension he would have felt for your humble servant if he had had no daddy. But the lesson was a good one, for it taught me, like the Irishman, that the best way "to avoid danger was to meet it plump in the face." . . .

During my residence at St. Joseph [Florida], my father and mother followed their wayward son, built a house next to mine. My mother died there [1848], and my father died about six months after in Apalachicola [1849]. He never recovered from the blow caused by my mother's death, had her body buried in the yard near the house, and used to pray at her grave daily, though he was never before religiously inclined.

My mother was a very religious woman, a strict conformist to all Jewish customs, and the day before, though in apparent health, she seemed to have a premonition of her death. I tried to rouse her and made her go to walk with me. On the way we met an old Irishwoman on whom she had been accustomed to bestow charity. She took her aside and talked with her, and the Irishwoman told me that she gave her $1 and told her to take that and remember her. The next day was [my daughter] Nina's birthday and she promised me, if she was well, she would throw off her depression and give her a party. But she felt that a calamity was impending over us. We parted that night, and she told Eliza [my wife] to be sure to take care of [Raphael Moses's] father. This I did not then know.

The next morning I went over as usual to see her, but she had not been out of her room, and father said he supposed she was washing. I knocked at the door and, receiving no answer, made our boy [Negro servant], Joe, go in at the window, and alas, mother was on the bed—dead. Her shrouds were on the bureau, and on a slip of paper was written, "Where the tree falls, let it lay," intimating, I suppose, that she did not wish her remains to be carried to Charleston to be laid in the Jewish cemetery.

She had her best linen sheets on the bed and every indication that she expected her room to be visited by strangers. Knowing how scrupulous she was about Jewish rights [rites], Eliza, with her usual self-sacrifice, performed all the duties of preparing her for burial, and thus, at seventy-two, passed from earth as pure a spirit as ever dwelt in human form. God bless her memory. I know that she has gone to her reward, and feel that she still lives and loves us. . . .

II.   The Ethical Will of Deborah Moses, 1837

The State of South Carolina. In the name of God, Amen. I, Deborah Moses of the city of Charleston and State aforesaid, being deeply impressed with the conviction that the Almighty had blessed me beyond my deserts, I feel bound in humble gratitude to avail myself of the full possession of all my faculties to regulate and dispose of my worldly effects in a way that I deem most advantageous to those exclusively dear to my heart, and who claim both from nature and affection every effort on my part to secure my property which I hold and have possessed as a free dealer, to them and for their interest and future welfare should the will of God so ordain (which with humility of spirit I hope may be the case) that they should survive me. . . .

I request that no pomp or parade whatever may be exhibited over my last remains. A plain coffin of the most simple materials, and in due time a wooden head and foot post without any inscription whatever are all that I require. The wisdom of God has mingled us indistinctly with the earth; why then shall we take from the living to arrogantly perpetuate an ephemeral name. To be forgotten is the lot of all. I therefore require no mark of outward woe. Lay the earth quietly and with respect on me; I leave the rest to conscience, feeling, and duty. Mourn not beyond the hour sanctified by nature and true grief; the tears which spring from the heart are the only dews the grave should be moistened with. The dead receive sufficient honor in being called to face their God. . . .

Witness my hand and seal this fourteenth day of November, one thousand eight hundred and thirty seven.
Deborah Moses

22

The Kinship of All Jews
1818–1840

J ews are distinguished for their concept of kinship. Every Jew, says the Talmud, is responsible for every fellow Jew (Talmud Bavli, Sanhedrin 27b). This is why Jews are willing to help coreligionists who are impoverished or exposed to violence. The obligation is taken very seriously. Individuals help the indigent, communities assist one another; Jews are determined to aid oppressed Jews abroad. This is the concept of *kelal yisrael,* the Community of Israel. We belong to one another.

Mordecai Manuel Noah (1785–1851) embodied this concept in many of his activities as a Jew. Noah, the most distinguished Jewish layman in antebellum America, was a journalist, a diplomat, a sheriff, a judge, a dramatist, a Surveyor of the Port of New York, a proto-Zionist. He was concerned with the fate of his fellow Jews when still in his twenties; in 1818—still a young man—he called on World Jewry to arm itself, march on to Palestine, and reclaim it from the Moslems. Seven years later he proposed that a Jewish colony—Noah called it Ararat—be established on Grand Island near Buffalo, New York. He invited the oppressed Jews of Europe to migrate to free America and create a Jewish commonwealth of their own here. It was to be a state in exile, a training ground preparatory to the revival of the Third Jewish Commonwealth in the Holy Land. Though Ararat never housed a single Jew, Noah in the 1830s and 1840s continued to plead for a reborn Jewish homeland in Palestine.

Selection I is an excerpt from an 1818 address in which Noah foretold the conquest of Palestine by the Jews; selection II—also an excerpt—is his Proclamation defining the goals and structure of Ararat, this "government of the Jewish Nation"; selection III is a reprint of several paragraphs from the long address Noah made that same day when dedicating his new colony in Buffalo.

177

In setting out to establish a colony for persecuted European Jews, Noah also donned the hat of an empresario, a land promoter out to make a fast dollar. Yet he was unquestionably moved by the desire to help his people. Here, too, he was motivated by the concept of *kelal yisrael*. It was this same principle that prompted Joseph Jonas (1792–1869), a founder of Cincinnati Jewry, to send out letters of appeal to American, British, and West Indian communities and various individuals, asking them for money to help build a synagog in his city, the first organized Jewish community west of the Blue Ridge Mountains. His message was clear: we are Jews; we have a right to turn to you; it is your obligation to help us. Selection IV is a reprint of his appeal to the congregation in Charleston, South Carolina; it responded by making a grant.

When in 1840 the Moslem authorities in Damascus arrested and tortured many of the Jews in that community on the false charge of kidnapping a Christian monk and his servant and using their blood in the Passover ritual, European Jewry was shocked. (Similar false charges and arrests were made on the Turkish Isle of Rhodes.) The Damascus Affair was medievalism with a vengeance. Public meetings of protest were held in London in July of that year. It was not until the middle of August that American Jewry—obviously dilatory—organized protests in several American towns to denounce this calumny. Christians in several cities took the lead in calling such mass meetings. By the time the protests of the American Jews and their Christian allies reached Washington, President Martin Van Buren and Secretary of State John Forsyth had already taken action. They had written to John Gliddon, their consul at Alexandria, calling on him to remonstrate with the Pasha of Egypt who then controlled Syria. They urged the consul to do what he could to aid the imprisoned Jews in Damascus. This humanitarian effort on the part of the nineteenth-century U.S. government to aid foreign Jews was rare; bear in mind that the Jews of Damascus and Rhodes were not American citizens (selection V).

All this was in August even before the American Jews had dispatched their first protest to Washington. By that time the English government; European consuls in Egypt; Sir Moses Montefiore, the Jewish philanthropist; and Isaac Adolphe Crémieux, a notable French Jew, had induced the Egyptian overlord to retreat. By late August and early September the Jews imprisoned in Damascus had already been released. Before the end of the year the sultan in Constantinople had issued a decree exonerating the Jews from all accusations of ritual murder. Selection VI contains excerpts of the resolutions passed on August 27, 1840, by Jews and Christians who had met together in Philadelphia to raise their voices against the Syrian authorities.

The Damascus Affair marked a turn in American Jewish history. Outraged, the various American Jewish communities established committees of correspondence and appealed to Washington for help. By this very act they created a national American Jewish community by consensus. And when Sephardic Congregation Shearith Israel—the most prestigious in all America—refused to associate itself with the effort to help the Damascenes, the Ashkenazic congregations automatically assumed leadership. Symbolically at least, America's mother church surrendered its spiritual primacy in American Jewry. Most of America's synagogs were already Ashkenazic in origin; the Sephardic period had now run its course; the years from 1840 to 1920 would mark the domination of the "Germans."

I. Mordecai M. Noah, Proto-Zionist, April 17, 1818

Never were prospects for the restoration of the Jewish nation to their ancient rights and dominion more brilliant than they are at present. There are upwards of seven millions of Jews known to be in existence throughout the world, a number greater than at any period of our history, and possessing more wealth, activity, influence, and talents, than any body of people of their number on earth. The signal for breaking the Turkish sceptre in Europe will be their emancipation; they will deliver the north of Africa from its oppressors; they will assist to establish civilization in European Turkey, and may revive commerce and the arts in Greece; they will march in triumphant numbers, and possess themselves once more of Syria, and take their rank among the governments of the earth. This is not fancy. I have been too much among them in Europe and Africa—I am too well acquainted with their views and sentiments in Asia, to doubt their intentions. They hold the purse strings, and can wield the sword; they can bring 100,000 men into the field. Let us then hope that the day is not far distant when, from the operation of liberal and enlightened measures, we may look towards that country where our people have established a mild, just, and honourable government, accredited by the world, and admired by all good men. Let us not seek the errors of other faiths, but calmly and peaceably pursue our own, in which there are no errors. Let us respect and assist all religions which acknowledge God, and whose principles are justice and mercy. We, of all others, can hold out the hand of toleration; the time will come when the wanderer who has been led astray in search of other Gods, will acknowledge the unity and omnipotence of the God of Israel, when persecution shall cease, and the groan of oppression be heard no more. Between two good men professing different faiths, no difference exists; both are born equal—both have a right to worship the Almighty in his own way; the road to honour should be open to both, for both must pursue the same path to immortality.

II.   Noah's Proclamation to World Jewry, September 15, 1825

Whereas, it has pleased Almighty God to manifest to his chosen people the approach of that period, when, in fulfillment of the promises made to the race of Jacob, and as a reward for their pious constancy and triumphant fidelity, they are to be gathered from the four quarters of the globe, and to resume their rank and character among the governments of the earth;

And whereas, the peace which now prevails among civilized nations, the progress of learning throughout the world, and the general spirit of liberality and toleration which exists together with other changes favorable to light and to liberty, mark in an especial manner the approach of that time, when "peace on earth and good will to man" are to prevail with a benign and extended influence, and the ancient people of God, the first to proclaim His unity and omnipotence, are to be restored to their inheritance, and enjoy the rights of a sovereign independent people;

Therefore, I, Mordecai Manuel Noah, citizen of the United States of America, late consul of said States to the City and Kingdom of Tunis, High Sheriff of New York, counselor at law, and by the grace of God, Governor and Judge of Israel, have issued this my proclamation, announcing to the Jews throughout the world that an asylum is prepared and hereby offered to them, where they can enjoy that peace, comfort and happiness which have been denied them through the intolerance and misgovernment of former ages; an asylum in a free and powerful country, where ample protection is secured to their persons, their property and religious rights, an asylum in a country remarkable for its vast resources, the richness of its soil, and the salubrity of its climate, where industry is encouraged, education promoted, and good faith rewarded, "a land of milk and honey," where Israel may repose in peace, under his "vine and fig tree," and where our people may so familiarize themselves with the science of government and the lights of learning and civilization, as may qualify them for that great and final restoration to their ancient heritage, which the times so powerfully indicate.

The asylum referred to is in the State of New York, the greatest State in the American confederacy. . . . The desired spot in the State of New York, to which I hereby invite my beloved people throughout the world, in common with those of every religious denomination, is called Grand Island, and on which I shall lay the foundation of a City of Refuge, to be called Ararat. . . . Grand Island may be considered as surrounded by every commercial, manufacturing and agricultural advantage, and from its location is pre-eminently calculated to become, in time, the greatest trading and commercial depot in the new and better world. To men of worth and industry it has every substantial attraction; the capitalist will be enabled to enjoy his resources with undoubted profit, and the mechanic cannot fail to reap the reward of enterprise in a great and growing republic; but to the industrious mechanic, manufacturer and agriculturist it holds forth great and improving advantages.

Deprived, as our people have been for centuries of a right in the soil, they will learn, with peculiar satisfaction, that here they can till the soil, reap the harvest, and raise the flocks which are unquestionably their own; and, in the full and unmolested enjoyment of their religious rights, and of every civil immunity, together with peace and plenty, they can lift up their voice in gratitude to Him who sustained our fathers in the wilderness and brought us in triumph out of the land of Egypt, who assigned to us the safekeeping of his oracles, who proclaimed us his people, and who has ever walked before us like a "cloud by day and a pillar of fire by night" [Numbers 9:16].

In His name do I revive, renew and *reestablish* the government of the Jewish Nation, under the auspices and protection of the constitution and laws of the United States of America; confirming and perpetuating all our rights and privileges, our name, our rank, and our power among the nations of the earth, as they existed and were recognized under the government of the Judges. And I hereby enjoin it upon all our pious and venerable rabbis, our presidents and elders of synagogues, chiefs of colleges and brethren in authority throughout the world, to circulate and make known this, my proclamation, and give it full publicity, credence and effect. . . .

A capitation tax of three shekels in silver, per annum, or one Spanish dollar, is hereby levied upon each Jew throughout the world, to be collected by the treasurer of the different congregations, for the purpose of defraying the various expenses of re-organizing the government, of aiding emigrants in the purchase of agricultural implements, providing for their immediate wants and comforts, and assisting their families in making their first settlements, together with such free-will offerings as may be generously made in the furtherance of the laudable objects connected with the restoration of the people and the glory of the Jewish nation. A Judge of Israel shall be chosen once in every four years by the Consistory at Paris, at which time proxies from every congregation shall be received. . . .

I recommend peace and union among us; charity and good-will to all; toleration and liberality to our brethren of every religious denomination, enjoined by the mild and just precepts of our holy religion, honor and good faith in the fulfillment of all our contracts, together with temperance, economy, and industry in our habits.

I humbly entreat to be remembered in your prayers; and lastly and most earnestly I do enjoin you to "keep the charge of the Holy God," to walk His ways, to keep His statutes, and His commandments, and His judgments, and His testimonies, as it is written in the laws of Moses, "That thou mayest prosper in all thou doest, and whithersoever thou turnest thyself" [Deuteronomy 29:9 and Joshua 1:7].

Given at Buffalo, in the State of New York, this second [third] day Tishri, in the year of the world 5586, corresponding with the fifteenth day of September, 1825, and in the fiftieth year of American independence. By the Judge, [Noah] A. B. Seixas, Secretary, Pro tem.

III.   Noah Launches the Colony of Ararat at Buffalo, September 15, 1825

Brothers, Countrymen, and Friends:

Having made known by proclamation the re-establishment of the Hebrew government, having laid the foundations of a city of refuge, an asylum for the oppressed in this free and happy republic, I avail myself of that portion of my beloved brethren here assembled, together with this concourse of my fellow citizens, to unfold the principles, explain the views, and detail the objects contemplated in the great work of regeneration and independence to which it has pleased the Almighty God to direct my attention. Truth and justice demand that I should candidly state the motives that have induced me to aim at higher objects than mere colonization. The world has a right to know what inducements have led to this declaration of independence, and what measures are contemplated to carry the design into successful execution. The peace of mankind, the security of persons and property, the changes incidental to the revival of the Jewish government, the progress and effect of emigration, and all those vicissitudes arising from change of climate, new laws, new society admonish me to be explicit in my declaration, and candid in my statements. . . .

Looking forward to a period of regeneration and to the fulfillment of the prophecies, the Jews have preserved within themselves the elements of government in having carefully preserved the oracles of God assigned to their safe keeping, and the time has arrived when their rights as a nation can be recognised, when, in the enjoyment of independence the light of learning and civilization, and the obligation of industry and morality, they can cultivate a friendly and affectionate understanding with the whole family of mankind and have no longer enemies on earth.

In calling the Jews together under the protection of the American Constitution and laws, and governed by our happy and salutary institutions, it is proper for me to state that this asylum is temporary and provisionary. The Jews never should and never will relinquish the just hope of regaining possession of their ancient heritage, and events in the neighborhood of Palestine indicate an extraordinary change of affairs. The Greeks are almost independent of the Ottoman Porte [the Turkish government].

The Turkish sceptre becomes weaker daily. Russia will march upon Constantinople. The Egyptians are cultivating the useful arts and are encouraging commerce and agriculture. The Turks, driven beyond the Bosphorus, may leave the land of Canaan free for the occupancy of its rightful owners, and the wealth and enterprise of the Jews may make it desirable for them to retain [regain?] their former possession by and without the consent of the Christian powers who, more enlightened, and consequently more tolerant, may be duly impressed with a sense of justice due to an injured and oppressed people.

Called together to the Holy Land by the slow, but unerring finger of Providence, the Jews, coming from every quarter of the globe, would bring with them the language, habits and prejudices of each country. Assimilating only in religious doctrines, and divided on temporal affairs, they would present innumerable difficulties in organizing under any form of government, and the diversity of opinions and views would create factions as dangerous and difficult to allay as those fatal ones which existed in the time of the first and second Temples. It is in this country that the government of the Jews must be organized. Here, under the influence of perfect freedom, they may study laws—cultivate their mind, acquire liberal principles as to men and measures, and qualify themselves to direct the energies of a just and honorable government in the land of the Patriarchs. . . .

Why should the parent of nations, the oldest of people, the founders of religion, wander among the governments of the earth, intreating succor and protection when we are capable of protecting ourselves? The time has emphatically arrived to do something calculated to benefit our own condition and excite the admiration of the world; and we must commence the work in a country free from ignoble prejudices and legal disqualifications —a country in which liberty can be insured to the Jews without the loss of one drop of blood. . . .

IV.   Cincinnati Jewry Asks Charleston Jewry for Aid in Building a Synagog, July 3, 1825

To the Elders of the Jewish Congregation at Charleston:
Gentlemen: Being deputed by our congregation in this place, as their committee to address you in behalf of our holy religion, separated as we are and scattered through the wilds of America as children of the same family and faith, we consider it as our duty to apply to you for assistance in the erection of a house to worship the God of our forefathers, agreeably to the Jewish faith; we have always performed all in our power to promote Judaism and for the last four or five years, we have congregated where a few years before nothing was heard but the howling of wild beasts and the more hideous cry of savage man. We are well

assured that many Jews are lost in this country from not being in the neighborhood of a congregation; they often marry with Christians and their posterity lose the true worship of God forever. We have at this time a room fitted up for a synagogue, two manuscripts of the law, and a burying ground, in which we have already interred four persons, who, but for us would have lain among Christians; one of our members also acts as *shohet* [slaughterer to provide kosher meat]. It will therefore be seen that nothing has been left undone, which could be performed by eighteen assessed and six unassessed members. Two of the deceased persons were poor strangers and buried at the expense of the congregation, one of whom was brought to be interred from Louisville a distance of near 200 miles.

To you, gentlemen, we are mostly strangers and have no further claim on you than that of children of the same faith and family, requesting your pious and laudable assistance to promote the decrees of our holy religion. Several of our members are however well known both in Philadelphia and New York—namely Mr. Samuel Joseph formerly of Philadelphia, Messrs Moses and [Abraham] Jonas and Mr. Joseph Jonas. The two Mr. Jonas's have both married daughters of the late Rev'd Gershom Mendes Seixas of New York. Therefore, with confidence we solicit your aid to this truly pious undertaking; we are unable to defray the whole expense, and have made application to you as well as the other principal congregations in America and England, and have no doubt of ultimate success.

It is also worthy of remark that there is not a congregation within 500 miles of this city and we presume it is well known how easy of access we are to New Orleans, and we are well informed that had we a synagogue here, hundreds from that city who now know and see nothing of their religion would frequently attend here during holidays.

With sentiments of respect and esteem

We are

Gentlemen

Your obed't sev'ts

S. Joseph Cha[irma]n

Joseph Jonas

D. I. Johnson

Phineas Moses

I certify the above is agreeable to a resolution of the Hebrew congregation in Cincinnati.

July 3 1825   Joseph Jonas, Parnas [President].

V.   John Forsyth, Secretary of State,
Instructs the American Consul at Alexandria
to Intercede for the Oppressed Jews
in Damascus, August 14, 1840

Washington, August 14, 1840

John Gliddon, Esq.,
United States Consul at Alexandria, Egypt.

Sir: In common with all civilized nations, the people of the United States have learned with horror, the atrocious crimes imputed to the Jews of Damascus, and the cruelties of which they have been the victims. The President fully participates in the public feeling, and he cannot refrain from expressing equal surprise and pain, that in this advanced age, such unnatural practices should be ascribed to any portion of the religious world, and such barbarous measures be resorted to, in order to compel the confession of imputed guilt; the offenses with which these unfortunate people are charged, resemble too much those which, in less enlightened times, were made the pretexts of fanatical persecution or mercenary extortion, to permit a doubt that they are equally unfounded.

The President has witnessed, with the most lively satisfaction, the effort of several of the Christian Governments of Europe, to suppress or mitigate these horrors, and he has learned with no common gratification, their partial success. He is moreover anxious that the active sympathy and generous interposition of the Government of the United States should not be withheld from so benevolent an object, and he has accordingly directed me to instruct you to employ, should the occasion arise, all those good offices and efforts which are compatible with discretion and your official character, to the end that justice and humanity may be extended to these persecuted people, whose cry of distress has reached our shores, I am, sir,
Your obedient servant,
John Forsyth

VI.   Philadelphia Jewry Protests against
Persecution of Jews in Damascus,
August 27, 1840

PREAMBLE

The Israelites residing in Philadelphia, in common with those of other places, have heard with the deepest sorrow, that in this enlightened age the absurd charge of their requiring human blood, at the celebration of their Passover, has been revived, and that an accusation of this nature having been brought against their brethren at Damascus and the Island of

Rhodes, has been the cause of a most cruel persecution being waged against them, by order of the Musselman authorities, instigated, as it is feared, by one or more of the European residents.

They have learned also, with unfeigned horror, that several prominent men at Damascus have been seized by their ruthless persecutors and tortured till some confessed themselves guilty of a crime which they never committed; and others died under the most exquisite barbarities, which ignorant bigotry, urged by the love of plunder and hatred of the Jewish name, could invent.

Although the Israelites of Philadelphia, living in a land where, under the blessing of Providence, equality of civil and religious rights so eminently prevails, are not in any danger of persecution for opinion's sake: still they cannot rest while so foul a blot is cast upon their ancient and sacred faith, a faith on which both the Christian and Mahomedan religions are founded, and which is essentially a law of justice, of mercy, and benevolence; and they would deem themselves traitors to brotherly love and the rights of outraged humanity, were they to withhold their expression of sympathy for their suffering brethren, who writhe under unmerited tortures, and languish in loathsome dungeons, and to offer their aid, if practicable, to have impartial justice administered to them upon the present and any future occasion. The Israelites of Philadelphia have therefore met in public meeting, and

Resolved, That they experience the deepest emotions of sympathy for the sufferings endured by their fellows in faith at Damascus and Rhodes, under the tortures and injuries inflicted upon them by merciless and savage persecutors; and that, while they mourn for those upon whom such cruel enormities have been heaped, they cannot but admire the fortitude evinced by many of the sufferers, who preferred enduring every torture rather than subscribing to the falsehoods dictated by their vindictive enemies.

Resolved, That the crime charged upon the Israelites at Damascus, of using Christian blood for their festival of redemption from Egypt, is utterly at variance with the express injunction of the Decalogue and other parts of the Pentateuch, and incompatible with the principles inculcated by the religion they profess, which enjoins them to "love their neighbour as themselves," and "to do justice, love mercy, and walk humbly before God" [Leviticus 19:18 and Micah 6:8].

Resolved, That they will co-operate with their brethren elsewhere in affording pecuniary aid, if required, to relieve the victims of this unholy persecution, and to unite in such other measures as may be devised to mitigate their sufferings.

Resolved, That the thanks of this meeting be accorded to the consuls of those European powers, who made efforts to stay the arm of persecution, and who by this deed deserve well of the cause of suffering humanity.

Resolved, That this meeting highly appreciates the prompt and energetic measures adopted by our brethren in Europe, and elsewhere, for the promotion of the object of this meeting, and the noble undertaking of Monsieur Cremieux [French Jewish statesman] and Sir Moses Montifore [sic]—[Montefiore, Anglo-Jewish philanthropist] in coming forward not only as the champions of the oppressed, but also as the defenders of the Jewish nation; and this meeting expresses the hope that the God of Israel will shield and protect them [the prisoners], and restore them to their families in the enjoyment of unimpaired health.

The foregoing preamble and resolutions having been read, were unanimously adopted. . . .

A. Hart, Esq., [the publisher] then offered the following resolution, which was unanimously adopted.

Resolved, That we invite our brethren of Damascus to leave the land of persecution and torture, and to seek an asylum in this free and happy land, where all religions are alike tolerated—where every man is allowed to enjoy his own opinion—where industry prospers, and where integrity is sure to meet its just reward!

PART III

The German Period, 1841–1924

In American Jewish historiography the term German or Central European Jewry includes—or should include—the Jews of Europe who lived in Alsace, the German and Austrian lands, and the Baltic littoral. When these Jews started coming in numbers to America in the late 1830s, they found established communities stretching south from New York to New Orleans and west to the Mississippi. These conventicles held services, maintained Jewish schools—primitive to be sure—and provided aid and charity in almost all towns. But it was the German newcomers who built American Jewry into the second largest Jewish settlement in the world; they established hundreds of new institutions, entrenched Jewry, Judaism, and Jewish culture, and by 1850 were firmly ensconced on the shores of the Pacific. When they started coming here, there may have been about 10,000 Jews in the land; when the doors were finally closed to them, and many others, in 1924, American Jewry numbered some 3,500,000 souls.

It was during the 1870s that Jews from Eastern Europe, from the Slavic and Balkan lands, began arriving in substantial numbers; by the 1920s some 2,000,000 had landed on these shores. These immigrants were in secular terms of a lesser culture; they had been denied many social, cultural, and political opportunities in the lands whence they hailed. Though in America the newcomers built numerous institutions of their own, they were overshadowed by the earlier—"German"—settlers. The Central Europeans tried to impose their way of life on the "Russians"; this acculturational stance of the Germans was suspect, yet often secretly admired and finally adopted and adapted. By 1916 the newcomers were ready to move against their patrons and to seek autonomy or even control of American Jewry; by 1924 the rebellion was in full bloom. When the dust of conflict settled after World War II, neither the "Germans" nor the "Russians" had emerged victorious. The new American Jewish culture, the new leadership, reflected radical compromises.

189

23

The Coming of the Germans
1853–1880

The first Jew known to come to continental North America landed on Roanoke Island, in 1585. He was a "German," a Central European. By the 1720s these Germans, Ashkenazim, outnumbered the Sephardim, the Spanish-Portuguese Israelites, in North America. In the late 1830s Jews began leaving the German lands in substantial numbers, though theirs was never to be a mass migration. Most Central Europeans stayed home; they were convinced that Jews in German-speaking Europe had a future. Thousands, however, did leave after the revolutions of 1830 and 1848 proved abortive. The Metternichian Age was one of conservatism. Jews feared conscription; their right to move about freely and settle in the German lands was often limited; they were not always free to marry; the new industrialism was a threat to their traditional economy; the German guild system hemmed them in; anti-Jewish prejudice was constant. This was the push that impelled them to emigrate; American liberties and opportunities attracted them.

Thus, after the failure of the 1848 republican revolutions, there were German leaders who preached a gospel of "Up and On to America." When the émigrés landed in the 1830s and 1840s, thousands of Americans were streaming westward; the Jews joined them. The balladist, Henry Russell (né Levy), stirred thousands as he sang:

> To the West! To the West! To the land of the free
> Where mighty Missouri rolls down to the sea,
> Where a man is a man if he is willing to toil,
> And the humblest may gather the fruits of the soil.

190

Selection I is a letter written in 1853 by the immigrant Isaac Jalonick, who had settled in Belton, the county seat of Bell County, Texas. The county was only three years old. Jalonick was eager to reach out to Jews; at that time, there were not 1,000 Israelites in all of Texas. In selection II, translated from German, the immigrant Jacob Felsenthal invited his brother to join him in San Francisco: we'll both do well, he wrote.

Selection III reprints an article from *Die Deborah*—Isaac Mayer Wise's German-language weekly—in which the Cincinnati rabbi reviewed Jewish immigration from the 1830s to 1860; it was a glowing report of how America had embraced the émigrés. In selection IV, also a translation, the Bavarian Getty Bachman sat down to write a farewell note to her beloved Heinrich as he prepared to leave for America. It was a sad letter; she was losing a cherished son.

The stream of emigration from Central Europe was blocked in 1924. The immigration act of that year made it abundantly clear that newcomers were not wanted, certainly not if they came from Eastern and Southern Europe. The United States was no longer to be a haven and asylum for Europe's poor and oppressed.

I.   Isaac Jalonick of Texas Writes a Letter,
May 28, 1853

Belton, Bell Co., Texas, May 28th, 1853

Mr. Isaac Leeser.
Dear Sir:
It will surprise you, sir, to hear from such remoot part on the frontier of Texas. But it is as it shuld be, the prophicing must be full fild [the biblical prophecy that Jews are to be scattered throughout the world]. I am surry to say that I am a poor scolar; I cane not express my feeling with the pen when I accidently came in posestion of such valuible inphomation as containing in your valuble [newspaper] *Occident*. May the leeving God spair you that you may accomplish which you have undertakin to do. I am surry to say that I was igronent what was going on, all though I am in this countiry fifteen years. But nearly all that time was spent heur and in Mexcico and Califonia. I am happy, wery happy indeeth, to see that our true riligion has a poblick advocate. I cane not find words to express my feelings. You cane put me on your list of sobscribers. I would like to send you the pay in advance but hear we cane not obtain paiper muny when we please, and I live a long wais from the coust; as soon as I cane obtain paper muny I will rimit it to you. I find in the *Occident* that you are a bougt [about] to transilait the [Hebrew] Bible. I will all so send for one of them and if you have the transilation of the *machser* [High Holyday prayer book] I would be very glad to get it all so. The expence is not in my way.

I hope you will ansure this, and belive me to be a true Jew and a frend to our cous [cause],
Isaac Jalonick Address Isaac Jalonick . . .
Belton, Bell Co. Texas

II.   A California Immigrant, January 13, 1854

San Francisco, Calif., Jan. 13, 1854

Dear Brother,

It was a wonderful surprise to learn from a fellow named Liwey [Levy?] that you are in America! And also that you are living in Baltimore with a family named Herzog. I could not remember who the Herzogs are but it finally dawned on me that it must be Jacob Herz and his wife from Limburg!

How are you getting along and how's business? It's not great here since as you can imagine things don't just fall in your lap. Here I have learned what business means, and I have put up with a lot, especially in Panama. I was sick there for several months and had no money, not even enough to eat. As I got a little better I got various jobs to pay for board and room, which cost a dollar-and-a-half a day. I was too weak even to play my guitar.

But with God's help I got well, and after 4–5 months in Panama in that awful heat I was able to put away 120 dollars in gold which I earned in just 5 weeks. Then I was able to go to California! Luckily, through a doctor I know, I got a place on a steamer as a cook so I didn't have to pay any fare. Also I made a deal with Carl Reis and made some money in potatoes, which cost 1 schilling a pound. I don't have to tell you how expensive everything is.

I have now been in California seven months, in San Francisco, and am married! I have a fine wife and thank God things are going quite well. I have already taken in several hundred dollars. If you would want to come here then you and I and my wife would start up a nice cafe with music and singing every evening. Here a cigar costs 1 or 2 schillings each, and drinks the same, so there is money to be made. Also I am as well known in San Francisco as I was in Cologne. . . .

Write immediately if you are coming or not. If you don't have 50 dollars then let me know and I will send you the money. It would be better if you have the money and then I can put more into the business. In any case, answer by return mail so I can start arranging things. Don't buy a through ticket because it will cost 25 dollars more from Panama to San Francisco by steamer. Take a sailing vessel. As I said, write me by return mail. I won't leave you in the lurch. The sooner you come the better for you and me. An ordinary worker gets 4–5 dollars a day, so you can see how you'll do.

I imagine you already speak good English. So do I since my wife is American and doesn't speak a word of German. She was born in Boston and speaks a little Spanish. But here every language in the world is spoken. If you get to Panama, then go to the doctor whose name I have forgotten. He is a German. When you arrive in Panama go to the pharmacist—take your right, then left—he is also a German. They both know me; tell them you are my brother and ask their help to get you a job on the steamer so you won't have to pay passage. Don't stay in Panama long; it is very unhealthy. And don't eat too much meat. The sooner you leave the better. Do what is best for you.

Regards from my wife who is looking forward to meeting you.
Your brother,
J. Felsenthal

Best wishes from me to Jacob Herzog and his wife and son and wish them luck.
Jacob

III.   America: A Land of Milk and Honey, 1860

How wonderfully, how very beneficially conditions have changed since 1837! In those days, when a Europe-weary Jewish journeyman used to tie up his valise and say: "I am emigrating to America," it meant that he, too, was a black sheep good for nothing at home and no loss. If a stout-hearted youth, tired of dealing in second-hand goods and snail-paced commerce, came to his parents and said "I feel within me the power for something more substantial; let me go across the sea," the parents wept and resisted, as if their son were going to the other world, from which they could hope for neither reunion nor return. If an educated Jew, because of discriminatory laws had no prospect of either a good position or a good future, expressed his determination to go live in the land of freedom, the father used to bewail the money he had spent in vain on his education, and the aristocracy could not comprehend at all how an educated man could so lower himself that he could prefer the distant America, the land of the uneducated, the land of the blacks and Indians, to beautiful Europe.

How conditions have changed! These unnoticed artisans, these youthful adventurers have since then become the supporters of their kinfolk in the old fatherland, the founders of unhoped-for happiness of their people, have become men of consequence and influence in the commercial Old and New World!

Many, very many of these beggarly-poor emigrants are nowadays at the head of business concerns that own enormous property, command unlimited credit and amass every single year an independent fortune in pure profit. And these gigantic fortunes have been honestly and uprightly acquired, no stain, no shadow, no blame clings to them.

These poor emigrants have become the props of their own people. How many parents who had to slave hard and bitterly, and saw facing them declining years full of cares, now live contented and carefree, through the plentiful largesses, that flow to them from their children in America. How many kindly old fathers and mothers exclaim like Jacob in the joy and gratitude of their heart: "Oh, if I were granted once more to embrace my child blessed of God, how sated with life I would then be able to die." And lo! Suddenly come the tidings: Your son is coming from America! And the youth who had departed as an ill-starred fellow, as a beggar, comes back for a visit to his paternal home; and the parents hardly recognize him again, and he tells the story of his good fortune and his abundance; and they marvel, and the whole place hearkens and exclaims: "The stone which the builders rejected hath become the foundation—the cornerstone!" [Psalm 118:22].

And then there are other poor emigrants, who have written to their brothers and sisters, enclosing generous sums for passage in their letters. And they have married off their sisters well and taken their brothers as partners in their businesses, so they are all faring well, superlatively well. And then one or the other of the sons went abroad and fetched the parents so they might be able to rejoice in the good fortune of their children.

And the aged country-Jews come; the father with his silver-mounted pipe and the coat that he has been wearing for ten years, and the mother with her wig and prayerbook for women. . . .

To be sure, not all of them have reached such heights; particularly those who came over accompanied by families or those who in the old fatherland had never learned to look out beyond the old fence in Wolfenku-kuksheim [East Podunk], have never succeeded as they might have dreamed during the voyage across the ocean. Yet we can count hundreds of the former group. The signs of their enterprises blaze in all the big commercial cities of the Union such as New York, Philadelphia, Cincinnati, St. Louis, New Orleans, etc.

IV.   Heinrich Bachman Leaves for America, September 30, 1880

11 P.M., Sept. 30,
Night, eleven o'clock, 1880.

My dear good Heinrich, *may you live to be a hundred* [Hebrew]:
The long expected has come to pass, your trip to America. You realize, my dear son, the pangs I suffer at the thought of your going. But it is your wish and so shall it be. May the Almighty guide and protect you from all evil and be with you always. Put your trust in Him and everything will

work out. Be good, as you always have been, good and kind, and you will get along everywhere. Dear Heinrich, do not forget our beloved religion. It will bring you comfort and consolation, patience and endurance in trials, whether it be your fate to be rich or poor. Always keep God before you and in your heart.

You are going out into the wide world far from parents and family. Don't be discouraged, for you are endowed with so many good qualities, and my heart tells me that God's blessing will accompany you in all that you propose to do. Commit your way unto the Lord and you will be successful. Be careful in all that you undertake, and particularly in your associations. Guard your health, know that it is the greatest gift on earth.

I would like to and I could say much more to you, dear Heinrich, but it is very hard and distressing for me. Therefore I can only say, finally: Go with God and may it be well with you. Be ever cheerful and put to good use all that you have been taught. Always consider very carefully what ever you do. Though a great distance separates us, my parental worry, my motherly thoughts of you, will never cease as long as my loyal heart beats. The thought that our separation will be of short duration is my only consolation in my great pain.

And so, my dear Heinrich, I bid you adieu. Write me and let me know everything that you experience and that happens to you. Do not play with the idea of settling so far away from us, and let me live in the expectation of not being without you too long. Tears come to my eyes; you will therefore have to excuse my poor writing although you know I have such good intentions.

Your ever faithful mama,

Getty

Amen, good luck, and blessing [Hebrew]

P.S. Tomorrow marks the advent of your twentieth birthday and the start of your big journey. May everything be for the best. Good luck, blessing, and prosperity!

24

JEW HATRED AND GENERAL GRANT
1862–1870

R are is the period in nineteenth-century American life when Jews did not experience some political disabilities. This country was a land of immigrants and most of them carried anti-Jewish prejudices in their baggage when they landed. As late as 1841 four states limited the rights of Jews to hold public office: New Hampshire, Rhode Island, New Jersey, and North Carolina. In the 1850s the U.S. government signed a treaty with the Swiss Confederation despite a provision curtailing the privileges of American Jews who sought to carry on trade in some of the Helvetian cantons. As early as 1832 the Americans signed a pact with the Russians, a treaty by whose terms all Americans doing business in Russia were required to submit "to the laws and ordinances there prevailing, and particularly to the regulations enforced concerning commerce." All Jews in Russia suffered severe political and economic disabilities; the same laws were imposed on visiting Israelites from the United States. American Jewish citizens who had been born in Russia were subject to military service on their return. American Jews were often not even permitted to enter that country; their American passports were not honored.

The restrictions under which Jews—natives and visitors—labored in Switzerland remained until the 1870s, but the U.S. government exhibited more sensitivity to Jewish citizens. Despairing of ameliorating Russia's attitude toward American Israelites, this country abrogated its treaty with Russia in 1911. When in 1885 Austria refused to accept the Christian, Anthony Keiley, as the American minister because his wife was a Jew, the United States refused to withdraw his name.

More distressing were the local Sunday laws to which the Jews had to conform. Well into the twentieth century, Jews—and Christian

Sabbatarians—were compelled to submit to ordinances denying them the right to work or to do business on Sunday. This meant that Sabbath observers were not permitted to seek their livelihood for two of the seven days of the week. The Sunday laws had plagued them since the 1650s in New Amsterdam. These were local ordinances, but in yet another way were Jews offended by their own national government. In 1921 and 1924, the United States passed immigration laws that imposed quotas on all Eastern and Southern Europeans who sought to immigrate to the United States. The numbers of those admitted to this country were cut radically. Slavs, Italians, Greeks, and Jews were not wanted.

Despite the objections of Jews and other concerned citizens, many public schools in the country read from the New Testament, opened sessions with prayer, and observed Christmas in the classroom. They refused to accept the fact that juridically the Christian religion was not the established church in the United States. In many instances these practices violated court decisions and most state and federal laws. There is no question that even today some school administrators and teachers continue to breach the laws that separate church and state.

When during the Civil War Jewish soldiers were not permitted to enjoy the ministrations of their own rabbi-chaplains, American Jewry appealed to the authorities and the offending statute was speedily emended (1862). Here in the United States the most distressing anti-Jewish act was the issuance of General U. S. Grant's General Orders No. 11, which expelled Jews from the areas occupied by the Union Army on the lower Mississippi (1862). Grant complained that "the Jews" were buying cotton from the Confederate enemy. This was true of some Jews, as it was of numerous non-Jews; army personnel and Grant's father engaged actively in this trade. We will never know exactly what motivated the general and his staff to issue General Orders No. 11. Many individuals, non-Jews in the main, were profiting from this lucrative—and, in fact, necessary—traffic in cotton: the soldiers had to be clothed! So the Jews of Paducah, Kentucky, were thrust into exile. When General Orders No. 11 was brought to the attention of President Lincoln he responded by rescinding it immediately.

Despite his anti-Jewish order, Grant appears to have been no Judeophobe. As an early nineteenth-century Christian, he had been taught to look askance at Jews; as a Christian he was also taught to relieve the distress of the suffering and oppressed. The selections chosen reveal the motivations that, apparently, induced Grant to issue General Orders No. 11. They also make clear the reaction of the Washington authorities. Here too we have Grant's disavowal of his expulsion edict and his concern for the suffering Jews in Rumania. Benjamin Franklin Peixotto, a committed Jewish leader, was appointed by him as consul to Rumania. President

Grant and the Jews hoped that Peixotto would keep the brutal Rumanians in check. The president gave Peixotto a holograph note to present to Carol, the ruler of the country. It was an appeal for humane treatment of the monarch's subjects (selection II).

I. General Grant's Orders Discriminating against Jews, November 9, 1862 to September 14, 1868

A

BY TELEGRAPH FROM LAGRANGE [NOV.] 9. 1862

[Jackson, Tenn.]

Maj. Gen. Hurlbut,
    Refuse all permits to come south of Jackson for the present. The Israelites especially should be kept out.
    What troops have you now, exclusive of Stevenson's brigade?
U. S. Grant
Maj. Genl.

B

La Grange, Tenn.
November 10, 1862

General Webster,
Jackson, Tenn.
    Give orders to all the conductors on the road that no Jews are to be permitted to travel on the railroad southward from any point. They may go north and be encouraged in it; but they are such an intolerable nuisance that the department must be purged of them.
U. S. Grant
Major-General

C

Holly Springs, Miss.
December 8, 1862

General Orders. No. 2
    On account of the scarcity of provisions, All Cotton-Speculators, Jews, and other Vagrants having no honest means of support, except trading upon the miseries of their Country, and in general all persons from the North not connected with the Army who have no permission from the General Commanding to remain in this town, Will Leave in twenty four hours or they will be sent to duty in the trenches.
    By order of Col. John. V. D. Du Bois.

D

Head Quarters, 13th Army Corps.
Dept. of the Tennessee
Oxford, Dec 17th 1862

Hon. C. P. Wolcott
Asst. Secty of War
Washington, D. C.
Sir:

I have long since believed that in spite of all the vigilance that can be infused into Post Commanders, that the Specie regulations of the Treasury Dept. have been violated, and that mostly by Jews and other unprincipled traders. So well satisfied of this have I been at this that I instructed the Commdg Officer at Columbus [Kentucky] to refuse all permits to Jews to come south, and frequently have had them expelled from the Dept. But they come in with their Carpet sacks in spite of all that can be done to prevent it. The Jews seem to be a privileged class that can travel any where. They will land at any wood yard or landing on the river and make their way through the country. If not permitted to buy Cotton themselves they will act as agents for someone else who will be at a Military post, with a Treasury permit to receive Cotton and pay for it in Treasury notes which the Jew will buy up at an agreed rate, paying gold.

There is but one way that I know of to reach this case. That is for Government to buy all the Cotton at a fixed rate and send it to Cairo, St Louis, or some other point to be sold. Then all traders, they are a curse to the Army, might be expelled.
I am, Sir, Very Respectfully
Your Obt Servant
U. S. Grant
Maj Genl.

E

Head Quarters 13th Army Corps
Department of the Tennessee.
Oxford, Miss. Dec. 17th 1862

General Orders No. 11(12)

I. The Jews, as a class, violating every regulation of trade established by the Treasury Department, and also Department orders, are hereby expelled from the Department.

II. Within twenty-four hours from the receipt of this order by Post Commanders, they will see that all of this class of people are furnished passes and are required to leave, and any one returning after such notification, will be arrested and held in confinement until an opportunity occurs of sending them out as prisoners unless furnished with permits from these Head Quarters.

III. No permits will be given these people to visit Head Quarters for the purpose of making personal application for trade permits.

By Order of Maj. Genl. U. S. Grant

Jno. A. Rawlins

Ass't Adj't Genl.

F

Paducah, Ky., December 29, 1862

Hon. Abraham Lincoln, President of the United States

General Order No. 11 issued by General Grant at Oxford, Miss., December the 17th, commands all post commanders to expel all Jews without distinction within twenty-four hours from his entire Department. The undersigned good and loyal citizens of the United States and residents of this town, for many years engaged in legitimate business as merchants, feel greatly insulted and outraged by this inhuman order; the carrying out of which would be the grossest violation of the Constitution and our rights as good citizens under it, and would place us, besides a large number of other Jewish families of this town, as outlaws before the world. We respectfully ask your immediate attention to this enormous outrage on all law and humanity and pray for your effectual and immediate interposition. We would especially refer you to the post commander and post adjutant as to our loyalty, and to all respectable citizens of this community as to our standing as citizens and merchants. We respectfully ask for immediate instructions to be sent to the Commander of this Post.

D. Wolff & Bros.

C. F. Kaskel

J. W. Kaskel

G

War Department
Washington, January 4, 1863

Major General Grant,
Holly Springs, Miss.
    A paper purporting to be General Orders, No. 11, issued by you December 17, has been presented here. By its terms it expels all Jews from your department.
    If such an order has been issued, it will be immediately revoked.
H. W. Halleck
General-in-Chief

H
Circular

Hdqrs. Thirteenth A.[rmy] C.[orps]
Dept. of the Tenn.
Holly Springs, Miss.
January 7, 1863

    By direction of General-in-Chief of the Army, at Washington, the general order from these headquarters expelling Jews from the department is hereby revoked.
    By order of Maj.-Gen. U. S. Grant
Jno. A. Rawlins
Assistant Adjutant-General

I

Galena, Ill., September 14, 1868

Hon. I. N. Morris [Congressman from Illinois]
Dear Sir:
    I am in receipt of a letter of Mr. A. Moses of the third instant, enclosing one from you, bearing same date. My first inclination was to answer Mr. Moses, because you desired it; then I thought it would be better to adhere to the rule of silence as to all letters. Were I once to commence answering all political questions asked of me, there would not be time between now and the third of November [the date of the presidential election] to get through. Mr. Moses, I think, will readily understand this. In regard to Order No. 11, hundreds of letters have been written to me about it by persons of the faith affected by it. I do or did not answer any of the writers, but permitted a statement of the facts concerning the origin of

the order to be made out and given to some one of them for publication. *I do not pretend to sustain the Order.*

At the time of its publication, I was incensed by a reprimand received from Washington for permitting acts which Jews within my lines were engaged in. There were many other persons within my lines equally bad with the worst of them, but the difference was that the Jews could pass with impunity from one army to the other, and gold, in violation of orders, was being smuggled through the lines, at least so it was reported. The order was issued and sent without any reflection and without thinking of the Jews as a sect or race to themselves, but simply as persons who had successfully (I say successfully instead of persistently, because there were plenty of others within my lines who envied their success) violated an order, which greatly inured to the help of the rebels.

Give Mr. Moses assurance that I have no prejudice against sect or race, but want each individual to be judged by his own merit. Order No. 11 does not sustain this statement, I admit, but then *I do not sustain that Order.* It never would have been issued, if it had not been telegraphed the moment it was penned, and without reflection.

Yours truly,

U. S. Grant

II.   President Grant Pleads on Behalf of the Persecuted Rumanian Jews, December 8, 1870

Executive Mansion,
Washington, D. C.
December 8, 1870

The bearer of this letter, Mr. Benjamin Peixotto, who has accepted the important, though unremunerative position of U.S. Consul to Roumania, is commended to the good offices of all representatives of this Government abroad.

Mr. Peixotto has undertaken the duties of his present office more as a missionary work for the benefit of the people he represents, than for any benefit to accrue to himself—a work in which all citizens will wish him the greatest success. The United States, knowing no distinction of her own citizens on account of religion or nativity, naturally believes in a civilization the world over, which will secure the same universal views.

U. S. Grant

25

THE JEW AS CITIZEN
1862–1888

The years between 1841 and 1924 are in a way the most important decades in American Jewish history. The basic Jewish institutions were then either established or expanded. In 1841 there were at the most twenty-five congregations or conventicles; in 1924 there were well over twenty-five hundred synagogs or prayer groups. By the 1920s individual Jews had occupied all political offices except the presidency; wealthy Jews like Julius Rosenwald had given millions to charity; Abraham A. Michelson was the first American Nobel laureate in the sciences (1907). Notable Americans since Washington's day had welcomed Jews; ever since 1840 the United States government, impelled by humanitarian concern, had moved to help oppressed Jews in Asia, North Africa, and Europe. There was no land more hospitable to the Jew than this country; here the Children of Abraham were able to fulfill themselves.

But there were problems. Most Americans were Christians; though this country was juridically non-Christian, few citizens doubted that this was a Christian state. They expected the Jews—a minuscule minority—to conform to the Christian way of life. In 1841, four states still prohibited their Jews from holding high office; for a brief period rabbis were not authorized to serve as chaplains in the armed forces (1861); American treaties permitted discrimination against Jewish Americans; the Sunday laws compelled Jews to close their businesses on the first day of the week; the evangelicals in Congress sought constantly to baptize the Constitution, to declare Jesus the real ruler of the nation; colleges, fraternities, private schools, barred the door to the Children of Israel; many corporations would not employ them, and in 1915 some of the best citizens of Marietta, Georgia, lynched a Jewish businessman, Leo Frank.

There are literally dozens of important selections that could be employed to reflect the good and the bad that the Jew here experienced in the eighty-three years before the Immigration Act of 1924 passed. I have arbitrarily chosen only three selections to reflect the nature of American Jewish life during these eight decades—the period of German domination—when Jews of Central European origin dominated Jewish life in this country. In selection I, Phoebe Levy Pember (1823-1913), the matron of the Confederate army's Chimborazo Hospital in Civil War Richmond, recounted her experiences with a patient. She was an aristocrat, the daughter of one of the leading citizens of Charleston and later Savannah, Jacob Clavius Levy. She had married out of the faith; she was in no sense traditional in observance; Phoebe was an acculturated Jew well on the way to assimilation. In selection II, Rabbi Isaac Mayer Wise, ever conscious of the encroachments of the state on his rights as an American Jewish citizen, came to grips with the problem of church and state (1872). Denigration of the Jew during this period was constant. Henry Ford, the automobile manufacturer, emerged as an anti-Semite. He spent millions in a national campaign to destroy the good name of his Jewish fellow citizens; his approach was defamation through insinuation; he turned many against the Jews (1920–1927). In 1888 a Greek immigrant, Telemachus T. Timayenis (1853–1918), published anonymously a paperback which he called *The American Jew*. The Minerva Publishing Company, his press, printed several anti-Jewish works. This propagandist had set out to build a large-scale anti-Semitic movement in this country such as was then flourishing in France and Germany. Henry Ford in his paper, *The Dearborn Independent*, and in his brochure series, *The International Jew*, sought to avoid crudities; Timayenis waded in with a bludgeon (selection III).

I.   Matron Pember Makes Her Rounds in the 7000-Bed Confederate Army Hospital, 1862

. . . Pleasant episodes often occurred to vary disappointments and lighten duties.

"Kin you writ me a letter?" drawled a whining voice from a bed in one of the wards, a cold day in '62.

The speaker was an up-country Georgian, one of the kind called "Goubers" [peanuts] by the soldiers generally; lean, yellow, attenuated, with wispy strands of hair hanging over his high, thin cheek-bones. He put out a hand to detain me and the nails were like claws.

"Why do you not let the nurse cut your nails?"

"Because I aren't got any spoon, and I use them instead."

"Will you let me have your hair cut then? You can't get well with all that dirty hair hanging about your eyes and ears."

"No, I can't git my hear cut, kase as how I promised my mammy that I would let it grow till the war be over. Oh, it's onlucky to cut it!"

"Then I can't write any letter for you. Do what I wish you to do, and then I will oblige you."

This was plain talking. The hair was cut (I left the nails for another day), my portfolio brought, and sitting by the side of his bed I waited for further orders. They came with a formal introduction: for Mrs. Marthy Brown.

My dear Mammy:

I hope this finds you well, as it leaves me well, and I hope that I shall git a furlough Christmas and come and see you, and I hope that you will keep well, and all the folks be well by that time, as I hopes to be well myself. This leaves me in good health as I hope it finds you and—

But here I paused, as his mind seemed to be going round in a circle, and asked him a few questions about his home, his position during the last summer's campaign, how he got sick, and where his brigade was at that time. Thus furnished with some material to work upon, the letter proceeded rapidly. Four sides were conscientiously filled, but no soldier would think a letter worth sending home that showed any blank paper. Transcribing his name, the number of his ward and proper address, so that an answer might reach him—the composition was read to him. Gradually his pale face brightened, a sitting posture was assumed with difficulty (for, in spite of his determined effort in his letter "to be well," he was far from convalescence). As I folded and directed it, contributed the expected five-cent stamp, and handed it to him, he gazed cautiously around to be sure there were no listeners.

"Did you writ all that?" he asked, whispering, but with great emphasis.

"Yes."

"Did I say all that?"

"I think you did."

A long pause of undoubted admiration—astonishment ensued. What was working in that poor mind? Could it be that Psyche had stirred one of the delicate plumes of her wing and touched that dormant soul?

"Are you married?" The harsh voice dropped very low.

"I am not. At least, I am a widow."

He rose still higher in bed. He pushed away desperately the tangled hay on his brow. A faint color fluttered over the hollow cheek, and stretching out a long piece of bone with a talon attached, he gently touched my arm and with constrained voice whispered mysteriously:

"You wait!"

And readers, I *am* waiting still; and I here caution the male portion of creation who may adore through their mental powers, to respect my confidence, and not seek to shake my constancy. . . .

II. "First Americans and Then Israelites":
An Editorial in *The American Israelite*,
August 23, 1872

"We are first Americans and then Israelites," is one of those common-places set afloat, without due consideration, merely in opposition to certain Roman Catholic declarations [claims made for papal power by Vatican I]. It is a phrase and no more, which we can accept with due modification only. "First my God and then my country," is no bad motto. It means, I and my conviction are identical. Without it, I am a slave of a person, a corporation, a state, a law, a body of laws; a slave after all. No honest man can or will sacrifice his conviction to any earthly advantage or human institution; if he does, he is no longer a free and responsible moral agent. There is a law higher than all made by man, and my conscience is the authority to its proper recognition. Therefore, in all matters touching the peace and prosperity of society, the administration of justice and the preservation of personal liberty, I am a citizen first, and the duties I owe to my country must be performed first and last.

But if I am an American, a Russian, or a Chinese, and that government to which I owe allegiance enacts laws or imposes duties contrary to my conviction of first principles, more is demanded of me than I can give, and I am an active or passive rebel, in order to save my manhood; for first of all things I am a man. As an Israelite I must have a conviction of first principles in religion. If my government enacts laws or imposes duties contrary to that conviction, I am an Israelite first and would treat my country as being in a state of rebellion against me; because I and my conviction are identical, and I can not sacrifice it without renouncing my manhood, which no government has a right to demand. The right of every government is limited by the rights of the person, one of which is freedom. If Congress would enact laws imposing upon the citizen atheism, or upon the Jew the Christian dogma, I would be an Israelite first, and in rebellion against my country, whatever means I would select to have that law or laws revoked. As things stand now, I am also an Israelite first and a citizen then; because my duties as a man and an Israelite are continual, almost without any interruption, while my duties as a citizen are but temporary and periodical. I am a loyal citizen, because it does not prevent me being an Israelite according to my conviction: There is certainly some sense in this mode of reasoning, the quintessence of which is, that no country has a right to demand the surrender of manhood, and every man is a man first, and so is every Israelite an Israelite first, and then a citizen, in all cases of first principle. Therefore first my God and then my country is as good a motto as any, and justly qualifies the phrase of our caption.

III.   Keep the Jews Out of America
[By Telemachus T. Timayenis], 1888

The Jew's soft hands and curved fingers grasp only the values that others have produced. Wherever the Jew is allowed to establish himself, dishonesty takes the place of honesty; immorality, of virtue; disease, of health; sluttishness, of cleanliness; anarchy, of order. One has but to study the social and political history of the different nations in Europe, during the last fifty years, to discover the poisonous work of the Jew. He has sapped the foundations of every government. He has reduced France from a nation of first rank to a second-class power. He has made Russia to writhe under incessant internal revolutions. He has ruined Turkey. He has so thoroughly impregnated England with his own Jewish cowardice, that England's martial spirit has sadly deteriorated. He is now carrying out his work of deterioration and destruction in the United States. From the time when the Jew first appeared upon the face of the earth, to this day, history does not record a single invention that can be claimed by the Jews. . . .

They began life in the New World as itinerant venders of cheap notions [goods]. For their petty stock in trade, consisting of pencils, pens, stockings, pocketbooks, and of all manner of odds and ends, they were trusted; but every night they were obliged to make returns of sales made to the one who had supplied them with the goods. Gradually they increased their little capital, and next they became receivers of stolen goods; and, to this day, it is the Jews who control this peculiar industry in all our cities. They established pawnshops, made advances for which an exorbitant rate of interest was charged, exercised every manner of usury, and introduced crookedness and theft in all transactions. They established petty stores, stocked them with an insignificant amount of cheap goods, insured them far beyond their actual value, and shortly afterward set fire to them, collected the insurance, and repeated this crime from time to time throughout the country. Thus they grew rich.

The crime of incendiarism, previous to the advent of the Jews, was with us, comparatively speaking, unknown. The Jews mulcted the insurance-companies of vast sums of money before the companies became aware of the fraud practised upon them. It is a matter of record, that many of the leading insurance-companies to-day hesitate, and often refuse, to insure the stock of any one having a Jewish countenance or a Jewish name. . . .

Let us turn into Wall Street, and look at the Jews there.

In the feverish atmosphere of the "Street," with its mad excitements, its wild speculations, its covetous "corners," greedy "combinations," and tricky "booms"; with its manifold opportunities for double-dealing, treachery, wholesale despoiling, rascality, misrepresentation, and deceit, the Jew feels happy and thoroughly at home.

The two leading lusts of the Jew's life are lechery and money. In Wall Street, men think of nothing, care for nothing, talk of nothing but money; and in this atmosphere which rings with the perpetual cry of money, money, money, the Jew revels with all the intoxicated rapture of a voluptuary plunging to the ears into some licentious debauch. And as he plots and plans, and intrigues, and cheats, amid the hoarse roar of money-making, and the crash of crumbling fortunes, he feels that he is following out the true bent of his nature; he is truly happy. The "Street" is the Jew's paradise. . . .

Next to his lust for money, the strongest passion in the Jew is his licentiousness. This, like every other vicious trait of which the Jew is possessed, takes a peculiarly prominent and objectionable form.

The average Jew is disgustingly bawdy in his talk, and interlards his conversation with filthy expressions and obscene words. On the verandas at summer-resorts, in hotel-corridors, in the lobbies of theatres, on steam-boats, on railway-cars, and in public places in general, the Jew indulges in this repulsive peculiarity, to the great annoyance and disgust of respectable Christian women and decency-loving Gentile men. This was one of the habits which made him so objectionable at summer-resorts, and has led to his practical exclusion from almost every first-class summer-hotel in the land. . . .

The Jew drummer [travelling salesman] is one of the most assiduous patrons of houses of prostitution throughout the country. Without the Jew clientele, it is safe to say that fully sixty-six per cent of the houses of ill-fame in the various cities of the United States, excepting, for certain obvious reasons, New York and Chicago, would be compelled to go out of existence. Not only is the Jew a liberal patron of these houses of prostitution, but such is the insatiability of his carnal appetites, and to such an extent does he give rein to his lasciviousness, that his debauches only too frequently exceed the ordinary limits of lust. These certain hideous and abhorrent forms of vice, which have their origin in countries of the East, and which have in recent years sprung into existence in this country, have been taught to the abandoned creatures who practise them, and fostered, elaborated, and encouraged, by the lecherous Jew! . . .

If the Gentiles in this country would combine, and refuse to deal with the Jews, if Gentiles would refuse to buy any goods manufactured by Jewish firms, if American women would absolutely refuse to patronize Jewish stores, these blood-sucking Shylocks would speedily be relegated to their natural sphere of action, "the old-clo'" business, and underpaid womanhood would no longer be forced to the streets for subsistence. Remember, by encouraging the Jew in business you indirectly promote vice, degrade womanhood, and dwarf the business prosperity of the country.

We repeat it once again: this country is in danger on account of the rapid growth of the Jews among us. Their number is daily increasing in New York, and the same is the case of every one of the large cities in America.

We warn all against the Jew. We are in danger from the hideous swarms of Jews, who besiege us like famished wolves, and who crowd every business, every channel of commerce, in this country.

It is high time for the people of this country to arouse themselves, and to realize what it has cost them to welcome to this home of the Aryan race the disgusting pariahs of Israel.

There are to-day over a million Jews who gnaw the resources of the United States. Remember that there is always a limit to the wealth of a country, however rich she may be.

These Jews, whether financiers, doctors, judges, journalists, book-sellers, managers, lawyers, brokers, keepers of pawnshops, receivers of stolen goods, professors, or rabbis, one and all, secretly and tenaciously agree among themselves in striving to fill every post of honor and responsibility, with one of their coreligionists.

In the streets, in the theatres, in the restaurants, in the hotels, one smells the Jews everywhere and on all sides. . . .

It is high time to put a stop to the disembarking of the rapacious hordes of Israel who swarm to our shores.

There should be a loyal exchange between the immigrant and the native.

In the case of the Jew there has never been any loyal exchange; in fact, there has been no exchange at all. He takes all, gives nothing.

One million of Jewish mouths—and what mouths!—a million mouths of parasites!

§§§§§§§§§§§§§§§§§§§§§§§

26

THE SECULAR CULTURE OF THE AMERICAN JEW
1855–1896

There were always cultured, educated Jews, men and women, in every period of American Jewish history. Abigail Billah Levy Franks (1696–1756) was a highly intelligent woman. She could not always spell accurately, but was a voracious reader of good literature. A number of eighteenth-century immigrants wrote good English letters; a few owned extensive libraries. In the course of the nineteenth and early twentieth centuries, as the Jews here grew to become the second largest Jewish settlement in the world, literally hundreds of Jewish men and women distinguished themselves for their attainment in the arts and sciences. There were poets and dramatists, scholars in the social and physical sciences, college professors, and even a Nobel laureate in the field of physics. Ludwig Lewisohn was a widely read author; Edna Ferber won a Pulitzer Prize as a writer of fiction—this at a time when the Jews in the United States numbered but 3.4 percent of the total population (1920s).

In 1855, Philip Phillips, an Alabama lawyer, wrote an essay *On the Religious Proscription of Catholics.* He set out to attack the American Party, the Know-Nothings, who hoped to advance their political fortunes by denigrating Catholics. Phillips (1807–1884) served in Congress (1853–1855) and later practiced law, primarily before the United States Supreme Court. The article—here excerpted—appeared originally in the *Mobile Register* (selection I). Although once active in Charleston's Reformed Society of Israelites (1820s), Phillips in later years evinced little interest in Jews and Judaism; he was, however, no assimilationist.

In 1896 Ida Henrietta Hyde (Heidenheimer, 1857–1945), a native of Iowa, received a Ph.D. degree at Heidelberg in Germany. She was the first woman—so it would seem—to receive this diploma at a German school of higher learning. Thus she prepared the way for other women who wanted to pursue their graduate studies in that country. She was also the first female admitted to Harvard Medical School's research laboratory. Later she served as professor of physiology at the University of Kansas (1905). In matters of religion she affiliated with Felix Adler's Society for Ethical Culture. In selection II—excerpted—Hyde describes her tribulations in Germany as she sought and won the right to receive the coveted Ph.D. degree.

I. On the Religious Proscription of Catholics, By Philip Phillips, July 4, 1855

Washington, July 4, 1855.

My dear sir:

I readily comply with your request to give you my impressions of the last development of political events. Nothing appears to me more interesting to the country than the recent demonstrations of the "Know Nothings," at Philadelphia and Montgomery, against the Catholics. In their national platform they [the Know-Nothings] declare that "Christianity, by the constitutions of nearly all the States, by the decisions of the most eminent judicial authorities, and by the consent of the people of America, is considered *an element of our political system.*" The application of this is not very apparent. But if it was intended to assert, as I presume it was, that in the Federal Constitution, which forms the bond of our Union and constitutes the "political system" of the United States, there is any such element incorporated, either by expression or necessary implication, then I deny the truth of the proposition. There is nothing clearer than that in the formation of the Constitution it was intended emphatically to exclude all connection with any religious faith whatever.

Separation of Church and State, eternal divorce between civil and ecclesiastical jurisdiction, were cardinal principles with the sages and patriots to whom not only we, but all mankind, are indebted for this model of a republican government. No, my friend; they possessed too much wisdom and practical good sense to be content with a mere feeble imitation of the existing order of things. They distinctly saw the evil fruits which the conjunction of political and religious power had everywhere produced, and in the discharge of the high duty intrusted to them—the highest that men could be charged with—they determined to profit by the example, and inaugurate a "political system," whose dominion should be exclusively confined to the political relations of its constituents, acknowledging in the eyes of the law the perfect equality of all sects and faiths, and leaving the whole subject of religion, and its requirements, to the dominion of that Higher Tribunal which alone can search the hearts and judge the motives of men. . . .

It is in your remembrance that many years ago a large and respectable body of citizens petitioned against Sunday mails. They evidently proceeded upon the idea that this was a Christian government, and that the violation of the Christian Sabbath was a sacrilege the government was bound to put an end to. Congress rejected the petition, and this action was approved by the country. Now, this approval could only rest upon the denial of the proposition that "Christianity was an element of our political system." But, my dear sir, whether right or wrong on this head, it must be evident that the assertion of this principle in a political platform, precluded by a solemn "acknowledgment of that Almighty Being who rules over the universe, and presides over the councils of nations," was a mere self-sanctification, intended to appeal to the religious feelings of the country, that they might the more easily be drawn into the vortex of political strife, and combined for what is declared to be one of the great objects of the movement—"resistance to the aggressive policy and corrupting tendencies of the Roman Catholic church in our country by the advancement to all political stations—executive, legislative, judicial, or diplomatic—*of those only who do not hold civil allegiance, directly or indirectly, to any foreign power, whether civil or ecclesiastical, and who are Americans by birth, education, and training.*"

Having first asserted that Christianity was "an element of our political system," do you now perceive how smoothly the inference is drawn that a pure Christianity requires the exclusion of Catholics from the rights of citizenship. . . .

Religious intolerance is as old as the history of man. In this country, where freedom and equality, under the shadow of the law, walk hand in hand throughout the land, intolerance lies dormant in the breast, or, when excited into action, shrinks from the public eye. It is, however, fully entitled to the "bad eminence" of being the first in the history of our country which has dared openly to stimulate this feeling for political objects: thus, in the name of Christianity itself, laying the train to light the torch of religious persecution.

If the leaders in this crusade were religious fanatics, we might respect their sincerity, though we denounced their action. But who are they? The Whig and Democratic parties are said to have become *corrupt*. But this new party, as you see, is very much controlled by the *scum* which the agitation of the old ones has thrown off. Look around, my dear sir, and inquire how many of those leaders have been noted for their piety, or characterized by devotional feeling, who now flaunt their religious robes in the face of every passer-by. How appropriately may they be described—

With smooth dissimulation skilled to grace,
A devil's purpose, with an angel's face.

I do not doubt the sincerity of the great mass of those who have been deluded into these lodges. I believe the mass of all parties to be honest; but I also believe that the great majority of their leaders are impelled by the hope of obtaining from a new organization the political promotion which they despaired of receiving from the old ones. . . .

Yours, most truly,

P. Phillips

Jno. Forsyth, Esq.,

Editor of *Register*, Mobile, Ala.

II.   Before Women Were Human Beings: Adventures of an American [Female] Fellow in German Universities of the 1890s, By Ida H. Hyde, 1893–1896

Early in the last decade of the nineteenth century, a polemic between two European professors, pertaining to the development of an organism they were investigating, led to bitter personal criticisms that finally appeared in print. The controversy aroused the interest of embryologists in this country, particularly a student in Bryn Mawr College, who, without knowing of these professors, was conducting experiments on the very problem about which the dispute centered. The results obtained by the student in her investigation corroborated those published by one of the disputants, Professor Goette of the University of Strassburg. When Goette was informed of this fact he was very much elated. Eager to have his interpretation of the results strengthened and the investigation of the problem variously extended, he invited the student to come to the University of Strassburg and continue study of the subject in his department. This invitation came to me as a complete surprise. Unfortunately it seemed impossible at the time to accept the tempting suggestion. But suddenly a way was unexpectedly opened through the splendid offer of the European Fellowship awarded in 1893 by the Association of Collegiate Alumnae for study in foreign universities. Thus in a short space of time and in a most extraordinary manner the realization of the dream to work in the promised halls of Strassburg University became a reality.

At the time the European Fellowship was awarded, it was not known to my professors nor to me that universities in Germany were not coeducational institutions, and that women had never studied in the University of Strassburg; in fact, that they had not been permitted to matriculate in any German university. Therefore we on this side did not appreciate the full significance and importance of the departure when Professor Goette, director of the Zoology Department in the University of Strassburg, graciously invited a woman student of Bryn Mawr College to work in his

department. It was not until I had worked many days in the splendid laboratory assigned to my private use that it dawned upon me that I was occupying a unique position, and that I was regarded by the students, faculty
members, and their wives as a curiosity. In the university circle the news
quickly spread that an American "woman's rights" freak, a blue stocking
and what not, had had the boldness and audacity to force entrance into
the college halls. At *Kaffee Klatchen* she was served for gossip and dissec-
tion. It was not unusual for a professor, student, or *diener* [attendant],
seemingly by mistake, to open the laboratory door, look frightened, and
quickly retreat. Or students would congregate at the windows of the botanical building opposite the laboratory, and from sheer curiosity stare
across at my windows, greatly to the annoyance of the professors in both
buildings. My hostess, the wife of a professor of mathematics, occasionally invited me to accompany her to social affairs. At a dinner that we attended I met the charming wife of Professor Goltz, one of the most distinguished physiologists in Europe. Frau Professor Goltz was deeply
interested in learning of the great independence enjoyed by women and
women students in America. In the course of the conversation I remarked
that I had specialized in physiology and had been assistant to and conducted investigations under Dr. Jacques Loeb, one of Professor Goltz's
former assistants, from whom I had a letter of introduction to her husband. I ventured to inquire whether she thought Professor Goltz would
allow me to work in his department. My heart sank when she replied that
her husband was bitterly opposed to the admission of women to the Phys-
iological Institute, the more so because it belonged to the Medical School,
where women were taboo. . . . Professor Graf Solms, the director of the
Botanical Department, announced that as chairman of the examining
commission he refused to allow a woman to take the examination [for a
Ph.D. degree in Strassburg]. . . .

When an American friend, engaged in publishing her late husband's
manuscripts with the help of Professor Rosenbusch, the noted geologist in
the University of Heidelberg, heard of Graf Solm's action, she urged me to
try to obtain the degree in Heidelberg. But first I wished assurance that the
university would actually grant me the degree. . . . I dispatched the official
petition blank to the Dean on January 11, 1894, to be presented to the faculty. Accompanying the petition were all of my letters and credentials and
a personal letter in which I begged to be informed whether there existed
any faculty ruling against admitting women to the examination for the
doctor's degree. A special meeting of the faculty was called to consider the
petition. All members were present and took active part in the prolonged
discussion. It was recognized that the questions asked in Miss Hyde's petition were for the first time in the history of the university presented for
definite official action. After much discussion, two motions were voted.

(1) Women are admitted to the examination for the degree, under the same conditions outlined in the official regulations for men candidates, with the provision that women are required to study in the University of Heidelberg in preparation for the examination. (2) A faculty rule does not exist against admitting women candidates to the examination for the doctor's degree. . . .

The first steps taken in following the Dean's advice were to call on Professor Butschli, Director of the Comparative Anatomy and Zoology Departments, and Professor Victor Meyer, Director of the Chemistry Department. Both courteously welcomed me to their departments. However, they suggested taking some subject other than physiology, which I had chosen for the third subject required, since physiology was given in the Medical School, where [Wilhelm] Kuhne, professor of physiology, had recently announced in a public lecture that women's place was in the home and not in the university. They advised securing an interview with him at once, since the pre-semester faculty meeting, to which my petition must be submitted for approval, was scheduled for the following day. Without delay I called on Professor Kuhne and presented a letter of introduction from his friend and colleague, Professor Goltz of Strassburg. He seemed a giant, seated in a huge armchair at a table in a spacious library. Without rising he expressed pleasure in receiving the letter and meeting me. When I told him that I was greatly interested in physiology, he kindly offered the use of his library, and asked what books he might send to my address. He expressed approval in the choice of books. I then told him that I expected to work in the departments of Professor Butschli and Meyer, and wished to know if, after physiology had been sufficiently mastered, he would examine me in that subject for the degree. He appeared to regard the question as a joke, and laughingly said, "Certainly, if that time should ever come!" As he rose to show me out, he casually remarked that his conference hours were Saturday morning in his laboratory, where the books might be returned and where he would be pleased to discuss them with me. I hastened to tell Professor Meyer the result of the interview. He expressed great surprise, and assured me that since Professor Kuhne had given his promise, he was obliged to fulfill it. He also aided me in preparing the petition that was to be presented the following day for faculty action. . . . But at the [faculty] council meeting Professor Kuhne had announced that he must be excused from giving the examination, and furthermore that he refused to let "skirts" enter his lecture room or laboratory. . . .

At an early hour of a spring morning in 1894, I entered the new Zoological Institute of the University of Heidelberg, selected a back seat in the lecture room, and was assigned to a well equipped laboratory. Over the table I hung a picture of the Grand Duke of Baden, writing below it

"Dankbarkeit erzungt Ehrfurcht und Gehorsamkeit" [Gratitude evokes veneration and obedience],—an answer to the fear expressed by the Duke, that
"if women became better educated, they would no longer respect, honor,
and obey men, as they should." (The picture still hung there when I visited the laboratory thirty years later.) In the Chemistry Department I was
greeted by Professor Meyer, who placed my name on one of the most desirable places, where the experiments and demonstrations could most readily be observed. Seemingly all was going well. But how to approach
Kuhne without making an irretrievable mistake was a question that constantly haunted me. What if he should refuse to admit me to the lecture
and laboratory courses in physiology? How would it be possible without
attending them to prepare for the finals? . . .

During the ensuing weeks most of my thoughts were stained in blood.
But when I came to the conference and begged to report on the topics
dealt with in the books, Kuhne, seemingly annoyed, inquired if I had
heard that the professor of botany would admit me to his department, I replied that I had come to Heidelberg to study physiology and had just received word that the Phoebe Hearst fellowship for study abroad had been
awarded me. I therefore felt in duty bound to make a success of my work
in the university, and hoped he would assist me to that end. I was dumb-
founded when he rose, opened the door to the general laboratory, and
beckoned to his assistants. He introduced me with the remark that I was
determined to study physiology, and since he refused to let me attend his
lectures, perhaps they would undertake to help me attain my object. They
said that with his consent they were willing to try. On the following
morning, the medical students who crowded the physiology lecture room
wondered why the two chief assistants were occupying the front seats.
This was the first time in the history of his instruction that Kuhne was
honored by the presence of his associates in the lecture room. To his
amazement and satisfaction they were actually taking notes. The notes
were taken for me, to be copied for study in preparation for the finals. Six
hours daily were devoted to the subject. In the opinion of the instructors,
this schedule followed for at most six semesters should prepare me for the
most rigid examination. During these months of arduous work, the
thought haunted me that Kuhne would do all in his power to frustrate my
purpose. He bitterly resented the gossip aroused among his colleagues by
the stand his assistants had taken, and he resented being an unwilling agent
in permitting "skirts" to enter the Medical School.

Finally the morning of the first lecture in chemistry arrived. On
reaching the building, I was dismayed to hear an uproar within, and awakened to the realization that I was late. The door of the lecture room was
closed. As I stood before it, the chills ran up and down me, and my courage
failed. It was impossible for me to face the excited crowd of noisy students.

Turning to leave as quickly as possible, I saw students rushing upstairs. I realized that if I failed then it would require more courage to enter the classroom the next day. The students jostled each other and hastened by, leaving me standing in the open doorway. A silence followed, so profound you could hear a pin drop. The men stood seemingly transfixed in their various attitudes. I never knew how I got to my seat. The blood was rushing to my head, and in the hush I distinctly heard an American voice say, "We shall next have them in the jury box." To hear those taunting words in my profound embarrassment from an American would have proved too disheartening if the remark had not been instantly censured with hisses and scraping of feet by the German students who heard it. And to the credit of the Heidelberg students it must be said that in all the time of my attendance at the university, they always treated me with the greatest courtesy....

As a matriculated student at the University of Heidelberg I devoted two years in preparation for the doctorate toward which my researches and thesis had already been accepted and credited in the Natural Sciences and Mathematics Faculty. While working here it was gratifying to meet women graduates from Russia and America, who were now admitted under the finally established resolutions not only to the lectures but also to the laboratories.... At last the day arrived when in formal attire, according to custom, it behoved me to call upon and invite the professors to the examination. The invitation was graciously accepted, but Kuhne said only that he hoped to be present. This implied uncertainty was very trying.... The examination lasted until ten o'clock when the *pedell* [beadle] entered, showed me to the anteroom, and asked me to wait until the professors had left the hall. While adjusting my wraps, I heard discordant voices issuing from the hall, and feared the worst. When the *pedell* opened the door, some of the members, among them Butschli and lastly Kuhne, came toward me, extending their congratulations. The ordeal was over! My friend was awaiting me in a cab at the entrance to the building. She kindly inquired if she might have my professors taken to their homes. Butschli accepted the offer, saying his wife was anxious to hear the result of the game, and to see me in the gown which she had heard I had made for the occasion. The Frau Professor seemed so very pleased that I had come. Excitedly she asked her husband how Kuhne had behaved. He answered that I had deserved *Summa Cum Laude*, but that the "brute" had objected to giving a woman that honor. Finally a compromise had been agreed upon, and a new term, *Multa Cum Laude Superavit* [praiseworthily excellent in many things], with the title, Doctor of Philosophy and the Natural Sciences, was conferred upon me [February 12, 1896]....

I was the first woman to obtain the Ph.D. of Heidelberg not as a courtesy but as a *bona fide* university student in the Natural Sciences and Mathe-

matics Faculty who had met in every detail the requirements of that institution's decree of March 7, 1894. The university, be it said to her honor,
had established a precedent of far-reaching importance.

27

THE JEW AND THE ECONOMY
1861–1895

The so-called German period of American Jewish history, 1841–1924, was marked by tremendous advances in American industry and banking and by the rise in America of an extended middle class. The Jews—a small group, to be sure—rose with others and achieved a measure of affluence. Some Jewish apparel manufacturers made money during the Civil War. Between August 1, 1861, and December 6 of that year Mack, Stadler & Glazer of Cincinnati manufactured 191,548 garments for the Union troops. Here are some estimates of New York Jewry's participation in several wholesale lines (1887). Bear in mind that at least one-third of the country's Israelites then lived in America's leading industrial mart:

Manufacturers of clothing	$55,000,000
Jobbers of jewelry	30,000,000
Wholesale butchers	25,000,000
Wines, spirits and beer	25,000,000
Jobbers of leaf tobacco	15,000,000
Manufacturers of cigars	15,000,000
Manufacturers of cloaks	15,000,000
Importers of diamonds	12,000,000
Leather and hides	12,000,000
Manufacturers of overshirts	10,000,000
Importers of watches	6,000,000
Artificial flowers and feathers	6,000,000
Importers and jobbers of furs	5,000,000
Manufacturers of undergarments	5,000,000

Lace and embroidery importers	4,000,000
Manufacturers of white shirts	3,000,000
Manufacturers of hats	3,000,000
Manufacturers of caps	2,000,000
	$248,000,000

In 1890 a survey of 10,618 Jewish families in the United States disclosed that 6,622 households had one or more servants. Jews owned retail stores in every state and territory of the Union. In 1928 Julius Rosenwald's mail-order house, Sears, Roebuck & Company, had more than 11,000,000 customers who had bought goods from it.

Thousands of newcomers started life as peddlers; more often than not peddling was a bitter experience. In 1861, young Louis Gratz (1839/43–1907) of Inowrazlaw, Posen, Prussian Poland, peddled and suffered and then joined the Union Army as a volunteer. In less than two years he was to become a regimental commander. His rise, however, is in no sense typical (selection I). In later life, a successful lawyer in Knoxville and Louisville, he seems to have moved away from Jews and Judaism. Another immigrant, Lazarus Straus of Talbotton, Georgia, also began as a peddler; his three sons became notable Americans: Oscar (1850–1926) was Theodore Roosevelt's Secretary of Commerce and Labor (1906-1909); Isidor (1845–1912) and Nathan (1848–1931) moved on from crockery to control of the R. H. Macy department store. In selection II, Isidor recounts how the family acquired a share in a Brooklyn emporium that was to become Abraham & Straus.

By the 1890s Jewish women here in the United States were beginning to reach out in many areas of endeavors; they were determined to be somebody. Undoubtedly they were influenced by the rise of women in the larger American world. In selection III we have the story of Jewish businesswomen who rose to success in a man's world.

I. From Peddler to Regimental Commander, By Louis Gratz, 1861–1862

Scranton, November 25, 1861

I will start from the moment I came to America, and you will learn from my short biography that America is the only country where one can make his fortune although in a variety of ways. When I came to this country all my property amounted to ten dollars. In addition, I did not understand the English language, and I had neither relatives nor friends. By pure accident I was introduced by a young man to a poor Jewish family of good reputation with whom I lived as a guest paying two and a half dollars a week. Living in this way did not solve my problem; however, I had at least found some people who did not cheat me and who provided me with cheap though poor food.

I wasn't particularly happy, and I felt also very depressed, for I had not learned any trade. I could not expect to become a bookkeeper, even to get a very small position in a business, for who would accept a young man without any other recommendation than his good looks, a young man completely unfamiliar with the language and the customs of this country? In addition, eight weeks on a sailing vessel under every imaginable deprivation had very much weakened my physical and intellectual strength. Although I had the intention of forgetting all my comfortable and easy past after my departure from Europe, and of concentrating my efforts towards the single goal of becoming a rich man—a goal only possible by hard work, toil, and economy—the execution of this plan was harder than I had thought. Everybody whom I asked for advice gave me a discouraging reply. I began to realize, only too clearly, that there is money lying around on the streets of America, but that it is very difficult and hard to pick it up. A young man, who had induced me to emigrate, and who, despite the fact of having more money, promised to work together with me, deserted me after a few days because he had found a position in a shop through the recommendation of one of his relatives. I visited my cousin Louis Basch, but I was coolly received; a question as to how things were at home was his only interest in me.

However, it was necessary for me to do something. My ten dollars was sufficient for four weeks; after that I would be without a penny. During those days I approached one person after another, willing to work for almost nothing, but, unfortunately, people believe that a young man cannot be any good who looks respectable and pretends also to be respectable, but yet is willing to take any small job.

Having spent two and a half dollars for board and lodging during the first week, I was compelled to buy some notions for the remaining seven dollars—fifty cents had been spent for small expenses—and to peddle them. My "splendid" stock in trade consisted of shoelaces, stockings, thimbles, needles and pins. This was to be the cornerstone of my fortune of the future, and besides I would have to make enough to eat, drink, and buy clothes, especially shoes.

The first day's attempt at peddling was made in New York. From early in the morning until late in the night I climbed up and down stairs, until finally I made enough to pay for board and lodging for a single day. You can imagine how difficult it was for me to make even that much dealing with notions, for I could barely memorize the English names and prices of my stock, and I could not answer any other question. After having peddled for a week in New York, I had scarcely made enough for my board and lodging. The merchant from whom I bought my articles, seeing how I struggled, advised me to go to the country, and was even willing to loan me merchandise to the value of five dollars. Naturally, I accepted this offer and started at the beginning of the next week.

The first day I did well; I made little more than I needed for food, although I ate only breakfast and supper, and as cheaply as possible. On the second and third day I also earned the money I needed for my living, but it rained on the fourth. I was compelled to spend the entire day at the inn. When the rain did not stop the next day, I returned to New York, because it wouldn't cost me so much to live there. There are not as many good roads here as back home. The roads here are of sand and clay and a little rain is sufficient to transform them into mud. It was on a path like this that I had to walk twenty-five English miles with my pack on my back, and sinking into the mud up to my knees.

My dear friends, for the first time in America it was difficult for me to endure these hardships and privations. I finally dragged myself into New York, and the result was a fever and an injured foot which, however, I ignored. I was well aware that my material conditions did not permit me to become sick. So the next day I peddled again in New York. Although I had not eaten during the whole day, I felt too sick in the evening to take any food. In addition, my foot was so badly hurt and swollen that I could not walk. I went to bed, and a full eight days passed before the fever disappeared. But the foot! The people with whom I lived did not know, naturally, that I was so poor, otherwise they would not have kept me any longer. My financial situation did not permit me to stay in bed for six weeks. That period, according to my doctor, was absolutely necessary for the recovery of my health. I did not have money enough to pay for my food, and even less to pay for the doctor and his expensive prescriptions. I had to make up my mind to go to a hospital for the poor where medical treatment, medicine, and food were free of charge.

My dear friends! You cannot imagine what I suffered during the six weeks which I had to spend in the hospital among sick people of all kinds and under loathsome conditions. Twice a week the doctors of the hospital operated on my foot, and, in my opinion, made it only worse. I could not understand their reason. Probably the doctors did it in order to find out how a negligible wound could cause so much irritation and swelling. I can only stress that after six weeks I left the hospital on my own initiative, physically and mentally more ill than before I had entered it. From the hospital I returned to the people with whom I had formerly lodged. There a doctor promised to cure me completely within four weeks, and all that for a fee of five dollars. I preferred to spend my last penny for such treatment and even to go into debt rather than to stay longer in the hospital.

And so I submitted myself to this treatment by Dr. Berg. To put it briefly, after four weeks I had recovered, but was as poor as a church-mouse. I had to pull in a notch in my belt, for my hosts had reduced the cost of my board, and therefore I had to eat less.

During this time I met a young man whom I had known before in [my native] Inowrazlaw and who worked as a clerk in New York. After my complete recovery we agreed to peddle together. I was very happy, since the young man had about fifty dollars, and I was entitled to fifty per cent of our common profit. Eight days later I left New York with my young companion for Carbondale, a city in Pennsylvania. In the meantime I had improved my English somewhat, studying with great zeal until late in the night. Our stock had at least a value of fifty dollars. We had some success working very hard, but then suddenly war broke out in America. You must have learned about this war from your own newspapers, so it is not necessary for me to go into detail.

Business came to a standstill, all public works were stopped, and after the call of the President to defend the country with arms, all the young folks flocked to the colors. Carried away by the general enthusiasm, I became a soldier. I studied English with great zeal until I could talk fairly fluently. Since I had the good will of my superiors, I became a noncommissioned officer in a few weeks. However, the way to a higher position was barred to me, because I had to write and read English perfectly to get such an appointment. I started again, sometimes studying through the better part of the night, and all this without any help, since I did not have enough money to hire a tutor. Now I am able to speak, read, and write English well. In the meantime our enlistment term, fixed for a period of four months, expired. Everybody had believed that this war would last only four months. We had been sworn in for this period only and were discharged on its expiration. However, the war was far from being finished, and therefore the President issued a second proclamation asking for soldiers for a period of three years.

Through the intervention of several high-ranking personalities, who had become interested in me, and possibly also because of the fact that I had shown courage several times during my first enlistment, I was introduced to Secretary of War [Simon] Cameron and was examined by him. I had used my time profitably to study military tactics whenever I had a moment, and so I became a first lieutenant in the cavalry of the United States. The name of my regiment is the Lochiel Light Cavalry. The name of my colonel is E. C. Williams, and that of my squadron commander is E. G. Savage. I have been given the promise of a captaincy as soon as possible, and therefore I am doing my best to make myself worthy of the commission.

We are now with our regiment in Washington; in a few days we will leave for the theater of war. Formerly a peddler, barely able to make a living, I have now become a respected man in a respected position, one filled by very few Jews.

I have been sent by my general to enlist new recruits and so I am today in Scranton, a city in Pennsylvania only twenty miles away from Carbondale, where I had peddled before. Before this no one paid any attention to me here; now I move in the best and richest circles and am treated with utmost consideration by Jews and Christians.

My dear ones, I beg you with all my heart not to be angry because I have gone to war. The dear Lord can also save me from this as He has saved me from many other perils. And should it be my destiny to lose my life, well I will have sacrificed it for a cause to which I am attached with all my heart, that is: the liberation of the United States. My beloved parents, brothers, sisters, and relatives will be taken care of. Should I fall in battle, use the enclosed address of my bank, where I have deposited my salary; should I survive well I shall return to Germany and live with you.

II.   The Strauses Expand Their Department Store Holdings, By Isidor Straus, January 1893

When I found that my father had no intention of returning South [after the Civil War], and that he therefore had to start life anew, I saw that my duty was to stay with him and add my mite to his efforts. But one thing I made up my mind to without long hesitation—that was, if we were to establish ourselves, it would be better to start in the chief market, rather than a secondary one, and so I had very little difficulty in persuading father that New York was preferable to Philadelphia. This was in the fall of 1865.

Father's chief reliance for the means with which to pay his indebtedness for merchandise purchased in the spring of 1861, and capital with which to start in business, was the cotton he had stored in the South. The difficulty in bringing the cotton to New York, owing to the confusion of conditions everywhere throughout the South, and the interruption to transportation facilities, compelled him to postpone taking steps for going into business until he could realize on his cotton. I think it was the early months of 1866 before that was accomplished.

In the meantime, the price of the staple had fallen to about half what he could have realized in the fall of 1865. Pending this interval, father used the time, as far as his available means permitted, in calling on his creditors and paying what he owed. The large amounts he had to postpone paying until the cotton reached New York.

I recall one incident in connection with his calling on his creditors which is worth recording. There was a dry goods house of George Bliss & Co. to whom he was indebted to the amount of four to five thousand dollars. When my father called to pay his indebtedness, Mr. Bliss talked with him on various topics, and the following conversation ensued. Mr. Bliss asked my father how old he was and what he intended doing. My father replied that his age was fifty-seven and that he hoped to start life afresh, by going into the wholesale crockery business. Mr. Bliss then said: "Mr. Straus, I don't think you are fair to yourself to deprive yourself of the slender means you tell me you possess by paying out your available resources. Wait until you are in a fair way of being established, and I don't propose to take your money. Pay me one-third cash, and I can well wait on you one or two years for the other two-thirds." It was certainly a most kindly concern, evidently engendered by appreciation of the honorable purposes of a man well-advanced in years, who would not consider his self-interest before discharging what he considered to be his first duty—the payment of his debts.

Mr. Bliss appeared to be particularly moved to such unusual generosity towards a comparative stranger, as he saw in my father a demonstration of the keen sense of integrity which I infer was the reverse of what his experience or, perhaps, better expressed, his prejudice had led him to expect, for I recall his saying that he had seldom found a Southern merchant who was willing to sell his negroes to pay his debts, from which I drew the conclusion that in considering a merchant of the South as to his worthiness for credit, the Jew or the newcomer, which were interchangeable terms, was always viewed with that suspicion which did not attach to the native-born. It made a great impression on me to observe, during this interview, how a feeling of compunction seemed to have overtaken a fair-minded man by a proof of the highest integrity which he found where he least expected it, while it had been absent, probably, in cases which came to his mind, in many Southern merchants whose pedigree and apparently chivalrous exterior caused him to look for it as a matter of course. I could see unmistakable signs how in Mr. Bliss's mind there came a realization of the erroneous basis which had theretofore governed the average estimate of the moral element that entered into the consideration when extending credit, and, therefore, an irresistible desire to make amends for a blind prejudice which evidently had possessed him.

That I was correct in this diagnosis of the mental change, if not remorse, on the part of Mr. Bliss, an event which occurred twenty-eight years later clearly proved, and even if I narrate it so out of chronological order, I deem it proper to do so here.

It was in January, 1893, that we had to make financial preparations to purchase the interest of Mr. Wechsler in the [department store] firm of

Wechsler & Abraham [of Brooklyn], in case certain contingencies developed. To this end I called on the United States Trust Co., and my friend Mr. John A. Stewart, the president, offered instantly to take $500,000 of our firm's paper on six months with three renewals at five percent. A few days later I asked him what his directors said to this transaction. He answered that only one of the directors, Mr. George Bliss, spoke up and asked whether the firm was in the crockery business, and on receiving an affirmative reply, Mr. Bliss said: "Well, if the old man is still in the firm, he is good for anything to which he will put his name."

III.   Successful Businesswomen, 1895

Of women who have made good their claim to compete in the fields of business activity, . . . I know of no better example than the subjects of this sketch, the Rosenfield sisters of New York city, proprietors of the largest stenographic and typewriting establishment in the United States.

The father of these young women, Joseph Rosenfield, a Bavarian by birth, came to this country at the age of eighteen and settled in New Orleans. His polished manners and winning personality gained for him a host of friends and at twenty-two he obtained a position of trust with the New Orleans branch of the house of Rothschild. . . .

Zerlina Rosenfield, elder member of the firm, graduated from the St. Louis High School with special distinction. Business interests finally necessitated the removal of the family to New York, where a few uneventful years elapsed. Then sickness and misfortune invaded the happy home. With stern necessity staring her in the face, Zerlina, the eldest daughter, took an inventory of her marketable accomplishments. She found that she was a good penman and mathematician and possessed a fair knowledge of bookkeeping. She finally secured a temporary position as assistant bookkeeper after which she entered a publishing house where she remained seven years. She then decided to identify herself with the stenographic and typewriting business, and, familiarizing herself with all classes of work, she soon ranked among the ablest women law stenographers in New York City.

Laura Rosenfield, junior member of the firm, also attended the St. Louis public schools but was graduated from a New York seminary. After the death of the parents, Laura decided to adopt her sister's profession. She succeeded in securing desk room in a prominent theatrical exchange. Naturally bright and quick, she was not slow in grasping the favorable situation. Her one machine soon gave place to two, then four and so on until desk room would no longer suffice and large offices were taken. About this time, the largest contract ever awarded for typewriting was given to the two sisters, a contract competed for by all the copying offices in Washington and New York city. This work was the compilation of a legal index covering 375,000 pages or about 11,000,000 words. Work of such magnitude required cooperation, and a partnership was formed in 1889 between Zerlina and Laura Rosenfield. To-day these enterprising women have six thoroughly equipped typewriting offices with from forty to fifty typewriting machines. In addition to their facilities for typewriting and stenographic work, they associated with them several compilers and translators of both modern and classic languages which makes the execution of dramatic, literary, legal or commercial work in the English or other languages possible.

To a query of mine regarding the secret of their success, Miss Zerlina Rosenfield responds as follows:

"Perhaps the true secret of our success lies in our unity. Three striving for the same goal can obtain infinitely more than if each pursued a separate avocation.

"I manage the down town offices and my sister Laura the uptown, the character of the business being quite distinct. My sister Laura is, according to the general verdict, the most popular woman in the profession. Her firmness and keenness in deciding business problems would do credit to an old and able financier.

"Our younger sister Alice, an expert stenographer, has an interest in both the finances and glory of the firm and strives, as far as possible, to keep all the work in the family. Hence it rarely becomes necessary to call in outside assistance.

"We are never too busy nor too tired to take an order. We are always ready for an emergency. We never have to send a customer elsewhere for assistance of any kind.

"We have a staff of thoroughly competent, reliable, and ladylike assistants who attend to their work not alone as a matter of duty, but because they like it. These are some of the reasons why the firm Z. & L. Rosenfield, although one of the last in the field is not the least."

We have here a brief sketch of the remarkable business career of three young and inexperienced girls, who carved out their fortunes simply by energy and unremitting hard work, tools within easy access of everyone, irrespective of sex or condition. Asking no favors, devoid of any extraneous influence, endowed with but the usual quantum of brains, they have by sheer pluck, persistency, and faithful work rapidly risen to the heights of their profession. Nor has this eminence been obtained at the sacrifice of any truly good or womanly quality.

※※※※※※※※※※※※※※※※※※※※※

28

THE ATTEMPTS TO CREATE
A NATIONAL AMERICAN JEWISH COMMUNITY
1841–1906

There has never been an organized national Jewish community in the United States. (There is none today!) Every congregation was ipso facto a community and when there was more than one synagog in a town then there were multiple communities. The shock of the Damascus Affair (1840) and the constant attacks on Jews in the American press prompted Isaac Leeser, the hazzan of Mikveh Israel in Philadelphia, to join with others in the efforts to create a national community based on Orthodoxy (today we might say: Modern Orthodoxy). He hoped to unite and elevate Jewry through a national representative assembly, a rabbinical or quasi-rabbinical court, and a system of elementary and advanced schools (selection I). Later in 1845 Leeser renewed his appeal for union; in this he was joined in 1848 by Isaac Mayer Wise; but no one ever succeeded in uniting America's synagogs; every congregation insisted on complete and absolute autonomy, independence. All forms of hierarchy were suspect.

In 1859 following the Mortara abduction case in Italy—when a Jewish lad was taken away from his natural parents—a national Board of Delegates of American Israelites was established; it never enlisted the support of the majority of the country's local communities and in 1878 was absorbed by the Union of American Hebrew Congregations. This latter Union, an association of synagogs, now amended its constitution and set out to concern itself also with the civil rights of Jews in all lands. The new defense arm was called the Board of Delegates on Civil and Religious Rights. The successes of the new Board were not notable; its budget was tiny; it had a one-man staff; most American Jews refused to recognize this defense agency. However, the Board and the Union did succeed in completing and publishing a census of American Jewry which had been conducted in 1878. The results of this census are summarized in selection II.

The influx of thousands of East European Jews into this country and the continuing persecution of Jews in North Africa, Asia, Russia, and Rumania made it imperative that a national association be established in this country that would provide financial relief and aid all Jews to secure political rights or to defend those they had already secured. The murder of Jews in Kishinev, Russia, in 1903, shocked American Jews and forced them to take speedy action. Almost immediately at least a half-dozen individuals and associations came forward insisting that a powerful national American relief and protective association be created. Leading Jews here—"Germans" and natives—were determined to establish a national organization that would protect American Jewry and aid needy and oppressed Jews abroad. Louis Marshall, the New York lawyer and communal leader, wrote his friend Rabbi Joseph Stolz of Chicago expressing his views on the nature of a new proposed national American Jewish defense and relief agency (selection III). As a result, the American Jewish Committee, a congeries of devoted notables, was established in 1906.

I.   The First Formal Attempt to Organize All of American Jewry, July 12, 1841

PLAN

ARTICLE I

The Ecclesiastical Authority

Section 1. The delegates of the different congregations, as hereinafter described, or of as many as may come into the measure, shall elect at their first meeting, or as soon after as practicable, three gentlemen of undoubted moral and religious character, who are duly learned in the written and oral law, who shall have the authority conferred upon them by their election, to act in, and decide on all cases of religious inquiry, and to determine all questions laid before them, according to the law, and the approved rabbinical authorities: the members of this Central Religious Council not to be at any time subject to any authority abroad, nor under the control of any congregation, except in cases of misdemeanour, and wilful false decisions, in which cases, one or all of such offending parties, are to be removed by the delegates of the Union as above; and a majority of the delegates present shall be required for a vote of suspension for a period of from three to twelve months, and a majority of two-thirds for a suspension for a longer period, or expulsion from office. . . .

Sect. 4. The hazanim [ministers] of all the congregations of this Union, are to be ex officio associates of the Board, provided always, that nothing is to prevent the delegates from electing a hazan to be a member of the Central Religious Council, if he be duly qualified for the office in character and capacity.

Sect. 5. In a place where no one of the members of the Central Religious Council resides, the hazan, or hazanim, or other persons in whom the community have confidence, may decide in any emergency, but the decision must also at once be transmitted to the Central Religious Council for their approbation.

Sect. 6. Any party deeming himself aggrieved by the decision of any one member of the Board, or any other person acting under an emergency, may appeal to the whole Central Religious Council, whose decision by a majority shall be final.

Sect. 7. The associates as above provided, shall merely have power to speak at a meeting of the members of the Central Religious Council, but not to vote. . . .

Sect. 9. As the authority herewith delegated is merely advisory, the Central Religious Council shall never exercise the power of excommunicating any one, for any offence whatever; nor to possess the right of summoning any individual who, in their opinion, might be guilty of any transgression of the Mosaic Law; but shall merely designate the offences which of right deprive any offender from the usual Jewish rights and privileges.

Sect. 10. The privilege of performing the marriage ceremony being the right of each congregation, the customary authority heretofore exercised by the Hazanim remains inviolate; nevertheless the party to be married has the option of selecting the hazan or any member of the Central Religious Council to perform said ceremony.

Sect. 11. The congregations belonging to the Union shall not elect any shochet [slaughterer], who has not been examined as to qualifications by one or more members of the Central Religious Council; and it shall be the duty of the respective shochetim belonging to this Union, to be examined once at least in three years by one or more of the Central Religious Council, for which examination no fee whatever is to be required.

Sect. 12. No shochet is to be suspended for frivolous reasons; and if any member of the Central Religious Council should find it his duty to exercise this prerogative, he must state the reason for so doing in writing to the person so suspended.

Sect. 13. It is expected that the Central Religious Council will watch over the state of religion, and use every proper occasion to exhort the people in sermons or lectures; and whenever any member of the Central Religious Council wishes to address any congregation, he shall have the privilege so to do, upon giving notice to the Parnass of said congregation.

Sect. 14. Whenever a new hazan is to be elected, he must be examined as to his qualifications by one or more members of the Central Religious Council, so as to prevent any incompetent person being forced upon the respective congregations; and if any congregation should elect a hazan who has not obtained a certificate of the Board, or who has been rejected by them, such hazan shall not be admitted an associate of the Central Religious Council.

Sect. 15. The superintendence of the schools is herewith vested in the Central Religious Council and the above associates, and it is made their duty to report any delinquency in the teachers to the Board of Control, as hereinafter mentioned.

ARTICLE II

The Schools

Section 1. As soon as practicable, schools for both sexes are to be established in every town where Israelites reside, and the teachers are to be paid out of a common local fund, and on no account to receive any pay or fee whatever from the parents.

Sect. 2. Whatever rates for education it may be necessary to charge, are to be paid to the local treasurer of this Union, who is to pay the amount of salary which may be agreed upon, to the teachers, upon warrant of the local president.

Sect. 3. The system of education is to be strictly Jewish, and is to embrace,

a. Hebrew reading, grammar, translation, catechism, Biblical commentaries, and at least an introduction to the Jewish Oral Law, and if possible, an elementary knowledge of the Talmud.

b. English grammar, composition, elocution, arithmetic, writing, singing, geography, universal history, history of the Jews, history of England, and history of the United States.

c. For the higher classes, in addition to the above, Hebrew composition, Talmud, general Jewish literature, Latin, Greek, French, German, Spanish, mathematics, natural history, natural philosophy, moral philosophy, political economy, and chemistry.

d. Any other useful matters to be added as occasion may require.

Sect. 4. The government of the schools is to be moral throughout, and on no account can any cruel punishment be permitted.

Sect. 5. A High School for education in the higher branches is to be established in some central point whenever practicable, in which the branches enumerated under c are to be taught; and where young men are to be educated in such a manner, that they may be fit for the office of hazan, lecturer, and teacher; and young women be educated for the high calling of female instructors; and all persons educated in our schools are to have the preference if any vacancy occurs, for any office in the gift of this Union.

Sect. 6. No teacher to be appointed, whether Jew or gentile, who has not been examined by one or more members of the Central Religious

Council in the first instance, and afterwards by the local president, treasurer, secretary, and hazan, as to capacity and moral worth: Provided, That the distance from one of the members of the Central Religious Council be not above 300 miles, in which latter case the local authorities may temporarily appoint a teacher or teachers, till one of the members of the Central Religious Council visits the place, when the teacher or teachers must be examined by him; and if an Israelite, he is to be examined also as regards religious knowledge and conformity.

Sect. 7. Though it may be found requisite to charge for education to those able to pay—yet no person, who brings evidence of his inability to pay, shall have his children or wards refused admission into our schools, provided he or she sign a pledge to send them regularly to school at least three months in the spring, and four months in the winter. . . .

The Union

Section 1. It is recommended that all regularly organized congregations in America do elect delegates to meet at Philadelphia on the 7th day of November, 1841, for the purpose of carrying the above recommendation into effect.

Sect. 2. The ratio of representation to be as follows: Every congregation numbering fifty male seat-holders or under, to send one delegate; from fifty to one hundred and fifty, two delegates; from one hundred and fifty to three hundred, three delegates; and one additional for every two hundred additional seat-holders.

Sect. 3. All votes of delegates shall be decided by the majority, under the usual parliamentary restrictions and regulations.

Sect. 4. The delegates shall be empowered to elect, in the first instance, the members of the Central Religious Council, and to fill all vacancies therein from time to time, provided always that the persons to be elected be duly qualified.

Sect. 5. They shall assemble, after the first organization, every two years, on the 4th Sunday after the first day of Passover, and remain in session, by daily adjournments, till all the business before them be duly transacted, or postponed to another meeting. . . .

Sect. 7. The delegates shall be appointed by the respective congregations in the manner they may themselves direct.

Sect. 8. The delegates shall elect a president to preside over them, and a secretary to keep the minutes, whose offices are to continue till the next general meeting.

Sect. 9. In addition to the above officers, they shall elect, at every biennial meeting: one vice-president, one corresponding secretary, one treasurer, four councillors, who, together with the president and recording secretary shall constitute a Board of Control to direct the affairs of the Union in the vacation of the assembly.

Sect. 10. In addition to the above Central Board, each town shall elect a president, treasurer, and secretary, to take charge of all local matters and moneys for local school purposes, but it shall be their duty to report every six months in full to the Central Board of Control.

Sect. 11. The biennial meetings shall be held alternately, unless otherwise ordered; first at Philadelphia, next at New York, and lastly at Baltimore. . . .

Sect. 14. The delegates in general assembly shall have power to deliberate on all subjects, which may tend to the general welfare of the Israelites, with the exception of matters properly belonging to legal points of the Mosaic law, which shall be left, as is reasonable, with the Central Religious Council.

Sect. 15. They shall devise ways and means to defray the expenses attending the execution of this plan, and to fix salaries and other outlays properly coming under the object of the Union.

Sect. 16. They shall not interfere directly or indirectly in the internal affairs of the congregations, except to offer their advice when any thing should be undertaken in opposition to the law and the commandment, and to judge between contending parties, if such should unfortunately arise in our congregations.

II.   The First National Census of American Jewry, 1878

States, Terr'ty	Congs.	Members	School Children	Census
Ala.	8	254	257	2,045
Arz.				48
Ark.	4	165	150	1,466
Cal.	12	613	678	18,580
Col.	1	31	35	422
Conn.	3	169	170	1,492
Dak.				19
Del.				585
D.C.	3	144	158	1,508
Fla.	1		20	772
Ga.	7	313	266	2,704
Id.				85
Ill.	10	567	675	12,625
Ind.	14	378	469	3,381
Ia.	3	91	65	1,245
Kans.	2	56	56	819
Ky.	4	285	368	3,602
La.	13	495	372	7,538

Me.	1		500
Md.	1	32	62	337
Balt.	13			10,000
Mass.	9		317	8,500
Mich.	6	263	276	3,233
Mn.	1	28	16	414
Miss.	8	239	194	2,262
Mo.	5	506	313	7.380
Mont.				131
Neb.	1	20	35	222
Nev.	1	29		780
N.H.				150
N.J.	8	229	193	5,593
N.M.				108
NYState	32	1,021	1,239	20,565
NYC.	20	2,351	1,998	60,000
N.C.	2	65	72	820
Oh.	19	442	506	6,581
Cinc.	5	572	535	8,000
Ore.	2	60	65	868
Pa.	18	511	505	6,079
Phila.	8	1,458	1,395	12,000
R.I.	2	105	55	1,000
S.C.	3	110	171	1,415
Tenn.	7	271	340	3,751
Tex.	7	210	293	3,300
Utah				258
Vt.	1	19		120
Va.	8	291	405	2,506
Wash. Terr'ty				145
W.Va.	2	58	54	511
Wis.	3	95	99	2,559
Wyo.				40
	278	12,546	12,886	229,064

[The census, published in 1880, discloses that there were also four Jewish fraternal orders with a total membership of 44,267 men; some of the national lodges had female auxiliaries. There were five Jewish hospitals, eleven orphan asylums and homes, twenty-five Young Men's Hebrew Associations, sixteen periodicals in English, German, and Yiddish. One of the magazines, the *Sabbath School Visitor*, was aimed at children and adolescents. There were 278 congregations; 118 were in the Reformist Union of American Hebrew Congregations; some of these, however, were Orthodox or Conservative in their ritual.]

III.   Organizing the American Jewish Committee, By Louis Marshall, January 12, 1906

January 12, 1906

To the Rev. Dr. Joseph Stolz

I am in receipt of yours of the 9th inst., which only reached me this morning. The notice for the consultation, of which you have received a copy, had already gone out, but as you will see from the nature of the notice, that it is not a notice for a conference, but only for a meeting for the purpose of consultation, the very thing that your letter indicates that you are anxious to have with some or all of the gentlemen who have been invited to be present at the consultation.

Among the rabbis who have been so invited, besides yourself, are the following: Dr. [David] Philipson, Dr. [Maximilian] Heller, Dr. [Joseph] Leucht, Dr. [Emil G.] Hirsch, Dr. [Adolph] Guttman, Dr. [Henry Pereira] Mendes, Dr. [Judah L.] Magnes, Dr. [Jacob] Voorsanger, Dr. [William] Friedman, and Dr. [Edward] Calisch. If there are any others whom you would like to have invited, let me know at once and I shall be very glad indeed to extend an invitation to them, provided there shall not be too many.

Among the laymen who have been asked to attend, besides those whose names are signed to the invitation, are Dr. [Cyrus] Adler, Judge [Mayer] Sulzberger, Mr. [Jacob] Schiff, Oscar S. Straus, Mr. [Adolf] Kraus, Mr. [Max] Senior, Dr. [Harry] Friedenwald, Mr. [Adolph] Rich of Milwaukee, Mr. [Jacob] Furth, Mr. [Isidore] Newman, Mr. [Samuel] Grabfelder, Mr. [Lewis] Dembitz, and Simon Wolf.

I think out of a total of fifty-five who have been asked to attend, only fifteen are residents of New York.

I greatly appreciate everything that you have said as to what your committee [the Reform Rabbinical Committee on National Organization] has done, and am very glad that you have taken up the subject. What I am trying to accomplish is, to get order out of chaos, and to united all elements that might possibly seek to father a national movement with the result that discord instead of union would be the rule. Dr. Voorsanger has attempted to organize one movement, Dr. Magnes another, Dr. Mendes a third, the Central Conference [of American Rabbis] a fourth. Mr. Kraus believes that the B'nai B'rith affords a panacea for all ills, and the East Side [with its Slavic newcomers] is bristling with organizations, each national in scope and zero in accomplishment.

It has therefore occurred to me and to my associates, that before any scheme is launched, those who have the welfare of Judaism at heart should come together, merely for the purpose of comparing notes, with a view of ascertaining whether or not there is a possibility of promulgating a plan which will be generally acceptable, and which will accomplish the objects which all of us have sincerely at heart.

What I am trying to avoid, more than anything else, is the creation of a political organization, one which will be looked upon as indicative of a purpose on the part of the Jews to recognize that they have interests different from those of other American citizens. I conceive that there can be but two tenable theories on which the Jews have the right to organize: first, as a religious body, and secondly, as persons interested in the same philanthropic purposes.

Obviously, it will be an absolute impossibility for the Jews of the country to unite as a religious body having ecclesiastical and disciplinary powers. It could be impossible to afford to such an organization, the authority and sanction which are essential to successfully carry out such a scheme.

We can, however, all unite for the purpose of aiding all Jews who are persecuted, or who are suffering from discrimination in any part of the world on account of their religious beliefs, and we can at the same time, unite for the purpose of ameliorating the condition of our brethren in faith, who are suffering from the effects of such persecution and discrimination directly or indirectly.

Whether it will be wise to go beyond this, I seriously doubt. Whether, if it were attempted, much harm would result, I strongly believe.

As you will see from some of the names which I have mentioned, it is my idea to bring into this organization, everybody who, if outside of it, would be a freelance, and a power for evil. It is better, therefore, to bring into the organization men of every shade of opinion.

I do not believe it to be feasible to organize upon the basis of existing organizations. There would be much inequality and injustice if such a plan were adopted. We must, in some way or other, go back to the people, and organize on the theory of democracy. While the beginning would be troublesome, I think, in the end, the results accomplished would be most excellent.

I shall expect Dr. Philipson on the 18th, and hope to have a very pleasant interview with him, to which I may possibly invite some other of our friends.

One reason for fixing the time for consultation in the early part of February is, that Mr. Schiff [Jacob H. Schiff, the banker] whom I consider an important factor, expects to leave for Japan in the early days of the month, and will doubtless be gone for two or three months. Furthermore, if we delay action until next summer, the probabilities are that nothing can be accomplished for another year, and by that time there will be less enthusiasm than there is at present, and the chances are that things will run

along in the same rut in which they have been permitted to travel for many years, with the result that a few self-appointed spokesmen are constantly muddling affairs and do infinite mischief. . . .
Louis Marshall

29

JUDAISM UNDER THE GERMANS
1873–1902

In 1841 there were twenty-some Jewish congregations in the United States; in 1924 there were at least 2,000 conventicles and synagogs, the vast majority Orthodox. In 1873 the Cincinnati laity, pushed by Isaac M. Wise, established the Union of American Hebrew Congregations. It was a relatively small organization. The Board of Delegates of American Israelites, a synagogal association established in 1859, was already moribund. The preamble and constitution of the new Union was careful to avoid all reference to theology, ideology; union—and a nonadjectival Judaism—was an end in itself. All Jewish religionists were welcomed (selection I).

In accordance with the directives of the Union's constitution, the Hebrew Union College opened its doors—in a subterranean vestry—in 1875; its first class graduated in 1883, on July 11. A triune celebration was held on that great day: the college graduation, the tenth anniversary of the Union's founding, and a national assembly of the Rabbinical Literary Association. The climactic moment was the banquet that very night. The menu is a feast in itself (selection II). Seven different wines were served; four biblically forbidden foods—shellfish and frogs—were dished up. This became known as the Terefah (unclean) Banquet. Two rabbis walked out; others pushed the forbidden food aside. The Jewish caterer had not erred; there were no pork products on the table. Shellfish! Most natives and many newcomers had been eating these tidbits for years. This was not the first congregational terefah dinner.

Two years later, in 1885, a number of America's Reform rabbis met together and hammered out a radical statement, the Pittsburgh Platform, which climaxed three decades of ecclesiastical conferences. A lay and rabbinical group meeting in Cleveland in 1855 had remained well within the ambit of Orthodoxy, but several liberal ministers, pontificating at Philadelphia in 1869, had broken with tradition; the men who met in Pittsburgh unhesitatingly cut the cord that tied them to the halakhah, the age-old "Orthodoxy." By the 1880s it was obvious to these still-dominant Germans that the incoming East European traditionalists would swamp the Reformers. The Pittsburgh Platform was to serve as a defiant proclamation of the liberals who felt themselves threatened by this "invasion of the Vandals" (selection III). America's Orthodox Jewish clergy and even left-leaning traditionalists were shocked by the 1885 break with the past. Losing faith in the neutrality of the Union of American Hebrew Congregations and the Hebrew Union College (they had never forgotten the Cincinnati Terefah Banquet), they responded by creating the Jewish Theological Seminary, which was rooted in the age-old gospel of rabbinic Judaism. When, fifteen years later, the seminary threatened to collapse, a group of New York Jews—mostly Reformers of German background—rechartered and financed it. In the new organic statute which the sponsors issued, they avoided saying that it was to be an Orthodox institution (selections IV and V). Their prime goal was to occidentalize New York's Jewish ghetto dwellers numbering now close to half a million. Solomon Schechter, a native Rumanian and a modernist scholar of international distinction, was brought over from England to serve as head of a brilliant faculty. Twelve years earlier the New York *Jewish Messenger* had published a letter by Ray Frank (1864/65–1948), a woman who nursed ambitions to become the country's first female rabbi. She had received little encouragement from the all-male rabbis. Her critique of the contemporary American rabbinate is most interesting (selection VI).

Despite the fact that the seminary barely managed to stay alive, the clergy who supported it—acculturated traditionalists—met in a national conference in New York City in 1898 and adopted a statement of principle for this new Jewish congregational union. It was intended as a reaffirmation of Orthodoxy, and a repudiation and denunciation of the Reformist Pittsburgh Platform (selection VII). A few years earlier, in 1895, the Central Conference of American Rabbis sitting in solemn assembly had implicitly reaffirmed the 1885 Pittsburgh statement by rejecting authoritative Jewish canon law. The 1898 declaration may well be traditional Jewry's answer to all Jewish religious radicals. After all many of America's Jews had been shocked by the 1885 Platform; the Board of the Hebrew Union College and even Isaac Mayer Wise—an ardent devotee of the Pittsburgh proclamation—had thought it wise to back away publicly from the new Torah that came out of that city.

I. The Constitution of the First Permanent National Jewish Association of Synagogs, July 9, 1873

PREAMBLE, CONSTITUTION, AND BY-LAWS,
OF THE UNION OF
AMERICAN HEBREW CONGREGATIONS

PREAMBLE

The congregations represented in this convention, in faithful attachment to the sublime principles of Judaism, and in consciousness of Israel's sacred duties, feel impressed with the conviction, that in order to discharge these obligations beneficially, a closer union of the congregations is necessary. To this end, under the protection of benign Providence and the laws of our country, we hereby establish this sacred covenant of the American Israelites, as set forth in the following:

CONSTITUTION

Name

Article I. The body hereby constituted and established shall be known as "The Union of American Hebrew Congregations."

Object

Article II. It is the primary object of the Union of American Hebrew Congregations to establish a Hebrew Theological Institute—to preserve Judaism intact; to bequeath it in its purity and sublimity to posterity—to Israel united and fraternized; to establish, sustain, and govern a seat of learning for Jewish religion and literature; to provide for and advance the standard of Sabbath-schools for the instruction of the young in Israel's religion and history, and the Hebrew language; to aid and encourage young congregations by such material and spiritual support as may be at the command of the Union; and to provide, sustain, and manage such other institutions which the common welfare and progress of Judaism shall require *—without, however, interfering in any manner whatsoever with the affairs and management of any congregation.*

II. The Terefah—Unkosher—Banquet, July 11, 1883

MENU
Little Neck Clams (half shell)
Amontillado Sherry

Potages
Consommé Royal

Sauternes

Poissons
Fillet de Boeuf, aux Champignons
Soft-shell Crabs
à l'Amerique, Pommes Duchesse

St. Julien

Salade of Shrimps
Entree
Sweet Breads à la Monglas
Petits Pois à la Francaise

Diedescheimer

Relevee
Poulets à la Viennoise Asperges Sauce
Vinaigrette Pommes Pate

Roman Punch

Grenouiles à la Creme and Cauliflower
Roti
Vol au Vents de Pigeons à la Tyrolienne
Salade de Laitue

G. H. Mumm Extra Dry

Hors D'Oeuvres
Bouchies de Volaille à la Regeurs
Olives Caviv, Sardeiles de Hollands
Brissotins au Supreme Tomate
Mayonnaise

Sucres
Ice-Cream
Assorted and Ornamental Cakes

Entréments
Fromages Varies
Fruits Varies
Café Noir

Martell Cognac

III.   The Pittsburgh Liberal Religious Platform, November 16–18, 1885

1. We recognize in every religion an attempt to grasp the infinite, and in every mode, source, or book of revelation held sacred in any religious system the consciousness of the indwelling of God in man. We hold that Judaism presents the highest conception of the God-idea as taught in our

Holy Scriptures and developed and spiritualized by the Jewish teachers, in accordance with the moral and philosophical progress of their respective ages. We maintain that Judaism preserved and defended, midst continual struggles and trials and under enforced isolation, this God-idea as the central religious truth for the human race.

2. We recognize in the Bible the record of the consecration of the Jewish people to its mission as the priest of the one God, and value it as the most potent instrument of religious and moral instruction. We hold that the modern discoveries of scientific researches in the domain of nature and history are not antagonistic to the doctrines of Judaism, the Bible reflecting the primitive ideas of its own age, and at times clothing its conception of divine providence and justice dealing with man in miraculous narratives.

3. We recognize in the Mosaic legislation a system of training the Jewish people for its mission during its national life in Palestine, and to-day we accept as binding only its moral laws, and maintain only such ceremonies as elevate and sanctify our lives, but reject all such as are not adapted to the views and habits of modern civilization.

4. We hold that all such Mosaic and rabbinical laws as regulate diet, priestly purity, and dress originated in ages and under the influence of ideas entirely foreign to our present mental and spiritual state. They fail to impress the modern Jew with a spirit of priestly holiness; their observance in our days is apt rather to obstruct than to further modern spiritual elevation.

5. We recognize in the modern era of universal culture of heart and intellect the approaching of the realization of Israel's great Messianic hope for the establishment of the kingdom of truth, justice, and peace among all men. We consider ourselves no longer a nation, but a religious community, and therefore expect neither a return to Palestine, nor a sacrificial worship under the sons of Aaron, nor the restoration of any of the laws concerning the Jewish state.

6. We recognize in Judaism a progressive religion, ever striving to be in accord with the postulates of reason. We are convinced of the utmost necessity of preserving the historical identity with our great past. Christianity and Islam being daughter religions of Judaism, we appreciate their providential mission to aid in the spreading of monotheistic and moral truth. We acknowledge that the spirit of broad humanity of our age is our ally in the fulfillment of our mission, and therefore we extend the hand of fellowship to all who operate with us in the establishment of the reign of truth and righteousness among men.

7. We reassert the doctrine of Judaism that the soul is immortal, grounding this belief on the divine nature of the human spirit, which forever finds bliss in righteousness and misery in wickedness. We reject, as

ideas not rooted in Judaism, the beliefs both in bodily resurrection and in Gehenna and Eden (Hell and Paradise) as abodes for everlasting punishment and reward.

8. In full accordance with the spirit of Mosaic legislation, which strives to regulate the relation between rich and poor, we deem it our duty to participate in the great task of modern times, to solve, on the basis of justice and righteousness, the problems presented by the contrasts and evils of the present organization of society.

The conference adopted the following resolutions on the proselyte and Sunday service questions:

Inasmuch as the so-called Abrahamitic rite [of circumcision] is by many, and the most competent, rabbis no longer considered as a *conditio sine qua non* of receiving male Gentiles into the fold of Judaism, and inasmuch as a new legislation on this and kindred subjects is one of the most imperative and practical demands of our Reform movement, be it

Resolved that a committee of five, one of them to be the president of this conference, be entrusted with framing a full report to be submitted for final action to the next conference.

Whereas we recognize the importance of maintaining the historical Sabbath as a bond with our great past and the symbol of the unity of Judaism the world over; and whereas, on the other hand, it can not be denied that there is a vast number of working men and others who, from some cause or other, are not able to attend the services on the sacred day of rest; be it resolved that there is nothing in the spirit of Judaism or its laws to prevent the introduction of Sunday services in localities where the necessity for such services appears or is felt.

IV.   The Preamble and Constitution of the Jewish Theological Seminary, May 9, 1886

PREAMBLE

The necessity having been made manifest for associated and organized effort on the part of the Jews of America faithful to Mosaic Law and ancestral traditions, for the purpose of keeping alive the true Judaic spirit; in particular by the establishment of a seminary where the Bible shall be impartially taught, and rabbinical literature faithfully expounded, and more especially where youths, desirous of entering the ministry, may be thoroughly grounded in Jewish knowledge and inspired by the precept and the example of their instructors with the love of the Hebrew language, and a spirit of fidelity and devotion to the Jewish law, the subscribers have, in accordance with a resolution adopted at a meeting of ministers held Shebat 25, 5646 (January 31, 1886), at the synagogue Shearith Israel, New York, agreed to organize The Jewish Theological Seminary Association, and to adopt for its government the following Constitution and By Laws:

CONSTITUTION

ARTICLE I

Name

This Association shall be known as the Jewish Theological Seminary Association.

ARTICLE II

Object

The purpose of this Association being the preservation in America of the knowledge and practice of historical Judaism, as ordained in the Law of Moses . . . and expounded by the prophets . . . and sages . . . of Israel in biblical and talmudical writings, it proposes in furtherance of its general aim, the following specific objects:

1. The establishment and maintenance of a Jewish Theological Seminary for the training of rabbis and teachers. . . .

V.   The New Charter of the Jewish Theological Seminary of America, February 20, 1902

The People of the State of New York, represented in Senate and Assembly, do enact as follows:

Sec. 1. Jacob H. Schiff, Leonard Lewisohn, Daniel Guggenheim, Mayer Sulzberger, Cyrus Adler, Simon Guggenheim, Adolphus S. Solomons, Felix M. Warburg, Philip S. Henry and Louis Marshall, and their associates and successors, are hereby constituted a body corporate by the name of the Jewish Theological Seminary of America, in perpetuity, to be located in the City of New York, for the purpose of establishing and maintaining a theological seminary for the perpetuation of the tenets of the Jewish religion; the cultivation of Hebrew literature; the pursuit of biblical and archaeological research, the advancement of Jewish scholarship; the establishment of a library, and for the education and training of Jewish rabbis and teachers. Such corporation shall possess the general powers prescribed by the general corporation law of the State of New York, except as the same are inconsistent herewith.

VI.   What a Jewish Girl Would Not Do if She Were a Rabbi, By Ray Frank, May 23, 1890

To the Editor:

Living in the "far West," your paper asking for replies to—"What would you do if you were a rabbi?" did not reach me in time to answer that interesting question, had I chosen to do so.

But I trust you will not think it too late to answer the question in a slightly different form, and one which is, I think, familiar to most minds. What I would not do if I were a rabbi.

First, if I were one of the elect, one who deemed myself worthy to expound the law to men created like myself with an understanding, and a small but mighty organ termed by physiologists the heart, why, then I would not, if I were a rabbi, endeavor to impress the nature of my calling by loud and shallow words, nor by a pompous bearing unbecoming the man of God. I would not say to my fancied inferiors, *"I am the rabbi,"* and you must therefore do this or that; but I would reach their actions through their hearts.

I would try and remember that example is better than precept. I would not imagine myself a fixed star around which lesser lights must move.

I would try the effect of a gentle demeanor, a quiet voice, an earnest will, and a helping hand. I would learn if an unfailing courtesy and a positive sincerity were not sufficient to announce and impress my high vocation to the stranger and to the sinner.

I would not, if I were a rabbi, consider a stylish residence, fine garments, including a silk hat, not any of the jewels representing the original twelve tribes, as absolutely essential to keeping up my position as a "priest of the temple." I would not make a business matter of my calling otherwise than for the good of my congregation or for humanity in general.

I would not say my services are worthy a salary of so much per annum because I do this or that, or because I preach oftener or more learnedly than Mr. A. or Rev. B.; but, after satisfying my own wants in a modest way, I would use amounts expended on "high living," on cigars, cards, and other pleasantries toward enlightening the ignorant of my people—if not in my own town, where perhaps they are blessed with both intelligence and wealth, then I would use it for the poor and oppressed abroad. I would be more like Judah Asheri; less like one type of Hebrew satirically mentioned as "Solomon Isaacs." [Judah Asheri was a very philanthropic medieval scholar; "Solomon Isaacs" was a late nineteenth-century contemptuous stereotype of the Jew.] It is, indeed, difficult nowadays to note the difference between the rabbi and his friend the clothier, or the broker; his dress, his diamonds, his language, his very walk is not bookish but business; is not piety but pence.

I would not, if I were a rabbi, attempt to be a politician, for religion and politics do not and cannot under existing circumstances walk hand-in-hand. I would not degrade my holy office by assuring any ward political "boss" that for a consideration I could capture the votes of my co-religionists, "because being the rabbi, they will do as I tell them," as one rabbi of my acquaintance is said to have remarked.

If I were a rabbi and the holidays were at hand, I would not make "stock" of my seats in *schule* [synagogue]; or in other words, I would not sell religion in the form of pews and benches to the highest bidder.

I would not treat disdainfully the moneyless fellow who comes on Rosh Hashanah, Yom Kippur, or Pesach to drink at the fountain of our faith, but alas! finds that unless he can pay for his drink of religion he must either go thirsty or beg it.

During the last holiday season a poor but faithful son of Israel travelled many miles afoot (he was a peddler) that he might reach a certain city before the morning services for Rosh Hashanah began. Weary and dusty he hastened to the synagogue, drawn thither by the teachings of childhood and an undoubted sincerity to be in God's holy temple.

When our shabby countryman entered, the *schule* was crowded almost to the doors by those who had *bought* religion at so much a seat; with difficulty the fellow found a resting place; but no sooner was he in it than the rabbi's aid-de-camp, the shamus, requested him to pay two dollars and a half for the privilege of saying his own prayers in the place dedicated to God. Now it so happened this poor peddler had not the amount; so after having the attention of scores of more fortunate brethren called to his case, he was finally refused a *seat*—no, not in Heaven, but in a fashionable *schule*. I'm glad, very glad, that *schules* are but depots in one of the big way stations on the road to Paradise. Yet one cannot but regret that the ticket agents are not more thoughtful.

If I were a rabbi, I would not refuse any man a ticket for Heaven.

If I were a rabbi, I would not frequent such public places as street corners, cigar stands, nor business houses, until I was conspicuous only when absent.

I would not, were I a rabbi, canvass the town with tickets for a party if the funds went toward my own high salary. I would prefer less salary and have no soliciting to do.

If I were a rabbi of what is termed the Reform type, I would not be funny or sarcastic at the expense of my orthodox brother. If I were orthodox in my ideas, I would not apply harsh names nor deny a state of future bliss to my brother of modern opinions.

If I were a rabbi, I would not direct my sermon to the costliest sealskin, handsomest bonnet, and smallest brain, but I'd divide my attention, as well as my remarks, among my audience.

If I had a Sabbath-school, I would so conduct it that each boy and girl should see in my conduct that which I preached in my sermon.

I would not correct evil-doers among children by physical pain, inflicted because "they do so in the old country." I would not, while an incumbent of one position, be on the "lookout" for another with a bigger salary, unless I felt I could do more good in the one than in the other.

I would not, at a wedding, be the first at the feast and the last to leave the wine; it looks too carnal for a rabbi.

There are many other things, too numerous to mention, which I would not do.

One thing more, and I have done. Were I a rabbi, none should insult my manhood by offering to pay me for praying at a funeral; nor would I dare accept money, unless for charity's cause, for any service I might do the living in memory of the dead.

Were I worthy to offer up a prayer for the departed, that worthiness and the honor of petitioning the King of Kings, the consciousness that I was an ambassador to the Court of Courts, the thought of pleasing the afflicted, would all be ample pay.

Would that the spiritual mantle of [the biblical prophet] Elijah was more often donned, or at least thrown over the very material broadcloth of our modern rabbis.

Women are precluded from entering the Holy of Holies; but it is a great satisfaction to contemplate *what we would not do* were the high office not denied us.

Ray Frank
Oakland, Cal., May, 1890.

VII.   Principles Adopted by the [Orthodox] Jewish Congregational Union of America, June 8, 1898

This conference of delegates from Jewish congregations in the United States and the Dominion of Canada is convened to advance the interests of positive biblical, rabbinical, and historical Judaism.

We are assembled not as a synod, and therefore we have no legislative authority to amend religious questions, but as a representative body, which by organization and co-operation will endeavor to advance the interests of Judaism in America.

We favor the convening of a Jewish synod specifically authorized by congregations to meet, to be composed of men who must be certified rabbis, and (a) elders in official position (cf. Num. 11:16), (b) men of wisdom and understanding, and known among us (cf. Deut. 1:13), (c) able men, God-fearing men, men of truth, hating profit (cf. Ex. 18:21).

We believe in the divine revelation of the [Hebrew] Bible, and we declare that the prophets in no way discountenanced ceremonial duty, but only condemned the personal life of those who observed ceremonial law, but disregarded the moral. Ceremonial law is not optative; it is obligatory.

We affirm our adherence to the acknowledged codes of our rabbis and the thirteen principles of [the medieval philosopher-theologian] Maimonides.

We believe that in our dispersion we are to be united with our brethren of alien faith in all that devolves upon men as citizens; but that religiously, in rites, ceremonies, ideals, and doctrines, we are separate, and must remain separate in accordance with the divine declaration: "I have separated you from the nations to be mine" (Lev. 20:26).

And further, to prevent misunderstanding concerning Judaism, we reaffirm our belief in the coming of a personal Messiah, and we protest against the admission of proselytes into the fold of Judaism without milah and tebilah [circumcision and baptism].

We protest against intermarriage between Jew and Gentile; we protest against the idea that we are merely a religious sect, and maintain that we are a nation, though temporarily without a national home; and

Furthermore, that the restoration to Zion is the legitimate aspiration of scattered Israel, in no way conflicting with our loyalty to the land in which we dwell or may dwell at any time.

30

Jewish Education and Culture in the German Period
1855–1915

Under the tutelage of the "German" Jews here, American Jewry was to grow from a few frontier settlements to the second largest Jewish community in the world. The Jewish educational pattern, fixed by the 1840s, would prove persistent; there were Hebrew tutors (rebbes), congregational schools that taught the Sacred Tongue, and private institutes, often excellent, for boys and girls. There were, ultimately, dozens of Sunday schools; in 1886 these were loosely joined together in the Hebrew Sabbath School Union under the patronage of the Union of American Hebrew Congregations. As early as the 1860s the United States could boast of hundreds of colleges—controlled by the states or the churches—but American Jews had only one, Leeser's Maimonides College in Philadelphia, a religious seminary that closed its doors after a few years (1867–1873). Attempts had been made in the United States ever since the 1820s to establish Jewish academies or colleges; Isaac M. Wise's Zion College, which was to be a secular college with a Jewish theological faculty, opened at Cincinnati in 1855, but failed to survive; the first permanent Jewish institution for higher learning was the Hebrew Union College (1875), a rabbinical school; it was followed in 1887 by the Jewish Theological Seminary.

On the whole, secularism in matters cultural tended to crowd out the religious. Except for the Sunday schools, the Jewish elementary schools were dependent on tuition; public schools were free. Jewish immigrants here had their own newspapers; there was even one for women, *The American Jewess*. Scholarly magazines devoted to Hebraic and Judaic studies had been appearing since 1880. Literary societies, disguised under the name of the Young Men's Hebrew Association, flourished no later than the 1850s;

Maimonides Library opened its doors in 1852; ultimately it was to house no fewer than 20,000 volumes. Although two previous attempts had failed, the 1880s saw the rise of the Jewish Publication Society; the American Jewish Historical Society and the Jewish Chautauqua organization were to make their appearance in the 1890s. The latter reached out to the Jews in the hinterland, bringing them a wealth of Jewish life and knowledge. The greatest achievement of American Jewry was its publication of the monumental twelve-volume *Jewish Encyclopedia*. There was nothing like it, even in Europe.

Jews, immigrants and natives, made rapid strides in the fine arts, in the social and physical sciences. True, they were hampered because university appointments were rare; Jews were not wanted. Yet there were poets, essayists, artists, scholars. Women, too, were making their way; they wrote for America's best magazines. In 1883 Emma Lazarus gave the world her magnificent sonnet, "The New Colossus." Apart, however, from *The Jewish Encyclopedia* and an English translation of the Hebrew Scriptures, achievements in the Jewish area were in no sense major. When, in 1921, then a young Hebrew Union College instructor, I wanted to further myself in the field of Jewish studies, I had no choice but to cross the Atlantic to Germany, the home of the Science of Judaism—even though in those days German Jewry was only one-sixth as large as its American counterpart.

The Polonies Talmud Torah in New York's Shearith Israel was probably the country's oldest Jewish all-day school. Its rules and regulations for the year 1855 appear in selection I. During the years 1859–1862, the Rumanian-born world traveler, writer, and genteel schnorrer Israel Joseph Benjamin (1818–1864) visited the United States and recounted his experiences in that country. In selection II, translated from the German, he describes the young American Jewish woman of his day. Two generations later, Louis Marshall (1856–1929), one of the country's most distinguished Jews, wrote to Benno Lewinson reproaching him for not supporting the suggestion that a chair of Hebrew be established at the College of the City of New York (selection III). Here we have the great Marshall at his best. Strangely enough, a generation later, he did not favor the instruction of Classical and Modern Hebrew at Hunter College; the intense anti-Semitism of the 1920s probably induced him to move cautiously. One of Marshall's opponents in the struggle for leadership in the American Jewish community was the Boston corporation lawyer, Louis D. Brandeis (1856–1941). In 1915 Brandeis, who had lived most of his life as a marginal Jew, published an essay in the *Menorah Journal*, "A Call to the Educated Jew." Here he made an eloquent appeal, asking the young college Jews of his day to embrace Jewry and the new Zionism. There can be no question, Brandeis deserves to be regarded as a Born Again Jew in ethnic pride, not religious observance (selection IV).

I. A New York City Jewish Day School, April to May, 1855

Rules and Regulations of the Polonies Talmud Torah School
(Attached to the Congregation Shearith Israel)
Rev. J. J. Lyons, Superintendent and Hebrew Instructor

1.

The school will be held daily (Sabbaths, Festivals, month of August, and such other times as the committee may authorize excepted) from 9 to 3 o'clock, from 1st May to 1st November and from 9 to 2 o'clock from 1st November to 1st May. On Fridays and days preceding festivals and Sundays, the school session shall end at noon. Sundays will be devoted to Hebrew instruction.

2.

The teachers and scholars [students] will be required to be in their places or seats 15 minutes before the hour for opening; and teachers will not leave for 10 minutes after the classes are dismissed for the day.

3.

The school shall be opened daily by one of the committee, the superintendent, or in his absence, by the next teacher in rank, by reading a portion of the Scriptures.

4.

Every scholar will be required to preserve strict order, decorum, to be cleanly in person and dress, and to obey the directions of the superintendent and teachers.

5.

Applications for admission of pupils (not under 6 years of age) must be made in writing to the committee, and may be left with any member of the committee, or with the superintendent at other times than school hours and will receive immediate attention.

6.

The terms for instruction in Hebrew and English will be from two to four dollars per quarter, according to the grade of class, payable in advance. Application for gratuitous instruction to be made in writing to the committee, who alone will be cognizant of the same.

7.

There shall be a recess daily from quarter before 12 to quarter past 12 o'clock for girls, and from 12 to 1 o'clock for boys, but neither teachers nor scholars will be permitted to leave the premises. A recess for each class for 15 minutes may also be allowed at other times than enumerated in the discretion of the superintendent.

8.

The course of instruction, until otherwise ordered, shall be as follows, divided in appropriate classes:

Hebrew

Reading, writing, grammar, translating, prayers and the Scriptures, and in Bible history.

English

The alphabet, conversations on common things, spelling, reading, arithmetic, grammar, geography, history, composition, writing on slates, and penmanship.

The course of studies will be extended to higher branches as soon as the revenue from the school or other sources will permit the employment of additional teachers.

9.

The superintendent shall keep a daily record of admissions and attendance of pupils.

10.

The school quarters to commence 1st May, 1st August, 1st November, and 1st February. Scholars entering at any intermediate period will be charged proportionally.

11.

The committee have the right to dismiss scholars for inattention, improper conduct, uncleanliness, or any cause affecting in their opinion the good government of the school. A scholar being dismissed will have the proportion of the quarter's pay returned.

12.

Improper behaviour, want of punctuality, wilful injury to books, &c. will cause the dismissal of the pupil; and pupils will be required to replace articles lost or injured while in their use, if furnished gratuitously.

13.

A register shall be kept of the time of the arrival, departure and absence of each teacher.

14.

Any complaint against teachers or others connected with the school to be made in writing, to the chairman of the committee.

15.

Examinations shall be had semi-annually, to which parents and guardians will be invited.

16.

Books and stationery will be furnished at cost, and if desired gratuitously, application to that effect must be made in writing to the committee.

17.

Scholars, it is expected, will attend service regularly in the Congregation S.I.

Isaac Phillips
Asher Kursheedt
Simeon Abrahams, M.D.
New-York, Nissim, 5615   Committee of the Board of Trustees

II.   The Education of Jewish Women in America, By I. J. Benjamin, 1859–1862

Of all the inflexible demands which his religion and his duty make on each Israelite, the first and foremost is to give his child a good education; to equip it for the journey through life and give it the means to find its way. The American schools, of which we are about to speak, certainly guarantee this in part; but it is much to be regretted that, because they exclude all religion and confessions of faith—not with an unwise purpose—I must say with the deepest regret that the study of the Holy Scriptures, particularly, is much neglected among the daughters of Israel.

Jewish boys after a fashion—for that is the established way—are instructed in their religion, as is also the case with the sons and daughters of Christians. The Jewish boys attend some Hebrew school or other, or are instructed privately; but in this respect, what does the situation look like for the daughters of Israel? What a great difference! How sad is the provision for the religious instruction of these Jewish housewives and mothers of the future! How little do they learn of their duties towards God and man! What do they know of what our faith requires and of the commandments that they must obey as daughters of Israel? Should not those who are to perform the holiest religious duties be thoroughly prepared for such performance? These duties are indeed many and noble and it is with regret and astonishment that one learns that half of the American Jewesses are at present unable to undertake and fulfil worthily the place in life for which they are intended; nevertheless, it is unfortunately all too true. And why? *The reason for this lies in their neglected education.*

To throw more light on this statement and confirm the truth of it, let us describe the upbringing that the American Jewish women of today receive, and then let us proceed to show how the evil may, and should be remedied.

The mother of a little girl, a good-hearted, rather well-to-do woman, let us say, will try to impress on the young spirit of her child as much good instruction as ever she can. This private care lasts until the child is five.

Then the child, it is obvious, must be sent to a public school or, what is more respectable, to a so-called "institute." Accepted by the "institute," the child begins the usual course of studies, makes the acquaintance of girls of other religions and has friends among them, and may well, without any objection or even realization of its significance, kneel during morning prayers which are arranged for those of other faiths, before classes begin. After school, she studies her lessons for the next day or, like all children, plays. Upon going to bed or arising in the morning, she may very likely recite for her mother some Hebrew or English prayers; but as for Judaism, the child experiences nothing and knows nothing.

In this manner the girl continues to be brought up until she is fifteen, except for the unimportant difference that in time she leaves the institute to attend a high-school or college. On her fifteenth birthday a new life begins; the longed-for day arrives at last; Papa and Mamma have promised her that on this day she shall be free and shall leave school, and she "graduates," to her great joy. What useful knowledge has she gained during this time? Extremely little in fact. She has spent ten years of her precious life among all kinds of books, and with all that, she has not advanced in the least; the time is lost, indeed, forever. What she has learned is of no use to her and of no profit. She does not know how to sew, has no knowledge of household affairs, and still less of higher things. Ask her who has created her, who clothes her, who gives her her daily bread; and she may have the correct answer—perhaps, but it is more likely that she will say: "That was not in my book."

Her good parents have increased their wealth during these ten years and have taken the commendable resolution that their daughter should not forget all that she has learnt. Accordingly, they provide her—to complete her education—with a music-teacher, a singing-teacher, a drawing-teacher, and a governess to continue the practice of French; the latter also teaches her how to sew, knit and the like; and to give it all a final touch, they assign a teacher to give her Hebrew lessons. He must make her acquainted with the alphabet of a language in which, as a child, she should have lisped the name of God. She will find this last teacher, as is only to be expected, a bore. She will find Hebrew too dull and also too difficult; she will weep over her lessons so that her yielding parents, who will be touched by her tears and moved to pity, will give the teacher notice—he whom they should have engaged first and dismissed last. But they took the opposite course, out of their own lack of true religious feeling, and so they engaged him last and, again, dismissed him first.

Since, in this manner, the girl has come to the end of her religious upbringing, she continues to recite in English the few prayers which she has learnt from her mother. Should she, quite by accident, attend synagogue, she takes a book in the same language. Her other teachers soon share the same fate as her former Hebrew teacher. Because of the parties, balls, soirees, and so on, which have now become the important questions of the day for her, and at which she remains until the last, the girl becomes full of whims, her mind is distracted. She listens to the chatter of young men and all thought of study and the desire for it is gone. The young lady—she will no longer permit herself to be called a girl—believes that her upbringing is now completed in every respect, considers herself qualified to take her place in the world, able to make a man happy and become a Jewish mother. . . .

III.   Louis Marshall Questions the Place of Hebrew in Public Education, May 12, 1908

May 12, 1908

To Benno Lewinson

You are entirely correct in the statement of yours of this date, that I would naturally expect your support for the plan of establishing a Chair of Hebrew at the College of the City of New York [of which you are a trustee]. I am not, however, surprised at the non sequitur which follows, that you will not be able to give such support; nor is it cause for astonishment, that Mr. Lee Kohns agrees with you. [Kohns was also a trustee of the college.]

It has been my observation, that whenever anything can be done to add to the self-respect of the Jewish people, to develop in them the consciousness of manhood, to foster those ideals which present to the world that for which they are truly admirable, the strongest opposition, is always to be found in the Jewish ranks. They are more Bourbon than the Bourbons, more anti-Semitic than the professed Aryans, more fearful that it may be suspected that they have Jewish sympathies, than Haman himself. . . .

You say you cannot consistently vote in favor of a chair for the study of Hebrew language, literature and history, because your institution is strictly a college, and that you are constantly resisting persistent efforts to introduce university features.

It is true, that you are not a university; but I have ascertained, that there are more than a dozen institutions which, in their college courses, teach Hebrew.

You say, that the study of Hebrew is not properly a part of the curriculum in such an institution as yours. It certainly is as much a part of such a curriculum, as Latin and Greek, French, German and Spanish, botany or zoology, or any of the sciences. I have been informed that the study of Italian has recently been introduced.

You concede the educational value of the study of Hebrew. It certainly is fully as great as that which flows from pursuing either of the subjects just enumerated. It has, moreover, a cultural value, which is fully as important. It is the language in which the world's greatest ethical teachings, its most enduring moral precepts, its most powerful lessons in human conduct, have been uttered. It has a literature which began thirty centuries ago, and which is today as full of life, vigor and power as almost any of the modern languages. It is not a dead tongue, but a living one. It is spoken by thousands of cultured men and women throughout the world. I do not refer to Yiddish, but to classic Hebrew speech.

Do you not believe that a student in your college, who is able to read the Pentateuch, or the Psalms, or the Prophets, in the original, will receive as much mental discipline, intellectual culture, and moral advancement, as he would from the reading of [Greek classics like] Anabasis, or the Iliad, or a play of Euripides, or of Aristophanes, or, for that matter, from the reading of [classical Latin writers like] Ovid, or Horace, or Juvenal?

Can there be any sound objection to the substitution of Hebrew for Greek, at the election of your students? Is it not true, that a student who conscientiously prefers the study of Hebrew, will derive greater benefits from his studies, than one who is practically driven to the study of Greek, for which he has no sympathy, and toward which he may have an antipathy? There may be a hundred students in your college, who desire to pursue their Hebrew studies in preference to Greek. What logical answer can there be to the proposition that they should have the opportunity for doing so, in view of the fact that the subject is one which has been recognized from time immemorial as coming within the purview of collegiate education?

Your second objection, which you term a personal one, is, that because more than seventy per cent of the students at the college are Jews, by enabling them to study Hebrew, your institution will thereby become Jewish. You say, that a great many of the non-Jews are leaving the institution. It is, therefore, conceivable that, at some time, ninety-five per cent of the students may be Jews. The logic of your suggestion is, that so long as you keep from your curriculum the study of Hebrew, you will have prevented that awful imputation to be imposed upon the City College.

Suppose that seventy per cent of your students were French, or Italian, would you hesitate to establish professorships of French or Italian literature, assuming that your regular curriculum did not include those subjects? That would not make your institution any the more or any the less French or Italian. But because there is a demand for the study of Hebrew by the Jewish students of your institution, you complacently assert, that, notwithstanding the educational, cultural and moral value inherent in the study of Hebrew, that demand must be disregarded, because, forsooth, the institution, which is now recognized by you to be well-nigh Jewish, would become the subject of criticism, because it affords to its students the opportunity of familiarizing themselves with the most sublime products of the human mind.

I have a higher opinion of my fellow-citizens, than to attribute to them views implying so narrow an outlook. I am sure that they will concur in the opinion, that the students in the City College should be permitted to develop along those lines, which will aid in making them the most useful members of society; that they would welcome the introduction of such courses as would enable the Jewish boys of the City College, to familiarize themselves sufficiently with Hebrew to enable them to become teachers of their own people, instead of half-baked lawyers and quack doctors, and prevent the creation of an artificial chasm between the Jewish boy born in America, and his foreign-born parents, due to the fact, that they move in different spheres, and, therefore, fail to thoroughly understand each other. To my mind, nothing would contribute so much toward bridging this chasm, as the intelligent study of Hebrew by the Jewish students of the City College, who are rapidly becoming agnostics, and are disposed to regard with contempt their progenitors.

If you for a moment think, that, by keeping Hebrew out of your curriculum, you will induce what you call "the sons of nice Gentile families" to become students in the City College, and to "cultivate friendships" with the Jewish boys who are now there, you are woefully mistaken. I would much prefer to develop "nice Jewish boys" out of the material which you now have, and I know of no better contribution that can be made to that end, than to let them know and feel, to let the public know and feel, that there is something of value, from an educational, cultural and ethical standpoint, in the language, literature and history of the Jewish people,

I shall probably have my labor for my pains. It is quite likely that the Jews will continue to be apologetic in this matter, as in others, and that they will earn the contempt of others, by the contempt which they evince toward themselves. They would rather bask in the smiles of apparent approval of their Gentile friends, who, in their heart of hearts, have naught but feelings of derision for those who abdicate that sense of dignity, and that devotion to principle, the cultivation of which is the only means of gaining the genuine respect of our fellow-citizens.

In conclusion let me say, that, whether you favor this proposition or not, I shall continue to urge it year after year, if necessary, until it is favorably acted upon.

[Louis Marshall]

IV. Louis D. Brandeis Addresses the Educated Jew, January 1915

. . . Our intellectual capacity was developed by the almost continuous training of the mind throughout twenty-five centuries. The Torah led the "People of the Book" to intellectual pursuits at times when most of the Ayran peoples were illiterate. And religion imposed the use of the mind upon the Jews, indirectly as well as directly, and demanded of the Jew not merely the love, but the understanding of God. This necessarily involved a study of the Laws. And the conditions under which the Jews were compelled to live during the last two thousand years also promoted study in a people among whom there was already considerable intellectual attainment. Throughout the centuries of persecution practically the only life open to the Jew which could give satisfaction was the intellectual and spiritual life. Other fields of activity and of distinction which divert men from intellectual pursuits were closed to the Jews. Thus they were protected by their privations from the temptations of material things and worldly ambitions. Driven by circumstances to intellectual pursuits, their mental capacity gradually developed. And as men delight in that which they do well, there was an ever widening appreciation of things intellectual.

Is not the Jews' indomitable will—the power which enables them to resist temptation and, fully utilizing their mental capacity, to overcome obstacles—is not that quality also the result of the conditions under which they lived so long? To live a Jew during the centuries of persecution was to lead a constant struggle for existence. That struggle was so severe that only the fittest could survive. Survival was not possible except where there was strong will—a will both to live and to live a Jew. The weaker ones passed either out of Judaism or out of existence.

And finally, the Jewish capacity for hard work is also the product of Jewish life—a life characterized by temperate, moral living continued throughout the ages, and protected by those marvellous sanitary regulations which were enforced through the religious sanctions. Remember, too, that amidst the hardship to which our ancestors were exposed it was only those with endurance who survived.

So let us not imagine that what we call our achievements are wholly or even largely our own. The phrase "self-made man" is most misleading. We have power to mar; but we alone cannot make. The relatively large success achieved by Jews wherever the door of opportunity is opened to them is due, in the main, to this product of Jewish life—to this treasure which we have acquired by inheritance—and which we are in duty bound to transmit unimpaired, if not augmented, to coming generations.

But our inheritance comprises far more than this combination of qualities making for effectiveness. These are but means by which man may earn a living or achieve other success. Our Jewish trust comprises also that which makes the living worthy and success of value. It brings us that body of moral and intellectual perceptions, the point of view and the ideals, which are expressed in the term Jewish spirit; and therein lies our richest inheritance.

Is it not a striking fact that a people coming from Russia, the most autocratic of countries, to America, the most democratic of countries, comes here, not as to a strange land, but as to a home? The ability of the Russian Jew to adjust himself to America's essentially democratic conditions is not to be explained by Jewish adaptability. The explanation lies mainly in the fact that the twentieth century ideals of America have been the ideals of the Jew for more than twenty centuries. We have inherited these ideals of democracy and of social justice as we have the qualities of mind, body and character to which I referred. We have inherited also that fundamental longing for truth on which all science—and so largely the civilization of the twentieth century—rests; although the servility incident to persistent oppression has in some countries obscured its manifestation.

Among the Jews democracy was not an ideal merely. It was a practice —a practice made possible by the existence among them of certain conditions essential to successful democracy, namely:

First: *An all-pervading sense of the duty in the citizen.* Democratic ideals cannot be attained through emphasis merely upon the rights of man. Even a recognition that every right has a correlative duty will not meet the needs of democracy. Duty must be accepted as the dominant conception in life. Such were the conditions in the early days of the colonies and states of New England, when American democracy reached there its fullest expression; for the Puritans were trained in implicit obedience to stern duty by constant study of the Prophets.

Second: *Relatively high intellectual attainments.* Democratic ideals cannot be attained by the mentally undeveloped. In a government where everyone is part sovereign, everyone should be competent, if not to govern, at least to understand the problems of government; and to this end education is an essential. The early New Englanders appreciated fully that education is an essential of potential equality. The founding of their common school system was coincident with the founding of the colonies; and even the establishment of institutions for higher education did not lag far behind. Harvard College was founded but six years after the first settlement of Boston.

Third: *Submission to leadership as distinguished from authority.* Democratic ideals can be attained only where those who govern exercise their power not by alleged divine right or inheritance, but by force of character and intelligence. Such a condition implies the attainment by citizens generally of relatively high moral and intellectual standards; and such a condi-

tion actually existed among the Jews. These men who were habitually denied rights, and whose province it has been for centuries "to suffer and to
think," learned not only to sympathize with their fellows (which is the essence of democracy and social justice), but also to accept voluntarily the
leadership of those highly endowed morally and intellectually.

Fourth: *A developed community sense.* The sense of duty to which I have
referred was particularly effective in promoting democratic ideals among
the Jews, because of their deep-seated community feeling. To describe the
Jew as an individualist is to state a most misleading half-truth. He has to a
rare degree merged his individuality and his interests in the community of
which he forms a part. This is evidenced among other things by his attitude toward immortality. Nearly every other people has reconciled this
world of suffering with the idea of a beneficent providence by conceiving
of immortality for the individual. The individual sufferer bore present ills
by regarding this world as merely the preparation for another, in which
those living righteously here would find individual reward hereafter. Of
all the nations, Israel "takes precedence in suffering"; but, despite our national tragedy, the doctrine of individual immortality found relatively
slight lodgment among us. As Ahad Ha-'Am so beautifully said: "Judaism
did not turn heavenward and create in Heaven an eternal habitation of
souls. It found 'eternal life' on earth, by strengthening the social feeling in
the individual; by making him regard himself not as an isolated being with
an existence bounded by birth and death, but as part of a larger whole, as a
limb of the social body. This conception shifts the center of gravity not
from the flesh to the spirit, but from the individual to the community; and
concurrently with this shifting, the problem of life becomes a problem not
of individual, but of social life. I live for the sake of the perpetuation and
happiness of the community of which I am a member; I die to make room
for new individuals, who will mould the community afresh and not allow
it to stagnate and remain forever in one position. When the individual
thus values the community as his own life, and strives after its happiness as
though it were his individual well-being, he finds satisfaction, and no
longer feels so keenly the bitterness of his individual existence, because he
sees the end for which he lives and suffers." Is not that the very essence of
the truly triumphant twentieth-century democracy? . . .

31

American Jewish Philanthropy in the German Period
1871–1923

In the 1840s most good-sized Jewish communities had at least one charity organization; Philadelphia and Cincinnati had several; New York City, about forty. If mutual aid societies are included as social welfare institutions, then New York City in 1917 had 2,300 such institutions. By the year 1900 American Jewish towns of size swarmed with autonomous philanthropic agencies that provided for the needs of their subscribers. Here is a sample list, by no means complete: Hebrew benevolent societies, male or female; a woman's organization that sewed garments for the poor; Passover relief organizations; hospices; hospitals; homes for tuberculars, for the aged, and for orphans; trade schools for men, women, and young folk; institutions to help immigrants; Young Men's and Young Women's Hebrew Associations; settlement houses; agricultural and colonization congeries.

Less than a decade after the California Gold Rush started, San Francisco established a sick-care and burial society, the Merciful Brothers Association (1857); its forty-page printed constitution and bylaws included a brief code of parliamentary law, certainly a contribution to Americanization, to the orderly conduct of a society's business session (selection I). Sadie American (1862–1944), a noted social worker, was, together with Hannah Greenebaum Solomon, one of the prime founders of the National Council of Jewish Women. For many years she was corresponding secretary. It was at the Jewish Women's Congress, held at Chicago in 1893, that Miss American made the appeal and offered the resolution that brought the council to birth. The resolution and brief excerpts from her appeal—including a New Testament reference—are selection II.

The armies that marched through Russia and Poland in World War I brought death and destruction to thousands. Moved by the distress in Eastern Europe and the desperate situation of Palestine's Jews, Louis Marshall, head of the American Jewish Committee, published a call to his fellow Jews to come to the aid of all war-stricken coreligionists. His plea of September 1, 1914, led to the organization of the American Jewish Joint Distribution Committee, a consortium of American Jewry's Orthodox, labor unions, and middle-class (largely Reform) elite who were determined to help fellow Jews (selection III). Some time after June 30, 1921, the "Joint" published a brief statement listing the overseas Jewish communities it had succored and the monies it had expended; the total was $38,121,433.10. This was, indeed, a remarkable showing (selection IV). American Jews—many of whom were immigrants—were sending millions of dollars—their sacrificial savings—to assist fellow Jews out of a sense of kinship. One of these immigrants, a German Jew who had come to these shores as a lad of eighteen, was the millionaire banker, Jacob H. Schiff. In November, 1918, shortly after the World War I armistice, Schiff wrote to Julius Rosenwald, the Sears, Roebuck magnate, and suggested that they initiate a half-a-billion dollar program to rebuild devastated Europe. Schiff was thinking of Europe as a whole, not of his coreligionists alone (selection V).

Fed up with an almost daily solicitation for funds from numerous charities, Jewish social workers preached the gospel of combining welfare institutions and raising money for them at one fell swoop once a year. Thus the federation movement came into its own in Boston and Cincinnati in 1895–1896, though the merger of social welfare agencies and a single fund-raising campaign had actually started in Chicago as early as 1859. In selection VI, Solomon Lowenstein, the executive head of New York's Federation for the Support of Jewish Philanthropic Societies, reports as chairman of a committee of the National Conference of Jewish Social Service (1923). The committee was evaluating the federation movement.

I.   Constitution of Chebra [Society] Achim Rachmonim, December 24, 1871

ARTICLE I

NAME OF THE SOCIETY

This society shall be known by the name of "Chebra Achim Rachmonim" (Brothers of Benevolence), and shall consist of at least fifteen members.

ARTICLE II

All books and writings of this Society shall be kept in the English language, but in making of motions, or speaking on any subject, either German or English may be used, on permission being given by the president.

ARTICLE III

CANDIDATES

Section 1. Persons who desire to join this society must be of the Hebrew persuasion, and have resided six months in San Francisco, must have attained the age of twenty-one years, and not have exceeded the age of forty-five; be corporally and mentally well, of good moral character, and if married, such marriage must be in accordance with the Jewish rites. . . .

Sect. 4. Every candidate proposed to become a member of this Chebra, shall, by receiving due notice from the secretary, go to the physician of said Chebra, as directed for examination. . . .

ARTICLE V

DUES AND BENEFITS

Section 1. Every member must make a monthly payment of one dollar, and contribute to all extra expenses enumerated in the by-laws.

Sec. 2. Every member entitled to the benefits of this society, who through sickness is unable to attend to his business, shall receive all such benefits stated in the by-laws, medical treatment and medicine, and if necessary, day and night watch.

Sec. 3. In the event of the death of a member in good standing, the sum of one hundred ($100) dollars shall be appropriated to defray the funeral expenses under the supervision of the president.

Sec. 4. The widow of a deceased brother, in good standing, who has been a contributing member for two successive years shall receive a monthly benefit of twelve ($12) dollars out of the funds of the society as long as she remains a widow and possesses a good and moral character.

Sec. 5. Six months after the funeral of a member, if entitled thereto, a tombstone shall be erected with the inscription *Achim Rachmonim;* the cost of such shall not exceed thirty ($30) dollars. If near relations live in this city, a communication shall be first sent to them upon this subject.

Sec. 6. If a member's wife, or child under the age of fifteen years, dies, he shall be paid out of the funds of the society, sixty ($60) dollars in the former, and twenty-five ($25) dollars in the latter case, for the payment of the funeral expenses.

Sec. 7. Every member keeping full *shiva* [the seven-day mourning period] according to Mosaic rites, and in accordance with such ceremony, absent from business, shall receive ten ($10) dollars out of the funds of the society. During this time he shall also be entitled to a *minyan* [prayer service] in which case the secretary shall summon ten members in rotation, including an officer, to attend daily, morning and evening.

Sec. 8. All extra expenses stated in sections 3 and 6 of this article, must be raised by the members, and placed to their accounts.

Article VI

Loss of the Rights of the Society and of the Membership

Section 1. Members suffering sickness through immorality, intemperance or affray, shall not receive any benefits from the society.

Sec. 2. Members who have been convicted of any criminal offence shall be expelled from the society; also, such who at their admission made false statements concerning their age or physical condition. Members who have not been married according to the Jewish ritual shall not be entitled to any benefits of the society. . . .

By-Laws

ARTICLE III

Duties of the President

. . . The president shall sign all orders drawn on the treasury, keep the charter, and bring the same to every meeting; he has the power with assistance of the first and second trustee to draw ten dollars on the treasury of the society for the relief of a distressed member; in case a larger sum be required, further action thereon shall be had by the Chebra at the next regular meeting. He shall adhere strictly to the duties of a chairman, and have special charge over the Sick and Burying Committee; he shall answer all questions addressed to him in a moderate manner, and at the expiration of his term of office, he shall deliver to his successor all effects entrusted to his hands. . . .

ARTICLE XI

Duties of the Sick Visiting Committee

Section 1. This committee shall consist of the board of officers of this Chebra, and the chairman thereof shall be the president. It shall be the special duty of this committee to visit the sick of this Chebra on the following days: president on *Sunday;* treasurer on *Monday;* first trustee on *Tuesday;* second trustee on *Wednesday;* third trustee on *Thursday;* fourth trustee on *Friday;* vice-president on *Saturday.*

To observe that they are well taken care of, and if such is not the case, they shall give notice to the president, and if he, upon consultation with the doctor of the patient, finds it necessary, he shall send a proper nurse to attend the sick brother; in urgent cases the secretary shall send one of the Burying Committee as an additional watch. All expenses incurred thereby shall be paid out of the funds of the society, and an equal assessment for such expenses levied upon the members every three months.

Sec. 2. At the decease of a member, the president shall see that all the Burying Committee be present, and that the proceedings are conducted according to the Mosaic rites; wherefore, if such signs should appear, the same should forthwith be made known by the member of the committee watching. It belongs to the duties of the chairman of this committee, to see that this is faithfully complied with. The *tahara* [cleansing of the corpse] and funeral shall be conducted by this committee, under the supervision of the president, in a proper and becoming manner. The same shall also take place if a male child of one of the members under the age of fifteen years should die.

Sec. 3. Eight members shall be appointed as a Burying Committee of this society by the president, to attend all deaths of this society, and in consideration thereof they shall be relieved from attending to *minyan*.

ARTICLE XII

Duties of the Investigating Committee

Each member appointed to the Investigating Committee shall make diligent inquiries regarding the proposed candidate, speak personally with the same, and report the result thereof in writing at the next regular meeting. . . .

ARTICLE XVI

Dues

Section 1. Each member shall pay one ($1) dollar monthly, in advance, and all assessments levied by the society for watching with sick brothers. (Art. V, Sec. 1 of the constitution.)

Sec. 2. In case of a funeral of a member in good standing, an assessment of one ($1) dollar, of his wife fifty cents, and of a child twenty-five cents, shall be paid by every member to cover the funeral expenses. . . .

ARTICLE XVIII

Physician, Druggist, and Surgeon

The physician, druggist, and surgeon, shall be nominated in the month of October, elected at the election of officers, and commence their duties on the first of January following. The physicians [sic], to be elected, must be known as a good and practical physician, and be in possession of a diploma as a graduate, to the satisfaction of the society. Further conditions between them and the society shall be stipulated in the contract between the two parties.

ARTICLE XIX
Benefits

Section 1. Every member, if taken sick, shall be entitled, besides physician and medicine (Art. V, Sec. 2, Constitution), to a weekly benefit of five dollars, to begin from the day of his report to the president; provided that he is not in arrears, or his sickness does not originate through immorality, or a concealed disease at the time of his acceptance. Only a member who has belonged twelve months to the society is entitled to the above mentioned benefits.

Sec. 2. A sick member unable to obtain good attention and care at his residence, may, by the consent of the physician and the president, be removed to some proper place at the expense of the society.

Sec. 3. A member taken sick out of this city, but within the states of California, Oregon, Nevada and Washington Territory, shall be entitled to a weekly benefit of seven dollars and fifty cents ($7.50), if he has notified the secretary of his departure, by sending weekly statements of the attending physician and the authorities of the place, mentioning the sickness and its origin, to the president.

Sec. 4. A member keeping full *shiva*, shall receive a benefit of ten ($10) dollars, provided he be in good standing and has been a member of the society for twelve months. (Art. V, Sec. 7, of the constitution.)

Sec. 5. Only in cases where it can be proven that the physician of the society neglects a patient, it shall be the duty of the president to provide the same with another competent physician, at the expense of the society. In all other cases the patient shall only be entitled to the services of the physician of the society; but, if the latter considers it necessary, a second physician shall be consulted, at the expense of the society.

Sec. 6. The patient has to obey strictly all prescriptions of his physician, or he will lose all benefits of the society. . . .

II. Organizing the National Council of Jewish Women, September 7, 1893

. . . This Congress would not be complete without some record of what many Jewish women have done, and are doing. Therefore, an attempt has been made to bring into a short, presentable form, the present work of Jewish women. . . .

There are in existence several working girls' clubs [in New York City] for evening instruction and one—the Working Girls' Alliance—for mutual improvement and culture. This is a self-supporting institution, and is a pioneer in a field that should be actively and energetically worked.

In New York and in other cities during the past few years have been formed in the various congregations what are known as Sisterhoods. They teach the value of personal service, and practically show it in visiting the sick and poor, in providing and teaching creches [nursery schools] and kindergartens.

Their work is divided into four sections:

(1) Visiting the poor;

(2) Work in Kindergartens, etc.;

(3) Work in Sabbath Schools and sewing classes, combining religious and practical work; and

(4) Work among working girls.

Prevention is their watchword, as it must come to be that of us all. The first three of these sections are in most active operation. Work among working girls is being pushed but has assumed no such proportions as it should and will.

In addition to these sisterhoods, there exists in Baltimore a society doing much the same work but on a different plan. The organization, known as the Daughters in Israel, is an organization composed of small bands of ten, each doing the special work itself decides upon; its small size insures all workers and no drones. Among the good things brought into existence through its instrumentality are visiting among the needy, dressmaking classes, the establishing of a fresh air fund for the care of sick children, the instituting of a temporary home where Russian immigrants are cared for during a few days till they can find employment; mothers' meetings, at which kindly advice on home matters is given to poor mothers and at which they are also taught to sew; a small kitchen-garden or household school, and a working girls' club for social approach. This club holds meetings every Saturday evening; often there are informal talks by some outsider on popular subjects, such as physiology, etc. Here, too, their sympathies have been quickened for those *most* unfortunate in this world—the sick and absolutely poor—and they find that out of their small means they still have enough to give something of money, of time, and of friendliness, to help those poorer than themselves. The Daughters seek to procure employment for specially talented girls. They have extended their influence even to children. There is one band that gives such things as children prize —fruit, and flowers, and candies, and good food for the mind in entertaining books. The Daughters in Israel may feel they have indeed deserved to be told, "Well done, thou good and faithful servant" [Matthew 25:21].

There are, too, in Baltimore, congregational societies "for promoting the interests of the congregations," furnishing prizes and entertainments for their Sabbath School children and decorations for the synagogue on Holy Days. There is the night school of the Hebrew Literary Society, arranged primarily to meet the needs of adult immigrants, to teach them English and act as an Americanizing influence. For the more advanced pupils here, the history of the United States is taken as a textbook, and some have this year been reading [Charles and Mary] Lamb's *Tales from Shakespear[e]*, with frequent passages from the great bard himself. Sunday evening lectures in winter are a feature of this school; but the best feature is the fact that it is partially supported by the small tuition fee of thirty cents a month, paid by the pupils, and giving them that feeling which is only theirs who know that they are not a burden nor a drag on others.

In Philadelphia, the institutions deserving special mention are a Wayfarers' Lodge, established by Russian women for the temporary housing and feeding of their persecuted brethren driven to seek new homes; the Household School, providing as an adjunct to itself weekly inspiriting entertainments; and the Personal Interest Society, composed of women, each of whom looks after some one family, inculcating principles of thrift, and cleanliness and culture, and seeing that the children get all the benefits of education open to them.

In Rochester, beside the general run of societies, there is one for encouraging and distributing good reading among children, a club giving monthly entertainments, a musical society, and a Shakespeare class.

In St. Louis, the Mothers' Club, and the Pioneer Society, a society established for mutual culture and improvement, must be mentioned.

In Detroit stands forth pre-eminent the Woman's Club, established on the fine principle of bringing rich and poor, women of all social conditions together in frequent meetings, that they may learn to know and to help one another. Sewing classes, readings, lectures and general social intercourse are its work; and it has proved its practicability and elevating tendency through the several years of its existence. . . .

There are among the Jewish women various benefit and secret societies, such as the Treue Schwestern [United Order of True Sisters], whose purpose is mutual aid in cases of sickness and death, and noble friendship and endeavor, together with some charitable work among the very poor.

There is in existence, too, a society called Sons of Zion with branches called Daughters of Zion, whose aim is (I read from the report), "To propagate the national idea among the women of Israel by meetings, lectures on history and literature, and a circulating library.

"Secondly, to assist Jewish colonization in Palestine, with the special aim of colonizing the Russian Jews. These societies, comprising in all about 30,000, exist in Russia, France, Germany, England, and a small number in America, as the Americans think not at all on this subject."

The existence of this society will be a surprise to many of us; yet, while we do not in the least share in the national idea, in fact, scarcely comprehend it and strongly oppose it, we can all see here in the colonization of Palestine another chance of bringing happiness to the persecuted of our religion. . . .

To the sewing of garments for the poor, by the poor, I also desire to call attention. In New York there exists a Young Ladies' Society which gives work to the very poor, to be sewed for distribution by the Hebrew Relief Society. But the like society in London is on a higher round [rung] of the ladder, since it arranges that the poor work directly for the poor, and be paid by them. This work should be copied.

There are three institutions in my own city [Chicago] which I must, however, mention. Though not entirely woman's work, women have done more than their one-half share in starting, managing and providing for them, and working in them—and therefore I include them.

In addition to the general run of philanthropic societies in which women are interested, we have the Jewish Manual Training School—the model of its kind in the United States, and an institution of which we are justly proud. We have the Elise Frank Fund, of which we are equally proud, for its application of funds to the support and bringing up of orphans in private families has proved so successful that it has demonstrated this manner of caring for the parentless to be no longer an experiment, but a finer, a better and, to the practical, a more economical way of solving this great question. In this country, this fine woman, following the plan laid out by the late lamented Dr. [Samuel] Hirsch, of Philadelphia, is the first woman to apply money to this purpose.

In addition to this there is about to be formed, a Social Settlement of Jewish Young People. While it will be non-sectarian, welcoming all co-workers, and doing its work among whom it may find, yet its main purpose is the elevation of the Jews in whose midst the settlement will be situated. Its work will not be charitable, but philanthropic. The distinction between these terms should always be carefully noted. The raising of the people from their outward and inward degradation, the helping of working men and women, girls and boys, to learn, to cultivate themselves—to play and relaxation and recreation—that is their mission—to inculcate the principles of independence, of self-dependence, of self-reliance; by living and working directly among them to become their friends, not their benefactors nor patrons, and thus to teach and to influence them as only personal contact can teach and influence. . . .

Miss American, of Chicago, then presented the following resolution:

Resolved, That we, Jewish women, sincerely believing that a closer fellowship will be encouraged, a closer unity of thought and sympathy and purpose, and a nobler accomplishment will result from a widespread organization, do therefore band ourselves together in a union of workers to further the best and highest interests of Judaism and humanity, and do call ourselves the "National Council of Jewish Women." Seconded and adopted.

III. Louis Marshall and the American Jewish Committee Organize a Relief Organization during World War I, September 1, 1914

A meeting of the Executive Committee of the American Jewish Committee was held yesterday at which communications were received from various parts of the world concerning the condition of the Jews in consequence of the late Balkan war and of the present general war raging in Europe.

It was decided to appropriate $2,500 for the benefit of the Jewish orphans at Sofia, Bulgaria, who had lost their parents during the late war.

Cablegrams were received from Hon. Henry Morgenthau, the American Ambassador at Constantinople, and from other reliable sources, indicating that the Palestinian Jews were confronting a serious crisis in consequence of the discontinuance of contributions which have hitherto been received by them from their brethren in the several European lands which are now at war with each other.

It was reported that the destruction of a number of flourishing colonies was threatened, unless financial assistance was at once forthcoming. The sum of $50,000 was stated to be immediately required to relieve the situation and that a responsible committee had been formed, of which Dr. Arthur Ruppin, of Jaffa, was the chairman, for the purpose of administering the funds that might be forwarded, for the establishment of a free loan society and for the support of families which, because of the fact that their bread-winners had been called into the army, were in a destitute condition. The committee appropriated the sum of $25,000 for this purpose, Mr. Jacob H. Schiff adding $12,500 to this sum, and it being understood that the Zionist organizations would undertake to secure the remaining $12,500 needed to carry on this relief work.

The committee then considered the effect of the war upon the Jews of Russia, Germany, Austria, the Balkan States, and other parts of the world, the assistance of whom it was believed would inevitably demand serious consideration from their co-religionists, especially in the United States. In order to cope with the serious problems which in all probability must soon be dealt with, a sub-committee was appointed to gather authentic information with regard to the situation of the Jews who might be affected by the existing calamity, and to make recommendations as to ways and means by which necessary and adequate assistance might at the proper time be rendered to all sufferers, without discrimination. The committee proposes to call upon other organizations to co-operate with it to aid in the formulation and carrying out of plans for the accomplishment of results commensurate with the immensity of the problem.

IV. Joint Distribution Committee Statement Showing Funds Appropriated for the Relief of Jewish War Sufferers, November 1914 to June 30, 1921

Country	Amounts appropriated since inception of Committee November 1914
Abyssinia [Ethiopia]	$ 11,704.80
Alexandria, Egypt (refugees)	58,851.55
Algiers, Tunis and Moroccco (refugees)	9,000.00
Austria-Hungary (prior 1920)	2,881,591.10
Austria	899,425.79
Baltic Provinces [Lithuania and Latvia]	66,317.04
Belgium	2,500.00
Bulgaria and occupied territory of Serbia (prior 1920)	26,600.00
Central Europe	388,451.53
Czecho Slovakia	316,008.73
Danzig (refugees)	10,012.25
Denmark	1,700.00
France (refugees)	12,996.55
Germany	424,765.32
Greece, Turkey, Serbia and Syria (prior 1920)	1,365,884.88
Greece (matzoths)	19,000.00
Holland (refugees)	92,115.70
Hungary	480,092.63
Italy (Matzoths, war prisoners, refugees)	29,998.99
Japan (refugees)	125,002.50
Jugo-Slavia (refugees)	35,000.00
Latvia	117,392.36
Lithuania	214,384.29
Palestine	5,194,502.06
Persia	35,700.00
Poland, Lithuania and Kurland [Latvia] (prior 1920)	11,522,007.09
Poland	5,409,379.97
Roumania	2,023,415.65
Russia (prior 1920)	4,000,300.00
Russia and Ukraine	1,168,448.72

Siberia (refugees, war prisoners)	498,494.41
Spain (refugees)	18,000.00
Switzerland (refugees)	37,281.77
Syria	49,956.34
Turkey	349,541.06
Miscellaneous, not classified	2,575.26
Paid to ORT, Paris, on account of $100,000 tool appropriation	44,008.95
Medical commission on account of $200,000 general appropriation	179,024.91
Total	$38,121,433.10

V.   Jacob Schiff and Julius Rosenwald's Plan to Restore Devastated Europe after the Armistice of World War I, By Jacob Schiff, November 21, 1918

Nov. 21, '18

Julius Rosenwald, Esq.,
c/o Messrs. Sears, Roebuck & Co.,
Chicago, Ill.
Dear Mr. Rosenwald:

Mr. [Jacob] Billikopf [the social worker], to my great gratification, has been able to tell me that he found you practically fully restored again, upon his recent visit to Chicago, and may I hope that, notwithstanding this, you will henceforth take things a bit easier, so that you may not risk another break-down.

I had a very similar experience at just about your age and I have found that by doing things systematically and taking periodical vacations, I could retain my health, after it had been restored, without any difficulty. We need you and we are selfish enough to be deeply interested in your well-being.

You will no doubt remember that in the summer of 1916, when we were rummaging over Mt. Desert Island [Maine], we discussed—rather prematurely then—the re-building of the devastated places of Europe, and you then said to me you would be willing to contribute a considerable amount—I believe you said a million dollars—whenever such a project could be made to take form; I then said to you I thought I could be counted upon to do something similar. More than two years of added war and destruction have passed since then. America, which in 1916 was neutral, has itself had to take up arms to prevent liberty and freedom from becoming extinguished in Europe and perhaps in the world. European nations have become impoverished, and what you and I discussed in the summer of

1916 is no doubt more imperatively necessary to be undertaken now, through American initiative, than two years ago, for, notwithstanding the great sacrifice our country has brought, its great resources will before long have restored the fortunes and income of its people.

It has occurred to me—and I have not discussed this with anyone else thus far—that it might be proper at this time for you and me to take the initiative and pledge $1,000,000—each toward a fund of $500,000,000—to be raised by the American people for purposes of restoration in Europe. The way I would suggest proceeding is that we address the President [Woodrow Wilson]—rather promptly, to enable him to act before he goes to Europe [for the Peace Treaty]—making the offer (not for publication, however, until he can see his way to act favorably upon it), and suggest to him that—if this meets with his approval—he name an "American Commission for Restoration in Europe," of which he is to be the Honorary President, for the raising of a minimum amount of $500,000,000—and for taking in hand the carrying out of the object in view.

Perhaps, however, it might be still better to first see whether we cannot obtain a number of additional $1,000,000 pledges from such men as Cleveland Dodge, Arthur James, J. P. Morgan, George F. Baker, Henry Ford, etc., etc., before we approach the President, but then we should likely not be able to do this prior to the President's departure, and as he is likely to stay in Europe some time, the carrying into effect of the project might have to await his return and suffer considerable delay, when it is of importance for the cause itself that prompt action be taken.

If you were strong enough, I would suggest that you visit Washington and seek a short interview with the President, in place of our addressing him in writing, for, while I do not think that I [as a Republican] am "persona non grata" in [Democratic] Administration circles, I am sure you are "persona grata" to a greater extent than I am, and could more readily secure a bit of the President's time than, at this time, when he must be so greatly overburdened, I should be able to do.

Awaiting your reaction upon this (using an expression I have adopted from Friend Billikopf), I am, with cordial greetings both to Mrs. Rosenwald and you—in which Mrs. Schiff would join, were she here with me, Most sincerely yours,
Jacob H. Schiff

VI. Federating Charities and the Creation of an Overall Jewish Community, By Solomon Lowenstein, May 13–16, 1923

. . . . In the opinion of your committee, it can fairly be claimed that the Federations have been successful in improving the financial methods of our communal agencies, in securing a larger measure of support and a more intelligent, just, and efficient distribution of the funds thus realized. It may also be fairly claimed that as a direct result of the Federation movement, there have come about improved standards in the work of the various constituent organizations, amplification of the content of their work, and an expansion of the fields of activity.

It cannot be said so surely, however, that the Federations have shown themselves to be resourceful in meeting new needs, in showing initiative in the establishment of new organizations to solve persistent problems, in enlisting the efforts of existing agencies, or in providing reserve or capital funds for the rehabilitation of antiquated plants or the construction of new institutions. Nor have they been altogether successful in their efforts to secure the hearty cooperation and active participation of all the elements making up the Jewish body politic.

Experience has proved that in practically every instance in which a Federation has been founded upon sound and approved plans, the initial increase in the amount of financial support secured has been great; that with proper organization and intensive effort, this sum can be increased annually both to meet natural losses due to death, business failure, and removals . . . and to provide a gradually increasing amount to meet greater costs of living and maintenance, legitimate expansions of activities, raising of standards, etc. In no instance does it appear that as yet the full financial resources of any given community have been realized; though the rate of growth of our communities naturally diminishes from year to year, there does not appear at the present time sufficient evidence to indicate that in any instance the maximum result has been achieved.

It would be presuming too much to claim that the improvement in standards of work of the various affiliated societies is due exclusively to Federation. The development of a class of professional social workers undoubtedly has much to do with the fact that Federations have helped develop social workers. Contact with non-Jewish agencies, offering in many instances examples of superior method and wider vision, has undoubtedly been a direct influence in the development of Jewish work. The increasing interest in social questions and the vast amount of study given them has been shared by Jew and non-Jew alike, and has much to do with the improvement of the technique of our various agencies.

But when all due allowance is made for these and other causes, it is undeniably true that by relieving the executive officers and the boards of control of our societies from a disproportionate and in many instances almost exclusive interest in the necessity for raising funds, there has been set free a reservoir of energy for concentration upon the problems of the work itself; this has brought about the marked improvement of which we are all conscious.

Moreover, the Federation movement has, though it must be admitted in varying degrees, unquestionably brought about a broad community spirit as opposed to a narrow institutional point of view, a recognition of the fact that our various forms of philanthropic effort are but individual expressions of different phases of one central communal problem, rather than independent, self-sufficient activities.

This broadening concept of the meaning of social work has had the effect of attracting large numbers of young men and women of superior education and ability to active participation in these communal enterprises —workers who would have stood aloof from mere absorption in the detailed administration of any single institution, no matter how worthy in itself.

On the other hand,it is alleged by many that this very factor is instrumental in diverting from the management of these essential agencies men and women who might have given themselves freely to their development, thus reducing the number of individuals joining in communal life. On the whole, however, it would not appear that this contention is justified. . . .

The great shortcoming of Federation has been that in many instances it has signally failed to organize the community. This is due to a variety of causes. In the first place, insufficiency of funds has too often restricted the Federation activities to those agencies already existing at the time of its organization and resulted in a great hesitancy in admitting new organizations. This has left outside the Federation list worthy institutions deserving communal support, and compelled them to meet the tremendous competition of a centrally organized body enlisting the financial support of the great majority of large givers in the community. . . .

But the chief cause of failure to create a comprehensive Federation must be sought in the lack of understanding and congeniality between the different national groups within the community itself. Too often the Federation has been merely a Federation of old-line institutions, ignoring completely or partially the new enterprises established by the more recent arrivals [the East European Jews]. Thus, there has been created unnecessarily a lack of unity which is destructive of any true manifestation of communal life. . . .

A recent study—by two of the members of the committee—of various Federations throughout the country shows that in the majority of instances, the newer groups in the community are either inadequately or not at all represented in the bodies controlling the Federation. We are witnessing on a much larger scale a renewal of the differences between the original Sephardi settlers and their immediate German successors. But whereas in the earlier period, these differences were of little importance because of the small numbers involved, today the problem is so huge as to require the coordination and understanding cooperation of every group in the community, if a real organization is to be achieved. This difference manifests itself throughout the communal structure. . . .

Moreover, there must be a frank recognition of the fact that if all elements of our community are to be represented and to participate in a thoroughgoing fashion in the philanthropic forms of communal expression, with a corresponding share of financial support, they must receive similar recognition in the purely social and recreational forms of organization. If we are to have real communal organization, there can be no place for snobbishness and exclusiveness. In this, as in other respects, all Jews are brethren.

This being granted, there remain, however, real questions as to procedure. It is conceded that the more recent additions to our ranks have not by reason of previous training learned the lessons of systematic organization to the same degree as have those who have been longer in touch with American conditions and methods of administration. Frequently, their institutions are not so organized as to make it advisable for them to enter at once without preliminary experience into the larger life of the Federation. In some instances, their premature inclusion in the Federation has been disastrous to both sides, and has hindered further development along the same lines. . . .

The obverse of the situation indicated above must also be recognized, namely, that as a result of the process of assimilation, there is annually a decrease in our ranks; year by year we find ourselves losing for communal purposes an increasing proportion of those men and women who by reason of heredity, tradition, and longer established residence, should for many years to come furnish the largest proportion of our active communal workers.

If the present diminution of immigration is to continue permanently, it will constitute an ever-increasing weakness in our endeavors to thoroughly organize our Jewish communities. It should also be said that your committee believes that one of the most important functions of the permanent committee, which it has recommended for the study of this entire question of organization, should be the deliberate and careful consideration of the probable effects of this immigration policy with reference to the field of what now constitutes Jewish social service.

It is manifest that under such conditions many of the needs now so pressing would lose much of their force, and money and energy would be set free for the fuller development of the work of the various institutions, possibly the elimination of a number of them, and the substitution of newer and more needed forms of work.

It is the definite opinion of your committee that the Federation represents but a stage in our communal development, and not the final form.

What that form may be, it is impossible at this time to forecast. Papers have been read at an earlier session with reference to two forms of activity which may indicate phases of this newer development—namely, district service and Jewish centers. . . .

The Jewish center offers much hope, if it can be made a democratic expression of all the needs of the community in which it is located, and if it endeavors to supply all such wants for family helpfulness, education—both religious and secular—recreation, cooperation with all existing special agencies, etc. This would no doubt do much to impress upon every member of the community his responsibility and his obligation. It is conceivable that such an organization, working in cooperation with a general community board which will outline policies for the entire city (to be applied locally through such centers) would constitute a form of organization much more immediate and efficient than is at present possible in the highly centralized way in which we endeavor to meet our communal needs. . . .

Questions that must be given very serious consideration before arriving at a conclusion in this matter concern themselves with the amount of financial support to be realized from the Jewish community. In places where the Jewish organizations are invited to join Community Chests, is it possible that the amount to be contributed by Jews will be greater or less than would be the sum realized by an independent Jewish Federation? Furthermore, would the amount contributed by Jews be fairly proportionate to their number and wealth in the community and also to the amount that they should receive for the support of their particular institutions—giving due regard to the obligation of the Jew to contribute to the various non-sectarian activities present in the community? Should the Jewish organization enter such Community Chests as independent units, or only after they have attained such complete local organization as will lead them to believe that they are prepared to enter on equal terms into a joint enterprise . . . ? [The Community Chest, which provides and apportions funds for all the charities in a town was inaugurated by Martin A. Marks of Cleveland in 1913.]

32

HOME AND SOCIALITY
1858–1897

D o not feel sorry for the Jews of the eighteenth and nineteenth centuries because they had no radio or television. Time did not hang heavy on their hands; they were not bored. Some eighteenth-century American Jewish boys and girls were given good training in music; David Franks was a member of a musical group which provided the accompaniment for staged operas. Individual Jews joined socioliterary organizations; business executives became respected officers in nineteenth-century eating clubs; as Yale students graduated they celebrated at balls and parties (1873).

The Jews of Newport, Rhode Island, had an eating and drinking club as early as 1761; Purim in Richmond, Virginia, was celebrated bibulously with ale, porter, gin, spirits, and brandy (1789). By the 1840s and 1850s the club life of the country's Jews was flourishing. New York's Harmonie Club was established in 1847; in many states and towns there were literary societies, Young Men's Hebrew Associations, and even an occasional library. Lodges, charity organizations, male and female, abounded; in all organizations sociability was as important as cultural and philanthropic activities. The ladies rejoiced in their bazaars and strawberry festivals (short cake!); there were Purim and charity balls, masquerades, piano and vocal recitals, evenings for elocutionary declamations. Everyone enjoyed wedding and bar mitzvah festival meals. The affluent visited Europe; afternoon teas and kaffeeklatsches were a staple. No gatherings, not even funerals, were devoid of their moments of fellowship.

In 1858 Benjamin Mordecai wrote Isaac Leeser, Philadelphia's leading Jewish clergyman, asking him to check the references of a Jewish woman who had applied for the position of governess in his family. Mordecai, one of Charleston's richest Jews, wanted an educated and refined woman who would fit into his home and serve as a moral influence on his children (selection I). At the age of sixty, Sophia Heller Goldsmith (1848/49 to ca. 1929) began to write her memoirs. By that time she and her husband Philip had built a successful national sporting-goods concern, MacGregor Sports Products, Inc. In selection II, Sophia describes her courtship and marriage in Chicago and Milwaukee in the 1860s. Eleven years after Sophia's marriage, Rabbi Isaac Mayer Wise, a widower, married Selma Bondi (1876), the daughter of the Reverend Jonas Bondi, a well-known New York City cleric and newspaper editor. He made an informal, "cute" announcement. His enemies—and they were legion—thought it in bad taste; his friends loved it; for them, Wise could do no wrong (selection III).

The Phoenix Club of Cincinnati had much in common with Newport's eating and dining club. In 1897 the Phoenix, already at least forty years old, published a new constitution (selection IV). It is an interesting and informative document, for it describes in considerable detail the nature of this typical institution of America's affluent Jews. Its last building (1873), still standing, could not be replaced in the early 1990s for less than $10,000,000. It is a classical illustration—an impressive one—of conspicuous consumption. The Jews had "made it" and they wanted their Gentile peers to sit up and take notice.

I. The Criteria for a Governess, By Mordecai Benjamin, November 28, 1858

Charleston, Nov. 28th 1858

Rev. Isaac Leeser,
Dear Sir:

Miss Esther Davidson of your city, who is an applicant for governess in my family, has referred me to you, in a recent letter, to testify as to her character and capacity, and, as the position she will occupy is one of importance, I trust that with your usual frankness and kindness you will give me ful particulars touching her character, disposition, and capability. As she will be the companion of my wife and the instructress of four of my children, three girls and one boy, whose ages vary from twelve to six years, it is highly important that I should be made acquainted with her antecedents.

I am anxious to procure the services of a lady who, while she is capable of teaching the varied branches of an English education, can also impart lessons in French, music, and painting; at the same time I desire one who will also be enabled to cultivate the moral sense, and while she improves the mind will also train the heart. In selecting such a person I should be governed in a great measure by the credentials of friends of the party, and if therefore your recommendation of Miss Davidson embodies my views and wishes I will take great pleasure in securing her services or that of any other person you may be pleased to recommend.

Anticipating an early and favorable response,
I remain
Very respectfully
Your ob'dt servant
B. Mordecai

II. Sophia Heller Goldsmith's Courtship and Marriage, By Sophia Heller Goldsmith, 1861–1865

. . . I grew to be a tall girl but slender. Between twelve and thirteen I went to swimming school [in Milwaukee]. In 1861, one summer day, not being able to take the usual hour at seven in the morning, which was our usual hour for instruction for girls, a friend and I went in the afternoon till four o'clock for girls. We rushed through dressing as it was time for the boys' turn. [I was] standing on the platform waiting for my friend as she came towards me, saying "Sophia, look at that handsome fellow." Of course I was not slow in doing same. I saw the back and profile of the young man with a black mole on his back. I answered: "O, Amelia, isn't he handsome?" He had turned so I could see his rosy face. We spoke about him on our way home and after that he was forgotten. . . .

At those times children gave ballads [ballets] in private charity balls. On one of these Saturday evenings, as before mentioned, I was as usual sitting next to mother opposite the door. The door opened opposite us and Uncle Pereles' wife and sons entered and, behold, my Phillip likewise. How happy I was! If he only could and would dance with me, were my thoughts. After their wraps were taken off they joined us. Mr. Goldsmith asked me to dance. I assure you he was a fine dancer. He and I enjoyed dancing together. For week after week we met every Saturday evening. I thought him handsomer every time I saw him. I was too young to realize anything else but his pretty face. In those days there were no letter carriers so I used to go to the post office. One day I met Mr. Goldsmith with a large tin notion box in one hand and a large heavy bundle of dry goods tied in a striped ticking on one shoulder, peddling. We were both embarrassed. One year passed. Then he took sick in a hotel with no one to care for him. He upbraided me because I did not call. The rich Uncle and Aunt Pereles had forgotten him. . . . The second year of our acquaintance came around; I went to school. Mr. Goldsmith gave up peddling. . . .

As I came to my brother's store [in Chicago] he told me he gave Mr. Goldsmith permission to take me for a drive. Mr. Alex Goldsmith, his wife, and young baby in one buggy, and I in another with Mr. G. We drove ten miles to the Insane Asylumn, which was also [a] home for old folks where Mrs. A. G. had a grandmother. That evening I went with Mr. Goldsmith to German theatre. During the acts he took out of his pocket an unusual large apple which he cut in two. In those days it was customary to do that and also to bring knitting. . . . Mr. Goldsmith took me to my first English performance. I was very nervous, as I had gone without my parents' knowledge, as in those days children always went with their parents' consent. I left for Milwaukee next day. Mr. G. requested me to correspond with him. I told him he would have to get permission from my parents first. It would be wiser if children nowadays showed so much regard for their parents' opinion; there would not be so many mistakes in marriages and other unhappy affairs of the present century. . . . Mr. G. proposed. I would not give definite answer until my parents were consulted. As I was determined not to break the vow made years ago, I put Mr. G. off from time to time with my excuse that I was too young, as I was little over fifteen years of age. At that time a girl of twenty was considered an old maid. Early marriages was the custom. . . . After a lengthy correspondence with my parents, Mr. G. at last received their consent to our engagement. Mr. G. could not leave his business at the time. Father came to Chicago to give us his blessing. . . .

My dear Phillip and I saw each other at least a couple of hours each day, after his store was closed. The parting came again. Weeks passed. Mother and I left Chicago [where we were visiting]. My parents consented to let the marriage take place, as we two children were lonesome for want of seeing each other. Your father was then only twenty-one, and I sixteen years and nine months on the wedding day. After three months' engagement our marriage took place August 27th, 1865, in the Temple Beneyeshurum on Fourth Street, Milwaukee, Wis., on a beautiful Sunday at 2:00 P.M. The sky was blue and silvery. Arriving at the temple, we found it filled to its capacity. I little realized the step I was taking, and when the choir began to sing, the tears rolled down my cheeks and I did not know whyfore. At home the table was set for fifty guests. Rabbi Faulk [S. Falk] was the minister and my former teacher. The following Tuesday, Aug. 29th, 1865, papa [Phillip Goldsmith] and I left for Chicago, where he had rented a large four-room flat for $25 per month, on State near Harrison, at that time a fashionable street.

My parents gave me a $300 check as a present, for which we bought furniture consisting of haircloth parlor set, bedroom furniture, and kitchen, and woolen, damask-upholstered chairs, and etc. And a piano and sundries were given me as a present on my following birthday, Nov. 16th.

Wednesday, the thirtieth of Aug., papa [my husband] took me to my future home, expecting many of our cases, etc. As I looked under the sink in the kitchen I was surprised to find a mother cat with five little ones. I was as happy as a child to play with them. Our first dinner in our home was ice cream and cake. I started housekeeping with $3 a week. Our house was gradually put in order, arranged prettily, and we were two happy children.

III.   Isaac Mayer Wise Announces His Second Marriage, April/May, 1876

The editor of the *American Israelite* has entered upon a life co-partnership with Miss Selma Bondi of New York, the daughter of the late Rev. Jonas Bondi, editor of the *Jewish Leader*. The articles of agreement were signed, sealed and delivered, Monday, April 24, in presence of Dr. Joseph Lewi and lady of Albany, N.Y., and the new firm. The Rev. Dr. A[dolph]. Hubsch of New York performed the ceremonies, and the Doctor's excellent lady said the necessary responses. [Dr. Wise's bride said yes!] The capital invested in the said firm, to be known hereafter as Isaac M. Wise & Lady, consists of all the editorials and directing abilities of the first party, and the executive and corrective abilities of the second party. The firm to be dissolved three days after death. It is understood that Dr. Wise will attend to editorial and outside business as heretofore, and Mrs. Selma Wise will direct the home affairs at 126 Dayton Street. In regard to sermons, it has been agreed that Dr. Wise continues to preach the sermons and deliver the lectures in the temple, and Mrs. Selma retains the privilege of delivering occasional curtain lectures [scolding the rabbi]; profits or losses to be shared equally, and no papers to be accepted or endorsed, especially no love letters, except by mutual knowledge and express consent. Friends are politely invited to call and inspect the new establishment.

IV.   Constitution of the Phoenix Club, Cincinnati, 1897

ARTICLE I

NAME

1. This organization, incorporated for social and literary purposes, shall be called the "Phoenix Club," and shall consist of such stockholders as shall be elected members according to the constitution. . . .

ARTICLE IV

DUTIES OF OFFICERS. . . .

4. Stage-Manager:—The stage-manager shall have control of all matters pertaining to the stage. He shall procure all requisite properties subject to the approval of the board of directors. . . .

Article VIII

DUES, ETC.

1. The annual dues shall be one hundred (100) dollars, payable in quarterly installments of twenty-five (25) dollars each in advance, on the first day of January, April, July, and October. Every person elected shall pay an entrance fee of fifty (50) dollars. Bills for supplies furnished to members of the Club, or its steward, shall be payable on the first day of each month. The bills for dues and supplies shall be payable in such manner as the board of directors may order. . . .

Article IX

RIGHTS AND DUTIES OF MEMBERS . . .

4. No member or visitor shall give any gratuity to an employee of the Club; nor shall subscription papers be exposed or circulated in the Club House.

5. All supplies, liquors, cigars, and provisions of any kind shall be purchased from the Club or its steward, subject to such rules as the board may adopt.

Article X

RENTING ROOMS

1. The board of directors may rent the auditorium and banquet hall floors to members, for weddings in their families, for one hundred (100) dollars. The board may adopt rules setting apart other rooms and facilities for the use of members renting, but the Kneipe [barroom], billiard room, smoking room, library, cafes and card rooms shall not be rented. The board of directors may grant without charge, to members, for weddings in their families, or for other purposes, the use of the banquet hall floor; but the minimum restaurant charge, when the banquet hall is used, shall be seventy-five (75) dollars. The members renting shall be responsible for all damages to the property of the Club. The use of the rooms shall be subject to such rules as the board of directors may from time to time adopt. . . .

Article XII

VISITORS, ETC.

1. A non-resident visitor may have extended to him, the privileges of the Club for one week, when introduced and registered by a member, who shall obtain for him, upon registering, a card signed by the secretary.

2. Monthly tickets entitling a non-resident to the use of the Club House, may be issued by the board of directors upon recommendation by a

member, and upon payment of ten (10) dollars a month. Non-residents shall not be permitted to attend entertainments without procuring special tickets from the board of directors, the price of which shall be three (3) dollars, except for New Year's evening entertainments, when the price shall be five (5) dollars. Non-residents to whom monthly tickets have been issued, must procure special tickets to attend entertainments in the same manner and upon the same terms.

3. When introduced by a member, a resident may be admitted to the Club House in accordance with the rules of the board of directors, but to entertainments once a year only, when provided with a stage ticket.

4. No special or stage ticket shall be issued to any person if two members of the board of directors object. No monthly ticket shall be issued to any person if three members of the board object.

5. The member introducing a visitor, shall be responsible for all supplies furnished him.

6. All persons residing, or engaged in business, in Hamilton and Butler Counties, Ohio, and Campbell and Kenton Counties, Kentucky, shall be deemed residents.

ARTICLE XIII

GAMES

1. The board of directors shall have full power to regulate all games in the Club House. . . .

RULES AND REGULATIONS FOR THE GOVERNMENT OF THE PHOENIX CLUB

1. All supper seats reserved and not cancelled by six o'clock P.M. on the day previous to the evening of an entertainment, will be charged to the members so reserving the same.

2. A person taking part in an entertainment of the Club, may have issued to him a stage ticket entitling a resident to attend such entertainment. Application for such ticket must be made to the board of directors at its regular meeting next preceding the evening of such entertainment. No stage tickets shall be issued for the New Year's evening entertainment.

3. All dues, assessments, and bills for supplies, shall be collected in the following manner: upon receipt of a bill from the treasurer for any obligations due the Club, it shall be the duty of every member to pay the same. All members who have not paid their bills by the 20th of the month, shall be notified by the secretary that they are delinquent, and that their names will be posted at the end of the month, unless their accounts be paid. The names of all members in arrears for thirty (30) days shall be posted on the bulletin board of the Club. Upon failure to pay any obligation within

thirty (30) days thereafter, action will be taken by the Club, as provided in Article VIII of the constitution.

4. No charge shall be made for the use of a billiard table, or bowling alley. No person shall use a table or alley for more than one hour, if same be wanted by others.

5. The bowling alleys may be reserved, upon application to the board of directors, for Monday, Tuesday, and Wednesday evenings by special parties, no one of which parties shall have the use of the alleys more than once in two weeks. On other evenings the alleys are subject to the use of the members of the club.

6. If any bowling club, to whom evenings have been set apart, does not use the alleys for two successive evenings, the privilege granted such bowling club may be revoked.

7. Except on entertainment nights, the Club House shall be closed at 12 o'clock midnight. On Saturday nights the Club House may be kept open until one A.M., but all games shall cease at 12 midnight.

8. The restaurant shall be open at 8 o'clock A.M. and shall close at 12 midnight. No meals shall be served unless the order be given before 11:30 o'clock P.M. On evenings of entertainments, the cafes shall be closed at 9 o'clock.

9. Non-members shall be allowed to participate in the following card games only: solo, pinnocle [sic], casino, hearts, sixty-six, euchre and whist [no poker].

10. No gambling paraphernalia shall be brought into the Club House.

11. Ladies are permitted to use the Kneipe on Monday, Tuesday, and Wednesday nights only; but at no time shall they be permitted to use the billiard room, library, or smoking room.

12. Persons, not members of the Club, residing in Hamilton or Butler Counties, Ohio, or Kenton or Campbell Counties, Kentucky, shall not under any pretext whatever, be introduced as visitors to the Club House by the same member more than once a year, except to the private dining rooms and reception rooms, provided for interviews with non-members, and such further exceptions as may be established by the House Committee, in case of private dinners and suppers.

13. Non-members of the Club may be admitted to private entertainments given in the private dining rooms. Meals for less than four persons shall not be served in a private dining room.

14. No refreshments from the restaurant shall be served in any of the rooms other than the dining rooms and cafes, except that cold refreshments may be served in the card rooms and Kneipe, and coffee in the smoking room.

15. No member or visitor shall be permitted to send a servant out of the Club House. On application at the office, messengers will be furnished at the expense of the sender. . . .

33

Kinship: Every Jew Is Responsible
for His Fellow Jew
1859–1906

American Israelites—like all other Jews—have a strong sense of kinship. They are concerned for the welfare of their fellow Jews, particularly if they are oppressed. In 1840 Jews here asked the United States government to intervene in Syria where coreligionists had been arrested and tortured on the false charge of ritual murder. There has not been a decade since that year in which American Jewry has not protested against the mistreatment of Jews in foreign lands. In 1858–1859 at least ten American Jewish communities protested because Pope Pius IX had refused to restore Edgardo Mortara (1851–1940), a child, to the bosom of his family in papal Bologna. Armed with a warrant, on a June night—the 23d or 24th—in 1859, the authorities in the Papal States seized young Edgardo; he never returned to his home as a Jew. When still an infant he had fallen ill; his pious Catholic nurse performed an emergency baptism; she trembled for the future of his immortal soul. Several years later, in 1858, when the Church discovered that the child had been baptized, it removed him and reared him as a Catholic. He grew up to become a priest and a professor of Catholic theology. The news of the abduction roused the world; Jews, Protestants, and even some Catholics hoped that His Holiness would let little Edgardo return to his parents. The Pope was adamant. Jews in Europe and in the United States remonstrated vigorously against the papal policy, though Catholicism as such, was not singled out for attack. The authorities in Washington refused to intervene with Pius IX, deemed an independent sovereign accountable only to his God and canon law. Selection I records the resolutions passed unanimously in San Francisco, January 15, 1859. The chairman of the meeting, Solomon Heydenfeldt, was a former California State Supreme Court judge.

286

That same year, American Jewry, hoping to increase its influence, established the Board of Delegates of American Israelites, the first Jewish national defense agency in the United States.

On November 21, 1905, Jacob H. Schiff, the banker, wrote Theodore Roosevelt's Secretary of State, Elihu Root, asking him to help Jews who were being hounded in Morocco. An international conference was about to meet in Algeciras, Spain, to discuss the future of Morocco. Schiff and his friends wanted the Great Powers to protect Jews and Christians who were then subject to gross abuse in that Moslem land. In his letter to Secretary Root, Schiff included an aide-mémoire dealing with the disabilities to which the Jews were then subject, de jure at least (selection II). At the Conference which met from January into April, 1906, the American representative made an appeal on behalf of Moroccan Jewry; it was favorably received. Inasmuch as Morocco was then a client state controlled by France and Spain, many of its oppressive laws were actually ignored in practice; the trouble was mainly in the backcountry where French and Spanish authority was weaker.

Schiff was more concerned about the East Europeans who were pouring into New York City than the problem of alleviating the distress of the Moroccans; he wanted to deflect the immigrant stream to the Gulf ports; a government immigration commissioner had suggested that this would be advisable. Elite metropolitan Jews were embarrassed by the presence of the arriving unacculturated Russian Jewish masses; Schiff knew that if the newcomers crowded into the east coast cities, anti-immigrant legislation was inevitable. Thus it was that he welcomed the proposal of the North German Lloyd Steamship Company—on the ships's trips to Galveston—to carry immigrants in their empty holds before they loaded up with cotton for the return trip. The newcomers were to be dispatched to the American South by the German Jews' Aid Society (Hilfsverein der deutschen Juden) and by Israel Zangwill's ITO, Jewish Territorial Organization (selection III). The Galveston Movement was not very successful; from 1907 to 1914 a mere 10,000 émigrés debarked at the Texas port where the Jewish Immigrants Information Bureau shipped them on to the backcountry. In the five years, 1904–1908, 642,463 Jewish newcomers, fleeing pogroms, had landed on the Eastern seaboard. By 1914 the Galveston Movement was dead; World War I had started; local immigration officials were hostile; and Schiff, disappointed, stopped footing the bill. Was the Galveston Movement a complete failure? The newcomers, settling in the interior, became nuclei for new Jewish communities. New York's Industrial Removal Office, 1901–1917, had shipped about 74,000 East Europeans into the interior; they settled in 1,731 towns.

I. San Francisco Jewry Appeals to the United States
Senate to Denounce the Abduction of Edgar Mortara,
January 15, 1859

The Mortara Abduction. We, the undersigned, feeling deeply incensed at the injury recently perpetrated upon Mr. Mortara of Bologna,
(Italy), in the abduction of his son, and recognizing the peril which attaches to the social and religious condition of all those antagonistic to the
Catholic faith involved in such a precedent, make this call upon the Israelites of San Francisco, and others of our fellow citizens whose sentiments
and sympathies are kindred to our own, to unite with us in mass meeting,
at Musical Hall, on Saturday evening, the 15th instant, at 7 o'clock, for the
purpose of publicly expressing their feelings upon this grievous wrong.

Henry Seligman, president Congregation Emanu-El; Israel Solomon,
president Congregation Sherith Israel; August Helbing, president Eureka
Benevolent Society; J. P. Davies, president First Hebrew Benevolent Society; L. King, president C.B.C.U.; M. B. Ashim, president I.O. [Indepen-
dent Order] Benai Berith.

At half past seven o'clock, Henry Seligman, Esq., called the meeting
to order.

Isaac S. Josephi, Esq., nominated the Hon. Solomon Heydenfeldt as
president of the meeting.

Mr. Heydenfeldt was unanimously elected, and, on taking the chair,
spoke as follows:

Fellow Citizens: The object of your meeting to-night has been made
known in the call which has brought you together. I am not fully acquainted with the transaction upon which you are here to express your
opinions. The details of it will, doubtless, be given to you by the other
gentlemen who are present. The general aspect seems to be that, on a recent occasion, in the town of Bologna, [in the papal-ruled part of] Italy, a
child of Hebrew parentage—an infant child—was snatched from the protection of his home by the ecclesiastical authorities, upon the pretence of
his having been admitted, by rites of baptism, to the faith of the Church of
Rome. The question does not appeal alone to the sect to which the child
belongs. It is a direct attack upon the principles of humanity and civilization [applause], and persecution of one, to-day, which may be the fate of
another to-morrow [applause]. It was an act of tyranny which, in the very
nature of things, must be adverse to the common sentiments of both Catholics and Protestants. It is strange, indeed, that, in the middle of the nineteenth century, we should be called upon to denounce such an outrage as
this—strange that, in the midst of this age of advancement, any man
should be molested in his own theory of the future or the past—strange
that we should still have an example of the existence of a power to enforce

religious faith. But, it may be asked, what good can come of this meeting here, and the passage of resolutions! The answer is, we are uniting our voices to those of the rest of the civilized world, in forming a grand public opinion against this invasion of the rights of humanity, of liberty, and the social relations of mankind [applause]. Our government may not have, according to the law of nations, the material power to stretch forth its hands with sufficient potency—rescue the child and restore him to the arms of his parents—but we have another power, which is irresistible—the power of public opinion, which if excited properly in this instance, the Mortara case will be the last of the kind that the world will ever see [applause]. . . .

Mr. Seixas Solomons then read the following preamble and resolutions:

On the 23d day of June last, Mr. Mortara, an Israelite, was forcibly bereft, by the authorities at Bol[o]gna, of the person of his youthful son, upon the allegation that he was baptized in the Catholic faith by a menial of the household, at a time when sickness had made probable the anticipation of his death, and that, by reason thereof, his guardianship, education and personal control ceased to be the prerogative of his Jewish parents, and belonged, of right, to the powers of the Papal Church.

The contemplation of such an act, at this period of the world's history, when civilization reveres the sanctity of the domestic hearth, and tenderly regards the holy affections of the human heart—when the intelligence of mind has unclasped the fetters which fanaticism had erewhile wrought about the freedom of conscience, stifling the aspirations of free and untrammeled devotion—when the progress of religion and the counsels of moral influence are teaching the recognition of personal liberty as an absolute right—at such a time, the contemplation of such an act moves the mind, in turn, with surprise at the boldness of the aggression, with sympathy for the bereavement of its unhappy victims, and indignation and abhorrence at the intolerance and oppression which would sacrifice the inalienable rights of humanity to a canon of the Church that was supposed to have long become obsolete and buried in oblivion.

The fell train of cruel and malignant persecutions which the records of the past disclose, when the red hand of sacrifice dictated absolute submission to the Church as the tenure of existence, and the political and natural prerogatives of mankind were absorbed in the usurped supremacy of the sacerdotal robes, are freshened in the memory and revived to the imagination, with all their associations of horror and disgust, until prudence and caution are awakened to the dread, if not the anticipation, of their repetition.

Public opinion, the great moral lever that controls alike the prince and the peasant, the mighty and the humble, the weak and the strong, is required to interpose against the dangerous assertion of power involved in such an act.

With this view and intent, be it therefore,

Resolved, That the Israelites and other citizens of San Francisco, in mass meeting assembled, denounce this act of the papal authorities at Bologna, as being sacrificial of the dearest rights of humanity—social, political, and religious.

Resolved, That we regard with apprehension and regret this revival of a power whose intolerance and oppression history and experience teach as prejudicial to mankind, and to a just enjoyment of their natural rights.

Resolved, That we appeal to the recognized intelligence, virtue, and humanity of the head of the Roman Catholic Church, to discourage the enforcement of a canon which is opposed to the enlightenment of the present century, and which must lead to consequences fraught with discord, evil, and danger.

Resolved, That we deeply sympathize with Mr. Mortara in his severe affliction, and are ready to contribute every means at our command necessary to effect the restoration of his child, and to secure the household of others from a similar visitation.

Resolved, That we fully appreciate the spirit of liberality and tolerance manifested by a large and enlightened portion of the Christian world in the expression of their disapproval of this act of tyranny.

Resolved, That a copy of the proceedings of this meeting be transmitted to our senators in Congress, with the request that they urge upon that body the moral power of our Federal Government, to co-operate with the several European powers in their endeavors to suppress religious intolerance and persecution, such as exhibits itself in the Mortara case.

Resolved, That a copy of these proceedings be transmitted to Sir Moses Montefiore, president of the London Committee of Deputies, as a response to the address made to the Israelites of America, dated October 25th, 1858. [Sir Moses asked the American Jewish communities to appeal to Washington to take action.]

Resolved, that the cordial thanks of this meeting be, and are hereby, tendered to the press for its liberal and kind co-operation in the cause of civil and religious liberty.

II. Jacob H. Schiff Intercedes for the Jews of Morocco, November 21, 1905

Dear Mr. Secretary [of State Elihu Root]: I have your valued communication of the 18th instant and thank you for the information therein concerning the expectation of the United States to take part in the international conference on Moroccan affairs.

I have also read with interest the programme agreed upon between France and Germany, of which you have been good enough to send me a copy. May I submit to you that it would be very desirable if our Government can see its way to do so, that, now that the Moroccan situation is to be made the subject of international discussion, the United States insist that, in any protocol which shall be adopted, there be inserted a condition of proper treatment of Moroccan subjects of other faiths than the Mohammedan? While the Jew is, in Morocco, subject to particular iniquities, I am informed that Christians and all other [non-Moslem] sects are great sufferers, in Morocco, from Mohammedan iniquities, and, as was the case in the Berlin and other Congresses when the participating powers insisted that the status of religious sects need be regulated by treaty, it appears to be most desirable that a similar course be followed in the coming international congress on Moroccan affairs. . . .

For your information I take the liberty to inclose herein a statement of the restrictions against Jews now existing in Morocco, which has been sent to me from Europe, which restrictions, when read by an American, appear most grotesque.

Thanking you in anticipation for giving this consideration, I am, with assurances of high esteem.

Most faithfully yours,

Jacob H. Schiff.

Jewish Restrictions in Morocco, especially in the Interior
A. Restrictions in Lodging and Dress

1. Moroccan Jews, with the exception of those living in harbor towns, must live in ghettos (mellah), the doors of which are closed at night.

2. Jews are compelled to wear a special garb, consisting of a heavy cap and heavy shoes. They are not allowed to wear any dress that could cause them to be taken for Mohammedans.

3. Outside of the mellah they must, as a sign of submissiveness, go barefooted and bareheaded. Where there are no mellahs, they must at least take off their head gear and shoes in front of the mosques.

4. Outside the mellahs they must go on foot and may not use animals to convey them. Neither may they carry canes. Even the old and sick may use a reed only for support. Humiliating and brutal indignities by Mohammedans are of daily occurrence. The Moorish part of the population often, as a pastime, throw burning coal, broken glass, old tinware, etc., on the places where the Jews have to pass, and then enjoy the sight of the wounds, burns, and pains to which the naked feet of the Jews are subjected. All this goes unpunished. In the Moorish quarters the Jew may not pass any side streets in order to avoid a road that is not easily passable, but must use a street which the Arabs do not frequent. In passing the native the Jews must go to the left, and if they do not do that, they must retrace their steps and make way in the manner prescribed. To such and similar vexations practices the Jews have to submit every day in the week.

5. Jews who are found outside the ghetto after sunset are, unless they have a permit, considered as outlawed, and liable to the grossest maltreatment, for which there is no redress.

6. Jews can travel or move only with special permission from the sheik. Jews travelling may not be accompanied by their wives and children, who are kept back as a sort of hostage for the husband's return. Jews who emigrate, if they can get permission at all to do so, must pay large sums as quit money. Emigrating women must pay twenty times as much as men, so that it is made impossible for families to remove.

7. Jews are not allowed to build their houses above a certain height.

8. As Jews are considered unclean by Mohammedans, they may not drink from public fountains or springs, nor get water from there. Neither may they make use of public baths; even bathing in the ghetto is not always permitted them.

B. Restrictions in Trade and Commerce

1. Jews may not own real estate outside of the ghetto.

2. They cannot have stores or shops in the Moorish quarters of the town where goods are sold to the Moorish population, such as clothing, shoes, silk, etc. Jews who are in these industries are therefore compelled to have their goods sold through native Mohammedans, which often entails considerable loss.

3. In case the Government warehouses, where grain and other articles are stored, are overcrowded, or if their contents are spoiled through being stored there too long, the Jews are compelled to buy such goods at the price at which the undamaged article sells.

4. Jewish provision dealers—as butchers, grocers, bakers, etc.—are forced to furnish their goods to officials gratis; if they refuse to do so, they are hampered in their business or ruined altogether.

C. Tributes in Money and Labor

1. Jews and their wives and daughters are forced to work for all public officials at all times, even on the Sabbath and holy days, and the pay they receive in return is far below the common wages. Women are often compelled during such work to have their heads uncovered, which orthodox Jews consider as sinful, as unchastity.

2. Jews are forced to perform labors which the Mohammedans think beneath them, such as the cleaning of closets and sewers or flaying, etc. Frequently they are forced by the Government to act as executioners.

3. When the heads of rebels are sent to town to be placed on exhibition at the public gate, the Jews are forced to salt such heads before they are exhibited; even on the Sabbath such labors are imposed upon them, and they lay themselves open to great cruelties, if they refuse to work on account of the Sabbath.

D. Legal Restrictions

1. A Jew may not testify in court; therefore a case of a Jew against a Mussulman is lost from the start. Consequently, in cases of dispute, the Jew must be satisfied to do what the Mussulman demands.

2. As a Jew cannot intrust his case against a Mohammedan to a Jewish counsel, he is obliged either to conduct his own case, or to engage a Mohammedan lawyer, or to lose on account of not being represented in court at all. No Jew may act as counsel for a Mohammedan.

3. Moreover, it is in the power of the Mohammedans to bring suit against a Jew and to have him convicted and severely sentenced by false testimony; and even if hundreds of Jews are ready to swear to the innocence of their coreligionist not one of them would be allowed to testify.

4. If a Jew is murdered by a Mohammedan, it is considered a sufficient punishment if the murderer pays a sum equal to about 1000 marks ($250). No other punishment awaits the slayer. He is simply imprisoned until his blood is paid, and the authorities pocket the larger part of the amount, while the family of the victim gets only a trifling sum. Often the murderer goes entirely free. A Moorish saying is: You may murder with impunity up to seven Jews.

5. The mere charge of religious desecration is punished by death; the charge of immoral intercourse with a Mohammedan woman, even if she be a prostitute, is punished by unlimited imprisonment; and it is permitted to beat the accused until he confesses; if, thus tortured, he confesses, or if Mohammedan witnesses testify against him, he is punished by death.

6. A Jew who is condemned to imprisonment or corporal punishment must pay the fee of all officials who are employed in this punishment, and if unable to do so he must, after he has served his term, remain in prison until this money is paid.

7. In prisons Jews are not kept in the ordinary prison cells, but in moist, underground holes.

8. If it should occur to a Mohammedan to maintain that a Jew has sworn off his faith, the Jew must become a Mohammedan, and if this Jew is found later to live according to the Jewish ritual, death by stoning or by fire awaits him.

E. Other Political and Social Restrictions

1. Jews are not allowed to follow liberal professions.

2. They are not permitted to bear arms; when they travel, therefore, they are exposed to robbery and murder without being able to defend themselves or their property.

3. Jews must pay a head tax to be dispensed from military service; when paying this money, they have to suffer all manner of humiliations. The most frequent one is that they are struck on the head.

4. Jews cannot hold any official or public position. (Some exceptions to this have occurred, without this, however, aiding the bulk of the Jews.)

III.   Origin of the Galveston Movement, By Jacob H. Schiff, October 25, 1906

October 25, 1906

Dear Mr. Zangwill:

I had a conference yesterday with Messrs. Cyrus Sulzberger, Oscar Straus, and Professor [Morris] Loeb upon the project about which we have been recently corresponding, and we had reached the conclusion that the [Industrial] Removal Office at New York, with the experience and connections it has already secured, would be well in position to undertake the carrying out of my project, as far as the labor on this side is concerned.

With this in view, it is proposed that the Removal Office create an organization at New Orleans or Galveston, not both, to receive arriving immigrants and at once forward them to their destination, which latter is to be previously arranged for through the New York organization of the Removal Office. To accomplish this properly, it is thought that the Removal Office should have sixty days' previous notice of the initial embarkation of emigrants for New Orleans or Galveston, and that the first shipment should not exceed 500 persons.

It would be left to the ITO, allied in this, as I hope, with Dr. Paul Nathan's Hilfsverein to father the movement in Russia, to gather the proposed emigrants, to arrange steamship routes, etc., and for any expense attached to this the funds would have to be found in Europe. On the other hand, I shall undertake to place at the disposal of the Removal Office the $500,000 which it is my intention to devote to the initiation of the project. Based upon the cost per head of carrying on the present removal work, which is steadily going forward, half a million dollars should suffice to place from 20,000 to 25,000 people in the American "Hinterland," and I believe, with the successful settlement of such a number, others would readily follow of their own accord, and that then a steady stream of immigration will flow through New Orleans and Galveston into the territory between the Mississippi River on the east, the Pacific Ocean on the west, the Gulf on the south and the Canadian Dominion on the north.

This project is now to a great extent in your own and your friends' hands, and I shall look forward with deep interest to see what can be done with it. . . .
Faithfully yours,
Jacob H. Schiff

PART IV

The East European Period, 1852–1924

The East European Jews who poured into America in the late nineteenth century came from Poland, Russia, Galicia, eastern Hungary, Rumania, and the Balkans. They had been arriving one by one since the 1650s. Asser Levy, the best known of the twenty-three refugees who landed in Stuyvesant's New Amsterdam, was the son of a Lithuanian Jew. They never stopped coming; by the 1870s there were at least two dozen "Russian" prayer bethels in New York City alone. By the time the exclusionary Immigration Act of 1924 had been passed by a panicky Congress, more than 2,000,000 East European Jews had landed on these shores. Though some achieved entry into the learned professions, many were to become proletarians, mechanics, petty tradesmen, or workers in the apparel factories. After forty years of wandering in the wilderness of unions and strikes the men and women who labored in the garment industry finally succeeded in creating four viable Jewish apparel unions. While papa bent over the sewing machine to sustain his brood, he encouraged each of the children to stay in school, to become *somebody*. His children shared his views; they were eager to rise in the economic and social scale; they were determined not to remain proletarians.

The year 1926 saw the publication of the first *Who's Who in American Jewry*. It included more than 3,000 bios of Jewish businessmen, lawyers, doctors, engineers, and a host of other professionals. Most of them were native East Europeans or the children of the new émigrés; they had all made their way into the middle-middle or upper-middle class; they were a successful lot. As the twenty-first century came shining over the distant horizon the descendants of these newcomers dominated American Jewry; they have imposed their nostalgically tinted way of life on Conservatism and neo-Reform.

34

JEWS AND THEIR VARIANT VIEWS
IN MATTERS POLITICAL
1906–1911

Rose Harriet Phelps Stokes (1879–1933) has been called a proletarian Cinderella. Even as a child of four, this Polish-born youngster had to help her mother make a living; she sewed bows on ladies slippers. No wonder she was concerned with the woes of the laboring
classes. When still very young she became a cigar maker in Cleveland. After the family moved to New York, to the Bronx, Rose succeeded in becoming an assistant editor of the Orthodox *Yiddishes Tageblatt*, the *Jewish
Daily News*, the oldest of all the Yiddish dailies. In 1905 she married an
aristocrat, James Graham Phelps Stokes, a Socialist. About a year later, in
1906, Rose wrote an article on the condition of American working
women. It appeared in the *Annals of the American Academy of Political and
Social Science*. Excerpts from it reflect her class-conscious Socialist approach
(selection I). In later years, after the Bolsheviks came to power in Russia,
Mrs. Stokes turned to Communism and barely escaped imprisonment for
her political views; she opposed America's entry into World War I and
thus came into conflict with the wartime Espionage Act. Though she had
but little formal schooling, Rose Stokes was to become a cultured woman,
a publicist, a poet, a painter. Her husband divorced her in 1925, and she
died of cancer in 1933 in a hospital in Frankfurt, Germany. Though not an
outstanding intellectual like the anarchist, Emma Goldman, she was a
gifted and courageous woman.

By 1911 most American Jews were probably immigrants of "Russian"
origin. When American Jewish citizens visited the Czarist empire, they
were subjected to disabilities, for Article I of the Russian-American treaty
of 1832 stipulated that American citizens in Russia had to submit to the
"laws and ordinances prevailing" in that land. Jews in the empire were

second-class citizens; accordingly all Jews who visited that country were automatically denied equality. American Jewish citizens of Russian birth who visited their families had experienced disabilities ever since the 1860s; on the whole, the American Secretaries of State and the American diplomatic representatives in St. Petersburg did not recommend breaking with the Russians over this issue. For more than a decade some American Jews and their political allies had been insisting that the treaty be denounced; by 1911 Jewry here moved forward vigorously. A group of notables met with President William Howard Taft on February 15 that year. The president initially refused to take radical action—he did not want to terminate the treaty—it would accomplish nothing, he insisted, and such action would merely make it more difficult to sell American goods in Russia. The president's statement disturbed the Jews who were meeting with him. As citizens they wanted their American passports to be recognized and respected. On February 20, Jacob H. Schiff, a banker who had participated in the White House Conference five days earlier, wrote Taft and chided him. Powerful bankers and Republican Party supporters like Schiff, the head of Kuhn, Loeb & Company, were not daunted even by presidents. Schiff's letter is selection II. On December 4, 1911, a representative from Manhattan presented a resolution in the House asking for the termination of the Treaty of 1832; it passed almost unanimously. Knowing it would also pass the Senate, Taft hastened to announce that he would terminate the treaty as of January 1, 1913. American Jewry had scored a victory not only because of its vigorous protests, but because the American people wanted their passports to be honored. Christian religionists here—both Catholics and Protestants—had no close ties to the Russian Orthodox Church, while most Americans were shocked by Russia's murderous attacks on Jews since the 1880s.

I. The Condition of Working Women, from the Working Woman's Viewpoint, By Rose H. Phelps Stokes, New York City, 1906

The topic, "The Condition of the Working Woman," itself suggests forcibly the chief evil which working women have to face. . . .

It must be perceived by even the casual observer that working women, as a rule, are permitted to retain but a portion of the value of what they produce; that they add more value to the material upon which they work than they receive in payment for their labor; that the average working woman produces, on the whole, more than she consumes, and that the excess is consumed by those who produce insufficient for their own maintenance, and who would probably resent being called working women; yet who are thus as dependent as any pauper is upon the labor of others. In other words, much of the hardship of the working classes is consequent upon the fact that they are obliged not merely to support their own families, but to contribute, whether they will or not, to the support of other families which live in idle luxury upon the products of working people's toil. It is the nearly universal recognition of this fact among the working people of our country that leads more than all else to strikes and industrial disturbances, to ill-will, to class hatred, and to that craving for larger justice which underlies the socialistic program. . . .

An enormous majority of working women live and labor under conditions inimical to health and happiness. Nearly one-third of the deaths among working women between the ages of twenty and forty-five occur from tuberculosis alone, and these deaths are due almost always to needlessly bad conditions of tenements and shops. The bad conditions are maintained, usually, by people of the employing and propertied classes, who prefer to continue them rather than suffer such slight curtailment of revenue as improvement might cause. . . .

Throughout the length and breadth of our land the terrible question faces our people: Shall the health and lives of our workers continue to be jeopardized and sacrificed to swell the income of the few?

The working girl does not object to the accumulation of wealth when accumulation harms no one; but her soul cries out in revolt against the callousness and heedlessness of those who in their mad greed for gain ignore the conditions under which the gain is produced. She sees herself and her sisters struggling ten or twelve or fourteen hours a day under conditions destructive to health and to progress, in order that the incomes of employers and their families may be large enough to sustain them in luxurious living. She and her working sisters see the daughters of their employers lead idle and self-indulgent lives upon profits wrung from the health and strength, and often from the virtue of those who must ignore industrial injustice or starve. "By what right," she cries, "whether divine or human, am I and my sisters compelled to exhaust body and soul that other human beings may be idle and wasteful, and even destroy their own souls in vicious and thoughtless living?"

The working woman sees the women of the employing class mock the teachings of their great religious leader [the biblical Moses] by manifesting everywhere, contrary to His injunctions, pride, vain glory, and hypocrisy. Instead of "remembering the Sabbath day to keep it holy" [Exodus 20:8] they choose that day of all others to "make broad their phylacteries and enlarge the borders of their garments" [Matthew 23:5], and to ignore His injunctions to humility and consideration of one's fellows. [It is interesting and ironic here to note that she does not hesitate to cite a New Testament passage which severely criticizes Jewish religious leaders.]

"Love thy neighbor as thyself" [Leviticus 19:18] sounds hollow and derisive to the working girl, who on the Sabbath day, and many other days, sees wealth and fashion "pass by on the other side" in all their show and glitter, while the victims of greed and oppression lie sick and poverty stricken in tenements close by.

As to the subject of religion, it is difficult for the working girl to rely upon its teachings, when on every hand she sees the wicked, the dishonorable and the covetous in high places, and the majority of honest workers abased, and compelled by circumstances beyond their control to toil and suffer excessively; particularly is it difficult for her to respect those churches in which "uppermost seats" are bought and paid for, like so much merchandise, with money unjustly earned. The working girl who received her first Christian precepts from a hard-working mother may have a deep and abiding respect and love for Jesus and His teachings, and faith in the ultimate triumph of right, but she cannot respect that false religion miscalled Christianity, and those false teachings of its preachers, which confine themselves to blasphemously singing praises of God while repudiating the great commandment to "Love they neighbor as thyself." For there is no loving one's neighbor as one's self, says the working woman, where one's self lives in wealth and luxury and affluence while one's neighbor, like the victim in the parable, lies robbed, wounded, starved and dying on the Jericho road, priests, churchmen and pharisees seeing his affliction, but "passing by on the other side." . . .

More fellow-feeling is what the world most needs, more true sympathy, more determination to promote justice and right living, by being just and living right one's self; more readiness to subordinate one's personal desires in consideration of the needs of one's fellows, and of the underlying causes which occasion those needs; more of the sort of charity which leads the individual not merely to offer aid to those who suffer, but to search out and remove from human environments the needlessly harmful conditions and the far-reaching manifestations of human greed and injustice that usually underlie the conditions to which, in last analysis, most of the suffering is due.

II. Schiff, the Banker, Chides Taft, the President: American Jewish Citizens Experience Political Disabilities, By Jacob Schiff, February 20, 1911

Hotel Poinciana,
Palm Beach, Florida,
February 20, 1911.

Mr. President:

I desire to take the first opportunity I can find since leaving Washington to thank you for the courteous hospitality extended to me, with others, at your family luncheon table last Wednesday and to assure you of the great pleasure it was to meet Mrs. Taft and your daughter.

I wish I could say that the "Conference" which followed the luncheon, and to which you asked us, had turned out equally satisfactory. It could scarcely be termed a *Conference*, as expressed in the invitation. It was rather a call to the White House for the purpose of acquainting those who had been asked with the final conclusions you had reached concerning the Russian Passport question, and as to which your Republican Party and you personally had given such clear and positive assurances during the campaign in which you were elected to the Presidency.

The main reasons, which as you explained, led you to the conclusion that it was impractical to further act upon the pledges were:

First: That Russia's failure to live up to its obligation under the treaty of 1832 to honor the American Passport, through an application of a faith test, had though constantly protested against, been permitted to continue for so long a period of time, that it was now too late to enforce the only logical remedy, the abrogation of the treaty.

Second: That special interests had in the course of time acquired rights, and that commercial relations had become established which might be jeopardized, if existing treaties with Russia were denounced.

Third: That it was moreover feared, that in case of such action on our part, pogroms and massacres of Russian Jews, such as shocked the world in 1905, might be repeated.

As to the last horrible prospect, those at the Conference undertook to assure you, that we were ready to take the responsibility upon our own shoulders; that the Russian Government having by its cruel treatment of its Jewish subjects forced the Jew all over the world into an attitude of hostility, it was recognized by our coreligionists that in such a situation, as in war, each and every man, wherever placed, must be ready to suffer, and if need be, to sacrifice his life.

The fact that certain trade interests, notably the Harvester and Sewing machine industries we assume, might be the losers from the abrogation of the treaty under which we live with Russia, but which on her part she ignores whenever this suits her, will, I believe, be hardly accepted as a good and substantial reason for the maintenance of the treaty on our part, by the gross of the American people, who not only quickly resent insult to what our flag represents—equality for and justice to all who live under it, but desire moreover their Government to adopt a firm attitude in the defense of the rights of every American citizen. The fact that the denial of the rights by Russia has heretofore been permitted to continue without positive remedial action, except repeated protests, is hardly a good reason why at some time our long patience should not come to an end. Nor has Russia at any time heretofore ignored our treaty rights in such flagrant and insulting a manner, as she now does, when she goes so far as not to hesitate to publicly announce that an Ambassador of the United States, when he confesses the Jewish religion can not enter her dominions, except as an exceptional favor and by a special permit [Schiff had Oscar S. Straus in mind]. And this is the same Russia which during the past few days has actually threatened China, which it is true, is weak, with war, because the latter as Russia claims, is ignoring the rights of a few Russian traders, secured to them under an old treaty, which until recently, as is stated, had not been considered of any value.

I am writing this, Mr. President, while away from home without consulting with those with whom I called on you, upon your invitation last Wednesday, so that the responsibility for this communication is entirely mine. Because of this, I may repeat that I am personally overcome with a feeling of disappointment and sorrow, that from what you have said at our recent meeting, you are apparently of the opinion that no further consideration need be given the party and personal pledges which have been made.

If what is generally meant by a *Conference*, as it was expressed in the invitation, had taken place, and if in its course we should have been asked, what in face of your own conclusions, we can yet advise to be done, we would likely have repeated the suggestion we made to you some eight or nine months ago, that all negotiations through our Ambassador in St. Petersburg be terminated, and that further demands upon Russia to live up to her treaty obligations, be accompanied by the firm request, that discussions and negotiations be carried on in Washington. The Court atmosphere at the Russian Capital appears to affect our Ambassadors in a manner, which is not conducive to the most effectual representation of such interests as are involved in this controversy; and we might further have said that something might be accomplished if the high-minded attitude taken by Representative Herbert Parsons, in the questions at issue, should receive the support of the administration, instead of otherwise. It is well to add here, that Mr. Parsons has, as far as I know, consulted none of us in what he has done and was, as he has assured me, solely impelled in offering his resolution, by the mortification he had long felt, that Russia should be permitted to offer such constant insult to the American people. [On February 10, 1911, Parsons introduced a resolution asking for the termination of the 1832 Russian-American treaty].

Notwithstanding the present discouragement we have received, I have the unshakable belief that at some time public opinion, that most emphatic voice of the American People, will compel the Government to

resent the continuous insult to them which Russia has only too long been permitted to inflict by the non-observance of its treaty obligations.
Very respectfully,
Jacob H. Schiff.
To the President,
Washington, D. C.

35

THE EAST EUROPEAN JEW AS CITIZEN
1918–1924

The East Europeans—the "Russians" who fled to America in large numbers from the 1880s on—were not exempt here from anti-Jewish prejudice. This they shared with the Jewish natives. The decade of the 1920s was especially bad for all Jews here: Henry Ford spent millions attacking them; they were denied jobs and kept out of colleges as students and as instructors. At the insistence of all Jews here, the State Department protested—diplomatically, to be sure—against the persecutions of Jews in Russia and Rumania, but in 1924 Congress and the people finally decided to close the portals of America to East Europeans, Balkans, and Levantines—not only Jews, of course. Non-Nordics were not welcomed; indeed they were deemed racially inferior. Even native-born Jews and their acculturated immigrant confreres had looked with disdain on the incoming Russians, Poles, and Rumanians. These newcomers were different, uneducated, uncouth, poor, but nevertheless they were Jews; they had to be helped. Jewish leaders, early in the century, initiated a policy of dispersal to the backcountry, Americanization, vocational training, and occidentalization in religious practices. Seeking to aid the immigrants, American-born Jews were eager to help, though patronizing; there can be no doubt that they were dedicated to the task of succoring their fellow Jews both here and abroad.

The incoming East European Jews made rapid progress; they acquired culture; many became affluent; they fled from the core city ghettos on these shores. Meyer London, a native of Lithuania, went to Congress (1915). The radicals among the immigrants, socialists and anarchists, took the First Amendment seriously; they believed in freedom of speech and the press. When America turned against the Bolshevik government in

World War I, four American Jewish anarchists published handbills object-
ing to this country's intervention in Soviet Russia (1918). They were convicted of sedition and sentenced to prison; the three men were to serve
twenty years, the woman fifteen years, though later they were pardoned
and deported to Russia. Most immigrant Jews were utterly devoted to
America and its political policies. They had suffered abroad; here they felt
at home. Despite the problems they encountered, America was for them a
land of opportunity; they were willing to fight for it. Three citations document the bravery of those soldiers who were awarded Congressional Med-
als of Honor in World War I (selection I). Selection II is Abraham Kroto-
shinsky's own account of how he risked his life to save the remnants of
two battalions of New York's 308th Infantry, Seventy-seventh Division,
who were being annihilated by German artillery fire. They went into position with 679 effectives; they came out with 194.

The Immigration Act of 1924 disturbed American Jewry. The East
European émigrés, who had fled from despotic Czarist Russia, were dismayed. In their civic classes in the Jewish settlement houses they had listened starry-eyed to Jefferson's sonorous affirmation: All men are created
free and equal and they are endowed by God with the unalienable rights of
life, liberty and the pursuit of happiness. Now on May 26, 1924, in this
year of grace, the Congress had in effect passed a "racially" discriminatory
law. About six weeks later, on July 4, three of New York's Yiddish dailies
looked back to Jefferson and the Continental Congress, brooding over the
changes that had taken place since the Declaration of Independence had
first been proclaimed 148 years earlier. These papers were the Orthodox
Yiddishes Tageblatt, the liberal bourgeois Der Tog, and the Communist
Freiheit. (The Socialist Vorwaerts published no special Fourth of July editorial.) It is worth noting that on this Fourth of July, the Yiddish-lan-
guage Tageblatt and Tog both published their editorials in English; the
Freiheit in Yiddish. It was forty-three years since the pogrom victims had
first landed at Castle Garden; they were now completely Americanized;
they wanted their beloved country to be whole, just, and without blemish
(selection III).

I.   Heroes Awarded the Congressional Medal of Honor during World War I, September to October 1918

A

GUMPERTZ, SYDNEY G.

Rank and organization: First Sergeant, United States Army, Company
E, 132d Infantry, 33d Division. *Place and date:* In the Bois-de-Forges,
France, 29 September 1918. *Entered service at:* Chicago, Ill. *Birth:* San Ra-
phael, Calif. *G.O.* [General Orders] *No.:* 16, W.D. [War Department]

1919. *Citation:* When the advancing line was held up by machinegun fire, Sergeant Gumpertz left the platoon of which he was in command and started with two other soldiers through a heavy barrage toward the machinegun nest. His two companions soon became casualties from bursting shells, but Sergeant Gumpertz continued on alone in the face of direct fire from the machinegun, jumped into the nest and silenced the gun, capturing nine of the crew.

B

KAUFMAN, BENJAMIN

Rank and organization: First Sergeant, United States Army, Company K, 308th Infantry, 77th Division. *Place and date:* In the forest of Argonne, France, 4 October 1918. *Entered service* at Brooklyn, N.Y. *Birth:* Buffalo, N.Y. *G.O. No.:* 50, W.D., 1919. *Citation:* He took out a patrol for the purpose of attacking an enemy machinegun which had checked the advance of his company. Before reaching the gun he became separated from his patrol and a machinegun bullet shattered his right arm. Without hesitation he advanced on the gun alone, throwing grenades with his left hand and charging with an empty pistol, taking one prisoner and scattering the crew, bringing the gun and prisoner back to the first-aid station.

C

SAWELSON, WILLIAM

Rank and organization: Sergeant, Company M, 312th Infantry, 78th Division. *Place and date:* At Grand-pre, France, 26 October 1918. *Entered service at:* Harrison, N.J. *Birth:* Newark, N.J. *G.O. No.:* 16, W.D., 1919. *Citation:* Hearing a wounded man in a shell hole some distance away calling for water, Sergeant Sawelson, upon his own initiative, left shelter and crawled through heavy machinegun fire to where the man lay, giving him what water he had in his canteen. He then went back to his own shell hole, obtained more water, and was returning to the wounded man when he was killed by a machinegun bullet.

II. Abraham Krotoshinsky, a Polish Immigrant, Rescues the "Lost" Battalion, By Abraham Krotoshinsky, October 7–8, 1918

As I look back at it now, it all seems strange. I ran away from Russia and came to America to escape military service. I hated Russia, its government, its people, and particularly its cruel and inhuman treatment of Jews. Such a government I refused to serve.

From the small town of Plozk, now Poland, I landed in 1912 in the New World, with all the hopes and dreams of the average immigrant. I walked the streets of New York City somewhat in a daze, not understanding the language, and my mind awhirl with the greatness, the hustle, the brightness, the confusion, the things of beauty and the things of ugliness which all go to make up a great city.

Soon the newness wore away, and what was left was a comfortable, happy feeling. Here I was conscious of a freedom which I had never known in Russia. I could feel it in everything, and everything was sweet and precious to me. "This is a great land; it is my land," was the thought that beat against my head even as the big Irish cop good-humoredly watched me for the strange figure I must have presented.

I found work as a barber, which brought me into intimate contact with a great variety of people, which all the more intensified and hastened this process of Americanization. By the time of America's entrance in the war in 1917, I was an ardent patriot. I was among the first to be called to service, and this time, unlike my previous experience, I welcomed the chance.

It was with thoughts such as these that I began drilling at Camp Upton: "America has done much for us Jews. It has given us freedom and an equal chance, which is the only thing, and no more, that the Jew has ever wanted or wants. This is a tolerant and a good country." America, my adopted land, was always more precious to me than the land of my birth, in which I considered myself an alien and an outsider.

I made some good chums in the army. The men in the ranks all mixed. There was a feeling of brotherhood and comradeship. Race and color lines were broken as we tried to make life livable and pleasant.

Some weeks of training and the Seventh-seventh Division, of which I was a member, was packed into ships and sent off to Europe. Despite the vigorous routine, which included kitchen duty, drilling, and guard duty, the men had enough time to feel miserable and gloomy [during the voyage].

We sailed into Great Britain without mishap, the fear of a submarine sending us under water not having materialized. When we landed, the company's spirits revived. We were entertained, feted and dined. "War is not so bad after all," we were saying.

Shortly after, we were sent to relieve the gallant men of the Forty-second (Rainbow) Division, who were battling near the Lorraine sector. Now we were part of the war. The first night we were in the trenches we saw a gesture made by the Germans we shall never forget. Over their trenches they shot up in leisurely fashion a balloon broadcasting this message: "Good-by, Forty-second! Hello, Seventy-seventh!"

From the Lorraine sector we moved on to the Chateau Thierry front, to take part in the first real drive by an all-American army. The Americans fought courageously and "tigerishly." An idea of the fierceness of combat can be had from the fact that it was necessary for our division to seek replacement three times. The sights I saw there will be better left untold. But it hurts, no matter how hardened you may be, to see your buddie right next to you bleeding and torn. It hurts to see dead men and dead animals piled up together. As for the strictly military part of the Chateau Thierry drive, which is now history, we accomplished our purpose in that we crushed the morale of the Germans and reached our objective.

But the story which you want me to tell, I suppose, is my connection with the Lost Battalion in the Argonne Forest. I have told it time and time again, and yet people want to hear it again. I wonder why? What I did, it seems to me, was nothing heroic, nothing deserving of all this fuss, and a stunt which I carried out because I wanted to, and had the next one been as lucky as I, he too would have been able to do it.

As a matter of record, we should begin with the drive of Nov. 2, 1917 [September–November 1918] when the Americans tried to clear out the Argonne Forest, which was infested with German machine guns. The attack our army made was a concerted and brave one, but it was ably met by the machine-gun fire of the Germans. Our battalion, under Colonel [Major Charles W.] Whittlesey, followed behind the main attack, and made sure that all machine-gun nests were cleared. All of a sudden firing on the German line stopped. We thought we had the enemy running, and we followed up our advantage by crossing the German first-line trenches and settling ourselves in the second—and, by gosh, if we weren't trapped!

The Germans, by this clever ruse, had led us into their own territory, and were now busy surrounding us and opening fire upon us from the front and the back. It should be explained that in all there are three lines of trenches. Further, the Germans had inclosed us with barbed wire, so that we could not fight our way out. Added to this, our communications with headquarters were severed, and, to make matters worse, the Americans, not knowing of our plight, concentrated fire on our trenches as well as upon the German lines.

We were in the analogous situation of being attacked by all armies.

Our losses, as you can imagine, were frightful. Of the 700 men in our battalion, only 180 survived. Without food or water, with ammunition greatly reduced, our only hope remained in getting in touch with the main branch of the American division. For five days and nights man after man left the shelter of our bombarded lines and crawled out into the open, only to serve as doomed targets for the deadly fire of German marksmen.

Thirty-six men in all plunged into the open, but all were either killed or captured.

Our situation appeared and was desperate and hopeless. Despite that, we refused to surrender. One of our messengers, captured by the Germans, was blindfolded and given a note to take back to our commander. This note, written by a German captain, named Kaiser [Lieutenant H. Prinz], who formerly lived in Milwaukee [Seattle], begged our commander to "Surrender in the name of humanity." Our German friend was emphatically told to "go to Hell." [This answer is apocryphal.]

Again a request was made for volunteers. I stepped forward. Another soldier with whom they sent me out was forced to return soon after. I continued alone. I started out at daybreak, but it did not take me long to be aware that I was a target for the Germans. I ran across an open space, down a valley and up a valley into some bushes. I remember crawling, lying under bushes, digging myself into holes. Somehow or other—I don't know how to this day—I found myself at nightfall in German trenches. I saw several of them smoking cigarettes. I knew that if they knew of my visit the greetings they would have extended to me would not be any too friendly. I hid under some bushes, lying prone and acting dead. A German, who, judging from the pressure, never knew anything about a reducing diet, stepped on one of my fingers, but I kept myself from making any outcry. Later I crawled into another deserted German trench. You can imagine the thrill I got when I heard good English words spoken. No music ever sounded better. But even now I had to face the problem of first convincing them I was a friend, and second, of entering the lines as I did not know the password. I began shouting, "Hello! "Hello!" After several minutes of yelling, a scouting group of American soldiers found me and took me to headquarters, where I delivered my message, giving them the position and condition of our battalion.

"We need medical assistance and food," I told them.

Orders were immediately given to stop firing on the Americans, and I was sent ahead with a relief squad which carried medical supplies and food. When we reached our company, they were certainly surprised to see me. I have been asked, just exactly what did they do? In the first place, let me say they didn't cheer, despite what men may do in the movies under similar situations. In the war hardly anybody ever cheered. If they escaped death today, they figured they may not be so fortunate tomorrow. But to say that the boys weren't happy was also not true. Their faces lit up; there was good spirit and optimism in the air. It was a revived bunch, able to smile a little once more.

Now I had time to take stock of my disabilities. I discovered I was gassed and wounded, something to which I didn't pay attention before. I was sent to the hospital. On my return to the company, I was informed that I had been awarded the Distinguished Service Cross, which was personally presented to me by General Pershing.

The award of the Cross surprised me, but I was even more surprised by the fuss they made about me when I landed in America. I delivered that message without thinking of being a hero or anything like that. It was in the course of duty, and it was nothing more than anybody else would have done, were he in my place.

When I came back to America, Nathan Straus made it possible for me to make a reality of a life-long ambition. I had always been a Zionist, and it was one of my day-dreams to be able some day to establish myself there. Mr. Straus was kind enough to help me settle on a farm in Palestine. I married there, and it is there where my two children were born. But I didn't have enough capital to make a living from the farm, and we had to come back to America, where President Coolidge issued an executive order making me eligible for any Civil Service position. I am now working in the Post Office Department, and devoting all my extra time to promoting the work of the Jewish Veterans of the Wars of the Republic, of which organization I hold the post of Chief National Aide.

It is veterans such as we who want peace and value peace, but it is veterans such as we who will be ready to go to the aid of our country should the need arise. But pray to God that the need should never arise!

III.   Independence Day in the Ghetto, July 4, 1924

A

IS OUR FAITH TO PROVE AN ILLUSION
YIDDISHES TAGEBLATT (THE JEWISH DAILY NEWS)
BY L. L. BRIL

My Dear Uncle Sam:—

This is the Fourth of July, the glorious Independence Day, and it is fitting that an American citizen, one of your nephews, not by birth but one by choice, by adoption, should address you,

I have lately read a book by one of your most distinguished nephews, Samuel Walker McCall, one time Governor of the State of Massachusetts. This book, entitled *Patriotism of the American Jew*, contains a paragraph which on this day I very much want to impress upon your mind.

Speaking of conditions in America Governor McCall, who, alas, is no longer among the living, says:

> There is operating a program which is sordid, which is calculated, which coordinates with powerful resources. Patriotism is preached. Shamefully different is the object aimed at. It has been with brave reluctance, with a sense of civic humiliation, that I have been brought to a realization of

these facts—the nearness of menaces—thrusting on me an unmistakable national duty. . . . The time to oppose is at the outset. It may begin in ignorance, but, if its evil meaning is made clear, it can only be continued in open disregard of consequences the most deplorable.

I ask you, my dear Uncle Sam, to read these words very carefully and to ponder over them very thoughtfully.

Two great national [political] conventions have met and formulated their programs, one of which the people of this country will have to choose within a few months. I have read the documents very very closely indeed, scanning every line, not missing a word, and it has dawned upon me that we have drifted far, far away from the foundations laid down by our fathers. I doubt whether you will be able to recognize your own nephews, whether you will see in them that relationship which every American should have toward you.

Changing America! True, the old flag still waves and we still sing "My Country 'tis of Thee." But it would seem as if the old flag does not connote the same thing and that the old national anthem has assumed a new significance.

The flag was born, was woven so that its folds might protect all. It is not the flag of East or West or North or South, but the flag of East and West and North and South. "My country," did not mean the narrow country for me alone, but of all.

You will tell me, my dear Uncle Sam, that times change and with the changing times new meanings are given to the old things and the ancient symbols. This is only partly true. Fundamental principles never change for if they do, there comes an end to the whole fabric, its foundations being undermined.

I told you a moment ago that I was your nephew by choice, by adoption. With the exception of the aboriginal Indian, the only true native American, all your nephews are yours by choice. And there comes to my mind the thought of why we chose you as uncle.

We selected you, dear Uncle Sam, because we were tired of old world ideals, such as they were, of old world jealousies and hatreds, of the old world spirit of destruction. We came here because we felt that here under your guidance, there might be developed a new civilization based on the broadest humanity. Here there would be an end to the religious prejudices and racial animosities which have made of the old World a slaughterhouse. We gave more than lip-worship to you. We gave you ourselves and our children so that this country might live as an exemplar to the rest of mankind.

Is our faith to prove an illusion? Are our hopes to be dashed to the ground, shattered beyond repair?

My dear Uncle Sam, you are a wonderful man. You have accomplished so much. I pray you do not be untrue to yourself, do not be false to your great, God-inspired ideals.

I want you to be not alone materially free, physically emancipated, but spiritually free as well. Do not turn back lest your stature becomes dwarfed.

Your loyal nephew,

L. L. Bril

B

The Declaration of Independence Addressed the World
Der Tog (The Day)

Independence. That has no meaning. What our independence from Europe indicated, what we have forfeited and what we may still regain.

"This," said an American politician recently [Congressman Albert Johnson of Washington State], "is America's new Declaration of Independence." And "this" was the Johnson Immigration Bill [Immigration Act of May 26, 1924].

To such strange uses may honorable terms be put, and so far may men's concepts sink.

When the American revolutionaries issued their famous document, the Declaration of Independence, they did not mean thereby simply to assert the secession of the thirteen states as a matter of political expediency. They meant a great deal more than that. They based their action on an eternal principle. And they did not address their Declaration of Independence to England: they addressed it to the world at large.

In fact, they were not revolutionaries in that they introduced a new principle, or sought a new order of government; they were asserting ancient rights; they were rebels, rather than revolutionaries; they were citizens defending themselves.

But whether they intended it or not, they did launch a venture which was a revolution in the history of mankind—or at least promised one. The American revolution did not consist in the repudiation of English rule, and the Declaration of Independence did not refer to the British Government alone. There was a wider significance in the emergence of America. And that wider significance was dimly foreseen by the founders of this Republic.

America was to be independent of Europe not simply in government, but in ideals. Here was a state which was founded on a concept, not a state which sprang out of the interplay of races, but out of the assertion of a principle.

The European countries were the products of blind forces; they issued, unplanned and chaotic, out of the welter of the races which broke up the Roman Empire. They were born in hatreds, animosities and wars; they continued their existence in the same spirit.

But America was created for the sustaining of a principle. To be an American was to subscribe to the democratic principle. There was no question of ancestry or of social standing; there was no question of nobility or plebs. To be an American meant to live in this country and to subscribe to the principles on which the state was founded; there was no other test; there could be no other test from the nature of the ideal.

And herein America became independent. This was true independence, spiritual independence. It was independence of the idea that a Government is an ethnic instrument, that political institutions are the reflex of racial instincts, that to be a member of a certain country one had to have a certain ancestry.

This independence from the ideals of the old world America maintained with a remarkable degree of firmness for nearly a century and a half. The country was open to all men. To be an American meant only one thing: to subscribe to the ideals of the country and to obey its laws.

Thus arose the concept of Americanism—which was a distinct thing that other countries did not know. There is no such thing (in this particular sense) as Englishism or Germanism or Gallicism. Americanism meant not descent, but acceptance of an ideal.

Of course there were attempts to drive the country out of the historic and unique path—as for instance the Know-Nothing movement. But these attempts failed. The ideal stood firm. And toward the end of the nineteenth century Byrce could still write in his famous book: "The American is unique in this: that when he says he loves his country he means he loves its constitution."

And this is the independence that is threatened now, and which in the last few years has been desperately attacked and compromised. What [Congressman Albert] Johnson called "The new Declaration of independence," was actually the return to the old racial ideal of a state. Far from being a new Declaration of Independence, it was a mortal blow struck at the old one.

C

THE FOURTH OF JULY: A HOLIDAY FOR THE BURIAL OF IDEALS
THE FREIHEIT (LIBERTY)
BY P. RYLAND

Today is the Fourth of July. It is the 148th year since the Declaration of Independence was signed. It laid the foundation for an independent republic of the United States. The Declaration was a political document, emanating from a people who resisted their foreign rulers, revolted and battled until they were independent. Perhaps even more important than the political aspect of the Declaration are the principles laid down in its introduction; it maintained, for the first time, the right of all peoples to independence and republican self-rule, and this at a time when there was not a single republic in the whole world.

The entire document was written by Thomas Jefferson, the first and only radical free-speaking president the United States has ever had. The issue that made the Declaration immortal is the following: rulers receive their authority from the consent of the people who are ruled and when a government threatens the power of the people it is their right to dispense with its leaders and to introduce a new political system, built upon foundations which will best guarantee the people security and the welfare of the masses. In this same Declaration it is maintained that the people not only have the ineluctable right to change the government, but to move against the authorities with arms if the rulers refuse to abdicate peacefully. The author of the Declaration, Thomas Jefferson, worked closely with the famous radical freethinker and revolutionary of the eighteenth century, Thomas Paine. Both of them were profoundly influenced by the materialistic French views of the encyclopedists who through their work prepared the ideological foundations for the great French Revolution. A special strong influence on the authors of the Declaration of Independence was exerted by Jean Jacques Rousseau and his writings, particularly his Social Contract in which he, Rousseau, established that the ruler has the right to rule because he has derived his authority from the people. The entire compact is a voluntary one and therefore can be nullified.

When the Declaration of Independence was worked out not all battlers were ready to accept the philosophical and political beliefs of the radicals. Particularly vehement was the resistance of the Middle Atlantic colonies, from Virginia north to New York. However, because of the fact that the English government had brought in a large army, the Americans had to move fast. They had to make a decision. The result was that the conservative dissenters compromised and the Congress of the Colonies accepted the Declaration. The delegation from New York had from the very beginning objected to the Declaration; however after three days it finally signed the document.

This is all a short history of the Declaration of Independence. The next one hundred and forty-eight years after the acceptance and celebration of the Declaration is the history of how the Declaration and its principles have been put to shame and mocked. The people of the United States have driven out their foreign rulers but they have in turn accepted oppressers and bloodsuckers. These leeches assume the pose of great patriots.

They celebrate every year the Fourth of July, a holiday of independence; they are happy in the pompous speeches they make, pleased that they have buried the principles of the Declaration so deep in the earth that no resurrection will ever revive them.

36

THE NEW IMMIGRANTS—
THE EAST EUROPEANS—
ACQUIRE SECULAR CULTURE
1902–1947

Around the year 1902 Hutchins Hapgood, a reporter for the *New York Commercial Advertiser*, collected and published his impressionistic sketches of Lower East Side Jewry. Since then this work, *The Spirit of the Ghetto*, has been reprinted several times; it is a classic. In selection I, he describes the thoughtful, idealistic, radical female intellectual as he learned to know her. His friend, the socialist Abraham Cahan, a fellow reporter, was his mentor as he moved south of Fourteenth Street. Later, Cahan was to edit the Yiddish *Forward*, destined to become the greatest foreign language paper in the United States. He was not only the country's most eminent Yiddish editor but also an English litterateur of distinction. All in all Cahan was one of New York's most influential citizens.

The very year that "Hutch" collected his articles, a young native of Russia began teaching mathematics in the preparatory division of the City College of New York. This was Morris Raphael Cohen (1880–1947), a Harvard Ph.D. Ten years later he turned to his métier, philosophy, an intellectual discipline that he loved. Cohen was an unusually gifted teacher; in the course of the next thirty-five years, before he passed away, he exercised a profound influence on the students who were privileged to hear him. He became a national figure; a number of America's notable intellectuals were his friends and admirers. Selection II contains excerpts taken from a biography of this philosopher prepared by an eminent legal scholar, Dr. Milton R. Konvitz, Professor of Law at Cornell University. *Who's Who in American Jewry, 1926* offers ample evidence that literally thousands of East European Jewish citizens were successful professionals.

I.   Cultured Russian Women Émigrés,
By Hutchins Hapgood, October 1902

As we ascend in the scale of education in the Ghetto we find women who derive their culture and ideas from a double source—from Socialism and from advanced Russian ideals of literature and life. They have lost faith completely in the orthodox religion [Rabbinic Judaism], have substituted no other, know Russian better than Yiddish, read Tolstoi, Turgenef and Chekhov, and often put into practice the most radical theories of the "new woman," particularly those which say that woman should be economically independent of man. There are successful female dentists, physicians, writers, and even lawyers by the score in East Broadway who have attained financial independence through industry and intelligence. They are ambitious to a degree and often direct the careers of their husbands or force their lovers to become doctors or lawyers—the great social desiderata in the matchmaking of the Ghetto. There is more than one case on record where a girl has compelled her recalcitrant lover to learn law, medicine or dentistry, or submit to being jilted by her. An actor devoted to the stage is now on the point of leaving it to become a dentist at the command of his ambitious wife. "I always do what she tells me," he said pathetically.

The career of a certain woman now practising dentistry in the Ghetto is one of the most interesting cases, and is also quite typical. She was born of poor Jewish parents in a town near St. Petersburg, and began early to read the socialist propaganda and the Russian literature which contains so much implicit revolutionary doctrine. When she was seventeen years old she wrote a novel in Yiddish, called "Mrs. Goldna, the Usurer," in which she covertly advocated the anarchistic teachings. The title and the sub-theme of the book was directed against the usurer class among the Jews, and were mainly intended to hide from the Government her real purpose. The book was afterwards published in New York, and had a fairly wide circulation. A year or two later her imagination was irresistibly enthralled by the remarkable wave of "new woman" enthusiasm which swept over Russia in the early eighties, and resulted in so many suicides of young girls whom poverty or injustice to the Jew thwarted in their scientific and intellectual ambition. She went alone to St. Petersburg with sixty-five cents in her pocket, in order to obtain a professional education, which, after years of practical starvation, she succeeded in securing. With several degrees she came to America twelve years ago and fought out an independent professional position for herself. She believes that all women should have the means by which they may support themselves, and that marriage under these conditions would be happier than at present. Her husband is a doctor, and her idea is that they are happier than if she were a woman of the old type, "merely a wife and mother," as she put it. She maintains that no emotional interest is lost under the new regime, while many practical advantages are gained. Since she has been in America she has furthered the Socialist cause by literary sketches published in the Yiddish newspapers, altho she has been too busy to take any direct part in the movement. . . .

The woman referred to, as well as many others of the most educated class in the quarter, some of them the wives of socialists, doctors, lawyers or literary men, are strongly interesting because of their warm temperaments, and genuine, if limited, ideas about art, but most of them are lacking in grace, and sense of humor, and of proportion. They are stiff and unyielding, have little free play of imagination, little alertness of ideas, and their sense of literature is limited largely to realism. Japanese art, for instance, as any art which depends on the exquisiteness of its form, is lost on these stern realists. They no more understand the latest subtle literary consciousness than they do the interest and eloquence of a creature who makes of herself a perfect social product such as the clever French woman of history.

But the charm of sincere feeling they have; and, in an intellectual race, that feeling shapes itself into definite criticism of society. Emotionally strong and attached by Russian tradition to a rebellious doctrine, they are deeply unconventional in theory and sometimes in practice; altho the national morality of the Jewish race very definitely limits the extent to which they realize some of their ideas. The passionate feeling at the bottom of most of their "tendency" beliefs is that woman should stand on the same social basis as man, and should be weighed in the same scales. This ruling creed is held by all classes of the educated women of the Ghetto, from the poor sweat shop worker, who has recently felt the influence of Socialism, to the thoroughly trained "new woman" with her developed literary taste; and all its variations find expression in the literature of the quarter.

II. The Impact of Morris R. Cohen,
a Cultured East European Immigrant,
By Milton R. Konvitz, 1947

Several days after the death of Morris Raphael Cohen on January 28, 1947, an editorial in *The New York Times* stated that long before his death Professor Cohen had become "an almost legendary figure in American philosophy, education and the liberal tradition." His wise and scholarly works, the editorial continued, were well known not only to professional philosophers but to lawyers and judges—including [U.S.] Justices [Oliver Wendell] Holmes, [Louis D.] Brandeis and [Benjamin Nathan] Cardozo, who were his intimate friends.

Professor Cohen also had won renown as a great teacher; according to the *Times*, "Several college generations of students at the College of the City of New York knew him as a contemporary Socrates who asked ruthlessly searching questions and persisted in questioning until he evoked such answers as the rational mind could assent to." But he was a gadfly to more than his students: "He was one of the most celebrated conversationalists of intellectual circles in our time, at once ironical and genial. He was, through his students, many of them in positions of major importance in law, industry, education and government, a deep and wide influence on American life."

The editorial noted two special qualities by which one might measure the nature of Professor Cohen's philosophical temper and achievements; namely, "the wide human range of his learning and interests, and his concern for precision and intellectual rigor. . . . He insisted on the necessity and the possibility of a rational discovery of the principles implicit in human existence and experience. He was a liberal in his warm and wide sympathies and his awareness of human tragedy in our time, but he was never taken in by sentimental or fanatic cliches. He was as critical of the rigidities and the emotionalisms of the left as he was of the right." . . .

All his life Cohen maintained an active interest in social problems and social reform. Social injustices aroused his hatred and put him in a fighting mood. He never forgave [Franklin D.] Roosevelt's imposition of the embargo against the Spanish Republic. Always taking his stand for freedom of thought and inquiry, freedom of discussion and criticism, he opposed Communism and the Russian dictatorship. He did not believe that the "proletarian" dictatorship was necessary as a "temporary" expedient. "The plea that the denial of freedom is a temporary necessity is advanced by all militarists. It ignores the fact that, when suppression becomes a habit, it is not readily abandoned. . . . When the Communists tell me that I must choose between their dictatorship and Fascism, I feel that I am offered the choice between being shot and being hanged. It would be suicide for liberal civilization to accept this as exhausting the field of human possibility." . . .

A fundamental tenet of his liberalism is that an individual may never assume that he has the whole truth in his possession. Moral humility, tolerance, a belief in the scientific method, freedom of speech and inquiry—a faith in these qualities of mind and action was at the heart of his liberalism.

He did not believe in the inevitability of progress; with Justice Holmes he said that effort is one of the ways through which the inevitable comes to pass. His philosophy of liberalism was satisfied with the mere possibility of progress. But this mere possibility is all a man needs to provide the moral strength for his will, to engage in the fight for social reform. No social cause, however, will bring about universal salvation. The achievement of universal suffrage, popular education or some other end greatly desired brings in its train new disappointments. But despair is not a permanent state of the emotions; new waves of hope arise, and so human history swings between the pole of growth and the pole of decay, between the pole of hope and the pole of despair.

Cohen's liberalism stands between these poles: it is not a set of dogmas or doctrines, but a process, a temper of mind. It means an open eye for alternatives, a questioning of all "self-evident" propositions, a faith in enlightenment "yet colored with a deep humility before the vision of a world so much larger than our human hopes and thoughts"; a readiness for new risks in new situations, "in which there is no guarantee that the new will always be the good or the true, in which progress is a precarious achievement rather than an inevitability"; a liberation of "the energies of human nature by the free and fearless use of reason." . . .

Although Cohen gave up a belief in a personal God, he did not give up the Jewish "ideal of holiness that enables us to distinguish between the good and evil in men and thus saves us from the idolatrous worship of a humanity that is full of imperfections." He might have called this "ideal of holiness" by the name of God, but he did not want to cause confusion or be misunderstood. He never returned to any supernatural beliefs, but if by religion is understood what he called "the realm of ideal expression," Cohen was a religious man.

Atheists, he said, are as a rule singularly blind "to the limitations of our knowledge and to the infinite possibilities beyond us. And those who called themselves materialists appeared to me to be shutting themselves off from philosophy, wisdom and the life of the spirit, which are certainly not material things. Those of my circle who rejected religion *in toto* seemed to me to be casting away the ideals that had sustained our people through so many generations before we had fashioned guide posts to our own lives that could stand up against the sort of buffetings that the old guide posts had withstood. In this some of us lost sight of the larger view that Thomas Davidson had taught, that we have no right to break away from the past until we have appropriated all its experience and wisdom and that reverence for the past may go hand in hand with loyalty to the future, 'to the Kingdom which doth not yet appear.' "

In [the seventeenth-century Dutch-Jewish philosopher] Spinoza Cohen saw a kindred spirit and in Spinoza's writings he found most clearly developed "the rational and tolerant attitude to the values of religion" for which he had been searching. If "religion consists in humility (as a sense of infinite powers beyond our scope), charity or love (as a sense of the mystic potency in our fellow human beings), and spirituality (as a sense of the limitations of all that is merely material, actual or even attainable), then no one was more deeply religious than Spinoza." In these passages Cohen is describing not only Spinoza's religion, but also—and especially—his own. . . .

The "larger vision" of Professor Cohen, especially after his retirement from the professorship at City College, encompassed many fields of interest. His eye saw through a "dome of many-coloured glass." He was a whole man; he sought the truth and was willing to open many doors in his search. Logical analysis was one door; scientific method was another door; history and tradition also were doors; active devotion to humanitarian causes was still another door; defense of freedom was another door; a religion of humility, charity or love, and spirituality was also a door. He did not always see all doors at one and the same time. But what man does?

He always sought, however, the larger vision and more often than is given to others he had the fortune to see his "father's mansion" in its totality. Yet can one honestly say that any mortal sees this totality? No; Cohen would say, no. For there is a "Kingdom which doth not yet appear"; there are "those human values that the process of time can never adequately realize or destroy." As his teacher William James said in *A Pluralistic Universe:* "the word 'and' trails along after every sentence. Something always escapes. 'Ever not quite' had to be said of the best attempts made anywhere in the universe at attaining all-inclusiveness."

Morris Raphael Cohen did not always agree with William James, but Cohen himself could have written these sentences. He had a sense of the infinite powers beyond any man's scope. His favorite form of expression was the question; his life was a quest. He worshiped no God, yet, like young Samuel, he lived a dedicated life. In the company of Morris Raphael Cohen, Mr. Justice Holmes once said, he felt the presence of a holy man.

37

THE EAST EUROPEANS STRUGGLE TO SURVIVE
1889–1924

Jews from Russia, Poland, Galicia, Rumania, and Hungary had been coming to the United States in increasing numbers ever since the 1850s. In the 1880s the stream was to become a torrent. A study of the occupations to which these newcomers turned proves rather conclusively that there were no economic avenues where they were absent; very many, however, were artisans, petty tradesmen, or laborers in the apparel industry.

In 1893 when America's acculturated Jewish women met in Chicago and organized the National Council of Jewish Women, Julia Richman (1855–1912) addressed them. Her subject was: "Women as Wage-Workers with Special Reference to Directing Immigrants." Excerpts of this talk are reprinted in selection I.

Miss Richman's analysis of the economic state of East European Jewish women is brutally frank, if not unsympathetic. She was a competent observer; she viewed the "Russians" intelligently, dispassionately; though she was concerned, she never seemed to forget that they were for her a different breed. Richman was one of America's notable educators; she was an innovator, an Americanizer, yet a Jew who identified with her people and their cultural aspirations.

Most American Jews of Miss Richman's generation were eager to ship the new immigrants to the backcountry, to settle them in colonies or on farms—anything to keep them away from the visibility of east coast urban centers. Dozens of such agricultural colonies were established, though not a single one was truly successful or proved permanent. Plowing was not—is not—the métier of the modern Euro-American Jew. With some exceptions, the men and women who landed at Castle Garden or Ellis Island preferred urban social ghettoes to rural challenges. They did not want to be exiled to the outback—dispersed! removed!—in order that bourgeois Jews might share in the reflected glory of horny-handed toilers in the sun. Bennie Greenberg of North Dakota, a successful farmer, thought otherwise; he was convinced that tillers of the soil could do well. His letter invites analysis; he did not deny that he had had several bad years (selection II). Ultimately Greenberg, too—so it would seem—made his home in New York City.

The new immigrants stayed in the East. They knew more about economics than the multimillionaire banker Jacob H. Schiff—they knew there was no future on the farm in a day when the native Americans were leaving rural America in droves. For thirty years these Russian immigrants wandered in America's economic wilderness working in apparel factories and sweatshops; they put in long hours for relatively low wages; they rebelled and went on strike; they were almost invariably unsuccessful; they were not good unionists. Their first real success came in 1910 when, with the aid of acculturated, concerned coreligionists, the nine-week strike of the cloak makers was won. The new contract was called the Protocol of Peace (selection III); the men and women in the trade now had to work only fifty hours a week. For that day this was a victory.

It has been estimated that by 1910 over 50 percent of the foreign-born Jewish wage earners were artisans or factory hands (this seems high) and that about 33 percent were in trade. There were then many thousands of Jews who were pushcart tradesmen, petty shopkeepers, and aspiring merchants. Selection IV is a brief description of a Lithuanian Jew who came here in the 1880s and retired after World War I. The last name of this West Virginia storekeeper was Marcus. His daughter and one of his sons were to become clerks; a second son was a successful haberdasher; a third taught history in a rabbinical college.

By the time the Immigration Act of 1924 went into effect the Jewish newcomers from the Slavic and Balkan lands were surviving economically. They had established over 2,000 mutual-aid societies—mostly landsmanshaften—to insure themselves against disaster. There was crime, there were desertions, but the majority succeeded in holding their families together and maintaining a modest standard of living, one that was higher than all other East European ethnic groups. Many fathers slaved to send sons and daughters to high schools and colleges; in the next long generation these papas—and mamas, too—would rear at least a dozen Nobel Prize winners. Most immigrants remained poor, but very few were paupers.

I. New York's East European Working Women,
By Julia Richman, 1893

Who are our women wage-workers? . . . Perhaps the simplest classification on practical lines would be in general terms:

Women engaged in professional work.

Women engaged in domestic service.

Women engaged in store or factory work. . . .

And now we come to the third class, "Women engaged in store or factory work." Perhaps this class comprises more grades of work than could
be classed under any other general head.

The manager of one large dry-goods house reports to me that he em-
ploys women as buyers, forewomen, dressmakers, milliners, saleswomen,
cashiers, stock-girls, office-assistants, bundlers, operators, addressers, and
scrub-women; while a manufacturer of tin toys uses female help exclusively for painting on tin, cutting tin, packing toys, making paper boxes,
and working foot presses. There are almost as many grades of woman's
work as there are branches in every style of factory work. A word, now
and again, is all that I can say in reference to these.

Saleswomen in large establishments are, on the whole, fairly well
paid; but this avenue is closed to the immigrant, until she shall have mastered the English language to such an extent that there is no room for misunderstanding between herself and her customer.

"Figures" [models] in wholesale cloak and suit houses are well paid;
their hours are short, their work never onerous, and "between seasons"
they have little or no work to do. But, perhaps, no other class of working
women in large cities is so directly placed in the way of temptation, and
the mother who lets her daughter, particularly if she be attractive and vain,
take a position as a "figure" [a model], has need of all our prayers added to
her own to protect her girl. You, who are doing such zealous work among
working girls, try to reach this class. God help them! They have need of
you. . . .

Probably, the manufacture of clothing and cloaks gives employment
to a larger number of immigrant Jewish girls and women than does any
other single industry in New York City, and, unfortunately, many, perhaps even most, of these women are compelled to run heavy machines, in
badly lighted, worse ventilated dens [sweatshops]. The manufacturer is
only indirectly to blame for this, owing to the pernicious "middleman"
system; and let me say right here that if *"the kindest proprietor in the world is a
Jew of the better class,"* there is no employer of our Jewish working girls who
shows less kind-heartedness to his employees than these Jews of the other
class, call them middlemen, or sweaters, or what you please. They are,
with few exceptions, so hard, so harsh, so grasping, so unreasoning, and so

unreasonable, that on several occasions, in my capacity as president of a Working Girls' Club, I tried to find better paying positions for some of these girls in order to take them away from shops owned or controlled by their own fathers. I recall one case distinctly—a girl, not over fifteen, whose father runs a shop for the manufacture of ladies' wrappers—over twenty machines in two small rooms lighted by kerosene lamps, the air vile, the language not less so, the employees paid by piece-work, laboring from seven in the morning until after ten at night, and for this, the girl I refer to received three dollars a week, of which she paid her father two dollars and a half for board. I saw her growing hollow-eyed, round-shouldered, narrow-chested, with a never-ceasing pain in the back. It was not until I found a place for her in which she earned six dollars a week, working daily from 8 to 6, that her father would let her leave his shop, and then only upon her promise to pay him four dollars a week for board. . . .

Almost all the female immigrants who come to this shore, through lack of knowledge as to the means by which they can swing themselves above the discouraging conditions which face them, sink down into the moral and intellectual maelstrom of the American ghettos, becoming first household or factory drudges, and then drifting into one of three channels: that of the careless slattern, of the giddy and all-too-frequently sinful gad-about, or of the weary, discontent wife.

We must disentangle the individual from the mass. We must find a way or several ways of leading these girls, one by one, away from the shadows which envelop them, if not into the sunshine of happiness and prosperity, at least, into the softening light of content, born of pleasant surroundings, congenial occupations, and the inward satisfaction of a life well spent.

Working girls' clubs are doing a grand work, but these clubs never reach the lower strata. There must be something before and beyond the working girls' clubs, something that shall lay hold of the immigrant before she has been sucked down into the stratum of physical misery or moral oblivion, from which depths it becomes almost impossible to raise her.

In this age of materialism, in these days of close inquiry as to the "Why?" of every condition, it has been claimed that the ever-increasing proportion of unmarried women among the Jews of America is largely due to the independent position women make for themselves, first, by becoming wage-earners, and second, through the development of self-reliance brought about by societies, working girls' clubs, and kindred movements. If marriage always meant happiness, and if celibacy always meant unhappiness, to make women independent and self-reliant would be a calamity. But, in the face of much married unhappiness and so much unmarried contentment, it is hardly pessimistic to wish that there might be fewer marriages consummated until the contracting parties show more discrimination in their selection of mates.

The saddest of many sad conditions that face our poor Jewish girls is the class of husbands that is being selected for them by relatives. It is the rule, not the exception, for the father, elder brother, or some other near relative of a Jewish working girl, to save a few hundred dollars, by which means he purchases some gross, repulsive Pole or Russian as a husband for the girl. That her whole soul revolts against such a marriage, that the man betrays, even before marriage, the brutality of his nature, that he may, perhaps, have left a wife and family in Russia, all this counts for nothing. Marry him she must, and another generation of worthless Jews is the lamentable result.

I wish it distinctly understood that there is no desire on my part to disparage matrimony; indeed, happy wifehood and motherhood are to my mind the highest missions any woman can fulfill; but in leading these girls to see the horror of ill-assorted marriages, I intend to teach them to recognize the fact that many of them may never find suitable husbands; and recognizing this fact, they must fill up their lives with useful, perhaps even noble work. Should the possible husband fail to appear, their lives will not have been barren; should he come, will a girl make a less faithful wife and mother because she has been taught to be faithful in other things?

And so I could go on showing how, in every direction, the harm and the evil grow, until the day will come when charity, even with millions at her disposal, will not be able to do good. It is easier to save from drowning than to resuscitate the drowned. Disentangle the individual from the mass; create a new mass of disentangled individuals, who shall become the leading spirits in helping their benighted sisters, and with God's help, the future will redeem the present and the past.

II.   A North Dakota Farmer, By Bennie Greenberg, April 22, 1897

Benzion P.O.
Ramsey Co[unty]., N. D.

Hon. Philip Cowen: I have read in your paper [the *American Hebrew*] about the colony at Vineland [he refers to the New Jersey Alliance colony]. I cannot help them financially, but I can advise them not to accept any assistance from anybody. Just try to overcome their misfortune. I know it by my own experience. I came to North Dakota in the spring of 1888. When I left Michigan I had a couple hundred dollars, but the expense for myself and family from Michigan to North Dakota took all of it. When I landed at the depot at Devil's Lake I had $2.50 left in my pocket. I took a pre-emption claim and I started farming. The first year we had a very fine crop, but a few days before harvesting a frost, and we lost all our crop. Of course we had hard times. We were assisted with provisions to live through. The next two years we lost our crop by drought, and the year '91 we had an abundant crop, the biggest that North Dakota ever had, but the winter set in so early that we could not thresh, and I lost $1,500 of grain that rotted in the shacks. A great many of our farmers lost their crops the same way, so you can see how much we had to stand. In the winter of '91 I lost six horses and four head of horned cattle, and now I have five good horses and harness, nine head of horned cattle, and all the farm implements; that is, plows, harrows, mower and rack, two self binders, a good lumber wagon, a pair of sleighs, a good frame house 18 by 24 with additional summer kitchen, a stable, and plenty of grain and all kinds of poultry, chicken, geese and turkeys, and all I owe on it is between $250 and $300. We make a fine living, and if we had taken assistance from anybody I do not believe we would have remained on the farm. But now I hope, if we get a couple of good crops, we will be well-to-do and I own 160 acres of land free from all incumbrance.

I hope you will print my letter so people should read it and know something about farming.

We have about twenty families in our colony yet.

From a Jewish farmer of the Colony Chananel.

Bennie Greenberg.

III.   The Protocol of Peace in the Cloak, Suit, and Skirt Trade, September 2, 1910

Protocol [record] of an agreement entered into this 2nd day of September, 1910, between the Cloak, Suit & Skirt Manufacturers' Protective Association, herein called the manufacturers, and the following locals of the International Ladies' Garment Workers' Union. . . .

Whereas, differences have arisen between the manufacturers and their employees who are members of the unions with regard to various matters, which have resulted in a strike, and it is now desired by the parties hereto to terminate said strike and to arrive at an understanding with regard to the future relations between the manufacturers and their employees, it is therefore stipulated as follows:

First: So far as practicable, and by December 31st, 1910, electric power be installed for the operation of machines, and that no charge for power be made against any of the employees of the manufacturers.

Second: No charge shall be made against any employees of the manufacturers for material except in the event of the negligence or wrongful act of the employee resulting in loss or injury to the employer. . . .

Fourth: No work shall be given to or taken to employees to be performed at their homes.

Fifth: In the future there shall be no time contracts with individual shop employees, except foremen, designers and pattern graders.

Sixth: The manufacturers will discipline any member thereof proven guilty of unfair discrimination among his employees.

Seventh: Employees shall not be required to work during the ten (10) legal holidays as established by the laws of the State of New York; and no employee shall be permitted to work more than six (6) days in each week, those observing Saturday to be permitted to work Sunday in lieu thereof; all week workers to receive pay for legal holidays.

Eighth: The manufacturers will establish a regular weekly pay day and they will pay for labor in cash, and each piece worker will be paid for all work delivered as soon as his work is inspected and approved, which shall be within a reasonable time.

Ninth: All subcontracting within shops shall be abolished.

Tenth: The following schedule of the standard minimum weekly scale of wages shall be observed:

Machine cutters	$25.00
Regular cutters	25.00
Canvas cutters	12.00
Skirt cutters	21.00
Jacket pressers	21.00
Under pressers	18.00
Skirt pressers	19.00
Skirt under pressers	15.00
Part pressers	13.00
Reefer pressers	18.00
Reefer under pressers	14.00
Sample makers	22.00
Sample skirt makers	22.00
Skirt basters	14.00
Skirt finishers	10.00

Button-hole makers. Class A, a minimum of $1.20 per 100 button-holes; Class B, a minimum of 80 c per 100 button-holes.

As to piece work, the price to be paid is to be agreed upon by a committee of the employees in each shop, and their employer. The chairman of the said price committee of the employees shall act as the representative of the employees in their dealings with the employer.

The weekly hours of labor shall consist of fifty (50) hours in six (6) working days, to wit, nine hours on all days except the sixth day, which shall consist of five hours only.

Eleventh: No overtime work shall be permitted between the 15th day of November and the 15th day of January, or during the month of June and July, except upon samples.

Twelfth: No overtime work shall be permitted on Saturdays except to workers not working on Saturdays, nor on any day for more than two and one half hours, nor before 8 A.M. nor after 8:30 P.M.

Thirteenth: For overtime work all week workers shall receive double the usual pay.

Fourteenth: Each member of the manufacturers is to maintain a union shop; a "union shop" being understood to refer to a shop where union standards as to working conditions, hours of labor and rates of wages as herein stipulated prevail, and where, when hiring help, union men are preferred; it being recognized that, since there are differences in degrees of skill among those employed in the trade, employers shall have freedom of selection as between one union man and another, and shall not be confined to any list, nor bound to follow any prescribed order whatever.

It is further understood that all existing agreements and obligations of the employer, including those to present employees, shall be respected; the manufacturers, however, declare their belief in the union, and that all who desire its benefits should share in its burdens.

Fifteenth: The parties hereby establish a joint Board of Sanitary Control, to consist of seven (7) members, composed of two nominees of the manufacturers, two nominees of the unions, and three who are to represent the public; the latter to be named by Meyer London, Esq., and Julius Henry Cohen, Esq., and in the event of their inability to agree, by Louis Marshall, Esq.

Said Board is empowered to establish standards to sanitary conditions, to which the manufacturers and the unions shall be committed, and the manufacturers and the unions obligate themselves to maintain such standards to the best of their ability and to the full extent of their power.

Sixteenth: The parties hereby establish a Board of Arbitration to consist of three (3) members, composed of one nominee of the manufacturers, one nominee of the unions, and one representative of the public, the latter to be named by Meyer London, Esq., and Julius Cohen, Esq., and in the event of their inability to agree, by Louis Marshall, Esq.

To such Board shall be submitted any differences hereafter arising between the parties hereto, or between any of the members of the manufacturers and any of the members of the unions, and the decision of such Board of Arbitration shall be accepted as final and conclusive between the parties to such controversy.

Seventeenth: In the event of any dispute arising between the manufacturers and the unions, or between any members of the manufacturers and any members of the unions, the parties to this protocol agree that there be no strike or lock out concerning such matters in controversy until full opportunity shall have been given for the submission of such matters to said Board of Arbitration, and in the event of a determination of said controversies by said Board of Arbitration, only in the event of a failure to accede to the determination of said Board.

Eighteenth: The parties hereby establish a committee on grievances, consisting of four (4) members, composed as follows: two to be named by the manufacturers, and two by the unions. To said committee shall be submitted all minor grievances arising in connections with the business relations between the manufacturers and their employees. . . .

International Ladies' Garment Workers' Union.

Abraham Rosenberg, President

John A. Dyche, Gen. Secry-Treasurer.

Approved Meyer London, Atty for Union. Julius Henry Cohen, Atty for Manufacturers Assn.

IV. A Small Town Émigré Merchant, By Jacob R. Marcus, 1889–1924

By the 1890s the East European Jews were in the majority in this country. At the very latest, they had begun coming here in the eighteenth century. Haym Salomon, broker to the Office of Finance, to the consul general of France, and to the treasurer of the French Army during the days of the Revolution, was a Polack, and Mordecai M. Mordecai, who operated a whisky still in Pittsburgh before the Revolution, was a Litvak. The "Russians," as the East Europeans were called, arrived in vast numbers after the pogroms of the 1880s. I would like to describe the life of one of those "Russians" who landed at Castle Garden in 1889. He was a man whom I knew intimately, whom I loved and revered, but for personal reasons I forbear to identify him except by his first name, Aaron. He embodied within himself the quintessential history of the East European Jews who had established a community of their own in this land as early as 1852 and maintained it until the day the immigration gates were closed in 1924.

When Aaron arrived here at the age of twenty-four, he had already served the Tsar for five years as a grenadier in the Caucasus. There was no future for him in Russia. He had no secular education and was master of no craft. He was a dirt farmer, but the family had been driven off the soil, a large leased estate, by the May Laws of 1882. He turned his face westward, stopped in Hamburg long enough to trade his Yiddish patronymic for something more German, and then moved on to New York. His only capital on arrival consisted of a few rubles and a watch which he had won in the army as an expert rifleman. He was tall and strong, so he went to work as a manual laborer. He got a job as a matzo baker and wheeled bricks in a brick factory, but he had no luck. He learned to run a sewing machine only to be discharged when he sewed two left sleeves on a jacket. He was eager to make something of himself, but clearly New York was not for him.

Aaron bought a basket of notions, started out on foot, successfully eluded all the constables who tried to stop him, and peddled his way without a license to Pittsburgh. There the erstwhile farmer got himself a decent job in a machine shop owned by one George Westinghouse who made it his business to know the names of all his employees. Aaron married a Pittsburgh girl who had come from his home town in the province of Kovno, and they began to rear a family. When the panic of 1892 threw him out of his job, he turned to peddling again, ultimately making his headquarters in the Youghiogheny Valley in a village across the river from Connellsville, Pennsylvania. He made a good living peddling clothing among the Slavic miners and the coke-oven workers and was soon the proud owner of a wagon and a team. When his youngest son was born, he named the boy after his favorite horse—which was a compliment both to the horse and to the boy.

The year 1900 found him in the steel mill town of Homestead where he opened a clothing store and prospered. Every Christmas his landlord gave him a bottle of rye whiskey, and that lasted Aaron a whole year till the next bottle arrived. Driven by ambition, he moved to Pittsburgh and opened a small department store, but lost everything in the panic of 1907. Undiscouraged, he started over again, followed the Slavic millworkers to Wheeling, West Virginia, and there helped establish an Orthodox synagogue which he served as president. He was now clean shaven, an American citizen, a subscriber to the local daily and to the New York Yiddish *Morning Journal*. Ever on the search for the fortune that always seemed to elude him, he moved south into the hill country, and by 1915, the second year of World War I, had established himself in a village in central West Virginia where the mines were working full time. He was the first and the last Jew to live in Farmington, a hamlet of about 800 people.

In this isolated spot, he achieved a measure of success and a modest affluence. He helped establish an Orthodox synagog in the neighboring community of Fairmount and tried to keep a kosher home. He had a cow, a horse, a stable full of chickens, and a vegetable and flower garden. He used an old straight razor to *shecht* [slaughter] his chickens, but when he was not looking, his boys used the wood axe to decapitate the squawking hens. In moments of leisure he would call his sons about him, open up the family Bible, read a passage in Hebrew from the major prophets, and express his admiration for the social justice message of those great religious figures. Even so, he was no political or economic liberal. He had a complete and utter contempt for socialists, anarchists, and communists, and like most respectable middle-class businessmen he voted the straight Republican ticket religiously. As his daughter and three sons grew up, he realized there could be no future for them in that village where his oldest son attended the Methodist Episcopal Sunday School and played the violin in the church. He pulled up stakes, moved back to Pittsburgh, joined a right-wing Conservative congregation, and spent his declining days as an observant Jew. These are "the short and simple annals" of a Russo-Jewish American.

38

The Kehillah of New York City and the American Jewish Congress
1914–1918

The typical Jewish community has almost always been a congregation: it is a local group with common interests. Attempts had been made to unite multiple Jewish synagogs and groups ever since the late eighteenth century. Jews in New York City banded together for a time to send money to Palestine (1832); their clergy did succeed in establishing a permanent Board of Ministers (1881); a congregational union, the Association of American Orthodox Hebrew Congregations, did not long survive (1887). In an article in the September 1908 issue of the *North American Review*, the Police Commissioner of New York City, Theodore A. Bingham, said that perhaps half of the criminals his men arrested were Jews. The local Israelites denied the accusation and were successful in securing a retraction, but they were fully aware that among the 800,000 coreligionists in town there were some—too many—who were violating the law.

It was the view of the local Jewish leaders—East Europeans, "Germans," and natives alike—that an organization was needed to weld the newcomers together, to Americanize them, to strengthen their loyalty to their traditional values. These elitists set out to coopt all the organizations in town; there were literally thousands. It was their hope that union would bring power, security, moral control, and improvement. Thus the Jewish Community (Kehillah) of New York City was established in 1908–1909, under the aegis of the American Jewish Committee, one of the country's important Jewish organizations. It was hoped, too, that Kehillahs would be established in other large towns, and some were. New York's "Jewish Community" reached out in all directions; it aspired to influence almost every aspect of the immigrant's life and activity. On April 5, 1914, the governor of New York State signed the charter incorporating the Kehillah (selection I). The charter avoided stressing the intent to create a "community"; the city and the state might feel that their authority was in jeopardy. On November 8 of that year Rabbi Judah L. Magnes, chairman of the executive committee, presented his report for the year 1913–1914 (selection II). It is typical in that it revealed the many-faceted program of this ambitious organization. The Kehillah was a bold concept. It failed because immigrant Jews refused to be disciplined; they were too individualistic; they had disparate vested interests, World War I preempted their attention, and by 1922 the Kehillah was dead. Uniting Jewry has almost always been an exercise in futility unless the state intervened and imposed its will. The Kehillah movement was motivated by the desire of the East European Jewish leaders and their German sympathizers to create a structured, democratic, all-inclusive local Jewish community.

The effort to bring to birth a compact national Jewry bore some fruit: by the early 1900s the Jewish religious denominations, the social workers, the women, the antidefamation activists, the welfare associations, the culture advocates, the educators, and the Zionists were all organized nationally; but there was still no one overall institution that tied them together; there was no coordinated national American Jewish community.

The constant ill-treatment and the continuous outrages in Russia and Rumania induced many Jews here—both native and immigrants—to push for a powerful national organization that would embrace all American Jews and would have the power to influence the United States government to intervene on behalf of oppressed European Jews. In part at least, it was this desire that explains the rise of the American Jewish Committee in 1906. Then came World War I; the welfare, the very lives of millions of Jews was threatened. Because England, France, and Russia were imperiled, the United States government was in a position to exercise world hegemony; it was obvious that it would have a decisive voice in the writing of the peace treaties after the Germans and their allies were defeated. The Zionist leaders who hoped for a homeland in Palestine now linked up with the Jewish immigrant masses who were determined to improve the lot of their dear ones in Eastern Europe. These newcomers wanted real equality for Jewry in Russia and Poland. Real equality spelled out as "minority rights." It was no "equality" to go to Christian-oriented public schools or to keep shops closed on the Christian Sabbath, on Sunday. Jews wanted the right to their own schools, their own culture, their own language, their own way of life. By 1915 the Zionists and the "Russians" here had created a Congress Organization Committee to present their demands for Palestine and for minority rights in the Slavic and Balkan lands.

The American Jewish Committee at first refused to go along with the Congress; its leaders knew—and they were right—that this was in effect a revolt of the American Jewish masses against the Germans and natives; the Eastern European newcomers demanded more than autonomy; they wanted to control American Jewry through a democratically elected assembly. The issue was joined. By the autumn and winter of 1916 a compromise was hammered out; the American Jewish Committee leaders and their cohorts agreed to go along with an overall Congress. They would support the struggle for a Jewish homeland in Palestine and minority-national rights in Eastern Europe. However—and this is important—the Congress was to be but a temporary one; it was to make its report and to adjourn sine die, permanently. The American Jewish Committee—so it hoped—would then resume its leadership role. The Congress elected its representatives—there were some 400 delegates but only twenty women! —and the agreed upon program, summarized below, was adopted when the Congress met December 15-18, 1918 (selection III). At Paris and at San Remo, 1919-1920, the Zionists received what they sought; the Jews were given a home in Palestine; minority rights were imposed by the Great Powers on the new East European states . . . and speedily disregarded or rejected. The adjourned American Jewish Congress made its report in May 1920 in Philadelphia; the Congress was disbanded and, contrary to agreement, immediately reinstituted. Now the American Jewish Committee had a new rival. One overall national Jewish communal organization? Never!

I. Charter of the Kehillah (Jewish Community) of New York City, April 5, 1914

AN ACT TO INCORPORATE
THE KEHILLAH OF NEW YORK CITY.

The People of the State of New York, represented in Senate and Assembly, do enact as follows: . . .

Sec. 2. The objects of said corporation shall be, to stimulate and encourage the instruction of the Jews residing in the city of New York in the tenets of their religion and in the history, language, literature, institutions and traditions of their people; to conduct, support and maintain schools and classes for that purpose; to publish and distribute text-books, maps, charts, and illustrations to facilitate such instruction; to conduct lectures and classes in civics and other kindred subjects; to establish an educational bureau to further the foregoing purposes; to conduct religious services and support, maintain and establish temporary as well as permanent synagogues; to adjust differences among Jewish residents or organizations located in said city, whenever thereunto requested by the parties thereto, by arbitration or by means of boards of mediation and conciliation; to maintain an employment bureau; to collate and publish statistical and other information concerning the Jewish inhabitants of said city and their activities; to study and ameliorate their social, moral and economic conditions, and to cooperate with the various charitable, philanthropic, educational and religious organizations and bodies of said city for the promotion of their common welfare. . . .

II.   Rabbi Judah L. Magnes, Chairman of the Jewish Community of New York City, Presents His Annual Report, November 8, 1914

To the Members of the American Jewish Committee:
The Jewish Community (Kehillah) of New York City, the constituent of the American Jewish Committee in its Twelfth District, has the honor to report the following summary of its activities for the period since the holding of the last annual meeting of the American Jewish Committee. . . .

A.   EDUCATION

The Bureau of Education, under the direction of Dr. S. Benderly, continues to demonstrate its unique value for the community, and is making its influence increasingly felt. It has a Department of Investigation, Collection, and Attendance, a Text-Book Department, and an Extension Department. It conducts three preparatory schools, supervises institutional schools and its affiliated Talmud Torahs, and co-operates in the training of teachers with the Teachers' Institute of the Jewish Theological Seminary. During the past year the Bureau has aroused the interest of hundreds of Jewish high school girls in matters Jewish; these girls have been organized, and many of them are fitting themselves to become teachers of Jewish subjects, meantime making themselves helpful to the Bureau in a variety of ways. As a result of a tour made by a representative of the Bureau of Education, the Bureau is in touch with Jewish schools in forty cities in different parts of the country. These schools turn to the Bureau for text-books, methods, and advice.

B.   RELIGIOUS ORGANIZATION

1. *Vaad Horabbonim, Board of Rabbis.* At the last convention it was resolved to make this Board independent of the Kehillah, in the belief that the organization of the Orthodox section of the community would be facilitated by such action.
2. *Provisional Synagogues.* Three provisional synagogues were conducted over the recent holidays under the auspices of the Kehillah. [Temporary synagogs were established during the High Holy Days.]

3. *Ghet* (Jewish Divorce). A joint committee of the Kehillah, the Board of Rabbis, and of the National Desertion Bureau has considered the legal problems connected with the issuance of the Jewish divorce, and is endeavoring to work out a method whereby the rabbis may issue the decree of divorce without violating the law of the country. [Some Orthodox Jews failed to get a civil divorce after securing a religious divorce; others remarried without a civil ceremony after receiving a religious divorce.]

4. *Milah (Circumcision).* It is planned to constitute a board of physicians and rabbis which should certificate competent mohelim [circumcisers], in order that Jewish children may be safeguarded from the dangers of unhygienic treatment.

5. *Mikwehs (Ritual Baths).* Investigations of a number of mikwehs has shown them to be a menace to the public health owing to lack of proper sanitary arrangements. The Kehillah has enlisted a number of sanitarians and rabbis to co-operate with the Department of Health as an advisory committee.

6. *Sabbath and Holiday Observance.* Difficulties are constantly arising in connection with Sabbath observance because Sabbath observers are not permitted to carry on their business on Sunday. It has hitherto been impossible to secure the passage of a much-needed law to this effect.

The usual efforts have been made to secure leave of absence from Federal and City Departments, public service corporations, etc., for Jewish employees over the High Holidays. Correspondence has been had with various colleges and universities in order to have due note taken of the dates of Jewish holidays when examinations are set.

C. SOCIAL AND PHILANTHROPIC WORK

1. *Committee on Philanthropic Research.* The Kehillah is endeavoring to constitute a Committee on Philanthropic Research, which is to serve as a laboratory for the study of philanthropic needs, and for the assembling of such authoritative information as would both prevent the founding of unnecessary institutions and would show what philanthropic needs were at the present time not dealt with. A careful consideration of the merits of a federation of charities would be well within the scope of this Committee. [This federation was established in 1917.]

2. *Industrial Relations.* A Committee on Industrial Relations has been established within the Kehillah, which has two representatives, Dr. Paul Abelson and Dr. Leo Mannheimer, at work. A new trade agreement has been arranged in the fur industry, guaranteeing peace for the next two years and a half. A representative of the Kehillah has acted as Chairman of the Furriers' Conference Committee for the past two years. A tentative agreement has been drawn up in the men's and youths' clothing trade for a period of one year, which provides that the terms of a permanent collec-

tive agreement shall be worked out in the course of the year, and that in the meantime all matters in dispute shall be brought before the Clothing Trades Commission for adjustment.

3. *Employment Bureau.* The Employment Bureau handled 4599 individual cases during the year, for whom 4260 positions were found. The Bureau devotes itself especially to securing employment for those who are seriously handicapped.

4. *Protection of East Side Depositors.* Immediately after the closing of several East Side banks by the State Banking Department, the Kehillah formed a Depositors' Protective Committee, to keep in touch with the State Banking Department, in order that the depositors might be guided and their interests protected.

5. *Welfare Committee.* The Welfare Committee organized in July, 1912, has accomplished large results in dealing with vice and crime on the Lower East Side. Its unremitting and intensive work has been done in cooperation with the Police Department and other city authorities.

6. *Oriental Jews.* The most urgent need of the Oriental community is a *Haham Bashi*, or Chief Rabbi. The salary of the *Haham Bashi* is to be raised by the New York Foundation, the Baron de Hirsch Fund, the Kehillah, and the Oriental Community.

7. *Good Name of Immigrant Peoples.* A committee organized by the Kehillah, which includes representatives of all of the immigrant peoples in New York City, has secured the suppression of many objectionable advertisements, moving picture films, and theatrical performances.

8. *Jewish Court of Arbitration.* At the present time innumerable petty cases are brought before the municipal courts by Jews and Jewish organizations. In order to decrease the amount of such litigation, the Kehillah is considering the establishment of a Court of Arbitration under its own auspices. It will also be the function of this Court to ensure a measure of justice for persons who have no redress before a court of law. [Such a court was established in 1920.]

Respectfully submitted

J. L. Magnes,

Chairman Executive Committee.

III. Resolutions of the American Jewish Congress, Philadelphia, December 15–18, 1918

Convening of American Jewish Congress; opened with prayer by Rabbi B. L. Levinthal, of Philadelphia; Col. Harry Cutler, chairman of Administrative Committee, calls Congress to order; Nathan Straus, chairman of Executive Committee, welcomes delegates, and outlines aims of Congress. Judge Julian W. Mack elected president of Congress by acclamation. Twelve vice-presidents elected: Louis Marshall, N.Y.C. [et al]. . . .

Resolutions adopted: (1) Extending greetings to the Jewish soldiers
and sailors of the United States and of their co-belligerents and expressing
gratitude and pride for their valor, and honor and respect for those who
fell; (2) Expressing appreciation of the British [Balfour] declaration and its
approval by the Governments of France, Italy, Greece, Serbia, and Holland, and pledging the co-operation of the Jews of America toward the realization of the aim of the declaration; (3) Expressing joy in the great victory of the forces of the United States and the Entente countries, and
congratulating the President of the United States on his exalted leadership
during the course of the war; (4) Demanding that the future of the Jews of
Roumania be surrounded with such protective measures and adequate
guarantees as will secure their rights; that all direct and implied anti-Jewish restrictions in Roumania be removed; that the Jews in Roumania be
granted the fullest political, civil, religious, and national rights, and that
the laws of naturalization be in theory and in fact the same for the Jews as
for the other inhabitants of Roumania; (5) To elect a delegation to leave
for Europe, where, in co-operation with representatives of the Jews of
other lands, it shall use its best endeavors to realize the objects of the Congress; that the delegation shall render a report to the Congress after its labors are completed; that president of the Congress summon the Congress
to receive report of delegation not later than one year after the Treaty of
Peace shall have been signed, and to transact such other business as may
come before it; that in the event the delegation requires further instruction, or new conditions arise, it may direct the president of the Congress to
summon a special session of the Congress; (6) Instructing delegation to
Europe to co-operate with the representatives of other Jewish organizations, and specifically with the World Zionist Organization, to the end
that the Peace Conference may recognize the aspirations and historic
claims of the Jewish people in regard to Palestine, and declare that, in accordance with the British Government's [Balfour] declaration, there shall
be established such political administrative and economic conditions in
Palestine as will assure, under the trusteeship of Great Britain, acting on
behalf of such League of Nations as may be formed, the development of
Palestine into a Jewish commonwealth; (7) Calling upon the American
Union of Roumanian Jews and upon the Federation of Roumanian Jews of
America to refrain from sending any commission for the purpose of working independently on behalf of the Roumanian Jews, but to work in that
respect through the executive agencies of the Congress; (8) Suggesting
that Peace Conference "insert in the Treaty of Peace as conditions precedent to the creation of the new or enlarged states, which it is proposed to
call into being," clauses expressly providing that

(a) all inhabitants of the territories of such states, including war refugees who shall return to them, "shall for all purposes be citizens thereof";

(b) for a period of ten years from the adoption of this provision no law shall be enacted restricting any former inhabitant of a state from taking up his residence in that state and thereby acquiring citizenship therein;

(c) all citizens, without distinction as to race, nationality, or creed, shall enjoy equal, civil, political, religious, and national rights and no laws shall be enacted or enforced which shall abridge such rights on account of race, nationality, or religion, or deny to any person the equal protection of the laws;

(d) the principle of minority representation shall be provided for by law;

(e) the members of the various national as well as religious bodies of the state shall be accorded autonomous management of their own communal institutions, religious, educational, charitable, or otherwise;

(f) no law shall be enacted restricting the use of any language and all existing laws declaring such prohibition are repealed, nor shall any language test be established;

(g) those who observe any other than the first day of the week as their Sabbath shall not be prohibited from pursuing their secular affairs on any day other than that which they observe; nor shall they be required to perform any acts on their Sabbath or holy days which they shall regard as a desecration thereof; (9) . . . Delegates instructed to demand citizenship and religious liberty for the Jews in Russia, Roumania, Poland, and the Balkans.

39

THE RELIGIOUS LIFE OF
THE EAST EUROPEAN IMMIGRANTS
CA. 1890–1916

By 1900 most American Jews were of East European origin; by far the largest number were Orthodox. New York City alone, in 1918, had 858 synagogs and prayer rooms; at least 800 were undeviatingly Orthodox; the liturgical pattern was "Russian." The Reformers, the elite, the affluent, could boast of but 200 congregations in all of America; the Conservatives were just beginning to find themselves; their overall organization, the United Synagogue of America, was not established until 1913.

For the Russians, the Poles, the Galicians, the Litvaks and Courlanders, the Rumanians, and the Hungarian newcomers, religion was a way of life, not a one-day interlude. Religion prescribed what was to be done—and it was done—from the moment one woke until one retired at night. There was a prescribed blessing for every occasion. When thunder boomed over a Burlington, Vermont public school, the Orthodox lads rushed to the cloak room, grabbed their caps, and recited in Hebrew: "Blessed art thou O Lord, our God, King of the Universe, whose strength and might fill the world." An Orthodox community in a city could boast of its synagogs, Hebrew schools, burial confraternities, kosher butcher shops and restaurants, male and female charities, ritual baths, and societies that read Psalms or studied rabbinic classics.

About the year 1890, Moses M. Zieve, a pious Jewish immigrant peddler, served as a volunteer preacher for a Minnesota Christian church. The brief description of this unique ministry was written by his granddaughter, Mrs. Theodore H. Gordon, of Merion Station, Pennsylvania (selection I). In 1894, some Camden, New Jersey immigrants established a combination synagog and mutual-aid burial society. Excerpts of the original Yiddish

constitution appear in selection II. Please take note of the democratic provisions in this organic instrument. In 1894, one of Jewry's eminent socialists made his home in the United States. This Russian had several names.
He seems to have been born with the name Benzion Novakhovichi, but is
best known by one of his pseudonyms: Morris W[or V]inchevsky (1856–
1932). As a socialist, a philosophic materialist, he was opposed to supernat-
uralism and religion. Winchevsky employed his talents as a poet and essayist to caricature sacred Hebrew religious documents; he wanted to emancipate Jewry from Judaism that he deemed to be an oppressive cult without
humanitarian goals. That is why he parodied the Mosaic Ten Commandments. The parody was published at Boston in 1895 in a Yiddish paper
called *The Truth* (selection III).

By the seventeenth century, European Jews had begun to publish Yiddish devotional works, primarily for women who seldom understood Hebrew. By 1852 a prominent American rabbi, Morris J. Raphall, had already
published in English a volume of translations of German petitionary prayers for women. Many European immigrant women in the United States,
especially those of the older school, were constant readers of their *tehinnot*
—supplications—in the home and the synagog. In one year alone, in
1916, the Hebrew Publishing Company of New York City published at
least three different volumes of *tehinnot*. Most of these works seemed to
have been prepared over the decades and centuries by men for the edifica-
tion of humble, unpretentious, docile Jewish wives. In all these writings
the woman is self-effacing—even self-abasing—always conscious of her
subordination to men—and this at a time when the American Congress
was about to adopt the Nineteenth Amendment granting suffrage to
women.

The supplication translated from the Yiddish in selection IV reflects
the misery of an *agunah*, an abandoned wife whose husband has disappeared without granting her a divorce. According to Jewish law, she can
never remarry as long as he is alive. Desertions were common in the New
York City Jewish community; in a period of about seven years, the Jewish
National Desertion Bureau handled 10,000 cases. The beautiful, sacrosanct, traditional Jewish home? Poverty destroys!

I.   Holy Moses, a Peddler, Brings the Jewish Gospel to the Gentiles, By Beryl B. Gordon, ca. 1890

My grandfather, Moses Menahem Zieve, came to this country in the
early 1880s from Lithuania where he had been a shochet, a ritual slaughterer. He left behind, to follow him some six years later, his wife and four
children: three boys and one girl, my mother.

After living in America for six years, he decided against pursuing his profession of shechitah. His visits to slaughtering establishments in New York, Chicago, and Los Angeles led him to the conclusion that his American coreligionists—he considered them "goyim," non-Jews by comparison with what he had known in Europe—would not or could not appreciate his meticulousness nor accept his high standards. He settled in Minneapolis and, for a livelihood, turned to peddling.

Grandfather's "territory" was the area out of Northfield, Minnesota, forty miles south of Minneapolis. When he set out on his trips he carried with him on his wagon, in addition to his goods for sale, his own utensils for preparing meals in accordance with the requirements of kashruth, ritual purity [the dietary laws]. Many week-ends he could not return to Minneapolis and spent the Sabbath in the home of a friendly farmer in Northfield. He would arrive at the farmer's house on Friday—or possibly Thursday night—in time to slaughter a chicken, do his Sabbath cooking, and make his personal preparations for the Sabbath. In the farmer's home, from sundown on Friday until dark on Saturday evening, he observed the Sabbath in the traditional manner. At twilight on Saturday a child in the family would go outside to watch for three stars and then come in to advise him: "You can smoke now, Moses."

The German immigrants who settled the area around Northfield worshipped together in a community church. For lack of funds, they had no regular preacher. On Sunday mornings, then, in this community church, my grandfather occupied the pulpit and preached to this German-speaking congregation. His language? A carefully selected non-Hebraic Yiddish. His subjects? The Torah portion of the week. And in serving this Christian community over many months, he won their gratitude—and an affectionate but reverent title. They called him "Holy Moses."

II.   A Camden, New Jersey Combination Synagog and Burial Society, 1894

INTRODUCTION

My Friend! Before you are accepted as a member of our *hevrah* [confraternity] I, as president, have the duty to acquaint you with the principles of our organization. The *hevrah* was organized for the purpose of maintaining Orthodox Judaism: to uphold the spiritual and moral values of our Jewish name, to visit the sick, to help and protect widows and orphans. A member should be helpful morally and financially to his fellow member in a friendly and brotherly way. The *hevrah* expects every member to cooperate to the best of his ability. We don't have any secret signs. We consider our words and our promises as a sign of brotherly love. Whatever takes place here must be kept secret. And, with this, I accept you and welcome you to our *hevrah*. I introduce you to our members and wish you luck.

Constitution of Congregation Sons of Israel of Camden, New Jersey

ARTICLE 1

Name and Purpose of the Hevrah

1. The name of the *hevrah* shall be: *Hevrah* Sons of Israel, Camden, N.J.

And that name can never be changed as long as there are ten good standing members, nor can it be dissolved. The *hevrah* [building] cannot be sold or moved without the consent of the seatholders.

2. The purpose of the organization is to be an Orthodox synagogue where daily services will be held. The Ashkenazi *nusach* [German version] will be followed. . . .

3. There should be a cemetery and a permanent *hevrah kaddisha* [holy society] with responsibility for caring for the dead and arranging for proper burial. . . .

ARTICLE 2

Introduction of New Candidates

1. Only candidates eighteen years and over can be accepted for membership; he must be Jewish and married in accordance with Jewish law.

2. When a member presents a candidate, he has to give his age, his address, and his occupation, and has to pay a fifty cent introductory fee.

3. The president shall then call a committee of three members and investigate the character and health of the family and bring a report to the next meeting. . . . [They want to be sure that the new family is not sick.]

5. The membership dues from applicants shall be $1.50 for those up to forty-five years of age. For those over forty-five years, the amount shall be a decision of the membership.

6. No member is entitled to any benefit during the first six months, with the exception of a cemetery plot. However, he must pay $2.00 for the first year.

ARTICLE 4

Membership Dues

1. Dues of $1.50 should be paid every three months. . . .

ARTICLE 6

Duties of the Officers

1. The president is obligated to be present at each meeting and to open the meeting promptly.

2. When a member is ill, the president is obligated to visit him once a week. He is also obligated to keep order at meetings, and to permit a member to speak on demand. . . .

5. When a member makes a suggestion that has support, the president must submit that suggestion to the membership for decision by majority vote. . . .

ARTICLE 10

Duties of the Gabbaim

1. The gabbaim [board members] must be present at every meeting and report on the synagogue income.

2. It is the duty of the gabbaim to see that there should be a quorum for the prayer services, to distribute the honors on the Sabbath and holidays, but not on the High Holy Days. . . .

ARTICLE 12

Duties of the Visiting the Sick Committee

1. During an epidemic, or in the event of a contagious disease, the president or vice-president are not obligated to visit the sick.

2. When it is necessary to stay with a sick person the entire night, the president and secretary should select two persons from the membership to stay with the sick patient from 10:00 PM until 4 o'clock in the morning; a substitute can be sent at his expense.

3. When the sick person is dying, the gabbai of the *hevrah kaddisha* should be notified immediately and he should send two men to be there until the person expires.

4. When a member dies, the members are obligated to show their last respects by following the hearse, wearing respectable clothes, until the outskirts of town. From there, the gabbai and the members of the *hevrah kaddisha* should follow the hearse to the cemetery.

ARTICLE 13

Duties of the Hevrah Kaddisha

1. The *hevrah kaddisha* must elect one gabbai on the 13th day of Kislev [December].

2. That gabbai must know which members are healthy and which are sick, and must give a report about the sick members at every regular meeting.

3. When someone dies, the gabbai must be there first, and must notify the president if he is entitled to any benefits.

4. The gabbai must see to it that the funeral is conducted according to the customs of Poland or Lithuania, and must arrange for ten members of the *hevrah kaddisha* to follow the hearse to the cemetery.

5. Pledges [gifts] made on the holiday of Shemini Atzeret and the last day of Passover belong to the *hevrah kaddisha*.

ARTICLE 14

Privileges of the Membership

. . . 3. If a member has any grievance against another member, he must not go to court before bringing it up before the *hevrah*, and the *hevrah* must try to settle it. . . .

7. When a member has Yahrzeit [anniversary prayer for the dead], he should notify the gabbai and the gabbai must provide a quorum for the prayer service.

8. Every member is obliged to buy one ticket for Rosh Hashanah and Yom Kippur [New Year and Day of Atonement services]. If he wants an honor he must purchase it. . . .

ARTICLE 15

Benefits of Membership

1. Every member in good standing has the following benefits: the right to demand visits in case of illness for himself and his family, if the president finds it necessary.

2. In case of the death of a child under the age of three the *hevrah* supplies a casket and a carriage; over the age of three an additional hearse. If a member or any of his family dies, the *hevrah* supplies a casket, two carriages, and a hearse.

3. A daughter is under her father's care [covered for insurance] until she marries; and a son until the age of eighteen. In that case all expenses are covered except shrouds.

4. The *hevrah* is obliged to provide a minyan [prayer quorum] during the shivah [week of mourning]. The secretary should select the minyan from the membership list, and if a chosen member does not come, he is fined $1.00.

5. If the amount in the treasury is over $100.00, the *hevrah* must pay $5.00 for shivah money. Also, when a member loses someone in Europe, he must be paid the $5.00.

6. The board of officers has the right to sell a plot to an outsider for a price that is satisfactory to the *hevrah*. The buyer must give security that by the end of the year he will put up a tombstone. . . .

III.   A Socialist Parodies the Ten Commandments, By Morris Winchevsky, 1895

I *I am the Lord thy god* and Mammon is my name. Heaven and earth, hear my word! Capital, I am thy soul and thy conscience. I cause starvation and I can bring gratification. I can make bitter or I can make sweet every bite you eat. I rule alone down below and up above. I can bring you peace or rivers of blood. I make the sun to rise and the snow to fall. I am the king and I am above all. Mammon is my name and money is my eternal flame.

II *Thou Shalt Have No Other Gods* . . . Don't dare to set up any other gods in my temple—it will hurt my feelings. I permit no other gods—or goddesses! A goddess makes me uneasy, especially the goddess of liberty—she is an obstacle to the enforcement of my laws, which are needed to protect us against our foes. And the goddess of equality is a troublemaker. Her place is more properly in the graveyard than in my temple! In a word, thou shalt have no other gods before me—and don't you forget it!

III *Thou Shalt Not Take My Name* . . . Never swear falsely unless by doing so you are adding to your bank account. In your business dealings you may do what the millionaires do so charmingly—tell a lie and then swear to it . . . ;

IV *Remember the Sabbath Day* . . . One day a week your employees shall do no manner of labor for you—and that includes your horse, your ox, your cow. If they protest, tell them to behave or you'll give them seven days a week rest. Get my meaning?

V *Honor Thy Father and Mother* . . . Especially if you have inherited all your gold and silver and oriental rugs from them. In this respect, the worker is luckier than you—he does not have the burden of this commandment, because after all, what does he own for which he should be thankful to his mother and father?

VI *Thou Shalt Not Murder* . . . No matter how vast your treasures, this is too heavy a sin to bear, my son. On the other hand, do not upset yourself if someone brings you the news that one of your workers has had his head split open by a machine in your factory. This is no worse than happens in a war—whether it be for gold or for revenge or even for a medal of honor.

VII *Thou Shalt Not Commit* . . . Avoid amorous interludes with women of your own kind—it interferes with your ability to augment your fortune. What do you need it for? There are many young women in the labor market who are willing to sell their talents—and some of them can dance and sing too. But don't go boasting about it all over town, lest the world begin to doubt you are the upright and Mammon-fearing citizen you're supposed to be.

VIII *Thou Shalt Not Steal* . . . Don't stoop to common thievery—it will lead to nothing but prison. And don't get involved with underworld characters—a partnership means your cut is only half. Stick to the big bankruptcies. If you play according to my rules, you'll stay out of trouble. Furthermore, you can swim in gold up to your neck if you set up trusts in the U.S. of A. Free countries let themselves be skinned alive without uttering a peep. They even help you weave the ropes to tie them up. On pain of death I command you: Don't be a petty crook!

IX *Thou Shalt Not Bear False Witness* . . . Don't bear false witness against your business associate. Don't tell tales out of school. You both have a common interest; to stand united for the status quo. But if you find yourself in court with him don't let him off easy simply because he's your friend. Don't take undue advantage of him either, if you hold the better cards, because you may both want to get together afterward and testify against the socialists who are trying to tear down my temple.

X *Thou Shalt Not Covet* . . . Do not covet your neighbor's servants, nor his mistress, nor his children. Avoid that like the plague, if you want to be the founder of new temples of Mammon. If you must covet, covet his millions, covet Vanderbilt's estates or Pinkerton's spies, covet Venezuela's oil or the tin of Bolivia. Don't waste such powerful emotions on unprofitable trivia. . . .

IV. A New Supplication for a Woman Whose Husband Has Deserted Her, 1916

God of mercy you who dwells in the high places, merciful Father who dwells in the heavens, whose eyes are always open and who takes care of all your creatures and particularly so of all human beings who have been created in your image. Pay attention also to me your servant and see my suffering. Help me, dear God, in my need and do not turn away your love from me, even as you do not deny your love to all your creatures, and even as you show mercy to all whom you have created. Your pity extends to all whom you have created; have pity also on me. Accept my prayer and answer me when I call upon you.

O Master of the World, you have said in your Holy Law that people should marry and bring children into the world. I have hearkened to your sacred call and I married according to the Law of Moses and Israel, just as you decreed. My husband did not amount to anything and he abandoned me; he disappeared and left me a widow, a deserted woman. I know, dear God, that it is you alone who unites couples. Without your holy decree no couple can be joined. It may well be that you did not consider me worthy;

perhaps it is because of my sins that I lost favor in my husband's eyes and he left me miserable and unhappy. I am now a foundering vessel adrift on the sea. There is no one to whom I can turn. I have no one to whom I can pour out the bitterness in my heart, except to you, O God, who is kind and forgiving, who is merciful and pardoning.

O God of mercy and forgiveness, God of pity and kindness, it may well be that I have sinned against you before my marriage. Perhaps after my marriage, I have not conducted myself properly as a Jewish woman should. Perhaps I have not properly observed all the commandments and the ordinances that you enjoined upon us women. Maybe I have sinned against you and against my husband, thinking evil thoughts—God forbid —and this is why you have punished me. So now I beg of you, dear merciful and gracious God, pity me, forgive my sins and turn back the heart of my husband to me. Maybe I did something to him; maybe I have not treated him with respect as a Jewish daughter ought to treat her man. O Master of the Universe, urge him to forget the evil which I have done him so that I may be acceptable in his eyes as I was when he married me and when I went under the marriage canopy. May he turn to me in love and may there be established among us, as it is written in your Holy Torah, "and they shall be one flesh"; man and woman shall be as if they were one body [Genesis 2:24]. And may there be only peace and quiet between us as long as we live.

If anyone is responsible for my misfortune, if evil men have led my husband aside from the straight road, if malicious tongues have inflamed him against me, I do not, indeed, require O Father in Heaven, that you should punish them because of this, but I do ask you to turn their hearts to good, that they no longer keep my husband from coming back to me. O Master of the World, induce him and my enemies to think no evil of me, so that I may live out my years with my husband in good fortune and in peace. Amen. Selah.

40

JEWISH EDUCATION AND CULTURE
IN THE WORLD OF
THE EAST EUROPEAN NEWCOMERS
1893–1918

The East Europeans who had been coming to the United States in considerable numbers brought with them their knowledge and love of traditional Hebrew literature, the Bible, the Talmud, and other classics. For them there could be no Judaism without—at the least—a reading knowledge of the Hebrew book of common prayer, the siddur. It was not too long (1885) before they began to modify the East European Hebrew schools for American use. By 1924, the end of the "Russian" period in American Jewish history, they had developed institutions and academies (yeshivot), schools for beginners, advanced students, adults, and would-be rabbis. The Rabbinical College of America would ultimately become Yeshiva University.

There were hundreds—more probably thousands—of privately owned heders, after-school elementary classes where Hebrew reading was taught; congregational and semicommunal schools (Talmud Torahs) began to abound. Those teachers who attended the metropolitan universities were influenced by the new pedagogical techniques. The Kehillah of New York City sponsored an innovative Bureau of Jewish Education (1910); there were several experimental private institutions of learning, and a few all-day "parochial" schools. The language of instruction in many institutions was Yiddish, but English was rapidly making its way. By 1925 the secular, Jewish Marxist lodges had begun to establish nontheistic Yiddish schools where history, ethics, and literature were taught. They were well attended. It must always be borne in mind that New York City never sheltered even a half of American Jewry; obviously there were numerous Hebrew schools in every state and territory. If there was no Hebrew school as such, there was always a "rebbi" who served as a private tutor.

In a brief autobiographical fragment, Ruth Sapinsky, the daughter of Russian Jewish immigrants, describes some of her experiences in New Albany, an Indiana city of about 20,000 inhabitants; there were only four other Jewish families in town (selection I).

Joseph Bovshover (1873–1915) was one of America's better known proletarian Yiddish poets, though by no means as popular as Morris Rosenfeld (1862–1923) whose poems describe the misery of those who labored in New York City's sweatshops. Bovshover, a Russian political leftist, came to the United States in 1891. An excellent student, he soon mastered English and within a few years of his arrival began publishing English poems in the anarchist magazine, *Liberty*. Writing under the pseudonym Basil Dahl, he wrote "The Departure," describing his emotions as he bade a last farewell to his tearful mother before departing for the New World (selection II).

Ruth Sapinsky, whom we have cited above, married a brilliant Harvard graduate, Henry Hurwitz (1886–1961). It was this man, a native of Lithuania, who in 1906—still a sophomore—helped establish the first Menorah Society. He and his associates set out to create a collegiate organization that would embrace and fuse the best in Hebraic and modern culture. Supported largely by native Americans of East European stock, the new organization took off and it became a national movement, calling itself the Intercollegiate Menorah Association (1913). In 1915 it began publishing the *Menorah Journal*, unquestionably the best Jewish periodical of its day. It emphasized the arts, history, literature, humanism. In later decades the national association started to decline; it refused to stoop in order to conquer; Hurwitz, the chancellor of the movement, far visioned but often captious, would not compromise his idealism. The rising Hillel Foundations on campus overwhelmed the Menorah societies; the Hillel houses emphasized sociability; by the 1930s the Intercollegiate Menorah Association was already in decline, a glorious failure (selection III). Did the ugly events in Germany threaten the hopes of young Jewish ecumenicals? Nazis were already parading even in this country.

In selection IV, Dr. Alexander M. Dushkin, a New York Jewish educator, describes the various East European types of Hebrew schools. In selection V, Dr. Samuel Margoshes tells us about New York City's Yiddish newspapers. These dailies, together with those in other metropolitan centers, constituted the country's largest foreign language press. The dozens of Hebrew magazines printed in this country found few readers; the masses spoke and read their beloved Yiddish. It was this tongue that tied the East European newcomers together despite bitter intraethnic prejudices. Hebrew, however, was to remain the language of ritual and religion. Indeed, there were numerous learned Hebraists in the big cities and even in smaller towns. There is reason to believe that the Yiddish-speaking newcomers west of the Hudson acculturated more speedily than those who lived in the east coast metropolitan ghettos; the backcountry Jews were numerically a minuscule group.

I. Growing Up in New Albany, Indiana, By Ruth Sapinsky, 1893–1906

By nine or ten I became somewhat more conscious of differences between my playmates and myself. None of them were Jewish. There were at the time only four or five Jewish families in the town. Only one had children about my age—the meek little rag and iron man and his booming-voiced wife, a menage decidedly out of social bounds. My cronies were flaxen-haired and blue-eyed, with names like Goodbub, Zimmerman and Beck. Their parents or grandparents had settled in New Albany several decades before to work at the skilled trades of boat building and glass making. The children attended mostly the German Lutheran and German Catholic churches. Their talk contained quite a few German expressions, since both at home and in their Sunday Schools German was spoken. I didn't understand German; my olive complexion and brown eyes and thick dark hair, I decided, bespoke a "Russian" origin; my "church" was in Louisville, and I explained to my best friends that it wasn't really called a church but a synagogue.

Anyway, it was due to my "church," I made clear to the inquisitive, that our meat was never bought at the local butcher's, that Father killed our chickens with strict regard to certain religious regulations, and our meat, "cow not pig," was delivered to us twice a week from Louisville. We never had butter and milk when meat was served at our meals, and for one whole week in the spring, I explained, to commemorate the delivery of our people from bondage in Egypt, all bread even to the tiniest crumb must disappear from our homes and we must eat of the crackly unleavened squares my schoolmates called "matches."

However, there was no explaining why we didn't celebrate Christmas, since our store in December was gay with tinsel and red bells and the show-windows crammed with Christmas gifts of all descriptions. I early learned to use considerable guile in order to show off Christmas gifts to my playmates. Luckily my December birthday (which always brought gifts from my brothers and sisters), and Hanukkah (when Mother gave each child a present), and a gaily boxed scarf or belt I regularly purloined from the store, built up for me a fairly satisfactory stockpile of "Christmas gifts."

My eagerness to celebrate Christmas came simply from a longing to be like everybody else, certainly not from any dearth of holidays in the Jewish calendar. It is tempting to dwell on them all—Purim, Pesach,

Shabuoth, Sukkoth, Hanukkah—every one with its rich emotional associations, its special food delicacies, the parties and best dresses of china silk
and flounced challis.

Through the years Mother's weekly euchre club in Louisville was her
chief social outlet. The club consisted of her relatives and friends who had
also come to America as young girls and had shared the early poverty and
struggles of their hard-working men. Now, their husbands well established in trade and most of their children grown up, they could begin to
take life easy. The card games being not at all such dressy affairs as balls
and weddings, the women wore their second-bests of wool or silk, beaded
or lace-trimmed. Their coats in winter were of black seal (real or imitation); their earrings were diamond drops, some quite huge; and they wore
breast-pins of gold, set with large or chip diamonds, each according to her
husband's economic status.

On one occasion, an early May afternoon when "The Races" at
Churchill Downs in Louisville were as pervasive and inescapable as the
weather, the euchre club adjourned to the tracks. It was before the day of
the pari-mutuels. A tout prevailed on the ladies to make up a pool of ten
dollars for a bet on a horse. The horse won and Mother received two dollars as her share of the windfall. "Think of it—to make two dollars so
easy!" she exclaimed to the family that evening. "If I had known that
horse would surely win I would have put up another dollar." . . .

Mother didn't read the *Courier-Journal* nor trouble her head with politics. Her favorite paper (and what a favorite!) was the *Yiddishe Gazetten*, a
news and literary weekly from New York. It arrived, as a rule, on Friday
morning, and I would stop any game to run indoors with the precious *Gazetten*, so eager, I knew, was Mom to see her paper, her link with the great
outside world. On Fridays she was always up at six and busy with the *Shab-
bas* cooking and baking: three fat loaves of bread with the glazing of egg-
yolk atop them, huge cinnamon coffee cakes, the Friday night *gefuellte* fish,
the Saturday chickens. By eleven o'clock (when the mail arrived) she
could leave the steamy kitchen to the hired girl, repair to the screened
side-porch and lose herself in her paper. . . .

Aunt Dvorie, a widow with five small children, was "poor relations."
Her chief respite from her cares was to come from Louisville once a fortnight to spend the afternoon, have tea with home-made hartshorn cookies
in winter and lemonade and vanilla wafers in summer, and remain for supper. Between her and Mother there would be transactions involving gifts
of money (about which Father was not supposed to know too much), gifts
of clothes (both used garments and "seconds" from the store), and saved-
up copies of the *Yiddishe Gazetten*. It was when (as often) the ignorant
hired girl had used one of the serial's precious chapters to start the fire that
Mother, speaking in English but with many vivid Yiddish expressions for

immorality and sin, would supply the missing episode. Playing not far away from the two utterly absorbed women, I would drink in great gulps of sexy romance....

When my youngest brother Lee was ten, a teacher was engaged to come over from Louisville twice a week to give both of us instruction in Hebrew. Compared with present-day methods of teaching Hebrew as a living language—a progressive course with attractive books and art materials carefully designed for various age levels—our instruction was indeed medieval. We began with the *aleph-beth*, learned to recite by rote a few prayers and blessings, and then were plunged cold into portions of the Pentateuch and Prophets!

II. A Russian Jew Recalls the Day He Left Home, By Joseph Bovshover, ca. 1896–1897

It was in March. The sun stood low;
Beneath its crimson, warmer glow
The snow hath long begun to thaw
From roofs of shingles, tile, and straw.
The pendant circles melted fast,
And winter seemed to breathe his last,
But though the winter's gloom and blast
Were almost vanished in the past,
Which made all bosoms white and glad,
Mine was depressed and chilled and sad.
For I was soon to leave my home
Resolved to distant shores to roam
In search of that which to possess
I thought was bliss and happiness.

No more to walk the scented wood
Not far from which my cradle stood,
No more to measure with fond looks
The well-beloved familiar nooks
Of house and garden, yard and street,
The friends of youth no more to meet,
To see no more the faces near
Of parents well-beloved and dear:
Alas, this thought was hard to bear.
And yet, though hard, I could not tear
My heart away from its desire
Which was to 'scape, as from a fire,
The Czar's oppressed and knouted lands
And seek the happier, freer strands.

My mother wept, my sire grew pale,
And, like a leaflet in the gale,
I shook in all my limbs with fear,
Yet checked the course of many a tear,
Partly because I would not swell
The sad news of their last farewell,
And partly, too, because I wept
Full oft before, and waking kept
Long hours at night beside their beds,
Kissing in thought their hoary heads.

At last this parting hour drew nigh.
The sun was set, and on the sky
Where the horizon's bound expands
Red streaks of clouds like blood-tugged bands
Gleamed with an awful, ominous light
And filled my bosom with affright.
Like lump of lead were both my feet;
I clenched my fists, rose from my seat,
Grasped with one hand my coat and trunk,
And with the other, like one drunk,
Embraced both parents in the gloom,
Ran to the door, and left the room.
But when the open street I'd gained,
I stopped and turned and then remained
Some moments rooted on the spot.
For by the door of our poor cot,
All heedless of the evening's chill,
I saw my mother standing still,
Surrounded by some female friends
With drooping head and wilted hands,
But pale and trembling like a reed.
Alas, alas, my heart did bleed
To see her there, so lone and lorn,
Away from her, her youngest torn.
Mine eyes grew dim, my spirits sunk.
A while I thought to dash the trunk
Against the pavement, to return
To her whose heart I knew would yearn
For me with pure, maternal love.
But strong, resistless forces drove
Me suddenly from where I stood.
I left her. Was it right and good?

III. The Menorah Movement: A Synthesis of American, Hebraic, and Judaic Culture, 1906–1918

In October, 1906, the first of the Menorah societies was organized in Harvard University. In the eleven years that have elapsed the Menorah idea took hold of the students at other institutions, and similar societies arose throughout the country. Now there is a Menorah Society in practically every college and university in the United States where there are Jewish students in any number. In January, 1913, these societies organized themselves into the Intercollegiate Menorah Association which at present includes sixty-two undergraduate societies of American colleges and universities (including three in Canada). There are also six graduate or community societies.

The aim of the Menorah movement is to study and advance Jewish culture and ideals, and to prepare university men and women for intelligent service to the community. It has adopted the Menorah, the seven-branched candelabrum, as its name and emblem, because of its symbolic connotation of Jewish enlightenment and idealism.

The Menorah societies, however, are not religious organizations. No religious qualification whatever is made for membership. Men and women of various kinds of religious belief are appealed to and brought together upon a purely intellectual basis of study and impartial discussion. It follows, therefore, that the Menorah societies are neither Reform nor Orthodox. Indeed they are not sectarian in any sense, since the membership is open to Jews and non-Jews of all beliefs. Nor are the Menorah Societies Zionistic. Zionism is naturally one of the subjects of discussion and study by the societies, but no Zionistic propaganda can be carried on by them. Not only are the Menorah societies non-sectarian, but they are non-partisan on all Jewish questions as well as on all political and religious movements.

Membership in an undergraduate society is open to all members of its college or university. The test for membership is purely intellectual and moral. The Menorah societies are neither "fraternities" nor social organizations. There is therefore no social selection whatever in their composition.

The activities of the Menorah societies are carried on in a variety of ways. Regular meetings are held for the members and others who are interested. At these meetings lectures are given by scholars or laymen, Jewish and non-Jewish, on current Jewish questions, as well as on subjects in Jewish history, literature, religion, etc., followed usually by a general discussion. Forums are conducted which are devoted to all-sided discussion of current questions, the Menorah platform being open to the expression of every point of view. Special study circles are added to the regular courses of study. As stimuli to thorough study and research, the Menorah societies conduct prize competitions. Prizes of $100 have been offered for this purpose, at Harvard by Jacob H. Schiff, at Michigan and Wisconsin by Julius Rosenwald, at the College of the City of New York by Bernard M. Baruch, at Missouri and Washington by the late M. C. Reefer, etc. The aesthetic phases of Jewish life are presented to the students in the form of plays, concerts of Jewish music, and similar forms of expression. . . .

The influence of the Menorah movement upon the Jewish college students has been marked. It has promoted the sense of noblesse oblige among Jewish university men and women through more intelligent appreciation of their heritage and ideals and it has brought about a deeper understanding and respect for them on the part of the non-Jews. It has facilitated mutual understanding and cooperation between various groups of Jewish students by providing them with a common organization and a common ideal. It has stimulated students and graduates not only to study Jewish problems but to participate in Jewish life. It has provided non-partisan forums both within the universities and without, for the broader comprehension of Jewish issues and problems, especially in their relations to the general questions of the day. Finally, it has introduced a much greater interest in Jewish studies and in the Jewish humanities at our colleges and universities, resulting in the establishment of regular courses and instructorships at an increasing number of institutions.

IV.   East European Type Hebrew Schools,
By Alexander Dushkin, 1918

THE CHEDER, THE ELEMENTARY HEBREW SCHOOL

In America the cheder degenerated. Several causes contributed to this degeneration. In the small communities of Eastern Europe, where every individual and his activities were known, there was a general unofficial control and supervision of the cheder, exerted by public opinion. Every one knew the qualifications and abilities of each teacher. The teachers were therefore men of knowledge and good character, especially in the higher Pentateuch and Talmud schools. After several years of experience, either as an apprentice to some other teacher, or in his own school, the teacher usually acquired the most essential requisites in the teaching process: patience, devotion, and a pragmatic understanding of the child mind.

But in a large community like New York, it is not possible for public opinion to pay attention to particular efforts of individual teachers. Every person, qualified or unqualified, who wished to supplement his weekly earnings by keeping school, could do so without hindrance. Today, many of the New York chedarim are taught by men who were formerly teachers in Eastern Europe. These men came to this country too late in life to make new adjustments, and they therefore continued in the only occupation which they knew in the land of their birth. The lot of these earnest, mediaeval men, zealously trying to impart unwished-for knowledge to the unwilling youngsters of the New World, is a sad one indeed. But there are many other chedarim kept by those who are less worthy. These are usually ignorant men who spend their mornings in peddling wares or in plying some trade, and who utilize their afternoons and evenings for selling the little Jewish knowledge they have to American children, at so much per session (10c.—25c. per week, for 10 or 15 minutes' instruction daily). The usual procedure is for a group of boys to gather in the home of the self-appointed "Rebbi," and to wait their turn or "next." While one pupil drawls meaninglessly the Hebrew words of the prayer book, the rest play or fight, with the full vivacity of youth.

Another cause for the degeneration of the cheder lay in the economic condition of the parents. In Eastern Europe their educational standard had been high. But in this country the new immigrants were too much occupied with their daily struggle for existence to be able to devote much of their time to the question of the religious education of their children. The educational standard of many parents consequently decreased, so that elementary Jewish education, on the plane of the dardekei [elementary] cheder, began to suffice. The ideal of many parents came to contain but three elements: (1) fluency in the mechanical reading of Hebrew prayers ("*ivri*"); (2) knowledge of the Kiddush or Sabbath Eve benediction, and the Kaddish, or prayer for the dead; (3) ability to read the portion of the Torah assigned at the Bar Mitzvah initiation ceremony, and to deliver a "confirmation speech."

In the towns of Eastern Europe, the cheder was the only educational model before the child, and therefore its equipment, management and teacher lost nothing by comparison. In New York, the congested life of the tenement made the sanitary conditions of the cheder much worse than in the communities of Europe. The equipment continued to be as primitive. Many of the chedarim are still situated in unbelievable places: above stables, at the back of stores, in cellars, in garrets, and in similar well-nigh impossible locations. When the Jewish child compares this school to the highly developed public school, Jewish education suffers greatly by the comparison. There are estimated to be over 500 of these chedarim in this city. It is not possible to survey or to supervise them. They arise without notice, and usually disappear after a brief existence. Their only announcement is the sign on the front of the house, and in many cases even that is lacking to tell of their whereabouts.

As a direct outgrowth of the conditions which caused the degeneration of the cheder, came the great number of itinerant melammedim (teachers). The entire school equipment of the itinerant teacher consisted of a worn-out prayer book securely placed under his arm. He goes from house to house, bringing the cheder *to* the child, for in aim, content and method, the home instruction which he gives, differs in no way from that of the cheder. There are hundreds of these teachers in New York City. They are either maladjusted individuals, whose earnestness must not be underrated, or mercenary disbursers of *ivri* (Hebrew reading), who are an obstacle to the progress of Jewish education in America.

THE TALMUD TORAH, THE AFTERNOON HEBREW SCHOOL

In contradistinction to the degeneration of the cheder, the Talmud Torah underwent a transformation for the better in this country. It began on the European model, as an institution for the children of the poor. But it came to be housed in special school buildings, which the school laws of the state required to be sanitary and safe. Because of its situation in congested quarters of the city, it reached many pupils, and was therefore capable of developing a system of grading and school management similar to that of the public schools. The necessity for raising communal funds for its maintenance, brought it constantly to the attention of the Jewish public. These reasons caused it to develop into an educational institution which shows the greatest promise for the development of Jewish education in this country.

The first of the Eastern European Talmud Torahs was organized in 1862 by Rev. Pesach Rosenthal, and continued for 17 years. In 1879 it was discontinued for lack of funds, but began sessions again in 1881, and two years later, March, 3, 1883, it was reorganized as the School of the *Machzike Talmud Torah* (Supporters of Talmud Torah). The school began in two rented rooms at 101 East Broadway. It then moved to 83 East Broadway, and in 1886 purchased its present building at 227 East Broadway. This building and the adjoining one were remodelled as one school building capable of accommodating 800 pupils. It was for a long time the pride of the Eastern European Jews on the East Side.

At first the language in which the business of the Board of Directors was transacted, as well as the language of instruction in the classroom, was Yiddish. In 1899 English began to replace Yiddish as the language of instruction. This movement towards the Americanization of the Talmud Torah was aided by Mr. Jacob H. Schiff, who promised to give his support to the Talmud Torah, on condition that English be substituted for Yiddish. This was done, and a building fund was started by Mr. Schiff to erect branches of the Machizke Talmud Torah throughout the city. But only one branch was created, at 68 East 7th Street. . . .

The Machzike Talmud Torah served as a model for the Talmud Torahs which followed, and is therefore typical of all other such schools prior to 1905. Its object was "to instruct poor children gratis in the Hebrew language and literature, and to give them a religious education." But besides religious education, shoes and clothing were also provided for the children of the poor. A ladies' auxiliary, Malbish Arumim ("clothes for the naked") society, was organized in connection with the Talmud Torah, for this philanthropic purpose. The Talmud Torah was maintained, "firstly, from dues of members who pay from $3.00 and upwards per year, or proportionately monthly, and secondly, from donations and charity boxes, and such other incomes as the Board of Directors decide upon." Members and donors had the privilege of admitting two or three free pupils to the school every year. Besides this privilege, special religious solicitation and benefits were given to the members in case of sickness or death. . . .

The instruction . . . was carried on daily from 4 to 8 o'clock every afternoon of the week except Fridays, also from 2 to 5 on Saturdays, and from 9 A.M. to 3 P.M. on Sundays. Besides the afternoon classes, there were "day" classes, from 9 to 12 every morning, for young children below public school age. These classes were for the purpose of teaching young children the elements of Hebrew reading and some of the prayers. In the Machzike Talmud Torah these day classes were abolished in 1902, but they still exist in some of the other Talmud Torahs.

The curriculum of the Talmud Torah during this period was as follows: "(a) reading of Hebrew, beginning from A B C up to fluent reading, in accordance with the rules of Hebrew grammar; (b) Holy Scriptures and grammar; (c) benedictions and prayers, and translation of same; (d) meaning of holidays; (e) reading of the portion of the week (in the Bible) and the haftorah (prophetic portion), according to the accentual marks and notes, also the benedictions pertaining thereto; (f) Shulchan Aruch and Orach Chayim (the standard legal code); (g) decrees [doctrines] of the Jewish faith, and Jewish history. If the board of education finds it necessary to teach Talmud also, and they have the necessary means, they may open classes for its instruction."

While the Talmud Torah began as an institution for the education of the poor only, it soon modified this policy. The following year, after its reorganization, the mashgichim (inspectors) were ordered to determine which children could afford to pay for their tuition. The payment of tuition fees were made weekly or monthly; in a few instances the fees were paid by the season. There was a wide range of prices, and each particular case was decided indpendently by the mashgichim or by the secretary of the school. In the course of time, some of the directors of the institution began to send their own children as pupils. The Talmud Torah thus lost its charitable aspect to some extent, and gradually became a communal educational institution, for all Jewish children . . .

HIGHER YESHIBAHS

Besides the elementary yeshibah, the Eastern European Jews also brought with them the original idea of the yeshibah, as a higher Talmudical academy. In 1897 "arose" the Yeshibath Yitzchak Elchanan, the Rabbi Isaac Elchanan Theological Seminary. The term "arose" is used advisedly because this school was not "organized" until much later (1908). The manner in which the school originated is very significant of the social psychology of the immigrant Orthodox Jew from Eastern Europe. "Some pious Jews found out that there were a few young men who would like to devote their entire time to sit and study (the Talmud) if someone would provide them with food. These Jews, therefore, (themselves by no means opulent)" collected among themselves $5.00 every week, and gave two of these young men $2.50 per week each, if they would sit and study. Gradually the number of young men increased, and a school "arose." Apart from the "good deed" of encouraging young men "to study the Torah for its own sake," it was also hoped that the students would prepare themselves to act as rabbis. Practically no teachers were required, since these young men had previous Talmudical training. No school house was needed, a room for this purpose being set aside in the building of the Yeshibath Etz Chayim. No supervision was necessary, except that of the lay *mashgiach* (overseer), who made sure that the young men earned their "two and a half per week," by constant application.

But as the students became more Americanized, they realized that Talmudical study alone was not sufficient preparation for even the most Orthodox rabbi in this country. They began to demand that secular studies also be provided for them. Another cause for dissatisfaction arose from the fact that the directors opened several classes for younger boys. There was misunderstanding in this institution also, as to whether its aim should be to prepare well-versed immigrant young men for the American rabbinate, or to give Talmudic training to younger children. The dissatisfaction expressed itself again and again, and culminated in a "strike" of the students in 1906. An appeal was sent by them to the Jews of New York, demanding "(1) that they learn systematically the right thing at the right time; (2) that they be given permission to learn the Hebrew language, Jewish culture, (i.e. not only Talmud) and Jewish history; (3) that the program of studies include the English language, history, and the general sciences; (4) that they be taught oratory and public speaking; and (5) that their material support be so arranged as not to make it necessary for them to make special requests for every little thing needed." This quaint appeal was signed by "all the pupils of the Yeshibah." The students threatened to leave the institution in a body, and actually carried out the threat. They removed for a short time to a little "Klaus" (private synagogue of a "chevra" or society). But an agreement was finally reached. The Yeshibath Yitzchak Elchanan was limited to higher Talmudical studies, and the Yeshibath Etz Chayim was to be only an elementary Yeshibah. The other demands of the pupils were also met. Upon the new basis the Yeshibah was "organized" in 1908. At this time it was housed at 156 Henry Street. Recently, in 1915, it combined with the Yeshibath Etz Chayim, as the Rabbinical College of America.

V. New York City's Yiddish Press, By Samuel Margoshes, 1918

The Yiddish press in New York City differs in many essentials from the other divisions of the Jewish press. First, it has the peculiar distinction of having practically created its own reading public. Very few of the people who are now readers of the Yiddish papers in New York City, had ever read any journals while on the other side of the Atlantic. As Shomer [Nahum Meir Shaikevitch, 1849–1905], the noted Yiddish novelist, created a Yiddish-reading public by the publication of his novels, so the Yiddish papers taught the East European Jew in America to read newspapers by coming out every day for his special benefit. Then, too, the readers of the Yiddish papers being newly made readers, have read very little outside, perhaps of the chumosh [Pentateuch]. The Yiddish newspaper, therefore, is their only education and their chief educative influence. Here may be found the origin of the make-up of the Yiddish paper, which is radically different from that of the English newspaper. While the English newspaper is primarily organized for the conveying of news, the Yiddish paper must also be a literary journal, printing short stories, novels, articles on popular science, theology and politics. It explains also the marvelous influence of the Yiddish press. No other press in the world exercises such a monopoly on the mental content of its readers. While, for instance, it is possible for a political candidate in New York City to get elected in the face of the strong opposition of almost the entire English press, the election of any candidate on the East Side is impossible unless the Yiddish press favors him.

As to the power of reach of the Yiddish press, the circulation statistics tell a very interesting story. These figures were given to the Post Office on October 1st, 1917, by all the Yiddish dailies:

The Day	65,369
The Forward	148,560
The Jewish Daily News	55,000
The Jewish Morning Journal	87,322
The Jewish Daily Wahrheit	50,241

This gives us 411,492 [406,492] as the total number of copies of the Yiddish papers actually sold every day in the United States. . . .

But the Yiddish dailies, though an exceedingly important part, are by no means the entire Yiddish press. Besides the five dailies, there are twenty-four other publications in New York appearing in Yiddish— weeklies and monthlies, covering a wide range of topics and appealing to a multitude of readers. The Yiddish press practically runs the entire gamut of Jewish life in New York City.

All this goes to show how great and important are the powers wielded by the Yiddish press. But it is only fair to say that the influence exerted by it for the good of the community has been proportionate to the power it wields. As an instrument for the Americanization of the masses of Jewish immigrants settled on the East Side, the Yiddish press has been invaluable. Assuming at the very beginning an American character, the Yiddish newspapers have instilled in their multitude of readers the spirit of American life, making possible the intelligent citizenship and loyal American sentiment found on the East Side. The great usefulness of the Yiddish press is demonstrated also in the conscientious vigilance over the welfare of the community and in its fostering and encouraging of Jewish institutions which carry on the charitable and educational work of the Jewish community. In addition, the Yiddish press, by serving for so many years as a common channel for information and education of the large and heterogeneous Jewish masses of New York City, created that indispensable modicum of communal apperception without which no communal activity would be possible. If we add to this fact that the Jewish newspapers have guided the Jewish masses to an understanding and appreciation of modern literary forms, we have the outstanding features of the character of the Yiddish press.

It should be remarked, however, that this exercise of power is not unattended by certain abuses. But the latter are almost unavoidable when power is wielded as omnipotently as it is in the Yiddish press. The Yiddish press has not always been able to resist successfully the temptation to allure its readers with cheap stories of "sex" interest, and its attitude towards Jewish institutions and movements as well as prominent personalities has not always been noble and righteous. Very often the editorial staffs of the Yiddish papers have not been animated by that spirit of responsibility which should be theirs. But there has come to pass in the Yiddish press an unmistakable gaining of vision both in its conception of the community as a unit and in the understanding of the character of its great responsibilities; the Yiddish press is beginning to catch the spirit for which the Jewish Community of New York [the Kehillah] is organizing itself into a firmer and more Jewish life. This spirit, it may now be hoped, the Yiddish press will eventually fully embody.

41

The East European Newcomers Help Themselves
1892–1924

In the 1870s when the Russians, Poles, Litvakim, and Rumanians started coming to the United States in numbers they were in need of help; most were desperately poor. The native Jews and the "Germans" responded, grudgingly for the most part but effectively; the various "United Hebrew Charities" supported thousands; Americanization programs were inaugurated; the larger cities saw the rise of settlement houses, Young Men's and Young Women's Hebrew Associations, neighborhood centers, trade schools. The Reform Jews, the National Council of Jewish Women, welcomed the Russian children into their Sunday schools. Many of the newcomers resented the assistance they received; equating relief with patronization, they were determined to emancipate themselves; they preached and practiced the gospel of self-help. On their own they established lodges, hospices, hospitals—with kosher kitchens—homes for convalescents, orphans, the aged. They met and assisted immigrants as they landed at the docks. No matter how little they earned, they made sacrificial gifts during World War I to the American Jewish Joint Distribution Committee; the folks at home, in Eastern Europe, had to be succored. Their favorite association was the hometown mutual-aid society —the landsmanshaft—which offered them sociability, monetary aid, sick-care, a burial lot, and even a headstone. By 1917 New York City could brag of its 2,100 Jewish mutual-aid and economic agencies.

The Linas Hazedek of Hudson County, New Jersey, was established in 1892. Originally it was a hospice but in the course of time it provided its members with almost every type of assistance. Selection I contains excerpts taken from an updated constitution published in 1976. Many of the newcomers who landed here had come from villages where the homes and

363

kitchens were very primitive. They had to be taught how to keep house. Selection II is taken from the 1903 edition of the Jewish *Settlement Cook Book*. The East Europeans, daring and innovative in their philanthropy, were among the first to develop the free loan society. Selection III—written by Samuel Seinfel—testifies to the importance and success of this self-help institution. Out on the farms these immigrants—few though they were—pioneered in establishing a loan system and credit cooperatives.

Many arriving Jewish newcomers needed help. As early as 1884—just a few years after the Russian riots and killings—a group of Eastsiders in New York City opened a hospice for immigrants. By 1902 a number of Downtown Jews had established the Hebrew Immigrant Aid Society, the HIAS, and this name still persists although the society has changed its name several times and made a series of alliances. By 1909, after taking over the old hospice, the HIAS was well on its way to becoming an important philanthropic agency; ultimately over the decades, it developed into an international society reaching as far as Japan. Its job was to aid any Jew, anywhere, if he needed a new home. Jews are always in trouble and require the help of a skilled immigration agency. The HIAS met the émigré at the port, and helped find a relative to secure employment and aid him to become a citizen. New arrivals were urged to move west, advice which reflects the opinion and the prejudices of an advisory committee of American Jewish notables. About the year 1924, Albert Rosenblatt, a vice-president of the self-help Hebrew Sheltering and Immigrant Aid Society of America, summarized its activity (selection IV).

I.   Constitution and By-Laws of the Brotherly Benevolent Association Linas Hazedeck [Hospice] of Hudson County, New Jersey, February 5, 1892–1975

DECLARATION

We, the members of the Brotherly Benevolent Association Linas Hazedeck of Hudson County, Inc., realizing the importance of the heritage of the founders of our organization and being mindful of the changing world, do hereby adopt this document as our new constitution.

PURPOSE

To hold our Jewish community together and to build good American citizenship.

To strive for a better understanding and complete brotherhood among all peoples.

To give aid and comfort to its members.

To provide burial according to Hebrew law and to provide sick and disability benefits as prescribed in this constitution.

Article I

Sec. 1. The association shall be known as "Brotherly Benevolent Association Linas Hazedeck of Hudson County, Inc." . . .

Article IV

MEMBERSHIP

Membership shall be open to any Hebrew male between the ages of eighteen and forty-five.

He must be of good moral character and, if requested, must submit to a doctor's examination.

All applications must be signed by two members.

An applicant married out of the Hebrew faith shall not be accepted.

An applicant meeting the necessary requirements shall be balloted upon at a regular meeting and, if voted on favorably, shall be initiated.

Should a member marry out of his faith, he shall be stricken from the rolls.

He shall also be stricken if he converts from the Hebrew religion.

Upon application, the applicant's wife may not be pregnant.

A brother reaching his eightieth year, or having been a member for fifty consecutive years, shall become a life member and his dues shall be waived. He shall be entitled to all other benefits.

The wife of a member, or his widow, may attend all meetings and have the right to the floor; however, she may not vote.

Article V

DUES

The lodge shall by vote levy dues.

Dues shall be $14.00 per year. . . .

Article VI

. . . Should a member of the organization be in need and apply for assistance, the Welfare Committee shall investigate and if their findings warrant a grant, they may give up to $200.00. . . .

ARTICLE X

SICK BENEFITS

A member shall be entitled to sick benefits when:
1. He shall be ill.
2. He shall be confined to a hospital or other institution.
3. He shall be chronically ill.

A member who is ill must present a doctor's certificate showing the nature of his illness and the time he was under the doctor's care.

A member confined to a hospital does not need a doctor's certificate, but if he is convalescing, a certificate must be presented.

The hospitaler must be notified in all cases of sickness so that he may report to the organization.

Sick benefits shall be in the amount of $10.00 (ten dollars) per week for a period of not more than five weeks in any six month period.

A member having received sick benefits for two consecutive years, shall be deemed chronically ill and shall not be eligible for further sick benefits.

He shall be entitled to all other benefits of the lodge and his dues shall be waived.

ARTICLE XI

FUNERAL, ENDOWMENT, AND CEMETERY

Funeral Expenses

An allowance of $100.00 (one hundred dollars) shall be paid toward the funeral expenses upon the death of a brother's child.

Under this constitution a child is one under eighteen years of age and unmarried.

Endowment

The lodge shall have the right to investigate all claims.

The sum of $500.00 (five hundred dollars) shall be paid to the legal heirs of a brother upon his death.

Cemetery

The Linas Hazedeck provides burial ground for its members and their families. . . .

RULES AND REGULATIONS GOVERNING CEMETERY PROPERTIES OF THE LINAS HAZEDECK OF HUDSON COUNTY, N.J.

As approved by the committee and the lodge, April, 1975.

The lodge will furnish a grave without cost in the following cases:

1. A deceased brother.
2. The deceased wife of a brother.
3. The deceased widow of a brother who remains unmarried.
4. The child of a brother.

In all the above cases the grave shall be in the row immediately in use and shall be subject to all other rules herein recorded.

All burials shall be according to Hebraic law.

Headstones shall be erected within one year of interment.

The lodge may at its discretion withhold from the endowment fund or ask for funds to cover the cost of a monument.

Should the brother or his wife wish to reserve the grave next to an interment, payment for such reservation shall be the amount as set forth in these rules. . . .

RULES AND REGULATIONS FOR BOTH CEMETERIES AT RIVERSIDE CEMETERY AT ROCHELLE PARK, N.J.

The price for single graves to members shall be $100.00. The price of plots shall be $100.00 per grave for members. The price of graves for non-members shall be $150.00. The price of plots for non-members shall be $150.00 per grave. . . .

II.   Instructing an Immigrant Jewish Woman How to Keep House, 1903

TO CLEAR THE TABLE AFTER A MEAL.

Brush the crumbs from the floor. Arrange the chairs in their places. Collect and remove the knives, forks and spoons. Empty the cups and remove them. Scrape off the dishes—never set any food away on the dishes used for serving—pile them up neatly and remove to the place where they are to be washed. Brush the crumbs from the cloth and fold it carefully in the old crease, as it lays on the table. If the napkins are used again, place them neatly folded in their individual rings.

WASHING DISHES.

Have a pan half filled with hot water. If dishes are very dirty or greasy, add a little washing soda or ammonia.

Washes glasses first. Slip them in sideways, one at a time, and wipe instantly.

Wash the silver and wipe at once, and it will keep bright.

Then wash the china, beginning with the cups, saucers, pitchers, and least greasy dishes, and changing the water as soon as cool or greasy.

Rinse the dishes in a pan of scalding water, take out and drain quickly. Wipe immediately.

Then wash the kitchen dishes, pots, kettles, pans, etc.

A Dover egg-beater should not be left to soak in water, or it will be hard to run. Keep the handles clean, wipe the wire with a damp cloth immediately after using.

Kitchen knives and forks should never be placed in dish water. Scour them with brick dust, wash with dish cloth, and wipe them dry.

Tinware, granite ironware should be washed in hot soda water, and if browned, rub with sapolio, salt or baking soda. Use wire dish cloth if food sticks to dishes.

Keep strainer in sink and pour all dish water, etc., in it, and remove contents of strainer in garbage pail.

Wash towels with plenty of soap, and rinse thoroughly every time they are used.

Hang towels up evenly to dry. Wash dish cloths.

Scrub dishboards with brush and sapolio, working with the grain of the wood, rinse and dry.

When scrubbing, wet brush and apply sapolio or soap with upward strokes.

Wash dish pans, wipe and dry.

Wash your hands with white (castile or ivory) soap, if you wish to keep smooth hands, and wipe them dry.

Wash teakettle.

Polish faucets.

Scrub sink with clean hot suds.

To Build a Fire.

It is necessary to have:

1st, Fuel.—Something to burn.

2nd, Heat.—To make fuel hot enough to burn.

3rd, Air.—To keep the fire burning.

To Dust a Room.

Begin at one corner and take each article in turn as you come to it. Dust it from the highest things to the lowest, taking up the dust in the cloth. Shake the duster occasionally in a suitable place, and when through, wash and hang it up to dry.

In sweeping a room, sweep from you, holding the broom close to the floor.

III.   New York City Free Loan Societies, By Samuel Seinfel, 1917

It is generally conceded that poverty and its attending miseries, while not entirely curable, are to a large extent preventible. The really deserving poor, if rendered prompt and judicious relief without the stigma of charity, are eventually restored to the ranks of self-supporting, self-respecting members of the community. To effect this result is the purpose of the Free Loan Societies. It is justly claimed that the work of these societies has been of great value and far-reaching importance in the cause of preventive and constructive relief rendered to the deserving poor.

Loans do not rob the poor man of his self-respect; he does not feel degraded in receiving this form of help. What the banks do for the rich and middle classes, a Free Loan Society does for the small tradesman and mechanic. It relieves borrowers of great inconvenience and privation, prevents their falling victims to ravaging loan-sharks, and this is done without elaborate formalities or unnecessary delays and with a courtesy that is reciprocated in prompt and scrupulous repayment.

The oldest existing Free Loan Society in New York City, and, as far as is known in the United States of America, was organized in 1892 and is only twenty-five years in existence. But there were from time immemorial Gemilath Chasodim societies in every Jewish community in Europe. Though similar in purpose, loaning money without interest, these Gemilath Chasodim societies were in method and extent as unlike the Free Loan Societies in this country as the "Heckdesh" [hospice] of a small Jewish European town is unlike the modern, well equipped hospital.

In the year 1917, the several Free Loan Societies of Greater New York made about thirty thousand loans amounting to approximately one million dollars. About 77% of the amount and number of loans was made by the largest society with its three branches, located in Harlem, Bronx and Brownsville. This society loans in denominations of from $5 to $300. Most of the others loan in amounts up to $50, a few up to $100, and only one up to $200. All loans are made on notes endorsed by responsible people, without charge of interest or expense of any kind, the borrowers repaying the loan in weekly instalments.

The borrower of $10, $15, or $25 invariably wants his loan to pay over-due rent, doctors', grocers' or butchers' bills. In these cases, the loans are least effective; the borrower remains just as poor after the loan as before. The loans of $100 and over, however, are usually applied for by small tradesmen, students and young professional men. The small businessman through such a loan is enabled to retain his credit in the commercial world, and continue his struggle for independence. The same is true of the student and professional man.

Loans of larger denominations, therefore, accomplish the most constructive and durable good, and it is in this direction that the smaller societies should aim to improve and extend their work. A still greater and further reaching achievement would be the merger of all the Free Loan Societies of New York into one great society with branches in every Jewish section of the city. This would not only reduce the losses, small as they are, and the average cost per loan, but would eliminate the great and only evil now existing among them—duplication.

The achievements of the Free Loan Societies cannot fail to fill one with enthusiasm for the cause. From the immigrant who needs a footing in this new world to the troubled merchant who has to be tided over some difficulty in meeting obligations, all are relieved from embarrassment and humiliation, not in a spirit of pauperism, nor as objects of charity, but with courteous treatment and genuine desire to keep alive self-reliance, self-respect and independence. No better method has yet been evolved to solve so practically the great problem of pauperism. . . .

Hebrew Free Loan Society, Inc. (Established 1892)

Central Office, 108 Second Ave., Tel. 8516 Orchard

Branches: 69 East 116th St., 1321 Boston Road, Bronx; 1878 Pitkin Ave., B'klyn.

Established more than twenty-five years ago, this society has been the practical embodiment of the idea of self-help in charitable relief work. Instead of giving alms to persons who have found the struggle for a means of livelihood too severe, the society loans money in sums ranging from $5 to $300, to applicants, without distinction of nationality, religion or race, on notes endorsed by reputable businessmen, without charge of interest or expense of any kind, the borrower repaying the loan in weekly installments. Over 80% of the loans have been made without requiring that the endorsers have a commercial rating. The expenses of the office, and losses, are covered by members' dues and donations. The records of the society show that almost 97% of the loans are repaid by the borrower, and less than 2% by the endorsers. Of these 22%, over one-half is ultimately returned to the endorsers through the society, or through the borrowers themselves.

During the fiscal year January 1st to December 31st, 1916, the society made 24,330 loans, aggregating $711,940. The returns in weekly installments amounted to $704,087.07. Receipts for 1916 from members' dues, donations and bequests, totaled $45,009.92; expenses including all branches, $24,500.49. During the fiscal year, January 1st to December 31st, 1917, this society made 23,403 loans aggregating $765,400. The returns in weekly installments amounted to $745,105.50. Receipts from Federation of Jewish Philanthropic Societies, $36,904.20. Expenses including all branches $23,615.52. Losses on loans, $2,910.50. Total capital of the society amounts to $241,637.69. To meet the increased demands for free loans, two new branches have been opened during the last year, one in the Borough of the Bronx, at 1321 Boston Road, and one in the Borough of Brooklyn, at 1878 Pitkin Avenue. . . .

IV.   The Jewish Migration Problem—
How It Has Been Met, By Albert Rosenblatt,
Vice President, Hebrew Sheltering and
Immigrant Aid Society (HIAS), 1924

As a result of the religious intolerance which European Christiandom inherited from its pagan predecessors, the European Jew was seldom more than an alien in his native land. As an exile or stranger he therefore became a wanderer, ever seeking a place of refuge from religious persecution, a house where he could worship God in security and live in peace. American tolerance has made it possible for the American Jew to put into practice the Biblical injunction to extend the hand of friendship to the homeless and stranger, commonly known to us as Hachnosass Orchim (harboring strangers). This was accomplished by organizing the Hebrew Sheltering and Immigrant Aid Society of America, now known the world over as the HIAS.

In 1889 [1884], a few years after the first federal regulations for the admission of immigrants into the United States were put into force, a number of East Side Jews, who themselves knew what it meant to be strangers in a strange land, organized the old Hachnosass Orchim or the Hebrew Sheltering House. In Essex Street, two small rooms were rented and there the newcomer was received and given food and shelter, and sometimes a few dollars with which to start anew. From Essex Street, the Hachnosass Orchim moved to larger and more pretentious headquarters, at 210 Madison Street, where also a number of old folks were given a home. In 1904, the buildings at 229–231 East Broadway were purchased in order to permit the extension of the work of the organization.

Immigrant aid work, such as meeting the immigrants at Ellis Island, and interceding in their behalf with the government, had always been done by charity organizations. In 1902 the Hebrew Immigrant Aid Society was called into existence, although efforts in that direction previously made, had failed. Finally in 1909, the Old Hebrew Sheltering House and the Hebrew Immigrant Aid Society merged under the joint name of the Hebrew Sheltering and Immigrant Aid Society of America, with the headquarters at 229–31 East Broadway.

Thus in the new Home, with larger forces and greater recognition, began the up-building of the Society, gradually transformed from a purely local organization into one of national scope. Its objects and policies are as follows:

To facilitate the lawful entry of Jewish immigrants at the various ports in the United States; to provide them with temporary shelter, food, clothing and such other aid as may be found necessary; to guide them to their destinations; to prevent them from becoming public charges by helping them obtain employment; to discourage their settling in congested cities; to maintain bureaus of information; to take proper measures to prevent ineligible persons from emigrating to the United States; to foster American ideals among the newcomers and to instill in them through a knowledge of American history and institutions, a true patriotism and love for their adopted country; to make better known to the people of the United States the many advantages of desirable immigration, and to promote these objects by means of meetings, lectures and publications.

The Society now extended its activities. Shelter and food were still provided for immigrants and wayfarers. Immigrants were still met and distributed. Department after department was added—as the need arose—until a complete immigrant aid structure was built up.

Then a new endeavor was entered upon. With the coming of large numbers of Jewish immigrants, the Society was appealed to from all parts of the country. In several of the port cities Hebrew Immigrant Aid Societies had been established. It soon became apparent that if the highest kind of service was to be rendered to Jewish immigrants, there would have to be complete co-operation between the New York Hebrew Sheltering and Immigrant Aid Society and the several organizations in other parts of the country. At first there was loose co-operation; finally, however, the organizations in Baltimore, Chicago, Philadelphia, Seattle and San Francisco became branches of the Society. The Ellis Island Bureau was strengthened and enlarged.

The government officials, in charge of immigration affairs, quickly realized the importance and the value of the work done by the Hebrew Sheltering and Immigrant Aid Society of America. An office was opened in Washington with a resident representative. It was made clear to the government that the Society had a twofold function. First, to receive, guide, distribute and Americanize Jewish immigrants. Secondly, and no less significant, to discourage the coming into the United States of those who would not be permitted to enter under law. For this purpose, it established co-operation with Jewish organizations abroad. It disseminated information broadcast. Through the press, by correspondence and by word of mouth the immigration laws were explained to immigrants and to those who wanted their relatives to join them.

The Society was, however, destined to branch out into activities that would take it beyond the borders of this country. This was the result of war conditions. During the early part of the conflict, when negotiations between this country and Eastern Europe were broken, Hias organized an international post office, receiving hundreds of thousands of letters from persons living abroad for their relatives here. Most of these people were the nearest and dearest, such as wives and children, fathers and mothers and brothers and sisters. Then came another development. It was discovered that immigrants were coming by way of Siberia through China into Japan and then into the United States. These immigrants were in a pitiable plight, and in order to afford them the aid that was absolutely essential for saving them from becoming destitute wanderers, a Commission was sent to Japan, and a home opened in Yokohoma and bureaus in Harbin, Irkutsk and Vladivostock. The result of this work was that these immigrants, the largest number of whom would have been completely lost, were saved.

The war had a most disastrous effect upon Jewish communities in Eastern Europe. Hundreds of thousands of men, women and children were made homeless. All trace of them was lost and the relatives here, in most cases a husband and a father, were powerless to give them any aid. Money was repeatedly sent, steamship tickets were purchased, but the reunion of families could not be effected. In response to a general appeal and with the consent and endorsement of the American government, Hias in 1920 sent its first Commission abroad. After studying the situation closely, headquarters were established in Warsaw, and work of reclaiming and reuniting the families began with the fullest measures of success. Hias has now been in Europe for nearly four years. Thousands upon thousands of human lives have been saved and millions of dollars transmitted.

Hias is still in Europe, organizing and helping European Jewry to solve its own problems.

In consequence of the enactment of the new immigration law [1924], thousands of Jewish emigrants, on their way to this country, were left stranded in various European ports and again Hias intervened. It sent a Commission of investigation abroad. This delegation which has just returned, succeeded in establishing relationship with European Jewish organizations so that new immigration centers may be found for those emigrants who cannot possibly come here and who under any circumstances cannot return to their native countries. In addition to going to Europe, Hias, too, took action in respect to the situation in Cuba, sending two commissions there and organizing immigrant aid work in Havana, by the establishment of a permanent committee and the opening of a home for immigrants.

Hias also interceded in the matter of having Jewish immigrants admitted into the Dominion of Canada, sending to that country several delegations with this end in view.

The survey indicates the far reaching activities of HIAS and the gradual but necessary extension of its work. Wherever there is the need, HIAS is sure to be there. It is recognized by our Christian brethren as well as by Jews, as the premier immigrant aid society in the world.

At its headquarters at 425 Lafayette Street, New York, the old Astor Library remodeled, HIAS since 1920 reaches out to wherever there are immigrants in need of aid and whenever an immigration problem has to be met.

Hias gives no financial relief. It gives advice and guidance and smooths the perilous path the Jewish wanderer has to tread. It is supported by voluntary contributions, having over one hundred and fifty thousand contributors in all parts of the United States. Its annual budget is of over half a million dollars. In some years its expenditure was approximately a million dollars.

In appraising the work of Hias, it must be borne in mind that the Jewish migration problem is unlike that of any other people. It is impossible to tell what may happen so far as the Jewish wanderer is concerned. A recasting of the map of Europe may have the effect of making thousands of Jews new nationals, or countryless altogether, so that Hias has ever to be on the watch.

A new law passed in this country or elsewhere may completely unsettle the situation, and so plans have to be reshaped and new policies framed in harmony with the law, to meet the new conditions.

If in the stormy days of the War and during the conditions arising out of that world catastrophe, there had been no Hias, it is no exaggeration to say that the disaster which befell our people would have been all the greater and perhaps beyond repair.

Thus out of a small beginning, the practice of the traditional "mitzvah" (sacred commandment) of "Hachnosass Orchim" (harboring strangers), there has grown this great organization known far and wide and wherever there are Jews, as the brotherly guide of the Jewish Wanderer.

42

THE SOCIAL LIFE OF
THE EAST EUROPEAN JEWISH IMMIGRANT
1905

To a degree the social life of Jews in America's small towns was limited. Only too often they were too few to create associations for sociability and entertainment, but life even for them was not one of boredom. The rites of passage gave them the opportunity to attend circumcisions, bar mitzvahs, weddings, and even post-burial wakes where an elaborate table was set. They went to the synagog—and gossiped—visited family and friends, made cheap railroad trips to neighboring towns (excursions), and never failed to read their favorite Yiddish newspaper. There were, however, few relationships with the older German Jewish settlers; the East Europeans and the Central Europeans constituted two disparate and hostile communities. The big cities offered much more in the social realm. The Hebraically learned met to study rabbinic literature; this was as much a friendly get-together as it was a religious and cultural experience. There were parties, picnics, beach visits; there were Jewish cafes, Yiddish theaters, lodges, and hometown societies, landsmanshaften. There were Zionist clubs and Marxist political organizations where comrades assembled to build a new world for Jews and mankind at large. The younger generation frequented the settlement houses; one could read a good book there and even take a shower. There were eloquent sermons in Yiddish for the parents; excellent lectures in English for the young and the aspiring.

The following account describes in detail the social life of the New York ghetto Jews. It is an excellent survey of the social and amusement activities of New York's Jewish newcomers, and, mutatis mutandis, in other large cities such as Philadelphia, Chicago, and Boston.

I.   Life on New York's Lower East Side,
By A. H. Fromenson, 1905

What saloons there are on the East Side [of New York City] do but an impoverished business and are dependent to a large extent upon the chance passerby. . . .

After all, it is in the "coffee saloon"—and where many times more tea is consumed than the beverage from which it takes its name—that the East Side finds recreation. Whether it is to play chess or checkers, or to discuss Karl Marx or Bakounine [the nineteenth-century Russian revolutionary Mikhail Bakunin], or to analyze Tolstoi or Ibsen, or to debate the relative merits and demerits of the naturalistic or romantic drama—or the wonderful coloratura of the last night's prima donna at the Metropolitan—(for all of these are included in the light converse of the East Side), or to denounce the critics of [Jacob] Adler, the [Yiddish] actor, or to excoriate the traducers of [Jacob] Gordin, the [Yiddish] playwright—these topics are handled best, thoughts come lucidly and words eloquently, over the glass of tea *a la Russe*—with a floating slice of lemon, and the cigarette.

It is estimated that there are between 250 and 300 of these coffee and cake establishments on the lower East Side, which figure is the best proof of the popularity of these "workingmen's clubs." Unlike the occasional liquor saloon on the East Side, they are absolutely independent of transient trade. The chance passer-by does not enter into the calculations of the proprietor, and is stared at as an intruder by the regular habitues. We have called these places "workingmen's clubs." They answer that description more truly and more pleasantly than the Bishop's tavern, for here there is an absolute guarantee of sobriety, and a free, democratic foregathering of kindred spirits. If one is up in the coffee and cake geography of the district, he knows where he may find the social and intellectual diversion most to his liking. It is each to his own; the Socialist has his chosen headquarters, the chess-crank his, the music-lover his, and so on right down the line. Some, indeed, combine two or three cults or fads, but even these have a *tendenz* [an inclination] which stands out clearly after the first clash of impressions.

Two or three of these "clubs" have considerable life in the afternoon, especially those in which the radical *literati* and journalists, the compositors on the Yiddish dailies, and students and insurance agents and others who have a few hours of the day to kill congregate. But, for the most of them there is no life until late in the evening. It is generally ten o'clock before the social phase manifests itself; if the "popular price" performance at the Metropolitan Opera House is a worthy one, or if there is something worth while on the boards in the Yiddish theatre, it may even be later before the roll-call would have a full response in certain of these places. The resort of the chess-player is naturally quiet enough, but the philosophers and critics are oracular and demonstrative. Often it is "mine host" who leads the discussion, or sits in judgment of the pros and cons. When he says his say, it is boldly, recklessly almost, viewed from the mercenary aspect of retaining his patronage. Nor does he fail to castigate a stubborn adherent of a contrary view. But the heat of controversy never assumes a petty, sulking character; to tear "mine host's" arguments to tatters, to utterly rout him at every point, is no mean accomplishment and worth hazarding many defeats, for generally he is very well informed on the topic under discussion. In fact, it is his known views and predilections that decide the character of his patronage. Thus, if his establishment is frequented by Socialists, it is fair to assume that he belongs to that political school; if his clientele is made up largely of musicians, he is an amateur critic or patron of the liberal art.

And where the cigarette smoke is thickest and denunciation of the present forms of government loudest, there you find women! One wishes he could write these women down gently. But to none would gentle words sound more strange than to the women of the radical coffee "parlor," who listen to strongest language, and loudest voices, nor fail to make themselves heard in the heat of the discussion. Yet it is hard to criticise them. The hall-bedroom is such a dingy, dreary place; the walls so close they seem to crush the unfortunate whose "home" is within its oppressive limits. The "coffee saloon" is light and cheerful; the noise is only the swelling chorus of spirits with whom they are in harmonious accord. If they are not the objects of fine courtesies and considerateness, they do not miss them; perhaps they never knew them. The stern realities of life, the terrible disappointment of thwarted ambition, the bruising friction of tradition and "emancipation," the struggle for existence,—all these have conspired to rob them of the finer attributes of womanhood. These are the stalwarts of the radical movements, the Amazons, or, as they have been dubbed, "die kaempferinen" [the battlers], whose zealotry rallies the flagging courage of their "genossen" [comrades]. Unromantic, perhaps, and yet we hear of them toiling, slaving, denying themselves until some man has won a degree and an entry into one of the professions. But, as they sit there in an atmosphere of tea-steam and cigarette smoke, one who does not know sees them only as unwomanly women; pallid, tired, thin-lipped, flat-chested and angular, wearing men's hats and shoes, without a hint of color or finery. And to them, as to the men, the time of night means nothing until way into the small hours. When one must sleep in a hall-bedroom there is no hurry about bedtime. . . .

Theatre-going is so much a habit with the Russian Jew in New York City that at the moment of this writing three theatres are deriving large profits from catering to it. All of these theatres, with seating capacities equal to the largest patronized by the non-Jewish elements of the city's population (one built for the specific purpose of housing a Yiddish stock company) are located within five minutes' walk of each other in the downtown Ghetto. Another, in the newer, but rapidly growing and more prosperous Harlem Ghetto, has failed. There were five Yiddish theatres up to a very recent date, and there may be that number again shortly. It is estimated that the patrons of the Yiddish theatres number from five thousand to seven thousand a night, and as performances are given on each of the seven nights in the week, with two matinees (Saturday and Sunday) the importance of the theatre as a source of amusement in the Ghetto may be realized. . . .

To-day Jacob Gordin is the dominant figure of the Yiddish stage, and his impress is the strongest. Some others, among them [Solomon] Libin and [Leon] Kobrin, have managed to get a hearing, and not without success, but they are disciples of Gordin, and at times have ventured farther than their master. Gordin has excellent literary skill and powers and, if he were tolerant of criticism and amenable to discipline, could become the greatest factor in the development of the Yiddish stage. But it would be absurd to grant him all that he and his followers claim for him. Although he has written many plays which he probably regards as greater, his "Yiddish King Lear" must stand out as indicative of his great possibilities if he had not chosen to become a philosopher and a problem play writer. What gives Gordin his greatest vogue, and what tends to confuse many of his zealotic followers, is his ability to write strong scenes. When at his best he has produced living, breathing entities, in contrast to the artificial, impossible creatures produced by his predecessors. His main faults are his stubbornly mistaken conception of "realism" and his persistent exposures of phases of life which are better left unrevealed. The consensus of opinion is that "God, Man and Devil" is Gordin's master-work. It is a combination of Job and Faust and its lesson is that even the most saint-like man may be tempted and fall. It has been witnessed and approved by college professors, and is unquestionably a lasting contribution to the literature of the drama. . . .

Unwittingly, the people themselves have been factors in lowering the tone of the Yiddish stage by fostering the pernicious system of "benefits." At one time or another, lodges and societies of the East Side, of which there are a countless number, will "buy a benefit"; that is, they will pay the management a certain sum of money, a little over half of the box-office receipts in the event of every seat being occupied; for this sum the benefit buyers are given tickets representing the extreme seating capacity and standing room of the theatre. A play is selected by the committee representing the organization to be presented on the night of the benefit. The tickets are sold by the members of the society and every dollar received over the price paid to the management is the society's profit. This is no philanthropy on the part of the theatre managers; on the contrary, it is good business. The theatres may be reasonably certain of "crowded houses" on Friday, Saturday and Sunday evenings and at the matinees on Saturday and Sunday afternoon, but the other nights of the week are not very lucrative. Without these "benefits" the theatres would have to run the risk of financial straits. It may readily be seen how these "benefits" could become a powerful weapon in the hands of the people, if properly directed.

It is on the "benefit" nights that the Yiddish theatre is best worth visiting, provided the play is not the thing. The audience is made up of family parties and neighbor-groups; from the grandsire to the infant and the boarder the whole tenement house is there with its luncheons and its bedlam. Half of the audience has never been to the theatre before, and would not have been there now, only they could not "insult" by not buying tickets, or because it is a "mitzvah" (good deed) to contribute to the good cause for which this "benefit" is given. And having earned the "mitzvah" why not partake of the earthly joy in its train? Here and there is the "veteran" theatre-goer, who may be a member of the society, or also could not "insult" by refusing to buy a ticket, or also wanted the "mitzvah" and all that goes with it. The veteran may be easily discovered, the centre of a group of novitiates explaining the play, naming the actors, criticising them audibly if they are lesser lights, telling where the laugh will come in and repeating lines lost in the noise. Altogether they are joyous occasions, these benefits. Presents are passed over the footlights to the "stars"; the officers of the society strut out before the curtain between acts and make "spitches"; the member who sold the greatest number of tickets has a gold-medal pinned on his palpitating bosom, and all bathe in a sea of ecstasy, with a feeling of good deeds well done, philanthropic purposes well served —if the "benefit" is a success.

Although the Yiddish drama is decadent, there is no evidence of a similar degeneracy among the people. As already pointed out, the value of plays like those written by Gordin and his disciples is due entirely to "strong" scenes and powerful acting. . . .

The ladies of the Ghetto are never "at home," but the welcome visitor is always sure of his glass of tea, his dish of preserves, and some fruit. There are no "Kaffee Klatches" here; nor [card games like] progressive euchres, or bridge-whists. Hospitality is simple, homely, genuine. There are no social circles; "social life" as that term is understood does not exist. "Parties" are given; not "coming out" parties, but "engagement parties," "graduation parties," "bar-mitzvah parties." The wedding, of course, is the big function. Hundreds of societies give dances and "receptions" (the latter being a more pretentious name for the former) during the winter, to which anyone may come if he can pay the price of a ticket and "hat check." Some societies couple entertainments with these receptions. The great social events are the "entertainment and ball" of the Beth Israel Hospital, the Hebrew Sheltering House and Home for the Aged, the Daughters of Jacob [a home for the aged], the Young Men's Benevolent League, and the New Era Club [a settlement house]. It is at these functions that the East Side makes its most gorgeous sartorial display, and it is by no means either a crude or cheap display. The women for the most part are as exquisitely clad as their sisters who visit the Horse-Show, and the diamonds worn at these affairs can be outblinked only by the collection on the grand tier at the Metropolitan Opera House. Strange as it may sound to many, the East Side is not all poverty and suffering. . . .

Owing to home-conditions on the East Side there is only such social life for the young folks as is made possible by organization membership, and as may express itself in the dances mentioned above, or in "open-meetings," indulged in by the "literary" societies, the Zionist societies, and the clubs in the settlements. In the summer time there are the picnics, which are dances in an open pavilion, with a few patches of grass surrounding it, all enclosed with a high fence. Much has been said against these "picnics" and it must be admitted that many of them are not very desirable. There is great need for healthy, wholesome recreation, for expression of the buoyancy of youth; and it is greatly to be regretted that the facilities for the things that help to make boys and girls better, purer men and women are so very few.

43

Anti-Zionism, Zionism,
Aid to Jews in Distress:
The Oneness of Jewry
1897–1921

No later than 1824 many cultured Jews in the United States believed that America was a Promised Land; they needed no other. They looked askance at the Jewish Restorationists who prayed for a speedy return to Palestine. The German Jews, who came later to these hospitable shores fleeing Central Europe with its disabilities, were dismayed when Theodor Herzl pleaded for a reborn Jewish state (1896). Zionism was disloyalty to America! Rabbi Isaac Mayer Wise was almost hysterical as he addressed the Central Conference of American Rabbis in Montreal on Tuesday, July 6, 1897, denouncing the new Jewish political philosophy (selection I). Many Jews in Europe and America, however, listened to Dr. Herzl. They wanted a Jewish state where there would be no anti-Semitism, where Jews could be themselves and live in peace. Influenced by a messianic tradition, most East European Jews in the United States embraced Palestine and Jewish nationalism. Meeting in Basel on August 30, 1897, the Zionists of all lands told the world that they wanted a new Jewish homeland (selection II). Twenty years later, 1917, the English promised to help the Jews reestablish themselves in Palestine (selection III). This Zionism was summarily rejected by most native American Jews; it gained very few adherents in their circles. But the cultured native-born Jew of Central European antecedents, Louis D. Brandeis, a distinguished public service advocate, joined the movement, giving it respectability. In his 1915 "Call to the Educated Jew" (selection IV), he appealed to the new generation of young Americans to support the cause of Zionism—the only solution to assimilation or what he called "national suicde." As early as the 1880s, the East European "Lovers of Zion" (Hoveve Ziyyon) had begun to colonize the Holy Land; Henrietta Szold (1860–1945), then living in New York City, created a female Zionist association to speed the restoration and to inspirit the American Jewish woman. She called it Hadassah after the biblical Esther. In 1921 Miss Szold, hard at work in Palestine, reported to a friend what she was doing to rehabilitate the land of her ancestors (selection V).

Zionism was always more than political nationalism; it was a movement to strengthen World Jewry by giving Jews a home where they could prosper culturally and spiritually. Zionism stresses the concept of the Oneness of Jewry. Every Jew in need has to be helped; this is not an appeal; this is not an option; this is a mandate. In 1914 when World War I erupted, American Jewry rushed to aid their East European coreligionists. Orthodox Russian immigrants in the United States responded immediately in the late summer of 1914, by establishing the Central Committee for the Relief of Jews Suffering Through the War (selection VI). A few months later, October 25, the natives and the acculturated German Jews—people of some substance—created the American Jewish Relief Committee (selection VII); a year later America's Jewish proletarians of East European background fashioned the Jewish People's Relief Committee of America. In 1915, the three groups, the immigrant Orthodox, the natives, and the Marxist labor leaders and their unions joined together to establish the Joint Distribution Committee of the American Funds for Jewish War Sufferers (JDC). The Jewish lions lay down with the lambs to help out other Jews whose plight was desperate. Obviously blood was thicker than Marxist dialectics. In 1917 the more affluent natives gave about $9,000,000; the Orthodox newcomers, about $2,000,000; the immigrants who worked in the shops and factories and who tended the tiny stores gave about $1,000,000. A small sum? These were the sacrificial nickels and dimes which impoverished men and women could ill afford to surrender. Relatively speaking the pushcart merchant who gave a quarter was as generous as Jacob H. Schiff, the international banker, but both gave because they were Jews responding to the anguished cries of fellow Jews (selection VIII).

I. Rabbi Isaac M. Wise Rejects Zionism, July 6, 1897

. . . I consider it my duty also, Rev. Colleagues, to call your attention to the political projects engaging now a considerable portion of our co-religionists in Europe and also in our country, especially in New York, Philadelphia, Chicago, and other large cities. I refer, of course, to the so-called "Friends of Zion," *Chovaveh Zion*, who revive among certain classes of people the political national sentiment of olden times, and turn the mission of Israel from the province of religion and humanity to the narrow political and national field, where Judaism loses its universal and sanctified ground and its historical signification.

The persecution of the Jews in Russia and Roumania and the anti-Semitic hatred against the Jewish race and religion, as it still exists in Germany, Austria, and partly in France [as revealed by the Dreyfus Affair], roused among the persecuted and outraged persons the hapless feeling of being hated strangers among hostile Gentiles. It was quite natural that this humiliating experience roused in their memory the glory of the past, when Israel was the great nation, the chosen people, and inspired in them the consolation, "we are the great nation yet." So the wronged man revenges himself on his oppressors generally with the pretense, "I am as good and better than you." Generally spoken it is true, the persecuted is always better than his persecutors.

This experience roused in those outraged men and women the old hope of restoration, the reconstruction of the Hebrew nationality, as in days of yore. The first step in this direction was the colonization of Palestine with Jewish agriculturists. This, of course, found favor and support among all good people, not indeed for the sake of Zion, but for the redemption of the persecuted, and with the conviction that these poor and neglected families can be redeemed morally and physically only by making of them honest and industrious tillers of the soil.

Idealists and religious phantasts took hold upon this situation, and made of it a general restoration of the Jews and their returning to the holy land, although the greatest number of Jewish citizens in the countries where they enjoy all civil and political rights loudly disavowed any such beliefs, hopes or wishes; yet the persecuted and expatriated from Russia and such other countries preached their new doctrine loudly and emphatically, and found advocates and friends also among Christians, more so even than among Jews. At last politicians seized the situation, and one of them, called Dr. [Theodor] Herzl, proposed to establish and constitute at once the Jewish State in Palestine [although Herzl's *Judenstaat* pamphlet had never mentioned Palestine], worked the scheme, and placed it so eloquently before the Jewish communities that the utopian idea of a Jewish state took hold of many minds, and a congress of all "Friends of Zion" was convoked to the city of Munich, to meet there in August next. [Actually they met in Basel, Switzerland.]

However, all this agitation on the other side of the ocean concerned us very little. We are perfectly satisfied with our political and social position. It can make no difference to us in what form our fellow citizens worship God, or what particular spot of the earth's surface we occupy. We want freedom, equality, justice and equity to reign and govern the community in which we live. This we possess in such fullness, that no State whatever could improve on it. That new Messianic movement over the ocean does not concern us at all. But the same expatriated, persecuted and outrageously wronged people came in large numbers also to us, and they, being still imbued with their home ideas, ideals and beliefs, voiced these projects among themselves and their friends so loudly and so vehemently, that the subject was discussed rather passionately in public meetings, and some petty politicians of that class are appointed as delegates, we learn, to the Basle Congress, and in each of those meetings, as reported by the press, so and so many rabbis advocated those political schemes, and compromised in the eyes of the public the whole of American Judaism as the phantastic dupes of a thoughtless Utopia, which is to us a *fata morgana*, a momentary inebriation of morbid minds, and a prostitution of Israel's holy cause to a madman's dance of unsound politicians. . . .

II. The Basel Program, August 30, 1897

Zionism strives to create for the Jewish people a home in Palestine secured by public law. For the attainment of this aim the Congress envisages the following means:

1. The promotion, on suitable lines, of the settlement of Palestine by Jewish agriculturists, artisans, and tradesmen.

2. The organization and unification of the whole of Jewry by means of appropriate local and general institutions in accordance with the laws of each country.

3. The strengthening of Jewish national sentiment and national consciousness.

4. Preparatory steps toward securing the consent of governments, which is necessary to attain the aim of Zionism.

III. The Balfour Declaration, November 2, 1917

Foreign Office
November 2nd, 1917.

Dear Lord [Lionel Walter] Rothschild
[President of the British Zionist Federation],

I have much pleasure in conveying to you, on behalf of His Majesty's Government, the following declaration of sympathy with Jewish Zionist aspirations, which has been submitted to, and approved by, the Cabinet:

"His Majesty's Government view with favour the establishment in Palestine of a national home for the Jewish people, and will use their best endeavors to facilitate the achievement of this object, it being clearly understood that nothing shall be done which may prejudice the civil and religious rights of existing non-Jewish communities in Palestine, or the rights and political status enjoyed by Jews in any other country."

I should be grateful if you would bring this declaration to the knowledge of the Zionist Federation.
Yours sincerely,
Arthur James Balfour
[British Foreign Secretary]

IV.   Louis D. Brandeis Appeals to America's Educated Jews to Espouse Zionism, January 1915

. . . In view of our inheritance and our present opportunities, self-respect demands that we live not only honorably but worthily; and worthily implies nobly. The educated descendants of a people which in its infancy cast aside the Golden Calf and put its faith in the invisible God cannot worthily in its maturity worship worldly distinction and things material. "Two men he honors and no third," says Carlyle, "the toil-worn craftsman who conquers the earth and him who is seen toiling for the spiritually indispensable."

And yet, though the Jew make his individual life the loftiest, that alone will not fulfill the obligations of his trust. We are bound not only to use worthily our great inheritance, but to preserve, and if possible, augment it; and then transmit it to coming generations. The fruit of three thousand years of civilization and a hundred generations of suffering may not be sacrificed by us. It will be sacrificed if dissipated. Assimilation is national suicide. And assimilation can be prevented only by preserving national characteristics and life as other peoples, large and small, are preserving and developing their national life. Shall we with our inheritance do less than the Irish, the Serbians, or the Bulgars? And must we not, like them, have a land where the Jewish life may be naturally led, the Jewish language spoken, and the Jewish spirit prevail? Surely we must, and that land is our fathers' land; it is Palestine.

The undying longing for Zion is a fact of deepest significance, a manifestation in the struggle for existence. Zionism is, of course, not a movement to remove all the Jews of the world compulsorily to Palestine. In the first place, there are in the world about 14,000,000 Jews, and Palestine would not accommodate more than one fifth of that number. In the second place, this is not a movement to compel anyone to go to Palestine. It is essentially a movement to give to the Jew more, not less, freedom—a movement to enable the Jews to exercise the same right now exercised by practically every other people in the world—to live at their option either in the land of their fathers or in some other county; a right which members of small nations as well as of large—which Irish, Greek, Bulgarian, Servian or Belgian, as well as German or English—may now exercise.

Furthermore, Zionism is not a movement to wrest from the Turk the sovereignty of Palestine. Zionism seeks merely to establish in Palestine for such Jews as choose to go and remain there, and for their descendants, a legally secured home, where they may live together and lead a Jewish life; where they may expect ultimately to constitute a majoriy of the population, and may look forward to what we should call home rule.

The establishment of the legally secured Jewish home is no longer a dream. For more than a generation brave pioneers have been building the foundations of our new-old home. It remains for us to build the superstructure. The Ghetto walls are now falling. Jewish life cannot be preserved and developed, assimilation cannot be averted, unless there be reestablished in the fatherland a center from which the Jewish spirit may radiate and give to the Jews scattered throughout the world that inspiration which springs from the memories of a great past and the hope of a great future.

The glorious past can really live only if it becomes the mirror of a glorious future; and to this end the Jewish home in Palestine is essential. We Jews of prosperous America above all need its inspiration.

V.   Henrietta Szold Helps Rebuild Palestine, October 7, 1921

Jerusalem, October 7, 1921.

[Addressee not given]

I can give you no idea of the bigness of the [Medical] Unit work in the field and in the office—actually and administratively. For the administration of the work we have an inadequate personnel, inadequate in number and in efficiency. The result is that everyone in the head office must work at a constant high pressure. Please picture me sitting from morning until night inside of a mountain of letters and notes which I myself create. I cast them out faster than they can be picked up and executed and carried to their destination. For one removed, I vomit forth a dozen.

But I'd rather tell you of my days away from the office. There were nine of them, during a tour of inspection through Upper and Lower Galilee. I touched at thirty-one points in which the Unit has some interest, either a doctor, or a nurse, or a sanitary inspector. That gives you an idea of the extent of our undertaking. I hasten to admit that it is not so intensive as extensive. I have been oscillating between these two poles, without being able to decide which should have been sacrificed to which. We cannot have both without a budget out of all proportion to the financial powers of the Zionist world. What the extent of our work should indicate to you is that the criticism made against it very freely before the [12th Zionist]

Congress at Carlsbad [Czecho-Slovakia], that we are doing nothing for the halutzim [cooperative farm settlers] and workingmen in general, the "productive" Jewish population, is false. Most of the thirty-one points are camps, workingmen's groups, colonies, etc.

Some of our critics went to the Congress with the intention of proposing that our hospitals be given up and all our available funds be devoted to the immigrants, the proper charge of the Zionist Organization. There is logic in this contention. Indeed, from my point of view, which is that everything of a public character ought to be thrown on the shoulders of the mandate government, the Medical Unit ought to cease to exist. Unless we make the government concern itself with us, it will never be our government in any sense of the word. The Zionist Organization pledged itself to take care of every immigrant for one year after his arrival. This, then, should be the extent of its medical task—logically.

But the course of Zionist development has not been any more logical than the rest of life has the habit of being. By force of circumstances, the Zionists have evolved a medical service which has served, and some time to come will continue to serve, as a standard to the government itself. The government establishments cannot compare with ours. And Jews being Jews, with a very proper regard for their bodies, must have a better service than the [British-controlled] Palestinian government can now give them. Then it is folly to think of abridging the Unit work—or to think of caring for the immigrant at the front without good, modern hospitals behind the lines. I should urge the Zionist Organization to make one magnificent effort and secure a great sanitary fund. The malaria-sanitary problem in Palestine is so well defined that it can be solved without residue in a short time and with not too much money.

First I'd like to tell you more about my trip, especially about the malaria-sanitary work, which, in a way, is the best we are doing. Most interesting of all is the anti-malaria experiment carried on since last March, by means of a fund of $10,000, the special gift for the purpose made by Mr. [Louis D.] Brandeis. The settlements at the north and south end of the Sea of Tiberias were chosen as the scene of the experiment. They comprise some of the well-known pest-holes of malaria. At Migdal Farm, for instance, a paradise—oranges, lemons, palms, bananas, almonds, and what not—with the anopheles mosquito playing the part of serpent—there were seventy-eight victims of malaria last summer, out of a possible eighty employees and laborers. You must consider what that means—on the average two attacks a season for each victim. Can you calculate the economic loss? This summer, so far—the malaria season ends only in December—the record is reversed: only two cases of malaria! In the whole region, comprising a population of about 1000 to 1200, there have been only five cases of malaria.

The results are all the more interesting because part of the population is shifting. It includes two road-builders' camps to which new forces from malaria-ridden sections are constantly being brought, and also it includes a few Arab villages which have been treated along with the Jewish settlements. The whole paraphernalia developed in Panama and Arkansas, etc., has been applied: petrolization of swamps, canalization and regulation, treatment of carriers, quinine prophylaxis under strict supervision, mosquito-nets, clearing of grassy spots that serve as breeding-places, etc. There is a microscopist on the spot, the doctors are enlisted for the therapeutic treatment, and a small corps of sanitary inspectors watch the swamps, execute the works, administer the quinine, look out for dripping faucets, etc. Result: the men sleep in the open, without nets, and remain unstung! It is a miracle.

When the money arrived in the spring for the purpose, we called a little conference of the physicians who had been in the country for more years than our Unit and who consider themselves malaria experts. The conference was to work out a plan of prevention within the limits of the budget. The best known among the physicians was rather contemptuous when he heard that the conference was expected to plan on a $10,000 basis. The Palestinians are very magnificent in their notions. Six ciphers is the minimum they are willing to manipulate with, especially when malaria is to be handled.

The experiment has proved conclusively that for three-fourths of Palestine the malaria problem is not a million-dollar engineering enterprise at all. In all but a few remote spots, it is a "thou-art-the-man" problem. The individual or rather the community of individuals can grapple with it. To be sure, there must be supervision, propaganda, education. I wish I could find time to write to Mr. Brandeis and give him a description of what has been done with his $10,000—which, by the way, has not been used up by a long shot.

It is such a pity I haven't time to keep in touch by correspondence with people in America. I have much material stored up, some of which would stimulate the interest of certain groups, and some of other groups. Do you know that in addition to the snug sum I carried with me from friends in America when I came here—it amounted to about $1300—to be applied as I saw fit, I have received $4150 since I am here for all sorts of purposes, named and to be named by me? Most of the sums came in response to letters of mine containing a bit of description of something or other out here. I never asked for money, never even thought of it. Isn't it a pity that I always get entangled in a multitude of administrative details?

You asked whether I have made friends with any of the Arab neighbors. Alas! the language difficulty. Three or four months ago a huge family took possession of the home next to us, which the head of the household has been building who knows how long. Since we have been here he has been working assiduously, but practically single-handed, laying stone upon stone, patiently. The whole harem down to the third generation visited us time and time again. We—that is, Sophia [Berger]—talked to them with the aid of the glossary in Baedeker. Sophia has some Arabic from her Red Cross days here. The trouble began when they talked back. Baedeker does not provide for the second half of the conversation. A week ago they invited us to a betrothal party. I am charitable to surmise that the men's part was interesting. In the women's apartment it was deadly dull. My only emotion was aroused by the sight of the sick babies nursing at their mothers' breasts—eternally. I wanted to pick them up—oh, but they were so dirty!—and carry them to my hospital.

VI.   American Orthodox Newcomers Pioneer in Helping Their East European Fellow Jews, By M. E. Ravage, August to October 4, 1914

Germany declared war on Russia on the 1st of August, and within scarcely more than a fortnight New York City witnessed the first conference on behalf of the victims. . . .

It was especially fitting that Orthodox Jewry should be the first to step into the breach. For it is this element along with another group which was later to be organized into the People's Relief Committee, which was bound by the closest ties of kinship to the sufferers abroad. Orthodox Jewry in America consists almost solely of Eastern Europeans—of the very people on whose behalf the relief expeditions of the past generation were instituted. For the most part, the victims of the present war are their own blood relatives. The funds which they collected went directly to care for the comforts of the brothers and sisters and the fathers and mothers of the donors. Moreover, this was the first great opportunity that this group had had of contributing materially and on an organized scale to the welfare of that part of the Jewish people which still remained under the yoke from which they had escaped.

How readily and magnificently they met this opportunity is now a matter of proud record. For the initial gathering of the 18th of August which was of a preliminary character, was followed a month later by a much more representative meeting at which plans for an organization were actually outlined and an immediate attempt made to rally kindred groups throughout the United States. It happened that the solemn season of the New Year and the Day of Atonement was approaching. Therefore the meeting proceeded to address telegrams to some hundred religious bodies in as many cities, urging them to turn the fast-days to account by issuing appeals to their respective congregations on behalf of the war sufferers on those days. Within two months of the outbreak of the war an establishment was actually in operation with offices in New York and with machinery for collecting funds installed in many ends of the country. The organization took the name of the Central Committee for the Relief of Jews Suffering Through the War.

These early meetings and the men and women who gathered at them gave the new organization the tone and temper which they have preserved through their honorable career down to the present moment. They set their stamp not only upon the types of the personnel in the organization, but to a very significant degree also they laid the foundations of its approach and its methodology. The Central Relief Committee had and still has its constituency in that element of immigrant Jewry which distinguishes itself primarily by its adherence to the ancient Jewish faith and tradition. On the one side it is flanked by the Reform group (which is Western European by origin), and on the other side by the great working mass whose affiliations are with the labor unions and kindred movements. The rank and file of the Central Committee are, socially and by tradition, the middle class. They consist in the main of the storekeeper and the small business man. Spiritually they belong in the camp of the traditional faith and ritual. Their leadership is preeminently to be found among the rabbis of the old dispensation and in a small but powerful group of intellectuals who constitute the modern prop of the synagogue. It is a middle class group not merely by antecedents and aspirations, but by the nature of its position in the Jewish community as well. It is a transition element standing as it does between the more Americanized Western Europe wing and the class-conscious idealistic working party of the Left. . . .

VII.   The Natives and the "Germans" Establish the American Jewish Relief Committee, By M. E. Ravage, October 25, 1914

The Central Relief Committee had been but a gauge of the state of feeling in American Jewry upon the outbreak of the European war and the calamity to the Jewish people abroad which it was bound to bring in its trail. It had been quite natural that the tragedy to the Old World ghetto should reecho first and most profoundly in its counterpart in the New. But ere long the wave of horror and sympathy spread to the remotest corners of the great Jewish community in America and gave impetus to an immense undertaking to cope with the emergency. On the 25th of October, 1914—less than three months after the opening of hostilities—Mr. Louis Marshall made the first attempt to enlist the organized effort of American Jewry in the great task. As the president of the most influential Jewish body in America—the American Jewish Committee—he invited the leading Jewish men and women in commerce, philanthropy and affairs to a meeting at the Temple Emanu-El. No more representative body had, I daresay, ever been brought together in the history of Jews in America. Platform and floor alike were crowded with men as well as women whose names have become known far beyond the confines of not only their racial group but of America herself. It was a meeting almost wholly of world figures—men noted for huge industrial and financial enterprises; men whose names had been for a quarter of a century identified with international benevolences, leaders in religion and jurisprudence, commerce and science—men for the most part whose names had become a word to conjure with in the remotest corners of the earth.

Little parliamentary claptrap marked the deliberations of this distinguished gathering. The business in hand was as clear as it was urgent, and there was in consequence a unanimity of purpose and procedure not always characteristic, alas, of Jewish public affairs. It required scarcely any time to crystallize an organization, and there developed no opposition or partisanship in the choice of its directing officers. The new body [the American Jewish Relief Committee] was conceived of as an off-shoot and a subsidiary of the American Jewish Committee. . . .

VIII.   The East European Proletarians Organize the People's Relief Committee, By M. E. Ravage, August 1915

At this point I must pause to narrate the origins of the third and last of the Committees. If the American and Central Committees were dramatic in their origin and career, the rise a year after the outbreak of the war of a third organization in the field, was hardly short of spectacular. The elements constituting the former organization were the traditional mainstays of charity. The membership of the latter were, if not givers of long standing, at least firm believers in the theory of benevolence. The seventy-five people on the other hand who congregated on the east-side one day in August, 1915, to institute the People's Relief Committee were the very leaders and formulators of the doctrine that all philanthropy is an irrelevance and an impertinence. Surely there was something striking and characteristic of the times that labor union officials, former socialist candidates, and radicals and semi-radicals of every stripe and shade should be themselves instrumental in the formation of a charitable society. In ordinary times these men had more than once led assaults upon the institutions of benevolence in their midst and had even gone so far as to discredit the motives of their supporters. All philanthropy, they had preached, was a screen devised by capitalists to mask their depredations and to salve their consciences. It was an instrument for misguiding the poor by blinding them to the causes of their poverty and inspiring them with a sense of gratitude toward their despoilers. It was a wedge in the solidarity of the proletariat designed to retard the triumph of the fullest democracy.

But these were not ordinary times. Therefore, contrary to the common belief that radicals are sticklers for theory, these leaders of labor faced reality with practical sense. Millions of women and children were perishing from hunger and exposure. Whoever might be at fault; whatever the sinister forces might be that were responsible for this vast misery, the first thought for sane men must be to devise methods for ameliorating it. Doctrinally, indeed, every attempt at relief might be a way of playing into the hands of the war-makers. But this was no time for doctrine. This was hardly in the category of usual benevolence. While whole peoples were being starved and tormented one could not sit back philosophically and wait for the victims to trace the origin of their sorrows in the hope that they might swell the ranks of the discontented with the present order of things. The immediate concern was inevitably to lighten as far as one could the burden of the sufferers; and for men with open eyes the immediate concern excluded for the time every other thought. . . .

But the People's Relief Committee extends its activities far beyond the industrial cities of the Eastern seaboard. Its branches and sub-committees operate in communities numbering no less than one hundred and fifteen municipalities scattered over three-quarters of the states of the Union. In these distant localities it is customary for the workmen's committee to work hand in hand with the local representatives of the Central [Jewish Relief] and the American [Jewish Relief] bodies. But everywhere their identity remains separate and distinguishes itself by its constituency, by its methods and by its fine spirit of generous helpfulness. It is a safe surmise that proportionately to income no element of Jewry in this country does its duty by the sufferers abroad more completely and at a cost of a more genuine sacrifice than they. This is the first time in history that the Jewish labor masses have had an opportunity to give substantial evidence of the love that is in them for their fellows [Jews]. They have responded to their opportunity with a nobility and an open-handedness which is incomprehensible and which cannot be forgotten.

PART V

Emerging American Period,
1925–1960

I n the late 1920s, after several years of frenzied speculation and fancied security, America plunged into a depression that was to last for several years. The panic evoked an outburst of anti-Semitism as political scoundrels saw opportunities to exploit the widespread misery and the stricken masses sought a scapegoat. The rise of Hitler in Germany and the spawning of little Hitlers in this country in the 1930s exacerbated an already unhealthy situation. The Germans were convinced that their pseudoscientific approach to the Jewish problem was the only correct one. Jews were inherently evil; they had no redeeming traits; they must be destroyed completely, annihilated. The stockpile of anti-Jewish prejudice here in the United States was already decades old. Jews were not welcome in some colleges and clubs. Anti-Jewish discrimination was encountered on all levels of the business world; the Sunday-closing laws continued to hurt observant Jewish businessmen and wage earners. The Immigration Acts of 1921 and 1924 had been directed against Jews and all Southern and Eastern Europeans.

Closing the portals to America was for European Jewry a death sentence more often than not. For American Jewry, however, it was not altogether a disaster, since it had the effect of spurring the diverse Jewish ethnic groups here to begin blending; ultimately, a new Jew would emerge; the "Germans" and the "Russians" as such were destined to disappear. Jews never became part of a larger American melting pot—if indeed there was one—but there was, very definitely, a Jewish melting pot. Out of diversity came forth unity—surely a gain. Even the Jew hatred of the 1930s was finally no unmitigated disaster; the Jews survived and ultimately prospered.

The Jews created a stronger structured local community—after all, American Jews now had much in common; there were even intimations of an overall nationwide Jewish organization. Locally the Jewish social-welfare federations grew strong; they raised millions, hundreds of millions, to aid Europe's suffering Jews; they gloried in the rise of the new settlements in Palestine and showered them with gifts. As American Jewry moved forward in the late 1930s, the new Jewish women began to make their presence felt. Because of their competence they exacted recognition.

American-born sons and daughters of immigrant families flocked to the colleges. They produced notable writers, poets, journalists, artists, musicians, entertainers, judges, congressmen, and Nobel laureates. Their immigrant papas built the make-believe world of Hollywood revolutionizing the recreational life of almost every human being; they dominated America's apparel industry and fashioned labor unions that were exemplary in their approach to the bosses and their solicitude for the toiling workers.

With the passing of the depression of the 1930s, the myriads of professionals, white-collar workers, and tradesmen achieved a degree of affluence. They moved upward from suburb to suburb. The rich built Jewish country clubs; the moderately successful patronized community centers. Magnificent new synagogs graced the golden ghettos. Exposed to acculturation, the new generation of Orthodox Jews modified—some even rejected—the faith of their fathers. The Conservatives, entrenched in tradition yet open to modernity, became the largest American Jewish denomination; the Reformers abandoned the nineteenth-century universalistic classicity, embraced Zionism, and set out as neo-Reformers to win over the native-born children of the East Europeans. Jewish education blossomed. Hundreds of all-day schools were opened; the scientific approach to Jewish studies was pursued in seminaries and colleges; by 1960 the United States could claim to be one of the world's greatest Jewish cultural centers.

No Jewry can ever hope to escape the impact of its environment. America's Jewish 3 percent of the population was pressured by the weight of the 97 percent of American Gentiles. Acculturation, intermarriage, and assimilation made inroads. Yet Jews survived and flourished in the open society of which they were an integral part. The 1960s brought intimations of better days. As blacks won concessions from a racist America, Jews rode in on their coattails; as a feared Soviet Union appeared to advance in knowledge and power, this country's apprehensive governing elite, recruiting all of its resources, opened doors—almost every door—to aspiring and ambitious youth. In the strengthening of the Pax Americana, the Jew was a loyal ally.

In the decades after World War II, the Jewish historian had begun to realize that a new Jewry was in a state of becoming. The "Russians" and the "Germans" were long gone; a new Jew was born, a highly educated, a relatively affluent, college-trained man or woman who was not unsympathetic to the ritual and practices which characterized traditional Judaism. The conservative political atmosphere, sponsored by the postwar Republican Party and the turn to the right of the American hoi polloi, encouraged many Jews to reject assimilatory and universalistic trends. Israeli war victories and Jewish ethnic nationalism beclouded the old concept of the Mission of Israel: the spiritual salvation of all mankind. In these postbellum years of change and advance, American Jewry—so it seems—was not fully conscious of the horrors of the Holocaust. Is it possible that America's Jews did not even wish to confront the almost unbelievable, the greatest tragedy in all World Jewish history? When in the last quarter of the century they finally realized what had happened to fellow Jews in Central and Eastern Europe they surrendered themselves almost frantically to the study of the Holocaust. This evil incarnate threatened to dominate the thinking, the feeling, the total being of Jewish scholars and intellectuals. Nothing was so important.

If there were any doubting Thomases who looked askance at the new State of Israel even they were now convinced of the imperative need of a political haven where any Jew could go as of right.

44

Acceptance and Rejection
1932–1952

B y the middle of the twentieth century, American Jewish citizens were enjoying the numerous opportunities which, probably more than in any other country on the face of the earth, were offered them by the United States. Thousands had achieved affluence, if not wealth; they sat in the halls of Congress, on the Supreme Court, in the cabinets of Presidents, and presided as governors over the destiny of states. Few men, if any, were more respected during the 1930s than Supreme Court Justice Benjamin Nathan Cardozo (1870–1938), a committed Jew. In the 1950s, Professor Morris Raphael Cohen of the College of the City of New York summed up Cardozo's ideological approach:

> The main features of Cardozo's, like those of any sound philosophy, are essentially simple, though it needs genius and energy to see their implications and to carry them out consistently. The first point is that law is not an isolated technique, of interest only to lawyers and to litigants, but that it is an essential part of the process of adjusting human relations in organized society. The second point is that the law of a growing society cannot all be contained in establishing precedents or any written documents, important as are continuity with the past and loyalty to the recorded will of the people. In the law as a social process, the judges play a determining role, having the sovereign power of choice in their decisions. It was in this emphasis on the judicial process that Cardozo's thought centered.
>
> The third point, the logical corollary to the foregoing, is that to meet his responsibility for making the law serve human needs the judge cannot rely on legal authority alone, but must know the actual facts of the life about him, the psychologic and economic factors which determine its manifestations, and must thus keep abreast of the best available knowl-

edge which those engaged in various social studies, researches, or investigations, can supply. . . . The law arises to meet social needs and can maintain itself in the long run only if it serves those needs justly to the general satisfaction of the community. The Sabbath was made for man, and not man for the Sabbath.

It is well to bear in mind that, in 1938, when Cardozo died, Father Charles E. Coughlin, the eloquent Detroit radio priest, was relentlessly attacking Jews. There has hardly been a decade since the Declaration of Independence in which the civil rights and liberties of the Jews in America were not threatened, to some degree at least. As late as 1953, U.S. Senator Ralph Edward Flanders of Vermont introduced a joint Senate resolution proposing an amendment to the Federal Constitution to the effect that "this nation devoutly recognizes the authority and law of Jesus." Had his amendment been adopted, Jews would have become second-class citizens. Under the guise of police laws, some Orthodox Jews were for decades compelled to keep their places of business closed on Sunday. Thus, these Sabbath observers lost Sunday also—an economic disability. Today Sabbatarians are not punished if they work on Sunday, the first day of the week. Well into the mid-twentieth century, Jews, blacks, and some other groups suffered discrimination in the area of employment. Several states, however, passed fair employment laws that helped remedy this problem. New York State's antidiscrimination act of March 12, 1945—the Ives-Quinn Bill—is an outstanding example. A coalition of blacks, Jews, liberals, and various minority groups made this law possible.

Beginning with the year 1882, Congress had begun to restrict immigration; ultimately Jews *as Jews* were to become one of the prime targets of the legislation. Many Americans were xenophobic; they had been so even in colonial days. Newcomers were often deemed inferior, hence less desirable citizens. In 1921, 1924, and 1952 Congress passed quota laws; aliens were to be admitted according to race and nationality. In 1905, governmental records disclose that 153,748 Jews—mostly East Europeans—landed on these shores; in 1932, after the quota laws were in operation, only 1,747 were admitted. Congress made its decision largely on the base of "race." Nordics—tall Caucasians possessing long heads, blue eyes, and light skin and hair—were deemed desirable, regarded as superior. East Europeans, Balts, Russians, Lithuanians, Poles, Galicians, Hungarians, Rumanians, Balkans, Italians, and Jews typified a lesser breed whose numbers must be limited! In 1924, all told, about 154,000 aliens were to be admitted; Great Britain was to be allotted 65,000 visas, Greece, 308. The Immigration and Nationality Law of June 1952—the McCarran-Walter Act—also set out deliberately to restrict the number of East Europeans admitted, especially Jews. This Nordic race theory accepted by Congress was a pseudoscientific concept; today it is discredited by all reputable anthropologists. American Jewish children of East European origin—often anything but Nordic in appearance—proceeded to garner Nobel Prizes far in excess of their numerical proportion in the population.

Despite the fact that the United States is not juridically or constitutionally a Christian country, even today there is hardly a community where individual teachers in the public schools do not breach the wall between church and state. Christian religious ceremonies and practices in the schools are often tolerated if not encouraged by the cities, states, and federal authorities—even by occasional decisions of the U.S. Supreme Court. School instruction is frequently sectarian, Protestant. Jews believe that religion must not be taught in the public schools; its place is in the home, the church, the synagog.

Selection I is an evaluation of the career of Justice Cardozo; selection II reproduces the essential paragraphs of the Ives-Quinn law; selection III excerpts the important paragraphs of President Harry Truman's veto of the McCarran-Walter Act. His eloquent protest, however, was overridden by a substantial majority in Congress and the statute became the law of the land until 1965, when the racially motivated national quota system was modified.

I. Justice Benjamin Nathan Cardozo, By Felix S. Cohen, 1932

Who is this man, Benjamin N. Cardozo? . . . With a rare unity of purpose, Benjamin N. Cardozo has devoted his life to an ideal of justice. The diligence, the patience, and the intensity with which he has, as a judge, consecrated his waking hours to the causes before him are proverbial. Even as a youth the call of his chosen vocation was clear and insistent. Graduating from Columbia with highest honors in 1889, at the age of nineteen, and winning his M.A. a year later, there was no time for more than a year at Columbia Law School. He was admitted to the bar at the age of twenty-one, and in his first argument before the Court of Appeals he won the praise of the court. Twenty-two years of private practice ended with his election on a Fusion ticket, in 1913, to the Supreme Court of New York. A month later he was appointed by Governor Glynn to the highest court of the State, the Court of Appeals. In 1917 his position on that court was confirmed by popular election, and in 1926 he was elected Chief Judge of the Court of Appeals. On March 3, 1932, he bade farewell to his associates on that court, and accepted the post of Justice of the Supreme Court of the United States.

Throughout this distinguished career, honored by public offices and ornamented by public awards, Justice Cardozo has borne himself graciously and with a humility as beautiful as it is rare in the seats of those who wield powers of life and death. This humility is more than the expression of a reserved, retiring temper of life. It is equally the product of a philosophical recognition that certainty is not the destiny of man, that our honest ignorance causes untold suffering, and that those who exercise the power of the state have need of what a distinguished disciple of Justice Cardozo, Justice Bernard L. Shientag, has called "a liberating skepticism, the power to stand up against dogmatic claims and the open mindedness and imagination 'to treat with reverence and humility every original hint and illuminating suggestion.'" . . .

With Baruch Spinoza, Benjamin Cardozo searches for a truth more universal than that of any creed. "The submergence of self," he writes, "in the pursuit of an ideal, the readiness to spend oneself without measure, prodigally, almost ecstatically for something intuitively apprehended as great and noble, spend oneself one knows not why—some of us like to believe that this is what religion means. True, I am sure, it is that values such as these will be found to have survived when creeds are shattered and schisms healed and sects forgotten and the things of brass and stone are one with Nineveh and Tyre."

Behind the badges of external faith there lie deeper ideals to which Benjamin Cardozo has been loyal, as a man and as a judge. In the passionate intensity and the courage of his quest for justice, there glows the spirit of Isaiah and Daniel and Amos. Characteristic of the ideals of his race is the devotion which he has submerged his whole being in his appointed task, denying himself recreation, foregoing the amenities of society, begrudging himself even the hours of rest.

The Jewish ideal of family solidarity illumines not only Justice Cardozo's personal life, and particularly his life-long devotion to his invalid sister, but as well many of his most noted decisions in the field of domestic relations. And in Justice Cardozo's defense of the right of Communists to hold and expound views he believes to be erroneous, he has given eloquent expression to the lesson which the whole history of Judaism exemplifies, the lesson of the futility of oppression and persecution directed to beliefs that men hold with sincerity and passionate conviction.

To get a true picture of the man who has never wilfully given cause for personal publicity, one must turn to Cardozo's own writings. In them and through them one gleans a glimpse of the ideals that have molded his judicial career.

Chief among these ideals is the vision of law as an instrument adaptable to the changing needs of a changing society.

> The process of judging is a phase of a never-ending movement and something more is exacted of those who pay their part in it than imitative reproduction, the lifeless repetition of a mechanical routine.

The legal philosophy of Justice Cardozo is marked by sensitiveness in which he has called "the agitations and promptings of changing civilization demanding outlet and expression in changing forms of laws, and a jurisprudence and philosophy adequate to justify the changes."

This sensitiveness, combined with the innate modesty of Justice Cardozo's spirit, has made him ready to admit that the history of government by the judiciary in this country has not been an unmixed blessing, that courts are not always properly equipped to deal with complicated social questions upon which they have assumed to pass, and that the legitimate growth of society has been hindered by reactionary decisions.

> Some of the errors of courts have their origin in imperfect knowledge of the economic and social needs to which a decision will respond. In the complexities of modern life there is a constantly increasing need for resort by the judge to some fact-finding agency which will substitute exact knowledge of factual conditions for conjecture and impression. . . .

Justice Cardozo, sitting on the bench of the United States Supreme Court, is not likely to join the ranks of those who have hindered or nullified, in the past forty years, important measures of basic social reform that Congress has passed, from the Income Tax Law and the anti-injunction provisions of the Clayton Act to the Child Labor Law and the Minimum Wage Law.

This does not mean that Justice Cardozo is a radical, even in the mild sense in which that term may properly be applied to Justice Brandeis. Indeed, the applause with which conservatives greeted President Hoover's choice seems well deserved if one considers some of the opinions which Justice Cardozo wrote for the Court of Appeals in labor injunction cases, in taxation cases, and in public utility cases. It may fairly be said that Justice Cardozo is inclined to look to the conduct of individual parties before the court, and to ignore less dramatic social and economic realities that demand, for their appreciation and understanding, a training in the use of social statistics and the data of the social sciences that only one American judge, Justice Brandeis, today commands. But the record of a year on the Supreme Court indicates that Justice Cardozo will join with Justice Brandeis and Stone in defending the right of Congress to deal with unprecedented problems of social maladjustment in ways that were not discussed on the floor of the Constitutional Convention in 1787. . . .

The ideal that Benjamin Nathan Cardozo has exemplified is an ideal that cannot be fixed in the stream of human events. If Justice Cardozo has envisaged a full ideal of government or society, the vision has not yet emerged to public expression. He has thought of the role of judge as that of a servant of the people, whose duty it is to enforce the community's ideas of goodness and justice rather than his own.

My duty as a judge may be to objectify in law, not my own aspirations and convictions and philosophies, but the aspirations and convictions and philosophies of the men and women of my time.

Thus it is that Justice Cardozo has ever sought the delicate adjustment, the honorable compromise between warring interests, without allying himself with any faction. Thus it is that of hundreds of New York lawyers who have been unsuccessful in their arguments before him, not one will be found who bears a personal grudge at defeat. In the voice of Cardozo one seems to have heard the passionless sentence of Justice . . . one can think of Justice Cardozo dealing with the enduring problems of the law in any civilization, faithfully pursuing, with all the instruments that intelligence, learning, honesty, and eloquence can afford, the ideals of the society about him. The measures in which Justice Cardozo speaks are not alien in any place nor ancient in any time—neither in twentieth century America nor in old Judea, neither in Soviet Russia nor in ancient Rome. There is in the soul of Benjamin Cardozo a wisdom that is ageless, a humanity that is nowhere foreign, a passion for justice that is, perhaps more fundamental than the dogmas which distinguish one social order from another. It may be that these things, too, will survive "when creeds are shattered and schisms healed and the things of brass and stone are one with Ninevah and Tyre."

II.   The New York Law against Discrimination, March 12, 1945

UNLAWFUL DISCRIMINATORY PRACTICES.

1. It shall be an unlawful discriminatory practice:

(a) For an employer, because of the age, race, creed, color or national origin of any individual, to refuse to hire or employ or to bar or to discharge from employment such individual or to discriminate against such individual in compensation or in terms, conditions or privileges of employment.

(b) For a labor organization, because of the age, race, creed, color or national origin of any individual, to exclude or to expel from its membership such individual or to discriminate in any way against any of its members or against any employer or any individual employed by an employer.

(c) For any employer or employment agency to print or circulate or cause to be printed or circulated any statement, advertisement or publication, or to use any form of application for employment or to make any inquiry in connection with prospective employment, which expresses, directly or indirectly, any limitation, specification or discrimination as to age, race, creed, color or national origin, or any intent to make any such limitation, specification or discrimination, unless based upon a bona fide occupational qualification.

(d) For any employer, labor organization or employment agency to discharge, expel or otherwise discriminate against any person because he has opposed any practices forbidden under this article or because he has filed a complaint, testified or assisted in any proceeding under this article.

2. It shall be an unlawful discriminatory practice for any person, being the owner, lessee, proprietor, manager, superintendent, agent or employee of any place of public accommodation, resort or amusement, because of the race, creed, color or national origin of any person, directly or indirectly, to refuse, withhold from or deny to such person any of the accommodations, advantages, facilities or privileges thereof, or, directly or indirectly, to publish, circulate, issue, display, post or mail any written or printed communication, notice or advertisement, to the effect that any of the accommodations, advantages, facilities and privileges of any such place shall be refused, withheld from or denied to any person on account of race, creed, color or national origin, or that the patronage or custom thereat of any person belonging to or purporting to be of any particular race, creed, color or national origin is unwelcome, objectionable or not acceptable, desired or solicited. Nothing herein contained shall be construed to bar any religious or denominational institution or organization, or any organization operated for charitable or educational purposes, which is operated, supervised or controlled by or in connection with a religious organization, from limiting admission to or giving preference to persons of the same religion or denomination or from making such selection as is calculated by such organization to promote the religious principles for which it is established or maintained.

3. It shall be an unlawful discriminatory practice for the owner, lessee, sub-lessee, assignee, or managing agent of publicly-assisted housing accommodations or other person having the right ownership or possession of or the right to rent or lease such accommodations:

(a) To refuse to rent or lease or otherwise to deny to or withhold from any person or group of persons such housing accommodations because of the race, creed, color or national origin of such person or persons.

(b) To discriminate against any person because of his race, creed, color or national origin in the terms, conditions or privileges of any public-assisted housing accommodations or in the furnishing of facilities or services in connection therewith.

(c) To cause to be made any written or oral inquiry or record concerning the race, creed, color or national origin of a person seeking to rent or lease any publicly-assisted housing accommodation.

(d) Nothing herein contained shall be construed to bar any religious or denominational institution or organization, or any organization operated for charitable or educational purposes, which is operated, supervised or controlled by or in connection with a religious organization, from limiting admission to or giving preference to persons of the same religion or denomination or from making such selection as is calculated by such organization to promote the religious principles for which it is established or maintained.

3-a. It shall be an unlawful discriminatory practice: . . .

(b) For any employer, licensing agency or employment agency to print or circulate or cause to be printed or circulated any statement, advertisement of publication, or to use any form of application for employment or to make any inquiry in connection with prospective employment, which expresses, directly or indirectly, any limitation, specification or discrimination respecting individuals between the ages of forty-five and sixty-five, or any intent to make any such limitation, specification or discrimination.

(c) For any employer, licensing agency or employment agency to discharge or otherwise discriminate against any person because he has opposed any practices forbidden under this article or because he has filed a complaint, testified or assisted in any proceeding under this article.

But nothing contained in this subdivision or in subdivision one of this section shall be construed to prevent the termination of the employment of any person who is physically unable to perform his duties or to affect the retirement policy or system of any employer where such policy or system is not merely a subterfuge to evade the purposes of this subdivision; nor shall anything in said subdivisions be deemed to preclude the varying of insurance coverages according to an employee's age.

4. It shall be an unlawful discriminatory practice for any person to aid, abet, incite, compel or coerce the doing of any of the acts forbidden under this article, or to attempt to do so.

III.   President Truman's Veto of the Immigration and Nationality Act of 1952, June 25, 1952

To the House of Representatives:

I return herewith, without any approval, H. R. 5678, the proposed Immigration and Nationality Act. . . .

Our immigration policy is equally, if not more, important to the conduct of our foreign relations and to our responsibilities of moral leadership in the struggle for world peace. . . .

I have long urged that racial or national barriers to naturalization be abolished. . . . But now this most desirable provision comes before me embedded in a mass of legislation which would perpetuate injustices of long standing against many other nations of the world, hamper the efforts we are making to rally the men of the east and west alike to the cause of freedom, and intensify the repressive and inhumane aspects of our immigration procedures. The price is too high and, in good conscience, I cannot agree to pay it. . . .

The over-all quota limitation, under the law of 1924, restricted annual immigration to approximately 150,000. This was about one-seventh of 1 percent of our total population in 1920. Taking into account the growth in population since 1920, the law now allows us but one-tenth of 1 percent of our total population. And since the largest national quotas are only partly used, the number actually coming in has been in the neighborhood of one-fifteenth of 1 percent. This is far less than we must have in the years ahead to keep up with the growing needs of our nation for manpower to maintain the strength and vigor of our economy.

The greatest vice of the present quota system, however, is that it discriminates, deliberately and intentionally, against many of the peoples of the world. The purpose behind it was to cut down and virtually eliminate immigration in this country from Southern and Eastern Europe. A theory was invented to rationalize this objective. The theory was that in order to be readily assimilable, European immigrants should be admitted in proportion to the numbers of persons of their respective national stocks already here as shown by the census of 1920. Since Americans of English, Irish, and German descent were most numerous, immigrants of those three nationalities got the lion's share—more than two- thirds—of the total quota. The remaining third was divided up among all the other nations given quotas.

The desired effect was obtained. Immigration from the newer sources of Southern and Eastern Europe was reduced to a trickle. The quotas allotted to England and Ireland remained largely unused, as was intended. Total quota immigration fell to a half or a third—and sometimes even less—of the annual limit of 154,000. People from such countries as Greece, or Spain, or Latvia were virtually deprived of any opportunity to come here at all, simply because Greeks or Spaniards or Latvians had not come here before 1920 in any substantial numbers.

The idea behind this discriminatory policy was, to put it baldly, that Americans with English or Irish names were better people and better citizens than Americans with Italian or Greek or Polish names. It was thought that people of West European origin made better citizens than Rumanians or Yugoslavs or Ukrainians or Hungarians or Balts or Austrians. Such a concept is utterly unworthy of our traditions and our ideals. It violates the great political doctrine of the Declaration of Independence that "all men are created equal." It denies the humanitarian creed inscribed beneath the Statue of Liberty proclaiming to all nations, "Give me your tired, your poor, your huddled masses yearning to breathe free."

It repudiates our basic religious concepts, our belief in the brother-
hood of man, and in the words of St. Paul that "there is neither Jew nor
Greek, there is neither bond nor free . . . for ye are all one in Christ Jesus"
[Galatians 3:28].

The basis of this quota system was false and unworthy in 1924. It is
even worse now. At the present time this quota system keeps out the very
people we want to bring in. It is incredible to me that, in this year of 1952,
we should again be enacting into law such a slur on the patriotism, the capacity, and the decency of a large part of our citizenry. . . .

Harry S. Truman

The White House, June 25, 1952

45

JEWS AND GENTILES
1928–1958

The American Jew—what proportion is he or she American? Jewish? Basically this Jew is all American, only occasionally conscious of his Jewish heritage, when wandering into a synagog or experiencing discrimination as a Jew. The decades from 1925 to 1960 were years of stress. Henry Ford continued to snipe at Jews in his Dearborn *Independent* until 1927 when he publicly apologized for his anti-Semitism. No dyed-in-the-wool pro-German racist, he was a yokel of limited vision who was set in his traditional prejudices. In the 1930s and 1940s, Hitler's Germany set out to destroy World Jewry; six million Jews were murdered. America's portals remained closed to Jewish refugees; the country was in the throes of a devastating depression; Americans would tolerate no large-scale immigration. Roosevelt, the consummate politician—determined to survive—refused to respond to the frantic entreaties of a desperate European Jewry. It is not really so surprising: twentieth-century polls disclose that there is still a substantial minority of Americans who do not care for Jews.

When in 1928 a little child in Massena, New York, was lost in a forest the mayor of the city and others asked the local rabbi whether Jews still sacrificed Christian children during their holy day season! Father Charles E. Coughlin, pastor of a church in Royal Oak, Michigan, tirelessly attacked Jews in his radio addresses (1938). He reached millions who were enthralled by his oratory. Like Ford, he believed or claimed to believe, that the Jewish Communists and international bankers were engaged in a successful conspiracy to rule and ruin the Christian world. It was not until the early 1940s during World War II that the U.S. government and Coughlin's archbishop put a stop to his tirades, now deemed subversive. A decade and a half later, during the years 1957–1958, seven Southern synagogs were bombed, or subjected to attack, by bigots and terrorists—a chapter in the civil rights struggle of that generation. Far more serious were the disabilities to which Jews were exposed until the 1960s: most Ivy League universities set out to limit the number of Jews admitted; many places of accommodation, hotels, and apartment houses were closed to them; clubs and fraternities boycotted Jews; Christian religious practices persisted in public schools; thousands of employment agencies refused to place Jewish applicants.

Yet despite all this anti-Jewish activity the Jews persevered; prejudices, disabilities, only served as a spur; they set out to excel. There were Christians—laymen and clergy—who struggled gallantly to defend Jews. During World War II (1945) in Reims, France, a Methodist clergyman, acting in the absence of a "Jewish" chaplain organized a Passover eve dinner for about 3,000 Jewish soldiers. He wrapped himself in a prayer shawl, put on a skullcap, and struggled through the Hebrew!

Selection I is a letter of Mrs. John D. Rockefeller, Jr., asking her three sons to reject all forms of religious and racial prejudice. Born Abby Greene Aldrich, the daughter of the Rhode Island Senator, Nelson W. Aldrich, she had strong social welfare interests, which are reflected in this letter. The second selection is a typical anti-Semitic screed. There were literally dozens of anti-Jewish agitators during this period; none, with the exception of Ford and Coughlin, had a large following. A wartime letter written by Sidney Rabbinowitz on April 26, 1943, three days before he was mortally wounded at Hill 609 in Tunisia appears in the third selection. As he lay dying, he plucked his "last letter" from his pocket; it was found tightly clutched in his hand when his body was recovered. Sidney, an employee of R. H. Macy of New York, was twenty-one years of age. Selection IV contains an excerpt from a detailed report of the Chicago Bureau on Jewish Employment Problems; the final document briefly describes the work of a Christian minister who prepared blind Jewish boys for their bar mitzvah ceremony (selection V).

I.   The Righteous Gentile, By Abby G. A. Rockefeller, January 1928

January, 1928

Dear John, Nelson and Laurance:

For a long time I have had very much on my mind and heart a certain subject. I meant to bring it up at prayers and then later have it for a question to be discussed at a family council; but the right time, because of your father's illness, has never seemed to come.

Out of my experience and observation has grown the earnest conviction that one of the greatest causes of evil in the world is race hatred or race prejudice; in other words, the feeling of dislike that a person or a nation has against another person or nation without just cause, an unreasoning aversion is another way to express it. The two peoples or races who suffer most from this treatment are the Jews and the Negroes; but some people "hate" the Italians, who in turn hate the Jugoslavs, who hate the Austrians, who hate the Czecho-Slovaks, and so it goes endlessly.

You boys are still young. No group of people has ever done you a personal injury; you have no inherited dislikes. I want to make an appeal to your sense of fair play and to beseech you to begin your lives as young men by giving the other fellow, be he Jew or Negro or of whatever race, a fair chance and a square deal.

It is to the disgrace of America that horrible lynchings and race riots frequently occur in our midst. The social ostracism of the Jew is less brutal, and yet it often causes cruel injustice and must engender in the Jews a smouldering fire of resentment.

Put ourselves in the place of an honest, poor man who happens to belong to one of the so-called "despised" races. Think of having no friendly hand held out to you, no kindly look, no pleasant, encouraging word spoken to you. What I would like you always to do is what I try humbly to do myself: that is, never to say or to do anything which would wound the feelings or the self-respect of any human being, and to give special consideration to all who are in any way repressed. This is what your father does naturally from the fineness of his nature and the kindness of his heart.

I long to have our family stand firmly for what is best and highest in life. It isn't always easy, but it is worth while.

Your Mother

[Mrs. John D. (Abby) Rockefeller, Jr.]

II.   The Gentile Declaration of Independence from the Jew Dictatorship, Jew Mongers, Jew Monopolists, and the Jew "Secret Controls" in the United States, Gentile Protocols, 1941

I PLEDGE MYSELF to do all in my power to VOTE OUT and help keep ALL JEWS out of political offices and positions of authority.

I PLEDGE MYSELF to EXPOSE the JEWS who change their names to conceal their JEWISH RACIAL IDENTITY in order to gain FAVORS and TRUSTS which would not otherwise be granted.

I PLEDGE MYSELF to EXPOSE the fact that COMMUNISM is nothing more than a scheme for JEW CONTROL originated by JEWS and PROMOTED and INTRODUCED into the United States by JEWS.

I PLEDGE MYSELF to AVOID purchasing foodstuffs or any kind of merchandise manufactured or sold by JEWS as a precaution against being POISONED or CHEATED.

I PLEDGE MYSELF to KEEP AWAY from JEW DOCTORS, JEW DENTISTS, JEW DRUGGISTS, or JEWISH-CONTROLLED HOSPITALS or INSTITUTIONS.

I PLEDGE MYSELF to AVOID any JEW judge, JEW jury or JEW lawyer in any litigation wherein GENTILE INTERESTS are involved.

I PLEDGE MYSELF to HELP PROSECUTE and expose JEW murderers, thieves and criminals along with their PAID ASSASSINS.

I PLEDGE MYSELF to EXPOSE and BOYCOTT all those concerns who hire JEW REFUGEES, thereby ROBBING the GENTILE Americans of THEIR JOBS.

I PLEDGE MYSELF to SUPPORT MEASURES to take from the JEWS and INTERNATIONALISTS their CONTROL of OUR MONETARY SYSTEM.

I PLEDGE MYSELF not to be MISLED by propaganda dispensed by the JEW-CONTROLLED press, radio and movies.

I PLEDGE MYSELF to OPPOSE any JEW ACTIVITY in our churches, schools, universities, clubs, labor unions and all other organizations.

I PLEDGE MYSELF not to DIVULGE any SECRET to any JEW which would be used in any way DETRIMENTAL to the welfare of a GENTILE.

I PLEDGE MYSELF to EXPOSE the JEW SLACKERS for the army who AVOID service for any cause, whether by "PHONY" EXAMINATION by a JEW doctor, graft, fraud, cowardice, or otherwise.

I PLEDGE MYSELF to REPORT to the proper officials or some recognized patriotic organization ANY JEW who lives in, or entered the United States ILLEGALLY.

I PLEDGE MYSELF to OPPOSE allowing our GENTILE AMERICANS to fight other GENTILES and DIE for some JEW CAUSE, whether HERE or in some FOREIGN COUNTRY.

I PLEDGE MYSELF to OPPOSE and EXPOSE any GENTILE who "FRONTS FOR," "CONNIVES WITH" or who "CARRIES THE BANNER" for a JEW CAUSE detrimental to GENTILES.

I PLEDGE MYSELF to go to the AID and ASSISTANCE of any GENTILE who has been cheated, mistreated or discriminated against by JEWS.

I PLEDGE MYSELF to READ and DISCUSS these "GENTILE PROTOCOLS" with my friends, neighbors and fellow workers.

I pledge myself to help *distribute* or *reproduce* this literature and make distribution—typewritten, carbon copies, mimeograph copies, planograph, printed or hand written copies.

WHEN ALL OTHER GENTILES KEEP THESE PLEDGES AS I DO,
IT WILL BE THE MEANS OF BRINGING ABOUT
AN IMMEDIATE "GENTILE PROSPERITY" IN THE UNITED STATES
THAT WILL AMAZE THE MOST SKEPTICAL.

III.   A Young Jewish Idealist, By Sidney Rabbinowitz, April 26, 1943

April 26, 1943

Dear Pa and Adele:

This is my last letter to you. I am keeping it in my pocket, and if I should be killed, I hope somebody will mail it to you.

Ever since I arrived in North Africa, I have been moving closer to the front. I finally got here yesterday, Easter Sunday.

We have just been told that we are moving up to the front lines in a few hours. Tonight or tomorrow morning I will be attacking the Germans. In case something happens to me, I want you both to know how I feel now.

I'm not scared or frightened. I feel tense, but I suppose that is to be expected. If I get shot, I would rather be killed than horribly wounded.

I'm only worried about how sad you would be if I get killed. But I hope you will also be proud that your son gave his life for the greatest cause in the world—that men might be free.

Pa, if I caused you heartaches and disappointments, I'm sorry. You'll never know how much I have always loved you, and how much more I love you now. Please take care of your health, for my sake.

Adele, whatever good qualities I may have, I owe to you. You were always kind and helpful, and you understood me better than anyone else did. I'm proud to call you "Mother." I leave you all my love.

To both of you, I want to say that you were the best parents in the world and I love you both. I hope God will take good care of you.

There is so much I wanted to say to you when I see you again; about how I was going to take care of you in the future and how I would make you proud of me.

Well, you will have something to be proud of anyway.

Do you remember, before I became a soldier, how I used to say that I wanted to do something to help make the world better?

Now I have the chance. If I die, at least I will know that I died to make the world a better place to live in.

I'll die, not as a hero, but as an ordinary young man who did all he could to help overcome the forces of evil.

I don't have time to write a letter to anyone else. So please give my love to Midge and Ben, Ralph and his family, Willie and the Rosenbergs, and all our friends and relatives. But most of all, give my love to Bobby and Larry. Please don't let them forget their uncle. I've always been so proud of them and I like to feel that they were proud of me, too. I hope they grow up in a peaceful world and become fine men.

God bless you both. I'll always love you.

Your devoted son,

Sidney

IV.   Jewish Unemployment Problems, Chicago, Report of Activities, October 1954

"Plenty of religious preferences—Nordic a must"

"This is a Gentile firm"

"No religious preferences as long as they are of the Nordic race"

"We want Christian girls"

"Says is desperate, but not desperate enough to hire Jews"

"We like the German-Scandinavian home-type girls"

"Can't use any Matzo-ball queens"

"A Jewish girl wouldn't be comfortable here—we like a compatible group"

"Protestant only—no Catholics, Jews or Orientals"

"We don't hire any of the forbidden race [Jews] or the African Brotherhood"

"Protestant preferred—will take a Catholic in a pinch"

These are typical of thousands of similar restrictive specifications which appeared on job-orders placed by Chicago employers during the past year, dramatically emphasizing the continuing seriousness of employment discrimination against Jews. Through documentary evidence made available to the Bureau on Jewish Employment Problems, specific information was obtained on the hiring practices of nearly 4,000 business firms in Chicago. Three out of ten of these firms specified "No Jews" when placing job-orders with employment agencies during 1953, and one out of four of all clerical job-orders barred Jews.

The President's Committee on Government Contracts created by Executive Order to bring about compliance with the non-discrimination provision of government contracts has been impressed by the conclusiveness of the Bureau's data and has worked effectively with us in dramatically eliminating discriminatory policies and practices in important Chicago business firms. The wealth of detailed information now in the Bureau's possession has permitted the application of this and other new techniques in increasing the effectiveness of our case-activity with employers and employment agencies.

JOB DISCRIMINATION AGAINST JEWS: THE FACTS

During the past year the Bureau conducted a unique analysis of the hiring practices of Chicago employers. The data on which this analysis was

[were] based consisted of job-orders placed with commercial employment agencies during 1953 and 1954 by business firms in the Chicago area. Close to 20,000 job-orders were analyzed together with referral, placement and other records of the employment agencies. No such information has ever before been gathered anywhere in the country. The Bureau's analysis reveals the following facts about current job-discrimination against Jews:

1. 3700 or 20% of all job-orders contained employer specifications which barred Jews from consideration. In some agencies the proportion of discriminatory job-orders was found to be close to 30%. Nine out of ten jobs covered in the analysis were for routine clerical positions. Despite the severe shortage of such workers during all of 1953, one out of four of those jobs were [was] closed to Jews at the express direction of the employer or his representative.

2. A total of 995 Chicago business firms or 27% of all firms surveyed were found to have placed discriminatory specifications directed against Jews on job-orders filed with commercial employment agencies. The listing of these firms reads like a "Who's Who of American Industry."

3. The 27% of firms which discriminate and the 20% of job-openings which are closed to Jews represent minimum figures. Employment agencies advise that a substantial proportion of firms which hesitate to frankly state restrictions to them, do in fact discriminate when Jewish workers are referred by the employment agencies. . . .

7. Although close to 3700 job-orders were found to contain restrictions against Jews (and as well against one or another racial, religious or ethnic group), in only three orders were preferences for Jews, or barriers to non-Jews expressed. Moreover, a substantial proportion of those firms which stated positive standards of merit hiring on their job-orders were found to be Jewish-owned.

8. An encouraging finding of the survey was the large number of firms previously contacted by the Bureau because of discriminatory practices, whose job-orders were found in the survey to not only be free of discriminatory specifications, but also to contain expressions of a positive identification with merit practices.

9. A negative note uncovered in the analysis of this data was the number of sizeable and well-known Jewish-owned firms whose job-orders contained barriers against Jews. In many of these cases, the responsibility for the discrimination was attributed by our employment agency informants to subordinate personnel department officials, but it is significant that despite the Jewish ownership of many of the firms, such officials feel secure in pursuing a discriminatory policy. . . .

V.   The Jewish Braille Institute of America, Inc., November 13, 1958

Serving the religious and cultural needs of the Jewish blind
101 West 55th Street, New York 19, New York
By Jacob Freid, Ph.D., Executive Director

November 13, 1958

Mrs. Hilda Weingart
919 Polk Boulevard
Des Moines, Iowa.
Dear Mrs. Weingart:

Would you be good enough to rush two copies of the Blessings before and after reading from the *Torah* to Father H. J. Sutcliffe, 1155 East 32nd Street, Brooklyn, 10, New York. Father Sutcliffe is preparing a young boy, Robert Gehlmeyer, for Bar Mitzvah. Robert is the son of a non-Jewish father and a Jewish mother who, on his own initiative, has asked to be Bar Mitzvah. Father Sutcliffe who was taught Hebrew Braille by our Institute, and who is now a Semitic scholar, will teach Robert his Blessings before and after the Torah. That is why two copies are required. . . .

With every good wish.
Sincerely yours,
Jacob Freid

46

JEWS AND THE WORLD OF THE SECULAR SCIENCES
1944–1955

Beginning in the second quarter of the twentieth century, many Jews turned to secular intellectual pursuits. Once the immigrants Americanized themselves, the gifted ambitious ones, the intellectuals, prepared themselves for professions; the native-born children of the newcomers devoted themselves to social, biological, and physical sciences as well as the arts. The accomplishments of this relatively small group were soon marked; they began to stand out in the graphic arts; individuals among them brought the fine arts to the world of the cinema; the theater, musical comedy, and symphony orchestras reflected their influence. Many of America's notable physicians and medical researchers were Jews; atomic energy was a field that invited the attention of J. Robert Oppenheimer, Lewis Strauss, Bernard Baruch, David E. Lilienthal, Edward Teller, and a host of Jewish physicists.

Roman Jakobson of Harvard and the Massachusetts Institute of Technology was at home in twenty-five languages; Morris Raphael Cohen, a polymath, was an educator, a philosopher, a mathematician, and a student of jurisprudence. Johnny Marks wrote a song which he called "Rudolph, the Red-Nosed Reindeer"; he sold about one hundred million copies. Peter Carl Goldmark invented the long-playing record and the first practical color television system; it was Admiral Hyman George Rickover who pushed the United States Navy relentlessly till the first atomic-powered submarine slid down the ways; Albert Kahn built a company of architects and engineers that constructed about one thousand factories for Henry Ford and erected industrial structures in more than 150 cities; Emanuel Haldeman-Julius published "Little Blue Books"; there were close to two thousand titles; he sold over 300,000,000 copies at five cents each.

Selection I describes briefly the career of the Russian-born Selman Abraham Waksman (1888–1973), the soil microbiologist who was primarily responsible for the discovery of streptomycin and other antibiotics and was in 1952 awarded a Nobel Prize in physiology and medicine. Selection II emphasizes the Jewish aspects of the career of Albert Einstein (1879–1955), the physicist, best known for his theory of relativity. Einstein won a Nobel Prize (1921) before settling in America; he had taught in Switzerland, Czechoslovakia, and Germany before his immigration in 1933. A member of the Institute for Advanced Study in Princeton, Einstein was a Zionist, a committed Jewish ethnicist, and—before the rise of Hitlerism in Germany—a pacifist. It was Einstein who warned President Franklin D. Roosevelt that the Germans were working on the atom bomb and urged that America anticipate this threat.

I. Selman Abraham Waksman and His Miracle Mold, By Al Bohling, 1944

When Selman Abraham Waksman was a youth in the little Ukrainian village of Priluka, he became fascinated with the soil. The cycle of life posed deep, important questions for him; "What is life?" "How does it begin?"

Waksman decided the answers could best be found in a study of medicine. But in the first decade of the 20th century, Russia was no place for such work. In 1910 he and four friends decided to try their luck in the United States.

The young Waksman spent his first winter in America with a cousin, on a five acre farm near Metuchen, N.J. The next spring he made perhaps the most important decision of his life, to visit Dr. Jacob Lipman, another Russian immigrant, who was the director of the New Jersey agricultural experiment station at Rutgers University.

Acting under the advice of Lipman, Waksman abandoned a medical career and sought to find his answers in the soil. He enrolled at Rutgers, in New Brunswick, N.J., and the long quest began. That study culminated 32 years later in the isolation of streptomycin, one of the most spectacular of the antibiotics. It brought hope of cure to tuberculosis sufferers. It also brought the Nobel prize in medicine to its discoverer last month [1952].

In the war winter of 1941–'42, Waksman's work almost was halted. A Rutgers official, seeking ways to trim a tight budget, suggested firing the scientist. His playing around with microbes had not paid off, the official contended, and this would be a good way to save $4,620 a year, his salary.

If Rutgers had succumbed to this temptation, the university would have been robbed of one of the greatest bonanzas in research history. Less than two years later streptomycin was isolated. To date the financial gain to Rutgers has been about three and one-half million dollars and is mounting at a rate of from $500,000 to $1,000,000 a year. . . .

Waksman, at 64, is a quiet retiring person. He might well have retained all the profits and become a millionaire. Instead, he turned over the patent with the simple comment:

"Rutgers won't let me starve."

In fact, Rutgers has been feeding the scientist since his graduation in 1915, except for a two year stint at the University of California, where he obtained his doctor's degree. In 1918 he returned to New Brunswick as a microbiologist at the New Jersey agricultural experiment station and a lecturer in the agricultural college, and immediately plunged into the research he had begun as an undergraduate.

In 1915, Waksman and R. E. Curtis had isolated a microbe known as streptomyces griseus, after the Greek for "white twisted fungus." Much earlier, scientists had become interested in microbes and the soil. Generally, the beginnings are attributed to Louis Pasteur. It was observed that if a disease ridden corpse were buried, the place of burial would not become a polluted area. Billions of microbes would come in to police up the spot, destroying or nullifying harmful effects.

The question then was, if these same microbes could be introduced into the human body, would they not attack and destroy the source of disease? The knowledge that certain microbes had the power to destroy others was applied by Waksman to human disease in 1932, when he undertook to study the fate of tuberculosis microbes when exposed to the action of microbes in a handful of soil.

He set up two problems. One was to isolate a microbe which would stop the growth of or destroy the "hard, waxy, water repellent walled microbe" which caused tuberculosis. The second was to discover a microbe which could destroy a dangerous microbe without at the same time having a harmful effect on the human or animal body.

In 1940, actinomycin was isolated. It was amazingly successful in destroying microbes, but was very efficient also in destroying the animal into which it was injected. Another selective agent was found. It, too, had the effect of eventually killing the animal. But the trail was growing warmer.

Mathematically, the search could have gone on indefinitely. The variety of micro-organisms is believed to be infinite. A break came in 1943, when two promising strains of the old streptomyces griseus were isolated, one from the throat of a sick chicken, the other from a manured field.

The results against the tuberculosis bacillus were effective, but the strains became less vigorous. Intuition, based on the belief that "the soil itself is the power plant of all life," motivated Waksman to plant the microbes in rich earth. This idea paid off. The new generation was more powerful than the parent.

There were other setbacks, new hopes, thousands of tests still to be made. Late in 1944, small quantities of the drug were sent to the Mayo clinic for tests. A short time later the Army joined in.

Finally, the news broke. Success in the treatment of tuberculosis made the drug a sensation. New hope was offered the 500,000 American sufferers. Today experimentation continues, with the hope that streptomycin may provide a means toward the eventual disappearance of the dread disease.

There are two ironic twists to the Waksman saga. One is that Russian boasts of inventiveness here apply, for Waksman was born in Russia. But he was forced to travel to America for the chance to fulfill his mission. The other is that a man who rejected medicine as a field has received the Nobel prize for medicine.

II.   Albert Einstein and His Jewishness, By David M. Szonyi, 1979

Of the three Jews who have played a crucial role in shaping the central ideas of our modern life and culture—Einstein, Marx and Freud—only Einstein—both publicly and privately—was extensively and intricately involved in coming to terms with his Jewish identity. As this month marks the centennial of his birth (March 14, 1879) it is fitting we examine the Jewish forces which played a role in influencing the life and thought of our century's greatest scientist.

The young Albert was neither very knowledgeable of, nor very involved in, Jewish liturgy, ritual and customs; his parents, Herman and Pauline Einstein, as assimilated Bavarian Jews, had sent their son to a Catholic elementary school in Munich. Though he was for a time "intensely religious, both spiritually and ritually . . . and he took it amiss that his parents were lax in their Jewish observance" (biographer Banesh Hoffmann), this period was short-lived. Einstein apparently was never *barmitzvahed* and his first wife Mileva was Greek Orthodox; near the end of his life, he requested that, contrary to halachah (Jewish law), he be cremated after death (which came to him at Princeton in 1955.)

In the Gymnasium (German high school) Einstein chafed against the compulsory nature of Jewish religious instruction, and went on to eschew what he saw as Judaism's over-emphasis on the legalistic and compulsory. Between 1920 and 1924, his rebellion against an imposed religious or communal discipline was expressed by his refusal to pay the "mandatory" Jewish communal tax in Berlin, although he did make a voluntary "contribution" for welfare needs, and during these years became a committed Zionist.

For in this period Einstein had begun to confront his deepest feelings about being a Jew, as well as his emerging sense of his obligations to his heritage. One trigger was a visit in 1919 from a Zionist group; shortly after he became committed to the cause. By 1920, when his theories on relativity were proven, he was subjected to vicious anti-Semitic attacks; his theories first were called part of a "Jewish conspiracy," then of a "Jewish Communist plot." And shortly after winning the Nobel Prize (in 1921), he accepted a request from Chaim Weizmann to go to America on a fund raising tour on behalf of Jews in Palestine and the Hebrew University. In 1923, he visited Palestine and delivered the inaugural address at the Hebrew University.

A strong spokesman for human rights, Einstein fought publicly throughout the '30s for the cause of Jews in Germany, fleeing that country himself in 1933. At the 1939 World's Fair in New York, which heralded the technology of the future, he opened the Jewish Pavilion. . . .

Although Einstein was not particularly observant, he was unquestionably proud of his Jewishness. In his two major collections of non-scientific writings, there are major sections on Jewish themes, and he gives succinct voice to the roots of his Jewish pride:

> The pursuit of knowledge for its own sake, an almost fanatical love of justice and the desire for personal independence—these are the features of the Jewish tradition which make me thank my stars that I belong to it.

Einstein exulted in the prophetic ideal of *tzedek tzedek tierdofe* ("Justice, justice shall you pursue"—Deuteronomy 16:20), which he expressed this way:

> The bond that has united the Jews for thousands of years and unites them today is, above all, the democratic idea of social justice . . . [as expounded by] Moses, Spinoza and Karl Marx.

As an internationalist and one who sometimes alluded to the "Judeo-Christian tradition," Einstein rejected the idea of the "chosen people." Like Hermann Cohen, the leading German-Jewish pre–World War I thinker, he valued Judaism primarily for its ethical teachings, not for classical texts, halachah or customs and holidays. The Torah and Talmud he viewed as "merely the important evidence of the manner in which the Jewish concept of life held sway in earlier times." . . .

Einstein's negative conception of a personal, transcendental, commanding God was strikingly similar to that of Freud in *The Future of an Illusion* (1920). According to Einstein, "the Jewish God is simply a negation of superstition, the imaginary result of its elimination. It is also an attempt to base the moral law on fear, a regrettable and discreditable attempt." All people might share the joy in the beauty and grandeur of the world expressed by the psalmist, he added, but "to tack this feeling to the idea of God seems mere childish absurdity."

A pacifist most of his life, Einstein saw this idea as largely rooted in the Jewish commitment to the supremacy of the intellect and language over the forces of power and coercion. Addressing a 1929 meeting of Berlin Jews, he remarked that "Jewry has proved that the intellect is the best weapon in history. Oppressed by violence, Jewry has mocked her enemies by rejecting war and at the same time has taught people." If Einstein did not see the Jews as the "chosen people," he sometimes spoke and wrote of them as though they were, or should become, what might be called "the exemplary people," calling on them, "true to the ethical teachings of our forebears, [to] become soldiers in the fight for peace, united with the noblest elements in all cultural and religious circles."

But the most important and most influential manifestation of Einstein's Jewishness was his Zionism. Indeed, his 1921 "conversion" to the movement, and specifically his accompaniment of Chaim Weizmann on a fund-raising trip to America, were as important to European Zionism as Louis Brandeis' 1917 endorsement of the idea of a "Jewish homeland" was to American Zionism. In both cases the involvement of a prestigious intellect provided what had been a minority and seemingly marginal movement new "clout."

What motivated Einstein's relatively late (he was 42 in 1921) involvement in Zionist affairs was, as was mentioned earlier, the anti-Semitism he encountered upon returning to Germany from Switzerland in 1914. . . .

> When I came to Germany fifteen years ago, I discovered I was a Jew, and I owe this discovery more to Gentiles than Jews. . . . I saw Jews basely caricatured and the sight made my heart bleed. I saw how schools, comic papers, and innumerable other forces of the Gentile majority undermined the confidence even of the best of my fellow Jews, and this could not be allowed to continue.

Then the August, 1920 meeting of "German physicists" who inveighed against "Jewish physics," i.e., Einstein's theory of relativity.

Influenced by the Russian-Jewish philosopher and polemicist Ahad Ha'am ("One of the People," the pen-name for Asher Ginzberg), Einstein saw a Jewish homeland in Palestine more as a spiritual and cultural center which would regenerate Judaism, than as a "normalized" state or simply a refuge for oppressed Jews. For him, Zionism represented nothing less than "the reawakening corporate spirit of the whole Jewish people," as he wrote in 1933. In an appeal to Hungarian Jews on behalf of Keren Hayesod a year later, he summed up his vision of Palestine as a regenerative force in Jewish life:

Palestine will be a center of culture for all Jews, a refuge for the grievously oppressed, a field of action for the best among us, a unifying ideal, and a means of attaining inward health for the Jews of the whole world.

Like Martin Buber, his fellow refugees (the late philosophers Erich Kahler and Hannah Arendt), and the idealist Zionists of the Bar Kochba university student group he had befriended while teaching in Prague around 1910, Einstein was particularly sensitive to the "Arab problem." In a letter written in early November, 1929—only a few weeks after Arab pogroms killed 133 religious Jews in Safed and Hebron, and at a time when rage, panic and confusion reigned in Zionist circles—he nevertheless insisted that

Without an agreement and cooperation with the Arabs we shall not succeed. There can be no talk of forcing the Arabs from their land.

As he had incurred the hostility of German nationalists for his original involvement with the Zionists, so Einstein was sharply criticized by many religious and Revisionist Zionists (followers of Vladimir Jabotinsky and, after 1940, Menachem Begin) for focusing too much on solving "the problem of living side by side with our brother the Arab in an open, generous and worthy manner," as he put it in a 1931 newspaper article.

In general, then, Einstein's Zionism was highly idealistic. As late as 1938, in a speech before the (American) National Labor Committee for Palestine, he asserted that

The essential nature of Judaism resists the idea of a Jewish state with borders, an army and a measure of temporal power no matter how modest. I am afraid of the inner damages Judaism will sustain—especially from the development of a narrow nationalism.

However, with ever darker clouds gathering over Germany and all of Europe, he added that, "If external necessity should after all compel us to assume this burden, let us bear it with tact and patience." . . .

It was hardly surprising that, following Weizmann's death in 1952, David Ben-Gurion invited Einstein to become Israel's second president. In declining (Einstein had too many scientific commitments to honor at Princeton's Institute for Advanced Studies and elsewhere, and did not see himself as a national leader), he observed that "my relationship to the Jewish people has become my strongest bond, ever since I became fully aware of our precarious situation among the nations of the world." This awareness was the basis of his 35 years of intensive practical and polemical activity on behalf of a safe and just Jewish homeland in the Middle East.

In sum, far more than Marx, and significantly [even] more than Freud, Einstein "exuded" his Jewishness. With his sometimes absentminded or distracted intellectuality, his intense eyes, shock of white hair and large forehead, Einstein in fact created the stereotype of the ultimate "Jewish scientific genius." And, in addition to his love of pranks and sailing, Einstein had at least as great a love for classical music, books, letters and good conversation; some might say he possessed the post-Emancipation, European-Jewish "craving for culture." His widely known traits of modesty and generosity were in a way typical of the Jewish tradition of . . . "compassionate children of compassionate parents." Of course, his persona as a scientist and pacifist-socialist-internationalist were of great importance in shaping Einstein the private and the public man. But seen in perspective, Einstein's Jewishness seemed to have played a predominant role in influencing his self-perception, his ideals and his myriad non-scientific activities.

47

THE ECONOMIC WORLD OF THE AMERICAN JEW
1922–1966

By the 1920s thousands of Jews of immigrant stock had been in this country for a half century. Many were culturally integrated; many more were already entrenched in the American economy. Because of purely fortuitous—historical—circumstances Jews had staked out special fields of commercial activity where they could survive comfortably. They flocked to the largest cities, the obvious nurseries of wealth, where opportunity beckoned. By the 1920s the Jews—mostly immigrants— were moving away from industry. Very few were pick-and-shovel men; a substantial number were skilled artisans; very few were dirt farmers.

Gifted individuals received national recognition for what they had accomplished. Louis Blaustein and his son Jacob built the American Oil Company (Amoco); they erected the first drive-in gasoline stations; David Sarnoff fashioned the Radio Corporation of America; Louis Jay Horowitz, as president of Thompson Starrett Construction Company, erected skyscrapers that changed New York's skyline; the Levitts bought 1,200 acres of Long Island potato fields and built Levittown, a city of 40,000 people and 10,000 houses; a new home was finished every fifteen minutes. Joseph H. Cohen (Gelatin Joe) of Woburn, Massachusetts, was the president of the Atlantic Gelatin Company, the world's largest manufacturer of that product; Isaac Gilman, a paper mill owner, turned a Vermont village into a model industrial town; the grateful inhabitants changed its name from Fitzdale to Gilman. All of these entrepreneurs were of East European immigrant stock. Jewish businessmen were leaders in radio, broadcasting, the cigar industry, the cinema, distilling.

Above all, they controlled the all-inclusive apparel industry; although Jewish workers had begun to leave the industry in droves, Jews still dominated the apparel unions; Jews were the employers, the owners, the distributors. David Dubinsky was president of the International Ladies' Garment Workers' Union (ILGWU); Sidney Hillman led the Amalgamated Workers of America. In Roosevelt's time the several "Jewish" unions were an integral part of the liberal New Deal coalition; for a brief period Hillman was one of America's most influential politicians. The Jewish unions —there were several—now laid less emphasis on socialist goals; they had become an integral part of the American body politic; unionism, not Marxism, was the basic issue. In certain respects the large clothing unions were exemplary. They furthered collective bargaining; their concern was hours, wages, clean factories; union leaders cooperated with the owners, the manufacturers; they had common goals. Hillman, Dubinsky, and their numerous Jewish colleagues were in the van of those union leaders who sought to provide their followers with unemployment insurance, pensions, housing, and their own banks. The ILGWU developed a remarkable Union Health Center that had about 90,000 members. Unionism for the Jewish members was a way of life; they had their own lodges, their Yiddish press, literature, and afternoon schools. The ILGWU spent millions in the Pocono Mountains, to build Unity House, a thousand-acre vacation resort with a dining room that fed 1,100. Come the Revolution— and it came—we will eat filet mignon—and they did!

The Jews of those mid-twentieth century decades flocked to the professions; the men—and some women, too—preferred law and medicine; the women no longer pedaled sewing machines in factories; they worked in offices and crowded school rooms as teachers. Most Jews, however, were in commerce and trade. Husbands and wives by the thousands operated small shops and stores; they were retailers; the more successful were jobbers and wholesalers; the truly gifted among them built department stores. Under the tutelage of Julius Rosenwald, Sears, Roebuck & Company became one of America's leading commercial enterprises; after a fashion its catalogue was the Bible of the common man.

Selection I tells the story of a twelve-year-old Brooklyn Jewish girl, Tillie Lewis (b. 1901), who took a job in a factory folding kimonos; they paid her $2.50 a week. Ambitious, she conjured up a brand new business, and when she was sixty-five years of age, she sold Tillie Lewis Foods for $9,000,000. Selection II recounts the story of a Polish immigrant, Samuel Goldwyn (1882–1974), who did as much as anyone to raise the cultural level of the American cinema industry.

I.   Tillie Lewis, Industrialist, By Caroline Bird, 1934–1966

Defense contracts [during World War II] enabled new small enterprises in many industries to survive their growing pains and grow big. One who made good use of this opportunity was one of the first women to get a cannery going in California. Manpower was short on the farms and in the canneries, but the armed forces were begging for more production, and the only way to deliver it was to find and train workers who had never seen the inside of a cannery.

During World War II, this woman stood along the assembly line of her plant personally showing new workers how to peel Italian tomatoes. When they couldn't do the delicate operation fast enough she tried canning tomatoes in their skins. It worked and other hard-pressed canners followed her lead.

Tillie Lewis (b. 1901) introduced the Italian tomato industry to California in the first place. One of a very small group of self-made enterprising women, she had long dreamed of growing, canning, and selling the small, tangy, pear-shaped tomatoes called pomodoros that make Italian spaghetti sauce unique.

She was born Myrtle Ehrlich in Brooklyn. Her father was a Jewish immigrant who ran a music store. Her mother died when she was a baby. She didn't like her stepmother, and nobody objected when Tillie quit school at 12, lied about her age, and went to work folding kimonos at $2.50 a week for a Brooklyn garment manufacturer. When Tillie was 15, she married a grocer twice her age just to get away from home.

The way she likes to tell the story, the idea of growing pomodoros popped into her head the only time she volunteered, on a Sunday, to help take inventory for her husband. Looking over his stock, she wondered why the high-priced tomatoes and tomato pastes were all from Italy. Why couldn't these special tomatoes be grown in the United States? . . .

After she divorced her husband, she worked as a "customer's woman" for a stockbroker for a time and went to business school at night. Soon she was selling securities on commission, and she was good at it. In 1932, one of her gloomiest years of the Depression on Wall Street, she earned $12,000.

One day in 1934 she read on the office news ticker that Congress had imposed a 40 percent tariff on pomodoro imports. If she was to do anything about her long-cherished dream, she realized this was the time. She bought a new hat and a Berlitz book of lessons in Italian, and invested her savings in a second-class passage to Naples aboard the S. S. *Vulcania*.

On the way over she had the luck to meet Florindo del Gaizo, a Naples canner who was the leading exporter of pomodoros. He was interested in the tariff too, and feared that it would cut down on the 700,000 cases a year he sold in America. He was also fascinated by the little red-haired woman in the big hat who had never been in a cannery but talked confidently of growing and canning pomodoros in the United States. The courtly Italian toured her through his cannery, showed her pomodoros growing around Naples, and entertained her in his home.

She left happily two weeks later with a cashier's check for $10,000 and four bags of pomodoro seedlings. Under the arrangement with Florindo del Gaizo, he would send her canning equipment and an expert to install it. She would undertake to grow, can, and market Italian-style tomatoes in the United States, and for this she was to be paid a salary of $50 a week.

Florindo was the closest thing to a male sponsor Tillie ever had. "I will never forget him," she says. "He was the first person to believe in me."

She named their enterprise Flotill Products, Inc., a combination of his first name and her nickname, and, in commemoration of its casual launching, designed a trademark picturing a champagne glass and a sprig of pomodoros. She had never been to California, but she had the names of business people who might be able to help, and they suggested various sites for her to visit. The San Joaquin Valley looked like the best place because it had soil and climate much like that of Naples. She found a canner who agreed to pack on a cost-plus basis.

The first real snag was the reluctance of farmers to plant the seedlings she farmed out to them. They were used to growing round tomatoes, onions, and potatoes, and they didn't think pomodoros would grow in the San Joaquin Valley.

Tillie induced them to promise to plant enough to can 100,000 cases of whole tomatoes and 100,000 cases of tomato paste. Then she set out on a one-woman tour of the East to get wholesalers to buy the crop she expected. Before the tomatoes were even grown, the whole crop had been sold.

The pomodoros grew beautifully, but there weren't enough of them. The farmers had been so doubtful that the pomodoros would grow that they had not been willing to risk all their acreage on the new crop. Tillie had to answer to the angry wholesalers. The second year she had her own cannery in Stockton, the crop was bigger and there was a profit, but there were always problems. Tillie had to learn all about commercial canning. In the beginning, she used secondhand equipment that was always breaking down. Once, just when tons of tomatoes were waiting to be processed, a steam boiler stopped working. At the very moment Tillie was wondering what to do, the wail of a railroad whistle reminded her that locomotives produced steam.

"I called up the Santa Fe and asked how much they would charge to lend me a locomotive," she recalls. "The man who answered was sympathetic and said they would charge only the switching fee of $7.50. 'Good,' I said 'I'll take two.' The tomatoes were saved."

Florindo del Gaizo died in 1937, and to keep control of the enterprise Tillie had to borrow $100,000 to buy his stock. A vice president of the

Banco di Napoli in New York loaned her the money, and she gratefully said: "If I can ever do anything for you, please don't hesitate to call me." Pearl Harbor ended operations of the Banco di Napoli in New York, and in a letter the banker reminded Tillie of her promise. She sent him tickets to California for himself and his family and created the job of vice president and treasurer for him in the company. He held the post for 27 years.

In 1940, the AFL [American Federation of Labor] cannery workers struck her plant, though she was paying more than the union asked and providing additional benefits. The strike was settled with the help of Meyer Lewis, western director of the AFL, and a year later he became her general manager. Seven years later, they were married.

As an independent canner, Tillie had to find some way to establish consumer recognition of her brand name. One of her assets was the attention she attracted as the only woman canner in the business. Her own attempts to reduce led, in 1952, to the first artificially sweetened canned fruit. The diet pack turned out to be popular and profitable. When she sold her controlling shares in Tillie Lewis Foods, Inc., to the Ogden Corporation in 1966 for $9 million, she became that billion-dollar company's first woman director.

Each major American war has permanently liberated women from some restriction on their freedom. The Civil War had made it respectable for them to leave their homes to work in public. Their contribution to World War I secured them the vote. World War II offered married women the option of working for money when they needed it, and at the same time gave to industry a badly needed flexible labor reserve.

II.   Samuel Goldwyn: Cinema Perfectionist,
By Albin Krebs, 1922–1959

. . . In a distinguished career that spanned a half-century, Mr. Goldwyn became a Hollywood legend, a motion picture producer whose films, always created on a grand scale, were notable for those most elusive of traits—taste and quality.

Truly one of the last tycoons, who even looked the part, Mr. Goldwyn was a driving perfectionist, a man with a titanic temperament whose great gift was the ability to bring together, for each of his productions, the very best writers, directors, cinematographers and other craftsmen. . . .

Although he was one of the flashiest and most controversial of the independent producers, to the general public he was probably best known for his "Goldwynisms," the malapropisms, mixed metaphors, grammatical blunders and word manglings that included the now classic "Include me out" and "I'll tell you in two words—im-possible!" . . .

Among the more famous Goldwynisms were:

"An oral agreement isn't worth the paper it's written on."

"A man who goes to a psychiatrist should have his head examined."

"This atom bomb is dynamite." . . .

"People say that whenever I have a picture coming out I always start a controversy about something that gets into the papers," he said, "Well, in all sincerity, I want to assure you that as a general proposition, there's not a single word of untruth in that." . . .

Mr. Goldwyn was born Aug 27, 1882, in Warsaw. Little was known of his family background, but he was the son of poor parents who died when he was young. At the age of 11, the boy left Poland. After spending two years in England, he migrated to Gloversville, N.Y., where he took a job sweeping floors in a glove factory.

The youth already had the drive for which he was to become noted in Hollywood. By the time he was 17 he was the foreman of 100 workers in the glove plant and at 19 he went on the road as a glove salesman. Four years later he became a partner in the company, and before he was 30 Mr. Goldwyn was making more than $15,000 a year.

It was almost by accident that Mr. Goldwyn got into movie making. In 1910 he married Blanche Lasky, whose brother was a vaudeville producer. Mr. Lasky, at the urging of a lawyer, Arthur S. Friend, toyed with the idea of film making and tried to interest his brother-in-law in such a venture. Mr. Goldwyn, who had moved to New York, was cool to the idea until one cold day in 1913, when he stepped into a Herald Square movie house to warm up and, only incidentally, saw a Western starring Broncho Billy Anderson. He was impressed not only with the movie but also with all the dimes the management was raking in.

With the enthusiasm that was typical of him, Mr. Goldwyn took up the idea of forming a film company of his very own. He and Mr. Lasky each put up $10,000 and, between them, Mrs. Goldwyn and Mr. Friend, pledged the rest of the $26,500 capitalization for the new Jesse L. Lasky Feature Picture Play Company. . . .

The company set out to produce long films that told romantic stories, even if they took an hour to unfold. Most "flickers" at the time were two-reelers, lasting about 20 minutes.

The Lasky Company's first movie was a milestone in more ways than one. It was a five-reeler, the first feature-length movie, and one of the first films to be made in Hollywood. Called "The Squaw Man," it starred a well-known Broadway actor, Dustin Farnum, and it was directed by a young stage manager and unsuccessful playwright, named Cecil B. De-Mille, who had never worked on a movie before.

"The Squaw Man" was a tremendous success. . . .

In 1922, Mr. Goldwyn became an independent producer, convinced that he would never be able to get along with partners or boards of directors. "It's a dog eat dog in this business and nobody's going to eat me." . . .

George Cukor refused to work for Mr. Goldwyn at all, which so exasperated the producer that he is reported to have said: "That's the way with these directors—they're always biting the hand that lays the golden egg." . . .

When he wasn't haunting his sound stages, Mr. Goldwyn was out selling his pictures, both in this country and abroad. "I've got a great slogan for the company," he once said—giving birth to another Goldwynism —"Goldwyn pictures griddle the earth."

They not only girdled the earth, they were immensely popular. In a 20-year period before television started giving mass exposure to films, more than 200 million people paid to see Goldwyn productions. Many of the films were nominated for Academy Awards, but Mr. Goldwyn did not receive an Oscar for best picture until 1947 when "The Best Years of Our Lives" won all the major awards. Mr. Goldwyn was also presented, at that time, with the Irving Thalberg Memorial Award for his contributions to the film industry.

"Wuthering Heights" received the New York Film Critics Award in 1939 the year "Gone With the Wind" swept the Academy Awards. . . .

Mr. Goldwyn came out of semiretirement in 1959 to make his last film, "Porgy and Bess." Although he was already 78 years old, he held his chesty 6-foot-tall body erect, and his swinging walk seemed as always to be jet-propelled as he strode through his studio streets. His eyes deep-set in his rather plain face could still flash with anger, and his Polish-accented voice had lost little of its deep vibrancy.

In recent years, Mr. Goldwyn rented his studio to independent film and television productions, but he was not pleased with much of the product that emanated from there and other parts of Hollywood. He believed movies and TV had become trashy.

Summing up his career, Mr. Goldwyn said, "I was a rebel, a lone wolf. My pictures were my own. I financed them myself and answered solely to myself. My mistakes and my successes were my own. My one rule was to please myself, and if I did that, there was a good chance I would please others." . . .

48

The Overall Structured Community, Locally and Nationally, 1945–1949

Practically all Jewish organizations were determined to remain autonomous, but were severely shaken by the anti-Semitism of the 1920s and 1930s. Having little faith in the several nationwide Jewish defense agencies, they spontaneously created a local institution which they called the Community Relations Committee (CRC). All elements in the city were co-opted including the synagogs and the aspiring East European immigrants who were now coming into their own. Professionals were hired by the CRC to defend the Jewish community from all anti-Jewish forces. Thus, in effect, the locality's autonomous associations were welded into the semblance of a united, overall community. Realizing the need to plan for its future, this new community met in constituent assemblies and established a Jewish Community Council that was governed by a democratically adopted constitution. This council seemed a great advance in local Jewish governance, in integrating all Jews, but actually it was not what it seemed to be. The new council had no authority to levy taxes. It was dependent on grants from the Jewish Federation, the oligarchic organization that conducted the annual United Jewish Appeal drive. Power in the community remained in the hands of the Federation leaders, the 10 percent of affluent householders who gave the bulk of the money raised for overseas and local needs. Thus no authoritative all-inclusive local administrative agency came into being.

While the Jewish Community Council was struggling to become effective in the 1940s, the Zionist Organization of America set out during these World War II years to save the Jews of the Palestine Mandate, threatened with dismemberment by British and Arab interests. Patterning themselves on the American Jewish Congress movement of 1916–1920, the Zionists now called an American Jewish Conference into being (1943). Its goals were twofold: to salvage European Jewry in the coming postwar days, and to establish a Jewish commonwealth in Palestine. At the first session, the Conference *demanded* that Great Britain, the Mandatory power, move to establish a Palestinian Jewish commonwealth. Four years later the Conference formulated a plan for an overall structured American nationwide Jewish community (1947). Many members of the Conference, non-Zionists and Zionists alike, were convinced that such an organization was an imperative need, but the most powerful institutions—the Union of American Hebrew Congregations, the American Jewish Committee, the B'nai B'rith, the Jewish Labor Committee, the National Council of Jewish Women—would not surrender one whit of their autonomy. The new Plan, a compromise, bound its institutional constituents to nothing; even if it had been implemented the proposed new national assembly would have been impotent. The Plan died aborning in 1947, for in November of that year the United Nations agreed to give the Zionists a Jewish state in a partitioned Palestine. This was the death knell of the American Jewish Conference. The Zionists had what they wanted and now had no desire to encourage the emergence of a powerful American Jewish organization that might well overshadow the imminent Palestinian Jewish state; the non-Zionist organizations were equally happy; a national Jewish congress might have limited their scope and activities. There were no general sessions of the American Jewish Conference after December, 1947.

Selections I and II contain excerpts from the constitutions of the Jewish Community Council of Essex County, New Jersey (1945) and the Allied Jewish Community Council of Denver (1949). Selection III is the Plan for a permanent overall organization of American Jews (1947).

I.   Jewish Community Council of Essex County, N.J., 1945

ARTICLE I

CHARACTER AND PURPOSES

Section 1. *Character of Organization.* So far as possible, the Council shall seek to be representative of all Jews and all Jewish groups having a constructive interest in Jewish life, located in Essex County and its neighboring municipalities. It shall be a voluntary association, following democratic procedures and seeking the maximum participation of its membership.

Section 2. *Purposes.* The Council shall endeavor to perform the community responsibilities of the Jews of Essex County and its neighboring municipalities for the needs of Jewish life—locally, nationally and overseas. Specifically, the Council shall

A. assume general responsibility for the conduct and support of essential local services;

B. seek to coordinate or conduct, when desirable, all appeals for funds made to the general community; and

C. help to maintain the dignity and integrity of Jewish life by

1) developing an intelligent and effective understanding of Jewish problems and interests;

2) encouraging the amicable adjustment of differences among Jews or Jewish organizations, through conciliation or arbitration; and

3) safeguarding the civil, political, economic and religious rights to which Jews are entitled with all Americans.

ARTICLE II

Section 3. *Members of the Council.* Every adult Jewish contributor of $3.00 or more to the most recently completed fund-raising campaign of the Council shall be a member of the Council. . . .

II. Allied Jewish Community Council of Denver, 1949

PREAMBLE

Recognizing that a unity of purpose and a totality of program in Jewish Life is best achieved by the more democratic process of full representation, the Council hereby broadens its organization to include agency representation so that its purposes will be achieved democratically by and with the consent of the organizations and the Jewish Community at large.

ARTICLE I

NAME

Section 1. The name of this organization shall be the Allied Jewish Community Council of Denver.

ARTICLE II

PURPOSE

Section 1. The purpose of the organization shall be:

(a) To further the welfare of the Jewish Community of Denver; to determine and recommend matters of policy; to represent the community in all matters of general Jewish interest, other than religious, where concerted action is desirable.

(b) To unite the Jewish Community for the purpose of one centralized appeal, collection, and allocation of funds to Jewish causes; to determine which causes have a justified claim on the community for support; to eliminate frequent and separate appeals and solicitations on the community; to evaluate by approval or disapproval fund-raising drives or solicitations of funds, for Jewish causes in Denver.

(c) To engage in social planning in all fields of community service, and to take such steps as are necessary to implement such planning.

(d) To encourage the amicable adjustment of differences between individuals and organizations by providing the appropriate machinery for conciliation and arbitration.

(e) To coordinate the activities of agencies and services, and to review agency programs and make recommendations.

(f) To encourage good public relations within the Jewish community and the community-at-large.

ARTICLE III

MEMBERS

Section 1. Members will be of two types, as follows:

(a) Any adult Jewish resident of Denver or vicinity who has contributed a minimum of $10.00 to the Council.

(b) Any agency or organization meeting the qualifications set down in this constitution. . . .

ARTICLE XIV

CONSTITUENT AGENCIES

Section 1. Qualifications:

(a) Any Jewish organization, congregation, or functional organization composed of residents of Denver, purely local in its purposes, may be eligible for membership to the Council.

(b) Any group or organization of residents of Denver of not less than twenty-five (25) members representing any national or international organization may be eligible for membership. The number of delegates to which such organization is entitled shall be based on the numerical membership of the Denver group. . . .

III. Plan for a Permanent Overall Organization of American Jews, 1947

I. PURPOSE AND SCOPE

1. An organization, democratic in structure and representative of the American Jewish community, shall be established to secure and protect

rights and to promote the general welfare of the Jewish people, here and abroad; and to enhance the contribution of the Jewish community to American democracy.

a. In matters affecting the rights and status of Jews on the international scene, this organization shall act for American Jewry in all representations before the United States Government and its departments, intergovernmental agencies and the United Nations, and in all public relations connected therewith. The organization shall endeavor to cooperate with the organized Jewish communities of other countries and with such international Jewish agencies as are or may be established.

b. In all matters affecting the rights and status of the Jewish people with regard to Palestine and its upbuilding, the organization shall endeavor to cooperate with the Jewish Agency for Palestine, as the official spokesman of the Jewish people with respect to Palestine, and may request organizations and agencies engaged in activities in this field in the United States to submit reports periodically.

c. In the defense of Jewish rights in the United States and in opposing all anti-democratic forces and tendencies in American life and in combatting anti-Semitism in all its forms, the organization shall act through recognized Jewish agencies, affiliated with the organization, operating in these fields, without affecting their autonomy, it being understood that such agencies shall be invited to report to the organization periodically in order that the organization may be in a position to consider their policies and work, and recommend proposals to promote their objectives.

d. In the field of overseas relief and rehabilitation, the organization shall act through recognized Jewish agencies, affiliated with the organization, operating in these fields, without affecting their autonomy, it being understood that such agencies shall be invited to report to the organization periodically in order that the organization may be in a position to consider their policies and work, and recommend proposals to promote their objectives.

e. American Israel [American Jewry] is rooted in the great historic and religious tradition of our people and this organization, aware of our common spiritual heritage, in its program and activities, shall recognize and respect the right of individuals and organizations to adhere to this heritage in accordance with their own beliefs and practices. This organization shall not interfere with the autonomy of religious groups.

II. STRUCTURE

1. The organization shall be governed by a National Council which will decide its policies and elect an executive body to conduct its affairs.

2. The National Council shall meet annually at a time and place to be fixed by its executive body, and provision shall be made for special sessions of the National Council at the call of the executive body.

3. The National Council shall consist of not more than 750 delegates to be elected biennially in accordance with the rules of election approved by the Council. The election shall be supervised by a National Board of Elections to be named by the executive body. . . .

IV. PROCEDURE

The decisions of the National Council shall be deemed the views of the body as a whole but shall not be regarded as representative of the views of all affiliated organizations unless such organizations have ratified the action.

49

The Jewish Religion and Its Adherents
1937–1960

ere in the United States, Judaism as a religion and a culture was to experience changes in the decades after 1925. The three main denominations were still Orthodox, Conservative, and Reform. The right-wing group, the Orthodox, maintained its basic conviction: the Holy Scriptures and their rabbinic supplements are the word of God, hence binding and authoritative. Orthodoxy was, however, in no sense homogeneous; it included then, as it does now, several disparate, if not hostile, factions. One of them, securely rooted in Orthodoxy, is Hassidism, a pietistic sect that first rose in Eastern Europe in the eighteenth century. The Lubavitch Hassidim stem from the Russian town to which this particular movement traces its origins; it was there that they preached the gospel of *habad*, a Hebrew acronym for three words, wisdom, understanding, knowledge, concepts that they interpreted cabalistically. As has been true of other Hassidic groups, their leader is called the Rebbe. By the mid-twentieth century the Lubavitcher had a substantial following in Brooklyn; subsequently they gained followers almost everywhere.

The Conservatives were probably the largest Jewish denomination in North America by the late twentieth century. In theory they acknowledged the authority of the rabbinic codes; in practice they accommodated themselves to the need to survive comfortably in a religiously permissive America. They have no commonly accepted platform on which all Conservatives can stand. Their leaders, however, have published individual credos that have much in common. From Conservative ranks has emerged a deviant group, the Reconstructionists; their founder, Mordecai M. Kaplan (1881–1983), established in 1922 the Society for the Advancement of Judaism; it later gave birth to the Jewish Reconstructionist Foundation.

435

Rabbi Kaplan and his followers respected the ancient rituals and customs, but theologically and intellectually were most comfortable far over on the left; many were humanists. As nationalists they were committed to Zionism; some believed in the spiritual primacy of the State of Israel.

Close on the heels of the Conservatives came the third major denomination, the Reformers, for whom the Hebrew Bible and the rabbinic writings were historical and literary works, to be treasured reverentially, but not held religiously binding. The creed that still prevailed reflected the 1885 Pittsburgh Platform, though in 1937 it was modified by the Columbus Platform. In the 1937 Platform, the Reform rabbis agreed to work for a Jewish homeland in Palestine. Thus neo-Reform was advanced. As early as 1922, Rabbi Stephen S. Wise, a religious liberal, had organized the Jewish Institute of Religion, which avowedly sought a meeting ground between liberal traditionalism and Zionism. The Reform movement began turning to the right if only to capture the acculturated East Europeans and their college-bred sons and daughters. Judaism was now seen as more than ethical monotheism; it was recognized as a way of life. What the parents had rejected the daughters and sons cherished; not infrequently the grandchildren "made aliyah," they settled in the new State of Israel. The tolerance extended Zionism by the Central Conference of American Rabbis and the Union of American Hebrew Congregations annoyed thousands of Classical Reformers for whom the Pittsburgh Platform was something like the word of God. In 1942, they established the American Council for Judaism (ACJ), an association that rejected Zionism, Jewish nationality and folkishness: We are American citizens of the Jewish persuasion! The ACJ recruited thousands of the faithful. Unfortunately for them anti-Semitism in America and the Holocaust stimulated Jewish ethnicism. Israel was the only country where suffering Jews could go as of right; the American Council for Judaism declined precipitously.

This same century saw the growth of still another "sect," substantial in numbers. Isaac M. Wise once called its adherents "nothingenarians." These were civil religionists, who, though not affiliated, retained some ties to Jews and Judaism. This is a group that will not diminish.

In general there was an upswing in ethnicity by 1960. Jews genuflected in the direction of traditional folkways; they had been pushed to the right by Judeophobes in America, Europe, the Middle East, and North Africa. The United States wanted no Jewish immigrants; Germany, in the 1940s, killed any Jews on whom it could lay its hands; the Moslems drove them out from all their lands. Close to 700,000 went into exile in the lands where Islam was regnant.

Selection I reprints the pro-Israel statement in the 1937 Columbus Platform. Reformers acknowledged the need for this new Jewish commonwealth. Ever since 1930 the Reformers had begun making surveys of religious practices; they cultivated ceremonialism hoping to recruit the new Americans of East European stock who were reared Orthodox. Selection II contains a religious survey which was conducted by the National Federation of Temple Brotherhoods; it appeared as a news release and was published by the Jewish Telegraphic Agency in 1953. Selection III reflects the religious views of Simon Greenberg, a notable Conservative cleric. In selection IV Rabbi Menachem M. Schneerson, the Hassidic leader, insists that in Orthodoxy women are not treated as inferiors (1957). The fifth document—in story form—describes a typical Friday in an American Hassidic home (1959). In the final selection, VI, Rabbi Mordecai M. Kaplan expounds his concept of Reconstructionism. For him Judaism is more than a religion; it is a culture, a civilization (1960).

I. The Zionist Paragraphs in the Columbus Platform, May 27, 1937

Israel. Judaism is the soul of which Israel [the Jewish people] is the body. Living in all parts of the world, Israel has been held together by the ties of a common history, and above all, by the heritage of faith. Though we recognize in the group-loyalty of Jews who have become estranged from our religious tradition, a bond which still unites them with us, we maintain that it is by its religion and for its religion that the Jewish people has lived. The non-Jew who accepts our faith is welcomed as a full member of the Jewish community.

In all lands where our people live, they assume and seek to share loyally the full duties and responsibilities of citizenship and to create seats of Jewish knowledge and religion. In the rehabilitation of Palestine, the land hallowed by memories and hopes, we behold the promise of renewed life for many of our brethren. We affirm the obligation of all Jewry to aid in its upbuilding as a Jewish homeland by endeavoring to make it not only a haven of refuge for the oppressed but also a center of Jewish culture and spiritual life.

Throughout the ages it has been Israel's mission to witness to the Divine in the face of every form of paganism and materialism. We regard it as our historic task to cooperate with all men in the establishment of the kingdom of God, of universal brotherhood, justice, truth and peace on earth. This is our Messianic goal.

II. Religious Trends in Reform Jewry, 1953

St. Louis. . . . The 15th biennial convention of the National Federation of Temple Brotherhoods heard a report on the attitude of Reform Jews in this country toward intermarriage, Jewish education, religious ceremonies, and synagogue observances. The report, based on a survey conducted by the National Federation among members of Reform congregations, established the following facts:

1. Virtually all of America's Reform Jews want religious education for their children. The survey revealed that 66 percent want one day a week; 22 percent two days; 8 percent three days; and 4 percent four days.

2. Almost 75 percent want their children to be taught Hebrew; 51 percent want one day of Hebrew education a week, 34 percent two days, and 15 percent want more. Only one out of eleven American Reform Jews believe in Jewish parochial or day schools.

3. Bar Mitzvah, the traditional rite of inducting a boy of thirteen into the congregation, is practiced in varying degrees in 92 percent of the Reform temples, and 77 percent of the laymen answering the poll endorse this practice. The recently instituted rite of Bas Mitzvah for girls has spread to the extent that it is now observed in 35 percent of Reform congregations, and 41 percent of the Reform Jews answering the poll endorse this practice. More than 60 percent of the Reform temples confirm their children at the age of fifteen or older.

4. Eighty-four percent of the congregations light candles at Friday evening services; and an even greater percentage of the laymen, 90 percent, want this practice. Eighty-nine percent of the rabbis report that the Kiddush [the blessing over wine and bread] is sung in their temples, and 88 percent of the laymen like this practice.

5. A Friday night Torah service, a non-traditional practice, is conducted by 58 percent of the rabbis reporting, but 77 percent of the laymen reporting approve this practice.

With regard to marriage ceremonies, the survey showed that 56 percent of American Reform Jews prefer that marriages be held in the temple, as against 29 percent in the home, and 15 percent in public places. Eighty-four percent would sanction a marriage of a Jew with a former Christian who has been converted to Judaism. However, 53 percent are opposed to marriages between Jews and unconverted Christians.

Only 24 percent would insist upon the use of a chuppah [canopy], for a wedding, and only 16 percent would ask the rabbi to wear a hat during the wedding. Forty percent would expect that a glass be broken at the ceremony. Only 4 percent believe that a religious divorce is necessary, in addition to a civil divorce. Seventeen percent of those replying said they would employ only a mohel [traditional circumciser] for circumcision. Forty-three percent said they would insist upon a rabbi being present if a surgeon was employed.

One of the most interesting revelations of the survey is the large number of people who indicate that they attend temple services weekly. In fact, the same number of Reform Jews now attend services weekly, namely 31 percent, as attend monthly, and the percentage attending occasionally is much smaller, 26 percent, and those who attend solely on the high holidays, only 12 percent. Friday evening services are now conducted in the congregations of 92 percent of those reporting; 48 percent worship on Saturday morning and 8 percent on Sunday morning.

The survey reveals that 59 percent of Reform families say a blessing over the candles in their homes on Sabbath eve; 26 percent make Kiddush; 18 percent say grace before meals, but only 4 percent after meals. Only 7 percent say a prayer on awakening in the morning, but 33 percent pray at night before retiring. Only 2 percent use phylacteries. Only 8 percent keep kosher households; 20 percent won't mix milk and meat; 24 percent won't eat pork, but only 8 percent won't eat shellfish.

On the Sabbath, the vast majority of Reform Jews, 88 percent, keep their businesses open, 90 percent work, 99 percent ride, and 82 percent smoke. Seventy-four percent have a seder in their homes on Passover eve, 93 percent eat Matzoh [unleavened bread] during Passover, but 59 percent also eat bread. Twenty-one percent of the Reform Jews reported that they have Christmas trees at home, but only 54 percent are opposed to this practice. On the other hand, 81 percent kindle Chanukah lights in their homes, and 75 percent exchange Chanukah gifts. Forty-seven percent have m'zuzzahs [traditional amulets] on the doors of their homes.

III. The Conservative Movement in Judaism, By Simon Greenberg, 1955

The Conservative Movement in Judaism has been closest to the spirit of traditional, historical Judaism in that it did not define itself in dogmas or in publicly announced platforms. But it did create, develop or adopt a number of concepts, and made them peculiarly its own. Within our Movement these concepts entered into a unique combination of interrelations, and proved to be the spiritually and intellectually fructifying leaven in our midst. Though these have never been formally voted upon and accepted by us at any national convention, they are, nevertheless, now widely recognized as the real forces that have been at work among us. They are standards in every significant sense of that word, for in their light we have formulated policy and passed judgment on our own acts and the acts of others.

What are these concepts? How have they determined the character of our Movement in the past? How can they guide us in the future? I shall refer to four such concepts and discuss them briefly.

The first of these concepts, in terms of chronology and perhaps also of significance, was created by the German Jewish precursors of our Movement, by men like Leopold Zunz, Zechariah Frankel, Heinrich Graetz.

They spoke of "Judische Wissenschaft," which has been translated as "the Science of Judaism," but which I prefer to think of as "the Scientific Study of Judaism." Judaism, as we know, has always stressed knowledge. But since the rise of the modern scientific method and the modern study of history, knowing our tradition as our fathers knew it is not enough. The scientific study of Judaism calls for knowledge in terms of historical circumstance, of growth, development, and adaptation. It calls for full and complete knowledge, not knowledge limited to any one area or to any one era of Judaism—not knowledge of the Bible, the Talmud, the medieval codes, or the modern literary, legal or philosophical writings, but of all of them with equal thoroughness and equal reverence. It calls for first-hand knowledge of original sources in their original languages and not for knowledge about our heritage through secondhand media. . . .

The second concept which became a fundamental standard for the Conservative Movement in Judaism is the modern articulation of the thought, repeatedly expressed by the rabbis, that Judaism is not just one segment of life but instead embraces all of life. "Search the *Torah* again and again for you will find everything in it" [*Sayings of the Fathers*, 5:22], wisdom, history, law, ethics, truth, beauty, and goodness. That description of Judaism formulated some nineteen hundred years ago was challenged for the first time during the nineteenth century. In the struggle for equal political rights for Jews in central and western Europe, a group arose which sought to limit the scope of Judaism to a few metaphysical dogmas and ethical principles. It was primarily against this narrow, sterile view of Judaism that our Movement fought—and indeed continues to fight, for the battle is far from won. . . .

Hence it is no mere accident that our Movement was at all times completely and unwaveringly devoted to Zionism, to the effort to reestablish an autonomous Jewish community upon the soil of Israel. We were loyal to Zionism not only in days of distress but also in days of comparative ease, because Zionism to us was always more than another typical nationalistic movement of the nineteenth century, more than a philanthropic movement concerned merely with the rescue of the persecuted, more than merely an answer to anti-Semitism. We followed Ahad Ha'Am [Asher Ginsberg] in his analysis that not only were Jews threatened by anti-Semitism, but that Judaism was also endangered by the new social and political conditions which faced us after the French Revolution. To us Zionism represented, above all, the hope that in an autonomous Jewish state, Judaism would have the best possible environment within which it could again function as a culture or a civilization, affecting every aspect of life and stimulating every creative impulse to find expression within the framework of our tradition.

Our interests in the establishment of a Jewish state were therefore never exclusively or even primarily political or philanthropic. They were always, first and foremost, spiritual and cultural. . . .

The third concept which has always been indigenous to our Movement, and which was given new and unique expression in our midst, is the rabbinic concept of *K'lal Yisrael*, which Dr. [Solomon] Schechter translated in his striking phrase "Catholic Israel." There have been varying interpretations given to the terms "Catholic Israel" and *K'lal Yisrael*, but one thing is certain. Those who created those concepts sought to express thereby their inner desire to be identified not with any one sect or party in Israel, but with the whole of the Jewish people. . . .

The fourth concept that has consciously and subconsciously molded the Conservative Movement I would designate as "innovation without regimentation." It is contained in the Preamble to the Constitution of the United Synagogue of America, written by very wise, learned and loyal men, which enumerates the following goals:

> The advancement of the cause of Judaism in America and the maintenance of Jewish tradition in its historic continuity; to assert and establish loyalty to the *Torah* in its historic exposition; to further the observance of the Sabbath and the dietary laws; to preserve in the service the reference to Israel's past and the hopes for Israel's restoration; to maintain the traditional character of the liturgy, with Hebrew as the language of prayer; to foster Jewish religious life in the home as expressed in traditional observances; to encourage the establishment of Jewish religious schools, in the curricula of which the study of the Hebrew language and literature shall be given a prominent place, both as the key to the true understanding of Judaism and as a bond holding scattered communities of Israel throughout the world. It shall be the aim of the United Synagogue of America, while not indorsing the innovations introduced by any of its constituent bodies, to embrace all elements essentially loyal to traditional Judaism and in sympathy with the purposes outlined above.

By that statement the founders of the United Synagogue expressed their recognition of the fact that at no time in Jewish history, and least of all in periods of flux and transition such as ours, has there ever been a uniformity of practice and ritual. The exigencies of time, place, and community require their own adjustments. . . .

IV.   In Orthodoxy the Woman Is Not Inferior,
By Menachem Schneerson, May 27, 1957

As for the remarks that were made to you in respect of the place of the Jewish woman in Jewish life that it was "undemocratic," etc.—needless to say such charges are absurd.

The attitude of the Torah in so far as the place of the Jewish woman is concerned is clear. Suffice it to quote our Sages on the duty of the husband to respect his wife more than himself. . . .

And another: When G-d was about to give His Torah to the Jewish people, the Torah which is the very life and existence of our people, He told Moses to approach the women first, as our Rabbis commented: "Thus shalt thou say to the 'house of Jacob'—i.e. the women—and (then) tell the children of Israel—the men."

The charges that the Jewish woman is placed in an 'inferior' category are claimed to be based on the fact that the Jewish woman is relieved of those Mitzvoth [obligations] which have a time-element. This is nothing but a complete misunderstanding of the real issue. To mention but one explanation: Everything in the world has its specific functions and purpose. For example, the brain and heart are the two most vital organs in the human body. Would it make sense to say that the brain is inferior to the heart, because the former lacks emotional quality; or the brain is superior to the heart, because the latter lacks the power of reasoning? It is precisely upon the proper functioning of each that the existence of the organism is dependent.

Similarly, man and woman, each has a specific function to fulfill. The woman's function is to be a mother and to care for, and bring up the infants, when they require the mother's utmost attention. Hence, G-d has freed her from certain obligations which He has imposed on the man. What is not less important is the woman's duty to take care of the household and create the right Jewish atmosphere, etc. Thus, it is for reasons of priority rather than her inferiority that the Jewish woman has been relieved from certain Mitzvoth, which are connected with a time-element, so that they would not interfere with her vital specific functions.

As for the argument that a woman is deemed legally unfit in cases of evidence and certain other legal matters—the explanation is to be found in the fact (which is a necessary result of the above) that a woman has been gifted with an extra measure of natural emotion, for having to take care of infants and children in their early years requires extraordinary love, patience and softness of character. But an overly measure of emotionalism is a hindrance in legal matters, where strict and completely impartial judgment and reason are of essence. Therefore, as the Torah deals with average persons, and the average woman is obviously more emotional, the woman had to be disqualified from judgeship and similar legal matters, which have been placed on the shoulders of the man, who is less emotional and can be more objective. Clearly, there is no reflection here on the woman, as in the case of an analogy from the brain and heart, mentioned above.

Needless to say, that there are women who are more rational than men, and men who are more emotional than women. But, obviously, when the Torah lays down the Law, it must be based on the majority and average, not on the exception, or it would not be practicable.

It is difficult to enlarge in a letter on such matters, but I trust that the above principles will suffice to refute the baseless charges, and you will be able to find many more points in support of the truth that G-d's Law is perfect, and the ways of the Torah are pleasant and peace-full.

Wishing you success in strengthening Yiddishkeit and disseminating its practice and observance, and wishing you also a kosher and happy Pesach.
With blessing,
Menachem Schneerson

V.   Sabbath Eve in an American Hassidic Home, 1959

Every Friday, a miracle happens in my home. "What's the miracle?" you ask. I finish preparing for Shabbos just in time to light the candles! So this doesn't sound like a miracle to you? Well, you should only be in my house Erev Shabbos [Sabbath eve]. One week, the delivery boy was on strike. One week, the cleaning woman couldn't come! One week, an insistent salesman came into the house for a 2½ half hour demonstration!

Last week, I decided to be smart. I did all my cleaning and cooking on Thursday. When Friday came, I gave my husband and children breakfast, packed up their lunches, sent my husband to work, the older children to school, and I began to wash the breakfast dishes. Time passes quickly, and soon it was 11:00 o'clock. I was feeling very proud of myself. The dishes were done. The house was clean. The beds were made. The Shabbos meal was ready. Moishele, my 3 year old, was playing nicely in the yard. All I had to do, was to set the table for Shabbos. Who should think that this would take all day!

Just as I was about to take out the white linen tablecloth and spread it on the dining room table, my little Moishele marched into the house yelling for cookies. One look at the source of all the commotion convinced me that what my baby needed most, at the moment, wasn't a cookie, but a good scrubbing. My youngest son followed me into the bathroom, chatting away about all the wonders of the world he had discovered in our backyard. As my attention was concentrated upon cleaning up Moishele, I didn't listen too carefully to what he said. After throwing his clothes into the hamper, and rubbing the dirt off his body, I began to catch words, phrases, and then sentences of Moishele's soliloquy. Pants . . . pocket . . . earthworms! Oh, no! Earthworms in his pant's pocket, wandering around my hamper! I finished drying my son, wrapped him in a blanket, sat him at the kitchen table, said his brocho [Hebrew blessing] with him, gave him his egg, milk and cookie. Then I rushed back to the hamper, and gingerly took out the pants. Not an earthworm was there. I took the hamper and emptied all its contents directly into the washing machine. I was determined that nothing would upset the sparkling cleanliness of my home, especially Erev Shabbos.

I surveyed the scene. Moishele was munching his cookie, the washing machine was humming, and I still had plenty of time to set the table for Shabbos. I took the candelabra off the mantelpiece, and placed it on the new silver tray which Shlomeh, my husband, had recently bought for me. I was standing a moment, admiring the way that the candelabra and the new tray looked together, when the sound of rain reached my ears. Rain? But the sun was shining in through the window! I peered into the kitchen, and in that moment I remembered that I had forgotten to take the plug out of the sink. It was too late. The water from the washing machine was pouring out—out and onto the freshly waxed floor. Moishele was gayly taking a second bath in the foaming fluid.

Well, it was two hours before Shabbos, time enough to set the table, after cleaning up the mess in the kitchen. First, I pulled the plug out of the sink, then I picked up Moishele and put him back into the bathtub. To placate my dissatisfied infant, I made soap suds in his bath with a mild detergent. When he was calmly playing with the suds, I returned to the scene of the crime and Operation Mop Up.

Within a 1/2 hour all traces of the flood had disappeared. I took Moishele out of the tub and put him in to his bed for a nap. While he slept, I rewaxed the kitchen floor. As I completed this task, the front door flew open, and my two older sons came running in, arguing about who had reached the door first. When they paused to catch their breath I took the opportunity to tell them that I had some ice cream for them as soon as they were washed. A new race was on, and my two little Yeshiva [parochial school] boys, aged 5 and 7, were shortly seated at the kitchen table; their hands and faces reasonably clean. I answered "omein" [amen], when they said their brochos, and I watched them dig happily into their dixie cups.

At this moment, my husband came home from work. "One hour to Shabbos" he announced, as he went straight to the bathroom to shower. Well, I thought, I still have time to finish setting the table. I washed my two big boys at the kitchen sink, and then took them to their room to help them select and change into their Shabbos clothes. By the time the boys were ready, Shlomeh had come out of the shower. He dressed and prepared the tea for Shabbos. It was 15 minutes before the lighting of the candles. All I had to do was finish setting the table. Shlomeh and the children volunteered to finish setting the table while I washed up for Shabbos. In 15 minutes I was in the living room with fresh make up on, a clean kerchief on my head, and a new duster wrapped around me. The table was all set, candles, challos [Sabbath loaves], salt, kiddush cup, and even the silver-

ware. I lit the candles, said the brocho and kissed my family "Good Shabbos." Then Shlomeh took the boys to shul with him. When the door
closed, I happily collapsed into the living room chair.

Despite the day's events, we were miraculously able to receive the
Shabbos in time. At last, relaxed and unrushed, I thanked G-d for the peace
and ease of the Shabbos day.

VI.   Some Premises of Reconstructionism,
By Mordecai M. Kaplan, April 1960

Both Reconstructionism and Reform differ from Orthodoxy, which
assumes that the Jewish tradition is of supernatural origin and therefore in
substance immutable. And they differ also from Conservatism, which
maintains that the evolution of Judaism is merely an unfolding of spiritual
truths latent in the Mosaic Torah. Reform and Reconstructionism accept
instead the idea of *creative* evolution as applicable to Judaism. They realize
that in the past Judaism developed spontaneously and without full awareness on the part of its spokesmen. They assume therefore that nowadays
only deliberately planned evolution will enable Judaism to have a future.

All of the foregoing is part of the major premise in which those
two movements in Judaism concur. When it comes, however, to the
formulation of the minor premises, Reform and Reconstructionism part
company. . . .

The following are the minor premises of Reconstructionism:

1. "Judaism" is *not* synonymous with "Jewish religion."

2. Judaism is the *tout ensemble* of all the elements that go into the making of a civilization: the group life of a people centering in a particular
land, a continuing history, a living language and literature, religious folkways, mores, laws and arts.

3. Jewish religion is that aspect of this *tout ensemble* which relates it to
God as the Power that makes for salvation in this world, and which finds
expression in the celebration of the Jewish *sancta:* the events, both natural
and historic, heroes, texts, places and seasons associated with the manifestation of God.

4. As a civilization, Judaism is the product of more than a millennium
of the national life of the Jewish People in Eretz Yisrael [ancient Palestine]
and, with the establishment of the State of Israel, is now enabled to resume
autonomous existence in that land.

5. Outside Eretz Yisrael [State of Israel] Judaism can function in the
life of the Jew only as a secondary civilization, the primary one being that
of the country of which he is a citizen.

6. As a secondary civilization outside Eretz Yisrael, Judaism can flour-
ish only through the medium of local organic communities, ethically

functioning Jewish religion, and social and cultural intercourse with the Jews in Israel.

7. The revitalization of Jewish religion both in Israel and in the Diaspora is indispensable as a means of giving purpose and direction to the renaissance of the Jewish People.

8. For the Jewish religion to be revitalized it has to evolve a conception of God and of the salvation of man which, by virtue of its greater approximation to reality than any of the conceptions thus far advanced, is bound to be more effective than they have been in impelling man to live the good life.

9. Jews outside Eretz Yisrael, whose primary civilization is that of the country they live in, owe it to their Jewish religion to foster the spiritual significance of the heroes, events, places and seasons of that civilization, thereby fulfilling the mission of their own Jewish religion as well as expressing their loyalty to their country in terms of the religion of humanity.

50

JEWISH EDUCATION AND CULTURE,
1940s(?)–1966

J ewish education in all periods of American Jewish life was both informal and formal in nature. It may well be that the informal forces of learning and influence are more important. A Jewish ethnic press developed in five different languages; congregational libraries contained thousands of volumes; divers Jewish cultural associations were active in most large universities; educational programs were developed by the Conservatives and Reformers in well-equipped summer camps; the Jewish Welfare Board and the National Council of Jewish Women devoted themselves to cultural projects. The pulpit was instructional as well as hortatory. Hundreds of books rolled off the presses of Jewish and non-Jewish publishers.

Formal education was twofold: there were both secular and religious schools. The secular schools, often with Yiddish as the medium of instruction, were sponsored by East European fraternal orders; ideologically they leaned toward socialism and communism. Religion as such was taboo in their curricula, but they taught ethics, Jewish history, Yiddish literature, and Jewish customs. After the German pogroms in the 1930s and 1940s, the Yiddish fraternal orders "rejoined" American Jewry; their programs assumed a more Jewish cast. The schools of the Yiddish secularists were always small; the masses attended those established by the religionists. Professional Jewish educators made a gallant attempt to set up citywide, communally-supported schools. These bureaus of Jewish education were not accepted; most schools were congregational: Orthodox, Conservative, Reform. The children were taught Bible, rituals, prayers, current events, ethics, Hebrew. After 1948 when the State of Israel came into being, emphasis was laid on the new commonwealth and its culture. Religious

447

schools were either afternoon or Sunday schools; the Conservatives preferred the weekdays; the Reformers, the weekends. Few children continued their studies after they were bar mitzvah or confirmed. There were, however, a small number of Jewish religious high schools. Those who sought more schooling went to the relatively numerous teachers colleges, talmudic academies, and rabbinical seminaries.

Structured education was radically modified after 1940 when all-day schools (some called them "parochial schools") began to proliferate. Here the children—male and female—studied both Jewish and secular subjects. Though many of the new schools were oriented toward Orthodoxy, the Conservatives and later even the Reformers ultimately opened denominational institutions of their own. Funding came through tuition fees—they were private schools—but in the course of time the welfare federations were induced to grant substantial subsidies. Thus in a way, they were community schools; administratively, they were autonomous. Many reasons are offered for the rapid growth of the new schools. The founders maintained that they hoped to produce a cadre of leaders. Right-wing traditionalists feared the assimilatory impact of the public school system. The Holocaust pushed Jews to the right. Many wanted more Jewish education for their children; stubbornly they insisted on surviving as Jews. By 1928 the Torah-true Jewish devotees had established Yeshiva College; Brandeis University, a secular Jewish-sponsored school, opened its doors in 1948. Indeed by the 1960s one could begin life in a Jewish kindergarten and ultimately receive a Ph.D. degree without ever attending a public educational institution.

And what is Jewish culture in its more restrictive sense—literature, music, sculpture, and the graphic arts? Numerous Jews, both men and women, turned early to these artistic challenges. There were Jewish painters, sculptors, cartoonists. Some had been trained abroad; others were products of American academies. Were they notables? Notability is a highly subjective term; some of these practitioners had large and admiring followings. In music Jews were outstanding. Most Jewish musicians and music lovers turned to the worlds of the classics and musical comedy; but there was as well an ever growing interest in synagogal singing, both in English and in Hebrew. In the metropolitan areas the ghetto theaters were constantly introducing new Yiddish songs destined to receive wide acceptance. Israeli music, both in the synagog and the concert hall, won thousands of adherents.

And literature, prose, and verse? Despite the closing of the country's doors to Yiddish-speaking newcomers, this language was to remain very much alive for decades. There were poets, novelists, essayists, publicists, and journalists who reached thousands through the Yiddish papers and periodicals. Litterateurs who excelled in Hebrew, however, had scant future here; the gifted writers—the celebrated poet Gavriel Preil is a notable exception—left for Israel when the new state was firmly established. There were literally thousands of American Jews, men and women, who sought to become inhabitants of the republic of English-language letters. Their themes were often Jewish. By the 1950s a handful of these novelists, poets, and storytellers were being acclaimed as distinguished literary artists. Books, periodicals, and research associations documented the rise of America as a center for Jewish scholarship. There was no longer a need to trek to Germany, to the Berlin "Jewish University," to prepare oneself to teach in an American Jewish academy. *Juedische Wissenschaft*, the Science—the academic study—of Judaism, the production of works conceived in the historicocritical mode, had entrenched itself in the rabbinical seminaries by the middle decades of the century. Through numerous publications, mostly in English, American Jewry made its bid to exercise cultural hegemony over World Jewry.

By the sixth decade of the twentieth century the United States sheltered the world's largest Jewry. Most Jews here were content to remain Jews. With affluence came an interest in culture. Jews could not escape the impact of America with its amenities, its learning, its intellectual aspirations. They were interested in Jewish education even if not always enthusiastically. They maintained and created thousands of cultural institutions and associations. At first glance Jewish education was in chaos. Actually, Jews were comfortably ensconced in this welter; every group had its own cultural way of life; it had what it wanted, what it had created. There were over 2,000 schools in the country; funding them and the magnificent colleges and synagogs Jews built ran into the hundreds of millions of dollars. True, a substantial number of youngsters received no Jewish education, but there were still over 500,000 in Jewish classes; 50 percent were in the Sunday schools; 41 percent in the afternoon schools, a sparse 9 percent in the "parochial" institutions. Thirty states had Jewish newspapers; well over 100 periodicals were published in New York City; there was even one for farmers and one for the blind. Despite the cult of cultural disparity, they were all "Jewish"; this made for a heightened sense of community. And insofar as Jews learned something of their own tradition, they enriched themselves and the America of which they were a part. The boys and girls in the Jewish elementary schools identified as Jews and thus guaranteed their survival on this soil.

Among the American poets of Jewish background, Karl Jay Shapiro (b. 1913) stands out; he has been honored frequently for his literary artistry, receiving numerous awards including a Pulitzer Prize. The first selection is one of his Jewish poems, "The Mezuza." A separate volume, *Poems of a Jew*, was published in 1958. In World War II, Rabbi Jacob Philip Rudin served as a naval chaplain in the Pacific theater. To keep in touch with his congregation in Great Neck, Long Island, he frequently sent an Open Letter which was printed in the congregational bulletin. Selection II deals with Jewish "soul food." Culinary favorites play an important part in tying people together. Food is an intimate part of one's culture. The East Europeans love smoked meat; the German Jews prize mazzah *Kloesse* (dumplings); the Rev. Gershom Seixas, a Sephardi, drooled over his *albondigas*, his Spanish meatballs.

In 1948, a group of American Jews opened this country's first secular university to function under Jewish auspices. It is named after Louis D. Brandeis, the United States Supreme Court justice, who had passed away in 1941. After the German atrocities, many American Jews huddled together emotionally; they were shocked, frightened, angry. Their mood was exacerbated by the quota laws operating in America's Ivy League colleges. Despite their published disclaimers, Jewish colleges were, in no small degree, a reaction to prejudice. Selection III describes the new school after its first year with a pilot class. Many years before Brandeis opened its doors, a group of New York's "Russian" Jews, Orthodox traditionalists, established Yeshiva College (1928). Its prime purpose was to provide a carefully supervised modern education for the students of the Rabbi Isaac Elchanan Theological Seminary. In 1945 the college was chartered as a university; in 1954 it opened the Stern College for Women. Four years later, on the occasion of the first commencement, a number of Jewish and Gentile women gathered together to assess the role of contemporary females. Among them was an Orthodox Jew, Mrs. Allen I. Edles, president of the women's branch of the Union of Orthodox Jewish Congregations of America. Her address indicates eloquently that mainstream Orthodox American Jewish women had certainly distanced themselves from the men who centuries earlier had fashioned the daily Hebrew prayer: "Blessed be Thou, O Lord our God, King of the Universe, who has not made me a woman"—women, in this series of blessings, are counted with pagans and slaves (selection IV). Finally, selection V is a rationale for the separatist Jewish all-day school. It was written by Alvin Irwin Schiff (b. 1926), an Orthodox Jewish educator and a member of the faculty of Yeshiva University.

The motto of this Jewish university is: "Judaism (Torah) and Science"; its founders and friends are convinced that they have harmonized Orthodoxy and Modernity.

I. The Mezuza, By Karl Shapiro, 1940s(?)

A hand in morning banged the door,
    not hard but with a kindly fist,

splashing my mercurial dream
    to beads of light. I turned and thought
it has to be a Christian there
    banging at my bright front door,
and turned back to my sleep.
    Let him leave his literature, I said,
and put a pillow on my head.

Once on a secular afternoon
    two Adventists or Mormons came
(who always come in twos like nuns)
    to confront me or affront me.
I took their literature in hand
    and with a kind of smile assayed
to point the error of their way.
    Rather I pointed to the jamb
where I had tacked the doorpost prayer
    hidden in its small bronze case
to consecrate the house. I said
    that is the holy letter Shin,
that is the secret name of God;
    inside are praise and promises.
Sirs, when you see that talisman
    you really ought to skip that house.

They looked at it and glanced at it
    and nodding wisely went their way.

II. All I Could Think of Was a Hot Pastrami Sandwich, By Jacob Philip Rudin, March 1943

Dear Friends,

Everything that happens in war isn't grim and tragic. Amusing incidents occur, too. I want to tell you one which falls, I think, in that category. It was related to me by a Jewish Marine from Brooklyn. I am certain, however, that you would have discovered that fact for yourselves, without my telling you.

This happened on Guadalcanal [in the South Pacific], during the time when the fighting was heaviest and hardest. But I'll let the Marine talk for himself, although these, of course, are not his exact words.

"I was in a fox-hole not far from Henderson Field," he said. "The Japs were letting us have it with all the stuff they could throw at us. It was really a hot spot. Their big guns were banging away; planes were coming over and dropping their loads; bombs and shells were crashing all around us. The noise was indescribable and I never knew whether that particular breath I drew was going to be my last one.

"But honest, Chaplain,—and you will think I was crazy—all I could think of in the midst of that confusion and thunder, all I could think of was a hot pastrami sandwich. If I only had a hot pastrami sandwich! And right there in that fox-hole on Guadalcanal, I vowed that if I ever came away from the Solomons [Solomon Islands] alive, the very first thing I was going to do when I hit the good old U.S.A. was to buy myself the biggest hot pastrami sandwich in the country."

Well, the Marine was wounded in a subsequent engagement and he was shipped back to the States to a Naval Hospital here on the Pacific Coast, not very far from San Francisco.

"The big day came, Chaplain," the Marine continued, "and I was well enough to go on liberty. I went straight to the nearby town looking for my hot pastrami sandwich. Not a delicatessen in the place! So I went into a store and I asked where there was a good delicatessen, with real rye bread and real pastrami. The Jewish storekeeper told me that the closest one was in San Francisco and he gave me the address.

"It was too late to go that day; but I knew just where I would head on my next free day, you can be sure of that. So when I got my next liberty, I boarded the bus and was en route for San Francisco. All through the trip, I rehearsed how I would go into the shop; how I would look around and ask for the sandwich; how the fellow behind the counter would answer. In my imagination, I could see him cut two big slices of rye bread. I could smell the hot pastrami as he took it from the steamer and cut off thick and tasty pieces—not too fat and not too lean—just right, the way I like it. The only thing I couldn't make up my mind about was whether or not to put mustard on it. I finally decided that I would put some on one half of the sandwich and eat the other half plain.

"At last I arrived in San Francisco. I got my bearings and was soon walking down the street where the store was. I could see the sign, 'Delicatessen,' sticking out from the side of the building. I was there!

"I came to the door and turned the knob. It didn't budge. I tried again. No use. The door was locked. Then my eye caught sight of the neatly typed card in the corner of the door frame:

> In order to cooperate with the Government in conserving meat, I am observing meatless Tuesdays. Therefore, my store will be closed all day today.

But the story does have a happy ending. The Marine went on: "That soured me. I decided to wait until I could get a couple of days leave so that I could go down to Los Angeles. Which I did. There I found the delicatessen store I had been waiting for all these months. I went in and I ordered a hot pastrami sandwich that thick." He held his hands about four inches apart.

"And, Chaplain," he concluded, "do you know, it tasted so good that I didn't even know I was chewing."

Hot pastramily yours,

Jacob Philip Rudin

III. Brandeis University Is One Year Old, By Maurice L. Zigmond, 1949

America's first Jewish-sponsored, non-sectarian university has completed its initial academic year. After a difficult and critical period of preparation—there were times when the very life of the institution hung in the balance—Brandeis was formally dedicated on October 7, 1948, with Dr. Abram Leon Sachar, for 15 years National Director of the B'nai B'rith Hillel Foundations, and now Chairman of the National Hillel Commission, as its President. Two weeks later its doors were opened to a small "pilot" class of incoming students. . . .

Last fall, 107 students gathered to form a Freshman class which, in the opinion of the faculty members, was not qualitatively below the average of similar classes of colleges of the first rank. Once the University started to function and became better known through nationwide publicity, applications came in a steady stream. Thus, the second Freshman class, numbering about 150, which matriculates this fall, represents a selection from more than 900 young people who expressed a desire to attend.

The most frequent question asked about Brandeis—at least by Jews—concerns its "Jewishness." What is Jewish about the institution? How does Jewish sponsorship influence its operation, its character, or the content of its curriculum? When it is recalled that Brandeis is officially described as both "Jewish sponsored" and "non-sectarian," it will be apparent that the problem is not a simple one. Under Jewish sponsorship the initial steps were taken by Jews and, with a few exceptions, the subsequent supporters of the project have been Jewish. On the other hand, its non-sectarian complexion implies not only that people of all creeds (and races, too) are welcome as students and as members of faculty, staff, and Board of Trustees, but also that there will be no denominational emphasis in official activities or in the classroom. . . .

This policy of non-sectarianism is pursued with consistency and thoroughness at Brandeis. In its application blanks for the admission of students, the University goes beyond the precaution of seeking no information about religious and racial backgrounds. It refrains also from asking invidious questions relative to the maiden name of one's mother and the occupation of one's father. While it is known that a majority of the student body is Jewish, the administrative staff is not interested in statistics of this type. "Those institutions concerned with quotas and percentages must of necessity be preoccupied with such facts and figures," explains the Director of Admissions [who happens to be a non-Jew]. "They are of no importance to us here." The University Calendar respects the major Jewish as well as the major Christian holy days. Courses are geared to a five-day week schedule—there are no sessions on either Saturday or Sunday. A similar indifference to origins and creeds characterizes the selection of members of the faculty and staff. As the Board of Trustees reaches its full strength (21 members are authorized by the Massachusetts legislature), emphasis is being laid upon diversity rather than upon uniformity.

On the other hand, Brandeis gives to Jewish learning a rightful place in its curriculum. Thus Hebrew is to be found alongside of French, Spanish, and German in fulfillment of the "Language and Literature Requirement." Among the "Fields of Concentration" (to be developed in the upper classes) there is one entitled "Semitic Languages and Civilization." The University Library, whose first function is to serve classroom needs, is beginning to build what is expected to be an outstanding Judaica collection. But perhaps most significant of all, Brandeis does not hesitate to challenge age-old academic judgments. In those courses considering such matters, there is a conscious effort to revaluate the role of the Jew in the history of civilization. Without erring in the opposite direction, an attempt is made to correct the bias of textbooks which would limit the participation of the Jewish people in world culture to a paragraph on the "Old Testament," or of historians who would submerge the Jewish contribution within the anonymity of "Syrian" culture.

The "Jewishness" of Brandeis cannot be measured in quantitative terms. It is to be discerned not so much in tangibles as in intangibles. It is not a label; it is an attitude, a *weltanschauung*, an awareness of the wrongs done in the name of education and a determination not to tolerate them. Perhaps there is nothing Jewish about the pledge of the University that it "is open to all students who meet academic standards without reference to race, color, or religious affiliations," but is not any deviation from this principle justifiably regarded as anti-Jewish?

Brandeis, states the General Catalogue, "came into being because of the desire of the Jewish community to make a corporate contribution to American higher education." It would be foolhardy to attempt, at this early stage, to predict what the exact nature of that contribution will be over a long period of years. Many factors will influence the institution's future. We can only hope that those who guide it decades hence will be motivated by the same broad and liberal spirit as pervades the campus today. . . .

IV. The American Jewish Woman of Tomorrow,
By Mrs. Allen I. Edles, 1958

Never before in history have women been given such opportunity to assume leadership, and color the destiny of future generations of the American Jewish community. Never before have women risen so admirably to the occasion.

Women have emerged from their places in the kitchen, to their rightful places beside their fathers, brothers, husbands, and indeed, their sons. The past three decades have witnessed the opening of newer and wider avenues of education for women. The bedrock reality is that the world has finally recognized the immense influences exerted by women in the past. We have every reason to believe these influences will become even more intensive and extensive.

History is the inventory of human experiences, and who can gainsay that women have been an integral part of that history, having felt the pains of progress equally? These experiences have necessarily served as the proving grounds for living, living in this great complex web called "world." And so, through the ages, the participation of women in every phase of endeavor presents a balanced picture today, not one of unrealistic fantasy.

A woman no longer lives a passive existence, content merely to nod in assent to situations that affect her vitally; her voice is heard from every direction. Not only has she pursued the classic professions as law, medicine, education, and politics, but has valiantly pioneered in the newer professions including the specialized areas of medicine, as psychiatry, etc. There were many contributing factors to this so-called "coming of age," not the least important of which is the mechanized kitchen and prepared foods. This innovation has afforded the distaff side leisure time for use in furthering her education and increasing her skills. The result has produced a unique effort on present-day society. Women have produced a magnetic influence in many areas of living by their perception and innate abilities to coordinate efforts into useful and meaningful action. They encourage positive endeavors and gracefully accept challenges presented to them.

What does all this add up to? How impressive are these facts in relation to the future of the American woman? To me, this spells out continued development and intensified education for a far greater segment of women. Stern College [of Yeshiva University] is a cogent force in fostering and encouraging that development. Stern College represents foresight, courage, talent, generosity, and hard work. It now stands on the threshold of far-reaching successes through the training of its students, who will find their ultimate paths leading them to diverse parts of the world. These graduates will take with them the reinforced religious patterns strengthened at Stern College.

Heretofore, women's opinions were barely tolerated; today our enlightened society not only accepts, but invites comments and opinions from women. This is further encouragement to those reticent females who feared to tread in fields overrun and monopolized by males; those retarded females who subscribed to the theory that women should not and cannot compete with men. They even stressed the risks involved. These were our timid sisters who are now gleaning new strength from the successes of their more courageous co-workers. These over-cautious ones have now realized that the risks of inaction are infinitely greater.

Today, 6 out of 10 married women are gainfully employed. This is our barometer for tomorrow. Women have learned the art of balancing their home lives proportionately with their business or professional lives. Their homes are happier and their families have fuller lives because of the wider experience of the mother, who has ceased to live in a vacuum. Because of these extended opportunities for women, security has evolved into a family project, and is no longer a one-man job. Despite all this, we women do not seek to supplant the man's position, merely to supplement it.

V.   The Value of a Jewish Day School Education, By Alvin Irwin Schiff, 1966

The rapid, three-dimensional growth of the Jewish day school movement—the growth in number of communities sponsoring day schools, the number of new schools, and the increase in pupil enrollment—has engendered great interest in the educational values of this type of schooling.

One of the major reasons for the growth of the Jewish day school is its unique educational program. The Jewish community realizes that the day school is the most effective instrument for transmitting the Jewish heritage to our youth. The day school is, indeed, basic to the survival of the American Jewish community. Moreover, the day school is vitally needed to help furnish future professional and lay leaders for the American Jewish community.

It is to the individual child that the day school makes its most significant contributions. The measure of the day school's effectiveness and success lies in the values its program provides for its pupils.

In the Day School the pupil receives his Jewish and General education under one roof. He need not be burdened by attendance at two schools and by two academic schedules.

The Day School is particularly noted for its friendly atmosphere and the personal interest taken in the progress of each child. The teacher-pupil ratio is, happily and significantly, high. In the average Day School there are two teachers for every twenty-five children (excluding specialty instructors). Small classes facilitate individual guidance.

The Day School has demonstrated excellence in both Hebraic and General Studies achievement.

In the Hebraic studies it has shown that pupils can really achieve a high degree of proficiency in Hebrew language and literature, and a deep understanding of Jewish life and history. Moreover, Jewish spiritual values and positive Jewish attitudes are readily developed.

In the General Studies, pupils in the Day School compare very favorably with their peers in the public schools. Jewish Day School students usually score higher on standard achievement tests and win more scholastic awards than their public-education friends.

Exposed to both disciplines in a congenial environment, the child learns to integrate the traditional with the modern, the secular with the religious, his Jewish heritage with American civilization. Through meritorious educational attainment, in an enriched program, he grows intellectually and culturally; via a program of intensive Jewish study he grows spiritually. In all, he learns to be a good American Jew. He learns that to be a good Jew is to be a good American. On this frame of reference he builds a wholesome set of values. He loves Israel and wants to help it grow, as he loves America and strives to become a useful citizen in his native country. He is part of his Jewish people as he is part of American democratic experience.

For the Jewish child, the Jewish Day School spells out preparation for life ahead through daily, meaningful happy school experiences.

51

PHILANTHROPY AND PHILANTHROPISTS
1925–1986

There may well have been 10,000 Jewish societies in the United States; many were of a philanthropic nature. The associations that set out to help Jews were primarily of a local and overseas nature; some of them had national offices in New York City which aided and counseled them. Almost any local community could boast of its many charitable societies; some of them were hometown landsmanshaften catering to Jews of East European origin. There were benevolent societies, and sections, branches of women's organizations like the National Council of Jewish Women, Hadassah, and Pioneer Women. Most philanthropic agencies in a typical city were tied together by a local "federation" which included agencies for family care, health, vocational services, community centers, and retirement homes. Very important were the overseas agencies; in 1960 there were dozens of them if one included also the Zionist organizations which were geared to support the Jews of Palestine and after 1948, the State of Israel. The American Organization for Rehabilitation Through Training Federation (ORT) had several branches in the United States; the women's groups were the largest. They founded vocational schools for Jews in many foreign countries. Hadassah was noted for its medical work in the Holy Land; the United Hebrew Immigrant and Sheltering Aid Society (HIAS) assisted newcomers abroad and at America's ports of debarkation.

Most important of all was the American Jewish Joint Distribution Committee which devoted itself to the rescue and the rehabilitation of East European Jewry. It was in the year 1925 that the Joint Distribution Committee established the American Jewish Joint Agricultural Organization (Agro-Joint) to rehabilitate Russia's Jews who had been declassed by

458

the new Soviet government. The work of retraining Jewish businessmen and making farmers and artisans out of them—a nineteenth-century Utopian ideal—was entrusted to Dr. Joseph A. Rosen (1876/77–1949), an American agronomist who was a native of Moscow. He put thousands on the soil and founded artisan cooperatives, loan banks, trade schools, and health stations. Thus he rehabilitated millions—who were saved only to be decimated later by Stalin or murdered by the invading Germans (selection I).

During the years 1912–1914 Henrietta Szold founded Hadassah, later to become one of the world's largest women's organizations. Its goals were to bring good medicine to Palestine, advance Zionism, and further the Jewish education of America's Jewish women and youth. Hadassah, eminently successful, built and continues to support the Hebrew University-Hadassah Medical Center (selection II).

Ever since the 1920s there were two rival groups competing for the Jewish philanthropic dollar, the Joint and the Zionists. After some futile attempts at unity the United Jewish Appeal was permanently established in January 1939. The burning of the synagogs by the Germans on November 10, 1938 convinced the Jews here in the United States that they must work together. On April 2, 1939 Herbert H. Lehman of New York outlined the group's goals (selection III). The United Palestine Appeal concerns itself solely with Jews in the Holy Land; all other lands are helped by the Joint; provision in the Appeal is also made for immigration agencies. The funds raised by the United Jewish Appeal provide both for the philanthropic institutions of the American Jewish communities and the Jews in Palestine (Israel). The lion's share of all monies collected goes to the ancient homeland; indeed the constant crises in Palestine induce American Jews to give liberally thus providing adequately also for American local needs. Half of the money raised by the annual drive remains in this country; American Jews ride on the coattails of the Israelis. Over the years the United Jewish Appeal has raised billions in response to crises. American Jews give generously to fellow Jews in distress.

There were, in addition, innumerable instances of individual Jews giving liberally to Gentile causes, and there were even some Gentiles who gave generously to Jewish institutions. Selection IV recounts the kindness of Cary Grant, a noted Gentile movie star who was only too happy to make a generous gift to Jews in need. In 1956 Henry Allen Moe, secretary of the John Simon Guggenheim Memorial Foundation, presented his report for the years 1955–1956 (selection V). Mr. and Mrs. Simon Guggenheim established the John Simon Guggenheim Memorial Foundation to honor a young son who had died some three decades earlier. This was in 1926. The Foundation made fellowships available to brilliant men and women, giving them the opportunity to advance themselves in the arts and the sciences. The family poured millions into the Foundation; Simon Guggenheim (1867–1941), a former U.S. Senator, was a member of a clan that made an immense fortune, primarily in the mining, smelting, and refining of metals. The Foundation did much to advance learning and further international understanding.

I. Dr. Joseph A. Rosen Reports on Jewish Colonization Work in Russia, September 12–13, 1925

The Agro-Joint was incorporated July 21st, 1924, in accordance with a resolution adopted at a meeting of the Executive Committee of the Joint Distribution Committee, for the purpose of carrying out in an experimental way a project of settling on the land in Southern Russia a few hundred Jewish families in order to ascertain the possibilities of Jewish colonization in Russia on a large scale. *Our project has absolutely nothing to do with the ill-famed fable of an autonomous Jewish republic in Russia* [Birobidzhan in eastern Siberia]. *It had no political aspects whatever, and was merely an effort to help along a spontaneous movement, a genuine new line of reconstructive rehabilitation originated by the Jewish masses in Russia of their own accord, as a dire necessity brought about by the post-war and post-revolutionary economic conditions of the country.*

The results have exceeded our expectations and have more than justified a continued effort in this direction on a more extensive scale. With the $400,000 originally appropriated by the Joint Distribution Committee, we expected to settle, at the most, one thousand families. Later, your committee found it possible to double this appropriation and we have succeeded in putting on the land during this period, not one thousand, but over four thousand families, a population of over 25,000 souls.

While nominally a separate organization, the Agro-Joint is in reality a direct offspring of the Reconstruction Department of the Joint Distribution Committee Russian Unit. The program of the Reconstruction Department launched in the fall of 1922 and continued until August, 1924, including three main lines of activity; A. Agricultural Work; B. Loan Kassas [agency] for Artisans; C. Vocational Training Schools....

The general principle of our work with the settlers is to *eliminate all kinds of philanthropic and paternalistic tendencies.* We aim to put our relations on a strictly business basis, advancing all the funds in the form of loans in cash or kind. These loans must be refunded within a specified time, and bear interest at the rate of 3% per year. We make it clearly understood to the settlers that we are not assuming any responsibility or any obligations to take care of them for any length of time. We give them a start and are ready to give them competent advice and instruction, but they must then take care of themselves. We encourage them to become members of the local farmers cooperative organizations and wherever possible make use of the general government agricultural credit system. This, however, they can do only after they have been on the land not less than a year. . . .

The human material of the new settlers is of a surprisingly high quality. Not so many years ago it was my good fortune to spend a few years among the people who are settling the western prairies in the U.S.A., and I may say frankly that among these Jewish settlers in Southern Russia I was surprised to find pioneering material in no way inferior to the sturdy pioneers of the West. The spirit of the settlers is remarkable. Regardless of the very trying conditions they have to live under, without any conveniences whatever, in shanties or dugouts, often under the open sky, doing very hard work that many of them have not been accustomed to, they take it cheerfully and feel that the future is with them. . . .

CONCLUSIONS

1. Living conditions of the Jewish masses in Russia make it imperative for them to adapt themselves to the new environments and turn in as great numbers as possible to productive work.

2. Of all the forms of adaptation under present conditions in Russia land settlements offers the greatest advantages.

3. The results accomplished by the Agro-Joint fully justify continued effort in this direction on a large scale.

4. While there are presently some possibilities for helping a great number of Russian Jews within their accustomed occupations, and attempts should be made to make use of these possibilities, our main efforts should be concentrated on the land settlement proposition, as:

(a) This is a broad spontaneous movement originated by the Jewish masses themselves who see here a real chance of reconstructive rehabilitation.

(b) Time is of the very greatest essence in this matter and delay means (and I repeat this in full seriousness) a loss of opportunity unprecedented in the history of Russian Jewry.

(c) By concentrating our effort on one proposition we can accomplish with the same amount of money much greater results than by spreading over a variety of enterprises.

II. Hadassah President's Report,
By Rose G. Jacobs, 1937

This Jubilee year of Hadassah falls into a group of notable anniversaries within the Zionist movement, fifty years of Bilu [emigration to Palestine], forty years of [Zionist] Congress, thirty-five years of Jewish National Fund and twenty-five years of Hadassah.

Hadassah took shape and developed during a quarter of a century of world upheaval, when one crisis after another shook mankind and was tragically reflected in the Jewish history of the period. Before the War [1914] Jews happily settled in the western liberal countries, were outgrowing the effects of the old Ghettoes. These settlers were joined by large numbers driven by the pogroms in Russia. The period may be characterized as one of large and rapid migratory movements from the east to the west.

In Palestine there was a settlement of about 50,000 Jews, most of them of Oriental origin with a sprinkling of European settlers in the Baron de Rothschild colonies. The Zionist Organization was then small, struggling to compete with the alluring promises of the assimilationist theory as against the movement of return to the East—to Israel's historic birthplace. The Zionists were planning and hoping. The Jewish State meant a pattern as woven by Isaiah, Micah and Amos.

Zionism in America was insignificant, unpopular and resisted by Jews of influence and wealth. The Monroe Doctrine with its policy of American isolation was not helpful in winning adherents from among American Jews to a movement that concerned itself with centralization of Jewish interest in another country, Palestine.

During this period the emancipation of women was gaining ascendancy in America and finally the political franchise was granted to the women by the nineteenth Constitutional Amendment ratified in 1920.

These three factors—the persecution of the Jews in eastern Europe, the growing acceptance of Zionist ideology and the new social and political freedom gained by women—all gave impetus to women's participation in the Zionist movement as a new social movement. Henrietta Szold, a product of the best of Jewish tradition and American culture, profoundly influenced by the forces that strove for self-determination and social justice, created Hadassah, a medium for these forces for American Jewish womanhood.

The program launched for Hadassah embraced practical specific work in the field of health and social service in Palestine. This program had a two-fold characteristic; it was basic to the upbuilding of Zion and was of special interest to women. Thus Zionism with its profound significance, its aims and purposes was brought before American Jewish women.

Zionism, like all other movements, was profoundly affected by the war. Out of the destruction there arose new hopes and ideals and new slogans to popularize them. The principle of self- determination of small nations was supported by the universal recognition of the urge of self-expression by ethnic groups. Palestine became a focal point in the history of that time. Zionism emerged strengthened by the pledge of the Balfour Declaration, and immediately Zionists began practical activity for the reconstruction of Palestine. Hadassah came to the fore by taking part in the organization and sponsorship of the American Zionist Medical Unit. Comprised of a personnel of 44 doctors, sanitary engineers and nurses, with hospital supplies and instruments worth $50,000, the Unit was sent to Palestine in 1918 for health and healing. The Joint Distribution Committee cooperated by supplying large funds toward the initiation of the health work in Palestine.

Hadassah lent its organization to fight the epidemics that swept Palestine in the wake of the War. Hadassah became the agency for anti-malarial campaigns that were promoted by the Joint Distribution Committee and the Palestine Economic Corporation until [the British] Government took over the responsibility.

The Zionist Medical Unit, its name later changed to the Hadassah Medical Organization, gradually instituted a complete health system in Palestine, which at one time carried a personnel of 600, its annual budget from America rising from $100,000 to approximately $500,000 in 1929. From its inception, Hadassah has operated on the policy of sending 100 per cent of all funds collected for its Palestinian projects directly to Palestine without deducting anything for the administrative expenses of the organization. The membership dues cover all the administrative expenses for the collection of funds, for transmission of budgets, for an elaborate system of education and propaganda. Regularly throughout the year its books are audited by certified public accountants, whose certificate is published with our annual statement of accounts, showing in detail how the "100 per cent policy" is adhered to.

The practical work undertaken by Hadassah in Palestine had its counterpart in America in a quickened interest in the philosophy of Zionism which began when the Balfour Declaration was issued in 1917. To be sure, a variety of reasons motivated the active participation in the movement—sometimes philanthropic, sometimes cultural, but more and more a growing acceptance of Zionist ideology. Knowledge of Zionism, of Palestine and of international problems involved in the rebuilding of the Jewish Homeland has become increasingly widespread among women through Hadassah, bringing into the Jewish communities of America a deeper appreciation of Jewish values, a deeper grasp of Jewish problems, a broader understanding of causes and effects and an interest in a creative, positive Jewish outlook.

When Hadassah had been in existence ten years it organized Junior Hadassah for service to Palestine and for the education and preparation of young women in the United States for future leadership and membership in the mother organization. There are now 13,000 members in the Junior units responsible for sizeable budgetary commitments for Palestine undertakings.

As a further recognition of the importance and necessity of stimulating interest on behalf of Zionism among the youth, Hadassah has given substantial financial support to Young Judaea and has encouraged interest by its chapters on behalf of Young Judaea groups throughout the country.

Through Hadassah the Jewish women of America reached out for the opportunity of grappling with the problems confronting Jews the world over. The Zionist cause opened up new vistas of understanding and new avenues of service. New viewpoints expressed in sociology and political science gave impetus to the building up of a Jewish society in Palestine along progressive lines.

Beginning with the middle 20s and continuing to this day the need for Jewish migrations again became pressing. But everywhere frontiers were closed. Only Palestine held the magic key, admitting Jews as of right. And so they came from Poland, from Germany and from Roumania in large numbers. They came to work, to build, to create, to be free men. . . .

III.   Address of Governor Herbert H. Lehman at Emergency Conference of the United Jewish Appeal at the Harmonie Club, New York City, April 2, 1939

I am grateful that so many men and women have set aside this day to join with us in the consideration of the very grave and important problems that confront us. I thank you for your interest and for your attendance. We are gathered here today on what may well prove to be an historic occasion, the launching of the United Jewish Appeal for Refugees and Oversees Needs. I have called this meeting gladly because I have conceived it to be a duty and at the same time a privilege to take my part in this great effort and to invite your generous collaboration. . . .

The United Jewish Appeal proposes to raise this year at least $20,000,000 to be allotted to and administered by three organizations of great standing and responsibility: First, the Joint Distribution Committee, with which I have been more intimately identified perhaps than with any other Jewish body; the United Palestine, which collects funds for the enlarged Jewish Agency of which I was for some years a member; and the National Coordinating Committee Fund, Inc., which deals on a nation-wide scale with the sensitive problems of adjustment and rehabilitation of the new immigrants in this country. . . .

We are met today at a time when world affairs are in a more critical state than at any time within our memory. European civilization is teetering on the brink of a conflagration whose possibilities of destruction of all the things we hold dear, are infinitely grave. We are met here as Americans, grateful for the blessings of freedom and opportunity in the land we serve and love, and at the same time as Jews whose hearts are wrung with compassion for our suffering co-religionists in other countries as well as for all other victims of oppression.

The generous tradition of our country to lend aid even in distant lands, and the basic Jewish spiritual principle, which is at the same time the foundation of all religion, to provide for the destitute and the unfortunate, are blended harmoniously in this effort today. Time and again our government has indicated its concern over the fate of down-trodden, persecuted peoples. From these shores generous grants have been sent abroad, whether to the victims of natural disaster or of man-made sufferings. Conscious of our responsibility to live up to our civic, philanthropic and communal obligations in this country, we need have no reluctance, no fear, to give additional aid to our co-religionists, and to other victims of racial hatreds and brutal, unworthy attack.

Within the borders of our country we have nurtured neither hatreds nor exclusions. As a free people we may well share some of the blessings of that freedom with those less fortunate.

I have spoken of the American ideal of mercy and generosity to the oppressed. How splendidly do the three agencies in this United Jewish Appeal exemplify these noble ideals of extending hope to the hopeless, help to the helpless, and shelter and refuge for those who are driven from their ancestral homes.

It is a tribute to the intelligent and statesmanlike qualities of the officers of the Joint Distribution Committee, the United Palestine Appeal and the National Coordinating Committee Fund, Inc., that they have reached the significant agreement of 1939, whereby they pool their strength and fund-raising possibilities, unify their efforts and give to the communities of the United States as an inspiring example of harmonious and cooperative effort. . . .

The Joint Distribution Committee has since 1914 carried on the major and difficult task of bringing constructive assistance and emergency relief to hundreds of thousands of oppressed peoples in Eastern and Central Europe. It has built up notable and splendid projects of rehabilitation in many parts of the world. It has met every catastrophe with sympathetic understanding and with efficient intelligence. It has promoted and stimulated wide-range activities on economic service, in credit aid, in child care, in trade training, in medical and health work. It has never given up its solicitude for those great masses of Jews in Poland, Roumania and other countries who require aid in the lands in which they live. In addition, it has taken on the new and staggering burdens of helping the desperately oppressed Jews of Germany, Austria and other countries within the widening Nazi orbit of intolerance, to train and prepare themselves for emigration. The Joint Distribution Committee has cooperated with Catholic and Protestant Committees; it works closely with the Quakers, with the High Commissioner for Refugees, with the Intergovernmental Refugee Committee. It is in daily touch with important Jewish and non-Jewish bodies. Its painstaking, careful, thorough and comprehensive program and the variety of its service cover a greater range and extent of territory and of individuals than is recorded by any other philanthropic body of modern times. I may say, with the knowledge of twenty-four years of close association with its work, that it embodies the highest idealism, the most thorough and businesslike efficiency of operation, the highest standards of responsibility and trusteeship.

The United Palestine Appeal bespeaks support of the far-reaching programs of the Jewish Agency for Palestine. I am intensely interested in helping Palestine to be built up as a spiritual center, as a place of asylum for the homeless and the refugees, as a homeland for those who so desire. The people of Palestine, with restraint and dignity, have consistently proven themselves of the hardiest stock of pioneers. They have overcome one obstacle after another. They have built up the Holy Land for the benefit of all its inhabitants, Christian and Moslem, as well as Jew. They have shown themselves worthy, animated by the keenest desire to build up a self-supporting, self-dependent life. They have taken to their hearts thousands of hapless refugees from Germany and emigrants from other countries. The 450,000 Jews in Palestine deserve our cordial support in their problems. Already a land that has released the energies of thousands and thousands of exiles into useful and ennobling channels, it is our fervent hope that Palestine may be enabled to open its doors wider to the hopeless victims of European intolerance.

The National Coordinating Committee Fund, Inc., is a relative newcomer in these far-flung humanitarian and constructive activities. It has grown as the problem of the refugees has grown. With rare generosity, the President of the United States last year let it be known that this country, without altering its immigration laws in the least degree, would admit the full quota of immigrants from Germany, over 27,000 of them annually. Under the relentless pressure of the terror and the hatred that crushes them, they come here and will continue to come so long as the laws of this country permit, and so long as we deal effectively, tactfully and intelligently with these strangers in our midst. As human material the quality of these people is high. But they must be helped—adjusted to their new home, encouraged to contribute effectively to our common welfare. The question of employment must be resolved in such a way as not to prejudice our American labor. The immigrants must not be permitted to stay in congested groups in the large cities on the Atlantic seaboard. They must be resettled, trained, educated. Under no circumstances can we permit it to be said or intimated that any of these to whom this country has thrown open its portals are pensioners on the public purse. These are the delicate, sensitive, difficult problems for which the National Coordinating Committee needs and deserves substantial support. We shall be judged by the results which that committee can achieve.

In many years of philanthropic and welfare activities I have not found so ideal an amalgam of three great causes which supplement each other so well in every respect as are embodied in this United Jewish Appeal.

The aid we extend to the suffering and the oppressed is evidence that we are not insensitive to the basic humanity so sorely needed in this distracted world. It is part of our keeping alive the worth and value of what we possess. It is a gesture of sharing which says to the rest of the world, "Taste a little of our good fortune. Share with us in a blessing that is not merely of the bread but of the spirit. Take this aid which we give in token of a way of life by which a nation of free men live on the American continent. Be encouraged and have hope in these dark days. Human freedom and mercy and tolerance yet live on American soil." By the token of this hand of friendship and of mercy which we extend, we shall not allow that freedom to perish. We shall defend and cherish it and with God's help we will share some of its blessings with the millions who hunger for it across the seas.

While we talk, the need grows greater, the sufferings increase. The United Jewish Appeal, with all its plans and hopes to achieve, challenges us, our Jewish spiritual heritage, our American tradition of humanity. If in the past we have dealt mercifully and justly by those who sought our help, let me say that this united and high-visioned cause, dealing with suffering and persecution on the largest scale in modern history, challenges us to render the utmost in service, to give in infinitely larger measure, to pledge ourselves, by helping our brethren, to live worthily to the high privilege of being free men and Americans.

IV.   Once and For All, Cary Grant Is *Not* Jewish!
By Leo Gallin, 1986

"Did you know that Cary Grant is Jewish?" For the past 30 years this pleasant invention has been hurled at me in Los Angeles, in New York, in London and in Israel. As it happens, I am in a unique position to know that Cary Grant is *not* Jewish, any more than Shirley Temple changed her name from "Positively Synagogue."

How did this rumor start? About 1947 our Jewish Fund held a meeting in the Crystal Room of the Beverly Hills Hotel and Hollywood packed the place to hear Reuven Dafni, the great hero of rescue operations in World War II (later to be our first consul). Cary Grant, who was working at RKO with Dory Schary, strode into Dory's office and, feigning anger, asked why he hasn't been invited to the UJA meeting. Schary mumbled something about our limiting attendance to Jews because the pressure appeal might be embarrassing to others. Whereupon Grant, never short on humor or imagination, exclaimed: "But I AM Jewish!" and proceeded to invent a convincing story about a Jewish grandfather.

Having earned his right to be a prospect, Cary Grant appeared at the dinner, politely refused to accept a front table seat, and heard Dafni while seated on the step leading into the main hall. When the "pitch" came to his name, he pledged $10,000 (this was 40 years ago) and two days later his check was in our office. Ever since, this most gracious gentleman was not only responsive to our requests to appear on UJA or Bonds programs (usually to read a dramatic passage from the Bible), but invariably he insisted that we owed him no thanks; that it was truly an honor and privilege to help.

Many other top non-Jews in the industry gave us time, influence and money. George Seaton, a partner of Bill Perlberg of 20th Century, objected to our appeal being limited to Jews and insisted on soliciting the non-Jews personally, a task which he performed effectively year after year. Frank Sinatra and Jimmy Durante made many appearances for the Fund and were generous contributors as well. Glenn Ford spoke at local meetings and traveled out of state when his schedule permitted. And that beautiful lady, Barbara Rush, became one of our effective speakers and, like Cary Grant, thanked us for asking her.

Fund raising in the entertainment industry can be exciting; it can also be maddeningly frustrating . . . the greatest difficulty lies in the hierarchy of power, which gives primary position to the producer, with even the wealthiest actors, directors and writers far down the line. Since the producer is generally less accessible to community involvement, leadership of campaigns falls to good-hearted volunteers for secondary and tertiary lines of power.

In the late 1940s "top muscle" was brought into the campaign picture for a few years, by creating an Honorary Presidency of the Fund with Samuel Goldwyn as the first president. This made possible successful parlor meetings at top level and unheard of gifts of $100,000 each from Goldwyn, Joseph Schenck, Harry Warner, Jack Warner, Albert Warner (New York City) and MCA (Music Corporation of America). Once the ice was broken, Goldwyn was succeeded by Schenck, then by Jack Warner, each of whom brought success to his term. To rediscover top giving in the entertainment industry, our Fund must have the vision and the nerve to "go for the muscle." True, the old moguls are gone, but the new giants in movies, television and records are no less accessible.

Before we leave the "Moguls," the record . . . should be corrected. It is true that Goldwyn and the Warners were ". . . known for their generosity to Jewish causes . . ." but their glorious *mitzvah* wagon should not be loaded with men who were niggardly in their giving even in years of peak crisis. One of these "generous" men once made a million dollar "pledge" and then reneged, saying he had done that only to encourage others to give!

Had Eddie Cantor been an influential producer, the industry would long ago have set records in Fund drives. But Eddie was "only" an actor. Yet this great Jew not only gave of his means and talent; his mind and his heart worked for the people he loved. At any hour I could expect a call from Eddie: "Can you meet me at my home? We have to figure out what to do about this calamity." When an anti-Semitic British general issued a press release saying that fat, rosy-cheeked Jews were emerging from the camps with black-market money oozing out of their pockets, Eddie Cantor demolished him with a full-page ad in the *New York Times* (paid for by Eddie), reading: "I went to bed thinking Hitler was dead, and I awoke to hear his voice again."

Even though at times it seems that organizing the industry for UJF (United Jewish Welfare Fund) is like trying to form a bronze statue of mercury, the job can be done; it only takes courageous, subtle, and innovating methods. The entertainment world will not respond to stodgy, plodding organizing strategies. But given a truly dramatic "call to arms" the latent power of Hollywood will surface. The good Jews of the industry won't tolerate boredom, nor will they be sold by phony *kitsch* which is often the coin of their trade. But they can be inspired!

V. John Simon Guggenheim Memorial Foundation, 1925–1956

Founded in 1925 by Former United States Senator and Mrs. Simon Guggenheim, in Memory of John Simon Guggenheim, a Son, who Died April 26, 1922

The name John Simon Guggenheim embodied in the title of the Foundation is that of a dearly loved son who was cut off by death on April 26, 1922, just as he had completed his preparation for college. In this great sorrow, there came to Mrs. Guggenheim and myself a desire in some sense to continue the influence of the young life of eager aspiration by establishing a foundation which in his name should, in the words of the charter, "promote the advancement and diffusion of knowledge and understanding, and the appreciation of beauty, by aiding without distinction on account of race, color or creed, scholars, scientists and artists of either sex in the prosecution of their labors." . . . It is Mrs. Guggenheim's and my desire, in memory of our son, through the agency of this Foundation, to add to the educational, literary, artistic and scientific power of this country, and also to provide for the cause of better international understanding.

FROM SENATOR GUGGENHEIM'S LETTER OF GIFT
REPORT OF THE SECRETARY 1955–1956

A foundation is an aggregation of assets about which the law says two things: the first is that it may go on forever and the second is that it need not pay taxes. For these high privileges of perpetual and untaxed existence, the price of the law is that the foundation must be organized and administered for the public good, in accordance with the law of the land.

For it is the law of the land which determines what purposes are for the public good and, hence, may be valid purposes for foundations. No foundation can exist unless its purposes have the approval of that law, either under general law or under a special act of our legislature of that land.

It is well for foundations never to forget that they exist by virtue of the law of that land in which they are organized and operate, and that they must be managed to further purposes that the law deems for the public good. It is well for the public to understand the same: that foundations exist only to serve the public good and that all of them came into being by virtue of the law's approval of their purposes.

The John Simon Guggenheim Memorial Foundation was created, as a legal entity, by Special Act of the Legislature of the State of New York, duly passed by the Legislature and signed by Governor Alfred E. Smith, as Chapter 133 of the Laws of 1925. This is to say, in the words of the preamble to the Act, "The People of the State of New York, represented in Senate and Assembly" officially ask the seal of their approval on the purposes for which Senator and Mrs. Simon Guggenheim wished to use their money, which was—in the language of the Act—"for the purpose of receiving and maintaining a fund or funds and applying the same or the income thereof to promote the advancement and diffusion of knowledge and understanding and the appreciation of beauty by aiding without distinction on account of race, color or creed, scholars, scientists and artists of either sex in the prosecution of their labors. . . ."

The constant theme of the Foundation's Reports has been the theme of the expansion, in a long curve upward, of the dignity, and concomitant freedom, of men—through all the history of Western civilization from its Mesopotamian beginnings. Our convictions—which many doubters said could rationally be no more than a hope—has been that, for peoples who had ever known freedom of the mind and spirit, submission to tyranny would not long be tolerated, even if it had to be endured. . . .

It seems to be accepted doctrine that no man is indispensable. Perhaps this is true if the objective is the limited objective of mere survival; but, clearly, the doctrine has no basis in truth if the objective is something more or something different. All of the great break-throughs, to what we call progress, have been made by men who were, indeed, indispensable. To be clear about this it is necessary only to remember, for example, Shakespeare and Michelangelo, Franklin and Jefferson, Aristotle and Archimedes, the Curies and Einstein, Newton, Lorentz, Lavoisier, Claude Bernard—to name but a few giants among hosts of giants. . . .

Accepting doctrine or not, we are determined to continue our search for indispensable men. We shall search for the lone and often lonely seeker, the individual and not the group, for men of ideas and not for projects, for qualities of training, imagination and character in individual men and women. Group research has many values; but ideas will come from individuals. . . .

Henry Allen Moe
Secretary

52

The Jewish Social Background
1950s–1960

Outside of the recreational facilities available to the general public, the Jews had a social world of their own. In the larger communities the more affluent had their Jewish dining and country clubs. It was not that all Gentile clubs excluded them—many made them welcome—but Jews, a gregarious lot, enjoyed relaxing with their coreligionists. And for the less affluent? Synagog members had brotherhoods and sisterhoods; there was the Council of Jewish Women, the Hadassah, landsmanshaften, and a variety of Jewish lodges, enough to satisfy every taste. Intellectuals had their literary societies; younger folk were comfortable with their Greek letter fraternities and sororities. Old-timers met in the halls of the Jewish War Veterans.

The Jewish Community Center—largely funded by the local Federation—set out to be all things to all Jews. Its quarters were often magnificent; there was an indoor as well as an outdoor pool, a gymnasium, a large auditorium with a stage, a kitchen that served kosher or kosher-style foods; there were concerts, art exhibits, dramatic presentations, lectures on Jewish and general subjects. The centers have a problem; they seek to be cultural and educational institutions, to induce their clients to intensify their Jewish identity. In this effort they clash with the synagogs, which have staked their own claim to control of Jewish education. Today the synagogs still tend to dominate the religiocultural area; the centers are to a large degree still primarily social and recreational.

In selection I Arlene G. Peck, a well-known journalist, describes the social world and horizon of the Jewish girl in the 1950s (the term "Jewish American Princess" had apparently not yet come to be resented); in selection II, Irving Leibowitz, an Indianapolis journalist, took time out to write

472

a no-nonsense letter to his son on the occasion of his bar mitzvah. The final selection, a survey by Herbert Millman, a social worker, provides an introduction to the history and activity of the typical community center.

I. Coming-of-Age in the South: The Southern Jewish American Princess in the Fabulous Fifties, By Arlene G. Peck, 1950s

What was it like growing up as a Jewish American Princess? Specifically, what was it like as a Southern Jewish Princess during the mid-1950s when life and responsibility were different. Life in the South was slow, uncomplicated, and crime wasn't rampant. The only "grass" we knew about was what the yardman cut, and "pot" was something that people cooked in.

We were the pre-tease, before-blow dry generation who thrived on seeing and being seen and most of all, being considered "with it." Popular was the key word. Clothes were important—too important—and there were few among us who did not have a charcoal grey felt skirt with pink poodles connected by a chain, with a matching cashmere sweater set, and finished off with expensive foreign imported shoes and our ever-present, leather, collegian tweed pocketbook. We were the *super* princesses, indulged from the womb to the tomb and we reaped the benefits of our parents' success. We were the forerunners of today's Gucci-Pucci generation, the ones who today look chic wearing their hair pulled back at the nape of the neck with a rubberband and tied with a designer scarf.

Most of all there was *sorority*. Sorority is what separated the haves and the have nots. And, as the local southern Jewry was divided between the Reformed Jews (who had their roots in Germany) the Askanizie [sic] (who arrived later from Eastern Europe, usually with less money and less education [though, despite the author's definition, "Ashkenazic" applies generally to Central and East European Jews]) and the Sephardic or Spanish Jews (who were a close community and usually stayed apart from the rest), so were the sororities.

When September arrived and we received a "special" invitation from one of the elite sororities, "we had arrived!" Never again would we have to worry about sitting by ourselves at the lunch table. There was a special table for these select few. For the rest of our school career we majored in "friends" and minored in "popular." Somehow, for those who didn't sit at that table where the gods favored us from their lofty heights, life went on, but nowhere near as exciting. We were the girls who never got our hair wet or went camping. Even though we might play intramural basketball, we would never, but never, sweat! Horses sweat, people perspire, *but the sorority girl glowed!* Looking cute in adorable gym outfits was the name of the game—much more than winning.

After Friday night football games, the popular "in place" to be was "The Hang-out," a drive-in restaurant located near the local college campus. Only there was it permissible to be seen without a date. There were no singles bars because only "hussys" would frequent them. Rule one was *never give your right name*. There in the safety of our peers and fortified with a "class" fictitious name like Modine Gunch, we were flirtatious, suggestive, seductive and sexy. We were also teasers. Jeans were unheard of and we were so inhibited in those days, that we wore girdles when we didn't need them because it was unladylike to *jiggle*. In the "Gone With the Wind" tradition, a trip downtown during the daytime meant that the Southern Jewish Princess had to dress in heels and gloves. To be seen on the street smoking was for harlots only. Besides, it was more fun sitting on the floor of the girl's bathroom passing around an unfiltered cigarette. Luckily, our lungs survived high school.

Northern college men who headed South for their education were filled with mixed feelings about the Southern Jewish American Princess. True, they were spoiled and pampered, but the Southern Jewish family was hospitable and their daughters were also usually pretty. If they weren't, then along with their "coming out" party of sixteen, they would visit the plastic surgeon for their nose job. Of course, the orthodontist was doing a thriving business.

We dated at ridiculous ages. Invitations were sent out to girls who were thirteen and looked twenty. We coerced our parents into allowing the eye makeup and the high heels that to this day have crippled my toes. The standard argument was, "You've *got* to let me; *everybody does*, or *everybody has one*." Dates were made weeks ahead; one reason being that it was unthinkable to wear the same dress twice. It could be reconstructed, and time had to be allowed for a trip to the local seamstress where, what nature had forgotten, she would fix with ruffles and more ruffles. Even if you weren't, everyone looked well-endowed. And, it was because of those voluminous ruffles, and the layers of crinolines that were starched so they could stand alone, that anything but double dating was discouraged. It was just impossible to fit more than four people in the car. Looking back, that was probably the reason most of us returned home from the dance with our virtues intact. That, and the fact that it took half an hour to hook ourselves into our "merry widow" waist clincher bra!

Speaking of that, no sooner were we out of our training bras into the dating scene at the age of thirteen than we received our indoctrination from our mothers. There is an old joke of the Jewish grandmother who was walking her grandchildren down the street and came upon a friend who exclaimed, "Oy, your grandchildren are adorable! How old are they?" The reply was, "The lawyer is two, the doctor is four." In a sentence, this sums up our mothers' attitudes' regarding the kinds of boys who would be an acceptable Prince for their Princess. We were taught that lightning would strike if we even considered speaking more than casually to a boy who wasn't Jewish. Horror stories were told of girls who married outside the faith and every city had at least one scandal. It was as though a vacuum had swallowed them up, never to be heard from again and doomed to live alone, and, certainly, without her former southern Jewish Princess friends. Of course, conversion was acceptable because after all even Queen Esther married outside her faith. And, who could forget the love story of David and Bathsheba that was known by every Sunday school student?

I remember testing my mother's words when I arrived at college and was invited to a non-Jewish fraternity party by the captain of the football team. He called me on my "princess" phone (what else?) and I accepted . . . expecting to be struck dead before the evening was over. I went, but with the guilt feelings of a lifetime on my head.

Chris was adorable (all football players are named Chris or Jim), and we were dancing under the magnolias (it was a southern campus), sipping Purple Passion, which was, in reality, White Lightning passed off as grape juice, I decided to find out if "they" were right. I tugged at a ruffle and casually asked, "What do you want to do when you finish school?" He looked over at me with those nordic gorgeous blue eyes and said, "Er, Ah, er, I kinda thought I'd be a coach." I spent the rest of the evening asking the other nordic types who asked me to dance, what they wanted to be and the answers ranged from working for a large corporate company to chief executive at the local bank. This was the first time in my life I found out that the boys that I knew didn't have to be a doctor, lawyer, professional man, or go into his father's business. WASP's didn't have a quota system and could be anything they wanted!

Southern Jewish American Princesses were accustomed to having two live-in servants, their mothers and their fathers. Until I went to college, I thought that the good fairy came into my room and put clean sheets on the bed, pressed clothes in the closet and nice meals on the table. I was so impressed when I found out that there were girls in my dorm from the North who actually sewed and ironed shirts and knew how to get clothes whiter than white. (I failed that in college.) That's why it was so important that a Southern Jewish American Princess never married beneath her station, because then we might find ourselves with husbands who thought that we were spoiled . . . which we were!

We grew up thinking that everyone used fine cut crystal glass to keep our toothbrushes in. By seventeen, we had our first car, diamond ring and trip to Europe (chaperoned, of course). For those who followed the trend, marriage was at eighteen, to our first husbands that is.

And, today, what has happened to us "golden girls" of the fifties? We were the children of parents who were, for the most part, first-generations Americans. Their parents had fled the old country to escape the pogroms. Our parents were the products of the post-war years and were afraid to speak out about prejudice. They shut their eyes to the quota systems and "restricted" clubs and avoided facing issues that we are battling today. Because of this background, many of us have turned into stronger, or at least more vocal Jews. Our parents were afraid to speak out about the injustices lest the fears of the Holocaust happen again. Today, we know if we *don't* speak out, it *could* happen here. We are raising our children with a stronger Jewish identity and a feeling of ethnic pride. That "Special" time is gone, but it has been replaced with something that is better.

II.   "Treat Your Sister Like a Little Lady,"
By Irving Leibowitz, May 2, 1958

Dear Alan:

You are on the threshold of manhood. Tomorrow, as is customary in the Jewish faith [at the age of thirteen], you will be confirmed. We call it "Bar Mitzvah."

As a young man, now, you have certain rights and obligations.

You ask: "What can I do? Where can I go?"

I shall tell you. Go home. Study your lessons. Mow the lawn. Wash the car. Get a job. Read a book. Help your mother.

Get it out of your head that the world, and your parents in particular, owe you entertainment, recreational facilities, and a handsome living.

This is a time for you to grow up. Quit being a crybaby. Develop a backbone, not a wishbone. Treat your sister like a little lady.

Do not expect your parents or teachers or friends of relatives to make excuses for you, to protect you, to deny themselves needed comforts for your every whim and fancy.

Do not misunderstand. Your mother and I are proud of you.

We realize that a boy of your age is slow to take a bath, slow to study lessons, slow to come home on time, slow to help around the house, slow to feed Champ, and fast to run out of the house (and bang the door) to play basketball and baseball.

As a good Jew, you must remember your heritage . . . that you come from religious people who pioneered in liberty, learning, and law.

As a good American, you must remember, too, that you were born and brought up in this great nation that has made freedom for everyone a daily, living thing.

You must be prepared to live and give your energy and talents so that no one will be at war or in poverty, or sick or lonely again.

You must be prepared to fight, and die, if necessary, to protect this country that welcomes the oppressed of the world so that your own children may continue to live in freedom.

May God grant you the courage and wisdom and faith to be a man.

III.   The Jewish Community Center, By Herbert Millman, 1960

Jewish community centers have been part of the American scene since 1854. Originally set up as social and cultural organizations for older youth and known as Young Men's Hebrew Associations or Young Men's Hebrew Literary Associations, they were established in communities across the country under a variety of designations, including YM and YWHAs [Young Women's Hebrew Associations], Jewish educational alliances, Jewish settlement houses, and Jewish community centers. In the first decades of the 20th century one of their major aims was to help Jewish immigrants adapt to American life. Later the focus shifted to providing for the recreational and cultural interests of Jews of all ages, and most of the organizations accordingly adopted the name of Jewish community center. Some retained or even reverted to the designation of YM and YWHA in order to distinguish themselves from synagogue centers, which also often took the name of Jewish center or Jewish community center.

The National Jewish Welfare Board (JWB) is the national association of Jewish community centers and YM and YWHAs. In 1959, 437 such agencies and their branches held direct affiliation with JWB, which also served Canadian centers through an arrangement with the Canadian Jewish Congress. In 1959 JWB served 181 Jewish community centers and Ys holding full constituent membership in JWB, 41 branches of constituent centers, 105 associate and provisional members (mainly synagogue centers), 39 resident-country camps, 58 country-day camps located apart from centers, and 13 Canadian centers—a total of 437 separate facilities.

The center movement experienced its greatest growth after World War II, reflected in a substantial increase in membership, construction of new facilities, expansion of services, rise in budgets, and increase in professional personnel. The postwar period was also a time of self-examination for the centers and for JWB. Center philosophy was clarified in a *Statement of Principles on Jewish Center Purposes* adopted in 1948, following a survey directed by Oscar I. Janowsky for a commission headed by Salo W. Baron. The statement defined the functions of the Jewish community center as (a) an agency of Jewish identification, (b) the common meeting ground for Jews regardless of doctrinal, ritual, political, or social views, (c) an instrument for furthering the democratic way of life, and (d) a means of helping the individual Jew to participate in the life of the total community. While emphasizing the responsibility of the center in fulfilling its Jewish purposes, the statement also affirmed that participation in Jewish community centers should be open to all. . . .

In 1958 membership in Jewish community centers reached a high of more than 600,000, having grown steadily since 1947, when an enrollment of 458,000 was recorded. Boys and girls under 14 years of age were about a third of the membership, nearly a half were adults 25 years of age and older, and the remainder were between 14 and 25 years old. Males make up slightly more than half of the total membership.

Most of the centers followed the national policy of welcoming non-Jews. In a special study completed in 1959, seven out of every eight centers reported non-Jewish membership, the percentage ranging from less than 1 to less than 25, with an average of 5. Non-Jews participated in a wide variety of center activities, especially physical education, recreation, and formal classes. . . .

The principal method employed in the center program is known as social group work, an aspect of social work which seeks to help the individual achieve personality growth through experiences as a group member. It also seeks to help the group as a whole enhance its social understanding and responsibility. Most of the executives and key program positions in centers were filled by men and women trained in this discipline at schools of social work. In addition, centers employed persons trained in pre-school education, health and physical education, adult education, and other fields.

More than half of the center members participated in group activities and classes. In 1957 an aggregate of more than 16,000 groups was reported, including clubs, formal and informal classes, nursery schools, adult organizations, golden-age clubs, and gymnasium classes, but excluding daycamp and resident-camp groups. The average center had about 155 groups. The larger the membership of a center, the greater the number of groups.

There were more than 4,000—a quarter of all groups—clubs for children, youth, and young adults, of which in turn a fifth were units of national organizations such as B'nai B'rith and Young Judaea and the remainder were center-sponsored. Next in numbers came physical-education classes, which made up 22 per cent of the total, and classes (conversational Hebrew, world affairs, Jewish history, etc.) and special-interest groups (drama, crafts, photography, arts, etc.), which made up a fifth. The remaining groups were nursery-school classes, adult organizations, older-adult clubs, and councils and committees.

Besides the 55 per cent of the enrolled members who participated in such groups, another 25 per cent took part in other types of program, including lectures, concerts, young-adult and adult social gatherings, mass activities for children (holiday celebrations, movies, entertainments, etc.), and indoor and outdoor swimming. The remaining fifth used the recreation and game rooms (table tennis, bowling, billiards, checkers, chess, etc.), libraries, and lounges of the centers.

The center field, through JWB, periodically reviewed its position in respect to the opening or closing of center facilities on the Sabbath. In 1958 the policy that had been in effect for the previous decade was reaffirmed. This stated:

> JWB recommends that on the Sabbath, Jewish festivals and Jewish holy days Jewish centers shall conduct only such activities as are in consonance with the dignity and traditions of these days. Where no special programs can be maintained, the Jewish center shall be closed on the Sabbath, Jewish festivals and Jewish holy days.

A survey conducted in 1958 indicated that more than three- quarters of the centers remained closed on the Sabbath. Half of the other centers reported special *oneg shabbat* [Sabbath joy] programs including discussions, singing, and story telling. Fourteen centers reported that they opened their indoor or outdoor swimming facilities on Saturday afternoons and made their health clubs available. Other types of program reported included hikes and trips, library, picnics, formal classes, and music. Almost invariably, centers that opened on the Sabbath did so only on Saturday afternoon, except for religious services in the morning. Fourteen centers reported that they either made their facilities available to synagogues for religious services or conducted these themselves. . . .

53

The Holocaust, Israel, and American Jewry
1945–1950

In 1924 the United States government, the president, the Congress, the people closed their gates to many immigrants. The number of newcomers was radically limited; Jews, certainly, were not wanted. Palestine, under the British Mandate since the 1920s, was one of the few lands where Jews, fleeing East Europe, were admitted. In 1933 the anti-Semitic National Socialists German Workers' Party (Nazis) assumed control of Germany. It was its goal to annihilate the Jews; this is the Holocaust. Ultimately millions of Europe's Jews were murdered. Fearing the Germans in their drive to dominate the nations of Europe, North Africa, and the Middle East, the United States entered World War II. After Germany had been defeated, a Jewish chaplain, Rabbi Abraham J. Klausner, found himself in Dachau, a concentration camp, faced with the problem of helping displaced Jews there and in other camps located in the zone administered by the United States Army. His determination to help fellow Jews is reflected in the account of his experiences in Germany (selection I). In Klausner, the words *kelal yisrael*, kinship, became flesh, stark reality, and heroic devotion.

Klausner helped many of the Jewish survivors reach Palestine, then still under British Mandate. Two years later, November 29, 1947, England and the United Nations, unable to pacify the warring Palestine Arabs and Jews, partitioned the Holy Land between the two peoples. The Arabs refused to accept the areas allotted them. The hostilities that had characterized Jewish-Arab relations since the 1920s now eventuated into civil war. The Jews, surviving Moslem attacks, established the State of Israel on May 14, 1948; President Henry Truman recognized it almost immediately. That same day the Palestine Jews and the World Zionist Movement issued a Declaration of the Establishment of the State of Israel (selection II). They promised to write a constitution in a few months, one that "will uphold the full social and political equality of all its citizens without distinction of religion, race, or sex; will guarantee freedom of religion, conscience, education and culture." The proposed Constituent Assembly never met and never wrote a constitution. It could not, for no secular state would satisfy the scruples of the Orthodox Jews or the fears of the Zionists: giving all rights to the prolific and militant Moslems created the possibility that they might ultimately threaten the hegemony of the Jews.

There was tremendous elation in United States Jewry when the Israelis emerged victorious in the 1948–1949 civil war. Jews here were proud of the prowess of their Palestine fellow Jews and the achievements of the Israeli pioneers who had set out to conquer the soil. But no matter how happy the American Jews were, how dedicated to the support of the State of Israel, they did not—would not—emigrate in substantial numbers to the Old-New Promised Land. America was home; here they were determined to stay. This was emphasized at a luncheon in the King David Hotel, August 23, 1950 when Jacob Blaustein, chairman of the American Jewish Committee, met with David Ben Gurion, prime minister of the State of Israel, and discussed prime loyalties. Ben Gurion assured Blaustein: "To my mind, the position is perfectly clear. The Jews of the United States, as a community and as individuals, have only one political attachment and that is to the United States of America. They owe no political allegiance to Israel" (selection III).

I. Chaplain Abraham J. Klausner and Germany's Displaced Jews, By Abraham J. Klausner, 1945

Early in 1945, I was one of 250 replacement officers shipped overseas after the Battle of the Bulge, Hitler's final military gasp. The war was rapidly winding down as we moved into Germany, and there was little likelihood that we would soon be assigned to units. At loose ends, I took off for Rheims, U.S. Command Headquarters, where I obtained an assignment to a hospital outside Paris. The very next day I was ordered to report to the 116th Evacuation Hospital, somewhere. I took my bewilderment at the double assignment to the Chaplain's office in Paris. There I learned that a "prisoner of war" camp had been liberated in which there was a sizable Jewish contingent in need of a chaplain's services; thus the assignment to the 116th Evac. The first leg of my trip took me back to Rheims, where no one knew the location of the 116th Evac., except that it was attached to the U.S. Seventh Army headquarters, Augsburg. There, finally, a sergeant told us it was in Dachau in Bavaria.

Before nightfall, I was swallowed up in a hectic scene: medical personnel rushing about, intent on singular missions. There was no one to whom to report, and no demonstrable interest in my arrival, except for a word from a passing officer: "Find a cot and drop your gear." With the first cast of light, I was up and out of the building to meet the liberated. I saw them to my right: a threesome of gaunt figures dressed in the striped concentration camp garb, immobile, behind a high barbed wire fence. An officer, moving through a gate, flicked the remains of a cigarette toward the fence. Suddenly, all three figures were kneeling at the fence, their arms pushing through the wires for the cigarette butt. There it all began. Pain shot through me. These were my people, the liberated, reduced to competing for a butt. I quickly headed for the gate, where I was told to lift my arms to allow soldiers, armed with DDT insecticide guns, to pump the stuff through the sleeves of my uniform. The powder formed a cloud, briefly moving with me. I walked slowly, studying the rows of ugly barracks, at the same time fingering the cellophane envelopes in my pocket in which were small mezuzot [traditional symbols of Jewish identity] provided by the Jewish Welfare Board for distribution to soldiers. I thought of them as passports to the world inside the barracks.

I chose one door, and through a horrible odor entered a dimly lit barracks, unfurnished except for shelves lining the walls. On them some of the liberated were stretched; others stood as if frozen in their places. My entrance created no stir. Then one, and another, and others spied the chaplain's insignia on my uniform. Without any introduction, their words tumbling over each other, they asked me: "Do you know . . . ?" Places and people in the United States, their connections back into life. I forgot about distributing mezuzot. I felt totally useless. I was about to leave, lost in the unreal reality of that moment. Then a voice, thin, pleading, came from the darkness of a shelf. In deference, those clustered about me moved aside, as if to let the voice pass through. "I had a brother. He left our home for America and took up the work of a rabbi. . . ." The voice—I had heard it before. Wasn't it in the boxcar travelling across France and into Belgium? My own voice trembled as I said: "Yes, I know your brother. And he is here in Europe. I will bring him to you." Fearful of being seen in tears, I rushed out. I knew there was purpose in my coming to Dachau and I knew what I had to do.

But it was not all reunions and excitement and action. Each day, except Shabbat, the dead lying about the railroad tracks and the crematoria were piled into mass graves. Those who did not survive after liberation were trucked to the Dachau town cemetery and lowered into graves—new rows dug daily for the newly-dead from Dachau and from Allach. Each day I went to the cemetery, stood at the last filled grave and intoned the traditional words that appeased and argued the nature of destiny and that affirmed life—even there, even then.

A primary problem of the liberated Jews was to reestablish identity denied them for years and to recapture family and other relationships. They knew who they had been; they knew they were alive; they needed desperately to know who they were in 1945 and who would be with them in living relationships. Isolated, pocketed in a variety of impersonal installations, they had no way of finding out who else had survived the Holocaust. So I set myself to the task of collecting the names of survivors, beginning in Dachau and moving out as far and as wide as I could reach, directly and indirectly, through colleagues and the inevitable grapevine. These names were published in a mimeographed series entitled *Sh'erit Ha'Pletah* [the last survivors]. They were distributed to survivors and to interested agencies throughout the world. Many survivors were reunited with dear ones as a result.

Until July of 1945, the American Military's plan, supported by other governments and by the United Nations Relief and Rehabilitation Administration (UNRRA), was to repatriate as quickly as possible all foreign nationals, including Jews, regardless of their wishes. For Jews, the problem centered on the Army's persistent refusal to recognize Jews as a national group, not solely as a religious denomination; nor was the Army willing to recognize the implications of a unique Holocaust, leaving Jews totally alienated from the lands and peoples among whom they had lived before World War II, and where often they had been persecuted, especially in Eastern Europe. The reality of this problem hit me forcefully when, early in my Dachau days, I came upon a number of Hungarian Jewish women, a huddle of familiar figures. They were part of 1200 DP's [displaced persons] camped on the outskirts of nearby Munich, ordered to prepare to be moved back to Hungary. I told them: "Make no preparations, you will not move." That evening I visited their camp, told the captain in charge the people would not be moving, and it would be unwise of him to force the movement. The following morning I was summoned into the company of three ranking officers. One of them immediately upbraided my interference, and ordered me to facilitate the repatriation. I insisted that the Army was reducing liberated Jews to non-beings, arbitrarily shunting them about, depriving them of the opportunity to reestablish an identity and to obtain a living address. One of the officers, taken by my statement, recommended I be taken to the Commanding General and be allowed to state the case. On our way, in response to my inquiry about the origins of the insistent policy of moving the DP's, I was told that General George Patton, 3rd Army Commander, was intolerant of having DP's in his occupation area. (The intensity of his "intolerance"—which was deep animosity in fact—would not be revealed until after his removal from command of the 3rd Army, his subsequent death in an automobile crash, and the publication of his diary in which he likened Jews to "Hawaiians with broad noses, lacking in intelligence, a threat to the American policy in Germany.")

Upon our arrival, the Commanding General shunted us to his repatriation officer. He, visibly incensed, suffered my presence only to my first words, "the 1200 Jews," to which he retorted: "There are no Jews in the camp," and directed my attention to a chart listing nationalities in the camps. "No Jews," he emphasized. When I asked: "If there are no Jews, why those sixty trucks?" He ordered me out of his office. The refusal of the U.S. Military to recognize the special situation of the Jews ended with an order from General Eisenhower's headquarters in the summer of 1945 adding Jews to the nationality list, establishing separate Jewish DP camps (which already existed de facto, of course), and prohibiting forced repatriation of Jews. I took some pride in that order!

One day I was summoned by the Colonel in command of American troops in Dachau. He had received orders to evacuate all the liberated from Dachau, and he had no place to send them, especially those who were sick. He wanted to know if I could help. I said that if he would allow me whatever supplies I would ask for from the vast Dachau warehouses (German army materiel) and the right to an ambulance corps, I would help him in moving the Jews. There were cooperative DP officers and UNRRA officials. I made an arrangement to have other nationals transferred out of designated camps. We then moved the Jews of Dachau into those camps, in effect making the camps Jewish installations. The DP's organized themselves, held elections, and created a community in each camp.

Once we had Jewish camps, I could establish the Central Committee of Liberated Jews, the institution through which I coordinated my own efforts, which became in fact the central institution of all the Jewish camps and communities in the U.S. Zone of Germany. Our first offices were in the bombed building of the Deutsches Museum in Munich. The lumber for building stairs and office cubicles in a scarred exhibit hall, came from Dachau. The workers were from the 1200 who had refused to be transported out of the area. We assumed authority. We established tracing relatives, health, cultural and education departments, with DP's leading and staffing them. The Museum quickly became an active crossing point for the many Jews moving around Germany in search of family survivors. The walls of the Museum were a heartwarming and heartbreaking mosaic of names and addresses of survivors looking for survivors.

In establishing hospitals—at St. Ottelien, Gauting, and Bogenhausen —I had faced the problem of medical staffing. Searching among the survivors I found doctors but they were reluctant to commit themselves to practice in Germany, even temporarily. I felt I could be more successful with them if they had proper instruments of their art. I prepared a list of items —stethoscopes, ophthalmoscopes, and such—and sent it to the Joint Distribution Committee (JDC), again to receive the disturbing response, "unavailable." I wrote to the community of New Haven in which I had served briefly before entering the chaplaincy; I found the people eager, giving. Their response was immediate. At the High Holydays, 1945, my chaplain colleagues and I, unable to get proper clothing, food supplements, and other supplies via the JDC, undertook through our own Jewish GI's, their families at home, and communal publicity to have 11 lb. packages (permitted to be sent to soldiers in unlimited quantity) shipped to us. Thousands upon thousands were received. Warehousing and distributing what we received kept many DP's well-employed. This undertaking did, however, create a crisis in the offices of the JDC; many American Jews raised the question: Where was the JDC? A meeting was called of UN-RRA, JDC, Army officials and me. My role was brought into question. An UNRRA officer displayed a batch of travel documents for DP's bearing my signature, an act contrary to Army policy. Those documents were but one of a variety fabricated or "liberated" from Army sources used by me and other Jewish chaplains to facilitate travel of those intent upon returning to their home cities just long enough to search for news of family members. For this "crime," UNRRA with JDC support, sought to induce the Army to remove me from the scene.

The Allied military authorities were faced with another serious problem. Thousands of DP's were coming from East Europe into Germany, returnees, partisans, those who had been moved into Eastern Russia during the war, and those frightened by the Kielce pogroms. [Forty-two Jews were murdered in Kielce by the Poles in 1946.] The Army, adamant, stationed troops along the borders. In response, we operated a surreptitious transportation program through the borders. The arrivals were stuffed into the overpopulated existing camps over the objections of some UNRRA people. During the winter of 1945–1946 and into the spring work became even more complicated with the arrival of *shlichim*, delegates, volunteers from Palestine under the official aegis of the Zionist Jewish Agency, actually *Haganah*, Palestine Jewish fighting men. Their relationships with the Central Committee and with me, with the JDC and involved soldiers were intricate, as they worked to organize transports of Jews to Italy and to France, primarily, to board illegal ships to make the Mediterranean run to British-ruled Palestine after Jewish immigration had been curtailed. I did not ask for them or want them, but orders did come to me in 1946 to return to the U.S. for separation from the service. I obeyed, of course, for the time being. On a visit to General Hilldring, Assistant Secretary of State and a friend of our people, I asked to be returned to active duty and to Germany. The State Department, he indicated, had no objection, but could take no action until a request came from the European Command, highly unlikely. Senator Robert Taft of Ohio had no qualms, and "arranged" both the necessary request and other necessities. In short order, I was on my way back to Germany with orders to report to General Walter Bedell Smith, Chief of Staff to the Commanding General of our troops, in Heidelberg. In conference with him and with Rabbi Philip Bernstein, third advisor to the Commanding General, I learned of the change in Army policy which permitted the surge of Jews across the eastern borders into Germany. Many were being accommodated in camps north of Frankfurt, in the vicinity of Kassel. They wanted me there; I was more than willing.

By late 1946, Jewish DP camps had taken on a rhythm of their own. Internal organization was complete, from schools for children to day-care for the incredible number of newborn infants, to religious activity, Zionist parties (all of them) and a panoply of cultural expressions. I wrote a lengthy report on conditions in the Jewish community in the US Zone of Germany. It was received by all the relevant agencies and then was discussed in my presence by representatives of all major Jewish organizations. Prof. Wm. Haber, last of the advisors on Jewish Affairs, labelled the report "the words of a Zionist zealot intent on compelling the people into the illegal [Palestine] pipeline." Nahum Goldmann, representing Zionist institutions, agreed with that evaluation and went further. The liberated Jews were not the kind of people the Yishuv [Palestinian Jewry] wanted and they were not to be recruited. "Let them," he concluded, "be absorbed into the German economy." Rabbi Stephen S. Wise, visibly agitated, dissociated himself from Goldmann's remarks. The matter became moot shortly thereafter with the November, 1947, decision of the United Nations General Assembly to partition Palestine and create a Jewish State. On that day, the DP's of the Wetzlar camp asked me to represent them at a celebration, specifically to tell the Americans what the UN decision meant to the liberated, and to thank the Americans for all that had been done to keep them alive and to support them through the critical post-Holocaust years.

II. Declaration of the Establishment of the State of Israel, May 14, 1948

The Land of Israel was the birthplace of the Jewish people. Here their spiritual, religious and national identity was formed. Here they achieved independence and created a culture of national and universal significance. Here they wrote and gave the Bible to the world.

Exiled from the Land of Israel the Jewish people remained faithful to it in all the countries of their dispersion, never ceasing to pray and hope for their return and the restoration of their national freedom.

Impelled by this historic association, Jews strove throughout the centuries to go back to the land of their fathers and regain their statehood. In recent decades they returned by the hundreds of thousands. They reclaimed the wilderness, revived their language, built cities and villages, and established a vigorous and ever-growing community, with its own economic and cultural life. They sought peace yet were prepared to defend themselves. They brought the blessings of progress to all inhabitants of the country and looked forward to sovereign independence.

In the year 1897 the First Zionist Congress, inspired by Theodor Herzl's vision of the Jewish State, proclaimed the right of the Jewish people to national revival in their own country.

This right was acknowledged by the Balfour Declaration of November 2, 1917, and reaffirmed by the Mandate of the League of Nations, which gave explicit international recognition to the historic connection of the Jewish people with Palestine and their right to reconstitute their National Home.

This recent holocaust, which engulfed millions of Jews in Europe, proved anew the need to solve the problem of the homelessness and lack of independence of the Jewish people by means of the reestablishment of the Jewish State, which would open the gates to all Jews and endow the Jewish people with equality of status among the family of nations.

The survivors of the disastrous slaughter in Europe, and also Jews from other lands, have not desisted from their efforts to reach Eretz-Yisrael, in face of difficulties, obstacles and perils; and have not ceased to urge their right to a life of dignity, freedom and honest toil in their ancestral land.

In the Second World War the Jewish people in Palestine made their full contribution to the struggle of the freedom-loving nations against the Nazi evil. The sacrifices of their soldiers and their war effort gained them the right to rank with the nations which founded the United Nations.

On November 29, 1947, the General Assembly of the United Nations adopted a Resolution requiring the establishment of a Jewish State in Palestine. The General Assembly called upon the inhabitants of the country to take all the necessary steps on their part to put the plan into effect. This recognition by the United Nations of the right of the Jewish people to establish their independent State is unassailable.

It is the natural right of the Jewish people to lead, as do all other nations, an independent existence in its sovereign State.

Accordingly we, the members of the National Council, representing the Jewish people in Palestine and the World Zionist Movement, are met together in solemn assembly today, the day of termination of the British Mandate for Palestine; and by virtue of the natural and historic right of the Jewish people and of the Resolution of the General Assembly of the United Nations.

We hereby proclaim the establishment of the Jewish State in Palestine, to be called Medinath Yisrael (The State of Israel).

We hereby declare that, as from the termination of the Mandate at midnight, the 14th–15th May, 1948, and pending the setting up of the duly elected bodies of the State in accordance with a Constitution, to be drawn up by the Constituent Assembly not later than the 1st October, 1948, the National Council shall act as the Provisional State Council, and that the National Administration shall constitute the Provisional Government of the Jewish State, which shall be known as Israel.

The State of Israel will be open to the immigration of Jews from all countries of their dispersion, will promote the development of the country for the benefit of all its inhabitants; will be based on the principles of liberty, justice and peace as conceived by the Prophets of Israel; will uphold the full social and political equality of all its citizens without distinction of religion, race or sex, will guarantee freedom of religion, conscience, education and culture, will safeguard the Holy Places of all religions, and will loyally uphold the principles of the United Nations Charter.

The State of Israel will be ready to cooperate with the organs and representatives of the United Nations in the implementation of the Resolution of the Assembly of November 29, 1947, and will take steps to bring about the Economic Union over the whole of Palestine.

We appeal to the United Nations to assist the Jewish people in the building of its State and to admit Israel into the family of nations.

In the midst of wanton aggression, we yet call upon the Arab inhabitants of the State of Israel to preserve the ways of peace and play their part in the development of the State, on the basis of full and equal citizenship and due representation in all its bodies and institutions—provisional and permanent.

We extend our hand in peace and neighbourliness to all the neighbouring states and their peoples, and invite them to cooperate with the independent Jewish nation for the common good of all. The State of Israel is prepared to make its contribution to the progress of the Middle East as a whole.

Our call goes out to the Jewish people all over the world to rally to our side in the task of immigration and development and to stand by us in the great struggle for the fulfillment of the dream of generations for the redemption of Israel.

With trust in Almighty God, we set our hand to this Declaration, at this Session of the Provisional State Council, on the soil of the Homeland, in the city of Tel Aviv, on this Sabbath eve, the fifth of Iyar, 5708, the fourteenth day of May, 1948. David Ben-Gurion, Daniel Uster, Mordecai Brentov, Yitzchak Ben-Zvi, Eliyahu Berlin, et al., et al.

III.   David Ben Gurion and Jacob Blaustein
Agree that American Jewry's Prime Loyalty
Is to the United States, August 23, 1950

BEN GURION, THE ISRAELI PRIME MINISTER, ADDRESSES THE
AMERICAN NOTABLE, JACOB BLAUSTEIN

We are very happy to welcome you [Jacob Blaustein] here in our midst as a representative of the great Jewry of the United States to whom Israel owes so much. No other community abroad has so great a stake in what has been achieved in this country during the present generation as have the Jews of America. Their material and political support, their warm-hearted and practical idealism, has been one of the principal sources of our strength and our success. In supporting our effort, American Jewry has developed, on a new plane, the noble conception, maintained for more than half a century, of extending its help for the protection of Jewish rights throughout the world and of rendering economic aid wherever it was needed. We are deeply conscious of the help which America has given to us here in our great effort of reconstruction and during our struggle for independence. This great tradition has been continued since the establishment of the State of Israel. You, Mr. Blaustein, are one of the finest examples of that tradition, and as an American and as a Jew you have made many and significant contributions to the Jewish cause and to the cause of democracy. We are therefore happy on this occasion of your visit here as our guest, to discuss with you matters of mutual interest and to clarify some of the problems which have arisen in regard to the relationship between the people of Israel and the Jewish communities abroad, in particular the Jewish community of the United States.

It is our great pride that our newly gained independence has enabled us in this small country to undertake the major share of the great and urgent task of providing permanent homes under conditions of full equality to hundreds of thousands of our brethren who cannot remain where they are and whose heart is set on rebuilding their lives in Israel. In this great task you and we are engaged in a close partnership. Without the readiness for sacrifice of the people of Israel and without the help of America this urgent task can hardly be achieved.

It is most unfortunate that since our State came into being some confusion and misunderstanding should have arisen as regards the relationship between Israel and the Jewish communities abroad, in particular that of the United States. These misunderstandings are likely to alienate sympathies and create disharmony where friendship and close understanding are of vital necessity. To my mind the position is perfectly clear. The Jews of the United States, as a community and as individuals, have only one political attachment and that is to the United States of America. They owe no political allegiance to Israel. In the first statement which the representative of Israel made before the United Nations after her admission to that international organization, he clearly stated, without any reservation, that the State of Israel represents and speaks only on behalf of its own citizens and in no way presumes to represent or speak in the name of the Jews who are citizens of any other country. We, the people of Israel, have no desire and no intention to interfere in any way with the internal affairs of Jewish communities abroad. The Government and the people of Israel fully respect the right and integrity of the Jewish communities in other countries to develop their own mode of life and their indigenous social, economic and cultural institutions in accordance with their own needs and aspirations. Any weakening of American Jewry, any disruption of its communal life, any lowering of its sense of security, any diminution of its status, is a definite loss to Jews everywhere and to Israel in particular.

We are happy to know of the deep and growing interest which American Jews of all shades and convictions take in what it has fallen to us to achieve in this country. Were we, God forbid, to fail in what we have undertaken on our own behalf and on behalf of our suffering brethren, that failure would cause grievous pain to Jews everywhere and nowhere more than in your community. Our success or failure depends in a large measure on our cooperation with, and on the strength of, the great Jewish community of the United States, and, we, therefore, are anxious that nothing should be said or done which could in the slightest degree undermine the sense of security and stability of American Jewry.

In this connection let me say a word about immigration. We should like to see American Jews come and take part in our effort. We need their technical knowledge, their unrivaled experience, their spirit of enterprise, their bold vision, their "know-how." We need engineers, chemists, builders, work managers and technicians. The tasks which face us in this country are eminently such as would appeal to the American genius for technical development and social progress. But the decision as to whether they wish to come—permanently or temporarily—rests with the free discretion of each American Jew himself. It is entirely a matter of his own volition. We need halutzim, pioneers too. Halutzim have come to us—and we believe more will come, not only from those countries where the Jews are oppressed and in "exile" but also from countries where the Jews live a life of freedom and are equal in status to all other citizens in their country. But the essence of halutziuth is free choice. They will come from among those who believe that their aspirations as human beings and as Jews can best be fulfilled by life and work in Israel.

I believe I know something of the spirit of American Jewry among whom I lived for some years. I am convinced that it will continue to make a major contribution towards our great effort of reconstruction, and I hope that the talks we have had with you during these last few days will make for even closer cooperation between our two communities.

RESPONSE OF JACOB BLAUSTEIN

I am very happy, Mr. Prime Minister, to have come here at your invitation and to have discussed with you and other leaders of Israel the various important problems of mutual interest.

This is the second time I have been here since the State of Israel was created. A year and a half ago my colleagues and I, of the American Jewish Committee, saw evidence of the valor that had been displayed, and felt the hopes and aspirations that had inspired the people to win a war against terrific odds. This time, I have witnessed the great achievements that have taken place in the interval and have discussed the plans which point the road upon which the present-day Israel intends to travel.

I find that tremendous progress has been made under your great leadership; but also, as you well know, tremendous problems loom ahead. The nation is confronted with gigantic tasks of reconstruction and rehabilitation, and with large economic and other problems, as is to be expected in so young a state.

I am sure that with your rare combination of idealism and realism, you will continue to tackle these matters vigorously; and that with your usual energy, resourcefulness and common sense, you will be able to overcome them.

Traveling over the country and visiting both old and newly established settlements, it has been a thrill to observe how you are conquering the desert of the Negev and the rocks of Galilee and are thus displaying the same pioneering spirit that opened up the great West and my own country. It has been satisfying to see right on the scene, how well and to what good advantage you are utilizing the support from the American Jewish community. I am sure, too, that the American tractors and other machinery and equipment acquired through the loan granted by the Export-Import Bank will further contribute to the technological development of your country.

But more than that, what you are doing and creating in this corner of the Middle East is of vital importance not only to you and to Jews, but to humanity in general. For I believe that the free and peace-loving peoples in the world can look upon Israel as a stronghold of democracy in an area where liberal democracy is practically unknown and where the prevailing social and political conditions may be potential dangers to the security and stability of the world. What President Truman is intending to do under his Four Point Program, in assisting underdeveloped peoples to improve their conditions and raise their standards of living, you here to a large extent have been doing right along under most difficult conditions and at great sacrifice.

Important to your future, as you recognize, is the United States of America and American Jewry. Israel, of course, is also important to them.

In this connection, I am pleased that Mr. [Eliyahu] Elath has been here during our stay. As your Ambassador to the United States, he has rendered invaluable service in bringing our two countries and communities closer together.

I thought I knew it even before I came to this country on this trip, but my visit has made it still more clear to me—and as an American citizen and a Jew I am gratified—that the Israeli people want democracy and, in my opinion, will not accept any dictatorship or totalitarianism from within or from without.

Democracy, like all other human institutions, has its faults; and abuses are possible. But the strength of a democratic regime is that these faults and those abuses can be corrected without the destruction of human rights and freedoms which alone make life worth living.

There is no question in my mind that a Jew who wants to remain loyal to the fundamental basis of Judaism and his cultural heritage, will be in the forefront of the struggle for democracy against totalitarianism.

The American Jewish community sees its fortunes tied to the fate of liberal democracy in the United States, sustained by its heritage, as Americans and as Jews. We seek to strengthen both of these vital links to the past and to all of humanity by enhancing the American democratic and political system, American cultural diversity and American well-being.

As to Israel, the vast majority of American Jewry recognizes the necessity and desirability of helping to make it a strong, viable, self-supporting state. This, for the sake of Israel itself, and the good of the world.

The American Jewish Committee has been active, as have other Jewish organizations in the United States, in rendering, within the framework of their American citizenship, every possible support to Israel; and I am sure that this support will continue and that we shall do all we can to increase further our share in the great historic task of helping Israel to solve its problems and develop as a free, independent and flourishing democracy.

While Israel has naturally placed some burdens on Jews elsewhere, particularly in America, it has, in turn, meant much to Jews throughout the world. For hundreds of thousands in Europe, Africa and the Middle East it has provided a home in which they can attain their full stature of human dignity for the first time. In all Jews, it has inspired pride and admiration, even though in some instances, it has created passing headaches.

Israel's rebirth and progress, coming after the tragedy of European Jewry in the 1930s and in World War II, has done much to raise Jewish morale. Jews in America and everywhere can be more proud than ever of their Jewishness.

But we must, in a true spirit of friendliness, sound a note of caution to Israel and its leaders. Now that the birth pains are over, and even though Israel is undergoing growing pains, it must recognize that the matter of good-will between its citizens and those of other countries is a two-way street; that Israel also has a responsibility in this situation—a responsibility in terms of not affecting adversely the sensibilities of Jews who are citizens of other states by what it says or does.

In this connection, you are realists and want facts and I would be less than frank if I did not point out to you that American Jews vigorously repudiate any suggestion or implication that they are in exile. American Jews—young and old alike, Zionists and non-Zionists alike—are profoundly attached to America. America welcomed their immigrant parents in their need. Under America's free institutions, they and their children have achieved that freedom and sense of security unknown for long centuries of travail. American Jews have truly become Americans; just as have all other oppressed groups that have ever come to America's shores.

To American Jews, America is home. There, exist their thriving roots; there, is the country which they have helped to build; and there, they share its fruits and its destiny. They believe in the future of a democratic society in the United States under which all citizens, irrespective of creed or race, can live on terms of equality. They further believe that, if democracy should fail in America, there would be no future for democracy anywhere in the world, and that the very existence of an independent State of Israel would be problematic. Further, they feel that a world in which it would be possible for Jews to be driven by persecution from America would not be a world safe for Israel either; indeed it is hard to conceive how it would be a world safe for any human being.

The American Jewish community, as you, Mr. Prime Minister, have so eloquently pointed out, has assumed a major part of the responsibility of securing equality of rights and providing generous material help to Jews in other countries. American Jews feel themselves bound to Jews the world over by ties of religion, common historical traditions and in certain respects, by a sense of common destiny. We fully realize that persecution and discrimination against Jews in any country will sooner or later have its impact on the situation of the Jews in other countries, but these problems must be dealt with by each Jewish community itself in accordance with its own wishes, traditions, needs and aspirations.

Jewish communities, particularly American Jewry in view of its influence and its strength, can offer advice, cooperation and help, but should not attempt to speak in the name of other communities or in any way interfere in their internal affairs.

I am happy to note from your statement, Mr. Prime Minister, that the State of Israel takes a similar position. Any other position on the part of the

State of Israel would only weaken the American and other Jewish communities of the free, democratic countries and be contrary to the basic interests of Israel itself. The future development of Israel, spiritual, social as well as economic, will largely depend upon a strong and healthy Jewish community in the United States and other free democracies.

We have been greatly distressed that at the very hour when so much has been achieved, harmful and futile discussions and misunderstandings have arisen as to the relations between the people and the State of Israel and the Jews in other countries, particularly in the United States. Harm has been done to the morale and to some extent to the sense of security of the American Jewish community through unwise and unwarranted statements and appeals which ignore the feelings and aspirations of American Jewry.

Even greater harm has been done to the State of Israel itself by weakening the readiness of American Jews to do their full share in the rebuilding of Israel which faces such enormous political, social and economic problems.

Your statement today, Mr. Prime Minister, will, I trust, be followed by unmistakable evidence that the responsible leaders of Israel, and the organizations connected with it, fully understand that future relations between the American Jewish community and the State of Israel must be based on mutual respect for one another's feelings and needs, and on the preservation of the integrity of the two communities and their institutions.

I believe that in your statement today, you have taken a fundamental and historic position which will redound to the best interest not only of Israel, but of the Jews of America and of the world. I am confident that this statement and the spirit in which it has been made, by eliminating the misunderstandings and futile discussions between our two communities, will strengthen them both and will lay the foundation for even closer cooperation.

In closing, permit me to express my deep gratitude for the magnificent reception you and your colleagues have afforded my colleague and me during our stay in this country.

PART VI

The Flowering of American Jewry, 1960s–2000

The "American" Jewish period ushered in during the 1960s was a time of ambivalence marked by ferment and progress. World War II, followed by the Korean and Vietnam adventures, troubled and bewildered great numbers. Many blacks, frustrated by the resistance to their civil rights gains, turned their backs on their Jewish allies. Traditional values were scorned by many of America's youth; hysteria was never absent; the storm passed, but there were thousands of young men and women—Jews, too—whose shattered lives littered the landscape. Though anti-Semitism had gone underground after World War II because of the horrors of the Holocaust, American Jews did not relax. In the latter decades of the twentieth century, the national administration together with the Supreme Court, tried to reconcile a nonreligious federal Constitution and the ethos of a Christian people.

The closing decades of the twentieth century had their share of anxiety, but they were also good years, very good years. Women were coming into their own; they were gaining equality; they made new lives for themselves, earning money, achieving independence; they did not hesitate, when they deemed it necessary, to divorce their mates. The children! Always adaptable, they learned to live in divided homes. The new generation of adolescents flocked to the colleges, became professionals, produced notables in business and literature, acquired wealth, moved further out in the suburbs or returned to gentrified inner city neighborhoods, and sought comfort and new challenges in the far reaches of South Florida and the distant West. In the suburbs of America's large cities Jews created a new world of their own. They had their beautiful new sanctuaries, their charities, clubs, community centers, hospitals, retirement homes, even their own public relations agency. There were few synagogs without a good Jewish library. The religious schools were constantly improving. For those who wanted a return to tradition—and an escape from deteriorating public schools—there were Jewish all-day schools almost everywhere.

Relatively speaking Jewish culture flourished, with special classes, colleges, and magazines and newspapers. Almost every major American publishing house issued its own list of Jewish books. Though ritualism was embraced by many with fervor, religionists kept moving ideologically to the left; even the most Orthodox did so to some extent; the Reformers, liberals, were gaining large numbers at the expense of the Conservatives, who were struggling valiantly to maintain a precarious lead.

With cultural and financial advance came affluence, acceptance by Gentiles, intermarriage—and, often enough, assimilation, disappearance as Jews. Soviet and Israeli émigrés pouring in helped to maintain a numerical balance, but there was no assurance that these newcomers would or could fortify the established community. The core of America's Jewry is small but loyal. It is building strong Jewish institutions and even reaching out to Europe. American Jewry, universal in its reach, is facing the challenge of rebuilding suppressed communities in Central and Eastern Europe. Though American Jews are devoted to the State of Israel, they are not in "exile"; America is home. If Jews in this land have a vision—and many have—"Zion" is the hope of bringing heaven down to earth, of fashioning a Messianic Age for themselves and all mankind.

54

Equal Rights for Jews
1964–1980s

The Founding Fathers were almost obsessed in their determination to accord equal rights to all—white—citizens, regardless of their religion. Yet from the very start the new government was actually "Christian" because the people, the masses were at least nominally believers in the teachings of the New Testament. Christian prayers in Congress were routine; Sunday, the Christian Sabbath, was a day of rest. For Jews this meant an economic disability that would not be ameliorated till the second half of the twentieth century. New problems rose in the postbellum days, beginning with the 1870s. Newly rich Gentiles, insecure in their social status, encouraged hoteliers to deny Jews accommodations. As the German Jews and those of East European background acquired education and wealth, they became formidable economic rivals to the non-Jews. There was a push to deny Jews social acceptance as well as jobs. All this was serious. The problack revolution started in the 1950s; the Civil Rights Act of 1964 guaranteed blacks, among other immunities, equality in employment and accommodations. The Jews rode in clutching the coattails of the blacks. This civil rights law included all citizens, Jews, too. On the whole, under this new statute, Jews—especially Jewish women—fared better in employment than the blacks did. Inasmuch as the blacks *had* to be hired, the more the bosses looked at Jews, the less Jewish they looked.

The first amendment to the Federal Constitution states specifically: "Congress shall make no law respecting an establishment of religion." This simple statement has invited many interpretations. The government of the United States almost inevitably favors Christianity. There are millions today who want to make the United States a "Christian" country; they seek to harness the public schools to teach their version of evangelical

Protestantism; they want "to put God" back into the classroom. Numerous bills have been introduced into Congress—down to the present day—to amend the Constitution, to invoke Jesus Christ. Not one has passed as yet. In the 1970s and 1980s, religiopolitical conservatives—the so-called "Christian Right"—began to make an impress in matters of church-state relations. All-day (private Christian "parochial") schools are being given financial help. Orthodox Jewry has rushed in to enjoy these benefits; its right-wing Jewish all-day schools are expensive to maintain, but it insists on separate Jewish schools as a brake against assimilation. The Supreme Court, inclining to the right, has opened public school buildings for the use of religious groups (equal access); religious symbols may now be erected on public, tax-supported lands. The State's services to religious schools are a definite step toward church and state union. Christian holiday celebrations are not frowned upon in the schools even though for Jewish children any form of Christian religious activity in a classroom is coercive and leads to tensions. Always apprehensive, American Jewry suspects that the Supreme Court and the Washington government are chipping away at the barrier between church and state. The problem of keeping the two realms separate is further complicated by the fact that there are Jews who are beginning to accept Christian symbols as national American symbols. Jews as a body believe that the place of religion is in the home, the church, the synagog; the wall between church and state must not be breached. History has taught them that where Christianity plays an important part in government, Jews end up as citizens of lesser rights.

Selection I contains excerpts from the Civil Rights Act of 1964; selection II is an article by Jill L. Kahn which she has condensed from one in an Anti-Defamation League *Bulletin*. It is a good survey of the church-state problem in the 1980s.

I.   The Civil Rights Law of 1964, July 2, 1964

Be it enacted by the Senate and House of Representatives of the United States of America in Congress assembled, That this Act may be cited as the "Civil Rights Act of 1964." . . .

TITLE II—INJUNCTIVE RELIEF AGAINST DISCRIMINATION IN PLACES OF PUBLIC ACCOMMODATION

Sec. 201.

(a) All persons shall be entitled to the full and equal enjoyment of the goods, services, facilities, privileges, advantages, and accommodations of any place of public accommodation, as defined in this section, without discrimination or segregation on the ground of race, color, religion, or national origin. . . .

Title VII—Equal Employment Opportunity
DEFINITIONS

Sec. 701. For the purposes of this title—

(a) The term "person" includes one or more individuals, labor unions, partnerships, associations, corporations, legal representatives, mutual companies, joint-stock companies, trusts, unincorporated organizations, trustees, trustees in bankruptcy, or receivers.

(b) The term "employer" means a person engaged in an industry affecting commerce who has twenty-five or more employees for each working day in each of twenty or more calendar weeks in the current or preceding calendar year, and any agent of such a person, but such term does not include (1) the United States, a corporation wholly owned by the Government of the United States, an Indian tribe, or a State or political subdivision thereof, (2) a bona fide private membership club (other than a labor organization) which is exempt from taxation under section 501(c) of the Internal Revenue Code of 1954; *Provided*, That during the first year after the effective date prescribed in subsection (a) of section 716 persons having fewer than one hundred employees (and their agents) shall not be considered employers: and, during the second year after such date, persons having fewer than seventy-five employees (and their agents) shall not be considered employers, and, during the third year after such date, persons having fewer than fifty employees (and their agents) shall not be considered employers; *Provided further*, That it shall be the policy of the United States to insure equal employment opportunities for Federal employees without discrimination because of race, color, religion, sex or national origin and the President shall utilize his existing authority to effectuate this policy. . . .

DISCRIMINATION BECAUSE OF RACE, COLOR, RELIGION, SEX, OR NATIONAL ORIGIN

Sec. 703.

(a) It shall be an unlawful employment practice for an employer

(1) to fail or refuse to hire or to discharge any individual, or otherwise to discriminate against any individual with respect to his compensation, terms, conditions, or privileges of employment, because of such individual's race, color, religion, sex, or national origin; or

(2) to limit, segregate, or classify his employees in any way which would deprive or tend to deprive any individual of employment opportunities or otherwise adversely affect his status as an employee, because of such individual's race, color, religion, sex, or national origin.

(b) It shall be an unlawful employment practice for an employment agency to fail or refuse to refer for employment, or otherwise to discriminate against, any individual because of his race, color, religion, sex, or national origin, or to classify or refer for employment any individual on the basis of his race, color, religion, sex, or national origin. . . .

II.   Church-State Relations in America Today, By Jill L. Kahn, 1980s

Congress shall make no law respecting an establishment of religion. . . .
These ten words from the First Amendment to the U.S. Constitution have presented America's courts and legislators with some of the most difficult issues in constitutional law. This short phrase prohibits any government—be it Federal, state or local—from "establishing" an official religion or promoting religion. The establishment clause is a constitutional guarantee that the United States remains a country which embraces persons of all religious beliefs—and even non-beliefs.

The establishment clause has been described as the "wall of separation" between religion and government. Such a wall is necessary in order to preserve the integrity and independence of both religion and the state, as well as to safeguard our religious freedom. Supreme Court Justice Hugo L. Black asserted the authors of the First Amendment were motivated by the "belief that a union of government and religion tends to destroy government and to degrade religion."

The establishment clause at first appears to be easily understood; but, in fact, drawing the line between permissible and impermissible government activity is a thorny question which has produced a multitude of seemingly confusing court decisions.

Over the past (35) years, the Supreme Court has struck down Bible reading and prayer recitation in public schools, but approved secular courses which teach about the Bible. Released time programs in which religion classes are taught on public school premises have been held unconstitutional; released time classes away from public schools were upheld. State reimbursement for bus transportation, state loans of textbooks, and public financing of speech, hearing and psychological therapeutic services for parochial school students has been upheld by the Supreme Court; however, government reimbursement for parochial school teachers' salaries in secular subjects and state loans of instructional materials and professional staff to parochial schools has been found unconstitutional.

Despite the obvious divergence of these decisions, the concept of a "wall of separation" has remained firmly intact through the years. Recently, however, legislative activity and court decisions appear to be threatening its foundations.

The public school is becoming the most common target for efforts to promote religion. Even though the Supreme Court's ban on prayers and

Bible recitation is more than twenty years old, prayer cases are still coming before the courts.

In Alabama, Louisiana and Massachusetts, state laws were enacted authorizing or prescribing a period of prayer for students and teachers at the start of the school day. These statutes differed slightly from those struck down by the Supreme Court because they were either "voluntary" or did not prescribe a specific prayer.

The three statutes were nevertheless uniformly struck down by Federal courts, which ruled that even though the purpose of the prayer laws was secular, the effect was to impermissibly advance religion and to entangle government with religion in violation of the establishment clause.

A different attempt to skirt court rulings has been attempted by legislating "moments of silence" for contemplation, meditation or reflection, without specifying prayer recitation. Proponents of the "moment of silence" bills attempt to cloud their sectarian purpose by asserting that such periods merely ensure a quiet and orderly atmosphere at the start of the school day and that such discipline is good for children. Sponsors also emphasize the fact that children are not forced to pray, but may sit quietly in their seats. So far, the New Mexico, New Jersey and Tennessee "moment of silence" laws have been declared unconstitutional, while a challenge to an Oklahoma law is pending.

The courts have been especially careful in scrutinizing any type of religious activity in public schools, recognizing the impressionability of schoolchildren, the pervasive peer pressure and the child's perception of school authorities. Permitting students to pray in school is too easily seen by children as official approval of prayer and religion. Therefore, courts have found that by enacting "moment of silence" laws, the state has placed its imprimatur on religious activity in violation of the First Amendment.

Perhaps the most dangerous aspect of the "moment of silence" statutes is the potential for abuse which exists in implementing such laws. The vague nature of these laws was intended by sponsors to avoid the constitutional ban on prayer, but this ambiguity also forces teachers to decide what type of behavior will be allowed during the "meditation" sessions, how they will be conducted and who will lead the period. Leaving school officials to hammer out a constitutional application of the prayer laws, however, is hardly what the framers of the First Amendment had envisioned.

Another variation on efforts to promote religious activity in public schools is the advent of student religious clubs. In December, 1981, the Supreme Court ruled that a state university which allows student clubs the use of campus facilities must extend the same privileges to a group of students who wish to meet for religious purposes. Proponents of religious clubs have taken that decision, which was explicitly limited by the Court to the university setting, as an encouraging signal to promote student prayer and Bible reading in public high schools. Even though two Federal courts have held it unconstitutional for student religious clubs to meet on public high school grounds during school hours, this issue is still alive on the legislative and legal battlegrounds.

On the national level, two Federal bills and a constitutional amendment have been introduced in Congress which, in effect, authorize religious activity in public schools. Ostensibly these measures prohibit public schools from discriminating between different types of student clubs. Under the euphemistic banner of "equal access," these proposals would require schools which, for example, permit stamp collecting clubs, to also grant permission to students wishing to meet in order to pray or read the Bible.

The "equal access" language is clearly deceptive. By proposing that we treat religious worship equally with stamp collecting, these bills dangerously erode the religious values of our pluralistic society. Religion in this country is granted special protection and is kept separate from secular activity because in the past, the comingling [sic] of religion and government in Europe had led to religious persecution, prompting minorities to seek refuge in America.

The Supreme Court has characterized the government's position with respect to religion as one of "benevolent neutrality." Under this principle, churches and synagogues are tax exempt and receive public support such as police and fire protection. But always the courts must draw a line to determine whether accommodation to religion goes beyond "benevolent neutrality" and impermissibly advances religion.

Nonetheless, two recent decisions have upheld state action which directly benefits religion and religious institutions—a disturbing trend for anyone concerned about church-state separation.

In June, 1983, the U.S. Supreme Court held it was constitutional to allow Minnesota parents to claim a tax deduction for the cost of their children's tuition, textbooks and transportation. While the deductions are ostensibly available to all Minnesota parents, deductible expenses are generally incurred only if children attend private schools—90 percent of which, in Minnesota, are religiously affiliated. In upholding the Minnesota law, the Supreme Court refused to consider statistical evidence that 97 percent of parents taking advantage of the deductions had children in parochial schools.

Only a few days later, the Supreme Court upheld the Nebraska Legislature's 16-year sponsorship of a clergyman who was paid to open each legislative session with a sectarian, denominational prayer. The Court essentially decided that since the first U.S. Congress had approved legislative chaplains 200 years ago, the practice is constitutional.

The Supreme Court's decisions show a disturbing tendency to disregard previous tests used by courts to judge whether the church-state barrier had been crossed. The blurring of the line of distinction has been interpreted as a sign of encouragement by proponents of public sponsorship of religion.

For example, conflicts over community-sponsored Christian holiday displays have in recent years become bitter disputes which create ill feelings and community fragmentation and, increasingly, lead to lawsuits. One such case, involving a life-size nativity scene in Pawtucket, RI. reached the U.S. Supreme Court last fall. Several town residents argued that public funds are being used to finance a religious and denominational observance and that the government is advancing the beliefs of one religion contrary to the prohibition in the First Amendment.

Attorneys for the City of Pawtucket urged the Supreme Court to uphold the nativity scene display for the same reason the Court upheld the Nebraska chaplaincy—longstanding tradition. A depiction of Jesus in the manger is only a recognition of a "religious tradition" which is "interwoven with a secular celebration," they argued. Christmas is a "secular folk festival" in America they said, akin to Thanksgiving.

Many religious Christians who base their faith on the event depicted by the nativity scene view these arguments as insulting. The birth of Jesus represents the most fundamental belief of Christianity. No amount of rationalizing the "seasonal" or "cultural" aspect of Christmas mitigates the sacred nature of the scene of Jesus in the manger.

The overriding danger inherent in government sponsorship of creche displays is the clear message of rejection it sends to non-Christians.

Even more disquieting is the fact that the U.S. Government has defended Pawtucket's sponsorship of the religious display, arguing that the nativity scene is part of our "national culture."

Solicitor General Rex E. Lee told the Supreme Court that "exclud-[ing] the creche from our national consciousness is intellectually, and historically dishonest. . . . It is cultural censorship."

Ordinarily, the Justice Department will enter a case only if Federal law or policy is implicated or if it can offer special expertise on the issue before the Court. The Government's entry in the case in support of Pawtucket's nativity scene raises serious concerns over the status of religious plurality in the United States.

When the Government of the United States declares in court that Christian religious symbolism is part of the national culture, the millions of Americans who do not recognize the divinity of Jesus have cause for concern. The inevitable corollary to this proposition is that one must be Christian in order to validate one's standing as an American.

Viewed together, the "meditation laws," the attempts to allow religious practice in public schools through the "equal access" argument, and support for tuition tax credits all point to an alarming trend toward a mingling of religion and government. The Justice Department's support of the publicly-sponsored nativity scene can only be perceived as placing a government seal of approval on one religion—the religion of the majority.

If religious minorities are to retain the freedom promised to them in the First Amendment, the erosion of the wall of separation between church and state must be reversed.

55

The Jew as Citizen
1970s–1990

I t would seem that nearly all American Jews are more American than they are Jewish. Most Jews do not go to a synagog except for the High Holy Days. To be sure, the psyche, the substratum of one's being, is often determined by the Jewish emotional and spiritual heritage. The American Jew has gone far in American society. There has never been a moment in all Jewish history comparable to the present age. Jews are accepted. Two twentieth-century candidates for the American presidency had Jewish fathers, Senator Barry Goldwater and Governor Reuben O. Askew (Goldberg). Although at least 20 percent of American Jews, many of them aged, live on a bare subsistence level, the rest constitute one of the country's most affluent groups. Culturally, the 2.5 percent of Jews in the general population stand out; they win numerous Nobel Prizes. Christians are beginning to realize that the church for centuries was a Jewish sect; the Old Testament still constitutes ten-thirteenths of the Christian Bible. At least till 5 o'clock, Jews are accepted; when the offices close, Jews and Christians for the most part go their separate ways. This is their choice.

Unfortunately, the 1960s saw the rise of a New Left that made inroads into the ranks of the Jewish college students; the negative impact on its recruits will be felt for decades. Unhappy with government, political morality, and university discipline, despairing of an economy that tolerated hopeless poverty and a submerged black class, frightened, certainly, with the thought of confronting the challenge of their own careers, they responded emotionally, sometimes irrationally. The idealists among them were opposed to military intervention in Vietnam, Cambodia, and Laos in the 1960s and 1970s; they called for nuclear disarmament; they were appalled when Ohio State National Guardsmen—called in to stop disorder

—killed four students at Kent State University (May 4, 1970). The rebels rejected conformity and self-control; love, love was deemed all important; the individual and his or her unrestrained desires were seen as the measure of all things. Young Jews turned to sit-ins, to violence, and even to drugs. Successes in storming university bastions gave them and their non-Jewish cohorts a sense of power; this was heady wine. Discipline was rejected; traditional morality was gutted; the emotions were regnant. The New Left ushered in a far-flung psychic explosion that rocked the world's youth; and the end result for the individual was often disastrous. The individual wanted a New Heaven and a New Earth, but secured at best a planless Paradise; the surrender to unbridled individualism, to absorption with self, to anti-intellectualism could only lead to unreason and a universe of anarchy. Selection I reprints an article written by Dr. Alfred Jospe, former international director of the B'nai B'rith Hillel Foundations; it is an insightful analysis of the New Left of the 1960s and 1970s.

The shock of the New Left movement was exacerbated by other problems. A very substantial minority of American Gentiles persist in disliking Jews. Blacks, in the first half of the twentieth century, tended to form political alliances with Jews, but the alliances are no longer as firm as they once were. As blacks rose in the social scale they encountered Jews as rivals; many blacks, strengthened in self-esteem, are comforted by the thought that as Christians they can claim superiority to their Jewish neighbors. Out on the edge of the black world is a small body of militants who are outspokenly anti-Jewish. Blacks as a body—with a strong sense of kinship—hesitate to denounce their fellow ethnics who are given to Judeophobia.

Even more serious is the problem of intermarriage. Acculturation and social acceptance further interfaith courting. It is estimated that at least 40 percent of all Jewish marriages are with a Gentile partner; most of the children of these unions are ultimately lost to the Jewish community. The decline in numbers is made up, to some extent, by a swelling immigration of Israelis and Soviet Jews so that American Jewry continues holding its own numerically.

There are a few white Gentiles—a very few—who are truly anti-Semitic. Anti-Semitism, a nineteenth-century pseudoscience, maintains that Jews are inherently bad; they cannot be redeemed; they must be segregated, removed, destroyed. Selection II reprints an anonymous broadside circulated in Cincinnati during the 1980s. It repeats an age-old myth: Jews murder Christian children. Selection III contains an obituary that describes in detail the career of Arthur J. Goldberg, a former United States Supreme Court Justice and Ambassador to the United Nations. This document is historically significant because it makes a point that every Jew understands: In this country there are no heights that even the son of an impoverished immigrant Jewish peddler cannot scale. In December 1990, the membership committee of the Kansas City Country Club refused to admit a Jewish businessman who possessed impeccable credentials. Infuriated at this snobbery, a Gentile member, a notable golfer, resigned in protest, unleashing a storm of protests on the part of the city's Gentiles and Jews. The story of the Kansas City cause célébre is recounted in selection IV, which does not record that several days later the club authorities finally capitulated and accepted the candidate as its first Jewish member.

I.   The Campus: Conflict or Challenge?
By Alfred Jospe, 1970s

Anyone who wants to understand today's campus scene should be aware of several factors which dictate caution.

First, be sure to beware of generalizations. Do not trust anyone who claims he knows the American college student or who tells you what the American college student thinks or is like today. There is no such thing as the American college student. The college generation speaks not with a single voice but millions of voices. When you have nearly seven million students, it is obvious that they differ enormously in their capacities, their political views, their social concerns, their outlook upon life, their attitudes towards authority, politics, Judaism, the synagogue, sex—in everything that matters to them most or least. No generalization can capture this diversity of often contradictory views and attitudes. The only thing that is certain when we speak of today's college students is that no tag or label really fits them. Secondly, there is a general consensus that only a relatively small segment of the student population is actively involved in what has been termed "campus rebellion." Estimates range from 4–8%. . . .

Yesterday's dominant concerns were racial justice, civil rights, voter registration. Yet when a group of student leaders was asked at the end of a National Student Conference on Religion and Race not long ago whether they favored a follow-up conference, the majority felt that the race issue already was quite dead on campus and that sex was "the thing right now." For some time, poverty and housing were the issues. Shortly afterwards, Vietnam and the draft began to move into the center of student concern. New issues have been added more recently: "student power," "participatory democracy," black power. Life on campus has a peculiar tendency to outdate yesterday's absolutes. But whatever the changes, one thing is clear: large numbers of students—among them many of our best young people—reject the values, the moral order, the standards and goals of today's society. . . .

As a result, we have the striking phenomenon that some of our most dedicated and sensitive young people reject any relationship to organized religion and its institutions—in our case, to Jewish life and especially the synagogue. Many of them can be found in the forefront of the civil rights struggle, the drive for peace, and similar battles of our time, yet they turn their backs on the synagogue and other institutions in the Jewish community because they have the uneasy feeling that our synagogues all too frequently are economically conservative, that they are fearful of genuine social change, that they pay lip service to social ideals but shy away from redemptive action, and that they are preoccupied with trivialities and irrelevancies at a time when they ought to be more relevant than ever and speak out courageously on the issues of life and death in our time.

Jewish students share and participate in the rebelliousness which characterizes student life in general. Their actions and reactions are motivated by the same concerns that motivate their fellow students. But their attitudes are also shaped by other factors.

There are about 300–350,000 Jewish students at our American colleges and universities today. You will find every conceivable kind of attitude and conviction among them. There are students who stay away from the synagogue and there are students who pray like the hasidim do. There are Zionists, non-Zionists and anti-Zionists. There are students who are Jewishly illiterate and others who are Jewishly highly educated. Some students are militantly orthodox, others are just as militantly anti-religious. Any generalization would be incorrect. . . .

Our basic problem on campus and, indeed, in all of Jewish life is not outright rejection of Jewish identity or defection from it. Both exist but are far less extensive than we are frequently led to believe. Our overriding problem is a sense of uncertainty about the meaning and worthwhileness of the Jewish enterprise in the world—indeed, a sense of irrelevance of Judaism often based on ignorance and fortified by the absence of meaningful Jewish experiences. As one of my colleagues once put it, most students are not trying to escape from Judaism. It is Judaism that is escaping them. It will superficially engage their hearts, but it rarely engages their minds. . . .

Jewish education must, of course, concern itself with the problems and predicaments of Jews as Jews, with the particular social and psychological problems arising from the condition of Jewish life in the world. But a human being-born-Jew needs more than pleasant associations with his people. He must also be able to face courageously and intelligently the perennial questions which have troubled the hearts and minds of all men; the questions about life and death, suffering and evil, right and wrong, love and sex, and all other problems we must face as human beings. What does Judaism have to say to these questions that is meaningful and can provide guidance for our time? To what degree is it prepared to answer the questions of man as man? These are the issues to which Jewish education must still learn to address itself and to which it must find persuasive answers if Jewish distinctiveness is to be meaningful. . . .

I am neither justifying nor condoning excesses on the campus. The problems of our world are very real. Like many others, I share the concerns of our students and hope they will realize that not everyone over thirty is against them, just as not everyone under thirty is with them. Passionate partisanship, for or against specific political policies and moral positions, transcends the presumed or actual divide between the generations. We are united with them in insisting on the urgency of change. We feel, like they do, that society has to be regenerated.

But I hope they will also learn that one cannot escape reality—not by drugs, not by sex, not by withdrawal from reality, not by filthy language or demonstrations for the freedom to use four-letter words. Fundamental social change must ultimately be achieved not by violence, destruction or the denial to others of the right to be heard. It must be achieved through responsible and orderly processes, not through vandalism, outlandish acts and non-negotiable demands which are self-defeating.

And it is in this connection that I welcome the activism and rebelliousness of our students today, even though I disagree with much they do and say. After the silence on the campus during the past ten or fifteen years, I regard their concerns and activities as a sign of renewed involvement in the world, as proof that they have begun to care, as one of the most hopeful developments on the American scene in many years.

If these wonderful young passions and energies will find it possible to seek expression in socially responsible actions and directions, today's students will make an enormously significant contribution to the emergence of a healthy and democratic change in our society.

II.   Beware of the Jew, 1980s

PUBLIC NOTICE
ALL CHRISTIAN PARENTS:
THE SAFETY OF YOUR CHILDREN IS AT STAKE!
BEWARE!!!

The persistent rumors concerning the Jews' practice of a pagan form of "Human Sacrifice" known as "Ritual Murder," have unfortunately been proven true. Arnold S. Leese has published a book titled *Jewish Ritual Murder* which proves beyond a shadow of a doubt that the Jews are now, and have been for centuries, practicing the murder of little Christian children in order to use their blood in religious ceremonies of the Jewish Synagogue.

HERE IS THE UNFORTUNATE STORY:

WHEN—At this time of the year just before the Jewish Holy Day of Passover (April 16 to 23) fanatic Jews run the streets in a crazed search for Christian Blood!

WHO—Their favorite victims are young male children whom they take a fiendish delight in crucifying and bleeding white in the image of our Savoir [sic] whom they murdered so long ago.

WHY—Because according to secret Jewish ritual (which they will of course deny) they must have Christian Blood to mix with the dough of their Ceremonial Passover Bread. They believe that only by partaking of the blood of your children will they assure their own entrance into their heaven.

PROOF—The court records of all Europe are filled with well documented cases where the Jews were caught and convicted; nearly fifty such cases have been brought to trial in the last century alone. The Jewish arguments against the accusation are all more or less worthless; for example that all the accusations are brought by "Anti-Semites." How could anyone help being "anti-Semitic" if he knew that the Jews murder little Christian children and use their blood in pagan rituals? For further proof we suggest that you read Arnold S. Leese's book *Jewish Ritual Murder*.

FOR YOUR CHILDREN'S SAKE!

CAN YOU AFFORD TO SAY "THAT ITS NOT TRUE."

Distributed as a public service by
The American Committee for the Unfortunate
Truth About Our Jewish Brothers.

III.   Arthur J. Goldberg, 1908–1990, By Eric Pace

ARTHUR J. GOLDBERG DIES AT 81
EX-JUSTICE HELD TOP U.S. JOBS

Arthur J. Goldberg, who rose from humble beginnings in Chicago to become Secretary of Labor, an Associate Justice of the Supreme Court and then United States representative to the United Nations, was found dead yesterday morning in his apartment in Washington. He was 81 years old.

Dr. Michael Newman, Mr. Goldberg's physician, said the former Justice died late Thursday or early Friday of cardiac arrest from coronary artery disease. A maid found the body lying on a sofa.

Prof. Alan M. Dershowitz of Harvard Law School, who clerked for Justice Goldberg and was a longtime associate, said Mr. Goldberg had been active until his death on a human rights project with Mr. Dershowitz.

Associate Justice William J. Brennan, a fellow liberal who served with Justice Goldberg, said yesterday: "The nation suffered a grievous loss in the death of Justice Goldberg. He served his nation brilliantly as Secretary of Labor, Ambassador to the United Nations, and Justice of the Supreme Court. Another great contribution was his work as a lawyer in bringing together the major labor organizations of the country. Few had more admirers and loyal friends."

Warren E. Burger, the retired Chief Justice of the United States, said, "As a Justice of the Supreme Court, he was a balanced and thoughtful jurist."

A wrenching decision that was a turning point in his life occurred in 1965 when Mr. Goldberg gave up his lifetime appointment to the Supreme Court at President Lyndon B. Johnson's urging to assume the United Nations post. It was a decision he later said he regretted.

On the one hand, as Mr. Goldberg said years later, he believed that as U.N. representative he could reverse the Johnson Administration's Vietnam policy and bring about peace negotiations. On the other hand, it meant giving up a judicial position in which Mr. Goldberg's admirers believed he would have made a greater mark on American history.

"In all candor," Mr. Goldberg said on the day he was named to the United Nations post, "I would rather the President had not asked me to undertake this duty."

Three years later, the Justice-turned-diplomat resigned from the post, citing frustrations and disappointments, including "the limitations of the scope of my office" in regard to getting the United Nations involved in a Vietnam peace effort.

In 1970 Mr. Goldberg entered the race for Governor of New York as the Liberal-Democratic candidate, but he was soundly defeated by the Republican incumbent, Nelson A. Rockefeller.

Mr. Goldberg was an owlish, unimposing figure with remarkable energy and legal, judicial, and negotiating skills. Johnson praised him in his memoirs as "a skilled arbiter and a fair-minded man."

It was in 1961 that the Chicago-born lawyer, then general counsel of the United Steelworkers of America, was named Secretary of Labor by President John F. Kennedy. In 1962, Kennedy appointed him to the Supreme Court.

The self-made son of an immigrant carter, Mr. Goldberg did much, as a union lawyer, to bring about the historic merger in 1955 of the American Federation of Labor and the Congress of Industrial Organizations.

His legal work plunged him repeatedly into important decisions involving labor and management. Admirers recalled him as the leading labor lawyer of that day. He denounced the Taft-Hartley Labor Act, which empowered the Government to obtain an 80-day injunction against strikes that endangered national health or safety, and he was involved in court cases that tested it. He negotiated on the steelworkers' behalf in 1959 in a steel strike that lasted more than 100 days, and he achieved what was widely seen as a signal success for labor.

As Labor Secretary, he was energetic in striving to settle a wide variety of labor disputes. As Secretary, he played a role in the Kennedy Administration's celebrated confrontation with the steel industry. Early in 1962

Mr. Goldberg helped bring about a noninflationary settlement between the steelworkers and the industry.

But the United States Steel Corporation decided to raise prices, angering Kennedy. Then the Administration applied successful pressure on steel executives to back down on their prices.

Afterward, on the Supreme Court, he quickly became influential as an innovative judicial thinker whose arrival, to replace the more conservative Felix Frankfurter, tilted the Court toward liberal activism.

When Mr. Goldberg's time on the bench ended in 1965, a *New York Times* editorial praised "his tact, persuasiveness and ingenuity, his ability to arrange a compromise without sacrifice of principle, his activism, enthusiasm, and pragmatism."

Authorities have offered different explanations of why Johnson chose Mr. Goldberg for the United Nations. The President emphasized his desire to name a distinguished public figure to the post previously held by [the late] Adlai E. Stevenson. Others noted Johnson's wish to name his friend Abe Fortas, a Washington lawyer, to the Court. Mr. Fortas was named to the seat after Mr. Goldberg stepped down.

Mr. Goldberg said he was reluctant to leave the judiciary for the uncertain world of diplomacy. In making the shift, he became one of the few Supreme Court Justices to quit for reasons other than retirement.

In July, 1965, on the day he was named United Nations representative, he told reporters: "In all candor, I would rather the President had not asked me to undertake this duty. But it appears perhaps I can at this stage in our national life make a contribution, I hope, in this area of foreign affairs."

He did make a contribution, largely through dexterous negotiations with Soviet diplomats. But he achieved far less than he had hoped, which was to have a major role in efforts to end the Vietnam War. Many of his admirers felt that, in his years after quitting the bench, he made much less of a mark on his country's history than would have been the case had he retained his Court seat.

After he left the United Nations, he served as president of the American Jewish Committee, the nationwide human rights organization, in 1968 and 1969, and became a member of the Manhattan law firm of Paul, Weiss, Goldberg, Rifkind, Wharton & Garrison.

In 1970, after opinion polls suggested that he would be a strong candidate, he entered the race for Governor of New York. But he proved to be a lackluster campaigner and he was easily defeated by Mr. Rockefeller, a more practiced politician and a long-entrenched power in state politics. Mr. Goldberg received 2,158,355 votes, against the 3,151,434 for his rival.

In 1971, Mr. Goldberg returned to Washington where he resumed his career. He also did part-time teaching, was called in on international arbitration cases, and served in 1977 and 1978 in the Carter Administration as a United States Ambassador-at-large.

In that role he was chairman of the United States delegation to a follow-up conference, in 1977 in Belgrade, on the 1975 Helsinki agreements on human rights. At the 35-nation gathering, he voiced vigorous criticism of Eastern bloc nations on human-rights.

That advocacy echoed the lusty assertiveness of his early years, as Labor Secretary, when the Federal Government played an interventionist role in some labor-management matters.

In that post Mr. Goldberg put a high priority on efforts to ease and rationalize the process of industries' adapting to technological advances.

He also felt the Government had an obligation to affirm the importance to the nation of resolving crucial labor-management contract talks with implications for the state of the economy.

With Kennedy's support he acted on his own conviction that the Government itself should be vigorous in trying to settle labor-management conflicts that jeopardize national interests.

Early in his tenure as Labor Secretary, Mr. Goldberg helped resolve a New York harbor tugboat strike. He also intervened, and became a successful arbitrator, in a dispute between the Metropolitan Opera and members of its orchestra.

The arrival of Mr. Goldberg—a liberal, though not a rigid one—on the Supreme Court, then led by Earl Warren, proved to be a watershed. It led, in the opinion of most constitutional experts at the time, to a change in the course of the Court's rulings.

While Frankfurter was still on the Court, he was the leader of a five-Justice majority that favored judicial restraint, including respect for states' rights and deference to Capitol Hill.

But as an Associate Justice Mr. Goldberg became a member of a group, usually constituting a cohesive majority of the nine Justices, that extended the Court's writ into what had been deemed the spheres of the states or of Congress. This majority group was often termed activist or liberal.

As a Justice, Mr. Goldberg was also innovative. In 1964, in perhaps his most notable opinion, he wrote for the Court's majority in the case of Escobedo v. Illinois, striking down a conviction in a murder case in which the defendant had been denied the right to confer with his lawyer after his arrest.

Similar decisions ensued, and so did reappraisals of much of the nation's criminal justice system. Many police executives and prosecutors complained the court's rulings had placed excessive restrictions on them.

Despite Mr. Goldberg's misgivings about leaving the Court for the United Nations, he had some successes as the United States representative there. Some admirers felt his most significant achievement was his role in drafting Security Council Resolution 242, which was passed in November 1967 after the Middle East war that year.

The resolution calls for "a just and lasting peace in the Middle East," including "withdrawal of Israeli armed forces from territories of recent conflict" and respect for the right of "every state in the area to live in peace within secure and recognized boundaries." The measure has been a cornerstone ever since in diplomatic efforts to bring peace to the Middle East.

But he did not succeed in getting the United Nations involved in an attempt to bring about an acceptable end to the confrontation in Vietnam. In addition, behind the scenes, Mr. Goldberg had grave differences with Johnson over Vietnam policies.

But Mr. Goldberg did figure modestly in the history of how the United States came to get out of Vietnam. In mid-March 1968, a time when, as Mr. Johnson put it in his book *The Vantage Point*, "our total situation in Vietnam was under comprehensive review," Mr. Goldberg sent Johnson a memorandum. It suggested that the United States stop "the aerial and naval bombardment of North Vietnam for the limited time necessary to determine whether Hanoi will negotiate in good faith" in peace talks.

"I read the memo carefully," Johnson wrote. "Goldberg made a strong case for a total bombing halt, but not strong enough. I could not take the risk of such a move at that time. I continued to believe that the North Vietnamese would interpret it as a clear sign of weakness—an indication that we wanted to stop fighting and come home."

On March 20, 1968, Mr. Goldberg pressed his proposal at a meeting with Johnson and Presidential advisers. He did so at a time when there was much talk within the Administration of how to foster Vietnam peace talks. His suggestion was not acted on at the time, but eleven days later Johnson announced an unconditional and sweeping, but less than total, cutback in the bombing.

The roles that Mr. Goldberg played in Presidential policy making and international affairs were remote from the world of his boyhood. Arthur Joseph Goldberg was born August 8, 1908 in Chicago, the youngest of eight children of Joseph and Rebecca Goldberg, both of whom were born in Russia. The elder Mr. Goldberg, a former peddler, owned a blind horse and a wagon and delivered produce to hotels.

After studying at Crane Junior College and De Paul University, Arthur Goldberg entered Northwestern University Law School, graduating at the head of its class of 1929 and earning a doctorate, summa cum laude, in 1930.

He went on to practice labor law in Chicago until 1948, with time out for war service from 1942 to 1944, serving with the Office of Strategic Services and as an Army officer.

From 1948 to 1961, Mr. Goldberg was the Washington-based general counsel of the United Steelworkers and was active in negotiations toward settling major strikes in the steel industry.

He was also general counsel of the Congress of Industrial Organizations from 1948 to 1955 and in that capacity worked toward its merger with the American Federation of Labor. He was special counsel to the industrial union department of the A.F.L.-C.I.O. from 1955 until 1961....

IV.   Jews in the Kansas City Country Club, December 1990

NOTED GOLFER QUITS COUNTRY CLUB
AFTER JEWISH MEMBERSHIP IS DENIED

Kansas City, Mo. *(JTA) [Jewish Telegraphic Agency]*—A prominent Jewish resident's withdrawal of his application for membership in the Kansas City Country Club after learning it would be rejected because he is a Jew has stirred widespread indignation in this community and beyond.

The incident involving Henry Bloch, co-founder, chairman and chief executive officer of H & R Block, the nationwide tax preparation service firm, got national prominence this week when golfer Tom Watson resigned from the club in protest.

The five-time winner of the British Open and twice winner of the U.S. Open is not Jewish, but his wife, the former Linda Rubin, is and their two children are being raised as Jews. His act of withdrawal was praised by local and national Jewish leaders.

"They put a prominent Jewish person up for membership and his application was withdrawn," said Watson, who became a junior member of the club when he was 21 and has been a full member for the past six years.

"It's something I can't personally live with because my family is Jewish," he added. "I would hope the club would significantly change so some good people of any religion, race and sex could be members."

Bloch's application faced rejection in the club's secret membership committee despite being sponsored by three of the city's most prominent civic and business leaders. It was withdrawn before a vote.

"While many Americans would like to believe that discrimination in this nation is a thing of the past, Henry Bloch's recent experience with the Kansas City Country Club is yet another unpleasant reminder that this unfortunate phenomenon is still with us," Abraham Foxman, national director of the Anti- Defamation League of B'nai B'rith, said in a letter to Watson.

"We just wanted to let you know that for those of us in the trenches, your principled stance has been a source of inspiration," Foxman added.

The incident has focused attention on the last bastion of discrimination in this city's prestigious private clubs.

The barrier is perhaps the last to fall in a city where Jews were once prevented from living in certain suburbs, attending exclusive private schools, and joining most of its prominent social clubs.

A handful of Jews are now members of Mission Hills Country Club, Indian Hills Country Club, and Milburn Country Club. Jews, including Henry Bloch, have been allowed to join downtown dens like the River Club and the Kansas City Club for more than 20 years.

However the roadblock remains at the Kansas City Country Club.

Foxman sent a letter to its president, L. Chandler Smith, criticizing the club for discriminatory membership policies.

"In recent days your club has attracted some media attention you probably find unwelcome," the letter said. "We hope that in spite of this attention, or perhaps because of it, you will seriously reflect upon and consider changing the club policies which prompted one of America's leading golfers, Tom Watson, to be publicly critical."

"A closer examination of your club's practices may reveal that they are not only ill-advised, but also may be illegal," ADL's national director said.

Foxman said efforts to make changes in such discriminatory policies in Kansas City clubs would have to be made at the local level.

"Some places where the Jewish community doesn't see it as a priority or doesn't want to raise the battle cry, it remains. Sometimes it takes a Mr. Watson," he said.

Jerome Chanes, co-director for domestic concerns of the National Jewish Community Relations Advisory Council, said discrimination at country clubs is on the decrease nationwide.

NJCRAC is the coordinating organization for 13 national Jewish groups and . . . [dozens of] community relations councils.

"The issue of private club discrimination, along with other forms of discrimination, has been on the decline," Chanes said. "But that is not to say it isn't a problem."

Both Foxman and Chanes agreed that the best way to fight such discriminatory policies is at the local level.

While Watson and Bloch aren't commenting on the matter, the incident has been the talk of the Jewish community for the past week.

"Henry's a great person; they're a great family, and anybody should be proud to have them as a member of their club or organization," said Callan Cohen, head of the local chapter of the American Jewish Committee, which recently honored Henry and Marion Bloch with its 1990 Human Relations Award.

"I'm surprised that, at this late date, in 1990, this kind of thing is still lurking under the surface," Cohen said.

"We regret that those attitudes which we had hoped were out of fashion are still with us," said Judy Hellman, assistant executive director of the Jewish Community Relations Bureau of Greater Kansas City.

"We're sorry for the image it presents of Kansas City. And we appreciate Tommy Watson's actions and those of the members of the Kansas City Country Club who are trying to bring the club into the 20th Century," she added.

Jewish Federation of Greater Kansas City president Ann Jacobson also praised Watson's resignation from the club.

"It's important for people of conscience to stand up for what's right and resist discrimination when they see it or hear it," she said.

Kansas City Milling Company executive R. Hugh Uhlmann, one of the first Jews to join the River Club, praised the businessmen who sponsored Bloch's nomination.

They are Donald Hall, chairman of Hallmark Cards, Inc., James Kemper Jr., chairman of Commerce Bancshares, Inc., and Richard Green Jr., chairman of Utilicorp United, Inc.

56

THE SECULAR CULTURE OF THE AMERICAN JEW
1976–1978

By the middle of the twentieth century there was literally no aspect of the arts and sciences without at least a few Jewish practitioners. This is rather surprising, for most American Jews were the children or grandchildren of East European immigrants who had never had an hour of formal instruction in the public schools of Poland and Russia. The formidable accomplishments of their descendants is a compliment to America's educational system, if not a genuflection in the direction of Jewish genes. It is not easy to evaluate the store of knowledge of these new generations in two or three pages, but it is no exaggeration to state that the accomplishments of these men and women were impressive. Not a few achieved national and international repute. Dozens of Jews were called upon to head colleges and universities; Jewish scholars were frequently invited to serve as financial, scientific, and political advisors to American presidents.

In 1945 *Fortune* magazine made a survey of some of the country's young scientists. One survey found that 29 percent came from Jewish homes. In a descending scale, Jews were found in biology, medicine, chemistry, mathematics, psychology, and astronomy. One study of the twenty best young scientists in industry and in the universities revealed that five, 20 percent, were of Jewish origin, even though Jews in this country constitute but 2.5 percent of the population. These surveys were made in a decade when most Ivy League schools were still determined to limit the number of Jewish students admitted. Yale was no exception, but a few decades later a Harvard dean—a Jew—was offered the presidency of Yale. *America*, a Catholic weekly, deplored the fact that there were so few Catholic Einsteins or Salks; Jews, it surmised, were culturally productive because of the Jewish family's emphasis on learning.

The medieval and early modern Jew was not distinguished for his contributions in the plastic and spatial arts, but his mid-and late twentieth-century descendants turned to painting and sculpture with devotion and a considerable measure of success. Developing an aesthetic sense, the Jewish commonalty began to build magnificent synagogs in suburbia; individuals became notable for their collections of artistically fashioned ritual silver. Economists of distinction flourished; more than a half dozen American Jews received Nobel Prizes for their achievements in medical research; the three physicists most closely identified with the atom bomb, the hydrogen bomb, and the neutron bomb were all of Jewish birth; enthusiastic theatergoers hummed the lyrics and melodies of Jews who wrote operettas and musical comedies; hardly a metropolis was without its symphony orchestra, whose players and even conductors were often Jews. By the second half of the twentieth century some of the country's most eminent composers of classical music were of East European émigré stock. Playwrights and poets of national stature abounded; the metropolitan newspapers and several of the best national magazines were staffed or led by Jewish journalists and editors; some of them wielded tremendous influence for they were read daily by millions. *The World Almanac and Book of Facts* (1986) listed America's 25 Most Influential Women in 1985; eight were Jews; three were syndicated columnists; one was a women's rights leader who edited *MS* magazine; another was a novelist; still another was a historian; the director of the New York City Opera was born in Brooklyn; the Washington Post Company was chaired by the daughter of Eugene Meyer, the banker and publisher.

Jewish writers of stories and novels in English did not hit their stride until after World War II when nearly all of America's cultural avenues fell open to the Children of Israel (Soviet scientific advances had frightened the country's controlling elite.) Jewish litterateurs blossomed; several of them received national recognition. Jews were no longer denied the right to teach English in America's great universities. It is interesting to note that many of the country's eminent Jewish scholars, artists, scientists, and musicians evinced little interest in the rock whence they were hewn; Jews and Judaism apparently meant little to them; they were too wrapped up in their work, in their careers.

Saul Bellow (b. 1915) is one of America's most distinguished novelists. He began honing his skills while still a young journeyman; by 1953, he had won an award for the most acclaimed work of fiction published that year; he later received a Pulitzer Prize, and in 1976 he was crowned a Nobel laureate for his work. Now, after almost five decades at his trade, no one can doubt that he is a master craftsman. Bellow is an American writer who has concerned himself most frequently with Jewish characters and themes. He has written about Jews because he knows them best and thus can give free rein to his artistry. Jews do not frighten him. As a good American, he enjoys being a Jew, being himself. Selection I reprints an address he made in 1976 when he received the B'nai B'rith Anti-Defamation League Democratic Legacy Award. In 1977 Rosalyn Sussman Yalow became "the first American-trained woman to be the recipient of a Nobel Prize in any of the sciences"; she worked in the field of medicine and physiology. The following year the *Ladies Home Journal* offered her a special woman's award, but she rejected it; she saw it as a "ghetto" citation and wished to be honored as a scientist, not as a woman. In selection II, she describes the reason for her refusal.

I.   I Said That I Was an American, a Jew, a Writer by Trade, By Saul Bellow, November 14, 1976

How enviable it sometimes seems to have a brief and simple history. Ours is neither simple nor brief. You have honored me with an award, and my part in acknowledging this distinction with gratitude, is to make a short speech about America and its Jews, the Jews and their America. The difficulty of this obligation is considerable, for the history we share is full of intricate, cunning and gloomy passages; it is also illuminating and it is noble—it is a large piece of the history of mankind. Many have tried to rid themselves in one way or another of this dreadful historic load by assimilation or other means. I have, myself, never been tempted by the hope of waking from the nightmare of history in a higher state of consciousness and freedom. As much as the next man, I enjoy meditating on such things, but my instincts have attached me to what is actually here, and among the choices that were actually open to me, I have always preferred the liberal and democratic ones—not always in the popular sense of these terms.

When I read last summer in the *American Scholar* an article by Professor Sidney Hook on the great teacher and philosopher Morris R. Cohen, I was stirred by Cohen's belief that "the future of liberal civilization" was "bound up with America's survival and its ability to make use of the heritage of human rights formulated by Jefferson and Lincoln." Professor Cohen was no sentimentalist. He was a tough-minded man, not a patriotic rhetorician.

He arrived on the Lower East Side at the age of 12. He knew the slums and the sweatshops. His knowledge of the evils of American life was extensive and unsparing—the history of the Indians and of the Negroes, cruelty, prejudice, mob violence, hysteria, injustice. Acidulous is Hook's word for Cohen's criticism of the U.S.A. Cohen, says Hook, was not a nationalist. He knew that no one chooses the land of his birth. He placed his hopes in the rule of enlightened world law. But Cohen was in some ways piously

American. Now piety has become one of our very worst words. It used to be one of the best—think of Wordsworth's desire for "natural piety." Maybe we can do something to rehabilitate the term. Cohen accepted Santayana's definition of piety as "reverence for the sources of one's being." This emotion, says Hook, was naturally acquired by Cohen without ideological indoctrination or blinding.

I understand this without effort. Most of us do. There *are* people for whom it is entirely natural to despise the life that they were born in to. There are others, like myself, who suspect that if we dismiss the life that is waiting for us at birth, we will find ourselves in a void. I was born in Eastern Canada and grew up in Chicago. My parents were Jewish immigrants from Russia. They sent me to a *heder* [Jewish afternoon religious school]. They didn't want me out in the sandlots or playing pool in the poolroom. All these matters were discussed or disputed by us in Yiddish. But when I went to the public library, the books I borrowed were by [American writers] Poe and Melville, Dreiser and Sherwood Anderson. I did not bring home volumes of the Babylonian Talmud to read. I took myself as I was—a kid from the Chicago streets and the child of Jewish parents. I was powerfully stirred by the books brought home from the library, I was moved myself to write something.—These are some of the sources of my being. One could have better sources, undoubtedly. I could make a list of those more desirable sources, but they are not mine, and I cannot revere them. The only life I can love, or hate, is the life that I—that we—have found here, this American life of the Twentieth Century, the life of Americans who are also Jews. Which of these sources, the American or the Jewish, should elicit the greater piety? Are the two exclusive? Must a choice be made? The essence of freedom is that one makes the choice, if choices must be made, for the most profound of personal reasons. It is at this very point that one begins to feel how intensely enviable it is to have a brief and simple history. (But is there any such thing?)

In Israel, I was often and sometimes impatiently asked what sort of Jew I was and how I defined myself and explained my existence. I said that I was an American, a Jew, a writer by trade. I was not insensitive to the Jewish question, I was painfully conscious of the Holocaust, I longed for peace and security in the Jewish State. I added, however, that I had lived in America all my life, that American English was my language, and that (in an oddly universalist way) I was attached to my country and the civilization of which it was a part. But my Israeli questioners or examiners were not satisfied. They were trying to make me justify myself. It was their conviction that the life of a Jew in what they call the Diaspora must inevitably be "inauthentic." Only as a Jew in Israel, some of them told me, could I enter history again and prove the necessity and authenticity of my existence. I refused to agree with them that my life had been illusion and dust. I do not accept any interpretation of history that declares the deepest experience of any person to be superfluous. To me that smells of totalitarianism. Nor could I accept the suggestion that I repudiate some six decades of life, to dismiss my feelings for some of the sources of my being *because I am a Jew or nothing.* That would wipe out me totally. It would be not only impiety and irreverences, but also self-destruction.

But one need not hold long arguments with views that are so obviously wrong. What underlies the position that I have just rejected is the assumption that America is bound to go the way of other Christian countries and expel or destroy its Jewish population. But *is* it a Christian country like the others? The question almost answers itself as soon as it is asked —this nation is not, in the European sense, a recognizably Christian country. One could write many volumes on what America is *not.* However, there is no need, in a brief talk on an occasion such as this to make grandiose statements about liberal democracy. It is sufficient to say in the most matter of fact way what is or should be obvious to everyone. In spite of the vastness and oppressiveness of corporate and governmental powers the principle of the moral equality of all human beings has not been rejected in the United States. Not yet, at any rate. Sigmund Freud, I remember reading, once observed that America was an interesting experiment, but that he did not believe that it would succeed. Well, maybe not. But it would be base to abandon it. To do so would destroy our reverence for the sources of our being. We would inflict on ourselves a mutilation from which we might never recover. And if Cohen is right, and the future of liberal civilization is bound up with America's survival, the damage would be universal and irreparable.

II.   Rosalyn Yalow Refuses to Accept a Woman of the Year Award, By Rosalyn Yalow, June 12, 1978

There is no doubt that women are disproportionately underrepresented among the scientists, scholars and leaders of our world. The failure of women to have arrived at positions consistent with their potential has been due in large part to social and professional discriminatory attitudes.

Some women have felt the need to strengthen their own psyches by banding together in women's groups since they, quite properly, felt rejected by the leadership of the "male world." Others, recognizing the existence of the problem, thought that if we were ever to move upwards we must demonstrate competence, courage and determination to succeed and must be prepared to challenge and take our place in the Establishment.

In 1961 a Federal Woman's Award was established to honor outstanding women in the Federal Civil Service. This award was clearly in recognition of the fact that women were under-represented as recipients of other awards, presumably open to all in federal service, but generally given largely if not exclusively to men. I viewed this award as second-class and, when I was chosen to be one of the first six recipients, my initial reaction was to reject it.

I was prevailed upon to accept and did in fact use the recognition accorded me to point out that even more important to women than honors or super-grade positions was the requirement of equal pay for equal work. Women in Civil Service did not have many of the important fringe benefits given to men such as protection for their spouses and children in medical, pension and death benefits. In the succeeding years some of these benefits have been better equalized and women are moving up, though too slowly, to positions of greater responsibility in some, though not all, of the government services.

Increasingly women are beginning to receive a fairer share of recognition for their accomplishments. I was therefore delighted to learn last year that the Federal Woman's Award was to be discontinued; I hope permanently.

It is obvious that there are differences between men and women. There may be perhaps good reason for awards to an outstanding father or mother; or a great husband or wife; perhaps even for the best actor or the best actress—all these are clearly sex-related. We recognize that on the average men are taller and stronger than women, so that it might be reasonable to have sex-related awards for athletic prowess. However there are fields of athletics in which these physical differences may be irrelevant and for these there should be awards for the best athlete—with no modifying adjective.

It may well be that, taken as a group, men are more intelligent, imaginative and talented than women. I do not accept this hypothesis; certainly such differences are not manifest in the very young and the differences in apparent aptitude even in fields such as science which are demonstrable beginning in adolescent and young adult life are quite likely attributable to what I call social discrimination—the non-competitiveness shown by many or even most women because of social pressures.

However, even if this hypothesis were valid, there is sufficient overlap such that some women can and should be expected to be fully competitive with the most talented of men. I therefore deem it inconsistent and unwise to have awards restricted to women or to men in fields of endeavor where excellence is not inherently sex-related.

As the first American-trained woman to be the recipient of a Nobel Prize in any of the sciences I feel that I have a special responsibility. I know very well that this ultimate reward does not make me more competent, more knowledgeable or in any way more worthy than I was before this recognition. However it does make me more visible. Therefore I cannot conform to traditional stands with which I disagree even if it were easier for me to not "make waves."

I have decided not to accept the 1978 Woman of the Year Award in the category of New Scientific Community from the *Ladies' Home Journal* although it would perhaps have been more diplomatic to accept it. I think it more appropriate for me to take a positive stand by rejecting what Susan Jacoby would have called a "ghetto" award.

She stated, very wisely I believe, that "A ghetto job is a ghetto job as long as it is perceived by male executives—and by the woman they hire— as a job with a 'for women only' sign. It doesn't matter whether the salary is $50,000 or $7,500 a year. . . . The situation can only be changed by women who regard themselves and are regarded by others as being plain excellent—not excellent only in comparison to other women. . . . Women who have 'made it' are no longer pleased to be told that their achievements are remarkable for a woman."

To this statement those of us who are committed to full equality for women can only add, "Amen."

Women, and other groups who have been victims of discrimination, may yet have a long way to go before achieving full equality. There may remain the need for some among us to accept token jobs or token awards as a temporary expedient on the road upwards. But we must view these aberrations as being temporary, worthy only for self-destruction.

If we are to have a world in which all people regardless of sex, race or creed are considered equally worthy some must take a stand against such discrimination. I do—I am certain that many others have in the past and will in the future join me in this stand.

57

Making a Living in America

1973–1990

By 1960 most Jews in the United States were either the children or grandchildren of East European newcomers. On arriving, the grandparents had settled in a metropolis. They most likely had no choice, no money to move on farther. Mayhap they sensed the wave of the future and avoided rural life; by the 1960s only 8 percent of American men and women labored on the soil. The Jewish father may have been a proletarian; the son was determined to emancipate himself from the sewing machine. Jews stayed away from heavy industry; they were not wanted; the émigré had no capital. Jews were kept out of banking, insurance, communications, transportation, and utilities except on the lowest level. As late as the 1990s they were often not welcome in the executive suite. There are laws against exclusions because of race, religion, or ethnic background, but they are difficult to enforce. The Jewish newcomers and their children were fiercely ambitious; education opened the door to a career; college, to knowledge, to learning, a respected tradition. Rejection, anti-Jewish prejudices, only drove them to work harder.

There were always opportunities for the innovative entrepreneur willing to crawl into the interstitial spaces and there was never a lack of imaginative, daring individuals. It is literally true: no area of economic activity lacks at least a few Jews. A Jewish woman was determined to become a beauty expert; she succeeded in opening 450 boutiques in America's department stores. A young Jewish native of New Orleans tipped the scale at 268 pounds; he went on a diet, lost over 130 pounds, and acquired millions preaching the gospel of diet, exercise, health, and geriatrics. The license on his car read: Y R U FAT. West 47th Street, New York, has become a diamond trading center dominated by the Children of Israel; a youngster who started life as a street peddler became the country's most notable manufacturer of grape juice; a young Jewish lawyer would one day become the chief executive officer of Delaware's Dupont Corporation. In 1962 when Abraham Levitt, the house builder, looked back he realized that he and his sons had erected 62,000 homes; a Viennese newcomer— presumptively of Jewish stock, for he had fled Nazi Europe—built dozens of pulp and paper mills all over the world. By 1963 the company's capital investments were well over a half-billion dollars. The Central European Jewish refugees who came to America in the 1930s were the most distinguished and productive immigrants in all American history. Individual Jews have amassed great wealth in this country; some have gone to jail, but most are people of integrity and responsibility, honorable businessmen. There are families, clans, whose wealth reaches into the hundreds of millions; they own hotels, newspapers, magazines, distilleries, refineries, mines, retail chains, garment factories, broadcasting systems, real estate. At most only a dozen or so stand out for their huge holdings; the assets of Mr. Cohen or Mr. Levy of Main Street, are far less impressive.

Jews are found in light industry; they are still very important in the manufacture and sale of clothing. Basically, they are merchandisers; they sell consumer's goods and services; they exploit their personalities. They are in trade, they are managers, clerks, professionals in the fields of law and medicine; they labor in all the sciences, in all the technologies.

Max Stern, a German immigrant, came to the United States in 1926 with 2,100 canaries. He and his son Leonard Norman Stern built the Hartz Group, Inc., the Hartz Mountain Corporation. They sell pet supplies and own real estate, as well as the *Village Voice*, a weekly for which Leonard paid $55,000,000. Selection I describes how the Sterns made their money. In 1973, Leonard was reportedly worth at least $500,000,000. (In gloating over the riches of the billionaires and multimillionaires, nothing is ever said of bank loans.) Arthur Frank Burns (1904–1987), a native of Austrian Poland, arrived in the United States in 1910; he was to become one of America's highly respected economists, an advisor to presidents, chairman of the Board of Governors of the Federal Reserve System, and finally the American ambassador to West Germany. In a letter to a youngster about to become bar mitzvah, Dr. Burns tells the lad that money is not the main purpose in life (selection II). While America was celebrating its bicentennial in 1976, Art Buchwald (b. 1925), a very successful syndicated columnist, dedicated a letter to his father who had died in 1972. Buchwald's "pop" was one of the millions who never became wealthy, but in his own modest way helped to build the land he learned to love. Buchwald's letter to his father is a tribute to the teenagers who left Europe's poverty and rejection for an America that offered them freedom and opportunity (selection III).

Samuel Paley, an East European immigrant, like Arthur Burns and Pop Buchwald, was a cigar manufacturer who made a fortune. Thousands smoked his brand, La Palina. The son, William S. Paley (1901–1990), built the Columbia Broadcasting System, one of this country's great commercial and cultural institutions. Sally Bedell Smith's biography of this important enterpriser *In All His Glory*, was reviewed in the *New York Times Book Review* by Christopher Buckley (selection IV). It is an interesting and brutally frank critique of the man.

I. A German Jewish Refugee Entrepreneur Sells Canaries, Gerbils, and Guppies, By Roger Ricklefs, June 21, 1973

"A turtle is basically a 'shut up' pet," explains Leonard N. Stern, president of Hartz Mountain Corp., which used to sell turtles by the thousand.

"A kid goes into a store and says, 'I want a pet.' The mother says, 'Shut Up.' The kid says, 'But I want a pet.' The mother says, 'OK, we'll get you a turtle.'" The executive relates.

Since it was discovered that turtles often carry salmonella bacteria, Hartz finds its turtle business has collapsed. But Mr. Stern isn't worried. "Hamsters are replacing the turtle as the 'shut up' pet," he reports happily. Hartz hamsters not only sell for more money than Hartz turtles but also eat several times as much Hartz pet food, he says.

Such is the sweet life at Hartz Mountain. Pet trends come and go, but this pet concern gets richer year by year. The Harrison, N.J., company has steadily parlayed its world of gerbils, guppies, bird seed and Dog Yummies into the kind of situation that most executives can only envy from afar.

Sales hit $134 million last year. Profits exceeded 10 percent of volume and have doubled in the past four years. The stock sells on the American Stock Exchange for over 30 times last year's earnings per share. And the outstanding stock—72% owned by the Stern family—has an aggregate market value of just over $443 million. All this from products like canine ear wash, "Canary Fruit Treat," flea collars and rawhide dog toys that look like ice cream cones.

The formula is simple. While other growing companies acquire and diversify, Hartz saturates a few closely related, highly specialized markets. It applies mass merchandising and distribution techniques to tricky "products" like live animals. Unlike many big consumer-product concerns, Hartz avoids Madison Avenue, generates most of its advertisements within its own house, has no public-relations department, struggles for corporate obscurity, and rarely bothers with market research.

It just makes money.

Hartz especially makes money for the Stern family. Max Stern, founder, chairman and father of Leonard, has a compensation package that few 74-year-old executives can match: $250,000 a year for life. To make sure this isn't wiped out by inflation, the figure is also subject to a cost-of-living increase every two years.

As for duties, the company proxy statement says the elder Mr. Stern is "required to devote only such time to Hartz as he deems necessary." Actually, the fit and hearty Mr. Stern still devotes about 80% of his time to the concern and spends the rest on his philanthropic interests, Hartz says.

And in any event, few outside shareholders are grumbling about salaries because Mr. Stern invented the success formula. Following this formula, Hartz peppers its markets with practically every product they could possibly absorb. There are single dog dishes, double dog dishes, puppy dog dishes and dishes especially created for poodles. (The poodle bowl is slightly narrower than regular bowls, so that the poodle's floppy ears will flop outside the bowl rather than inside it. The poodle bowl is also recommended for cocker spaniels.) There are two sizes of the biscuit treat called Dog Yummies, one having larger Yummies for larger dogs. And there is a long list of pet books such as "Enjoy Your Beagle," "Enjoy Your Snakes" —even "Enjoy Your Alligator."

Hartz also offers three different kinds of dog shampoo—one that requires wet lathering, another that comes out of a bottle and is applied with a cloth, and a third that comes in an aerosol spray can. Some of these kill fleas, while others concentrate on making the fur lustrous.

The company also sells a "parakeet mirror" with a row of "counting beads." Parakeets, it seems, just love to look at themselves in the mirror and move the beads with their beaks, an official says. Owners often like to believe that the bird is "counting" the beads, somewhat like a human being working with an abacus, he adds.

Toys of all kinds proliferate at Hartz, and the company has developed a successful strategy in designing them. "Unfortunately, dogs and cats and gerbils don't have any money to spend—only their owners," an official explains. "So the question is, would the person want to buy the toy for himself?"

A key rule is that the *owner* must get gratification from the toy. "That means you have to get the pet to play with it. So we use scented materials to make the toys smell like liver or chocolate," the official says. "A lot of our ideas come from kids toys," he says. "Right now, I'm fascinated with yo-yos that light up. If we can make it safe, I'd really like to do something with a toy that lights up when it is rolled."

For all the gimmicks, the company sticks closely to products that can be sold cheaply to a mass market and rejects ideas like hair driers for dogs. It has also turned down an assortment of ideas for parakeet diapers.

Instead of test marketing, the company simply relies on its judgment and knowledge of pet owners. In one exception, it did test market a line of canned cat and dog food—and decided to shelve the whole project. Among other items in the line, the company even tried "French Cuisine Canned Dog Food" that looked like a stew, was made in France and came in a Gallic red, white and blue can. But the company decided that the market was overcrowded and that the price of meat is currently too high to make the venture promising, officials say.

Meanwhile, Hartz searches the world for other products. For instance, it goes to the Danish fishing port of Esbjerg for toy mice filled with catnip. While the Esbjerg men fish, the Esbjerg women sit at home filling the mice with the herb that excites cats. Hartz maintains buying offices in Hong Kong and Kobe, Japan, and has gone as far as Katmandu, Nepal to find new items.

Some of the company's tropical fish are caught in the Amazon River by South American tribesmen, floated down the river by canoe to jungle air strips and flown to Florida. The company also breeds fish at its 210-acre hatchery in Gibsonton, Fla., and ships them by air all over the U.S. and Canada. Hartz says it ships about one million fish a week (mostly retailing for under $1).

All this shipping causes problems. For instance, as water is heavy, the object in transporting fish by air is to pack them with as little water as possible. The solution: tranquilizers. Hartz drugs its fish before shipment to reduce their metabolism and thus reduce the amount of water required. (Apparently this unusual procedure is safe enough. The American Society for the Prevention of Cruelty to Animals hasn't any complaint with the company's handling of animals in general, a spokesman says.)

Shipping fish represents something of a diversification from the original Hartz business, which dealt exclusively in canaries. It all began in 1926 when Max Stern, then a young businessman in Germany, packed his bags and his 2,100 canaries and sailed for America. Previously in the textile business, Mr. Stern became worried about the inflation and financial turmoil that was rocking Germany at the time and decided to leave. A friend in the bird business suggested the American venture.

"I didn't speak much English, but I Americanized my thinking very fast," the soft-spoken, white-haired Mr. Stern recalls. "The birds that others were selling for up to $19 and $20 each, I decided to sell in volume for $5.95."

Just as some companies sell razors cheaply and make their real money on blades, Hartz tended to sell the birds for chicken feed and make big money on the bird seed and other products. The company also encouraged retailers to name the canaries after singing stars ranging from Caruso to Perry Como. Originally Hartz imported the birds from Germany and particularly from the Harz Mountains there. (The "t" in Hartz was added to make the spelling phonetic in English.)

The elder Mr. Stern says he soon turned to big variety and general merchandise chains, pushing his belief that mass merchandising of live pets could be feasible and lucrative. Even today, W. T. Grant Co., F. W. Woolworth Co. and S. S. Kresge Co. are Hartz's biggest customers by far.

To Americans of the 1930s and 1940s, the company was known largely for the Hartz Mountain Master Singers, a group of the company's supposedly most operatic canaries. Accompanied by organ music, the birds sang their hearts out on radio and prompted thousands of Americans to buy Hartz canaries.

Gradually, the company began to diversify, though strictly within the pet field. "I asked myself, why should we just create sales for canary cage makers? So we started making the cages ourselves," says the elder Mr. Stern.

Later the Sterns started Sternco Industries, Inc., another family controlled pet and pet-supply concern, which last month merged with Hartz Mountain.

During placid separate special meetings attended by a total of about 65 people last month, shareholders of both concerns approved the merger by margins that management found "gratifying"—99.6% for Hartz and 99.9% for Sternco. In this era of shareholder activism, only one young man, holding fewer than 10 shares, had any negative questions to ask.

Small wonder. Pro forma combined earnings of Hartz and Sternco climbed to a record $14 million, or 77 cents a share, last year from $11.7 million, or 68 cents a share, a year earlier and from $6.7 million, or 40 cents a share, four years earlier. Record sales of $134.5 million last year represented a rise from $118.7 million the previous year and from $80.1 million four years earlier.

And according to Leonard Stern, the 35-year-old, $175,000-a-year president of Hartz, the best may be still ahead. As he sees it, the bird business may see only moderate growth, but the small-animal, fish, dog and cat fields should thrive in the next several years, "I think you're going to see a company substantially bigger and substantially more profitable," he told Sternco shareholders. At the end of the meeting the shareholders gave management a warm ovation.

II. Economic Improvement Is Not the Only or the Main Purpose of Life, By Arthur F. Burns, May 4, 1976

Dear Elliot:

I'm a friend of your father's. Therefore I am also your friend. Your father may have told you that I'm the Nation's "money man." It gives me pleasure to send you the enclosed coin set to help you celebrate your *bar mitzvah*.

I wish I could be with you and your parents when you are called to read the *Torah*. But I must go off to Europe and discuss a few problems with my European counterparts. Our purpose, I should tell you, is not to make money for ourselves, but to help the great mass of people in our several countries to improve their economic conditions.

But economic improvement is not the only or the main purpose of life. That is especially true of the Jewish people. God gave us the *Torah* so that we may lead righteous lives, love our neighbors, and help the needy. Your *bar mitzvah* symbolizes the privilege of living by the noble teachings of the *Torah*. To the extent that you do so, you will enjoy God's blessing and bring honor to your parents.

With every good wish,
Your friend,
Arthur F. Burns
Enclosure

III.   A Letter to Pop, By Art Buchwald, July 4, 1976

July Fourth

Dear Pop:
It's been four years since you passed away at the age of seventy-nine. On this Bicentennial holiday, with all the hoopla and overkill, I am not taking the 200th anniversary of the country lightly, mainly because I know you wouldn't.

First, I would like to thank you for leaving your home in Galicia which you once explained was part of [Austrian] Poland, in 1910, when you were seventeen years old. I know it wasn't an easy trip for you. You had to cross Europe all by yourself, and then you had to find a ship in Rotterdam that would take you to New York City.

I've tried to imagine what it was like for a seventeen-year-old boy to arrive at Ellis Island without being able to speak a word of English. There were thousands like you, and fortunately there were people who came before you to help you through the maze of paper work and bewildering ways of New York.

You wound up on the Lower East Side with so many of your fellow-immigrants. They offered you a chance to go to night school, but you said you would learn English by reading every New York City newspaper every day. You kept reading them for sixty-two years and you seemed to know more about the country and the world than any of your children who had been "educated" in American schools.

I know you started out working in a raincoat factory fourteen or fifteen hours a day, and when World War I came you worked even longer. They wouldn't let you serve in the Army because [as an immigrant from Hapsburg territory] you were considered an "enemy alien."

Then you went into the curtain and drapery business—The Aetna Curtain Co. The business consisted of you, a man named Sammy who helped you hang the drapes, and a seamstress. "Gimbel's we're not," you used to tell me, much to my chagrin. But you did save enough money to bring your two sisters and a brother to America. And you did manage to get out of the Lower East Side.

"Making it in America in those days," you once told me, "was moving to the Bronx."

You even got as far as Mt. Vernon, when business was good, before the depression. Then during the depression it was back to the Bronx.

The thing I shall always remember is how you felt about the United States. You kept telling me there was no better place to live than America. And I could never appreciate this unless I was a Jew who had lived in Europe.

You were like so many foreign-born Americans—Jewish, Russian, Italian, Irish, German, Scandinavian and Greek—who considered this country the only land where your children would have a chance to become what they wanted to be.

You told me, "Everyone has dreams for their children, but here it's possible to make them come true."

Well, Pop, I just wanted you to know, as far as your children are concerned, you made the right decision when you left Poland. There are four of us, [who are like] all first-generation Americans whose mothers and fathers arrived here in more or less the same way.

I don't know if all those great men in 1776 had you immigrants in mind when they signed the Declaration of Independence and formed a new country, but even if they didn't they made it possible for you and millions like you to come to a free land.

So let the tall ships sail and the fireworks explode. We're probably overdoing it, but if you were here I'm sure you would say, "It's probably a good thing people remember what a great place this country is, even if it's going to cost the city a lot of money."

IV.   William S. Paley and the Columbia Broadcasting System: A Review of Sally Bedell Smith's *In All His Glory: The Life of William S. Paley*, By Christopher Buckley, November 4, 1990

"Why do I have to die?" the aging William S. Paley repeatedly asks of a somewhat helpless friend toward the end of Sally Bedell Smith's fascinating and exhaustive biography of the man who built the Columbia Broadcasting System. At this point, having kept company with Mr. Paley's ego for more than 600 pages, no reader is likely to be surprised at the old solipsist for having posed such a bizarre question, and so unphilosophically at that. If CBS'S corporate logo was its famous "eye," Mr. Paley's innermost being ("soul" seems not quite the right word) bore the indelible stamp of an "I." The friend "could give no answer except to reassure him that his mother had lived into her nineties." The reply was possibly ironic, as it was Mr. Paley's cold and unloving mother, Goldie, who by shunning her young son had forced him to turn to the larger world for constant, indeed unremitting, affirmation.

Still, a mother's coldness can account for, or excuse, only so much. If ever there were a man to confirm Lord Acton's axiom that no great men are good men, surely it was William S. (tellingly, he added the middle initial at the age of 12, for effect) Paley, who turned 89 this fall. One does not get the sense that Ms. Smith, the author of "Up the Tube: Prime Time TV and the Silverman Years," came to deconstruct the man, but rather that her superb and thorough reporting uncovered all the unpleasantness along with the greatness. "In All His Glory" is an impressive narrative history, not only of the man who pioneered the most important broadcasting network of its day but also of that technology's extraordinary impact on the United States from the 1920s to the present.

It is also a rich and vivid social history of Mr. Paley's world, peopled with everyone from Edward R. Murrow to Truman Capote, so absorbing that the pages turn themselves. Yet the William S. Paley that emerges from them is a toweringly small man: insecure, petty, jealous, ungrateful, snobbish, ashamed of his own Jewishness nearly to the point of anti-Semitism; a philanderer who cheated on his rather good wife even as she lay dying, a tyrannical father (on those rare occasions when he was present), a pathological liar; abusive, resentful, cruel, neurotic, hypochondriac, self-absorbed, tightfisted and greedy—in other words of the journalist David Halberstam, a close observer of the Paley phenomenon, "somewhat more pathetic than he really is."

Mr. Paley was also a genius, possessed of enough energy to propel a dozen brilliant careers, generous, thoughtful, vital and, above all charming. In the words of Frank N. Stanton, for 27 years the president of CBS (and without whom it is entirely safe to say, there would have been no CBS as we knew it), "He was too complex."

William Paley was born in Chicago in 1901, the son of a Russian Jewish immigrant, who eventually built his small cigar manufacturing company into a prosperous business. He went to the University of Pennsylvania's Wharton School of Finance and Commerce and into the family business. In 1927, his father, an uncle and some investors bought an interest in a shaky Philadelphia radio network called Columbia, with the notion of using radio to promote the sale of La Palina brand cigars. Cigarette smoking by newly liberated women was on the rise, and cigar smoking was in decline.

They had signed a contract with station WCAU in Philadelphia to advertise the cigars on a one-hour song-and-dance program hosted by a songwriter named Harry Link, "The La Palina Boy," but the cigars weren't moving. When the 26-year-old son returned from a European vacation, he was tapped to run the network. Furious that his father and uncle had bought it without telling him, he indignantly refused, saying, "I don't want anything to do with this pipsqueak radio network, this phony chain." He relented and produced a half-hour program called "The La Palina Smoker," featuring a husky female voice—"Miss La Palina," the only female guest at an all-male "smoker"—and a pack of wisecracking admirers. Sales jumped from 400,000 cigars a day to a million. The young Paley promptly put up $417,000 of his own money—that's roughly four million in 1990 dollars, making this something other than a rags-to-riches story—and ended up president of the pipsqueak network.

In his largely fictional 1979 memoir, "As It Happened," Mr. Paley would claim that it had all been his idea, right down to the detail that it was his father and uncle who had been on vacation in Europe. Ms. Smith refers to Mr. Paley's official version of his life's events throughout her book. After a while you can tell that she is about to refer to it whenever you come across "despite" or "contrary to." For Mr. Paley it was never enough to succeed; someone else must not have been there. A shame, unnecessary, for as Ms. Smith quotes a relative of one of his credit-grabbing victims, "if Bill Paley told the truth he would be a bigger man."

His greatest genius lay in programming, an instinct he had apparently developed while spending summer months selling candy in a Chicago movie theater and observing hits and flops, what worked and what bombed. In time CBS would become known as the "Tiffany" network—that is, synonymous with quality; but in fact his feel for popular culture—and his obsession with the bottom line—acted like Gresham's law on radio and later on television: bad programming drove out the good.

"While NBC opened the door to light entertainment by signing 'Amos 'n Andy' in 1929," Ms. Smith observes, "it was Paley who flooded his network with escapist fare and strident commercials. NBC had little choice but to follow suit." To be sure, there was quality programming, but it functioned as a facade behind which was a great deal of junk. In this sense, William S. Paley was one of the master architects of modern popular culture, a colossally dubious achievement.

Among his innovations were "block programming"—that is, grouping similar shows together—and the idea of developing programs independently instead of buying them from advertising agencies. Another of his great talents was his knack for recognizing talent and its paramount importance. Thus he set out to seduce—or steal, usually from his archrival, David Sarnoff of NBC, a man to whom he felt vastly inferior—such early stars as Fats Waller, Bing Crosby, Burns and Allen, Goodman Ace, Fred Allen, Will Rogers, Al Jolson, Nelson Eddy—you name them, he usually got them. His greatest acquisition was that of Jack Benny from NBC, a feat one contemporary wit likened to "getting Quebec away from Canada, so fixed had he been and for so long in the heaven of that richer and bigger network."

Sarnoff's failure to realize how important his stars were was his one blind spot, and Mr. Paley, with 20-20 vision for an Achilles' heel, was quick to exploit it. Shortly after the great Benny raid in 1949, Sarnoff is said to have called Mr. Paley and said, "Why did you do this to me, Bill? I thought we had an agreement not to raid each other's talent." After a long pause, Mr. Paley reportedly answered, "I needed them." Of course! CBS finally displaced NBC as the No. 1 radio network in 1949, capturing 12 of the top 15 prime-time shows—an advantage later carried to television.

He was not, despite the mythology he and his press agents so assiduously manufactured, a risk taker. On the contrary, he was more often timid to the point of fecklessness. He balked at setting up a radio news-gathering organization until a sponsor agreed to underwrite it. (With Mr. Paley, profit always, always came first.) He banned tape recorders from broadcasts, fearing that if Bing Crosby and other performers could record their shows they might try to distribute them independently. He actively obstructed the early development of television, fearing an encroaching effect on radio. "He was like a horse-and-buggy driver who couldn't fathom the Model T," Ms. Smith writes. "He didn't see any profit in TV at all," Mr. Stanton said. When Mr. Stanton's genius inventor Peter Goldmark came up with the first version of video, Mr. Paley once again vetoed the idea on the ground that it posed a threat to network broadcasting. But as with the early Philadelphia cigar promotion, once the reluctant Mr. Paley had seen the full potential of these profit monsters he was quick to climb on board—and to take credit for everything.

His reluctance could also extend to his primary area of strength, programming. When Fred Silverman, the whiz-kid CBS programmer of the '70s, introduced a show called "All in the Family," Mr. Paley initially hated the bigoted Archie Bunker. The show, of course, became a major hit, and thereafter Mr. Paley became its biggest fan. So much so, Ms. Smith reports, that when CBS commissioned an internal study that ended up showing that the program in fact reinforced bigoted racial attitudes, Mr. Paley ordered: "Destroy the study. Throw it out."

So much for the "Legendary Tycoon" of the book's subtitle. Ms. Smith's biography is equally fascinating for its portrait of "His Brilliant Circle," a group that included Edward R. Murrow, whom Mr. Paley eventually drove from CBS after Murrow's attacks on Senator Joseph McCarthy and other incidents that threatened something Mr. Paley greatly coveted: the ambassadorship to the Court of St. James's. (He never got it, and bristled when Richard M. Nixon, whose campaign coffers he had generously if hardly disinterestedly filled, gave the job to Walter Annenberg.) Others in the circle included David O. Selznick, Averell Harriman, Edith Piaf, Marietta Tree, Susan Mary Alsop, Duff Cooper, Herbert Bayard Swope, George S. Kaufman, Alexander Woollcott, Condé Nast, Errol Flynn; later on, it also included Truman Capote (who served Mr. Paley and his second wife, Babe, as house Pekingese, until he bit the hands that fed him in his infamous *Esquire* story "La Cote Basque, 1965"), as well as Slim Keith, Leland Hayward, Diana Vreeland, Pablo Picasso, the Rothschilds, the Windsors, the Guinnesses, the Astors, *le tout* de toot.

It was more of a universe than a circle, really, and admittance to it was nearly as restricted as admittance to the clubs, the Metropolitan of Washington among others, that would not admit Mr. Paley because of the simple fact that he was a Jew. All his life he strove toward a perfect assimilation, suppressing his Jewishness and marrying the quintessentially perfect, devoted and beautiful wife, Barbara (Babe) Mortimer Cushing of Boston, "the ultimate glowing Gentile" as one of her friends tellingly described her. Despite her flawless and lavish attentions to him, his interest in her waned after a few years and sexual relations ceased—perhaps, Ms. Smith suggests, to Babe's relief—as he turned his satyrical attention to an endless procession of mistresses, some classier than others.

The grass is always greener, in Mr. Paley's case, particularly on the lawn of his next-door neighbor in Long Island, John May (Jock) Whitney, chairman of The International Herald Tribune, race horse breeder, polo enthusiast and ur-WASP. Whitney shunned Mr. Paley for years, but eventually befriended him when Mr. Paley became his brother-in-law.

Ms. Smith describes a scene that one can only hope will be included in the made-for-television movie. Mr. Paley and Whitney kept up a gentle sort of rivalry. One night while the two were watching television at Whitney's manse, Mr. Paley wanted to change the channel. "Where's your clicker?" he asked, meaning the remote-control channel changer. "Jock calmly pressed a buzzer, and his butler walked up to the TV set to make the switch." F. Scott Fitzgerald, call your office.

To the end of his career, Mr. Paley remained a desperately insecure man: jealous of his wife's affection for her son from her first marriage; jealous of Frank Stanton, whom he disastrously hounded from CBS, thereby insuring the ensuing succession of catastrophes that have made the network now, as Mr. Stanton put it perfectly, "just another company with dirty carpets." Lear-like, Mr. Paley ultimately subverted and ruined CBS, the thing he loved above all else—besides himself—driving out Mr. Stanton's successors, undermining the company by leaking unfavorable reports about them to the press, meddling in programming even though his quondam powers had by now left him, fretting obsessively about his perks, his private jet, his helicopter, his office, unable to let go; gobbling down experimental, supposedly life-prolonging protein pills every half-hour, gorging on supposedly restorative cucumbers, unable to let go, even of life. For Bill Paley, "Why do I have to die?" was the perfectly logical question.

58

The American Jewish Community
1964–1986

The United States government is well structured; it can effectively control its citizenry; because of its wealth and power it even attempts to exercise world hegemony. Jewish leaders here, influenced, subconsciously at least, by the American pattern, have been reaching out for generations to dominate American and foreign Jewries. Though there are hundreds of national Jewish organizations, there are relatively few that are powerful. Among the few which at some point in their histories could be considered powerful are the Jewish Labor Committee, the American Jewish Congress, the Anti-Defamation League, the B'nai B'rith, the American Jewish Committee, the National Jewish Community Relations Advisory Council, the Council of Jewish Federations, Hadassah, the Zionist Organization of America, and the United Jewish Appeal, which collects and distributes the millions raised in the larger cities. The religious denominations are a group apart; their influence—while sometimes potent—is limited to their own partisans. The first six associations listed above are primarily civic defense organizations. The Council of Jewish Federations provides services of various types for about 200 social welfare agencies in about 800 separate communities. Until well into the 1960s the American Jewish Committee was very influential, but by 1966 the Conference of Presidents of Major Jewish Organizations (COP) had begun to emerge as a rival; by the 1990s this loose federation included over forty national societies, a substantial number of them Zionist. As the COP gathered strength, it concerned itself not only with the well-being of Israel—its original primary raison d'être—but widened its scope to help Jews in the United States and in all lands where they were threatened or oppressed.

American Jews of the 1980s and 1990s, to whom the national organizations addressed themselves, numbered about 5,500,000. Greater New York sheltered the largest contingent; Southern California and Southeastern Florida were the next largest communities. After World War II, Jews began flocking to Florida, Texas, Arizona, and California. California has made notable Jewish cultural advances, though most of the southern states have lagged intellectually. Ever since the 1950s American Jews have begun moving still farther out in the suburbs and exurbs. They are building beautiful homes and have created magnificent synagogs and schools, spacious well-appointed community centers, and multiacred country clubs. Local Jewry's most influential organization is the federation of philanthropies. As a rule the federation leaders are men and women of means (in which respect they resemble the members of the House and the Senate). Religious institutions remain for the most part beyond the federation pale, but the federation funds—if it does not control—the numerous social-welfare agencies, the community centers, and the Community Relations Committee; it subsidizes some of the local Jewish educational institutions and, frequently, the Jewish community newspaper. In effect it dominates the community. The money it raises annually is parcelled out by the United Jewish Appeal to its local, national, and overseas beneficiaries.

No later than the 1930s, the rising East European newcomers and the synagogs began pressing for recognition by the federation. Their instrumentality to achieve this end was the Jewish Community Council. By the 1990s, the federation, responsive to the insurgent petitioners, became somewhat more democratic, though in the final analysis, the federation, the Jewish Community Council, the Jewish Welfare Fund, and the United Jewish Appeal are controlled by the big givers. The average donor is not unhappy since, on the whole, the federations are well-run and millions are dispensed in support of good causes. Every town of size has literally dozens of societies of various hues; every contributor can join one or more and hope to be fulfilled emotionally and intellectually. As a rule, a consensus is usually reached in every town when all committed ethnicists unite to provide welfare services to support cultural and recreational institutions, to fight for civil and political rights, and to aid the suffering or persecuted abroad. In summary, however, no large town has a Jewish overall representative body comparable to a city council. Despite this acephalous, headless characteristic of the Jewish town government, the community prospers, offering a whole host of services that make provision for every man, woman and child. Selection I describes the services provided—through the federation—to the local, the national, and foreign Jewish communities; the people are the community; through scientific surveys we are privileged to know much about the everyday American Jew. Selections II and III contain highlights of surveys made in the 1990s of the Jewish communities of Boston and greater Kansas City.

I.   Services Provided by the Local Jewish Community, Locally, Nationally, Internationally, By S. P. Goldberg, 1964

Many types of Jewish communal services are provided under organized Jewish sponsorship. They are designed to meet those needs of Jews which are not exclusively individual or governmental responsibilities. Although the aim is to serve Jewish community needs, Jewish services may be made available to the total community where the nature of the service permits such extension.

Most services are provided at the geographic point of need, although their financing may be secured from a wider area: nationally or internationally. Geographic classification of services (local, national, overseas) relates to areas of operation. A more fundamental classification would be in terms of types of services provided or needs met, regardless of geography. On this basis, Jewish communal services would encompass:

1. Economic aid—furnished mainly overseas, since this is largely a function of government in the United States.

2. Migration aid—a global function, involving movement between countries, mainly to Israel, but also to the United States in substantial magnitude at particular periods.

3. Absorption and resettlement of migrants—another global function, involving economic aid, housing, job placement or retraining, and social adjustment. The complexity of the task is related to the size of movement, the background of migrants, and the economic and social viability or absorptive potential of the communities in which resettlement takes place.

4. Health needs—met mainly in general hospitals, some specialized hospitals and out-patient clinics in larger cities in the United States, including facilities for the chronically ill and aged. This also includes health facilities in Israel and, to a lesser extent, in Europe.

5. Welfare services—provided primarily through family counseling, child care, and care of the aged. Some of these services are maintained on a regional, as well as a local basis. They are rarely organized on a national basis except for coordinating and clearance services. Child care and care for the aged are also major activities in Israel.

6. Recreational services—furnished mainly in Jewish centers, summer camps, Hillel units on campuses, and other youth services furnished by B'nai B'rith.

7. Community-relations functions—maintained by a network of local agencies and a series of national agencies, some of which also operate on regional and local bases. Some national agencies also seek to provide aid to overseas communities in relation to civil rights.

8. Religious agencies—local congregations, national groups of congregations, and associated rabbinical bodies.

9. Jewish education—provided through congregational and other bureaus of Jewish education, specialized national agencies, *yeshivot*, teacher-training schools, and theological seminaries.

10. Vocational services—provided in larger communities in the United States through specialized agencies (Jewish Vocational Services and Vocational Service of B'nai B'rith), in sheltered workshops, and sometimes as part of family agencies; overseas in the form of vocational education programs conducted by ORT [Organization for Rehabilitation Through Training] and other agencies.

11. Cultural agencies—mainly specialized national agencies designed to make for more effective clearance of activities in each field of service among national and local agencies.

The cohesive elements in planning and financing these services are mainly federations and welfare funds, for local services, and federations together with national and overseas agencies, for nonlocal services.

Federations conduct annual fund-raising campaigns. Their planning function is related to the budgeting responsibility. After review of programs and finances, each federation distributes its campaign proceeds to those local, national, and overseas beneficiary organizations which are generally accepted as broad Jewish responsibilities.

II. The Greater Boston Area Jewish Ensemble, 1985

The Jewish population of the CJP [Combined Jewish Philanthropies, Boston's Jewish federation] area increased 10% between 1975 and 1985, and now totals 187,000. The number of Jews in Boston itself and in the communities to the northeast and southeast remained stable or decreased between 1975 and 1985. The Jewish population grew in the areas to the northwest, west, and south of Boston. The greatest percentage growth was in Newton and the towns from Sharon and Randolph south through Brockton. Forty-five percent of the Jewish population of the CJP area lives in Boston, Newton, and Brookline. Only 45% of Greater Boston's Jewish adults have lived in their current city or town for ten years or more. Sixty-two percent are likely to stay in the area for at least the next 10 years. Boston is [in its age groupings] the youngest Jewish community in the United States. Fifty-four percent of the adult population is under 40. The young adults who come to Greater Boston tend to remain here. Sixty percent of Jews in their 30s were here in 1975. Seventy percent of them expect to stay here for 10 years or more. There are 20% more Jews over age 70 than there were in 1975. Boston is having a Jewish "baby boomlet." For every 5 children between the ages of 6 and 10, there are 8 under the age of 6.

Forty-one percent are affiliated with synagogs, the same proportion as in 1975. The rates of synagogal affiliation are up for those over 65 and under-40 singles. For the first time, more Jews identify as Reform than any other group (42%). Thirty-three percent say they are Conservative, 4% Orthodox, and 14% express no preference. Eighty-three percent of children in the CJP area are receiving or will have received some form of Jewish education. Over 90% of them will receive it in afternoon and Sunday schools. The rate of intermarriage for first marriages has not changed in the past decade. Twenty-nine percent of first marriages in the 1980–85 period were to an originally non-Jewish spouse. The intermarriage rate for second marriages is 54%. Attending a Passover seder remains the most widely-observed Jewish practice, and lighting Chanukah candles is close behind. Sixteen percent are JCC [Jewish Community Center] members and 61% of JCC members belong to synagogs. About a third of adults have visited or lived in Israel. Ninety-five percent gave to some form of Jewish charity in the past year. Thirty-nine percent gave to CJP. About half of the CJP area, with 55% of the Jewish population, consists of home-owner communities, in which over two-thirds own their homes. Forty-five percent live in renter communities, where over two-thirds rent. Jews in the renter communities are more likely to be very young or very old, to be newcomers, to have lower median incomes and smaller households, and they are less likely to be married, have children, and give to CJP. Jews in the communities south of Boston are more likely to have been born in the metropolitan area, and they are less likely to have advanced degrees, or to have traveled to Israel. The highest rates of synagog affiliation are in the homeowner communities of Newton and the South Central-Brockton areas. Jews under 40 are more likely to live in sparsely Jewish neighborhoods, but more of them would also like there to be more Jews where they live.

There is a continuing high desire for the Jewish community to offer social services under Jewish auspices. About a third of households experienced family or marriage problems in the previous year, and 23% had vocational issues. Twenty-four percent of families with children reported serious problems or concerns about their children, and 33% of households with singles in them desired singles' programs. Twenty-three percent had an elderly relative who had difficulty managing on their own. Depending on the type of problem, from 30% to 80% sought help. The greatest need for help with family and vocational problems is felt in the lowest income households. Problems with elderly relatives are felt equally by all economic groups. Jews continue to postpone marriage; 63% of adults in their 20s are singles, and 23% of adults in their 30s have never married. Eight percent of Jewish adults in their 30s and 12% of the ones in their 40s are currently divorced. This is higher than ever before, although the proportion is smaller than in the general population. More than two-thirds of the currently divorced are women. Twenty-three percent of the Jewish households in Greater Boston have only one person. Households with 2 spouses and children are now only 24% of all households. Single parent households make up about 9% of all households with children. Sixty-two percent of Jewish women are in the work force, two thirds of them full-time. Sixty percent of women with children under the age of 4 are working.

III.   Data Highlights of Greater Kansas City Jewry, 1986

There are 22,100 individuals living in Jewish households in the greater Kansas City area. About 61% (13,360) of all Jews live in Kansas and 39% (8,740) live in Missouri. There are 8,900 households with one or more Jews in the Kansas City area. This represents about 1.8% of all households in the area. Sixty-one percent of the households are made up of 2 persons or less. Of that 61%, 22% are single person households and 39% are 2 person households. Fifteen percent of the married adults have been married once before. Almost 17% of the population is 65 and older, and of that 17%, almost 6% is older than 75. Jewish women in Kansas City wait longer than the general population to have children. Nationally, 30% of all 18 to 24 year-old women have a child; however, only 4% of the Jewish women in the Kansas City area in this age group have a child. When asked if they plan to have children within the next 3 years, 20% of the women said "yes"; 17% said they did not know; 63% said "no." Eighteen percent of the women aged 18 to 24 said they expect 3 children. The mean number of children expected for women 25 to 44 is 2.3. Because of the large proportion of women in their late 20s and mid-30s who are planning to have a child in the next 3 years, the Kansas City Jewish community should expect a "mini" baby boom.

About 40% of the households said that they might move within the next 3 years. Of those who are planning a move, most will be moving to or within Johnson County. Thirty-eight percent of the households have lived at their current residence more than 10 years, while 24% have been in their current residence 3 years or less. Thirteen percent of the Jewish households have moved to the Kansas City area since 1980. Forty-one percent of the respondents were born in the Kansas City area. Of the total population, 50% were born in Missouri and 9% were born in Kansas; 7% were born in New York and New Jersey; 22% in other states; and 1% did not answer. About 11% of the population was born abroad, primarily in Russia, Poland and Israel. Seventy-five percent of the adults older than 25 have some college education. Almost 20% of the adult population has an advanced degree. In 35–44 age group, 90% of the individuals have some college education. Five percent of the population is disabled to some extent, largely among the elderly population. Two percent need daily supervision. Thirteen percent of the adults were unemployed sometime during the last three years. Of these, a majority spent two weeks or less looking for work during the year prior to this Study. Twenty-one percent of the adults are classified in sales occupations, 25% are professionals, 32% are in managerial proprietorial positions, 14% are in clerical positions, and 10% are blue collar workers. Twenty-five percent of the workers are self-employed.

In Kansas City, most Jewish persons (88%) are not currently enrolled in a Jewish education program. About 25% of the adults said that they will take Jewish education classes in the future, and another 23% said that they might have some Jewish education in the future. Those between the ages of 25 and 44 are most likely to indicate a desire to take Jewish education courses in the future. The proportion of Jews who received a Jewish education approaches 95%. For those who received a Jewish education in the past, over half (57%) attended an afternoon Hebrew school. Most of the remaining Jews (25%) attended Sunday School in the past; 11% were in day schools; 5% were with tutors; and 2% were in other kinds of programs. Of those who received a Jewish education, 20% received less than 5 years, 41% received between 5 and 9 years, and 36% received 10 years or more. Three percent did not report the amount. Four percent of the households earn less than $10,000 per year and about 17% of the households earn more than $75,000 per year. The median income for the Jewish population is $37,000; the median income for Missouri residents is $28,000; and the median income for Kansas residents is $46,000. Seventy-five percent of the households are in owner-occupied living quarters. About 5% of the households live in condominiums. Only 3% of the households do not own any automobiles. About 12% of the households 65 or older have no automobiles.

Fifty-two percent of the households currently belong to a synagog or temple. Of those who do belong, 40% are Reform, 43% are Conservative, 14% are Orthodox and 3% are something else. Almost 9 out of 10 households currently belong, have belonged, or intend to join a synagog or temple in their adult life. About 10% of the adults never attend synagog or temple. Five percent of the households indicated they refrain from driving on Shabbat. Eleven percent of the households indicated they always buy kosher meat for the home. About 31% of all married households have a spouse who was not born Jewish. The intermarriage rate since 1976 is about 58%. Before 1976 it was about 23%. Sixty-two percent of the households where the spouse has not converted are not raising children as Jews. In all intermarried couples, about 25% of the non-born Jewish spouses have converted; however, only 75% were formal conversions. Included in the 22,100 total Jewish population are 3,000 non-Jews living in

Jewish households, usually children and spouses of Jews (2,100 who report another religion and 900 that say they have no religion). Twenty-two percent of those sampled have experienced anti-Semitism in the last 12 months. Almost all anti-Semitic experiences consisted of hearing anti-Semitic remarks.

59

AMERICAN JEWISH RELIGION ON THE EVE OF
THE TWENTY-FIRST CENTURY
1963–1990

Like Protestantism, modern Judaism can boast of—or deplore—its many religious denominations. Orthodoxy, in terms of praxis the oldest, maintains that the Mosaic Code with its rabbinic elaborations is divinely inspired. Most of America's traditionalist Jews—provided with good educations—are constantly making concessions to modernity; tradition is being whittled down. Striving desperately to survive, Orthodox leaders have developed a sophisticated media program, but mutual, often virulent hostilities toward one another characterize many Orthodox groups on the right. Despite propaganda claims to the contrary, Orthodoxy has declined precipitously in numbers of adherents, as is borne out by recent surveys.

Conservatism, now probably the largest of the country's Jewish religions, accepts the age-old teachings along with the implications of contemporary science. It hopes it has harmonized these two disparate cultural worlds. Today it tends to be increasingly "leftist" and egalitarian and is moving—not without controversy—to give women complete equality. It was the Conservative Movement that for decades served as a haven for Rabbi Mordecai M. Kaplan (1881–1983) and his humanistic philosophy of Reconstructionism. For Kaplan and his followers, Judaism is more than a religion; it is an organic civilization in which complete freedom is accorded every moral individual to think and act as he or she thinks fit. In theory no Jewish religious group, not even Reform Judaism, is more liberal. It was Conservatism, too, that initially accorded hospitality to the *havurah* devotees of the second half of the twentieth century. Reacting to the impersonality of the larger synagogs, religionists and "seekers" established *havurot*, fellowships, where small groups could meet, unburden their hearts and minds, and build a Jewish world of their own.

546

In 1988 the Conservatives issued a Statement of Principles, a booklet of fifty-seven pages. It is no credo; the statement merely held up a mirror to reality: this is what Conservatism believes and practices. Reform Jews still lean heavily on a one-page pronouncement made as early as 1885, the ultra-liberal Pittsburgh Platform, whose anti-nationalism was rejected in 1937 when the Central Conference of American Rabbis volunteered to aid in the upbuilding of a Jewish homeland in Palestine. Reform persists in its liberalism; the traditional law codes are viewed as literature, as guides, but are not held binding. By the 1950s, however, Reform was experiencing a revolution, not in theory—that remained constant—but in practice. Horrified by the Holocaust which demonstrated the extent to which the Gentile world rejected Jews, fired by Israeli nationalism, Reform Jews turned increasingly to traditional practices, to bar and bat mitzvahs, to the skullcap and the prayer shawl, to Hebrew language rituals. Liberal Judaism now had the best of both worlds: traditionalism *and* modernity. In 1942 Reform had spun off the antinationalist American Council for Judaism. Reacting to the Zionist politicization of the Central Conference of American Rabbis, many of its members established this new Council: it rejected Jewish "nationalism," Zionism, the concept of a Jewish State. A year later the Germans began killing Jews. Ultimately Israel was the only land where Jews could go as of right. It was imperative that Jewish refugees be saved. After the rise of the State of Israel—especially in the wake of the Six-Day War of June 1967—the Council was mortally wounded; today it is but a shadow of its former self.

Selection I reprints a letter that a Reform Jew, Jane B. Bloch, wrote to her son as she lay in an iron lung, her mattress grave; it reflects her religious faith. The second selection analyzes the problems of a divided Orthodoxy; the third is a brief autobiographical note by Sally Priesand, this country's first female rabbi; the next two, pronouncements, describe in some detail the state of the Conservative Movement in the 1970s and 1980s (selections IV). In selection V the Reform rabbis place themselves on record favoring abortions; the sixth selection describes the Havurah Movement; in the seventh, the American Council for Judaism, reaffirms, in 1983, a programmatic announcement made in 1963; in the last and final document the Central Conference of American Rabbis, overriding many objections, announces publicly that it will accept homosexuals as professional colleagues.

I.   The Faith of a Jewish Woman, By Jane B. Bloch, May 4, 1963

May 4, 1963

My dear Peter:

I have wanted to write you a special letter for a very long time.

I have wanted to tell you about all the things that have happened these past fourteen years—starting from the hot August days in 1949 when the hospital ward was filled—sometimes with death or physical destruction, or sometimes miraculously with returned health. These were the days of the polio epidemic.

I want to take you with me through those dim summer days and then through the many that followed in increasingly shining succession. . . .

We have not spoken together, you and I, much about God. Because I have felt so deeply, I have remained silent—too silent. And if you have felt, because my life has had little formal religion, that I have removed myself from deep belief, you would have been given reason to have concluded this.

I can only tell you that I have felt very close to God. In the very early days of my sickness, half-destroyed and understanding little, I began a prayer, and each night the same simple words returned again and again to me: "Grant me the strength, the courage, and the wisdom." There was no ending to the prayer, just those words, and the feeling that some spirit far greater than mine would hear me, and help me. And in my room over the years, this belief has grown stronger.

Although I know that there are disbelievers, I doubt that there are many men among us who in time of darkening trouble do not feel the need to turn to an unknown, but omniscient presence.

And in my room, thinking and believing, I have been restored. I share with you your deep feeling, and in a larger sense, like that calendar of time which I once feared, I am no longer torn when I acknowledge the force of my feelings. I have learned what I might not have learned had the hand of destiny not guided me into this different life. Or was it, perhaps, the hand of God?

And so, Peter, dear, the chapters come to an end, but the story continues. There are just a few things left to be said.

When the time comes, as it inevitably must, that you and I will again be separated, I shall meet this with the greatest possible freedom of spirit, because I know, despite our closeness and great affection, you will be equally prepared for any separation. You are young, and independent, and strong, and you will find temporary sadnesses breached for you by your own freedom of spirit. You will always go ahead, even while welcoming the memories of what I hope is perhaps a uniquely experienced and enriched past.

I know now the hurdles of the years that you have passed, and so I know too the hurdles you will pass in the future, and by this knowledge I am freed.

And so, we will continue to enjoy our tomorrows, you, and your father and I, each of us prepared in our own way for the future, and each of us supported by the bonds of our united pasts.

I have chosen to end my writing on an especially sun-warmed, summer day. The leaves are moving slowly in the beautiful tree outside my window, and the golden morning light throws shifting patterns into my silent room.

There will be many happy, sundrenched days ahead, and I will see you tomorrow and each sun-filled tomorrow thereafter.

And when there are no more tomorrows, we will have shared a splendid bond. And so as I began, with love, I end for now.

II.   The Many Voices of Orthodoxy,
By Michael Wyschogrod, December 19, 1966

The Central Conference of American Rabbis and the Rabbinical Assembly, together with their respective lay organizations, are the united voices of Reform and Conservative Judaism. There are no other rabbinic or lay organizations claiming to speak for Conservative and Reform Judaism. But this is not so in the Orthodox area. Here we have a whole host of organizations, all Orthodox, each with its own point of view and many rather critical of each other.

They can be grouped under three headings: right, left and center. To the right will be found the Yiddish-speaking Hasidim [mystical pietists] concentrated in the Williamsburgh section of Brooklyn but also well represented in other sections of that borough, such as Crown Heights and Boro Park and even extending to the semi-autonomous Hasidic community of New Square near Monsey, N.Y. A large part of this group looks to Rabbi Joel Teitelbaum of Satmer for its leadership; those that do tend to sympathize with the *Neture Karta* of Jerusalem in refusing to recognize the legitimacy of the State of Israel. Others among them have a more friendly attitude toward Israel. All of them, however, are Hasidic in that they wear the traditional garb of the Hasidim, have beards and *peyot* (traditional earlocks) and speak mostly Yiddish at home. Secular studies are kept to a minimum in their schools, with higher education totally ruled out on religious grounds. The activities of the English-speaking Orthodox are of relatively little interest to the Hasidim.

To the left of this group we find the Orthodox Judaism of the *Yeshivoth* [academies] other than Yeshiva University. Most of these, such as Torah Vodaath and Chaim Berlin, are located in Brooklyn but there are also well known senior *Yeshivoth* in Baltimore, Cleveland and Lakewood, N.J., among others. While Yiddish is very often the language of instruction in these schools, most of these students are native-born and speak English at home. The attitude toward secular education in these circles is reserved but not altogether negative. Many, if not most, of these students attend college, frequently the evening sessions of the municipal universities, and a fairly large segment enters the various professions. Leadership in this community is held by the *Roshe Hayeshivoth*, the heads of the various higher schools of Talmudic studies. These men are eminent authorities in rabbinic literature, products of the European *Yeshivoth* of the Lithuanian variety and therefore reserved in their attitude toward Hasidism. Politically, this group is represented by the Agudath Israel, a movement organized in Europe after the first World War to advance the interests of Orthodox Judaism. Unlike the *Neture Karta*, the Agudath Israel is represented in the Israel Knesset and from time to time has even participated in the ruling coalition. The Agudath Israel has for several years now published the *Jewish Observer*, an English-language monthly that sets forth the position of the organization in not unacceptable English.

Finally, there is the Orthodoxy clustered around Yeshiva University. While fully Orthodox, this group harbors no reservations toward secular learning. Instead, it strives for a synthesis of the best in the Jewish tradition and the rest of human culture. Through its journal *Tradition*, it has in recent years made an attempt to come to grips with some of the crucial intellectual and religious issues of the day. The graduates of Yeshiva University generally feel at home in the American Jewish community. They look for leadership to the president of the University, Dr. Samuel Belkin, and to Dr. Joseph B. Soloveitchik, professor of Talmud at the University and one of the few persons who combines standing as an old-fashioned *Rosh Yeshiva* with a Ph.D. in philosophy from the University of Berlin.

III.   The First American Woman Rabbi, By Sally Priesand, 1972–1975

On June 3, 1972 I was ordained rabbi by Hebrew Union College-Jewish Institute of Religion in Cincinnati, Ohio. As I sat in the historic Plum Street Temple, waiting to accept the ancient rite of *s'micha* [ordination], I couldn't help but reflect on the implications of what was about to happen. For thousands of years women in Judaism had been second-class citizens. They were not permitted to own property. They could not serve as witnesses. They did not have the right to initiate divorce proceedings. They were not counted in the *minyan* [quorum]. Even in Reform Judaism, they were not permitted to participate fully in the life of the synagogue. With my ordination all that was going to change; one more barrier was about to be broken.

When I entered HUC-JIR, I did not think very much about being a pioneer. I knew only that I wanted to be a rabbi. With the encouragement and support of my parents, I was ready to spend eight years of my life studying for a profession that no woman had yet entered. My decision was an affirmation of my belief in God, in the words of each individual, and in Judaism as a way of life. It was a tangible action declaring my commitment to the preservation and renewal of our tradition.

As one would expect, there were problems even as I worked toward ordination. Though Reform Judaism had long before declared an official religious equality between men and women, Reform Jews still believed that a woman's place was in the home. They no longer insisted that men and women sit separately during worship services. They allowed women to be counted in the *minyan* to conduct the service, to serve as witnesses on ritual matters. They demanded that girls receive a religious education equivalent to that provided for boys. They allowed women to become members of the congregation with the privilege of voting and they even permitted them to be elected to offices on synagogue boards. But they were not yet ready for the spiritual leadership of a woman.

Undoubtedly, many believed that I was studying at HUC-JIR to become a *rebbetzin* rather than a rabbi, to marry rather than to officiate. Four years passed (while I concentrated on my studies at the University of Cincinnati) before people began to realize that I was serious about entering the rabbinate. During that time, I felt that I had to do better than my classmates so that my academic ability would not be questioned. Professors were fair, but occasionally I sensed that some of them would not be overly upset if I failed. And when, in my fifth year, I was ready to serve my first congregation as student rabbi, some congregations refused to accept my services. Still the members of Sinai Temple in Champaign, Illinois, received me warmly.

My sixth year of study brought the beginning of a tremendous amount of publicity. When you are a "first," you are expected to be an expert in everything. Personal appearances, interviews, statements on contemporary issues—all are expected. Surprisingly enough, though I have always considered myself an introvert, I somehow managed to cope with these new pressures. It helped to know that by this time I had the support, or at least the respect, of most of the members of the college community. Dr. Nelson Glueck, the late president of HUC-JIR, was a particular source of strength. His courage in accepting me as a rabbinic student made possible my eventual ordination.

As my eighth and final year drew to a close, I was faced with finding a job. Some congregations refused to interview me. I was disappointed and somewhat discouraged by these refusals. But since I had not expected everyone to welcome me with open arms, I had prepared myself for this possibility. I knew that I needed only one acceptance and I never really doubted that I would find one synagogue ready to accept me.

The offer of a position as assistant rabbi at the Stephen Wise Free Synagogue in New York City was a blessing in the true sense of the word. I have been extremely well-received by the members of the congregation, and it has been my privilege to work with and to learn from Rabbi Edward E. Klein, the senior rabbi. My activities have not been limited to one area of the Synagogue. My duties include conducting worship services, preaching on Shabbat, teaching both in the Adult Institute and in the Religious School, supervising the youth program, advising a biweekly study group, lecturing to the Golden Age Club, counseling, officiating at life-cycle events, and attending all committee meetings. The only area in which people have shown any real hesitancy has been that of my officiating at funerals.

In addition to my congregational responsibilities, I have lectured extensively throughout the country—an activity which has shown me that congregations and rabbis are ready for change. Ten years ago, women were much more opposed to the idea of a woman rabbi than were men. Since then, however, the feminist movement has made a tremendous contribution in terms of consciousness-raising, and women now demand complete and full participation in synagogue life. This is a significant development because changes will not be made until we change the attitudes of people.

Men and women must learn to overcome their own psychological and emotional objections and regard every human being as a real person with talents and skills and with the option of fulfilling his or her creative potential in any way he or she finds meaningful. Women can aid this process— not by arguing but by doing and becoming, for accomplishments bring respect and respect leads to acceptance. Women must now take the initiative. They should seek and willingly accept new positions of authority in synagogue life.

It is still too soon to assess the impact of my ordination, but I would hope that it would at least mark a transition in our congregations, that sole involvement on the part of women in the synagogue kitchen and the classroom should move toward complete and full participation on the pulpit and in the boardroom as well.

When I accepted ordination on June 3, 1972, I affirmed my belief in Judaism and publicly committed myself to the survival of Jewish tradition. I did so knowing that Judaism had traditionally discriminated against women; that it had not always been sensitive to the problems of total equality. I know that there has been a tremendous flexibility in our tradition—it enabled our survival. Therefore, I chose to work for change through constructive criticism. The principles and ideals for which our ancestors have lived and died are much too important to be cast aside. Instead we must accept the responsibilities of the covenant upon ourselves, learn as much as possible of our heritage, and make the necessary changes which will grant women total equality within the Jewish community.

IV.   Conservative Judaism, 1978–1988

A: The Seven Principles of Conservative Judaism, By Robert Gordis, 1978

American Jewry is becoming increasingly conscious of its historic role, not only as the partner of the State of Israel and the defender of Jewish rights in the Soviet Union and throughout the world, but as the last major center of Jewish life in the Diaspora. In this sacred task, the movement popularly known as the Conservative movement has a significant role to play.

As a matter of fact, the founders of the Conservative movement, the youngest group in modern Judaism, had no wish to create a new alignment in Judaism. They sought, rather, to unite all Jews who had a positive attitude toward Jewish tradition, in spite of variations in detail. Nonetheless, life itself led to the crystallization of Conservative Judaism, *which is dedicated to the conservation and development of traditional Judaism in the modern spirit.*

Its basic attitudes may be set forth under seven headings.

1. Jewish tradition properly understood and intelligently interpreted, has sufficient vitality and capacity for growth to meet the needs of modern American Jews no less effectively than it served the great Jewish communities of the past, such as ancient Babylonia, medieval Spain, and Eastern and Central Europe in modern times.

2. The religious outlook and world-view of Judaism, with its faith in God and its concept of man, offer our distraught and confused generation a sane and courageous philosophy of life, second to none.

3. The Jewish way of life, embodied in the ritual and ethical *mitzvot* [commandments] of Judaism, far from being outmoded, is indispensable, both for the survival of the Jewish people and for the happiness and dignity of the individual Jew. The observance of the *mitzvot*, the Sabbath and the Festivals, daily prayers, Kashrut [dietary laws] and the home rituals are commandments, binding upon each Jew, male and female, young and old.

4. Jewish knowledge is the privilege and duty of every Jew, not merely of the rabbi and the scholar. A Hebrewless Judaism that has surrendered to ignorance and has ceased to create new cultural and spiritual values, is a contradiction in terms, and must perish of spiritual anemia. The regular study of Torah [Jewish lore] on whatever level is incumbent on every Jew, is a supreme commandment second to none.

5. Jews the world over, for all their differences in outlook, political citizenship, and status, are members of the Jewish people, sharing a sense

of kinship and a common history from the past, a common tradition and way of life in the present, and a common destiny and hope for the future.

6. The future of the Jewish people as a creative and self-respecting member of the human family is inconceivable without the rebuilding of security and peace in the Land of Israel, which has already brought home to its borders the scattered remnants of Oriental and European Jewry. Hence the support of the State of Israel and of its progress as a democratic Jewish commonwealth built upon the foundation of justice and equality, in which the body of the Jew will be safe and his spirit unshackled, is a cardinal *mitzvah* of Judaism in our day.

7. The sense of Jewish unity is thoroughly compatible with freedom of thought and difference of viewpoint. Whether one adheres to Orthodoxy, Reform, or Conservative Judaism, the noun is more important than the adjective. Conservative Judaism is grateful for the contributions that both Orthodoxy and Reform and many other movements have made to Jewish life, and seeks to encourage every manifestation of Jewish vitality and creative activity. . . .

B: *Emet Ve-Emunah:* Conservatism's "True Faith," 1988

The formulation of basic doctrine is a particularly difficult task for Conservative Judaism, far more than for its sister movements. Reform Judaism has denied the authority of Jewish law, so that each rabbi and each congregant is free to choose whatever elements of the tradition seem appealing in the name of "individual autonomy."

American Orthodoxy, divided into a dozen groups and factions, is theoretically united under the dogma that both the Written and the Oral Law were given by God to Moses on Sinai, and have remained unchanged and unchangeable through the ages. In fact, this promise of a safe harbor of absolute certainty in a world where everything may be questioned has been the source of the attraction that Orthodoxy has possessed for many of our contemporaries. This comes at a high price, however. The results of modern scholarship that reveal a long history of development in Judaism are ignored, and the challenges presented by modern life are disregarded when possible or minimized when it is not.

It is Conservative Judaism that most directly confronts the challenge to integrate tradition with modernity. By retaining most of the tradition while yet being hospitable to the valuable aspects of modernity, it articulates a vital, meaningful vision of Judaism for our day. Difficult as this task is, there is comfort in the observation of our Sages that *lefum tzaara agra,* according to the pain involved is the reward (Avot 5:24). . . .

The dignity of every human being has always been central to Judaism. This fundamental premise is derived from the biblical assertions in Genesis 1:27 and 5:11 that God created humanity, both male and female, in the divine image. The equality of the sexes is explicitly affirmed in the Conservative Prayerbook, in the blessing in which both men and women thank God for having been created in His image. Access to Jewish education for women has been a hallmark of Conservative Judaism since the days of Solomon Schechter. In almost all our synagogues, men and women are seated together. The *bat mitzvah* [initiating women as ritual equals] ceremony, now celebrated in virtually all synagogues, was originated in the Conservative movement by Professor Mordecai M. Kaplan. Over the years, our movement has encouraged women to assume roles of communal service and leadership both in a professional and in a lay capacity. In recent days, the discussion of the role of women has rekindled interest in some quarters in areas as diverse as *tohorat ha-mishpahah* [the system of family purity revolving around the use of the mikveh (ritual bath)], the creation of naming ceremonies for girls, and special women's observances of *Rosh Hodesh* [the first of the month in the Jewish calendar].

We are all convinced that justice and dignity for each human being can be achieved within the framework of Halakhah, thus obviating the inequalities which lead to situations like that of *agunot* (women who cannot remarry without their husbands' initiating divorce). After years of research and trial by the Committee on Jewish Law and Standards, the Conservative movement has provided satisfactory practical solutions to many of the knotty problems in this area.

There is a wide spectrum of opinion within our movement with regard to the role of women in Jewish ritual. Many believe that women should assume the full rights and responsibilities of ritual participation, including serving as rabbis and cantors. Indeed, the Jewish Theological Seminary now ordains women as rabbis and certifies them as cantors, and the Rabbinical Assembly accepts women as members. On the other hand, some within the movement believe that women today can find religious fulfillment in the context of traditional practice [accepting the restrictions on women imposed by Jewish law]. . . .

Throughout most of its history, Jewish life was an organic unity of home and community, synagogue and law. Since the Emancipation, however, Judaism has been marked by increasing fragmentation. Not only do we find Jewish groups pitted against one another, but the ways in which we apprehend Judaism itself have become separate and distinct. That unified platform upon which a holistic Jewish life was lived has been shattered. Participating in a majority culture whose patterns and rhythms often undermine our own, we are forced to live in two worlds, replacing whole and organic Judaism with fragments: ritual observance or Zionism, philanthropy or group defense; each necessary, none sufficient in itself.

Facing this reality, Conservative Judaism came into being to create a new synthesis in Jewish life. Rather than advocate assimilation, or yearn for the isolation of a new ghetto, Conservative Judaism is a creative force through which modernity and tradition inform and reshape each other.

During the last century and a half, we have built a host of institutions to formulate and express and embody our quest. As important as these are, they in themselves cannot create the new Jewish wholeness that we seek. In spite of the condition of modern life, we must labor zealously to cultivate wholeness in Jewish personalities.

Three characteristics mark the ideal Conservative Jew. First he or she is a *willing Jew*, whose life echoes the dictum, "Nothing human or Jewish is alien to me." This willingness involves not only a commitment to observe the *mitzvot* and to advance Jewish concerns, but to refract all aspects of life through the prism of one's own Jewishness, that person's life pulsates with the rhythms of daily worship and Shabbat and holiday. The moral imperatives of our tradition impel that individual to universal concern and deeds of social justice. The content of that person's professional dealings and communal involvements is shaped by the values of our faith and conditioned by the observance of *kashrut*, of Shabbat and the holidays. That person's home is filled with Jewish books, art, music and ritual objects. Particularly in view of the increasing instability of the modern family, the Jewish home must be sustained and guided by the ethical insights of our heritage.

The second mark of the ideal Conservative Jew is that he or she is a *learning* Jew. One who cannot read Hebrew is denied the full exaltation of our Jewish worship and literary heritage. One who is ignorant of our classics cannot be affected by their message. One who is not acquainted with contemporary Jewish thought and events will be blind to the challenges and opportunities which lie before us. Jewish learning is a lifelong quest through which we integrate Jewish and general knowledge for the sake of personal enrichment, group creativity and world transformation.

Finally, the ideal Conservative Jew is a *striving* Jew. No matter the level at which one starts, no matter the heights of piety and knowledge one attains, no one can perform all 613 *mitzvot* or acquire all Jewish knowledge. What is needed is an openness to those observances one has yet to perform and the desire to grapple with those issues and texts one has yet to confront. Complacency is the mother of stagnation and the antithesis of Conservative Judaism.

Given our changing world, finality and certainty are illusory at best, destructive at worst. Rather than claiming to have found a goal at the end of the road, the ideal Conservative Jew is a traveler walking purposefully towards "God's holy mountain."

V.   The Central Conference of American Rabbis: Resolution on Abortion Rights, June 23–26, 1980

In 1967 the Conference stated: "We strongly urge the broad liberalization of abortion laws in various states, and call upon our members to work toward this end."

The Conference reaffirms this position with the following comments:

A. Jewish legal literature permits therapeutic abortion.

B. The decision concerning any abortion must be made by the woman and not by the state or any other external agency.

C. We oppose all constitutional amendments and legislation which would abridge or circumscribe this right.

D. We call upon our rabbis and upon the Union of American Hebrew Congregations to strengthen their support of the Religious Coalition for Abortion Rights on national, state and local levels.

VI.   The Havurah Movement Comes of Age, By Jonathan Shenker, April 2, 1982

Enriched by a history that goes back 2,000 years, the rebirth of havurot—small fellowships of Jews devoted to a serious self-directed Jewish living—has only taken place during the last 20 years in the US and Canada.

Where once there were only a few, today there are literally thousands of havurot across North America—in urban centers, rural areas and suburbia. They take many forms, reflecting the diversity of Jewish life in America today, as well as a level of commitment uncommon in organized Jewish life.

The first contemporary havurot were formed in Whittier, Calif. in the late 1950s and in Denver in the early 1960s, all within the Reconstructionist Movement.

In 1968 the first unaffiliated havurah, Havurat Shalom, was founded in Somerville, Mass. Soon after, that a pathfinding experiment with havurot within a synagogue was begun by Rabbi Harold Schulweis of Temple Valley Beth Shalom in Encino, Calif. Both types of havurot—the independent, not connected with any synagogue or community center, and the synagogue affiliated—proliferated during the 1970s.

While they are different in many ways, "the vast majority of havurot share four basic features: small size, active participation of all members, an egalitarian/democratic approach and a Jewish rationale," according to Dr. Carl Sheingold, executive director of the National Havurah Coordinating Committee (NHCC).

The NHCC is an independent organization founded in 1979 which has organized conferences and study institutes and has published materials to aid the many havurot and the emerging havurah culture nationwide.

"As non-traditional as the structure may seem at first glance, the rational for a havurah is nevertheless a traditional one, that is, the dedication of its members to creating for themselves serious Jewish lives that are shared within a community." Dr. Sheingold continued. "Havurot are an important means of reaching unaffiliated and underinvolved Jews. For many they bridge the gap between family and the Jewish community."

Havurot have also played an important role in strengthening synagogues. Saul Rubin, the rabbi of a long-established Reform Synagogue, Congregation Mickve Israel in Savannah, Ga., recently wrote about the effect of the havurah program on the synagogue:

"Our previously 'cold' synagogue environment has suddenly become more warm and hospitable. The board has shifted away from trivia and toward problem solving; formerly passive members now hunger for Jewish leadership.

"And that's just the impact on the institution; the impact on the people has been even greater. . . . As the rabbi operates in a havurah setting, he relates to people whose creativity he respects, and he can encourage them to do even more."

Just over two years ago at Rutgers University in New Brunswick, NJ, the First National Havurah Conference gathered more than 350 individuals, describing themselves as "Reform," "Conservative," "neo-traditional," "Reconstructionist," and simply, "havurah," to share the common experiences of havurah-style Jewish community life. The conference was unique in that it succeeded for the first time in bringing together a diverse group of Jews, not to discuss an issue or support cause, but to support and learn from each other in shaping their personal, Jewish lives.

In an effort to continue the activities initiated by the Rutgers Conference, the NHCC based in New York, was founded in the fall of 1979. During the summer of 1980 and again in 1981, the NHCC sponsored the First and Second National Havurah Institutes and the Second National Havurah Conference, which were held at the University of Hartford in West Hartford, Conn.

At these events participants explored different havurah lifestyles, while studying traditional Jewish texts. The opportunity to study for a week in the characteristically participatory havurah style, with scholarly, dynamic teachers, drew several hundred havurah members and other interested Jews. There was, as in 1979, a sense of community among these varied people, reflecting a common need for serious study as an integral aspect of the renewal of their Jewish lives. Participants took home new insights, skills, ideas and techniques with which to enrich the activities of their own havurot and communities.

The summer institute marked the emergence of havurot as a distinctively American contribution to Jewish communal life. "In the years to come," wrote Jeffrey Oboler in *Congress Monthly*, "the havurah approach may help bring new life into those Jewish organizations and institutions that are no longer attracting new members. . . . The message of the havurah is a simple one, that Jews need to rediscover each other and be Jewish together."

These events also marked the further evolution of the broader meaning of the havurah approach. William Novak, in a *Moment* article about the 1980 Summer Institute characterized havurah Judaism as built on, among other things:

a re-emphasis on Torah study, integrating insights from psychology, literature, history and personal experience to make the text a "living document" for the participants;

full participation of men and women in all aspects of havurah activity;

group self-direction and skills sharing;

a resurgence of interest in Jewish theology and the making of midrashim (Jewish stories and parables by which Jews achieve greater insights into traditional texts and teachings). . . .

VII.   The American Council for Judaism Reaffirms Its Position, Summer 1983

The American Council for Judaism, assembled in its Annual Conference, marks the conclusion of twenty years of unswerving dedication to its principles. We reaffirm our historic belief that Judaism is a religious faith of universal values and insights, and that those voluntarily identifying with it form a religious fellowship of mutual interest and concern—a humanitarian concern for the welfare of our fellow Jews, which we deeply share with others, and which in no way represents a political attachment to those whom we would assist—in Israel or elsewhere. We reject the Zionist concept that, as Jews, there attaches to our religion an automatic, inherent political relationship to the nationalism of the foreign State of Israel.

We seek the continuing and expanding civic, cultural and social integration of Americans of Jewish faith into the total national life of the United States; we strive to offset all efforts to establish Jews in this country as a segregated, identifiable Israel-oriented political collectivity, separate and apart from their fellow Americans of other faiths. We regard such separation and withdrawal as a complete denial of the status which Jews have sought for themselves in America for over three hundred years.

We affirm that our homeland is the United States of America, just as it is the homeland of all Jews enjoying the privileges and responsibilities of American citizenship.

We insist that the nationalism of the State of Israel be confined to its citizens living within the boundaries of the State. We are determined to prevent the involuntary imposition of that nationalism on Americans of Jewish faith.

Finally, we are committed to the basic and demonstrable fact that no Jew, no group of Jews and no Jewish organization can speak for or represent all Jews.

Encouraged by the accomplishments of twenty years of service to those sharing our views, we are resolved to press forward the implementation of our cherished principles and beliefs, through positive educational programs, some already undertaken and others to be developed as needs arise.

We invite the support and cooperation of all Americans of the Jewish faith to whom our principles are meaningful and for whom our programs are in consonance with their lives as Americans and Jews.

VIII.   Homosexuals and the Reform Rabbinate, June 25, 1990

... The Committee is acutely aware that the inability of most gay and lesbian rabbis to live openly as homosexuals is deeply painful. Therefore, the Committee wishes to avoid any action which will cause greater distress to our colleagues. As a result, the Committee has determined that a comprehensive report is in the best interest of our Conference and the Reform Movement as a whole.

Publicly acknowledging one's homosexuality is a personal decision which can have grave professional consequences. Therefore, in the light of the limited ability of the Placement Commission or the Central Conference of American Rabbis to guarantee the tenure of the gay or lesbian rabbis who "come out of the closet," the Committee does not want to encourage colleagues to put their careers at risk. Regrettably, a decision to declare oneself publicly can have potentially negative effects on a person's ability to serve a given community effectively. In addition, the Committee is anxious to avoid a situation in which pulpit selection committees will request information on the sexual orientation of candidates. The Committee urges that all rabbis, regardless of sexual orientation, be accorded the opportunity to fulfill the sacred vocation which they have chosen. ...

We applaud the fine work of the gay and lesbian outreach synagogues, and we, along with the Union of American Hebrew Congregations, call upon rabbis and congregations to treat with respect and to integrate fully all Jews into the life of the community regardless of sexual orientation. ...

In Jewish tradition heterosexual, monogamous, procreative marriage is the ideal human relationship for the perpetuation of species, covenantal fulfillment and the preservation of the Jewish people. While acknowledging that there are other human relationships which possess ethical and spiritual value and that there are some people for whom heterosexual, monogamous, procreative marriage is not a viable option or possibility, the majority of the Committee reaffirms unequivocally the centrality of this ideal and its special status as *kiddushin* [sanctified marriage]. To the extent that sexual orientation is a matter of choice, the majority of the Committee affirms that heterosexuality is the only appropriate Jewish choice for fulfilling one's covenantal obligations. . . . A minority of the Committee dissents, affirming the equal possibility of covenantal fulfillment in homosexual and heterosexual relationships. The relationship, not the gender, should determine its Jewish value—*kiddushin.*

The Committee strongly endorses the view that all Jews are religiously equal regardless of their sexual orientation. We are aware of loving and committed relationships between people of the same sex. Issues such as the religious status of these relationships as well as the creation of special ceremonies are matters of continuing discussion and differences of opinion. . . .

The general subject of sexual morality is important. The Committee, in various stages of its deliberations, sought to discuss homosexuality within that larger framework. However, it concluded that while a comprehensive statement on sexuality and sexual morality was a desideratum, it was beyond the mandate of the Committee. Nevertheless, rabbis are both role models and exemplars. Therefore, the Committee calls upon all rabbis

—without regard to sexual orientation—to conduct their private lives with discretion and with full regard for the mores and sensibilities of their communities, and in consonance with the preamble to the Central Conference of American Rabbis' *Code of Ethics:*

> As teachers of Judaism, rabbis are expected to abide by the highest moral values of our religion: the virtues of family life, integrity and honorable social relationships. In their personal lives they are called upon to set an example of the ideals they proclaim. . . .

One of the original issues which brought the Committee into existence was a concern about the admissions policy of the College-Institute. President Alfred Gottschalk has recently set forth the admissions policy of HUC-JIR [Hebrew Union College-Jewish Institute of Religion.] The written guidelines state that the College-Institute considers sexual orientation of an applicant only within the context of a candidate's overall suitability for the rabbinate, his or her qualifications to serve the Jewish community effectively, and his or her capacity to find personal fulfillment within the rabbinate. The Committee agrees with this admissions policy of our College-Institute.

The Central Conference of American Rabbis has always accepted into membership upon application all rabbinic graduates of the College-Institute. The Committee re-affirms this policy to admit upon application rabbinic graduates of the College-Institute. Since its inception, the Rabbinical Placement Commission has provided placement services to all members of the Central Conference of American Rabbis in good standing, in accordance with its rules. The Committee agrees with this policy of the Rabbinical Placement Commission which provides placement services to all members of the Central Conference of American Rabbis in good standing, in accordance with the Commission's established rules.

Respectfully submitted. . . .

The Committee unanimously endorses this report as a fair reflection of four years of deliberation and urges its adoption.

60

Jewish Education and Culture
1961–1968

Despite the fact that professional educators were ringing their hands in despair deploring the plight of Jewish education in the late twentieth century, American Jews were exposed to a host of institutions which raised their cultural niveau. The Jewish Chautauqua Society dispatched rabbis to the colleges and universities of the country to preach the gospel of Jewish universalism; Brandeis and Yeshiva University made every effort to lure Jewish men and women to matriculate in their departments of Hebraica and Judaica. Every community of any size had an English-language Jewish newspaper; the Yiddish dailies had all died, but there were still Yiddish weeklies. Languages die hard: *Ha-Doar*, the Hebrew literary periodical, now more than eighty years of age, refused to give up the ghost, and indeed new Hebrew-language journalistic ventures appeared in America aimed at Israeli émigrés.

The Jewish Community Centers, all of which had cultural programs, were determined to persist as rivals of the most successful synagogs. The *havurot*, religiosocial fellowships, continued to rebuke and ameliorate the impersonality of the larger synagogs; there were dozens and dozens of these conventicles, a great many of them under synagog sponsorship. Whether they will survive the coming of the new century lies in the laps of the gods. Sunday schools, afternoon schools, and all-day schools flourished. The 1980s saw close to 500 Jewish all-day schools in the United States; they were holding their own despite the high cost of tuition. Parents, aware that standards in most metropolitan public schools were low, wanted a superior secular-*cum*-Jewish education for their youngsters. Even Beth Israel of Houston, which had once frowned on Jewish nationalism, opened an all-day school! Jewry's cultural and educational bastions were the religious seminaries, the teachers' colleges, the old-fashioned Talmud-teaching yeshivot; they were all alive and well, preaching their gospel of a Judaism that was now three thousand years of age.

Already by 1960 none of this was new. What fresh winds were blowing? A whole new crop of novelists, dramatists, poets, social scientists, and philosophers made their way to the center of America's cultural stage. Often they were not "Jewish" writers; they were Americans who happened to be Jews but they could not escape—and usually made no endeavor to escape—their Yiddish-speaking fathers and grandfathers. Among them were a handful of intellectuals who lived in a recondite world of their own where the Anglo-Saxon monosyllable was engulfed by the Latin polysyllable. But the genes that made them what they were went back to the sensitive Jews who wrote the biblical books of Proverbs and Ecclesiastes. This new generation of writers gave birth to two Nobel Prize winners, Saul Bellow and I. B. Singer, writers of novels and short stories.

During the heyday of Classical Reform—the early twentieth century—few if any "temples" taught the Hebrew of the prophets they professed to venerate, but by the last decades of the twentieth century a veritable revolution had occurred. The youngsters in all Reform synagogs and Sunday schools began to study Hebrew and to sing Hebrew songs, courtesy of the new State of Israel. This post-Holocaust turn to the ancestral language, this realization that Gentiles never forgot that Jews were different, spurred an interest in Hebraic and Judaic studies; there are today literally hundreds of universities and colleges where Jewish courses are taught; a host of men and women began writing dissertations on Jewish subjects; even the Hassidim of Brooklyn—entrenched in "Torah-true" traditions—furthered the cultural advance of their womenfolk by encouraging them to publish *Di Yiddishe Heim (the Jewish Home)*, a bilingual quarterly. The local social-welfare agencies began subsidizing Jewish cultural institutions and schools; they have accepted communal responsibility—in part at least—for the education of the young. This is—to be sure—an approach pregnant with problems, since the synagogs will never surrender control of the Jewish education of their youngsters.

In 1961, when selection I was printed, its author, Dr. Enoch Gordis, a medical internist, was engaged in scientific studies at the Rockefeller Institute for Medical Research. His article was one of several that appeared in a symposium on "Jewishness and the Younger Intellectuals" sponsored by the editors of *Commentary*. Apparently Dr. Gordis had come to terms with his heritage. On the other hand, Dr. John Slawson, the executive vice president of the American Jewish Committee in 1963, struggled with the problem of Jewish identity (selection II). The final document in this section dealing with Jewish education and culture was written in 1968 by David Dubinsky, once president of the International Ladies' Garment

Workers' Union. Dubinsky was responding to a query of some youngsters who had asked him to define himself as an immigrant American Jew.

I. A Scientist Remains within the Ambit of Judaism, By Enoch Gordis, April 1961

(1) Bigotry is less fashionable nowadays, due in part to relative prosperity, in part to frequent public presentations of intergroup problems. This change has no bearing on my attitudes toward Judaism.

(2) I refrain from the obvious detailed exposition of the combination of rebelliousness, *Selbsthass* [self-hate], and idealism which spawned the Jewish socialist, who, by the way, owed much to the tradition he despised. I believe there is no viable element in this movement, because being Jewish is now respectable in America and the welfare state has adopted much of the old socialist platform.

(3) Jewish culture has many subtle and indirect influences on American life. But to determine if in total they are significant, consider for a moment what would happen if all the Jews were to disappear from America. Except for the loss of a slight Yiddish tone to New York City, the change would be undetectable in that America which extends from the Atlantic to the far Pacific.

(4) The two words in defining a person's relation to his tradition, "historical reverence" and "obligation," are not equivalent. I may have great regard for a museum of antiquities and not want to fill my house with them. On the other hand, participation in cyclic rituals and institutional activities does not necessarily imply a genuine regard for the tradition they are supposed to be part of.

My present position is an often inconsistent mixture of conviction, habit, and weighted practical alternatives.

I am firmly rooted in the Jewish tradition, having grown up happily in a richly Jewish home. I believe that in four key respects Judaism is unsurpassed in Western religion. (A) It has consistently applied its ethical insights, for which its spokesmen showed a remarkable talent very early in history, to a variety of mundane matters, at the same time keeping its sights on distant goals such as universal peace. (B) It is *explicitly* tolerant of other points of view. (C) It makes minimum demands on credulity, and concentrates on the human, physical, and practical. Knowledge and action are paramount over faith. It is refreshingly free from cloying otherworldliness, emetic concern for the "soul," and biological nonsense. (D) It has led, in its adherents, to a frequent and attractive combination of attitudes: idealism and skepticism.

This much said for the "reverence," I now confess that my feeling of "obligation" has been attenuated for several reasons. (A) I can accept no theology, since theological assertions are invariably arranged so that experimental validation of their consequences is logically as well as practically impossible. (B) Ethical insights, in my view, are in principle derivable from many sources, so the Jewish religion and others are dispensable in this regard. I must also reject the theological concept of sin when applied to both unethical behavior, and, *a fortiori*, ritual disobedience. (C) I am impatient with institutional activities, and find the quality of verbal and musical expression in communal worship intolerably bad.

Pushed to their legitimate conclusion, these attenuating forces might render my "obligation" nil. For several reasons, however, I have not wished to throw out the whole structure despite its unacceptable philosophic foundation. (A) The holiday observances and many of the home rituals are beautiful, and like any art which has taken centuries to find its current expression, they ought not to be dismissed without seriously considering whether the loss is not greater than the gain in consistency. The values which the holiday stress and ornament are those to which I subscribe, despite my rejection of their "official" derivation. Deaf to any "divine imperative," I reserve the right to choose my observances. (B) A significant gap in the emotional resources of many modern children is their inability to feel reverence for anything. Reverence is an attitude which must be learned, and once learned, is transferred easily to new areas. Children learn it by seeing adults behave in a manner that suggests that solemn, important, and permanent things are being considered. Regarded in this light, the unacceptable philosophic basis for many observances should be occasionally neglected. (C) If the Jewish tradition is not indispensable for the derivation of ethics, it certainly has served as the vehicle for their transmission. The Jewish tradition is the one whose language I know, whose nuances I fathom, whose insights are expressed in a variety of contexts with which I identify. I can summon no other language to speak them to my children. I do not doubt, however, that my position leads to a gradual attrition of the specifically Jewish after a few generations, but for me, at present, there is no alternative.

(5) I believe that most Americans can lead a fruitful, decent, and happy life in any of the popular religious traditions. I have the uneasy feeling that in most cases, religious conversion in America in any direction reflects more on the emotional instability of the person involved than on the merits of the religions. Ignorance of one's own traditions is an ancillary cause. What my wife and I can do to repair the ignorance our children were born with and to make them secure, we will do. After that, the future is out of our hands, and I spend no more time worrying about conversion than about the possibility they may some day have diabetes.

(6) Israel has and will continue to have my sympathy. Israel, however, is not concerned with my sympathy except when it leads to financial support or useful pressure on Washington.

That the zeal of the "kibbutzniks" and other early settlers reflected the ultimate in the practice of Jewish ethics is obvious. It would be naive to expect anything other than what has happened: a thinning out of the initial idealism, and the emergence of racial bigotry, political machinations, and an excess of nationalism. Whatever the proportion of the wonderful and the less-than-wonderful in Israel—and the former predominates—it is meaningless to ask whether Israel "embodies" Jewish values more than America. Israel *is* the continuing Jewish tradition, the tradition which contains villains and fools, as well as prophets and scholars.

II.   The Quest for Jewish Identity in America, By John Slawson, June 2, 1963

One experiences great difficulty in defining the subtleties of our subject [identity], for is it not true, as Professor J. L. Talmon of the Hebrew University in Jerusalem once said, that "the links holding Jews together are—to use the words of Edmund Burke—as invisible as the air and as strong as the heaviest chains, and the Jewish ingredient imperceptible to the sense yet as effective in result."

Identity is one of the most important quests of man. Its realization is a lifelong development, beginning with childhood. It is in fact the consciousness of selfhood and the extension of the ego from the individual through the family to the more embracing groups—peer, religious, ethnic, and national. Freud refers to Jewish identity as "the individual's relatedness to the unique history of a people."

It has been aptly said that "the modern, emancipated Jew does not fully know what he is and much of what he does know, he cannot accept." Yes, today's Jew finds the contemplation of identity at times very painful because there are vast uncertainties surrounding it. There is a gap between the label and his own actuality, frequently an absence of authenticity which prevents a surefooted attitude toward selfhood.

The current concern with Jewish identity centers increasingly on how to achieve an integrated yet unassimilated status in the general American community. Indeed, to many leaders of Jewish communities, defense against assimilation now seems more urgent than defense against discrimination. The intensity of this new interest doubtless derives from the need, now more than in the past, for the individual Jew to formulate his own beliefs and support them from within. He can no longer rely on the non-Jew to tell him what he is; he must decide and affirm the fact for himself. Otherwise he will cease to exist as a Jew.

It should be noted that although assimilation always requires integration, the reverse is not true. Integration does not necessarily involve assimilation. Integration is working and interacting with others for common purposes. Assimilation is trying to forget that one is a Jew.

Of course the evolving character of Jewish group identity must be very largely determined by the overall pattern of group life in America. We should therefore examine the contours of that pattern for a few moments.

May I say at the outset that never, perhaps, in American history, has the prevailing social framework afforded as great an opportunity for the development of Jewish self-regard as exists today.

Pluralism, with all its implications for group identity, is no longer a theory in America; it is a fact. The election of Mr. [John F.] Kennedy [as president] marked America's entry into a new age distinguished by religious and ethnic pluralism and industrial urbanism. The Kennedy administration both symbolizes and ratifies this profound development. The pluralistic trend is gaining momentum even among Catholics; witness the proceedings of the current Ecumenical Council in Rome, the various pronouncements of Pope John XXIII, especially his last encyclical, and the marked changes in intergroup outlook and action among Catholics in the United States.

Jews today are Americans, not alone by citizenship, but by upbringing, outlook, taste, and even memories. Harry Golden's boyhood experiences on the East Side of New York are now regarded as no less American than Tom Sawyer's adventures on the Mississippi. Interestingly enough, certain features of American life have assumed what were traditionally considered Jewish traits—a sort of confluence of trends in the American character and traits generally attributed to Jews. Thus, it used to be said that Jews were peculiarly attached to middle-class pursuits and city life. But middle-class tastes and values now characterize the entire American population. Industrial urbanism and the technological revolution of our day have conformed the average American's socio-economic life to the very same patterns forced upon the Jew by exclusionary practices during various periods in his turbulent history. . . .

Secularism in the American environment is an important factor in determining whether the present-day climate favors the development of Jewish group identity. The predominance of secularism has been caused by a number of developments, past and present. Among them are the great migrations, the industrial revolution, the scientific revolution, the technological revolution, Darwin, Freud and the Atomic Age. We make a great error when we interpret secularism as a denial of God. It is by no means that, even though its connotation is civil rather than ecclesiastical. Secularism implies that religion is a private matter for the individual, that creedal commitments and theological doctrines are less important than inner convictions. Protestants who are not church-committed are still considered Protestants—and, as revealed in the census findings, so consider themselves. There is a basic agreement between the two traditions, religious and secular, on a common humanism and humanitarianism. This common affirmation of the dignity of man has protected America against fiercely anti-clerical and anti-secular movements. John Courtney Murray, the distinguished Catholic theologian, reluctantly speaks of secularism as a fourth religion—Protestantism, Catholicism, Judaism and Secularism.

For Jews especially, this secularist atmosphere is important because it makes possible the free development of a minority religion, such as Judaism, within the accepted framework of society. . . .

The Jewish tradition still speaks with vigor and relevance in the world today, not alone to Jews, but to all society. That tradition is the source of our identity. Acculturation to American society without loss of identity—either religious or religio-cultural, depending upon one's point of view—is the essence of Jewish integration.

Recognition of one's group identity instills a sense of surefootedness and tends to minimize feeling of uprootedness, unrelatedness, and aloneness in this modern mass society. It is essential to the unconditional acceptance of self, which in turn is basic to acceptance by others.

With a society hospitable to difference, and a vigorous tradition that has much to say to the modern world, it would appear that Jewish religious and communal leaders, social workers and educators, lay and professional, have both an opportunity and a responsibility to help the individual Jew to find the personal enrichment and sense of community that Jewish identity can give.

It is probable that we in America have put too much emphasis on eliminating or suppressing the differences which distinguish us from other American groups, as if we were trying to approach a mythical, non-existent American "type." Fundamental research on the problems surrounding Jewish identity would be of great value—influences from parents and others that shape the process of identity formation; the manifold ways in which Jewishness, in both its positive and negative aspects, becomes an intrinsic part of the self of the growing child.

I should like to end with the words of Rabbi Zusya of 18th century Chasidic fame, as narrated by Martin Buber. Rabbi Zusya, the Chasidic rabbi of great piety, explained to his disciples the meaning of identity in this manner: "When I face my Maker, I will not be asked, 'Why were you not Moses?' But I will be asked, 'Why were you not Zusya?'"

III.   My Jewishness Has Always Been a Source of Pride, By David Dubinsky, January 16, 1968

Seventh Grade
Temple Israel
35–38 East 3rd Street
Long Beach, California 90814

Dear young people:

I regret the delay in replying to your letter, but it was sent to an address where I have not lived for many years. When I did receive it, I was not in a position to reply immediately.

Thank you for choosing me as your example of the Jewish immigrant in the United States.

I arrived in this country at the beginning of 1911, alone. My brother, who had made the crossing earlier, took me into his home on the East Side of New York. But my dear parents never came to the United States. They were born in [Russian-ruled] Brest-Litovsk and lived out their lives in Lodz, Poland, where they had grown up, married and raised a family. At home we knew only that our forefathers had come to that place after much wandering. But who they were, who even my grandparents were, and whether we had sprung originally from the Sephardic or the Ashkenazi root of our people, were questions whose answers were lost in history. I knew only that my beloved father was an Orthodox Jew who worshipped the noted rabbi of Alexander. At that time there were two sects of Chasidism—one, followers of the Gerrer rabbi and the other followers of the Alexander rabbi.

My life in America has been rich in service and experience. I have encountered my share of anti-Semitism. Some of it has been conscious, willful or even mean. But I know that some of it has also been unintentional, reflecting the melding of many strains that go into our national character. While anti-Semitism is especially vicious, it is not a unique phenomenon in a nation that also experienced tragic anti-Irish, anti-Catholic, anti-German waves.

It has been my good fortune to have been associated for most of my adult life with a great union whose proud and justified boast is that within its ranks, for more than 70 years, Americans of many origins have worked to advance together. The International Ladies' Garment Workers' Union, in that sense, is a miniature reflection of a country which is uniquely a "nation of immigrants."

The fact of my being Jewish has made no difference. Nor did it make a difference in the case of Samuel Gompers, also a Jew, who was the founder of the American Federation of Labor on whose Executive Council I was, for a time, the only Jewish member.

The union and the labor movement which I serve have extended generous aid to the Jewish State of Israel and to its labor movement. I have played some part in rallying that aid because I felt it was both my humanitarian duty and my Jewish duty to support and strengthen a nation born in the shadow of the exterminating ovens. Differences of opinion were largely swept aside once the United Nations recognized this little country, and in the years since then, I, personally, and the ILGWU have continued support of a land where Jews are proving their ability to overcome new challenges.

Some people are bothered by their Jewishness; mine has always been a source of pride. Some people seek to escape from their Jewishness; I have always felt that no Jew can completely cease being a Jew. Some people capitalize on their Jewishness and even exploit it; for me Jewishness has helped but only in a deeply personal way.

I do not go to a synagogue. Nor do I observe the prescribed rituals. Yet I consider myself a profoundly religious Jew, one who is constantly aware of his Judaic heritage.

All my life and every inch of the way I have come I have felt that additional responsibility which only the Jew must feel. Upon him there rests continually the need to prove himself not only as an American—or as a citizen of whatever country in which he is at home. He must always prove himself doubly—as an American and as a Jew.

A Jew must do better, for if he fails there are those who will use his failure to magnify his individual fault as a fault of all Jews. But if he succeeds, if he "makes good," serves well, some part of the glory of his achievement rubs off on all Jews.

If I have served some larger cause, it has been that of rescuing, preserving and enhancing the dignity of the individual human beings who must work for a living. If I have been moved by any single principle, it is that we must do for others as we would have them do for us. The record clearly shows my concern, as a trade union leader, with both the spirit and the mechanics of ethical trust and conduct.

I have been able to do these things in a nation which has given freedom and opportunity to millions who have come to it with hope. I believe I have in this manner fulfilled to the best of my personal ability not only my duty as an American but my obligations as a Jew.

Sincerely yours,

David Dubinsky

61

MILLIONAIRES AND PAUPERS
1965–1984

J ewish philanthropy? This is what Jews give to the general and the
Jewish communities. Most money donated goes to non-Jewish institutions and colleges. The Jew is eager—perhaps overeager!—to document his devotion to America, but very substantial sums are also raised to
aid Jewish welfare institutions both here and abroad. The "federation"—
the local Jewish charities—provides for most social-welfare needs. It gives
grants to Jewish schools, to the university Hillels, the Community Center,
the Community Relations Committee—which works primarily with
Gentiles—and the vocational guidance association; it supports newly arrived immigrants and refugees. Its prime challenge, however, is to aid the
impoverished, the sick, the poor, the orphan, the emotionally disturbed. In
short the federation influences, if it doesn't control, almost every Jewish
social-welfare organization; only the synagogs remain beyond its ambit.
The relation between these two, synagog and federation, leaves something
to be desired. The money to fund the federation comes from the U.S. government (primarily as grants for refugees), from the local "non-Jewish"
Community Chest, and from local Jewry in the form of contributions.
Annually, the United Jewish Appeal (UJA), a national advisory association, works with the local Jewish Federation and Welfare Fund to help it
stage a money-raising campaign. The gifts received make provision for local, national, and overseas needs. The rich, the "big givers," millionaires,
give generously; the middle-class contributors give liberally and, in addition, provide the dedicated volunteers without whom no campaign can be
carried on.

Most local institutions have national counterparts which provide
guidance. The federation, per se, leans on the New York based Council of

Jewish Federations. The Council is powerful; no Jewish national congeries is more influential! It moves constantly toward centralization; obviously it believes that a united Jewry is a stronger Jewry. New York City
also houses the national headquarters of well over twenty other organizations offering guidance to agencies concerned with the well-being of
American Jewry. Women are increasingly important in the job of raising
funds, though this is not new; they have been active in relief for the impoverished ever since the first quarter of the nineteenth century. Today
America's Hadassah, the women's Zionist organization of America, sends
millions to further the medical welfare of Israel's inhabitants. A rival, in a
way, is the Women's American ORT (Organization for Rehabilitation
through Training). This branch of the World ORT Union is a prime
sponsor of vocational training schools in Europe, Latin America, and Israel. Women's American ORT has thousands of members, hundreds of
chapters. Its schools abroad train students in almost every field of endeavor
from hairdressing to electronics.

In recent decades women have been playing an increasingly important
role in the United Jewish Appeal. The beneficiaries of the UJA's annual
campaign are the American Jewish Joint Distribution Committee and the
United Israel Appeal. Most of the money they receive is sent to Israel to
provide social-welfare services. All told, American Jewry raises no less
than one billion dollars a year for Jewish philanthropic purposes in the
United States and overseas. This is an impressive record; at least 20 percent
of American Jews are in no position to make gifts of any consequence.

Selection I tells the story of a multimillionaire who gave liberally to
help student nurses; the second documents the work of a Jewish interest-
free loan society; the final selection recounts the odyssey of a Holocaust
victim who was helped by New York City's federation of charities.

I. The Shabby Millionaire, September 1, 1965

Trenton, Aug. 31—Dr. Leonhard Felix Fuld, a self-made multimillionaire and shy philanthropist who dispensed about $1 million annually,
died this morning at Helene Fuld Hospital. He was 82 years old.

Dr. Fuld, who lived much of his life as a recluse, was also a lawyer,
economist and expert in police administration and public health. He held
five degrees from Columbia University, all earned in a period of six years.

Dr. Fuld's fortune of about $25 million, which he made in real estate
and the stock market, is held in perpetual trust by the Helene Fuld Foundation, named for his mother. He set up the agency to promote his special
interest—the health of student nurses.

Form 1956 until he became ill last year, Dr. Fuld had lived in a modest house at 93 Fuld Street in North Trenton. The city had renamed the

street for him to honor his work at the Helene Fuld Hospital, to which he gave more than $2.5 million over the years. . . .

The scene was repeated in many hospitals on the East Coast in the last 35 years. A shabbily dressed old man with a Phi Beta Kappa key dangling by a gold chain from his lapel would appear in the reception room and inquire after the health of the student nurses.

He was often ejected, but when he was not, the hospital became the beneficiary of a new nurses residence, a scholarship program or even a new wing. More than 20 hospitals from Springfield, Mass., to Johnson City, Tenn., now have student-nurse facilities named for the donor.

The benefactor in each case was Dr. Fuld, a publicity-shy man whose life was an indelible mixture of the humane, the eccentric and the successful.

Dr. Fuld was forever surprising people, either by his knowledge or his gifts. Men who had dealings with him for years knew nothing about him except that he presented certified checks to their institutions from time to time.

For much of his life he lived with his sister, Florentine, in a tenement he owned at 130 East 110th Street [New York]. In 1956 Miss Fuld died of malnutrition at the Hospital for Joint Diseases, to which her brother had given money. Before she died she said she had not left the house in nine years.

The death of his only relative brought a change in the life of the thin, bowed, bald little man. He moved to Trenton and set himself up in a house. "I figured the time had come for me to start protecting myself a little bit more realistically for my future with people," he explained.

Thereafter he got around a bit more, often taking a train to visit one of his projects. Sometimes he traveled with a student nurse. At each project he would take out a worn black notebook and jot down the names of nurses who were ill. On his next visit, he would check to see if they had improved.

In the last two years he became increasingly ill and had to curtail his visits. When he did go, he traveled by hired limousine. For the last year, he was too debilitated to travel at all.

Dr. Fuld was born in New York City on Aug. 12, 1883. His father was a wholesale merchant. His mother, the former Helene Schwab, died in 1923. As a youth, he attended Public School 57, Public School 83 and Horace Mann High School.

In 1902 he entered Columbia and completed the requirements for the B.A. in one year. He earned a[n] M.A. in 1904, a Bachelor of Laws in 1905, a Master of Laws in 1906 and a Ph.D. in 1909.

During his time at Columbia, he told an interviewer many years later, he worked as secretary to Nicholas Murray Butler, the university's president.

In 1909 he became a civil service examiner for the city. He spent his days in the office and his nights in precinct stationhouses. "I felt, you see," he once said, "that the only way I could properly examine candidates was to actually see first hand what problems policemen faced."

In 1910 he produced a 1,100-page book entitled "Police Administration" that became a standard work. He was instrumental in the planning of the New York Police Academy. One of his last bequests, in 1963, was for advanced training of officers at the New Jersey State Police Academy.

Dr. Fuld worked for the city until 1918. In the next few years he held similar posts in Rochester and Washington. Then he was hired by Henry L. Doherty, the president of Cities Service, to set up a school for security salesmen.

It was this experience that gave him his knowledge of the stock market. He often said that he had to study at night to keep ahead of his students. From 1923 to 1945 Dr. Fuld was an evening instructor in economics and business administration at the Bernard M. Baruch School of Business and Public Administration of City College.

Dr. Fuld was always vague about how he made his money. He would only say that he put the precepts he taught into practice and that he never sold a stock once he bought it.

Some friends assumed that his initial capital was provided by a small inheritance. He held extensive real estate in East Harlem and elsewhere.

Dr. Fuld maintained a continuing interest in the dissemination of knowledge about the stock market, and was proud of his membership in the New York Society of Security Analysts.

In 1958 he bought one share of each stock sold on the New York Stock Exchange to be presented on his death to the Wharton School of Finance and Commerce at the University of Pennsylvania. He explained that in addition to the income, the school would obtain the financial statements of each of the companies and be able to send students to stockholders' meetings.

He managed all his own investments and wrote all his correspondence in longhand—about 5,000 letters a year. Some institutions to which he gave gifts recalled that they would receive postcards from him commenting on the bequest or, on occasion, announcing that it had ended.

Dr. Fuld was a tireless worker. He arose at 4 A.M. and did not retire until about 11 P.M. At his tenements, he often performed janitorial services.

Once, when he gave some land to the Hospital for Joint Diseases, he explained how he had gotten the tenants out of the houses to clear the way. He did not collect rent for four months, he said, and then announced that in a week he would be around to collect all the money owed to him. Before the deadline, all the tenants had fled.

He could not explain his interest in the health of student nurses beyond saying that they were often exposed to disease and he wanted to improve their lot. "I have never been in love with one, or jilted by one," he remarked.

Dr. Fuld's care for the well-being of the nurses was extensive. He provided air-conditioning for their dormitories, and recreation areas and swimming pools. He even paid for the installation of a traffic light in Trenton so they would be safe crossing the street. Five institutions have Fuld scholarship funds for girls who aspire to be nurses.

In 1962, Baltimore made him an honorary citizen because of his gifts to the Provident Hospital School of Nursing. He often lectured on the importance of health to student nurse gatherings and in 1961 he had the Burmese Ambassador to the United States come to Trenton to speak on student-nurse health in Burma.

Once an interviewer asked Dr. Fuld for a word of financial wisdom. "Here's something you must do," he replied. "Every month when you pay your bills, be sure to pay something to the most important person in the world—you."

II.   Interest-Free Loans to Immigrants, May 1, 1983

On a December evening in 1892, 11 men met at the Wilner [Vilna] Synagogue on Henry Street in Manhattan and pooled their savings—$95 —to establish a free loan society similar to those they had known in their native eastern European countries.

"They would lend out $5 to the next guy off the boat so he would load up a pushcart, make a few dollars to feed his family and slowly pay back the loan," said Nathan Belth, executive director of the Hebrew Free Loan Society. The loans were interest free, as the Old Testament prescribes.

The first year the society lent $1,205 in amounts of $5 and $10. By 1905, some 15,000 families, mostly Jewish immigrants living on the Lower East Side, had borrowed $364,480.

Today the society is still making interest-free loans to immigrants, giving out $2 million each year since 1976. Although the society still lends the majority of its money to Jews, it has been a nonsectarian organization since its founding.

The maximum loan of $750 is given to about 2,500 people each year.

"Often the loan is for an elderly person whose Social Security check is late or when a family has a sudden crisis like a large medical expense or a business problem," Mr. Belth said. We don't ask the reason but by the time they leave, we know what it is. The story just pours out. People feel they have to justify their request. "One woman needed to make the last installment on her daughter's cello. A first-rate one costs $10,000. We've helped a number of musicians."

The loans must be repaid in 10 months, 10 percent each month. They require a guarantee by a credit-worthy endorser.

On the 75th anniversary of the society in 1967, it reported that it had made loans totaling more than $52 million to more than 776,500 people. Since then the society has lent more than an additional $30 million.

Mr. Belth said that the rate of repayment was high. The society figures, he said, that last year all but $100 in loans were repaid, and those who did not pay them back were probably older people who had died.

Among the donors who had helped finance the efforts of the society was Jacob H. Schiff, a banker, who contributed $100 a few months after the society was formed. In 1896, Mr. Schiff sent his second contribution, $1,000. For the next four years, he contributed $5,000 annually. During his lifetime and that of his son, Mortimer, the Schiffs contributed well over $100,000.

Baron Maurice and Baroness Clara de Hirsch, neither of whom had ever been to the United States, donated $6,000 to the society in 1897. The de Hirsches had been organizers of free-loan societies in London, Paris, Cracow, Bucharest and other European cities. In addition, Mr. Belth said, over the years the society has received both small and substantial contributions from those to whom it had made loans.

Few people walk in off the street to the society's office at 205 East 42nd Street. Most people hear about the society through community and welfare organizations, including Catholic and Protestant missions and schools and universities.

Small, personal loans are still the society's main concern, but recently it has started some other projects.

In the early 1970s, it started a program of making three-year loans for up to $3,500 to members of the Lubavitcher community in the Crown Heights section of Brooklyn, who wanted to use the money as part of the down payment on their homes so they could maintain their base in the community. Mr. Belth said the society had made $380,000 in loans to 105 people for down payments. No money has been lost in the program, he said.

Another project provides loans for education in Jewish day schools. Last year, the society began a program of offering loans for college students.

III.　A Survivor of the Holocaust Has a Jar Brimming with Quarters, By Julian Mincer, December 9, 1984

"This is for anyone who comes to the door," said Esther as she lifted a pint jar brimming with quarters out of a wooden cabinet. "I never say I don't have anything if someone needs it."

Eight years ago Esther, a seamstress, had no money. Arthritis and deteriorating eyesight had forced her to stop working. Impoverished and sick, she turned to Self-Help Community Services, a member of the Federation of Jewish Philanthropies, one of the beneficiaries of The New York Times Neediest Cases Fund.

"If not for them I would not have pulled through until now," she said. "I went hungry for many years, but I don't any more."

Esther returned the jar to its shelf and sat down at an old brown table that faced an even older television set. The apartment in the Borough Park section of Brooklyn was warm, and she wore a short-sleeve blouse and faded pink-and-green slippers. A yellow scarf was the only remnant of her brief marriage. As she leaned over the table, numbers tattooed on her left arm in a concentration camp became visible.

"When I was in there I wanted to die," she said. "I wanted to end the misery."

A picture of Esther's parents, taken in 1906 while they were on a trip to the United States, hung on the wall opposite the television. Unfortunately, her parents did not stay. They returned to Czechoslovakia, and at the beginning of World War II, the Nazis deported all 90 members of her family, taking them by cattle car to Germany. . . .

At the concentration camps, the young and the old and the weak, including Esther's mother, were burned to death.

"We survived," Esther said, "because they didn't have time to kill us."

Toward the end of the war, the Nazis sent the remaining prisoners on a death march through Germany. They walked barefoot through the snow-covered countryside.

Despite the hunger and violence, daily beatings and inhumane conditions, she survived. Most of her family did not. The war ended, but Esther's pain and misery continue.

"My arthritis is here and here and here," she said, first pointing to her wrist, her hands and her back, which she rubs frequently because of the pain. "I am always in pain."

"For 15 years," she said, "I had nightmares every night and couldn't sleep. Even now I have them."

After the war, Esther found her only surviving brother, in Paris. It took her four more years to acquire the necessary documents and $180 ship fare to travel to the United States.

"When I arrived in America, I was too sick to live," she said. "I could hardly stand up."

Esther's medical problems made full-time work impossible. She worked as a seamstress and was paid for piecemeal work. Eventually, the pain in her hands and blurred vision from an eye injury forced her to give up her job.

With nowhere else to go, she turned to Self-Help Community Services. The organization, founded by a group of Quakers and Jews almost 50 years ago, serves 1,500 to 2,000 Holocaust survivors in the New York metropolitan region.

Self-Help social workers guided Esther through the bureaucratic maze. They found her subsidized housing and badly needed medical treatment. She now receives a regular Social Security check, and twice a week a home-care worker from the program cleans her apartment.

This time of year, Esther's arthritis is particularly bad, and she rarely leaves her apartment except to go to a nearby clinic for physical therapy. But in July Self-Help will send her to their summer program at Camp Ella Fohs in Far Rockaway.

"We are their last surviving relative," said Edith W. Bayme, a Self-Help social worker of people like Esther, "because many of them don't have any family."

62

Problems and Challenges
1964–1989

I t is obvious that the American Jew has lived in two worlds: an American one and a Jewish one. Every Jew here is at least 90 percent an American; at most he is 5 to 10 percent "Jewish." (This applies even to the Brooklyn hassid, the pietist, who is completely enveloped in the American environment during his work hours.) The English-language literary menu offered the Jew is a tempting one. Thousands of books of non-Jewish character are published each year; there are magazines to fit every taste; the *New York Times* prints all the news "that's fit to print," and the Los Angeles *Times* is not far behind.

Actually these newspapers serve as America's Jewish dailies, for they cater to the almost 2,000,000 Jews in Greater New York and the adjacent states and the 600,000 or so in Southern California. Jews—not as Jews but as cultured Americans—go to concerts, lectures, the theater. Of course there is always the possibility that the play one sees may be of Jewish interest. In 1982, Edward M. Cohen published a 125-page bibliography which he entitled *Plays of Jewish Interest*. When the Jewish American becomes conscious of his Jewish self, he realizes he must maintain good relations with the other 97.5 percent, the non-Jewish whites, blacks, and Asians whom he meets in his office or business from 8:30 in the morning till 5:00 in the late afternoon. More and more he is confronted with the challenge of coming to terms with the blacks, five times more numerous than the Jews in America. It is imperative that blacks look upon Jews as allies in their struggle to improve their lot; some, however, are Judeophobes, and some Jews are probably prejudiced against blacks. The arrival in the house of the weekly Jewish newspaper reminds the Jew that there is another world into which he was born. In 1989, Jewish magazines and weeklies were published in at least thirty states and the District of Columbia; some of them were multimillion dollar enterprises. There are well-edited periodicals for the Orthodox, the Conservatives, the Reformers, and the many thousands who are civil religionists. If the Jewish man or woman or child is prompted to read a Jewish book, a choice from hundreds of titles is available every year in English or Yiddish or Hebrew. The typical Jewish country club—there is one in almost every town of size—is too costly for most middle-class Jews, but membership in the local Jewish Community Center is well within their means. Middle-class Jews can enjoy the indoor pool, the health and fitness spas, the aerobic and dance studio, the Jewish lectures and plays, the automated bowling alley, the kosher or kosher-style snack bar. If they are New Yorkers they can spend a week or two in the Catskill Mountains at a Jewish hotel. This is especially important to those who are single and are thinking of finding a mate. The summer resorts are marriage marts and, if an individual is bashful, there are always the enterprising Jewish men and women, professionals, who will—for a fee—help find a mate. These modern *shadkanim* are computer experts; one punches a few keys and out pops the woman or the man of one's dreams. If there are marriages, there are divorces. The new breed of householder is the single man or woman; myriads of children learn to survive in broken homes.

The Jew, a social being, is fortunate, for he or she has a way of life that offers sustenance from the cradle to the grave, and beyond. (Actually the mother might have gone to a Jewish prenatal clinic; a synagog will say kaddish for individual Jews a century after their bones have turned to dust!) Judaism provides both boys and girls with birth and coming-of-age rituals; the marriage ceremony follows—replete with a photographer and a professional regisseur—topped off by a magnificent dinner dished up by a Jewish caterer. Jews revel in their own distinctive "soul food"; today ingenious bakers offer more than a dozen different kinds of bagels. There are many Jews who are determined to discipline themselves and find it easy to avoid pork and shell fish. Keeping kosher helps them identify themselves as Jews; they feel closer to the rock whence they were hewn, to their parents. During the Passover even the pet in the house may not eat any forbidden food, any leaven!

By the 1960s, after 3,500 years, Jewish traditions were shattered by the rise and spread of feminism. Egalitarianism changed the life of almost every Jewish woman; she is emerging as a human being insisting on her right to all the immunities and privileges of her counterpart male. The Jewish home is threatened; the family and family life are changing radically; no one, no one knows what the future will bring to this institution after years of encrusted, implacable controls.

The first selection, written by an Orthodox Jew, appeared in the *Commentator*, the undergraduate newspaper of Yeshiva College of New York

City; it attempts an analysis of Jewish-black relationships as they were in the 1960s. The second selection emphasizes the ever-increasing problems of divorce; the third and final selection deals with feminism and the emancipation of the Jewish woman, a truly revolutionary change in Judaism and Jewry.

I.   The Roots of Negro Animosity towards Jews,
By Steven Prystowsky, March 25, 1964

The question whether anti-Semitism exists among Negroes is, at first, very puzzling. Why should Negroes hate Jews?

Both groups are minorities. Both are discriminated against in housing, education, and employment. The battle for equality, therefore, is their fight. Furthermore for decades the Jewish people have participated in Negro movements dedicated to raising the status of the Negro by contributing funds and working for them. (The New York Urban League's major financial support comes from Jews. The president of the NAACP [National Association for the Advancement of Colored People], Arthur Spingarn, is Jewish.)

In addition, much of the civil rights progress that has been achieved in recent years can be attributed to the work done by Jewish anti-discrimination agencies. Organizations such as the American Jewish Congress and the Anti-Defamation League have been effective forces behind the drive for desegregation and fair-employment codes.

Thus, it comes as a surprise to the many Jews who support Negro freedom rides, sit-ins, and prayer marches that there are many Negroes who hate Jews. Negro anti-Semitism is, however, a reality. In fact, nobody denies the presence of anti-Semitism among Negroes; only its degree is questioned.

Negro middle-class organizations, like the NAACP, claim that anti-Semitism "is not widespread among Negroes nor is it nourished or passed as a working creed. . . . It is not virulent and exists among relatively few Negroes."

For purposes of analysis, I must discount these views as failing to portray the Negro temperament. The NAACP and similar organizations are middle class oriented whose views neither represent nor reflect the attitude demonstrated by the millions of Negroes living in ghettos where anti-Semitism is prevalent. Another factor which must be taken into account is the reluctance of these organizations to criticize Jews for fear they will withhold their moral and financial support from them. Thus I must concentrate my attention on the rank and file Negro and the communities in which he lives.

Anti-Semitism among Negroes in the United States is principally an urban phenomenon. As an active element it is virtually unknown in rural regions. It is the close relationship between these two minorities in the urban areas, especially in economic matters, that spawn Negro anti-Semitism. These ties include: 1. landlord-tenant; 2. merchant-consumer; 3. professional competition; and 4. competition between Negro and Jewish businessmen.

The closest relationship found between Negroes and Jews in Negro communities and a main cause of anti-Jewish feeling is that of landlord to tenant.

Houses in Negro neighborhoods are usually in need of repair. Despite such deplorable conditions—buildings are over-crowded, unsanitary, and dilapidated—Negroes pay comparatively higher rents than whites. Consequently, the landlords of these buildings are regarded with great contempt by the Negro populace. But it is the Jew who is blamed. Because these communities were formerly Jewish neighborhoods, plus the fact that many apartment houses are owned by Jews, Negroes tend to identify all landlords as Jewish and attribute all housing ills to the "gouging Jewish landlord."

Many Negroes state that they are anti-Semitic because "Jews own everything in sight." One Negro described his plight: "I pawn my watch at a Jewish store, I buy my food at a Jewish store, I go into a Jewish place of amusement, and I buy my clothes from a Jew." This is the economic situation Negroes have to cope with. Since these stores (grocery, hardware, liquor, etc.) are the only ones that will extend him credit, the Negro has no alternative but to shop there though the prices are generally higher than similar stores in white communities. As a result, Negro anti-Jewish feeling is generated.

Intense resentment is expressed by Negro professionals against their Jewish counterparts. The feeling is that Jewish professionals are of service to Negro clients and patients who rightfully belong to them [to the blacks]. They also charge that Jewish firms refuse to hire them and, instead, give employment to members of their own religion.

In governmental jobs there is much Negro antagonism towards Jews. Jews, because they have worked longer, are often found in superior positions while Negroes, on the other hand, are found in inferior positions. It is not unusual to find Negro school teachers working under Jewish principals or Negro social workers taking orders from Jewish supervisors.

The fourth cause of Negro anti-Semitism is the competition or lack of it between Negro and Jewish businessmen in Negro communities. Convinced that Jews can always outdo rival Negro businessmen, Negroes demand that Jews leave their neighborhood. . . .

James Baldwin, in *Notes of a Native Son*, describes the Negro view of the Jews of Harlem: "Jews in Harlem are small tradesmen, rent collectors, real estate agents, and pawnbrokers; they operate in accordance with the American business tradition of exploiting Negroes, and they are therefore identified with oppression and are hated for it. I remember meeting no Negro in the years of growing up who would really trust a Jew, and few who did not, indeed, exhibit for them the blackest contempt."

Traditional Christian belief that the Jews killed Jesus is another contributor to anti-Jewish feeling. "All of us black people," states Richard Wright, "who lived in the neighborhood, hated Jews, not because they exploited us, but because we had been taught in Sunday School that Jews were 'Christ Killers'. . . . To hold an attitude of antagonism towards Jews was bred in us from childhood, it was not merely racial prejudice, it was part of our cultural heritage."

Negro anti-Semitism is increasing with the growing tide of Negro militancy. The Black Muslim movement, a Negro cult emphasizing separation, is openly anti-Jewish and incites the latent anti-Semitism of its followers. The danger of the Muslims lies not so much in their extreme hatred for Jews but in that their hatred is being spewed forth by thousands of Negroes not associated with the movement. Should the Muslims become a major force there is no doubt that anti-Semitism will increase greatly.

The reasons for Negro anti-Semitism are paradoxical; they are the result of both truth and fiction. The fictional part is composed of traditional stereotypes and faulty generalizations lodged in the minds of Negroes by anti-Semitic propaganda.

Negroes refuse to judge each individual Jew by his deeds, but rather lump all Jews into one category characterized by the performances staged by a small minority. He sees one deceitful Jewish merchant and concludes that all Jewish merchants are deceitful. He believes that all landlords in Negro neighborhoods are Jewish because of the popular belief that Jews own most of the property in the area. Even when Jews are collectors for Gentile firms resentment is still directed against him. It is seldom realized by Negroes that most landlords, irrespective of the racial group to which they belong, are guilty of the same practices.

The stereotype of the Jewish store owner as an "exploiter" is common among Negroes. What Negroes refuse to consider is that wherever small businessmen exist prices are high. And the small businessmen in Harlem are no exception. They must charge higher prices if they are to make any profit. Their small-scale buying forces them to pay higher wholesale prices.

James Baldwin has written that "as society must have a scapegoat, so hatred must have a symbol. Georgia has the Negro and Harlem the Jew."

Jews are singled out because they are more easily identified as a group than Gentile landlords and merchants. The latter belong to many religious denominations and are more difficult to blame. As Whitney Young, head of the Urban League, pointed out: "What is mistaken for anti-Semitism is anti-white feeling." . . .

On the other hand, there are many Jews—too many—who, in fact, exploit Negroes. Jews own slum houses, and overcharge Negro tenants. This unfortunately, is true. This type of behavior does more damage to the Jewish image than one-thousand Jewish freedom riders or one-thousand Jewish members of the NAACP do to promote it. . . .

Jews are also guilty of discrimination and hypocrisy. Masquerading as friends of Negroes, they always talk about helping them improve their lot. But they only give Negroes token equality. They speak of equality, but do not practice it.

When Jewish realtors refuse to allow Negroes to move into their apartment houses for fear of losing their white tenants they are guilty of discrimination. When Jews move out of attractive neighborhoods en masse as a few Negroes move in they are guilty of discrimination. This sight becomes too difficult for the Negro to forget and understandably so. Who can blame Negroes for anti-Jewish feelings?

Relationships between Jews and Negroes will undergo difficult tests in the future. There will be many areas of conflict between the two minorities. Negroes will be moving into Jewish neighborhoods; Negro and Jewish businessmen will be competing for Negro consumers; and aspiring Negro politicians will challenge Jewish politicians for control in minority areas.

If the Jews want to reduce Negro anti-Semitism, or at least want to be sure that they are innocent victims rather than contributors, they must practice equality in deeds and actions, and not in platitudes. And this must be done daily. If not, they have only themselves to blame for fostering anti-Semitism among Negroes.

II.   Men Talk about the 2nd Time Around, By Jane Biberman, January 29–30, 1987

Not long after he was graduated from law school, George Meyerson [a fictitious name] met an extremely attractive young woman who fell in love with him. "I was 25," says Meyerson, "and I was conditioned by my family, friends and society to believe that the next logical step in my life was to get married and have kids. Since Ellen was nice as well as pretty, I got engaged without giving marriage much thought."

Now, 25 years and a divorce later, George consider his first marriage. "As time went on, I realized that we were two different kinds of people," he explains. "We shared few common interests and our taste in movies, books and music was completely opposite. I also realized that I was not the type of person to be happy with a typical domestic routine—living in a typical suburban neighborhood and going out Saturday night with other typical couples. I guess I was a maverick."

When his two children were in college and George could afford to do so, he got a divorce. "After the initial trauma of the separation, I really enjoyed being independent," he says. "I had a lot of girl friends, and I didn't want to get married again." George was content with his life for many years, "but as I approached 50, I gradually wanted to settle down again."

Not long ago, he remarried a woman he describes as totally unlike his first wife. "Ann is exceptionally easygoing and has a good sense of humor. She knows how to handle my moods and cope with my eccentricities. She also has a career, and we realize that we don't have to spend every minute together in order to be happy." In fact, George and Ann frequently take separate vacations, as he loves skiing and she prefers golf. "But we also enjoy doing many things together," he says. "Essentially we are both independent people who like to lead an unstructured life without too much routine."

Of course, with the maturity that comes with experience, George realizes that having grown children and an established career permits him to choose his lifestyle, rather than having one imposed upon him. However, he feels that he remarried for the right reasons: love and companionship. "I think it's a 50-50 proposition," he says. "You must have mutual physical attraction and a companionable mate. Because Ann is soft, kind and understanding, I, in turn, am a more considerate husband. It's not the kind of crazy love I felt in my 20s, it's much deeper."

Ed Gottlieb [fictitious name], like George Meyerson, married at 30 "because it felt like it was the right time." And although he says he and his wife had many things in common, they parted two years later because of conflicting goals. Ed wanted to stay in Philadelphia to pursue a career in journalism, while his wife, Ruth, was determined to live in New York, where she was committed to a life in the theater. Ed was deeply hurt by the divorce and was convinced he would never marry again, until a year later when he met Sarah.

"I liked her very much," he says. "And once again, I made an emotional, rather than an intellectual decision, to get married. In many ways, Sarah and I are different, but I feel that people's differences are more interesting than their similarities. Sarah is very goal oriented and I'm not, but we both want to share the important things in life with each other. Perhaps I was more realistic the second time around. I take what's offered and try not to expect the unreasonable. I accept the fact that the human being is prone to error. But underlying everything is a sense of romance and commitment."

Both George Meyerson and Ed Gottlieb consider their second marriages extremely gratifying. In a recent study conducted by psychologist Jesse Bernard 85 percent of remarried people rated their second marriages as very satisfactory. Citing these statistics, Center City therapist Dr. Martin Gelman says that some people learn a great deal from their first marriage because they have had some significant experience in understanding the basic ties that hold people together.

"Some of them are better able to share and forbear because they're more mature and have better information," he explains. "By virtue of being older, people who remarry generally change more slowly in terms of personality and are more firmly consolidated then when they were younger. Therefore, they are somewhat less likely to change and grow apart, as sometimes happens with younger mates."

The second time around, according to Gelman, people tend to be more realistic, rational and pragmatic in choosing their partners. "Unfortunately," he says, "the statistics indicate that the success rate of second marriages is about the same as first marriages: They last approximately seven years."

Gelman is quick to point out that statistics alone are misleading. "They provide one way of looking at groups, but not at individuals. However, the principles that bind relationships together in a fulfilling way do hold for most people. I'm speaking of such things as common values, common purposes, vowing some degree of autonomy to your mate."

He concludes that "all marriages have risk factors, especially if individuals marry in haste, marry for emotional factors alone, or marry too early and do not resolve their inner personal difficulties during their courtship. And that's just as true of second, as well as first marriages."

Whether it's the first, second or third time around, Gelman believes men "still place great emphasis on physical attractiveness, sincerity, honesty, compatible personality, trustworthiness and responsiveness."

Dan Opperman [fictitious name], a successful Philadelphia businessman, concurs. "My standards haven't changed since my first marriage ended 10 years ago," he says. "But I have a better understanding of the good values: kindness, concern, being other as well as inner directed." When he first meets a woman, Opperman tends to look for surface things, "like similar backgrounds and attractiveness" as a starting point. "But more and more," he says, "I want to find a really intelligent woman." Having led a full life as a bachelor, Opperman maintains that he would never marry simply for companionship. "There would have to be a strong emotional involvement."

According to Sally Green, a senior staff therapist at the Marriage Council of Philadelphia, divorced men who want to remarry are still looking for romance. "They want to be overwhelmed by feeling," she says.

"They want to really 'fall in love,' because they were disappointed the first time around." In Green's opinion, most men want to find a woman who is the exact opposite of their first wife. "For example," she says, "a man may complain that his first wife was domineering, so now he wants someone who is totally non-controlling. He thinks he has remarried someone different from his first wife; then, two years later, he comes in to us with the same complaint: His wife is too domineering. He fails to see that he may be making her into that kind of woman.

"A man can't simply change partners," Green explains. "He must change his own behavior, look below the surface. If he doesn't own up to his part in what went wrong with the first marriage, he is doomed to repeat it." In Green's experience, many people think that they've learned from the past, but in reality they tend to repeat patterns.

The success of a man's second marriage will depend, in Green's view, "on how well he has his act together." Her advice to men considering a second marriage is to be cautious. "A lot of men are afraid to be alone and therefore remarry too quickly. They are not looking out of pure eyes because they are too needy. I feel that it's a mature person who can live alone. So I would say take it easy, slow down and make sure you have emotionally separated from the first marriage. The majority of divorced people do remarry, and I think if they take an honest look at themselves, they can make enormous changes in their lives."

III. The Impact of Feminism on American Jewish Life, By Sylvia Barack Fishman, 1989

In tandem with other factors making for change in American society, feminism has had a powerful impact on the American Jewish community. Increasing numbers of American Jewish women pursue career-oriented educational programs and the careers which follow. Partially as a result, they are marrying later and having fewer children than Jewish women 25 years ago. Moreover, a majority of today's American Jewish women, in contrast to the pattern of the past, continue to work even when they are the mothers of young and school-age children.

These demographic changes have affected the Jewish community in several important areas. First, they have created a large population of single adults, including never-married and divorced persons, who are far less likely to affiliate with the Jewish community in conventional ways. Second, they have produced a population of beginning families who are, as a group, older and more focused than beginning families 25 years ago. Third, they have fostered a dual-paycheck work ethic among Jewish parents, which makes both men and women disinclined to volunteer time for Jewish organizations. Fourth, they have resulted in a client population of

Jewish children who are in need of child-care provision from birth onward, and a corresponding parental population demanding that the Jewish
community provide Jewish-sponsored child care for children of varying
ages.

Jewish religious life and Jewish culture have been profoundly transformed by Jewish feminism in all its guises. From birth onward, American
Jewish girls today are more likely than ever before in Jewish history to be
treated in a manner closely resembling the treatment of boys vis-à-vis their
religious orientation and training. Increasing numbers of Jewish girls are
welcomed into the Jewish world with joyous ceremonies, just as their
brothers become official Jews with the ceremony of Brit Milah
[circumcision]. American Jewish schoolgirls receive some sort of formal
Jewish education in almost the same numbers as their brothers. Bat Mitzvah has become an accepted rite in the American Jewish life cycle in all
wings of Judaism, with the exception of the ultra-Orthodox.

Jewish women are counted for minyanim [religions quorums] and receive aliyot [invitations to read the Pentateuch in public], in all Reform and
a majority of Conservative synagogues. Despite vehement attacks by some
Orthodox rabbis, women's prayer groups around the country give Jewish
women of every denomination the opportunity to participate in communal worship and Torah reading. College-age and adult Jewish women
take advantage of greater access to higher Jewish education, with increasing numbers of women augmenting their knowledge of traditional Jewish
texts. Reform, Reconstructionist, and Conservative female rabbis and cantors have been graduated and serve the Jewish community in pulpits and in
other positions. Women hold tenured positions in Judaica in universities
—including the Ivy League—and rabbinical seminaries. In addition, many
women find meaning in traditional and innovative Jewish feminist liturgy
and rituals. Through Jewish women's resource centers, networks, and
publications of all types, Jewish feminists communicate with each other
and increase communal understanding of Jewish feminist goals.

In the Jewish communal world, women assertively pursue both
professional and volunteer leadership positions in local and national Jewish organizations. During the past 15 years, the number of women in such
leadership positions has increased substantially, although neither the number of female executives nor the status and salary level of most of their positions comes close to matching that of male executives. Similarly, female
representation on communal boards has improved in the past decade but
does not come close to equaling that of men. Jewish women who express a
desire for a more equal distribution of communal power have been advised
by communal leaders that they must be prepared to fight aggressively for
that power, including litigation, where necessary.

Despite the mainstreaming of feminist and Jewish feminist goals within the American Jewish community, the relationship between feminism and Judaism remains troubled. Some elements in rabbinical and communal leadership have a "knee-jerk" anti-feminist response to any and all items on the Jewish feminist agenda. On the Jewish feminist side, there often exists a kind of tunnel vision which puts feminist agendas ahead of Jewish communal well-being and survival. . . .

To strong proponents of feminism, the multifaceted flowering of American Jewish women overshadows any communal difficulties which may result. Jewish feminists argue that the personal needs of female individuals are as significant as the personal needs of male individuals. If those needs must be sacrificed for the sake of the family, the community, or *kelal yisrael* [Jewry as a whole], they contend, women should not bear the burden alone. Women will no longer consent to be the "sacrifice" that guarantees the well-being of a male-centered community.

Remembering that women comprise, after all, at least one-half of the Jewish people, it seems appropriate for Jewish survivalists of all denominations to reconsider the validity of feminist goals case by case and to search for constructive ways in which to reconcile Jewish feminism with the goals of Jewish survival. It is hard to imagine what communal good could be served by religious and communal leaders rigidly adhering to an automatic antifeminist stance. On the other hand, it seems appropriate for Jewish feminists, to the extent that they are serious about Jewish survival, to weigh carefully the repercussions of proposed changes and to consider their responsibility to the community as a whole. Indeed, it is one of the achievements of American Jewish feminism that women are now in a position to examine these issues—and to make choices.

63

THE ONENESS OF WORLD JEWRY:
ISRAEL, VATICAN II,
THE HOLOCAUST, THE ETHIOPIANS
1964–1991

Those Jews who are conscious of their Jewishness are also profoundly influenced by the concept of *kelal yisrael*, the Oneness of All Jews. No Israelite can evade the responsibility to aid any or every Jew, anywhere. Here in the United States individual Jews must live exemplary lives if only because they will thus enhance the repute of their people. Concern for one's fellow Jews has induced Israelites throughout all of American history to make provision for coreligionists who have come on hard times. In such an approach, Jews on this continent were not unmoved by apologetics; they were apprehensive lest they be reproached by Gentiles if the Jewish poor became a burden on the larger general community. But the prime motivation that moved Jews to aid their Jewish neighbors was the belief that a Jew in distress must be taken care of by the Jewish community. This obligation cannot be evaded—and it was not. A Christian may well ignore the plight of Christians destroying one another in internecine strife, but if a Jew is beaten in Eastern Europe, the Jew in America is heartsick. Concern for a fellow Jew begins in the local community; the poor and the sick must be succored. To achieve this end, a widely ramified social-service structure was erected. To help America's Jews in every corner of the country, dozens of national institutions were organized to make provision for them medically, culturally, religiously; defense agencies, Jewish schools, colleges, and universities were established.

The more distant a Jew is, the more that Jew's welfare is a matter of concern. When the full horror of the Holocaust was sensed by American Jews, their devotion to Jews everywhere was intensified. Hadassah, the women's Zionist organization of America, collected millions to comfort the sick in the State of Israel; annually, the United Jewish Appeal and the

State of Israel Bonds raise about $1,000,000,000 to make life better for those Jews who have found shelter in the ancient homeland. The American Jewish Joint Distribution Committee takes care of Jews in thirty-some lands where there is need. It has not failed, also, to bring relief to the "Falashas"—the *Beta Yisrael*—Jewish sectarians whose roots in Ethiopia go back to pre-Christian days. The lion's share of all moneys collected goes to Israel; in the 1980s and 1990s Jews in the United States, without hesitation, pledged hundreds of millions of dollars in Operation Exodus to bring Soviet Jews to Israel—and to the United States—when the Soviet Union began to be restructured and, to some degree democratized. (The U.S. government generously shared part of the cost.) The Jews are well aware that Israel is the only country in the world where they, as Jews, are made welcome. American Jews take pride in the technical and economic achievement of the young State; they admire its army; they are pleased that the Hebrew University, the Haifa Technion, and the Weizmann Research Center are institutions of repute. It would be a blow to the morale of every Jew in the United States if the reborn State were crushed; Jews here are fiercely determined to keep it and its people alive.

Unfortunately, the Arabs in Palestine and in the Middle East have never accepted the Jewish State. They believe they have been dispossessed. It is worthy of note that as late as 1946, 64 percent of all Palestine inhabitants were Moslems or Christians; 31.8 percent, less than half, were Jews. After losing four major wars, the Arabs in the Middle East were still unreconciled to the Jewish presence. In the late 1980s and early 1990s, Palestinian Arab youth, fervently nationalist, resorted to harassment and petty violence. The disruption which followed was exacerbated by terrorist incursions from neighboring Moslem lands. Israel became a state under siege (at this juncture one cannot help speculating: Would there have been an Israeli commonwealth if the United States had not enacted the exclusionary immigration legislation closing American doors to Jews?)

Eliezer Livneh (b. 1902), an Israeli sociologist, educator, and legislator was not enamored of the Diaspora Zionism of his day (1964). Because of his love for sensitive American Jews, he wanted them to come to Israel and help inaugurate a spiritual rebirth in this land of their ancestors even though he feared that it was on the verge of becoming just another Levantine state (selection I). In 1965 the Catholic hierarchy meeting in Vatican II was prodded by America's Jewish activists to pass a resolution exonerating modern Jews of any guilt in the death of Jesus. These American Jews, because of their concept of *kelal yisrael*, hoped to diminish the impact of anti-Jewish prejudice in the Catholic world (selection II).

The accusation of deicide—Christkiller—has plagued the Jews for centuries. The greatest danger came in 1933 when the National Socialist German Workers' Party came to power. The leaders of the new Germans were determined to annihilate Jews; they succeeded. Most Israelites who fell into their hands were murdered. This is the Holocaust. Millions of Jews—and non-Jews too—lost their lives. This was the greatest calamity in all Jewish history. No later than 1979, President Jimmy Carter and the American people—sensitive to the horror of the mass murders by the German government in the 1940s—established a Commission on the Holocaust. The chairman appointed was Elie Wiesel (b. 1928), a Hungarian who was later to become a distinguished litterateur and a recipient of the Nobel Peace Prize. He had lost his family in the Holocaust and was incarcerated in a concentration camp when still a child. On September 27, 1979 he submitted his report on the Holocaust to the President, recommending the establishment of a museum. Why a museum? In a subtle—or not so subtle—fashion, Wiesel and his colleagues were telling the world "look what you have done!" The museum might well serve as a mirror to reflect the depravity of one anti-Semitic state and, at the same time, serve as a text to incite the nations of the world to measure up to their noblest aspirations (selection III).

Six years later Elie Wiesel appeared in the White House to receive the Congressional Gold Medal of Achievement. This was on April 19, 1985. It was at this very time that the then President Ronald W. Reagan had consented to lay a wreath on the graves of the German soldiers buried in a cemetery in the town of Bitburg. (Among the soldiers were some members of the Schutzstaffel, an elite group of soldiers fiercely loyal to the German National Socialists.) American Jewry was indignant. The President of the United States was, after a fashion, commending the Germans who had fought in a war that inflicted more than a million casualties on the American people. Wiesel reproached Reagan for his readiness to go to Bitburg. It was no light thing for an American citizen to chide the most powerful political figure in all the world (selection IV).

Though no American Israelite was executed by the Germans the impact of the Holocaust on American Jewry has been powerful, traumatic. The Jews of the United States are well aware that if this country had opened its doors to those persecuted human beings hundreds of thousands of lives could have been saved. The fact that Germany—one of the most "civilized" of all lands—used its power and its techniques to murder millions inclines many thoughtful Jews to believe that no country—not even the United States—is immune from the threats of murderous gangsters. Religious liberalism in the United States has suffered a blow. The Jewish denominations—all of them—have turned to the right; ritualism is in the saddle; myriads have abandoned the public schools for ethnic all-day institutions of learning; humanitarianism, universalism, liberalism—all have declined.

In 1990 a writer, Sholom Stern, was convinced that with the arrival of hundreds of thousands of Russians in Israel it would soon become the largest Jewish community in the world, destined for a glorious future; Israel was "standing on the threshold of greatness." Stern was almost euphorically enthusiastic. What he failed to see or say was that the Israel of tomorrow would probably not survive without the aid of American Jewry (selection V).

American Jewry evidenced its kinship for a relatively obscure Ethiopian Jewish sect in 1991 when it moved politically and financially to help save the *Beta Yisrael*. The non-Jewish Ethiopians referred to the Jews as "Falashas," "strangers," while the Jews in Ethiopia hold to the name "the House of Israel," *Beta Yisrael*. It is ironic; the Ethiopian Gentiles call them "strangers," though these Jews have lived in the land well over 2,000 years; they migrated there in pre-Christian times. It is their belief that they are descendants of a union between King Solomon and the Queen of Sheba. Centuries ago the Falashas were powerful and numerous, but persecution, enslavement, and mass conversion have decimated them. In 1969 the American Association for Ethiopian Jews set out to bring them to Israel. After some hesitation, the new Jewish republic began in the 1980s to fly them to the Promised Land in relatively large numbers. On May 24 and 25, 1991, in thirty-six hours the Israelis transported 14,500 of them to their ancestral homeland. Operation Solomon, as it was called, was a remarkable logistical feat. If the United States, in relation to its land mass, were proportionately to bring in as many immigrants as tiny Israel did in less than two days, it would have to admit about 6,000,000 men, women and children. In selection VI, Helen Davis describes the rescue of the *Beta Yisrael* in the last days of May 1991.

The American Jewish Joint Distribution Committee (JDC) was organized in 1914–1915 to succor the East European Jews, victims of the ravages of World War I. Unfortunately for Russian Jewry the rise of Communism in this powerful Slavic state required that the Jews, declassed, be helped if they were to survive. Millions were expended but even so the JDC was finally driven out of Eastern Europe, out of all the lands dominated by the Communists. As early as the 1960s the USSR slowly—almost imperceptibly—began to disintegrate. (Historians in a later generation will have to determine why this Marxist empire fell apart.) Desperately needing credits in the 1960s–1970s, Russia responded to the threats and promises of the U.S. government—and persistent Jewish agitation—by allowing some Jews to emigrate. The émigrés left for Israel or the United States; funding by America's United Jewish Appeal (UJA) helped make this resettlement possible. Pressed relentlessly by circumstances, and responding to the constant need for further credits from the United States, Mikhail Gorbachev (1985) introduced a policy of "openness" and "restructuring": anticapitalism was ameliorated; thousands of Jews were allowed to leave for the United States where they faced the challenges of Americanization and Judaization. Larger numbers, hundreds of thousands, found their way to Israel in Operation Exodus—freedom. All this in 1989–1990. The U.S. government and the UJA subsidized the Russian refugees who came to America's shores; the UJA also poured millions into Israel to help that State provide for the incoming Russians; in 1991 Jews of the United States promised to raise $900,000,000 to aid the settlement of the Slavic Jewish newcomers in the Promised Land of the ancient Hebrews.

That same year the USSR collapsed; in its stead a new federation of states began to take shape. The old USSR still sheltered at least 2,000,000 nominal Jews. American Jewry was and is determined to assist them and all East European Jews, communities that stretch from Czechoslovakia to the Pacific Coast. Emancipated from an antireligious Communist policy, the Jewish natives will have to reassess their attitude toward Judaism. Confronted with this new Russian Jewish problem, American Jewry will also have to analyze its options. Dr. Jacob R. Marcus of the Hebrew Union College has written an aide-mémoire to clarify the choices facing Jewry in the United States (selection VII).

I.   Does Zionism Have a Future, By Eliezer Livneh, 1964

. . . Let us first summarize a number of facts. Seven and one half million Jews in North America, Western Europe, and the British Dominions and in a number of other lands are satisfied with their condition. The *Aliyah* [emigration] from these countries is next to nothing, and the migration to them from Israel is noticeably greater than the *Aliyah*. These lands, especially the United States, Canada, France and Britain, absorb not only Israelis but also immigrants and refugees from lands where a "Jewish problem" or crisis has arisen. Since the beginning of the sixties they have received more Jewish immigrants than Israel, not only quantitatively but also qualitatively. Professional men, the fit and the healthy, have left these lands, especially North Africa, for new homes in the Diaspora, whereas a large percentage of the immigrants to Israel are handicapped, sick, old, and social misfits. . . .

How do the 7½ million Jews of the Western world of today (with the exception of Latin America) differ from the Jews of Russia, Poland, Roumania, Czechoslovakia, Austria, etc., of the past?

First of all, they lack a Jewish culture; their Judaism has become secular. Their estrangement from a religious, traditional way of life for the past two or three generations has demonstrated that there is no great significance to Jewish secular culture. With the exception of habits which are in the realm of mental reaction, urban Jews of the United States and Britain act like their Gentile neighbors of comparable status. The crumbling of the Ghetto, as a result of which the Zionist movement was formed, came to an end during the period of modern Western civilization. Jews of America, England, Canada, and Switzerland are, however, separated from society in general in different ways. By more or less subtle means society (we will not define it as Christian in order to avoid unnecessary problems) pushes them to separate domains. But within these separate limits Jews live the life of the non-Jewish environment—the same language, concepts, customs, and experience. The point is that both sides accept this reciprocal relation as proper and expedient. A "Jewish Problem" in the pre-Nazi sense does not exist there. The Jews of the West are sure that they will be able to continue where they are in the same form in which they live now—and they consider this the desirable pattern for their future. Jews are not "superfluous" in the American or British economy as they seemed to be in the Russian, Polish, etc. systems at the beginning of the development of capitalism. . . .

The average Western Jew does not fulfill the *mitzvot* [religious injunctions], does not want a separate Hebrew school, has no intention of speaking or reading Hebrew, does not invest his resources or savings in Israel, and neither considers *aliyah* for himself nor would he instigate such a movement for others in his community. When he establishes his Jewish identity (and not without pressure from the non-Jewish community) he seeks to do it in a superficial symbolic way which intrudes upon neither his substantive assimilation nor his roots in the Diaspora (which he is unwilling to view as Diaspora). A monetary contribution to Israel is the least demanding way of exerting oneself for Jewish life. For the Zionist, his donation was one link in a many-sided Jewish network. For the modern contributor, the act of giving is separate, dissociated from his over-all aims and motivations. It is merely an indulgence which aids him in carrying on his daily routine. . . .

After the state of Israel lost its Jewish-European background and its traditional horizons, more than its source of immigrants and active love of Zion was lost. Israel of today is becoming an outcast province of modern Western civilization, without Christian roots—one of the Levantine copies of the West, at the moment a relatively improved version. Is it any wonder that it is unable to exert any spiritual influence on world Jewry, to fill their void with a compelling guiding force? Is it surprising that Hebrew has no emotional or intellectual appeal? It is only natural in these circumstances that English has rapidly become the common language of Jews all over the world and in Israel. And I do not refer to language alone. The scale of values of Western Jews—their concepts and customs, their aspirations and way of life, from the home to the field of entertainment and leisure,—have become the standards and ideal of the Israeli masses. Spiritual decline precedes abandonment of Eretz Israel [Land of Israel]; the former becomes more and more entrenched even when there is no actual emigration. . . .

And what about the Jews of America and the West? Will their purpose always be the maintenance of a Jewish framework, impoverished in Jewish content? Will they continue to assimilate without losing their identity or will they slowly become extinct? Most certainly the aforementioned purpose will remain dominant for some time. But on the horizon we can see a few new signs.

A very small minority has begun to feel the imperfection and shame of Jewish existence in the free world. A yearning for perfection and a need for self-respect are always the lot of the few. They are beginning to recoil from the image of "Americans like all the Americans." They know that Americans—Protestants and Catholics—do not consider the Jews as such. And as for the Jews themselves, their emotions do not coincide with their public expressions. . . .

The more the prosperity of American Jews becomes stabilized and produces its anticipated psychological results, the greater will become the sensitivity of their spiritual elite, and the contradictions of their spurious existence will produce feelings of anger and perhaps embarrassment. Not because of economic hardship but in the footsteps of nauseating satiety the elite of Western Jewry will turn to Israel.

Moreover, as the economic, social, technological, and scientific achievements become greater and the standard of living rises and leisure increases and financial security is assured, the spiritual distress becomes deeper. A profound restlessness, a frustrating dissatisfaction and a restrained indignation seethe to a surprising degree. Among Western mankind there has not been for a long time a period so rife in pessimism in literature, art, and thought, as there is today.

Prosperity seems to produce evil, pleasure results in sickness, entertainment leads to despair, Eros disintegrates into perversion, togetherness accentuates loneliness. At the threshold of the conquest of nature, the conqueror reveals loss of thoughts. What use is there in travelling to space or to the planets if emptiness dominates the heart and there is no escape from the glaring terror within? Man cannot escape from himself, not even to the stratosphere. He is made, perhaps, to evaluate himself with regret for his past.

Western man turns to his own resources, or to other spiritual, religious, and esoteric sources to seek an answer to the streets of "the good life." A substantial number of Western Jews are in the forefront of success and progress. It would not be surprising if they were to be among the first to search for spiritual return. Will a portion of them not turn their eyes back to their own sources? Will they not seek in Zion, where the remnant of the nation and the tradition is rooted, the way to their source in order to re-establish the continuity of the thread which was broken and to bemoan the treasure which they forsook for the sake of the rags in which it was wrapped? The results of their search will be largely dependent on conditions in Israel.

A Levantine province which imitates either demonstratively or quietly the "good life" of America or of Italy will not reach the hearts of the elite of Western Jewry. But we will not deal here with this aspect. Our question is what form will the new groups of returnees to Zion take? It is certain that at first they will be a small and exceptional minority which will attack the worthless, contemptible life of the Diaspora which flourishes and they will steer clear of the familiar Jewish institutions, including the Jewish Agency and the Zionist Organization which is joined and blended with it. They will not need authorization or a contract from the government of Israel. They would not aspire to official recognition and they would not even honor it.

If a movement for return to Zion arises among Western Jews, it will be a new beginning, outside the Zionism of today and beyond the range of its concepts.

II.   The Catholic Church Reproves
Every Form of Persecution,
Nostra Aetate Declaration, October 28, 1965

Sounding the depths of the mystery which is the [Catholic] Church, this sacred [Vatican] Council remembers the spiritual ties which link the people of the New Covenant [Christians] to the stock of Abraham.

The Church of Christ acknowledges that in God's plan of salvation the beginning of her faith and election is to be found in the patriarchs, Moses and the prophets. She professes that all Christ's faithful, who as men of faith are sons of Abraham (cf. Gal. 3:7), are included in the same patriarch's call and that the salvation of the Church is mystically prefigured in the exodus of God's chosen people from the land of bondage. On this account the Church cannot forget that she received the revelation of the Old Testament by way of that people [the Israelites] with whom God in his inexpressible mercy established the ancient covenant. Nor can she forget that she draws nourishment from that good olive tree onto which the wild olive branches of the Gentiles have been grafted (cf. Rom. 11:17–24). The Church believes that Christ who is our peace has through his cross reconciled Jews and Gentiles and made them one in himself (cf. Eph. 2:14–16).

Likewise, the Church keeps ever before her mind the words of the apostle Paul about his kinsmen: "they are Israelites, and to them belong the sonship, the glory, the covenants, the giving of the law, the worship, and the promises; to them belong the patriarchs, and of their race according to the flesh, is the Christ" (Rom. 9:4–5), the son of the virgin Mary. She is mindful moreover, that the apostles, the pillars on which the Church stands, are of Jewish descent, as are many of those early disciples who proclaimed the gospel of Christ to the world.

As holy Scripture testifies, Jerusalem did not recognize God's moment when it came (cf. Lk. 19:42). Jews for the most part did not accept the Gospel; on the contrary, many opposed the spreading of it (cf. Rom. 11:28). Even so, the apostle Paul maintains that the Jews remain very dear to God, for the sake of the patriarchs, since God does not take back the gifts he bestowed or the choice he made. Together with the prophets and that same apostle, the Church awaits the day, known to God alone, when all peoples will call on God with one voice and "serve him shoulder to shoulder" (Soph. 3:9; cf. Is. 66:23; Ps. 65:4; Rom. 11:11–32).

Since Christians and Jews have such a common spiritual heritage, this sacred council wishes to encourage and further mutual understanding and appreciation. This can be obtained, especially, by way of biblical and theological enquiry and through friendly discussions.

Even though the Jewish authorities and those who followed their lead pressed for the death of Christ (cf. John 19:6), neither all Jews indiscriminately at that time, nor Jews today, can be charged with the crimes committed during his passion. It is true that the Church is the new people of God, yet the Jews should not be spoken of as rejected or accused as if this followed from holy Scripture. Consequently, all must take care, lest in catechizing or in preaching the Word of God, they teach anything which is not in accord with the truth of the Gospel message or the spirit of Christ.

Indeed, the Church reproves every form of persecution against whomsoever it may be directed. Remembering, then, her common heritage with the Jews and moved not by any political consideration, but solely by the religious motivation of Christian charity, she deplores all hatreds, persecutions, displays of antisemitism leveled at any time or from any source against the Jews.

The Church always held and continues to hold that Christ out of infinite love freely underwent suffering and death because of the sins of all men, so that all might attain salvation. It is the duty of the Church, therefore, in her preaching to proclaim the cross of Christ as the sign of God's universal love and the source of all grace.

III. Report to the Honourable Jimmy Carter, President of the United States, By Elie Wiesel, Chairman of the President's Commission on the Holocaust, September 27, 1979

Dear Mr. President:

It is with a deep sense of privilege that I submit to you, in accordance with your request, the report of your Commission on the Holocaust. Never before have its members, individually and collectively, given so much of themselves to a task that is both awesome and forbidding, a task which required reaching far back into the past as well as taking a hard look into the future.

Our central focus was memory—our own and that of the victims during a time of unprecedented evil and suffering. That was the Holocaust, an era we must remember not only because of the dead; it is too late for them. Not only because of the survivors; it may even be late for them. Our remembering is an act of generosity, aimed at saving men and women from apathy to evil, if not from evil itself.

We wish, through the work of this Commission, to reach and transform as many human beings as possible. We hope to share our conviction that when war and genocide unleash hatred against any one people or peoples, all are ultimately engulfed in the fire.

With this conviction and mindful of your mandate, Mr. President, we have explored during the past several months of our existence the various ways and means of remembering—and of moving others to remember—the Holocaust and its victims, an event that was intended to erase memory.

Our first question may sound rhetorical: Why remember, why remember at all? Is not human nature opposed to keeping alive memories that hurt and disturb? The more cruel the wound, the greater the effort to cover it, to hide it beneath other wounds, other scars. Why then cling to unbearable memories that may forever rob us of our sleep? Why not forget, turn the page, and proclaim: let it remain buried beneath the dark nightmares of our subconscious. Why not spare our children the weight of our collective burden and allow them to start their lives free of nocturnal obsessions and complexes, free of Auschwitz and its shadows?

These questions, Mr. President, would not perhaps be devoid of merit if it were possible to extirpate the Holocaust from history and make believe we can forget. But it is not possible and we cannot. Like it or not, the Event must and will dominate future events. Its centrality in the creative endeavors of our contemporaries remain undisputed. Philosophers and social scientists, psychologists and moralists, theologians and artists: all have termed it a watershed in the annals of mankind. What was comprehensible before Treblinka is comprehensible no longer. After Treblinka, man's ability to cope with his condition was shattered; he was pushed to his limits and beyond. Whatever has happened since must therefore be judged in the light of Treblinka. Forgetfulness is no solution.

Treblinka and Auschwitz, Majdanek and Belzec, Buchenwald and Ponar, these and other capitals of the Holocaust kingdom must therefore be remembered, and for several reasons.

First, we cannot grant the killers a posthumous victory. Not only did they humiliate and assassinate their victims, they wanted also to destroy their memory. They killed them twice, reducing them to ashes and then denying their deed. Not to remember the dead now would mean to become accomplices to their murderers.

Second, we cannot deny the victims the fulfillment of their last wish; their idée fixe to bear witness. What the merchant from Saloniki, the child from Lodz, the rabbi from Radzimin, the carpenter from Warsaw and the scribe from Vilna had in common was the passion, the compulsion to tell the tale—or to enable someone else to do so. Every ghetto had its historians, every deathcamp its chroniclers. Young and old, learned and unlearned, everybody kept diaries, wrote journals, composed poems and prayers. They wanted to remember and to be remembered. They wanted to defeat the enemy's conspiracy of silence, to communicate a spark of the fire that nearly consumed their generation, and, above all, to serve as warning to future generations. Instead of looking with contempt upon mankind that betrayed them, the victims dreamed of redeeming it with their own charred souls. Instead of despairing of man and his possible salvation, they put their faith in him. Defying all logic, all reason, they opted for humanity and chose to try, by means of their testimony, to save it from indifference that might result in the ultimate catastrophe, the nuclear one.

Third, we must remember for our own sake, for the sake of our own humanity. Indifference to the victims would result, inevitable in indifference to ourselves, an indifference that would ultimately no longer be sin but, in the words of our Commissioner Bayard Rustin, "a terrifying curse" and its own punishment.

The most vital lesson to be drawn from the Holocaust era is that Auschwitz was possible because the enemy of the Jewish people and of mankind—and it is always the same enemy—succeeded in dividing, in separating, in splitting human society, nation against nation, Christian against Jew, young against old. And not enough people cared. In Germany and other occupied countries, most spectators chose not to interfere with the killers; in other lands, too, many persons chose to remain neutral. As a result, the killers killed, the victims died, and the world remained world.

Still, the killers could not be sure. In the beginning they made one move and waited. Only when there was no reaction did they make another move and still another. From racial laws to medieval decrees, from illegal expulsions to the establishment of ghettos and then to the invention of deathcamps, the killers carried out their plans only when they realized that the outside world simply did not care about the Jewish victims. Soon after, they decided they could do the same thing, with equal impunity, to other peoples as well. As always, they began with Jews. As always, they did not stop with Jews alone.

Granted that we must remember, Mr. President, the next question your Commission had to examine was whom are we to remember? It is vital that the American people come to understand the distinctive reality of the Holocaust: millions of innocent civilians were tragically killed by the Nazis. They must be remembered. However, there exists a moral imperative for special emphasis on the six million Jews. While not all victims were Jews, all Jews were victims, destined for annihilation solely because they were born Jewish. They were doomed not because of something they had done or proclaimed or acquired but because of who they were: sons and daughters of the Jewish people. As such they were sentenced to death collectively and individually as part of an official and "legal" plan unprecedented in the annals of history. . . .

Our Commission believes that because they were the principal target of Hitler's Final Solution, we must remember the six million Jews and, through them and beyond them, but never without them, rescue from oblivion all the men, women and children. Jewish and non-Jewish, who perished in those years in the forests and camps of the kingdom of night.

The universality of the Holocaust lies in its uniqueness: the Event is essentially Jewish, yet in interpretation is universal. It involved even distant nations and persons who lived far away from Birkenau's flames or who were born afterward.

Our own country was also involved, Mr. President. The valiant American nation fought Hitler and Fascism and paid for its bravery and idealism with the lives of hundreds and thousands of its sons; their sacrifices shall not be forgotten. And yet, and yet, away from the battlefield, the judgment of history will be harsh. Sadly but realistically, our great government was not without blemish. One cannot but wonder what might have happened had the then American President and his advisors demonstrated concern and compassion by appointing in 1942 or 1943 a President's Commission to prevent the Holocaust. How many victims, Jews and non-Jews, could have been saved had we changed our immigration laws, opened our gates more widely, protested more forcefully. We did not. Why not? This aspect of the Event must and will be explored thoroughly and honestly within the framework of the Commission's work. The decision to face the issue constitutes an act of moral courage worthy of our nation.

The question of how to remember makes up the bulk of the Commission's report. Memorial, museum, education, research, commemoration, action to prevent a recurrence: these are our areas of concern. I hope that these recommendations will be acceptable to you, Mr. President, reflecting as they do the joint thinking of the members of the Commission and its advisors over a period of 7 months.

During that time, we held meetings and hearings and studied known and hitherto undisclosed material. Our hope was to reach a consensus among our diverse membership, which includes academicians and civic leaders, Christians and Jews, native Americans and survivors from the deathcamps who found a welcome and a refuge here and who now, as American citizens, enjoy the privileges of our democracy.

Special attention was paid to the opinions, views, and feelings of the survivors, men and women who know the problems from the inside and who ask for nothing more than the opportunity to show their gratitude. "Our adopted country was kind to us," says Commissioner Sigmund Strochlitz "and we wish to repay in some way by helping to build a strong and human society based on equality and justice for all." Their willingness to share their knowledge, their pain, their anguish, even their agony, is motivated solely by their conviction that their survival was for a purpose. A survivor sees himself or herself as a messenger and guardian of secrets entrusted by the dead. A survivor fears he or she may be the last to remember, the last to warn, the last to tell the tale that cannot be told, the tale that must be told in its totality, before it is too late, before the last witness leaves the stage and takes his awesome testimony back to the dead.

In the hope that you will enable this testimony to be brought to the attention of the American people, and the world, I submit the attached report to you, Mr. President.
Respectfully yours,
Elie Wiesel
Chairman
The Honorable Jimmy Carter
President of the United Sates
Washington, D.C. 20500

IV.   Elie Wiesel, Like a Prophet of Old, Chides President Reagan, April 19, 1985

Mr. President, speaking of the conciliation, I was very pleased that we met before, so a stage of the conciliation has been set in motion between us. But then, we were never on two sides. We were on the same side. We were always on the side of justice, always on the side of memory, against the SS [Schutzstaffel] and against what they represent.

It was good talking to you, and I am grateful to you for the medal. But this medal is not mine alone. It belongs to all those who remembered what SS killers have done to their victims.

It was given to me by the American people for my writings, teaching and for my testimony. When I write, I feel my invisible teachers standing over my shoulders, reading my words and judging their veracity. And while I feel responsible for the living, I feel equally responsible to the dead. Their memory dwells in my memory.

ALONE IN AN ORPHANED WORLD

Forty years ago, a young man awoke and he found himself an orphan in an orphaned world. What have I learned in the last 41 years? Small things. I learned the perils of language and those of science. I learned that in extreme situations when human lives and dignity are at stake, neutrality is a sin. It helps the killers, not the victims. I learned the meaning of solitude, Mr. President. We were alone, desperately alone.

Today is April 19 and April 19, 1943, the Warsaw Ghetto rose in arms against the onslaught of the Nazis. They were so few and so young and so helpless. And nobody came to their help. And they had to fight what was then the mightiest legion in Europe. Every underground received help except the Jewish underground. And yet they managed to fight and resist and push back those Nazis and their accomplices for six weeks. And yet the leaders of the free world, Mr. President, knew everything and did so little, or nothing, or at least nothing specifically to save Jewish children from death. You spoke of Jewish children, Mr. President. One million Jewish children perished. If I spent my entire life reciting their names, I would die before finishing the task.

FRAGILITY OF HUMAN CONDITION

Mr. President, I have seen children, I have seen them being thrown in the flames alive. Words, they die on my lips. So I have learned, I have learned, I have learned the fragility of the human condition.

And I am reminded of a great moral essayist. The gentle and forceful Abe Rosenthal, having visited Auschwitz, once wrote an extraordinary reportage about the persecution of Jews, and he called it, "Forgive them not, Father, for they knew what they did."

I have learned that the Holocaust was a unique and uniquely Jewish event, albeit with universal implications. Not all victims were Jews. But all Jews were victims. I have learned the danger of indifference, the crime of indifference. For the opposite of love, I have learned, is not hate, but indifference. Jews were killed by the enemy but betrayed by their so-called allies, who found political reasons to justify their indifference or passivity.

But I have also learned that suffering confers no privileges. It all depends what one does with it. And this is why survivors, of whom you spoke, Mr. President, have tried to teach their contemporaries how to build on ruins, how to invent hope in a world that offers none, how to proclaim faith to a generation that has seen it shamed and mutilated. And I believe, we believe, that memory is the answer, perhaps the only answer.

A few days ago, on the anniversary of the liberation of Buchenwald, all of us, Americans, watched with dismay and anger as the Soviet Union and East Germany distorted both past and present history.

Mr. President, I was there. I was there when American liberators arrived. And they gave us back our lives. And what I felt for them then nourishes me to the end of my days and will do so, if you only knew what we tried to do with them then. We who were so weak that we couldn't carry our own lives, we tried to carry them in triumph.

Mr. President, we are grateful to the American Army for liberating us. We are grateful to this country, the greatest democracy in the world, the freest nation in the world, the moral nation, the authority in the world. And we are grateful, especially, to this country for having offered us haven and refuge, and grateful to its leadership for being so friendly to Israel.

And, Mr. President, do you know that the Ambassador of Israel, who sits next to you, who is my friend, and has been for so many years, is himself a survivor? And if you knew all the causes we fought together for the last 30 years, you should be prouder of him. And we are proud of him.

Support for Israel

And we are grateful of course, to Israel. We are eternally grateful to Israel for existing. We needed Israel in 1948 as we need it now. And we are grateful to Congress for its continuous philosophy of humanism. And compassion for the underprivileged.

And as for yourself, Mr. President, we are so grateful to you for being a friend of the Jewish people, for trying to help the oppressed Jews in the Soviet Union. And to do whatever we can to save Shcharansky and Abe Stolar and Iosif Begun and Sakharov and all the dissidents who need freedom. And of course, we thank you for your support of the Jewish state of Israel.

But, Mr. President, I wouldn't be the person I am, and you wouldn't respect me for what I am, if I were not to tell you also of the sadness that is in my heart for what happened during the last week. And I am sure that you, too, are sad for the same reasons.

What can I do? I belong to a traumatized generation. And to us, as to you, symbols are important. And furthermore, following our ancient tradition, and we are speaking about Jewish heritage, our tradition commands us "to speak truth to power."

So may I speak to you, Mr. President, with respect and admiration, of the events that happened?

We have met four or five times. And each time I came away enriched for I know of your commitment to humanity.

And therefore I am convinced, as you have told us earlier when we spoke, that you were not aware of the presence of SS graves in the Bitburg cemetery. Of course you didn't know. But now we all are aware.

YOUR PLACE IS WITH THE VICTIMS

May I, Mr. President, if it's possible at all, implore you to do something else, to find a way to find another way, another site? That place, Mr. President, is not your place. Your place is with the victims of the SS.

Oh, we know there are political and strategic reasons, but this issue, as all issues related to that awesome event, transcends politics and diplomacy.

The issue here is not politics, but good and evil. And we must never confuse them.

For I have seen the SS at work. And I have seen their victims. They were my friends. They were my parents.

Mr. President, there was a degree of suffering and loneliness in the concentration camps that defies imagination. Cut off from the world with no refuge anywhere, sons watched helplessly their fathers being beaten to death. Mothers watched their children die of hunger. And then there was Mengele and his selections. Terror, fear, isolation, torture, gas chambers, flames, flames rising to the heavens.

But, Mr. President, I know and I understand, we all do, that you seek reconciliation. And so do I, so do we. And I too wish to attain true reconciliation with the German people. I do not believe in collective guilt, nor in collective responsibility. Only the killers were guilty. Their sons and daughters are not.

And I believe, Mr. President, that we can and we must work together with them and with all people. And we must work to bring peace and understanding to a tormented world that, as you know, is still awaiting redemption.

I thank you, Mr. President.

V. The Revolution American Jewry Is Sleeping Through, By Sholom Stern, February 1, 1990

The *gevalt* [murder] syndrome of always anticipating foreboding political consequences for Israel is a part of the psyche of many American Jews. We have difficulty accepting good news for Israel.

There is a statement in the Talmud that declares that the only difference between this world and the Messianic era is that during the Messianic era, the Jewish people will no longer be subjugated to the nations of the world. Presently the Jewish people have reason to feel good. For the political climate today is one in which Israel is, in a certain sense, on the brink of an era, which meets the afore-mentioned description of the Messianic era. A majority of the 150 countries currently belonging to the United Nations do not have any formal diplomatic relations with Israel. During the next two to three years, the balance will shift, and approximately 120 countries will have entered into diplomatic relations with Israel.

For with the process of internal democratization of the Eastern European countries, there will be a significant change in their foreign policy. Countries like the Soviet Union, East Germany, Czechoslovakia, Bulgaria and Poland, which currently do not have diplomatic relations with Israel, will change this. The ripple effect may eventually include many African countries, who are expected to follow suit. Today, more than ever before, Israel has an excellent chance of breaking the noose of isolation which has gripped her since she became a sovereign state in 1948.

In an address to a group of more than 100 rabbis who were attending an Israel Bonds Rabbinic Conference in Jerusalem in early January [1990], Binyamin Netanyahu, deputy foreign minister of Israel, said that, in his conversations with leaders of Eastern European countries who vilified Israel in the past, he has learned they now talk of establishing democratic governments that will be modeled after Israel.

With the shift of foreign policy of the Eastern European nations toward Israel will also come a much-needed new wave of tourism.

In the moral sphere, Israel will also be entering into a new era. For there is every indication that the United Nations resolution equating Zionism with racism will be rescinded. One cannot underestimate the salutary effect that revoking this resolution will have on the image of Israel in the international community. It is not stretching the bow of credulity to assume that the Arab nations will be isolated politically in a few years if they continue their stance of non-recognition of Israel.

But by far the best news which we have yet to awaken to is that Israel, during the next five years, will probably undergo the most massive aliyah [migration] in the history of Zionism.

We are now being told that during the next five years an estimated one million Russian Jews will emigrate to Israel. While some find such a prediction too high, the figure of a half a million Russian Jews emigrating over the next five years is now considered a sober estimate in many reliable circles. The forerunners to those that translated the Messianic dream of Jewish nationalism into a more contemporary framework, like Theodore Herzl, Moses Hess, Max Nordau and Leo Pinsker, all envisioned a Jewish state where the majority of the Jews of the world would live. While even the most optimistic figure of a massive aliyah from the Soviet Union will not create such a phenomenon in the next five years, the current aliyah is a giant step in the direction ultimately leading to the majority of world Jewry residing in Eretz Yisrael [the Land of Israel].

In an effort to belittle the massive aliyah from Russia currently under-way, there are those who contend that this aliyah is different from all pre-vious aliyot in that it brings to the State of Israel Jews who have little if any knowledge of Judaism or Zionism.

One must bear in mind what Chaim Weizmann once said. "They will come pulled and pushed." Some, like today's former prisoners of Zion—[Soviet Jews] Yosef Begun, Anatoly Shcharansky [Natan Sharansky], Yosef Mendelevitch and Ida Nudel—will come pulled by the dream of Zion as a center for world Jewry. But the majority will come pushed and driven by anti-Semitism.

A brief survey of the aliyot during the first 75 years of modern Zion-ism will reveal a pattern that has its parallel with what is taking place today.

In modern Zionism the first aliyah took place from 1882–1903 with 25,000 Jews entering Palestine. Some of them were consciously Zionist and had come under the influence or auspices of Chovevai Zion, lovers of Zion, or Bilu, an emigration society named after a Hebrew biblical acros-tic, "Bet Yaakov Lehu Vnelcha," The House of Jacob Let Us Go [Isaiah 2:5]. But the majority were refugees from Tsarist oppression.

The second large aliyah emigration wave took place from 1905–1914. There were 30,000 who then departed for Palestine. Possibly 80 percent of the second aliyah returned to Europe or continued on to America within weeks or months of their arrival.

The third aliyah, from 1919–1923, saw 37,000 newcomers coming into the land. Most of the immigrants were simultaneously fleeing revolu-tion, counterrevolutionary pogroms, and civil wars. The fourth wave, 1924–1928, brought 70,000 Jews into the land. Few of these newcomers were animated by Labor Zionist or even agricultural ideals. They were not pioneers. Some rescued a few thousand zlotys from their doomed little shops in Poland. They went to the cities. This group was responsible for making a city out of Tel Aviv. As late as 1921 there were only 3600 Jews who inhabited Tel Aviv, which then was a garden suburb of Jaffa.

The fifth and final aliyah took place between 1932 and 1935. And the Jewish population of the Yishuv [Jewish Israel] doubled its population from 185,000 to 375,000. The majority continued to come from Eastern Europe. Judeophobia of the Polish and Romanian governments made life all but insupportable for their Jewish populations. For the first time, some began to arrive as fugitives of Nazi anti-Semitism.

This skeleton-like survey of aliyot that took place before World War II demonstrates that the numbers that we are now talking about, by comparison, are vast. The first five aliyot saw a number of Jews coming into the land who had been raised on the Zionist ideology from youth. But the majority of them came pushed with no alternative. Our focus is blurred as long as we think of this new wave of Russian Jews [1980s and 1990s] immigrating to Israel as taking place because refugee status is no longer being accorded to them by the United States. Some will be pulled to Israel and others will be pushed. Both groups potentially can make enormous contributions. The real miracle taking place is that despite glasnost [openness] and despite perestroika [reconstructuring] there remains something in Russia that does not permit these Jews to entrust their future to Russia.

Those American Jews afflicted with the *gevalt* syndrome will argue that there is no way Israel can properly absorb a million Jews in the span of five years. What is overlooked is that Israel, from 1948 to 1950, a short span of two years, doubled its population from 600,000 to 1.2 million. Secondly, by saying that it is impossible for Israel to absorb such a large number, American Jews conveniently exonerate themselves of the responsibility of becoming partners in participating financially in the greatest exodus to Eretz Yisrael since Moses led the Hebrew slaves out of Egypt over 3200 years ago.

We are standing on the threshold of greatness. The news out of Zion couldn't be better. At the present time American Jewry is still in a deep slumber, unaware that the revolutions that have taken place in Eastern Europe this past year may yet pave the way for the greatest revolution in contemporary Jewish life.

VI.   Operation Solomon: Flying Ethiopian Jews to Israel, Bribes and Precision Helped the Rescue, By Helen Davis, May 24–25, 1991

"This is a great moment for all our people." The speaker was Israeli Prime Minister Yitzhak Shamir and he made the statement as the first of more than 14,000 Ethiopian Jews streamed into Ben-Gurion Airport last weekend in a heroic rescue operation that added a new chapter to the dramatic story of the modern State of Israel.

With one extended swoop, nearly the entire community of Ethiopian Jews remaining in that war-plagued African nation was plucked to safety in the top-secret "Operation Solomon"—an operation conducted with military precision under the tightest of security nets.

Lending an air of urgency to the operation was the backdrop of advancing Arab-backed Ethiopian rebels thought also to be harboring a grudge against Israel and Ethiopian Jews because of the Jewish state's past military aid to the collapsing Ethiopian regime.

Full details of "Operation Solomon" are unlikely ever to be revealed by the Mossad, Israeli's foreign intelligence agency, but sufficient information has emerged to construct a picture of the dramatic events that unfolded late last week.

Two key Israeli figures have emerged as principal players in the high-stakes drama.

The first is the accomplished Israeli diplomat Simcha Dinitz, former ambassador to the United States and now chairman of the Jewish Agency.

He was the link between Jerusalem and Washington, whose desire to play midwife to the birth of a new Ethiopia enabled the operation to take place. A letter from President Bush to Ethiopia's acting president urging him to let the Jews go helped pave the way.

The second—and even more dramatic Israeli role—was that played by Uri Lubrani, a shadowy figure and the former Israeli envoy to Iran who was first to spot that the Shah would not survive the onslaught of Islamic fundamentalism. More recently, it was Mr. Lubrani who recognized that the bloody, 14-year reign of Ethiopia's Mengistu Haile Mariam could no longer resist the Eritrean and Tigrayan rebels.

His task was to deal with the key officials of that dying, tyrannical regime which had re-established relations with Israel in 1989 and had dealt with the Jewish state on the basis of driving self-interest in the face of growing rebel military pressure.

Ethiopia's Jews were virtually hostages of the regime, which refused to let them leave in large numbers to insure a steady supply of badly needed Israeli military assistance. Mr. Lubrani's task was to cajole, promise and threaten the Ethiopian leaders, to do everything necessary to safeguard them until the rescue mission could be mounted.

"Operation Solomon" was finally activated last Tuesday, immediately after news filtered out that Mengistu had fled to the southern African state of Zimbabwe—an event believed to have been engineered by the United States.

By that time, virtually all of Ethiopia's remaining Jews had walked to the capital from their former homes in the war-ravaged, drought-stricken provinces of Gondar and Tigray. An estimated 4,000 died on the long, treacherous trek, easy prey to exhaustion, disease and roaming bandits.

Meanwhile, about 70 Mossad-trained, Amharic-speaking Ethiopian Jews who had escaped to Israel five years earlier during "Operation Moses" were returned to Addis Ababa, where they melted unobtrusively into the squalid refugee camps and shanty towns where 14,000 Jews had been concentrated.

The day after Mengistu fled, they moved into top gear.

One group left the camps to organize busses that would transport the Ethiopian Jews on the first stage of their journey to safety. A second group told inhabitants of the camps to prepare to leave.

The destitute, displaced remnant of Ethiopia's Jewish community, mostly barefoot and wearing traditional white robes, was about to be dispossessed of its last, precious belongings. They could not, they were told, take anything but the clothes they were wearing—no luggage except for personal religious articles.

At the same time as the Ethiopian end of the operation swung into action, Israeli Air Force transport planes took off from bases in the Jewish state for the three-and-a-half-hour journey to Addis Ababa.

On board were some 200 crack commandos, led by Israel's Deputy Chief of Staff, Maj. Gen. Amnon Shahak. They had already been briefed on their task: to secure the airport at Addis Ababa and ensure the safe arrival and departure of scores of flights that would follow almost immediately.

Less than 24 hours after Mengistu had fled, and with the sound of rebel gunfire clearly audible, fleets of busses, each accompanied by Mossad agents, had loaded their human cargo and were snaking through the deserted streets of Addis Ababa toward the Israeli Embassy compound.

At the international airport, the Israeli transport planes disgorged the commandos who knew every inch of the airport layout from their training in Israel. As they took up their positions, the Ethiopian police quietly left the area.

This was not a matter of luck or intimidation, but the result of another piece of careful planning: Israel had taken the precaution of handing the Ethiopian authorities $35 million in cash "to facilitate the operation."

"Our assessment was that the operation could not be carried out by force," said the Israeli official simply.

With the airport perimeter and buildings under Israeli control, the approaching Israeli planes prepared to land.

At the same time, the groups of Ethiopian Jews arriving at the embassy compound were quickly reorganized into fresh groups and once again put on the busses.

This time they were bound for the airport, where the first of the planes had landed and were waiting, engines still running, to take them to Israel.

For the next 21 hours, the 34 aircraft, packed more tightly with humanity than their designers had dared imagine, made a succession of round trips, landing at Ben-Gurion Airport every 15 minutes (because the operation took place over the Sabbath, rabbinic approval had been required.)

At one point in the operation, a total of 28 planes were in the air at the same time. One Boeing 747, its seats removed and its cabin floor covered with mattresses, carried 1,087 Ethiopian Jews, more than twice its normal maximum load and the largest number of people ever to travel in a single passenger airliner.

Some two-thirds of the immigrants were estimated to be children, and their number was swollen by no fewer than 10 infants who were born during the operation itself, including one set of twins.

Once in Israel, the new immigrants were processed and then taken to absorption centers, hostels and, in one case, to a hotel in Jerusalem for the start of yet another long and arduous journey.

For most, it was not only a journey from Ethiopia to Israel, from peril to safety, from exile to home, but also a journey from the 17th century to the 20th century; a replay of that remarkable event six years ago which captured the imagination of the world when 7,000 Ethiopian Jews had their first encounter with the modern world.

This week, another 14,000 embarked on a journey that will eventually take them, like previous waves of immigrants, into the mainstream of Israeli society.

"This is a great operation that has brought out the entire Jewish community from Ethiopia to Israel," Mr. Shamir, Israel's prime minister, declared triumphantly at Ben-Gurion Airport.

Meanwhile, other, more sober-minded Israeli officials estimated that in addition to the $35 million payoff to the Ethiopian authorities, "Operation Solomon" would cost a further $127 million: 7 million for the flights and the remainder—at a modest $8,500 a head—for the absorption of the immigrants.

For the time being, no one is counting the cost, but coming on top of the bill for absorbing the hundreds of thousands of new Soviet immigrants, Israel will sooner or later face a tough day of reckoning.

VII. Helping Jews in the Old Union of Soviet Socialist Republics, By Jacob R. Marcus, 1990s

The collapse of the Union of Soviet Socialist Republics was a historical event of cataclysmic significance, for the old Russia was the largest of all the earth's polities. We are concerned with its Jews—such as they were after some seventy years of rigorous Communist, anti-religious suppression. Russia's remaining Jews have the option of staying at home, going to Israel, or to some other land such as the United States. America's Council of Jewish Federations prefers that the would-be emigrants go to Israel—a relatively secure homeland—American Jewry will not insist that they come here; assimilating them would be an expense and a problem; this country's Jews have always looked askance at newcomers. Israel has already, enthusiastically, welcomed hundreds of thousands of Russian Jews; the Israelis need bodies, the beleaguered Jewish state of 5,000,000 is surrounded by 70,000,000 hostile Moslems. What is more to the point, Israel and many American Zionists are absolutely convinced that no Jewish community in the Diaspora has a future.

The Council of Jewish Federations favors settlement in Israel; they are well aware that American Jewry will always give generously to Israel and, what is equally important, half of the money raised by the United Jewish Appeal will remain in this country to support Jewry's local and national institutions. However, it may well be that the residual 2,000,000 Russian Jews may decide not to immigrate but to remain and build a new Jewish life for themselves despite East European's almost sacrosanct tradition of persecuting Jews.

An argument may well be made that it is vitally important that Russia's Jews remain and rebuild their communal life. No Jew in the world can be guaranteed inviolable security. It is imperative therefore that new Jewish settlements be established—or old ones rehabilitated—in order that there always will be multiple centers to provide Jewish continuity. The salvation of the Jews is omniterritoriality. The Talmud says, Pesahim 87b: God showed his goodness to the Jews by scattering them among the nations. The comment of the medieval scholar Rashi is enlightening: "If they are scattered they cannot all be annihilated at one fell stroke." Over the centuries, omniterritoriality has saved Jewry. There must be no land without some Jews. Russia's loyal Jewish traditionalists, who had never ceased to maintain a Jewish way of life, have already surfaced and established religious, educational, and cultural institutions, newspapers, theatres, and even a B'nai B'rith Lodge. The Jews who remain hope for a market economy of sorts and a new polity that will accord them genuine equality. They are already being helped by American Jewry's Joint Distribution Committee. All this is déjà vu. In the early twentieth century the Joint rehabilitated Russian Jewry and kept it alive for decades; now they have accepted a new challenge; they have to salvage a relatively small East European Jewry that once numbered 8,000,000 bodies and souls. There will be problems; Israel will compete tenaciously for the American philanthropic dollar; there will be much logic—and sound history—in their arguments.

Russian Jewry may well have a future; the Jews of America should and will help them. I repeat: it is imperative that Jews have "centers" everywhere.

64

The Onset of the Twenty-First Century:
The Future of the American Jew

Most frequently the future is but an extension of the past. Yet there are always "revolutions." Throughout the nineteenth century amateur prophets suggested that the Jew here had no future. They were wrong. The Jewish population has stabilized itself; though there is constant assimilation, there is compensation through immigration: Soviet émigrés and Israelis are pouring in. Jews here live in metropolitan communities, in the suburbs; they tend to abandon the inner city. In the larger United States they are still moving to the Sun Belt: the South, the New Southwest, and to California. At least 20 percent of all Jews in the United States are—and will continue to be—relatively "poor"; the rest, an extended middle class, are "comfortable," if not truly well-off. In matters of finance, making a living, Jews do better than their neighbors; they are white collar workers, professionals; their wives contribute substantially to the family budget. In the future the women will earn even more.

The lot of America's Jewish citizens in matters political is steadily improving; they are relatively numerous in Congress; men—and women too —have graced gubernatorial offices. A Jewish president! Years ago Barry Morris Goldwater and Reubin O'Donovan Askew—both sons of Jewish fathers—were presidential candidates. For decades Jews have voted for America's liberal parties because they are committed to the protection of minorities; Jews are always apprehensive. In matters of secular education no group in the country has a better record; in 1979, 29 percent of Gentile adults were college trained; the Jewish percentage was 56. Jews in relatively large numbers do graduate work, teach in the universities, and stand out as Nobel Laureates. Up to 5 o'clock, Jews and Gentiles work together in the marts of commerce; after 5 o'clock, they each retreat to their respective suburban ghettos. This is what the non-Jews want; this is what the Jews want; in social terms, America is distinctively pluralistic. This country's Israelites are completely acculturated; because of an increasing measure of social acceptance they intermarry in large numbers. As a medieval Jewish poet once wrote: "Love laughs at the paternoster."

So much for the Jew as an American. But what of the Jew as a Jew? Disparities are diminishing in the local Jewish community; the structure, almost all-inclusive, is constantly being strengthened; the town's Jews are Jewishly integrated. The national picture is different; unless the Good Lord provides a crisis, there is little overall national unity; there is no Jewish "congress." Jews are a fissiparous organism; they have always enjoyed thumbing their noses at Jewish national authority ever since King David's day when that maverick Sheba cried out: "Every man to his tents, O Israel" (II Samuel 20:1).

Things are different on the international level. Jews cluster together to help one another; God always provides crises to unite them; American Jews enjoy their role as generous donors to World Jewry. For generations at least, Jews in the United States will solicitously watch their coreligionists in the Soviet Union, Moslem North Africa, divided South Africa, unstable South America. The State of Israel is American Jewry's most pressing, most precious "Diaspora" client. Israel symbolically is World Jewry incarnate; the State must be buttressed, maintained at all costs. Yet, for all this concern, Israel is not—and will not be—American Jewry's arbiter; Jews here will not genuflect in the direction of Israel's secularists or its right-wing rabbis. Over 60 percent of all Israelites in this land have never been to Israel; America is home.

Jewish Americans stretch forth a helping hand to Israel and all distressed Jewries because of a sense of kinship, *kelal yisrael*. Despite constant internal squabbles, Jews *are* one, determined to survive everywhere, at all costs. This determination has been intensified by the increasing impact of the Holocaust's atrocities, by the realization that even here in the United States there is a submerged stream of anti-Jewish prejudice. Intelligent, perceptive Jews, a tiny 2.5 percent of the country's population, are always looking about for allies. They seem to have lost the blacks—almost 30,000,000 strong—many of whom are indifferent to Jewry's problems; indeed, some blacks are militant in viewing Jews as economic rivals. American Jewry works well with the Catholics who realize that the Children of Abraham can never threaten them religiously.

Concerned Jews, survivalists, are divided into two groups: those who are the synagog affiliated and the more numerous "unchurched." (The "unchurched" are not necessarily secularists.) Both groups belong to Jewish organizations, read a Jewish book or an American-Jewish magazine, give to Jewish charities, enjoy Jewish soul foods, and worry about Israel. They may not be conscious of it but they are comfortably ensconced in the local Jewish community; it guarantees protection, comfort, "insurance" for all eventualities. A sick Jew would often rather go to the Jewish Hospital than to Christ or the Good Samaritan. Jews never question the credentials of a kindred human being who says that he is a Jew, shares their anxieties, and rejoices in their achievements.

It has been pointed out above that the American Jews of the next century will be rooted in the culture and the economy of the twentieth century. The Jew has now been admitted unreservedly into America's academic community both as student and instructor. There were already in the 1990s no fewer than 50,000 Jews teaching in American colleges and universities; quotas directed against Jewish students have been scrapped. Reform Jewry has returned to ritualism and has more or less jettisoned its humanistically oriented classicism. By the early twenty-first century, Reform will, most probably, be the largest of the denominations. The Conservatives—now the leading Jewish sect—are moving to the left; in ideology and observance there is not much that separates them from the Reformers. Despite Orthodoxy's militant stance and claims it continues to decline. In Washington—where at most 40 percent of the Jews are synagog affiliated—only 2 percent align themselves with Orthodoxy; in New York City, where the traditionalists are strong, they number 13 percent of those who identify themselves as Jewish religionists. One would be well advised, however, to employ caution in evaluating religious statistics in community surveys. Some Jews—many?—are ashamed to admit that they are not affiliated; on the whole, Jews are not synagog-goers; the Christians have a much better record in church attendance.

The religious revolution is reflected in the rise of Jewish all-day schools, a turning away from the city's public elementary schools. The anti-Jewish American immigration laws and the Holocaust have induced many Jews to turn inward. Large numbers are sending their children to these new institutions of learning; in part, they are fleeing from the free common schools because standards are not being maintained. There is more to this break with the past. Among the Reformers, ritualism is in the saddle; they no longer glory in their classicism. Once proscribed by left-wing religionists, bar and bat mitzvahs bring crowds to the synagogs and enrich the caterers who serve the lavish dinners. Thousands now celebrate Hanukkah and Passover, symbols of political and religious freedom. Youngsters in the temple sing Israeli songs and intone Hebrew prayers; the Torah portion for the week is chanted by teenagers, wearing prayer shawls and skullcaps. Some disport themselves theatrically in their sacred vestments; others, spiritually reborn, reach out devoutly, mystically, to the Holy One, blessed be He. One suspects that the future lies with the younger religionists. There is no record of a Jewry ever having survived through secular leadership. These new young men and women are the guarantors of tomorrow's survival. To be sure they are few in numbers; but then this has always been true of the faithful; this is why ever since biblical days they have constituted the Saving Remnant.

Jewry in the twenty-first century will not experience substantial growth. Intermarriages eventuate in loss for the Jewish body politic, but then numbers are not really important: in the first quarter of the twentieth century German Jewry counted but some 600,000 souls, yet it exercised spiritual hegemony over World Jewry, some 15,000,000 strong. From all indications—statistical surveys made in the 1990s—American Jewry is surviving and prospering in an open society. Jews are Jewish because they prefer to remain Jewish; they are blending Americanism and Jewishness. Because of the fusion of these two cultures they are content, if not happy; they strive to become enlightened human beings. For them, patently, the United States is still "the land of unlimited opportunity."

Acknowledgments

I am grateful to the American Jewish Historical Society (AJHS) for permission to quote from its Proceedings as well as from many of its publications and its manuscript holdings, including all citations from the *Publications of the American Jewish Historical Society* (*PAJHS*).

I am grateful to the American Jewish Committee (post 1951) and The Jewish Publication Society (pre 1951) for permission to quote from the *American Jewish Year Book*.

I am grateful to The Jewish Publication Society (JPS) for permission to quote from many of its publications.

Of course, I am grateful to the American Jewish Archives (AJA) for use of its archival holdings and materials published in its journal.

Specific references to these and other sources, listed by chapter and selection number, for permission to reprint follow:

3.II. AJHS.

5.IV. Reprinted with permission of The Historical Society of Pennsylvania.

9.I-J, I-K, I-L. Reprinted with permission of the Newport Historical Society.

10.I. JPS.

10.II. Reprinted with permission of The Historical Society of Pennsylvania.

10.III. Reprinted with permission of the Newport Historical Society.

11.V. Reprinted with permission of the Newport Historical Society.

13.II. AJA.

14.III-A, III-B, III-C, III-D. Reprinted with permission of Edgar E. MacDonald.

15.IV. Reprinted with permission of The Historical Society of Pennsylvania.

16.I. JPS.

18.I. AJA.

24.I-A, I-B, I-C, I-D, I-E, I-F, I-G, I-H. *The Papers of Ulysses S. Grant.* Reprinted with permission of John Y. Simon, ed.

26.II. Reprinted with permission of the American Association of University Women.

28.III. JPS.

29.V. Reprinted with permission of the Jewish Theological Seminary of America.

31.III. Reprinted with permission of Dr. Charles Berlin.

31.V. Reprinted with permission of the University of Chicago Library.

31.VI. JPS.

37.IV. AJHS.

39.III. Reprinted with permission of *Jewish Currents.*

41.I. Reprinted with permission of Linas Hazaedek of Hudson County.

43.V. From *Henrietta Szold: Life and Letters*, by Marvin Lowenthal. Copyright 1942 The Viking Press, renewed © 1970 by Harold C. Emer and Harry L. Shapiro, Executors of the Estate. Used by permission of Viking Penguin, a division of Penguin Books USA, Inc.

44.I. Reprinted with permission of B'nai B'rith.

45.II. Reprinted with permission of Dr. Charles Berlin.

46.I. Reprinted courtesy of *The Kansas City Star.*

46.II. Reprinted with permission of the *Women's American ORT Reporter.*

47.I. Reprinted from *Enterprising Women,* by Caroline Bird. By permission of W. W. Norton & Company, Inc. Copyright © 1976 by Caroline Bird.

47.II. Copyright © 1974 by the New York Times Company. Reprinted by permission.

48.II. Reprinted with permission of the Allied Jewish Federation of Colorado.

49.I. Reprinted with permission of the Central Conference of American Rabbis.

49.III. Reprinted with permission of The United Synagogue of Conservative Judaism.

49.IV. Reprinted with permission of the Central Organization for Jewish Education.

49.V. Reprinted with permission of *Di Yiddishe Heim.*

49.VI. Reprinted with permission of the Central Conference of American Rabbis.

50.I. Reprinted with permission.

50.II. Reprinted with permission of Temple Beth-El.

50.III. Reprinted with permission of B'nai B'rith and Brandeis University.

50.V. Reprinted with permission of the Council for Jewish Education.

51.IV. Reprinted with permission of Leo Gallin.

52.I. Reprinted by permission of the author Arlene Peck and the editor Edith Blicksilver. *The Ethnic American Woman: Problems, Protests, Lifestyles,* © 1978 Kendall/Hunt Publishing Co.

52.II. Reprinted with permission of Scripps Howard.

54.II. Reprinted with permission of the *ADL Bulletin.*

55.I. Reprinted with permission of B'nai B'rith.

55.III. Copyright © 1990 by the New York Times Company. Reprinted by permission.

55.IV. Reprinted with permission of the Jewish Telegraphic Agency.

56.I. Reprinted with permission of Saul Bellow.

56.II. Copyright © 1978 by the New York Times Company. Reprinted by permission.

57.I. Reprinted by permission of the *Wall Street Journal,* © 1973 Dow Jones & Company, Inc. All Rights Reserved Worldwide.

57.III. Reprinted with permission of Art Buchwald.

57.IV. Copyright © 1990 by the New York Times Company. Reprinted by permission.

58.II. Reprinted with permission of the Combined Jewish Philanthropies of Greater Boston, Inc.

58.III. Reprinted with permission of the Jewish Federation of Greater Kansas City.

59.II. Copyright American Jewish Congress. Reprinted with permission.

59.III. Used with permission of Behrman House, Inc.

59.IV-A. Reprinted with permission.

59.IV-B. Reprinted from *Emet Ve-Emunah: Statement of Principles of Conservative Judaism.* Copyright © 1988 by the Jewish Theological Seminary of America, by the Rabbinical Assembly, and by the United Synagogue of America. Reprinted by permission of the Rabbinical Assembly.

59.V. Reprinted with permission of the Central Conference of American Rabbis.

59.VI. Reprinted with permission of the *Intermountain Jewish News.*

59.VII. Reprinted with permission of The American Council for Judaism.

59.VIII. Reprinted with permission of the Central Conference of American Rabbis.

Source Notes

1.

I. *The Jewish Historical Society of England*, Transactions, 4 (1899–1901):99–101. The spelling has been modernized.

II. *Publications of the American Jewish Historical Society*, hereafter *PAJHS*, 18 (1909):4–5, 19–21.

III. *PAJHS*, 18 (1909):4–5, 9–11.

IV. *PAJHS*, 18 (1909):4–5, 73–74.

V. *PAJHS*, 18 (1909):4–5, 8.

VI. *PAJHS*, 18 (1909):4–5, 19–20.

2.

I–III. Francis Newton Thorpe, comp. and ed., *The Federal and State Constitutions, etc.* (Washington, 1909), 3:1870, 1881; 5:2772, 2783–85, 3052, 3062–63.

IV. *PAJHS*, 1 (1892):93–98.

V. Franklin Bowditch Dexter, ed., *Extracts from the Itineraries and Other Miscellanies of Ezra Stiles, D.D., LL.D., 1755–1794* (New Haven, 1916), 16.

3.

I. B. C. Steiner, ed., *Archives of Maryland* (Baltimore, 1922), 41:202–4.

II. Leo Hershkowitz and Isidore S. Meyer, eds., *The Lee Max Friedman Collection of American Jewish Colonial Correspondence: Letters of the Franks Family (1733–1748)* (Waltham, Mass., 1968), 116–22.

III. *Publications of the Colonial Society of Massachusetts* (Boston, Mass.), 32 (1933–37):107.

4.

I. *PAJHS*, 12 (1904):103–4.

II. Peter Kalm, *Travels into North America, etc.* (Warrington, 1770), 1:145–46.

III. Moses Lindo to Mess'rs Sampson and Solomon Simson, April 17, 1770, MS, Brown Papers, Brown University Library, Providence, R.I.

5.

I. *Boston Weekly Gazette*, Oct. 22, 29, Nov. 5, 1754; cited in Lee M. Friedman, *Early American Jews* (Cambridge, Mass., 1934), 11–12.

II. "Indenture of Isaac Moses," Sheftall Papers, B. H. Levy Collection, Savannah, Ga.

III. Barnard Gratz to Michael Gratz, Nov. 20, 1758, Etting Collection, Historical Society of Pennsylvania, Philadelphia. Translation, except for minor changes, taken from Joshua N. Neumann, "Some Eighteenth-Century American Jewish Letters," *PAJHS*, 34 (1937):79–80.

IV. Isaac Delyon to Barnard Gratz, Sep. 24, 1760, Etting Collection, Historical Society of Pennsylvania, Philadelphia.

V. *Commerce of Rhode Island* (Boston, 1914), 1:96–97, Massachusetts Historical Society Collections, vol. 69.

VI. *PAJHS*, 23 (1915):31–35.

6.

I–III. *PAJHS*, 21 (1913):1–5, 74–75, 90, 93–94, 96–97, 100–101.

IV. [Draft constitution], Henry Joseph Collection of Gratz Papers, American Jewish Archives, Cincinnati, Ohio.

7.

I. *PAJHS*, 21 (1913):72.
II. *PAJHS*, 27 (1920):17–18.
III. *PAJHS*, 21 (1913):85–86.

8.

I. Isaac Pinto (translator), preface and exhortation to *Prayers for Shabbath, Rosh-Hashanah and Kippur or the Sabbath, the Beginning of the Year, and the Day of Atonements, etc.* (New York, 1766), iv.

9.

I-A. *PAJHS*, 21 (1913):72.
I-B. Ibid.
I-C. Hanne Lezade to Sir, Nov. 9, 1761, MS, Lyons Collection, no. 77, American Jewish Historical Society, Waltham, Mass.
I-D. *PAJHS*, 21 (1913):86.
I-E. *PAJHS*, 21 (1913):87–88.
I-F. *PAJHS*, 21 (1913):91.

I-G. Ibid.

I-H. Levy Michaels to the President and Elders of the synagoga in the City of Newyork, ca. 1765, Lyons Collection, no. 131, American Jewish Historical Society Library, Waltham, Mass.

I-I. *PAJHS*, 21 (1913):95.

I-J. Jacob Rodrigues Rivera to Nicholas Brown and Co., May 21, 1770, Brown Papers, The John Carter Brown Library, Providence, R.I.

I-K. Jacob Rodrigues Rivera to Nicholas Brown and Co., May 25, 1770, Brown Papers, The John Carter Brown Library, Providence, R.I.

I-L. Nicholas Brown and Co. to Jacob Rodrigues Rivera, May 29, 1770, Brown Papers, The John Carter Brown Library, Providence, R.I.

I-M. Hannah Paysaddon to Aaron Lopez, July 26, 1770, Champlin Collection, New York State Library, Albany, N.Y.

I-N. *PAJHS*, 21 (1913):107.

I-O. Michael Jacobs to Solomon Simson, Sep. 9, 1773, Lyons Collection, no. 122, American Jewish Historical Society Library, Waltham, Mass.

10.

I. *The Newport Historical Magazine*, 4:58ff., as cited in Lee M. Friedman, *Jewish Pioneers and Patriots* (Philadelphia, 1942), 199ff.

II. Miriam Gratz to Barnard Gratz, Aug. 26, 1769, Etting Collection, Historical Society of Pennsylvania, Philadelphia.

III. Esther Hart to Aaron Lopez, Sep. 3, 1773, Lopez Letters, Newport Historical Society Library, Newport, R.I.

11.

I. *PAJHS*, 27 (1920):177-78.

II. *Commerce of Rhode Island, 1726-1800* (Boston, 1914), 1:338.

III. *PAJHS*, 11 (1903):150-51. The original appeal was in Portuguese.

IV. Petition, May 5 Siran 5533 (1773), Minute Book, Archives of Congregation Shaar Hashamaim (Bevis Marks), London, England.

V. Isaac Lindo to Aaron Lopez, April 17, 1774, Lopez Letters, Newport Historical Society Library, Newport, R.I.

12.

I. Francis Newton Thorpe, comp. and ed., *The Federal and State Constitutions, etc.* (Washington, D.C., 1909), 1:3-6.

II. Lee M. Friedman, *Jewish Pioneers and Patriots* (Philadelphia, 1942), 144-45.

III. Thorpe, *Federal and State Constitutions*, 3:1686, 1689-90, 1700.

IV. Ibid., 5:2635-37.

V. *The Freeman's Journal*, Philadelphia, Jan. 21, 1784. Printed in Charles Edward Russell, *Haym Salomon and the Revolution* (New York, 1930), 301-3.

VI. Thorpe, *Federal and State Constitutions*, 2:957-62.

VII.   *PAJHS*, 2 (1894):108–10.

VIII.   Thorpe, *Federal and State Constitutions*, 1:19–35.

IX.   *Journal of the Assembly of the State of New York, 1787–1790* (New York), 66–67.

X.   There are many versions of this speech; see for instance *PAJHS*, 16 (1907):68–71; Joseph L. Blau and Salo W. Baron, eds., *The Jews of the United States, 1790–1840: A Documentary History* (New York, 1963), 1:29–32.

13.

I.   Frances Sheftall to [Mordecai] Sheftall, July 20, 1780, Sheftall Papers, B. H. Levy Collection, Savannah, Ga.

II.   Petition to the People of Philadelphia, April 30, 1788, Archives, Mikveh Israel, Philadelphia.

III-A.   *PAJHS*, 3 (1895):90–92.

III-B.   *PAJHS*, 3 (1895):91–92.

IV.   M. M. Noah, *Correspondence and Documents Relative to the Attempt to Negotiate for the Release of the American Captives at Algiers, etc.* (Washington City, 1816), 82ff.

14.

I.   Poems, Grace Nathan Papers, American Jewish Historical Society, Waltham, Mass.

II.   Charleston Section, Council of Jewish Women, *Secular and Religious Works of Penina Moïse, etc.* (Charleston, S.C., 1911), v, 177; Penina Moïse, *Fancy's Sketch Book* (Charleston, S.C., 1833), 97–98.

III-A.   Edgar E. MacDonald, ed., *The Education of the Heart: The Correspondence of Rachel Mordecai Lazarus and Maria Edgeworth* (Chapel Hill: University North Carolina Press, 1977), 111.

III-B.   Rachel Mordecai to George W. Mordecai, 6 Oct. 1831, Mordecai Papers, North Carolina Department of Archives and History, Raleigh. Printed in MacDonald, ed., *Education of the Heart*, 212.

III-C.   MacDonald, ed., *Education of the Heart*, 274.

III-D.   Ibid., 305–7.

IV.   *PAJHS*, 27 (1920):301–2.

V.   Poem, Joseph Lyons Diary, May 23, 1834, American Jewish Archives, Cincinnati, Ohio.

VI.   Octavia Harby Moses, *A Mother's Poems: A Collection of Verses* (n.p., 1915), 11.

15.

I.   *Freeman's Journal, or North-American Intelligencer*, Nov. 16, 1782; printed in *American Jewish Archives* (hereafter AJA) 27 (Nov. 1975 #1):208–9.

II.   "Advertisement," *South-Carolina State Gazette*, 6 Sep. 1794; printed in Barnett A. Elzas, *The Jews of South Carolina, etc.* (Philadelphia, 1905), 129–30.

III. *PAJHS*, 27 (1920):339–40.

IV. Sally Etting to Ben [Etting], May 19, 1825, Etting Collection, Historical Society of Pennsylvania.

V. Claim of Lewis H. Polock, United States-Mexico Claims Commission, 1848, November Term, Claim No. 159. Folder 18, National Archives.

16.

I. Edward Davis, *The History of Rodeph Shalom Congregation, Philadelphia,* 1802–1926 (Philadelphia, 1926), 15–21.

II. Hannah Adams, *The History of the Jews from the Destruction of Jerusalem to the Nineteenth Century* (Boston, 1812), 2:215ff.

17.

I. *AJA*, 27 (Nov. 1975 #2):239–42.

II. Letter, Rachel Lazarus to Parents, The Henry Joseph Collection of Gratz Papers, American Jewish Archives, Cincinnati, Ohio.

III. Discourse Delivered at the Consecration of the Synagogue of the Hebrew Congregation, Beth Shalome in the City of Richmond, Virginia, on the Last Day of Elul, 5582, Corresponding with Sunday, 15th Sept'r, 1822, By a Member of the Congregation (Jacob Mordecai, Esq.), 30ff., American Jewish Archives, Cincinnati, Ohio.

IV. Elzas, *Jews of South Carolina*, 161–63.

18.

I. Bertram Wallace Korn, *Eventful Years and Experiences: Studies in Nineteenth Century American Jewish History* (Cincinnati, 1954), 199–200.

II. To the Jewish Inhabitants of Philadelphia, March 8, 1835, Leeser Papers, American Jewish Historical Society Library, Waltham, Mass.

III. *PAJHS*, 42 (1952–53):399–404.

19.

I. An Israelite, *Israel Vindicated: Being a Refutation of the Calumnies Propagated Respecting the Jewish Nation etc.* (New York, 1820), 29–32.

II. Isaac Leeser, *Discourses on the Jewish Religion* (Philadelphia, 1866–1867), 2:172–76.

III. Isaac Leeser, *Claims of the Jews to an Equality of Rights, etc.* (Philadelphia, 5601 [1840]), 10–12.

20.

I. *The Constitution of the Female Hebrew Benevolent Society of Philadelphia* (Philadelphia, 1825–1838), 3–8.

II. *Constitution and By-Laws of the United Hebrew Beneficent Society of Philadelphia . . . Instituted . . . A.M. 5582, June 16, 1822* (Philadelphia, 1837).

21.

I.   "Memoir," Raphael Moses Collection, American Jewish Archives, Cincinnati, Ohio.

II.   Register of Mesne Conveyances and Judge of Probate, Charleston, S.C., Will Book, 45(1845–1851), 581–83.

22.

I.   Mordecai M. Noah, *Discourse Delivered at the Consecration of the Synagogue of Kehillah Kedoshah Shearith Yisrael in the City of New York on Friday, the 10th of Nisan, 5578, Corresponding with the 17th of April, 1818* (New York, 1818), 27–28.

II.   *PAJHS*, 8 (1900):106ff.

III.   *PAJHS*, 21 (1913):230ff.

IV.   *PAJHS*, 10 (1902):98–99.

V.   *PAJHS*, 8 (1900):143–44.

VI.   *Persecution of the Jews in the East, Containing the Proceedings of a Meeting Held at the Synagogue Mikveh Israel, Philadelphia, on Thursday Evening, the 28th of Ab, 5600, Corresponding with the 27th of August, 1840* (Philadelphia, 1840), 18–22, 29–30.

23.

I.   Isaac Jalonick to Isaac Leeser, May 20, 1853, Isaac Leeser Papers, Annenberg Research Institute, Philadelphia.

II.   *PAJHS*, 22 (1914):167–69. Translated from the German by Aaron Levine.

III.   *Die Deborah*, 6 (8 May 1861):38.

IV.   Getty Bachman to Heinrich Bachman, Sep. 30, 1880, Letters, American Jewish Archives, Cincinnati, Ohio.

24.

I-A.   *PAJHS*, 17 (1909):71ff. See also John Y. Simon, ed., *The Papers of Ulysses S. Grant* (Carbondale, 1977), 6:283.

I-B.   *PAJHS*, 17 (1909):71ff.

I-C.   *PAJHS*, 17 (1909):71ff. See also Simon, ed., *Papers*, 7:9, note 1.

I-D.   *PAJHS*, 17 (1909):71ff. See also Simon, ed., *Papers*, 7:56–57.

I-E.   *PAJHS*, 17 (1909):71ff. See also Simon, ed., *Papers*, 7:50.

I-F.   *PAJHS*, 17 (1909):117.

I-G.   *PAJHS*, 17 (1909):71ff.

I-H.   *PAJHS*, 17 (1909):71ff.

I-I.   *Occident*, 26 (Jan. 1869 #10):440–41.

II.   *PAJHS*, 24 (1916):13.

25.

I.   Phoebe Yates Levy Pember, *A Southern Woman's Story* (New York, 1879), 36ff.

II. "First Americans and Then Israelites," *American Israelite*, 23 Aug. 1872, p. 8.

III. Anonymous, *The American Jew: An Exposé of His Career* (New York, 1888), 5–7, 31–32, 81–82, 87, 133, 191–92.

26.

I. This article is reprinted from a brochure in the Phillips Collection, Division of Manuscripts, Library of Congress.

II. *Journal of the American Association of University Women* (June 1938): 226ff.

27.

I. *AJA*, 13 (Nov. 1961 #2):174–75.

II. Isidore Straus, *Autobiography* (New York, 1911). Typescript copy in American Jewish Archives, Cincinnati, Ohio.

III. *The American Jewess*, 1 (May 1895 #5):67–70.

28.

I. *Occident*, 3 (July 1845 #4):175–76, 3 (Aug. 1845 #5): 217–27; 6 (Dec. 1848 #9):421–36.

II. Board of Delegates of American Israelites and the Union of American Hebrew Congregations, compiler, *Statistics of the Jews of the United States* (Cincinnati, 1880), 55–59.

III. Charles Reznikoff, editor, *Louis Marshall, Champion of Liberty, etc.* (Philadelphia, 1957), 21–23.

29.

I. *Proceedings of the First General Convention, and Preamble, Constitution, and By-Laws of the Union of American Hebrew Congregations, etc.* (Cincinnati, 1873), 22–23.

II. *AJA*, 25 (April 1973 #1):20.

III. *Proceedings of the Pittsburg Rabbinical Conference, November 16, 17, 18, 1885, etc.* (n.p., 1923), 5ff.

IV. *Constitution and By-Laws of the Jewish Theological Seminary Association, etc.* (New York, 1886), 2–3.

V. Cyrus Adler, ed., *The Jewish Theological Seminary of America: Semi-Centennial Volume* (New York, 1939), 178.

VI. "What a Jewish Girl Would not Do if She Were a Rabbi," Ray Frank, *Jewish Messenger*, May 23, 1890.

VII. Isidore Singer, ed. *The Jewish Encyclopedia* (New York, 1901–1906), vol. 4, p. 217.

30.

I.   Rules and Regulations of the Polonies Talmud Torah School, Lyons Collection, American Jewish Historical Society, Waltham, Mass.

II.   I. J. Benjamin, *Three Years in America, 1859–1862* (Philadelphia, 1956), 1:85–87.

III.   Charles Reznikoff, ed., *Louis Marshall, Champion of Liberty* (Philadelphia, 1957), 894–97.

IV.   Louis D. Brandeis, "Call to the Educated Jew," *Menorah Journal*, 1 (Jan. 1915 #1):13–17.

31.

I.   *Constitution and By-Laws of the Chebra Achim Rachmonim* (San Francisco, 1872), 7ff.

II.   *Papers of the Jewish Women's Congress Held at Chicago, September 4, 5, 6 and 7, 1893* (Philadelphia, 1894), 218, 225–30, 264–65.

III.   Charles Berlin, ed., *American Jewish Ephemera: A Bicentennial Exhibition from the Judaica Collection of the Harvard College Library* (Cambridge, Mass., 1977), No. 31.

IV.   *American Jewish Year Book*, 23 (1921–22):269.

V.   Jacob Schiff to Julius Rosenwald, Nov. 21, 1918, Julius Rosenwald Papers, University of Chicago Library, Chicago, Ill.

VI.   Robert Morris and Michael Freund, eds., *Trends and Issues in Jewish Social Welfare in the United States, 1859–1952, etc.* (Philadelphia, 1966), 234–39.

32.

I.   Mordecai Benjamin to Isaac Leeser, Nov. 28, 1858, Isaac Leeser Papers, Annenberg Research Institute, Philadelphia.

II.   Marriage Announcement, Isaac Mayer Wise Papers, American Jewish Archives, Cincinnati, Ohio.

III.   *The Jewish Times*, May 12, 1876.

IV.   *Constitution, Phoenix Club, Cincinnati, 1897*. American Jewish Archives, Cincinnati, Ohio.

33.

I.   *Proceedings in Relation to the Mortara Abduction Mass Meeting at Musical Hall, San Francisco, California, January, 1859, etc.* (San Francisco, 1859), 3–5, 11–13.

II.   *Foreign Relations, 1905*, 680ff.; cited in *American Jewish Year Book* 8 (1906–7): 94–98.

III.   Cyrus Adler, *Jacob H. Schiff: His Life and Letters* (Garden City, New York, 1928), 2:98–99.

34.

I.   *Annals of the American Academy of Political and Social Science*, 27 (1906):627–37.

II.   Simon Wolf, *The Presidents I Have Known from 1860–1918* (Washington, D.C., 1918), 310–13.

35.

I.   Congress, House Committee, *Medal of Honor, 1863–1968*, 60th Congress, 2d sess., 1968, Committee Print 444, 449, 462.

II.   *The Jewish Tribune*, Jan. 1, 1929, p. 5.

III-A.   *Yiddishes Tageblatt*, July 4, 1924.

III-B.   *Der Tog*, July 4, 1924.

III-C.   *Freiheit*, July 4, 1924.

36.

I.   Hutchins Hapgood, *The Spirit of the Ghetto: Studies of the Jewish Quarter in New York* (New York, 1909), 79–85.

II.   *American Jewish Year Book*, 49(1947–48):49–66.

37.

I.   *Papers of the Jewish Women's Congress* (Philadelphia, 1894), 91ff.

II.   Philip Cowen, *Memoirs of an American Jew* (New York, 1932), 100–101.

III.   *Annals of the American Academy of Political and Social Science*, 69 (Whole No. 158, Jan. 1917): 183–96.

IV.   *American Jewish Historical Quarterly*, 58 (Sept. 1968 #1):15–22.

38.

I.   *The Jewish Communal Register of New York City, 1917–1918* (New York, 1918), 57–58.

II.   *American Jewish Year Book* 17 (1915–16): 377–79.

III.   Ibid., 21 (1919–20):186–88.

39.

I.   *AJA*, 17:179.

II.   *Constitution of Hevrah Sons of Israel in Camden, New Jersey (1894)*, English and Yiddish. The translation was made by Carol Frank Glatz and Leo Frank. Minor changes have been made in the translation.

III.   Max Rosenfeld, trans., *Jewish Currents* (July–Aug., 1981): 26ff.

IV.   *Shas Tehinnah, Rav Peninnim, etc.* (New York, 1916), 209–11.

40.

I. Ruth Sapin(sky) Hurwitz, "A Hoosier Twig," *Menorah Journal*, xxxv (Winter 1947) 1:111–26.

II. *AJA*, 7 (Jan. 1955 #1):104–6.

III. *The Jewish Communal Register of New York City, 1917–1918* (New York, 1918), 1211–13.

IV. Alexander M. Dushkin, *Jewish Education in New York City* (New York, 1918), 66–72, 76–78.

V. *The Jewish Communal Register of New York City*, 612–16.

41.

I. *Constitution and By-Laws of the Brotherly Benevolent Association Linas Hazedeck of Hudson County, Inc. Organized February 5, 1892. Revised and Effective as of January 1, 1976* (n.p., n.d.).

II. Mrs. Simon Kander and Mrs. Henry Schoenfeld, eds., *The Way to a Man's Heart Under the Auspices of "The Settlement"* (Milwaukee, 1903), 4–5.

III. *The Jewish Communal Register of New York City*, 689–92.

IV. *Jewish Forum*, Aug., 1924.

42.

I. Charles S. Bernheimer, ed., *The Russian Jew in the United States, etc.* (Philadelphia, 1905), 222–32.

43.

I. *Central Conference of American Rabbis Yearbook*, 7 (1897–98):x–xii.

II. Isaac Landman, ed. *The Universal Jewish Encyclopedia* (New York, 1939–43), vol. 1, p. 103.

III. *Universal Jewish Encyclopedia*, 1 (1939–43):45–49.

IV. *Menorah Journal*, 1 (Jan. 1915 #1):17–19; *Brandeis on Zionism: A Collection of Addresses and Statements by Louis D. Brandeis, etc.* (Washington, D.C., 1942), 59–69.

V. Marvin Lowenthal, *Henrietta Szold: Life and Letters* (New York, 1942), 191–96.

VI. M. E. Ravage, *The Jew Pays: A Narrative of the Consequences of the War to the Jews of Eastern Europe, and of the Manner in Which Americans Have Attempted to Meet Them* (New York, 1919), 35–39.

VII. *Ibid.*, 45–46.

VIII. *Ibid.*, 65–67, 73–74.

44.

I. *B'nai B'rith Magazine* (May 1933): 233, 249, 255.

II.   New York, *Law Against Discrimination* (1945), 1ff., art. 12, secs. 125–36.

III.   Veto Message of Harry S. Truman to Congress, 82d Cong., 2d sess., June 25, 1952, House Doc. 520, 8225–28.

45.

I.   Abby G. A. Rockefeller to John, Nelson, and Laurance Rockefeller, Jan. 1928, Letters, American Jewish Archives, Cincinnati, Ohio.

II.   Charles Berlin, ed., *American Jewish Ephemera: A Bicentennial Exhibition from the Judaica Collection of the Harvard College Library* (Cambridge, Mass., 1977), plate no. 23.

III.   Isaac E. Rontch, ed., *Jewish Youth at War: Letters from American Soldiers* (New York, 1945), 153–55.

IV.   News Release, Bureau of Jewish Employment Problems, Chicago, 1954.

V.   Jewish Braille Institute to Mrs. Hilda Weingart, Nov. 13, 1958. Marcus Collections, American Jewish Archives, Cincinnati, Ohio.

46.

I.   *Kansas City Star*, 1952, reprinted in *Milwaukee Wochenblat-Jewish Press*, New Year issue, 1954 (5715).

II.   *Women's American ORT Reporter* (March–April, 1979): 13ff., 18.

47.

I.   Caroline Bird, *Enterprising Women* (New York, 1976), 199–203.

II.   Albin Krebs, "Samuel Goldwyn Dies at 91," *New York Times*, Feb. 1, 1974, pp. 1, 34C.

48.

I.   *Proposed By-Laws of Jewish Community Council of Essex County* (Newark, N.J., [1945]), 1ff., typescript in American Jewish Archives, Cincinnati, Ohio.

II.   *Constitution of the Allied Jewish Community Council of Denver, 1949* (Denver, 1949), 1–2, 9.

III.   Ruth Hershman, ed., *The American Jewish Conference. Proceedings of the Fourth Session. November 29–December 1, 1947, Chicago, Illinois* (New York, 1948), 253–56.

49.

I.   *Central Conference of American Rabbis Yearbook* 48 (1937):98–99.

II.   *AJA*, 25 (April 1973 #1):56–58.

III.   Simon Greenberg, *The Conservative Movement in Judaism, An Introduction* (New York, 1955), 17–26.

IV. *Illustrated Bulletin of the Second National Convention of the Agudas Neshei Ubenois Chabad of the United States and Canada, 26th of Iyar, 5717* (Brooklyn, 1958), 6–7.

V. *Di Yiddishe Heim (The Jewish Home)* 1 (no. 2): 9–10.

VI. *CCAR Journal (Central Conference of American Rabbis),* 8 (no. 1): 3–5.

50.

I. Karl Shapiro, "The Mezuza," *Jewish News* (Detroit) June 23, 1978, p. 4.

II. *Bulletin of Temple Beth-El*, Great Neck, Long Island, March, 1943.

III. Maurice L. Zigmond, "Brandeis University Is One Year Old," *National Jewish Monthly*, Sep., 1949.

IV. Mrs. Allen I. Edles, "America's Leaders Look at Woman's Role Today," commencement address (Yeshiva University, New York, 1958).

V. Alvin Irwin Schiff, *The Jewish Day School in America* (New York, 1966), 264–65.

51.

I. Joseph A. Rosen, *Founding a New Life for Suffering Thousands. Report of Dr. Joseph A. Rosen on Jewish Colonization Work in Russia, etc.* (New York, 1925), 7, 40, 42, 47.

II. *Hadassah Silver Jubilee Year Book, 1937* (New York, 1937), 4–6.

III. Governor Herbert H. Lehman, Address at Emergency Conference of the United Jewish Appeal at the Harmonie Club, New York City, April 2, 1939.

IV. *The Jewish Journal of Greater Los Angeles* (Aug. 22–28, 1986): 12.

V. *Reports of the Secretary and the Treasurer John Simon Guggenheim Memorial Foundation* (New York, 1955, 1956), 12ff.

52.

I. In Edith Blicksilver, ed., *The Ethnic American Woman: Problems, Protests, Lifestyle* (Dubuque, Iowa, 1978), 14–16.

II. Irving Leibowitz, "Treat Your Sister Like a Little Lady," *Indianapolis Times*, May 2, 1958.

III. *American Jewish Year Book,* 61 (1961):92–94.

53.

I. Memoirs of Chaplain Abraham J. Klausner's experiences in Germany, 1945–1947. Copy in Marcus Collections, American Jewish Archives.

II. Israel Provisional Government. *Official Gazette* (Tel Aviv), May 14, 1948.

III. *American Jewish Year Book,* 53 (1952):565–68.

54.

I. Public Law 83–352, 85th Cong., (July 2, 1964), H.R. 7152.

II.   Jill L. Kahn, *Church-State Relations in America Today*, condensed from Anti-Defamation League *Bulletin,* 40 (10); reprinted in *Jewish Digest* (Feb. 1984): 19–22.

55.

I.   Alfred Jospe, *The Campus: Conflict or Challenge?* (brochure; Washington, D.C., ca. 1970), 4ff.

II.   This anonymous circular was distributed in Cincinnati in the 1980s.

III.   Eric Pace, "Arthur J. Goldberg Dies at 81. Ex-Justice Held Top U.S. Jobs," *New York Times,* Jan. 20, 1990.

IV.   "Noted Golfer Quits Country Club After Jewish Membership is Denied," *Community News Reporter,* Dec. 7, 1990, pp. 1–2. Published by the Jewish Telegraphic Agency.

56.

I.   Paper presented on receiving the Anti-Defamation League America's Democratic Legacy Award, Nov. 14, 1976.

II.   Rosalyn Yalow, Editorial, *New York Times,* June 12, 1978, p. A19.

57.

I.   Roger Ricklefs, "A German Jewish Refugee Entrepreneur Sells Canaries, Gerbils, and Guppies," *Wall Street Journal,* June 21, 1973, p. 40.

II.   Arthur F. Burns to Elliot, May 4, 1976, American Jewish Archives, Cincinnati, Ohio.

III.   *Jewish Digest* (Sep. 1976): 75–76. My thanks to Mr. Art Buchwald, Washington, D.C., for permission to publish this letter.

IV.   Christopher Buckley, *New York Times Book Review,* Nov. 4, 1990, pp. 1, 40–41.

58.

I.   *American Jewish Year Book,* 66 (1966):230–31.

II.   *The 1985 CJP [Combined Jewish Philanthropies of Greater Boston] Demographic Study. Highlights* (Boston, 1985).

III.   Gary A. Tobin, Robert C. Levy, Samuel H. Asher, *A Demographic Study of the Jewish Community of Greater Kansas City. Executive Summary, 1986* (Kansas City, Mo., 1986).

59.

I.   *American Jewish Archives,* 31 (July 1963): 80ff.

II.   Michael Wyschogrod, "The Many Voices of Orthodoxy," *Congress Bi-Weekly,* Dec. 19, 1966, pp. 9–11.

III.   Sally Priesand, *Judaism and the New Woman* (New York: Behrman House, 1975), preface.

IV-A. Max Gelb, ed., *Understanding Conservative Judaism* (New York, 1978), 215–17.

IV-B. *Emet Ve-Emunah: Statement of Principles of Conservative Judaism* (New York, 1988), 9–10, 47–48, 56–57.

V. *Central Conference of American Rabbis Yearbook* (New York, 1981), 90:73.

VI. *Intermountain Jewish News*, April 2, 1982.

VII. Clarence L. Coleman, Jr., "A Message from the President of the Council," *Issues* (summer 1983): 1.

VIII. "Report of the Ad Hoc Committee on Homosexuality and the Rabbinate, Adopted by the Central Conference of American Rabbis," Seattle, June 25, 1990. Printed in *Central Conference of American Rabbis Yearbook*, 100:107–12.

60.

I. *Commentary* 31 (April 1961): 323–24.

II. *Journal of Jewish Communal Service,* 40 (Fall 1963 #1): 17–25.

III. David Dubinsky to the seventh grade class at Temple Israel, Jan. 16, 1968, files of the International Ladies' Garment Workers' Union, New York; copy in Marcus Collections.

61.

I. "The Shabby Millionaire," *New York Times*, Sept. 1, 1965.

II. "Society Makes Interest-Free Loans to Immigrants," *New York Times*, May 1, 1983.

III. Julian Mincer, "A Christmas Appeal: Help for the Neediest Cases," *New York Times*, Dec. 9, 1984.

62.

I. *Commentator Magazine,* 59, no. 4 (March 25, 1964).

II. *Jewish Times/Jewish Exponent,* Jan. 29–30, 1987, weekly section, p. 17.

III. *American Jewish Year Book,* 89 (1989):60–62.

63.

I. Eliezer Livneh, "Does Zionism Have a Future?" *Tradition* (spring/summer 1964): 30–41.

II. Leon Klenicki, Eugene J. Fisher, Janet Laucher, *Celebrating the 25th Anniversary of the Vatican II Declaration Nostra Aetate (No. 4) on Catholic-Jewish Relations: Programs and Resources* (New York, 1990), 19–20.

III. President's Commission on the Holocaust, Elie Wiesel, Chairman, *Report to the President* (Washington, D.C., Sep. 27, 1979).

IV.   "Transcript of remarks by Reagan and Wiesel at White House Ceremony," *New York Times*, April 20, 1985.

V.   *Jewish Advocate*, Feb. 1, 1990.

VI.   *Detroit Jewish News*, May 31, 1991, pp. 24–25.

VII.   Original contribution by Jacob R. Marcus.

Index

Entries in boldface refer to the documents reproduced throughout the book. All other entries represent material from Dr. Marcus' explanatory text.